S0-AZO-667

PEOPLESOFT DEVELOPER'S HANDBOOK

PeopleSoft Developer's Handbook

Richard Gillespie

JoAnn Gillespie

McGraw-Hill

New York San Francisco Washington, D.C.
Auckland Bogotá Caracas Lisbon London
Madrid Mexico City Milan Montreal New Delhi
San Juan Singapore Sydney Tokyo Toronto

Library of Congress Cataloging-in-Publication Data

Gillespie, Richard
The PeopleSoft handbook/Richard Gillespie, JoAnn Gillespie.
p. cm.
ISBN 0-07-212394-X
1. PeopleSoft software Handbooks, manuals, etc. I. Gillespie, JoAnn. II. Title.
QA76.755.G55 1999
650′.0285′574—dc21 99-28609
CIP

McGraw-Hill
A Division of The McGraw-Hill Companies

1 2 3 4 5 6 7 8 9 0 DOC/DOC 9 0 4 3 2 1 0 9

P/N 0-07-212393-1
PART OF
ISBN 0-07-212394-X

The sponsoring editor for this book was Simon Yates, the editing supervisor was Penny Linskey, and the production supervisor was Clare Stanley. It was set in New Century Schoolbook by Victoria Khavkina of McGraw-Hill's Desktop Composition Unit in cooperation with Spring Point Publishing Services.

Printed and bound by R. R. Donnelley & Sons Company.

This book is printed on recycled, acid-free paper containing a minimum of 50% recycled, de-inked fiber.

CONTENTS

INTRODUCTION

The number of PeopleSoft implementations is growing like wildfire. In 1998, PeopleSoft overtook Oracle as the second leading provider of Enterprise software solutions, and a big reason for this growth is the strength and flexibility of its development environment. One of the most refreshing things about PeopleSoft is its commitment to deliver the best possible solutions to customers. PeopleSoft does not try to reinvent the wheel whenever they expand functionality; instead, they incorporate the best-of-breed third-party tools into their suite whenever possible. This is very evident in PeopleSoft's use of Tuxedo to move into a three-tier architecture, as well as in the use of reporting tools such as Seagate's Crystal Reports Pro and SQRibe's SQR. An advantage of using third-party tools is that it enables new technical developers to bring relevant skills and knowledge to the table at a greater speed.

With the focus and number of specific applications expanding every year, the functional aspects of PeopleSoft are far too vast for any one book to cover all that would be needed to become an effective functional team member. Functional PeopleSoft implementers are a unique new breed of developers. They usually possess specific business knowledge and have a detailed understanding of the modules they work with. On the other hand, technical PeopleSoft developers usually have a programming background in either COBOL or client/server technologies. They seldom have a detailed understanding of any one specific module; rather, they are proficient in developing graphical customizations, reports, and interfaces.

That being said, this book is geared to enlightening both functional developers who want a better understanding of the development environment and new technical developers who will soon be required to develop their own customizations. This book focuses on giving an in-depth overview of the primary development tools delivered in a PeopleSoft installation. The topics covered include the Application Developer, the Security Administrator, PeopleCode, the Process Scheduler, and third-party applications such as SQRibe's SQR and Seagate's Crystal Reports Pro that are bundled with PeopleSoft. The CD that is included with this book contains screen-captured movies that will illustrate the steps that are documented in the examples. If you are new to PeopleSoft, it is highly recommended that you take the time to view these movies. Each step used to create our fictional ordering application will be covered.

Part 1 of this book is a basic tutorial on the PeopleSoft environment, covering topics such as the navigational methods, effective dating concepts, and many of the fundamental PeopleSoft methods and objects.

Part 2 gives a detailed description of the requirements surrounding a fictional ordering application that will be developed in this book. The example is loosely related to an inventory-purchasing implementation. Necessary fields required for this implementation will be discussed. However, common field names that could be found in any module will not be created. Since this book is not intended to be a functional tutorial of any PeopleSoft application, it will not use application-specific objects or functionality. The example is not meant to be an ideal ordering process. It is used only to give you a feel for how you could solve a small-scale development task.

After the requirements of our example problem are laid out, the next step is to map the requirements to relational data objects.

Part 3 of this book explores PeopleSoft's data objects. Through definitions and examples, you will be shown all the major properties of each object. When we have completed the PeopleSoft data structures for the ordering example, we will then create the graphical user interface that will allow us to insert and update our data. The next step to cover before we can test our application is security. With the Security Administrator, we will create new users and classes with access to our new functionality. At last, we will then be able to test the beta version of our application. The first pass at the creation of our application will lack many of the features required for it to be a finished product.

After we have tested our example, the final chapter in Part 3 will introduce PeopleCode. With that knowledge, we will enhance our application with function libraries to include automatic number functionality to our panels.

The rest of the book covers several topics that could easily merit their own books. Part 4 explores the reporting features of PeopleSoft's Query and NVision and Seagate's Crystal Reports. In addition, Part 4 covers the reporting—as well as the importing and exporting—features of SQRibe's SQR. Appendix A discusses the Configuration Manager in detail. Appendix B discusses the Application Designer in Upgrade Mode.

Most of the chapters in this book first give an overview of the relevant topics and then explore them by continuing to build on the example that is described in Chapter 2. If you have access to a PeopleSoft development environment, it is highly recommended that you work along with the book. If you do not have access to a PeopleSoft environment, fear not; by running the screen cams on the CD, you should get a feel for how the example would be created.

—Richard Gillespie
JoAnn Gillespie

PEOPLESOFT DEVELOPER'S HANDBOOK

PART 1

PeopleSoft Application Environment Review

Part 1 of this book will help familiarize the reader with the People-Soft environment.

CHAPTER 1

PeopleSoft Environment Review

This book goes over key PeopleSoft elements in great detail. This chapter will first give a brief definition of each key element so that as each topic is discussed in greater detail, it will not be foreign to you. Once the key elements are defined, this chapter will discuss how to navigate through a PeopleSoft application from a user's perspective. Next, this chapter will go over the PeopleSoft actions that can be performed on the data in the database.

Definitions of Key PeopleSoft Elements

1. *Field.* A single entity of data. For example, name could be a field or age could be a field.
2. *Record.* A logical grouping of one or more field definitions. A record is similar to a row in an SQL (Structured Query Language) table.
3. *Panel.* A PeopleSoft screen that displays data from the database in an organized manner. There are various ways of displaying the data on the panel such as with radio buttons, edit boxes, and check boxes. A panel allows the user to update or display data.
4. *Panel group.* If not all the data in a certain category fit on one panel, the developer would create more panels. All the panels in this category would be placed in a panel group. This is done for organization purposes.
5. *Menu.* A menu is made up of panel groups and/or panels.
6. *Menu group.* A menu group consists of a list of menus pertaining to a specific topic.

Navigation

There are two major methods of navigating through PeopleSoft applications:

- Menu navigation
- Business process navigation

The main method of navigation is via menus. This is the default method, and it is always available.

Another method of navigation is Business Process Navigator Display. The Business Process Navigator is used to graphically give a user an ordered process to navigate the application.

This method is available only if (1) the developer created a Business Process while creating the application or (2) the user running the application has access to that Business Process.

If the Configuration Manager was run and the Navigator Display option was set to ON or FIRST, then the Business Process will automatically be displayed graphically if the above two conditions are true. Otherwise, if the Navigator Display option is OFF, the user could turn on the graphical Business Process display by selecting VIEW, NAVIGATOR DISPLAY, or BUSINESS PROCESS. Refer to Appendix A on the Configuration Manager for more details.

Signing on to PeopleSoft

Regardless of which navigation method is preferred by the user, the first step is to sign on to PeopleTools. To do so, select START, PROGRAMS, PEOPLESOFT, and PEOPLETOOLS, and enter the following information:

- Connection type—the database type to connect to (e.g., SQLBase, ORACLE, Application Server*).
- Database name—database where the PeopleSoft application is located.
- Operator id—PeopleSoft Application Operator (not the Database username).
- Password—operator passwords are set in the Security Administrator.

Figure 1-1 shows the options available on the login screen for PeopleSoft.

Menu Navigation

As stated above, menu navigation is the default navigation process. In other words, the user always has menus to turn to in order to get to a panel in the application regardless of whether the Business Process is being displayed graphically.

All the PeopleSoft screens contain a menu bar. The menu bar is unique for each screen. The menu bar contains menu-bar labels such as FILE, EDIT, GO, FAVORITES, USE, REPORT, and HELP. At the core of menu navigation are the GO and USE menu-bar labels.

---

*If you are working in a three-tier environment, you would select an Application Server to connect to and would not need to supply a database name. More and more companies are deciding to go with a three-tier architecture. This allows them to distribute the PeopleSoft client without any database client software. Depending on your licensing agreements and your level of support, this could be very appealing.

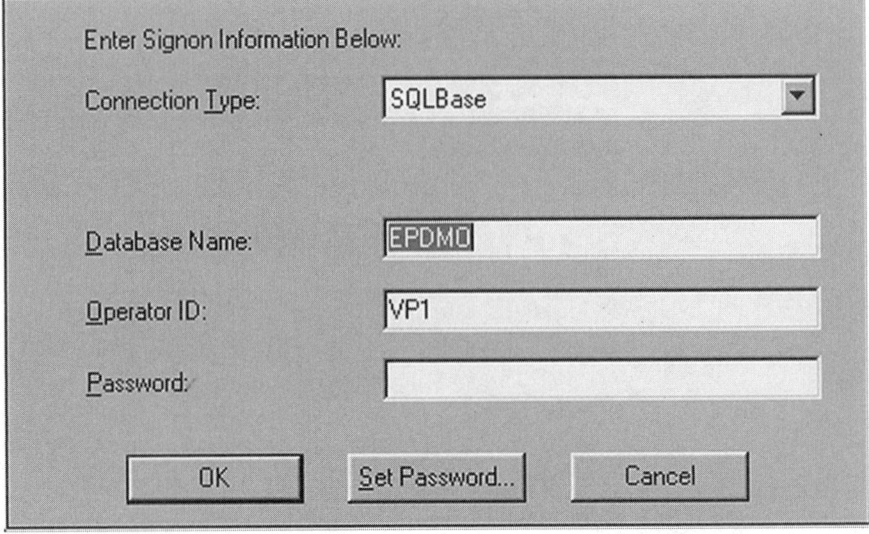

Figure 1-1
Login screen.

When the user clicks on the GO menu-bar label, a list of menu groups is displayed as shown in Figure 1-2. All menu groups that the current operator has access to will be displayed. A menu group consists of one or more menus. If the menu group consists of more than one menu, then the menu has a right arrow next to it. In this case, the user should move the cursor over to the right to see the complete list of menus in that group and click on the desired menu. Again, refer to Figure 1-2.

When a menu is selected, a new screen will appear. This screen will have the menu label of the selected menu at the top of the screen. This helps users know exactly where they are at any given time. In addition to the menu label changing, the menu bar may change to this menu's specific options.

When the user clicks on the USE bar label, a list of panel groups to which that user has access is displayed. A panel group contains one or more panels. Each panel contains data from the user's database tables. A user can perform actions on the data via the database panel. Therefore, to perform an action on data, the user must click on the USE bar label and then click on the desired panel group. If there is a right arrow next to the desired panel group, then a list of panels is displayed. At this point, the user should click on the desired panel. The panel will also have a right arrow on it. When the cursor is clicked on to the right arrow, a list of actions is displayed. The user should then click on the desired action.

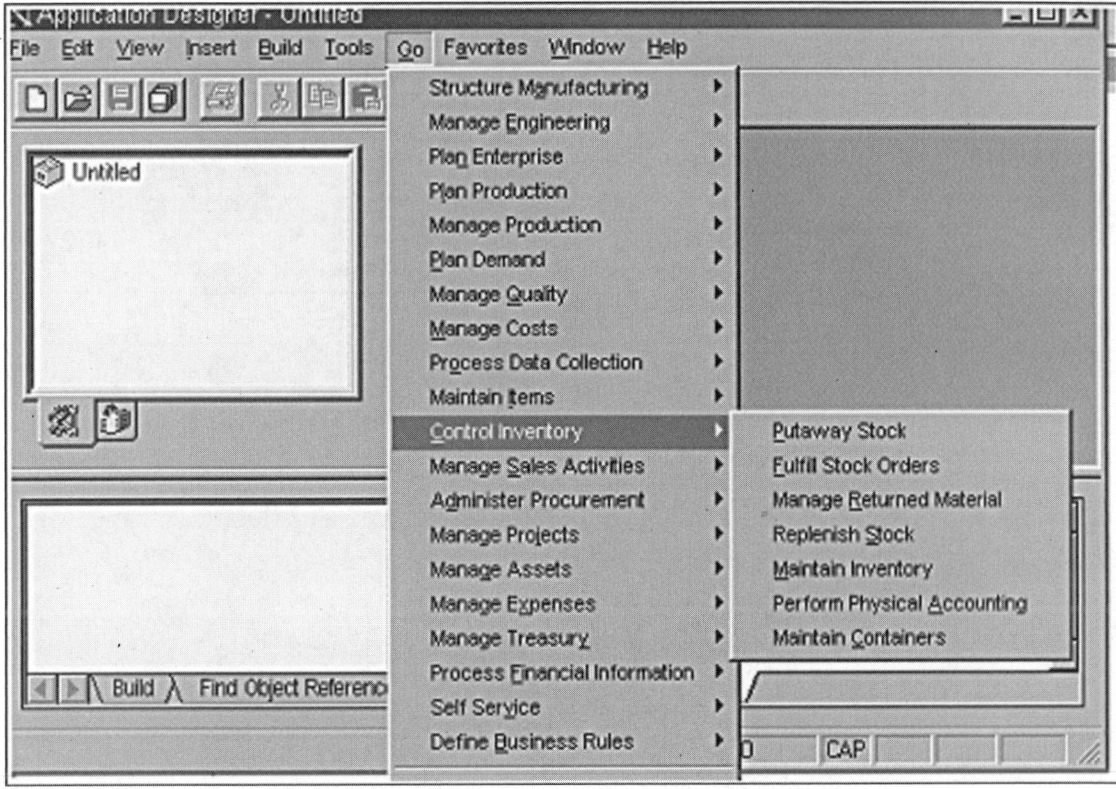

Figure 1-2 A list of menu groups appears when the GO bar label is clicked on.

Figure 1-3 shows an example screen of a possible USE menu selection.

Following is the complete list of actions that can be performed on data:

- ADD
- UPDATE/DISPLAY
- UPDATE/DISPLAY ALL
- CORRECTION

A user may or may not have privileges to perform all the possible actions on the selected data. This is why only a subset of the actions is shown in Figure 1-3. The actions that can be performed on the data are discussed in more detail later in this chapter.

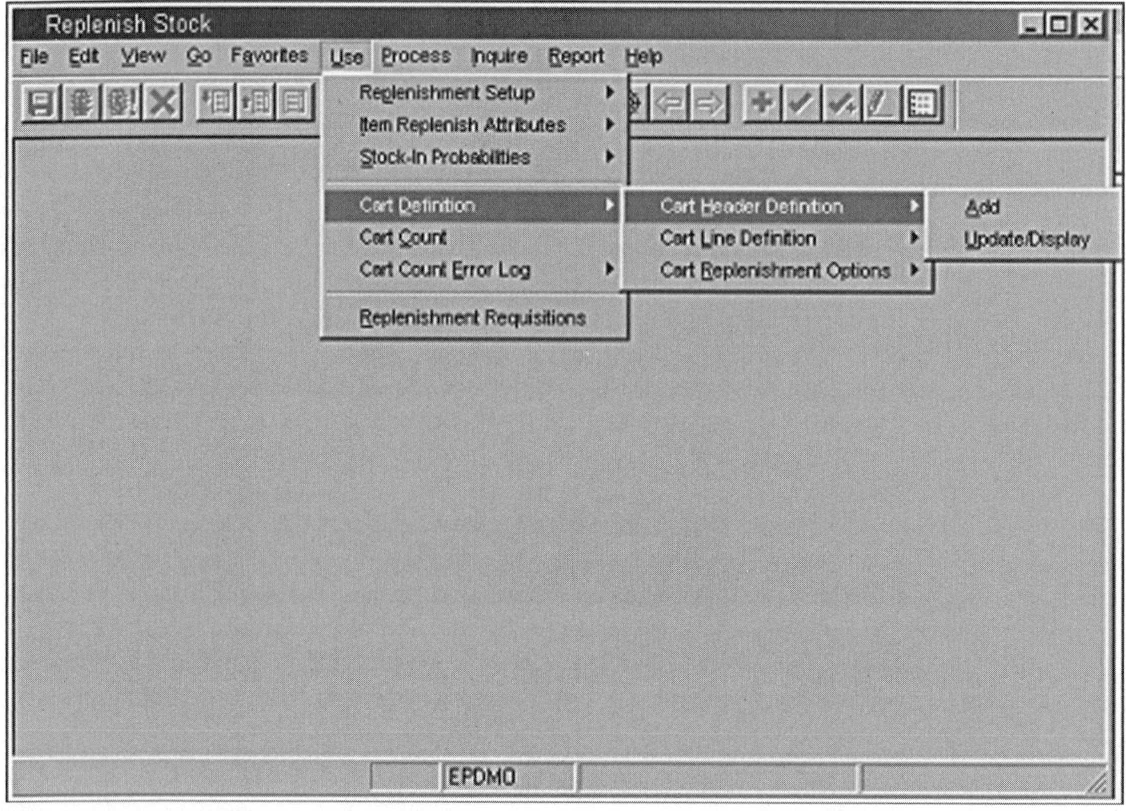

Figure 1-3 Sample USE menu selection.

Business Process Navigation

Another method of navigating through PeopleSoft applications is via Business Processes.

There are times when the actual business job at hand is so complicated that it is difficult for a user to know the correct steps needed to complete each task. In this case, a developer may have created a Business Process. Business Processes are created by the application developer in the Application Designer of PeopleTools. A *Business Process* is a graphical representation of all the tasks needed and the order in which they must be performed to complete a job. The Business Process displays graphically, and quite clearly, the steps the user must take to complete the Business Process and, in effect, get to the proper panels of the application in a particular order by double-clicking on icons.

This section concentrates on explaining the Business Process Navigation Display from a user's perspective. If the user has access to Business Processes and the Configuration Manager was run to set the Navigator Display option to ON or FIRST, then the Business Process will automatically be displayed graphically. Otherwise, if the Navigator Display option is OFF, the user could turn on the graphical Business Process display by selecting VIEW, NAVIGATOR DISPLAY, or BUSINESS PROCESS. The CHANGE WINDOW CONTENT icon (see Fig. 1-4) can be toggled to remove the Business Process Navigator graphical display and toggled again for it to return.

Figure 1-5 shows how to turn the Business Process Navigational Display option to ON.

When the graphical representation is displayed, the screen will show the Business Process map in tree format on the left side of the Business Process window. This map contains one or more Business Processes. Figure 1-6 shows the tree representation of a Business Process map on the left side of the window. It also shows the icons representing each Business Process that makes up the Business Process map on the right side of the window.

A Business Process is a complete task consisting of one or more activities. When a Business Process icon is selected, the activities that make up that Business Process are displayed. Figure 1-7 illustrates an activity icon. Figure 1-8 shows the activities that make up the selected Business Process.

An *activity* is one or more steps. Figure 1-7 shows an activity icon.

When an activity icon is double-clicked, the next screen that comes up is a diagram of all the steps that make up that activity. Figure 1-9 shows the new screen after the activity icon is selected. Figure 1-10 shows a step icon.

A *step* is one step in the Business Process. The step is associated with a predefined action that will be performed on data on one panel.

Figure 1-4
CHANGE WINDOW CONTENT icon.

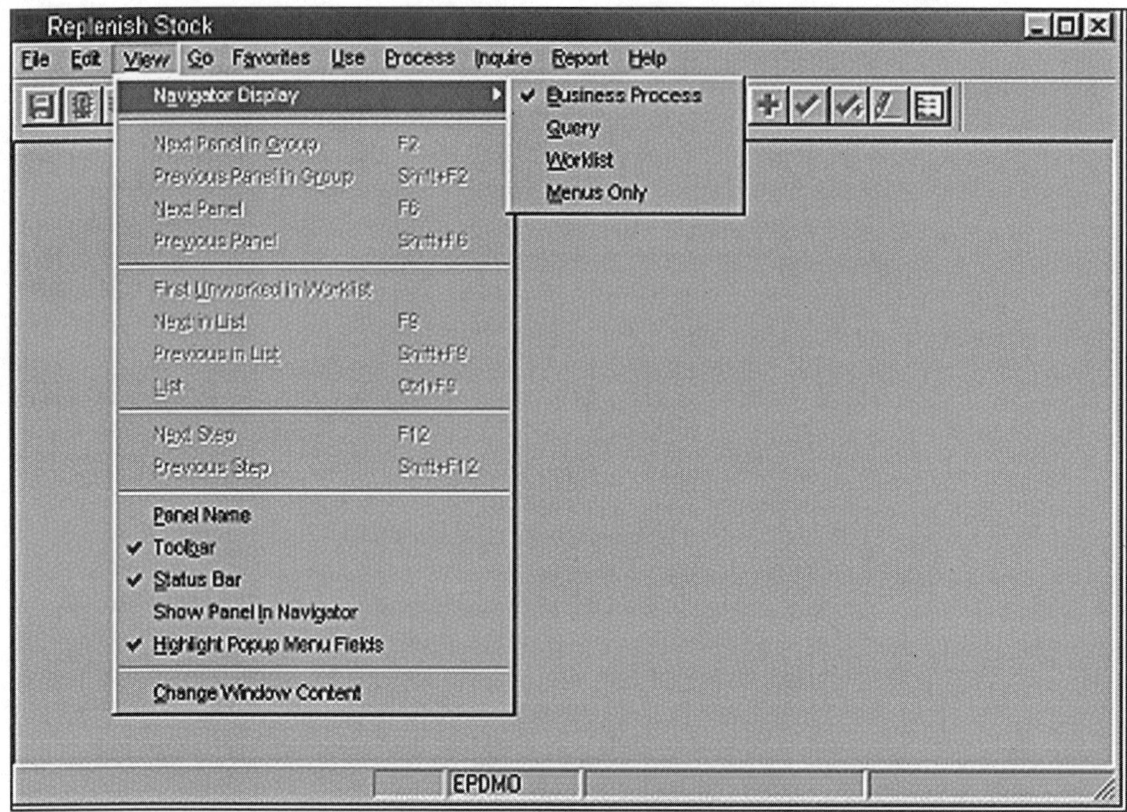

Figure 1-5 Turning the Navigator Display to Business Process.

Remember that when we were discussing menu navigation, there was a list of actions the user could select for a panel. The complete list of actions was ADD, UPDATE/DISPLAY, UPDATE/DISPLAY ALL, and CORRECTION. When a panel is accessed via Business Process Navigation, the user cannot choose an action. Instead, there is one action associated with a step. (Actions are discussed in greater detail later in this chapter.)

When a step icon in the Business Process Navigation Display is double-clicked, a panel may appear. (A panel is one way that a user can view the data in the database.) Whether a panel appears when a step icon is selected depends on what the step was programmed to do. For example, if the step is defined to ADD some data to the database, then a panel will appear which will allow the user to type in the data. If, how-

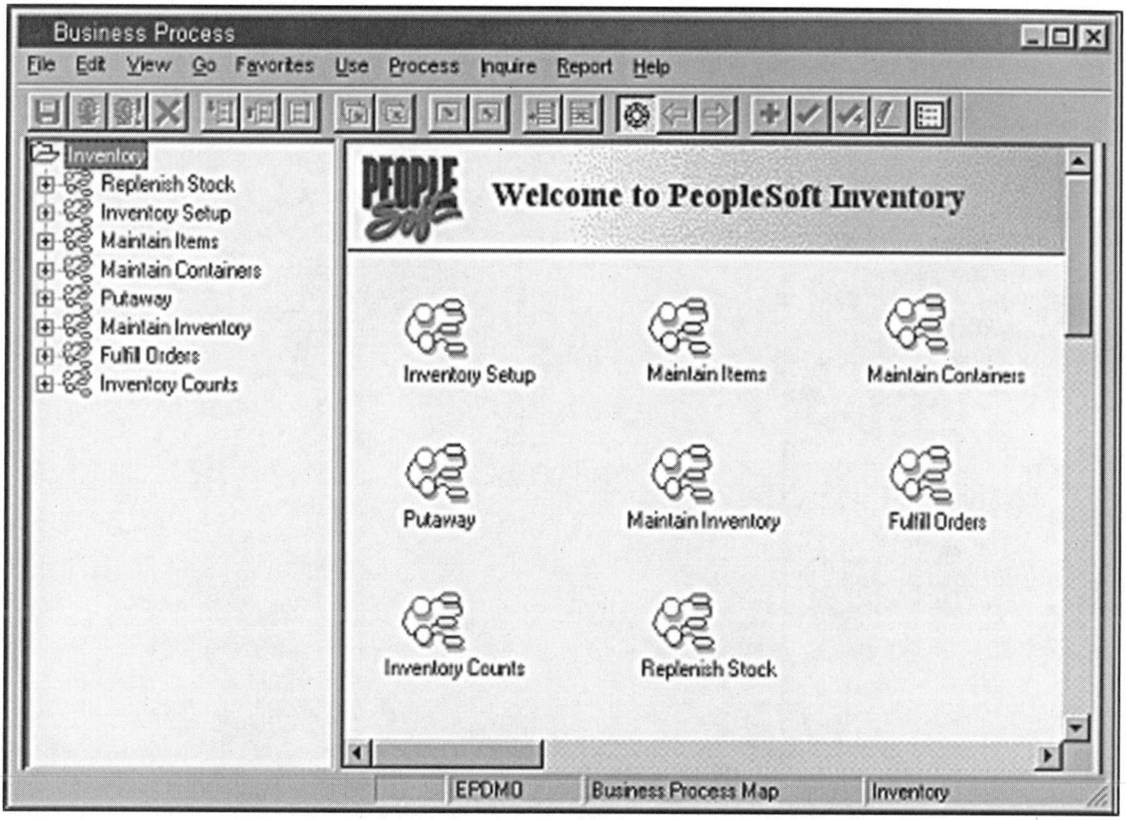

Figure 1-6 Business Process map.

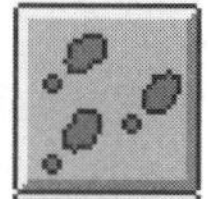

Figure 1-7 Activity icon.

ever, the action defined for that step is UPDATE/DISPLAY, then a search dialog will appear first. The search dialog box allows the user to narrow down the records of data that will be displayed on the panel. Figure 1-11 shows a search dialog that will be displayed after clicking on a step icon when the action is defined as a panel with the UPDATE/DISPLAY action.

After the user enters a value in the search field of the search dialog and double-clicks on the SEARCH button, the panel defined for the previ-

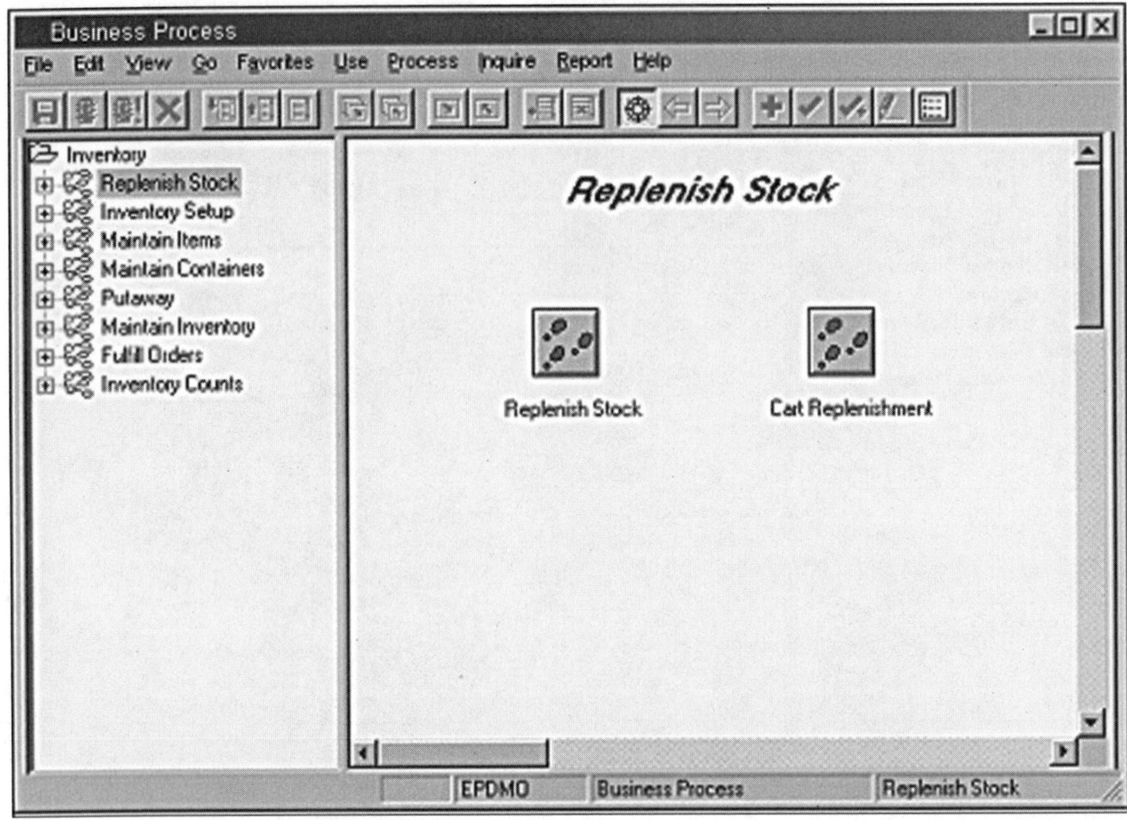

Figure 1-8 *All activities making up one Business Process.*

ously selected step will be displayed. This panel will contain the record data that match the value entered in the search field. Figure 1-12 illustrates the panel associated with the previously selected step. You can see that this panel contains the data that were entered in the primary key search dialog. Sometimes the primary key is difficult to remember because it may be just a four-digit code. In these cases, the developer may have set up the record to have an alternate search key. This means that the table could be searched using an alternate field (one that is easier for the user to remember). When a record is set up with an alternate search field, the search dialog box would have two boxes at its top. The top box contains the primary search field. The bottom box contains the

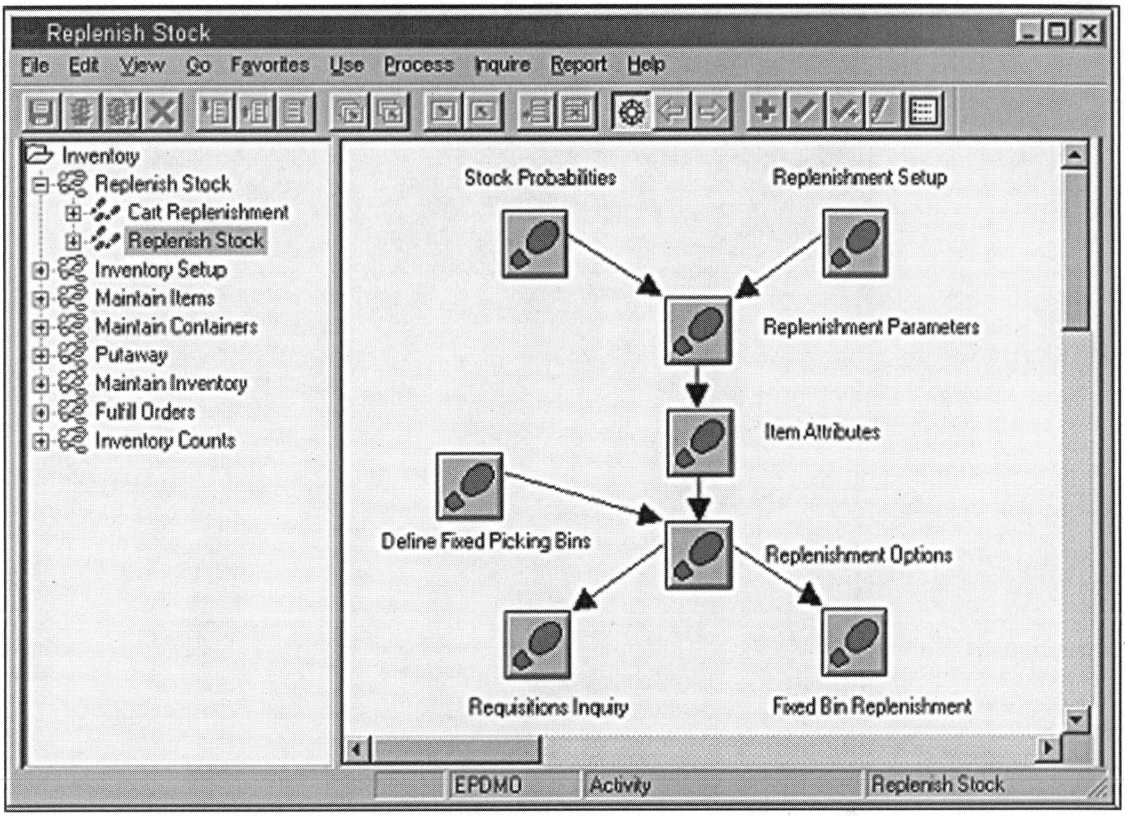

Figure 1-9 *All steps making up one activity.*

Figure 1-10
Step icon.

alternate search field(s). Note that Figure 1-11 does not contain an alternate search field.

To review, the right side of the Business Process window initially displays an icon for each Business Process in the selected business map. If a Business Process is selected, then the right side of the Business Process window will display all the activities that make up that Business Process. A user can continue to double-click on each graphical por-

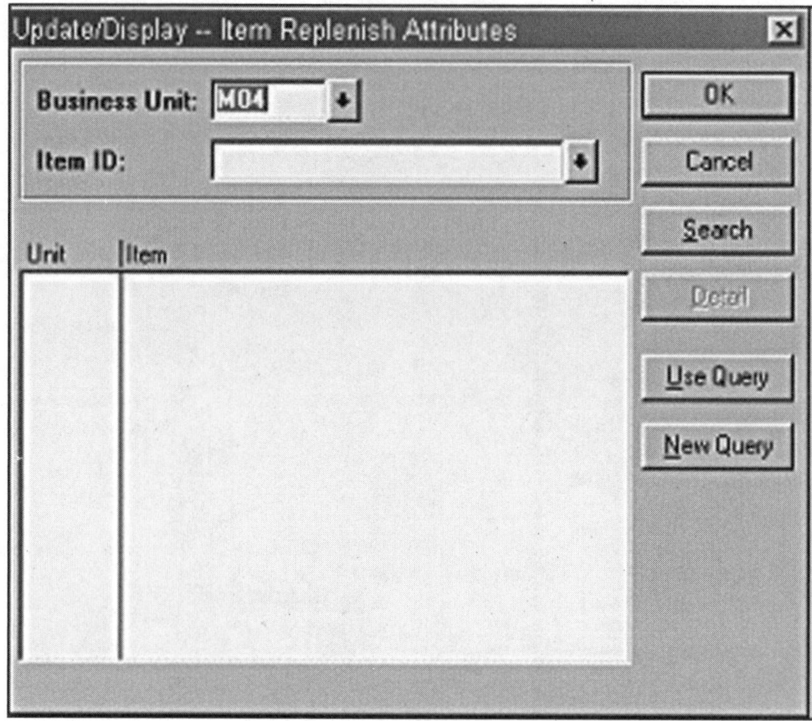

Figure 1-11 UPDATE/DISPLAY search dialog.

tion displayed on the right side of the Business Process window until the desired panel appears. Remember that for Business Processes, each time a panel is accessed, a predefined action will be performed on the panel.

An alternate way to get to the desired panel is to double-click on the Business Process map tree located on the left side of the screen. If a Business Process tree node is selected, then all activities that make up that Business Process are displayed in exactly the same way as when the Business Process icon was selected. In addition, if an activity tree node on the left side of the screen is selected, all the steps making up that activity are displayed on the right side of the screen in icon form.

Actions

Data are displayed on panels. When a panel is displayed, the user can view or modify the data via actions. Four actions can be performed on the data:

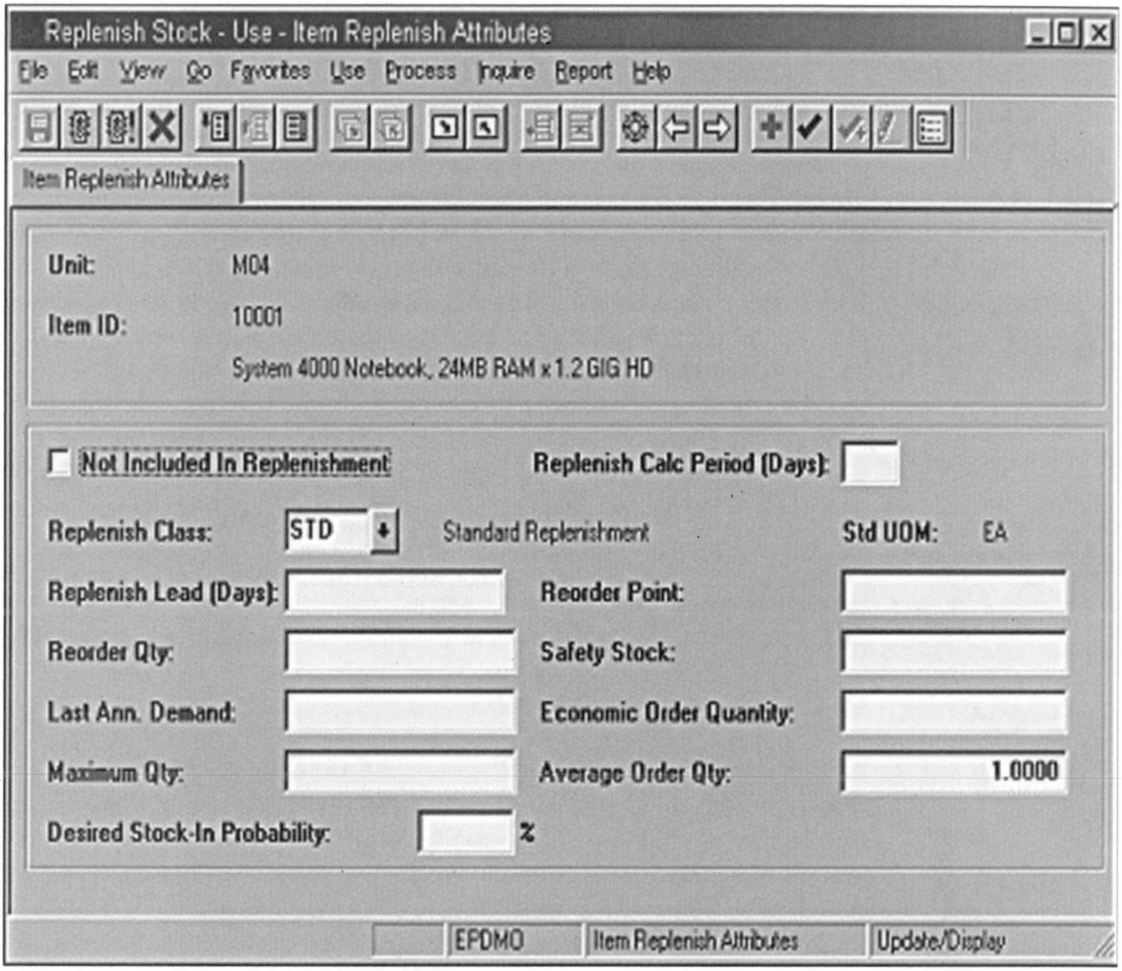

Replenish Stock - Use - Item Replenish Attributes
File Edit View Go Favorites Use Process Inquire Report Help
Item Replenish Attributes
Unit: M04
Item ID: 10001
System 4000 Notebook, 24MB RAM x 1.2 GIG HD
Not Included In Replenishment
Replenish Calc Period (Days):
Replenish Class: STD Standard Replenishment
Std UOM: EA
Replenish Lead (Days):
Reorder Point:
Reorder Qty:
Safety Stock:
Last Ann. Demand:
Economic Order Quantity:
Maximum Qty:
Average Order Qty: 1.0000
Desired Stock-In Probability: %
EPDMO Item Replenish Attributes Update/Display

Figure 1-12 Panel.

- ADD
- UPDATE/DISPLAY
- UPDATE/DISPLAY ALL
- CORRECTION

The ADD action allows the user to add data to the database. The UPDATE/DISPLAY, the UPDATE/DISPLAY ALL, and the CORRECTION actions allow the user to retrieve data from the database.

ADD Action

The ADD action is equivalent to an SQL insert, which means that it inserts a record into a table in the database. When the ADD action is selected, an ADD dialog box is displayed as shown in Figure 1-13. This dialog box displays the primary key labels, and the user must enter values for all parts of the primary key. Note that if the primary key was set up as a prompt table then a drop-down arrow appears. When the arrow is clicked on, a valid values box is displayed. If this happens, the user must select an entry from the valid values or type in a value that is listed in the valid values list. Otherwise, the ADD function will not complete since prompt tables are a means of data validation and only specific values are allowed. Once the primary key is entered, then the remaining (nonprimary key) data in the record can be entered as shown in Figure 1-14. Note that the primary key is grayed out. This indicates that the primary key cannot be modified when adding the record to the table.

Once all the required data are entered, the user must select FILE, SAVE in order to add the record to the database.

UPDATE/DISPLAY Action

The UPDATE/DISPLAY action will query the user for search criteria. The search dialog allows the user to enter both primary search keys as well as alternate search keys. The primary search keys are in the top square, and the alternate search keys are in the square below the primary search keys. Refer to Figure 1-15.

The user enters the search criteria and then clicks on the SEARCH button. All existing rows of data matching the search criteria will be displayed. After the search dialog has successfully returned rows of data, the user must select the desired row to be displayed. Once the desired row is selected, an UPDATE panel or panels will be displayed. The user

Figure 1-13
ADD dialog box.

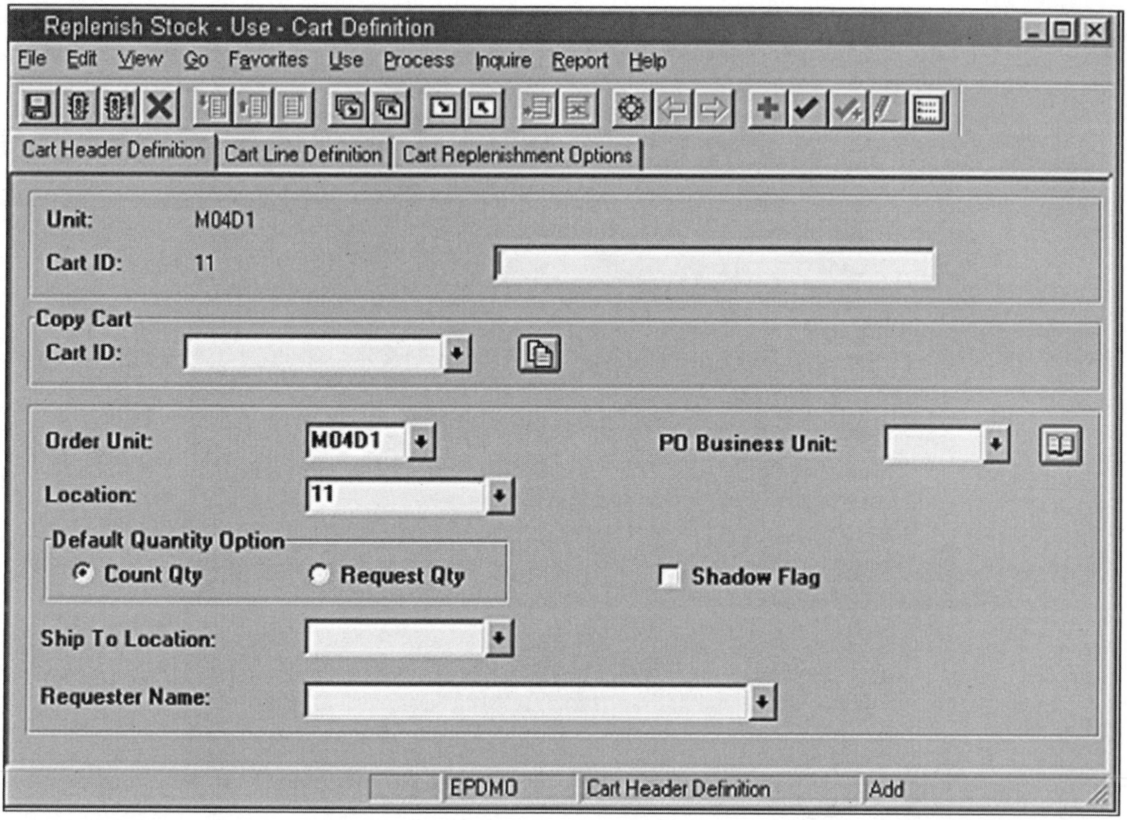

Replenish Stock - Use - Cart Definition

File Edit View Go Favorites Use Process Inquire Report Help

Cart Header Definition | Cart Line Definition | Cart Replenishment Options

Unit: M04D1

Cart ID: 11

Copy Cart

Cart ID:

Order Unit: M04D1

PO Business Unit:

Location: 11

Default Quantity Option

Count Qty

Request Qty

Shadow Flag

Ship To Location:

Requester Name:

EPDMO | Cart Header Definition | Add

Figure 1-14 Panel.

can simply edit the text to be changed. Once all the changes are made, the user must press the SAVE toolbar icon or select the FILE, SAVE menu option to save the changes to the database. Note that the SEARCH keys are grayed out and cannot be modified. An example panel is illustrated in Figure 1-16.

UPDATE/DISPLAY ALL and CORRECTION Actions

The UPDATE/DISPLAY ALL action and the CORRECTION action are used only on *effective dated tables*. In order to discuss these actions, we must first spend some time covering effective dated tables.

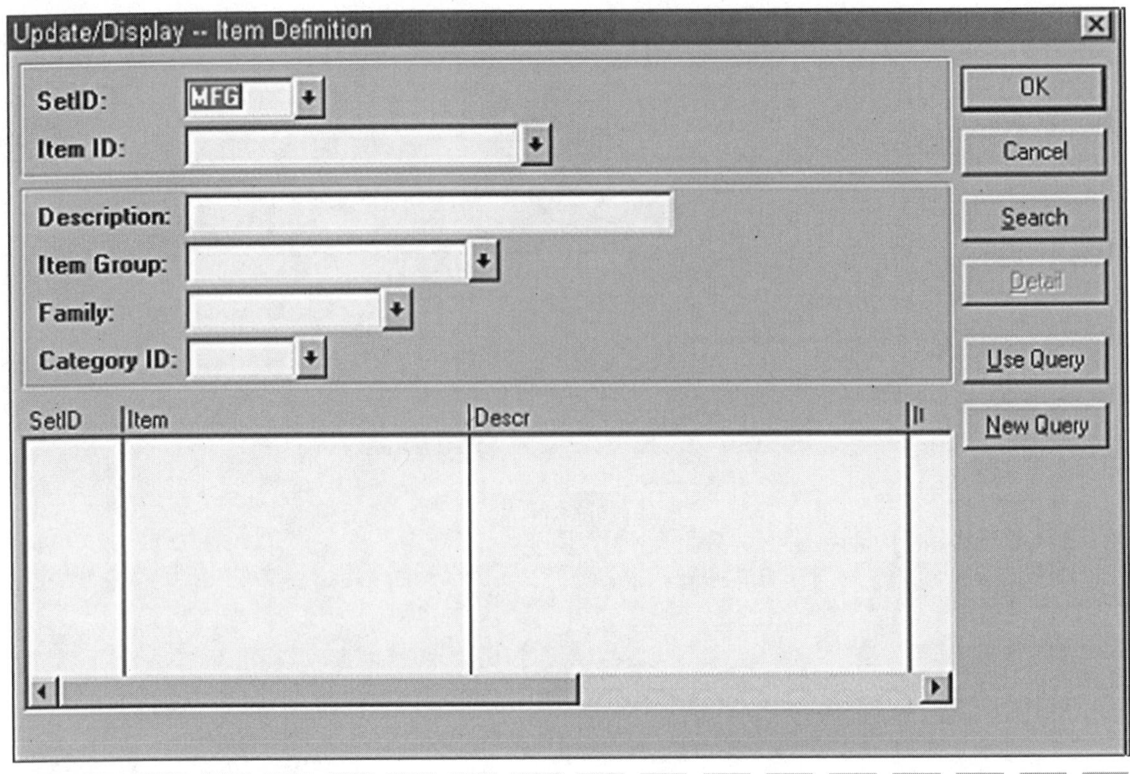

Figure 1-15 Update/Display dialog box.

Effective Dated Tables Effective dated tables always contain the *effective date* EFFDT field. It is this date that determines whether a row is considered a historical row, a current row, or a future row. An effective dated table contains only one current row. The current row is the one row in the table whose EFFDT is closest but not greater than the system date of the computer. Any row is considered *historical* if its effective date is less than the effective date of the current row. Any row is considered *future* if its effective date is greater than the system date. In addition to the effective date field, effective dated tables always have an effective date status. This status can be set to ACTIVE or INACTIVE depending on whether the row in the effective dated table is still active or not. Generally, prompt tables are effective dated tables because the application may have certain data that are only valid through a specific date or starting at a specific date.

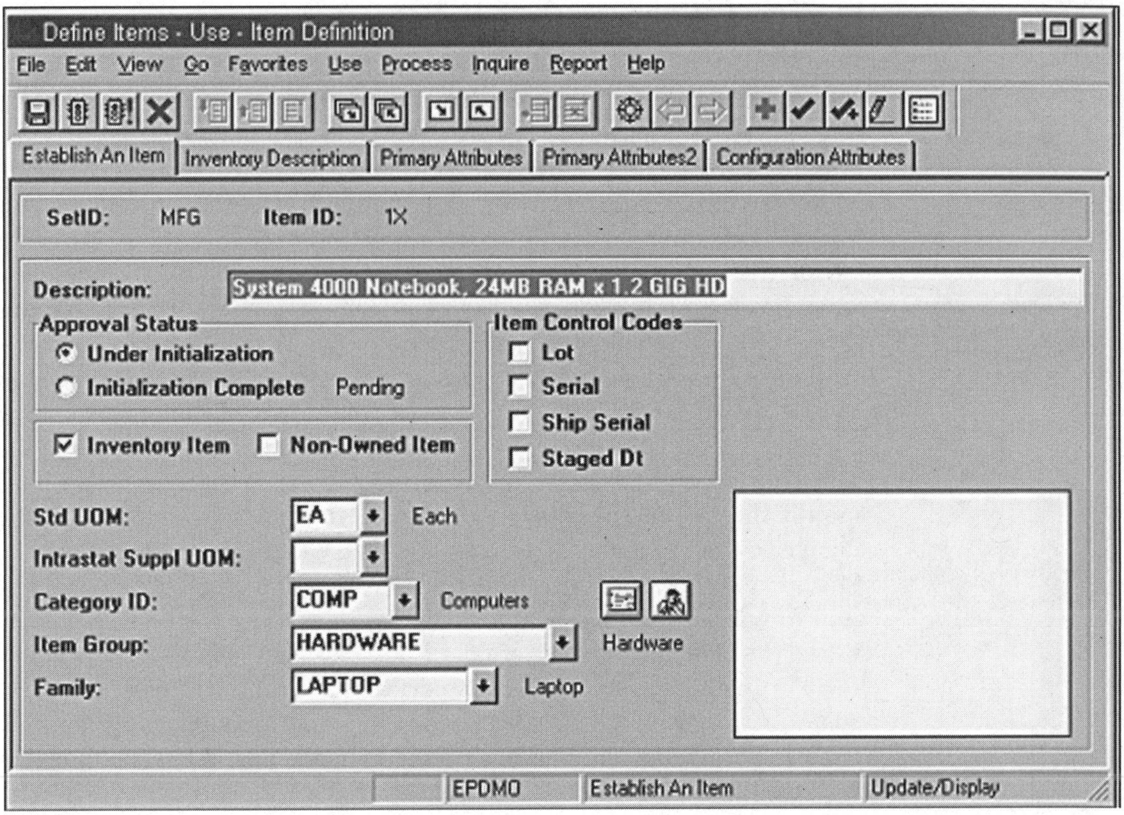

Figure 1-16 UPDATE/DISPLAY panel.

When the UPDATE/DISPLAY action is performed on an effective dated table, it allows the user to (1) view current and future rows, (2) modify future rows only, or (3) insert future rows or a new current row.

The UPDATE/DISPLAY ALL action can be performed only on effective dated tables. It allows the user to (1) view all rows of data (history, current, future), (2) modify future rows only, or (3) insert future rows or a new current row.

The CORRECTION ACTION also applies only to effective dated tables. It differs from the UPDATE/DISPLAY ALL function in that it allows the user to modify history rows as well as current or future rows from effective dated tables. It also allows the user to (1) view all rows of data (history, current, future), (2) modify all rows of data (history, current, future), or (3) insert all rows of data (history, current, future).

Scroll Areas

Some panels contain scrollable areas. Scrollable data on a panel come from one table. There may be more than one scrollable area on a panel. This indicates that the data on the panel come from more than one table. The user can insert a row into the scrollable area or delete a row from the scrollable area. To insert a row, the user hits the F7 function key or the insert row icon on the toolbar. This creates an empty row and the user simply enters the required data. Before the data are saved to the database, the user must save it. To delete a row from the scrollable area, the user must place the cursor on the row to be deleted and hit the F8 function key or the DELETE ROW icon. A dialog box asking the user whether the current row should be deleted is displayed. If the user selects YES, the row will disappear from the screen. The user should then save the changes by selecting FILE, SAVE to make the change to the database. Note that a primary key cannot be inserted or deleted from a panel using the F7 or F8 function keys. The *scrollable data* are detail data associated with a primary key. This functionality allows the user to add rows of detail data associated with that primary key. For instance, say the user is performing an UPDATE/DISPLAY operation on a panel and enters a primary key and a search is performed. The panel is displayed for the selected primary key. When the panel is displayed, there is a scrollable section that contains data relevant to that primary key. Now the user could decide to modify existing data and save them to the database or could insert an entirely new row of detail data. In the latter option, the user would need to hit the F7 function key and enter the data and would have to save this new row to the database by selecting FILE, SAVE. The detail data that is inserted are stored in a "child" table. The table containing the primary key is a "parent" table.

Data Validation

Data Validation ensures that the values entered into the system are valid values. Two means of accomplishing Data Validation in PeopleSoft are prompt tables and the Translate Table.

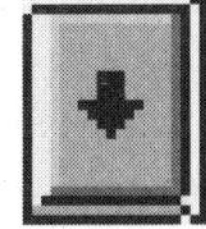

Figure 1-17
PROMPT button.

Prompt Table

A *prompt table* (also called *lookup table*) is used to validate data. When a field on a panel has a PROMPT button next to it, a prompt table has been set up for this field. This means that when the user clicks on the PROMPT button (Fig. 1-17), a list of valid values is displayed. If the field was set up to have Data Validation active (this is done on the EDITS tab of the Record Field Properties dialog box), then the user must select one of the values listed. The value entered in the field is then checked against all the valid values in the prompt table. If the field was not set up to have Data Validation active, then the list of values is needed only to assist the user with the field entry. The user can enter a value different from the value(s) listed.

There can be many prompt tables in the system. The number of prompt tables is determined by the developer and the requirements of the developer's application.

Translate Table

A *Translate Table* contains values used for Data Validation of a field. PeopleSoft databases have one Translate Table that all the fields in the entire database can share to store static variables for Data Validation. To take advantage of the Translate Table, a field must have a data type of character and be four characters or fewer in length. The values in the Translate Table are relatively static, and the recommended maximum number of variables for any one field is about 30. The Translate Table is an effective dated table with an effective status. This allows you to selectively turn ON or OFF values without having to delete them.

A real-world example of this is found in the Purchasing application. Out of the box, purchase orders have dispatch methods of print (PRN), fax (FAX), phone (PHN), and electronic data interchange (EDI). If the Purchasing Department that is going to use the new application does not utilize EDI, the developer could simply set the effective status to INACTIVE. This would then remove EDI as a possible selection when the users were defining a dispatch method for a new purchase order. If, however, there is an existing application that previously used EDI and as of a certain date EDI will no longer be available, then simply setting the effective status to INACTIVE is not sufficient. Instead, a new line would have to be added to the table with the date that EDI becomes INACTIVE and with the effective status set to inactive. This is true because any report that refers to EDI when it was active would have problems if the effective status were set to INACTIVE.

Figure 1-18 shows the Field Properties dialog box for the dispatch

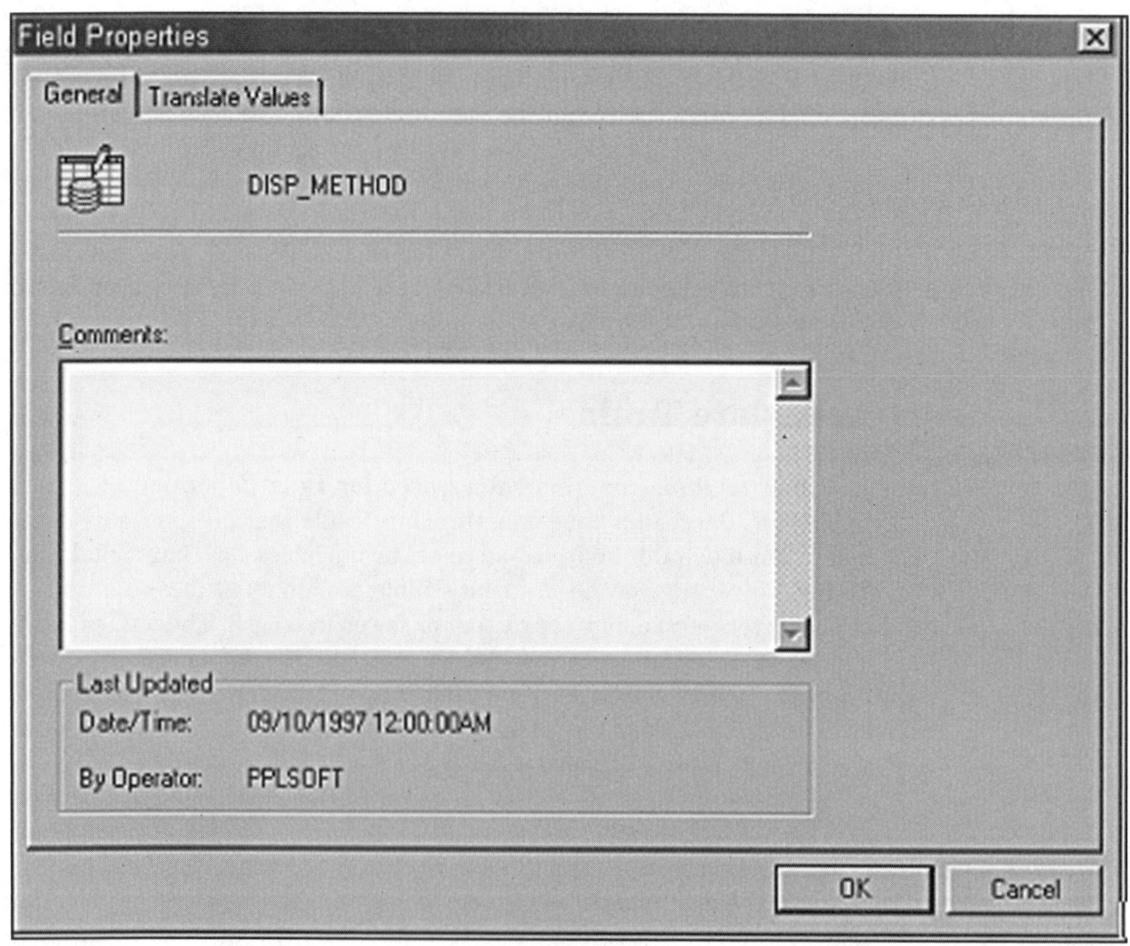

Figure 1-18 General tab of Field Properties dialog box.

method field DISP_METHOD. The Field Properties dialog box contains two tabs: a general tab and a TRANSLATE tab. Please note that a TRANSLATE tab is visible. This is because DISP_METHOD is a character with a length of less than five. Figure 1-19 shows the TRANSLATE tab. The TRANSLATE tab shows the available translate values for this field. In addition, note that there are three buttons allowing you to add, delete, or change the translate values. Figure 1-20 shows the Change Translate Table dialog box. This dialog box appears when the CHANGE button is

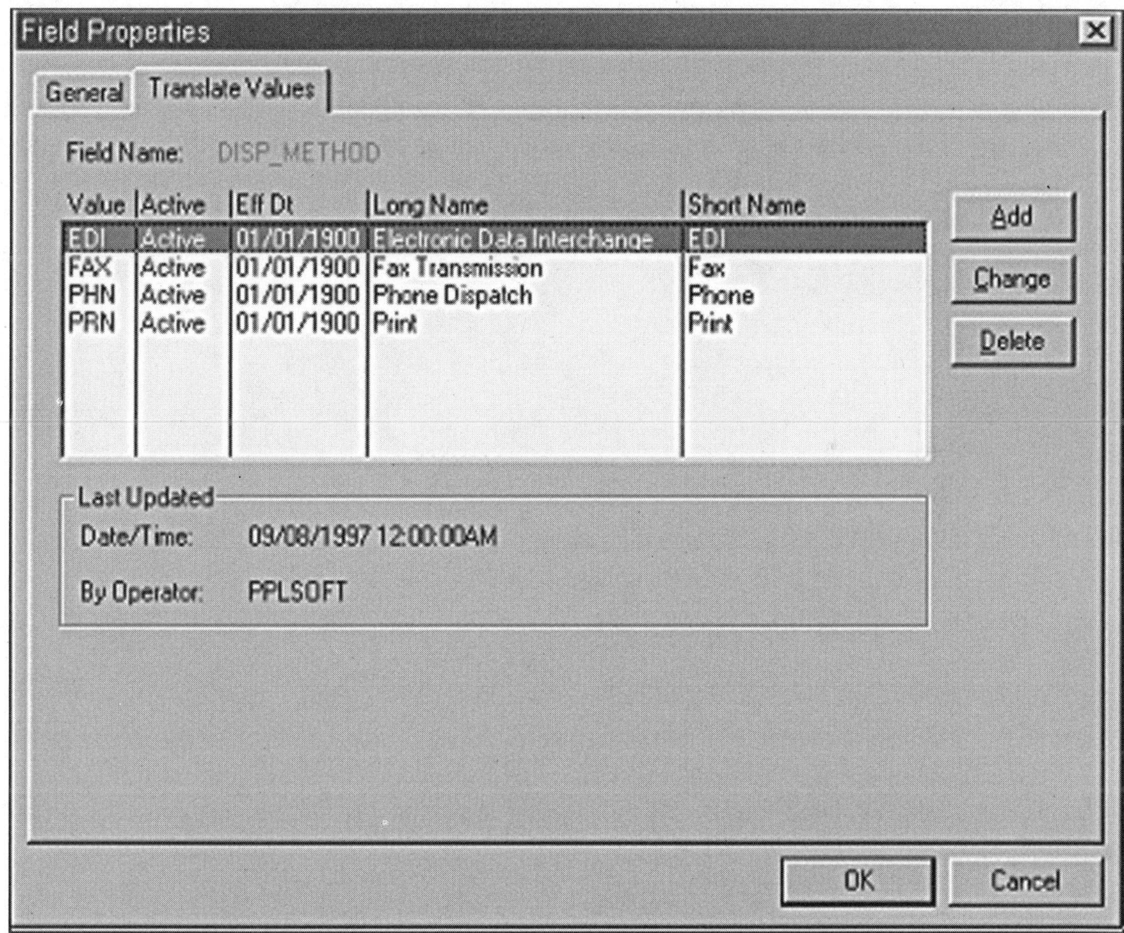

Figure 1-19 TRANSLATE VALUES tab of Field Properties dialog box.

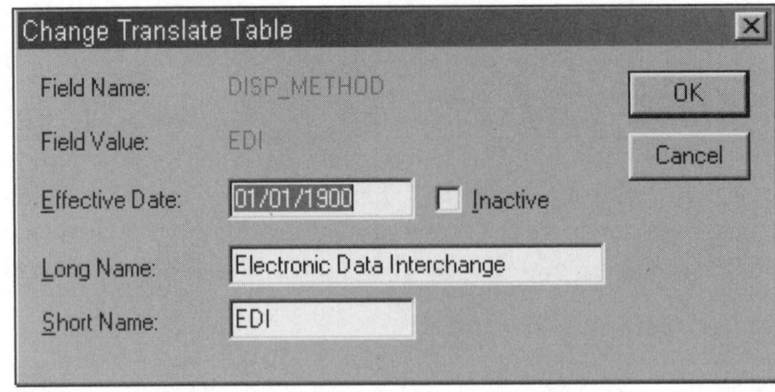

Figure 1-20 Change Translate Table dialog allows the developer to modify the definition of a translate value.

selected. The Change Translate Table dialog box displays one translate value definition for the field. The developer can modify the translate value definition by modifying the effective date, changing the value from ACTIVE to INACTIVE, or changing either the long name or the short name of the translate value.

CHAPTER 2

Application Designer Review

The Application Designer is PeopleSoft's integrated development environment (IDE). This is where the business application (project) is developed or upgraded. In this chapter, we review the development mode of the Application Designer. In Appendix B, the upgrade functionality will be discussed.

The Application Designer consists of three separate sections:

1. Project Workspace
2. Object Workspace
3. Output Window

The Project Workspace

The Project Workspace is located on the left side of the Application Designer screen. It contains the Project name and object definition folders. There is an object definition folder for each type of object that can be created. Our example shows a field folder, a menu folder, a panel group folder, a panel folder, and a record folder. If you double-click on the plus (+) sign next to the folder, a list of all objects in the project that are of that type will be displayed. To open an object, just double-click on the object, and it will be displayed in the Object Workspace area of the Application Designer.

In addition, there are two tabs on the project workspace:

1. A DEVELOPMENT tab, when selected, indicates whether the Application Designer is in development mode. Initially, we will have this tab selected while working on our warehouse example.
2. An UPGRADE tab, when selected, indicates the Application Designer is in upgrade mode. Note that Appendix B has more information on the Application Designer in upgrade mode.

The Project Workspace is where we will group all the objects that we will use to create our application. An object can be a field, a record, a panel, a panel group, a menu, or a Business Process map. Figure 2-1 shows the Project Workspace as a tree view containing fields, records, and panels.

The Object Workspace

The Object Workspace is located on the right side of the Application Designer screen. When an object is opened by double-clicking on it in the Project Workspace, the object's definition will be displayed in the Object Workspace area.

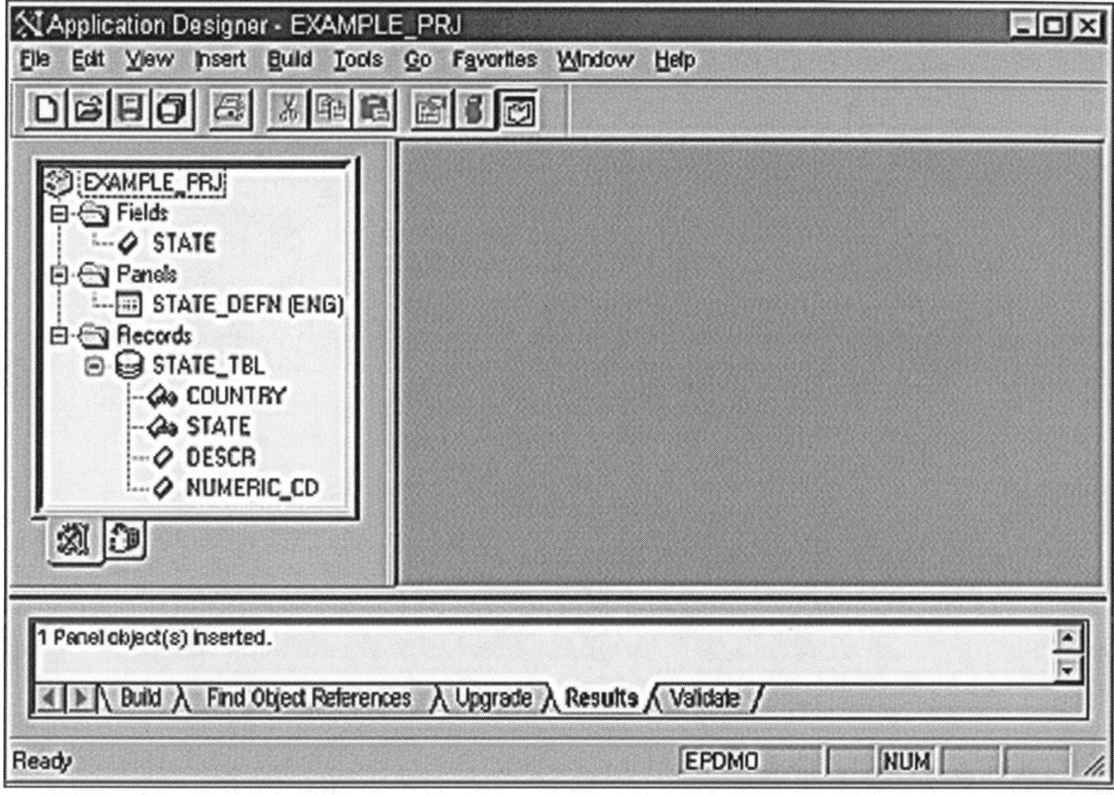

Figure 2-1 Project Workspace.

A developer could also open an object by selecting FILE, OPEN from the menu bar. When the Open Object dialog box is displayed, the developer selects the type of object from the list of object types. Once the object type is selected, the developer could narrow down the number of objects of that type listed by entering a name (or substring) in the selection criteria group. In other words, the developer could enter a search string and click on SELECT. When the search is completed, all objects with the search string in their names would be displayed as seen in Figure 2-2.

Once the complete list of possible objects of interest is displayed, the developer could double-click on one from the list, and that object's definition would be displayed in the Object Workspace as seen in Figure 2-3.

When creating new objects, it is possible to copy objects to other

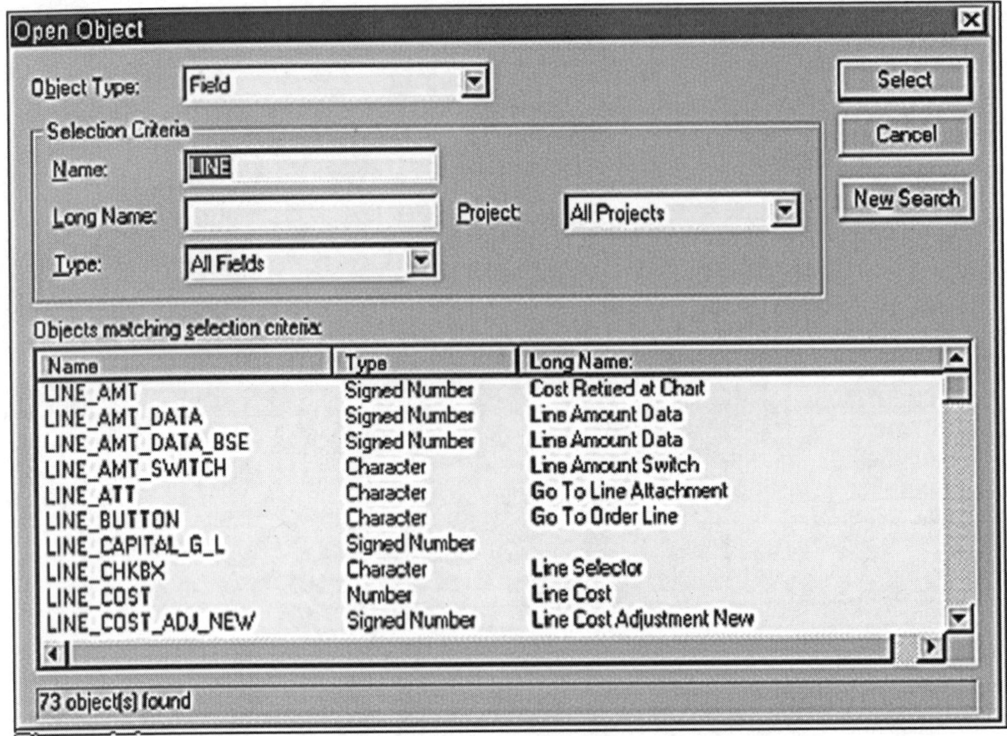

Figure 2-2 FILE, OPEN was selected. Selection criteria of LINE were entered. SELECT was clicked on. Objects matching the search criteria appear.

objects by the drag-and-drop method. "Drag and drop" is Windows terminology for simply placing your cursor over an object, pushing the left mouse button down and, while holding the mouse button down, moving or "dragging" the object that you selected to a new location.

To close an open object, either hit the X in the upper right-hand corner of the object or simply select FILE, CLOSE.

The Output Window

The Output Window is located at the bottom of the Application Designer screen. It contains status information or output from searches or other operations. A very useful feature of this window is that you can open ref-

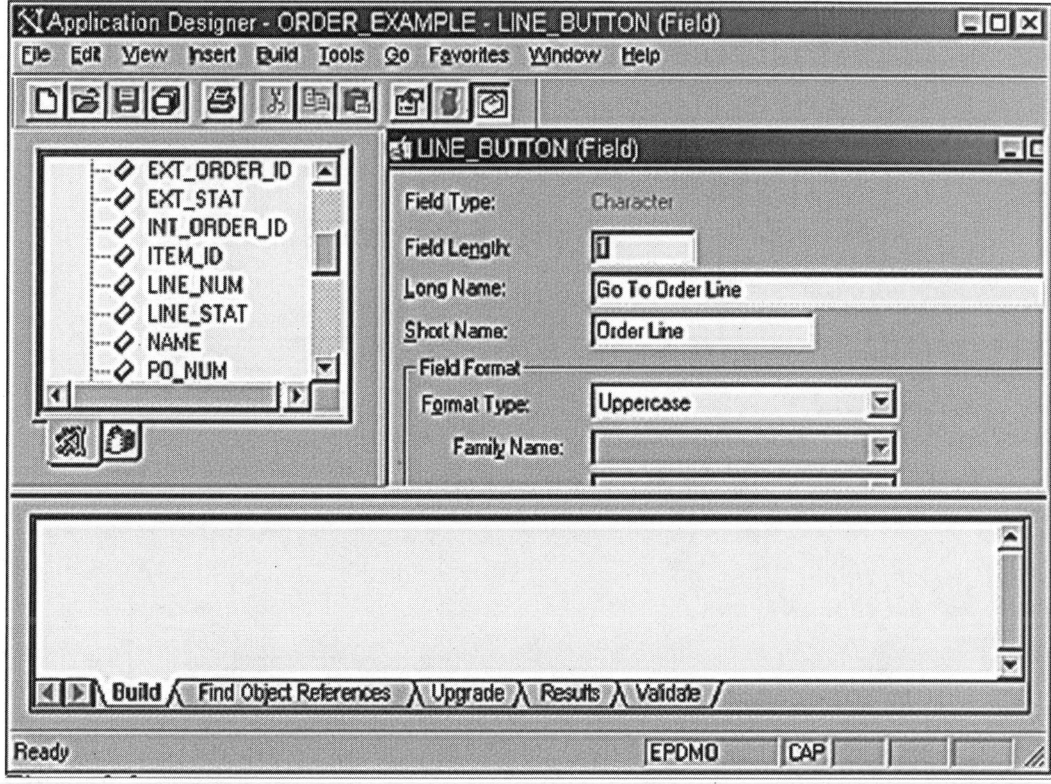

Figure 2-3 An example of an open object in the Object Workspace.

erenced objects by double-clicking on them in the Output Window. For example, when you search references of a field in other objects by selecting EDIT, FIND REFERENCES (Fig. 2-4), a list of records and panels will be displayed in the Output Window. The output indicates all occurrences of the searched field throughout the entire project. Figure 2-5 shows the output of an EDIT, FIND REFERENCES search. If you double-click on one of the returned values, its definition will automatically be opened in the Object Workspace.

Note in Figure 2-5 that there are tabs at the bottom of the Output Window. Each tab represents the type of output message that can be displayed in the Output Window. In this example, you can see that the output is in the FIND OBJECT REFERENCES tab

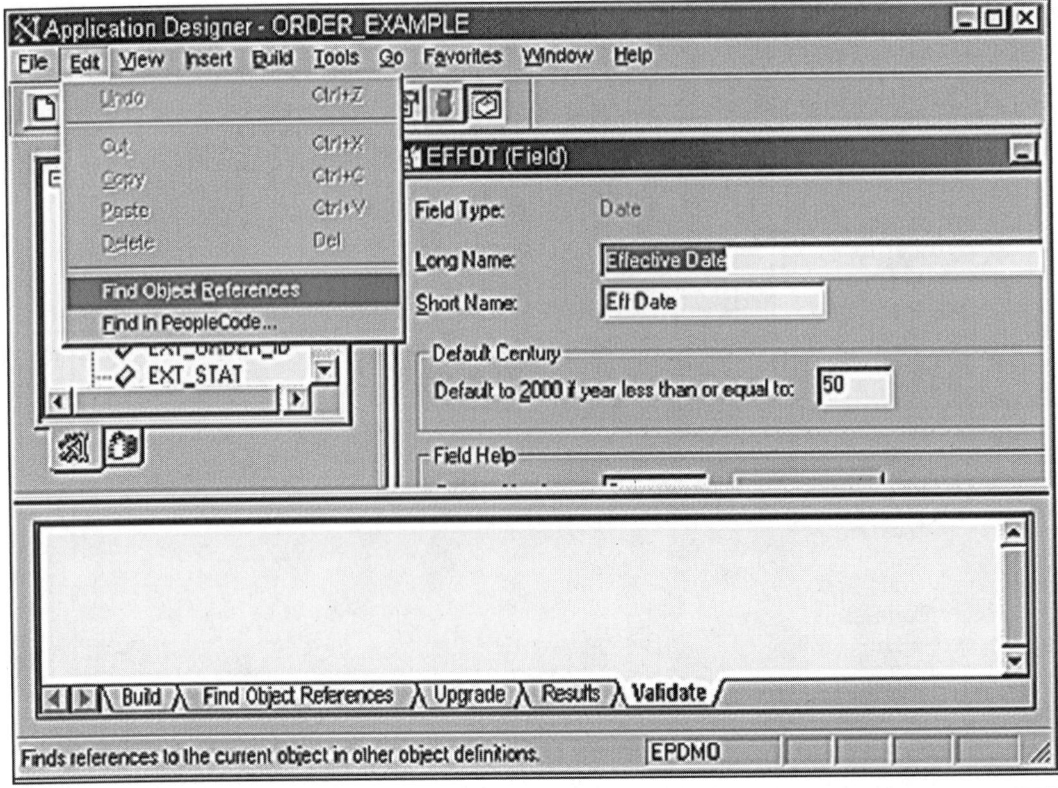

Figure 2-4 Finding object references.

Another example of the type of output that appears in the Output Window is during the build process of a record. During this process SQL files and log files are listed in the Output Window in the BUILD tab. A user can simply click on a log filename, and that file will be opened in a Text Editor for viewing errors that occurred during the build. The remaining output tabs are UPGRADE, RESULTS, and VALIDATE.

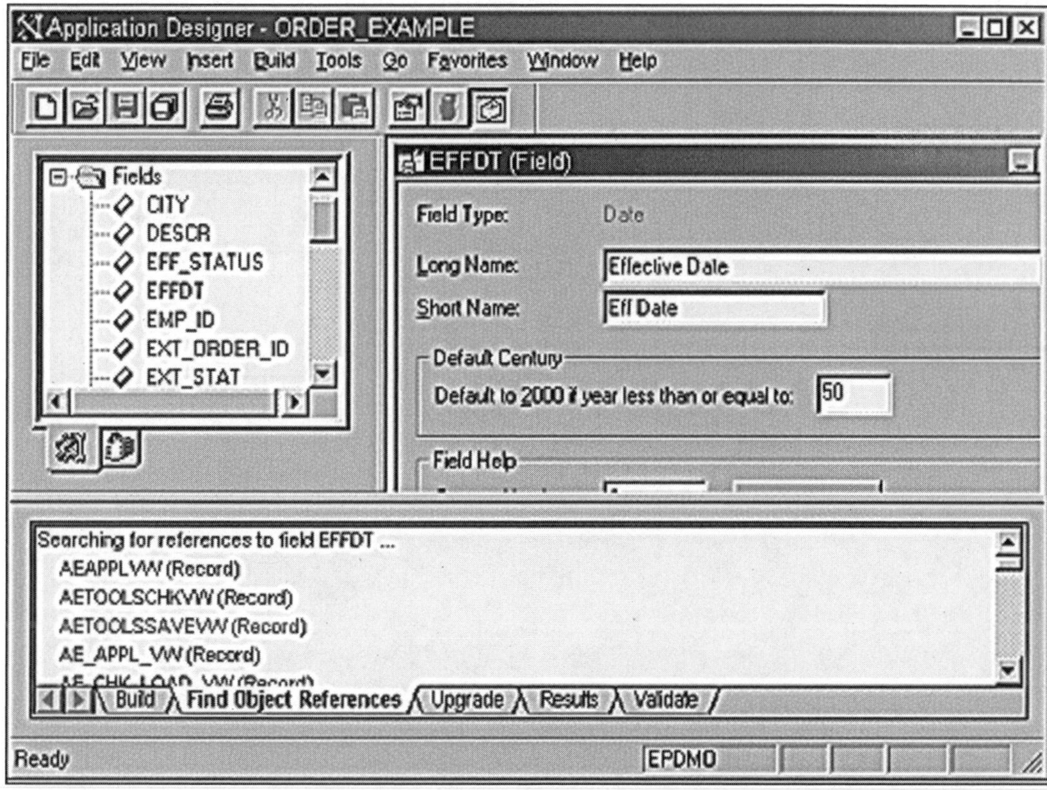

Figure 2-5 Output from FIND OBJECT REFERENCES appears in Output Window.

PART 2

Our Example Application

In this part, we will be developing a Warehouse Ordering application. This application is not intended to be a perfect solution to an inventory problem. Instead, it is a solution to a simple, fictional inventory problem, and its main goal is to teach the reader PeopleSoft. It is complicated enough to cover most of the PeopleSoft elements that the reader will need to know to develop good PeopleSoft applications. Again, the solution we are developing is not a real-world solution.

In addition, this part will go over each and every step necessary to create the application. This may seem redundant at times. But how many of us had a professor who said "Let's move on to the next example because the remaining steps in this example are obvious"? Guess what—the remaining steps are not always obvious to everyone. This book will review each step because what is obvious to one reader may not be obvious to the others. In addition, the best way to learn is sometimes through repetitiveness.

CHAPTER 3

A Warehouse Ordering Example

The fictional application we are going to develop will highlight many of the problems you will be asked to solve when you begin developing applications in the PeopleSoft environment. The Business Process we are going to create in our application consists of the following steps:

- An employee creates an internal order for material and submits it to a local warehouse.
- The warehouse personnel reserve material that is currently in inventory and create external orders for all other items.
- The external orders are forwarded to a purchasing group that will initiate a purchase order for the required material.
- On the specified date, the material is delivered to the manufacturing location entered on the original request.

Internal Order

The first step of the process requires that an employee (the requester) create an internal order for the desired material. The internal order consists of the following information:

Internal order id	Internal order identification number
Requested date	The date the requester filled out the internal order form
Requested by	The person requesting the material
Process date	The date that the material will be delivered to the requester
Process location	The location where the material will be delivered
Line number	A number (starting with 1) that is unique for each item
Material	Material requested
Quantity	Desired quantity of material (in units of measure)
Unit of measure	Unit of measurement

Figure 3-1 displays the internal order request form.

After the request form is submitted to the warehouse, all the requested items that are in inventory are reserved for the manufacturing process. The warehouse personnel will requisition any of the items that are not currently available in inventory from the Purchasing Department using an external order request. When the manufacturing process date arrives, the warehouse personnel are then required to deliver the material to the manufacturing processes location.

Throughout the entire procedure, the status of the material request must be available to the initial requester. This will be accomplished by creating a view-only panel with the fields shown in Figure 3-2.

The view-only panel contains the same fields as those on the internal

Internal Order ID: ________

Requested date: __/__/____ Process date: __/__/____

Requested by: __________ Process location: ____________

Line #	Material	Qty	Unit of Measure
__	______________		______
__	______________		______
__	______________		______
__	______________		______
__	______________		______

Figure 3-1 Internal order request form.

order form that the warehouse receives in an updatable form. The additional fields provide the following information.

- Overall status—overall status of all the material in the entire internal order.
- External order required—if an external order was required, this field will be checked.
- Line-item status—the status of the material on this line.
- Line-item promise date—the promised date for delivery of the material on this line to the warehouse.
- Line-item purchase order number—purchase order number for the material on this line.

The overall order statuses are

Internal Order ID: ________

Requested date: __/__/____ Process date: __/__/____ **Status:** ____

Requested by: ________ Process location: ____________

Line #	Material	Qty	Unit of Measure	**Ext**	**Status**	**Promise Date**	**PO #**
__	__________		______	__	_____	__/__/____	______
__	__________		______	__	_____	__/__/____	______
__	__________		______	__	_____	__/__/____	______
__	__________		______	__	_____	__/__/____	______
__	__________		______	__	_____	__/__/____	______

Figure 3-2 View-only panel with material status.

- New
- Canceled
- On order
- Ready
- Fulfilled

New is the initial status before a warehouse clerk has updated the order. *Canceled* will reflect the statuses of orders for processes that are no longer scheduled. *On order* indicates an order that currently has items to be delivered from an external supplier. *Ready* reflects orders that all the items have been reserved and the order is set to be delivered on the process date to the process location. *Fulfilled* indicates all orders that have been delivered to the process location.

The statuses for each item on the order are

- Reserved
- On order
- Fulfilled

Reserved indicates all items that are ready to be delivered to the processing location. It is set both for items that are in inventory when the order is initiated as well as for when externally ordered items have been received from the vendor and are ready to be delivered. *On order* indicates that an item is awaiting receipt from an external supplier. *Fulfilled* reflects all items that have been delivered to the process location.

External Order

The external order is placed by the warehouse clerk when the material requested by the engineer is not in stock in the warehouse. The external orders contain the following information:

External order id	The external order identification number
Requested date	The system generated date assigned when the original internal order was initiated
Required date	The date the requester needs the material
Buyer	Warehouse clerk filling out the external order
Vendor	Vendor
Line number	Line number from the original internal order
Material	Material to be purchased
Quantity	Quantity (in units of measure) of material to be purchased
Unit of measure	Unit of measurement
Status	Status of the line item being purchased
Promise date	Expected date that the material will be delivered from the vendor to the warehouse

- Purchase order # Purchase order number associated with the material being purchased

Figure 3-3 illustrates an external order.

The fields shown in bold in Figure 3-3 [the *buyer*, *vendor*, *status*, *promise date*, and *PO #* (purchase order no.)] are the fields that the purchasing group will update. This process is very similar to the internal order, except there is only one item for each external order. The *external order ID* is simply a concatenation of the *internal order ID* and the *line #* from the original request. The *vendor* is referenced from a list of "approved" vendors. The *PO #* is a reference to an actual purchase order sent to the vendor. The *promise date* is the expected delivery date.

The statuses for the item on the external order are

On order or Received

External Order ID: ________

Required date: __/__/___

Buyer: __________

Vendor:_________

Material   Qty   Unit of Measure   **Status   Promise Date   PO #**

______________   ______   ____   __/__/___   _____

Figure 3-3 External order form.

CHAPTER 4

A Relational View of the Warehouse Request Example

Now that we have a better understanding of the problem that we are going to solve, the first step is to identify all the entities, attributes, and relationships that will logically map to the Business Process. Throughout this section the terms *column* and *field* as well as *table* and *record* are used interchangeably. If you have a client/server background, you will be more familiar with the column table terminology. A big difference between the way PeopleSoft records are implemented and the way SQL implements tables is that PeopleSoft uses field definitions that exist as separate entities. This may not seem very clear now, but when we begin to create the PeopleSoft data objects, it should become evident.

The Main Tables in our Example

The two main tables we will create will be the Internal Order and the Internal Order Lines Tables. The external order information has a one-to-one relationship with internal order lines; therefore we can include its information in the Internal Order Lines Table. Both of these tables will make use of lookup tables to help ensure that the data stored in them are valid. Tables 4-1 and 4-2 show the tables and records and fields.

The Internal Order Table's *primary key* is `INT_ORDER_ID`. Each table must have a primary key in order to uniquely identify a row in the table. The field `INT_ORDER_ID` is what uniquely identifies the internal order in the Internal Order Table. The Internal Order Lines Table's primary key is a combination of its parent's primary key, `INT_ORDER_ID`, plus `LINE_NUM`. These keys allow us to uniquely identify one of the many rows that can be placed in the table. The Internal Order Table is the top-level table. The Internal Order Lines Table has a child relationship to the Internal Order Table. All this means is that for one of our child tables to exist, there must be an existing row in the parent table that it references.

TABLE 4-1

Internal Order Table

Column	Description	Data Type	Key	Valid Values
INT_ORDER_ID	Internal order id	Char(10)	X	
REQUESTED_DT	Initial date of the request	Date		=> Today
EMP_ID	Requester	Char(10)		Supervisor from the employee TBL
PROCESS_DT	Warehouse delivery date	Date		=> Today
PROCESS_LOC_ID	Delivery location	Char(10)		Location TBL
INT_STAT	Overall status	Char(1)		New
				Canceled
				On order
				Ready
				Fulfilled

TABLE 4-2

Internal Order Lines Table

Column	Description	Data Type	Key	Valid Values
INT_ORDER_ID	Internal order id	Char(10)	x	Internal order TBL
LINE_NUM	Line number	Number	x	
ITEM_ID	Material requested	Char(10)		Item TBL
QTY	Amount requested	Number		
UNIT_MEASURE	Unit of measure	Char(4)		Unit TBL
LINE_STAT	Line status	Char(3)		Reserved
				On order
				Fulfilled
EXT_ORDER	External order	Char(1)		Yes or no
EMP_ID	Buyer from purchasing	Char(10)		Buyer from employee TBL
REQUESTED_DT	Initial date of the request	Date		=> Today
VENDORID	Vendor id for supplier	Char(10)		Vendor TBL
PO_NUM	Purchase order reference	Char(10)		
PROM_DT	Promised date			=> Today
EXT_STAT	External order status	Char(3)		On order
				Received

The relationship between the Internal Order Table and the Internal Order Lines Table is one to many. This means that there can be multiple Internal Order Lines Tables for each Internal Order Table. We did not separate the external order into its own table since the requirements stated that there would only be one external order for a given internal order line. This will also give us a good example of how we can create records based on views in PeopleSoft.

The Prompt Tables (Lookup Tables) in our Example

We will now discuss the prompt tables that are required in our example. A *prompt table* is also called a *lookup table*. As discussed in Chapter 1, it is used to give the user a selection of valid choices when entering data in a field on a panel. The prompt tables we are creating will be used as lookup values for fields in the Internal Order and Internal Order Lines Tables. In the "Valid Values" column of the table descriptions for the Internal Order Table (Table 4-1) and the Internal Order Lines Table (Table 4-2), we have identified the fields that will utilize prompt tables for their data validation. Therefore, the prompt tables that we will create in our Warehouse Ordering application will be the

- Employees Table (see Table 4-3)
- Items Table (see Table 4-4)
- Locations Table (see Table 4-5)
- Vendors Table (see Table 4-6)
- Units of Measure Table (see Table 4-7)

With these tables, the concept of effective dating is introduced to our application. Refer to Chapter 1 for more information on effective dating.

TABLE 4-3

Employees Table

Column	Description	Data Type	Key	Valid Values
EMP_ID	Employee id	Char(10)	X	
EFFDT*	Effective date	Date	X	
EFF_STATUS*	Effective status	Char(1)	X	A = active; I = inactive
NAME*	Employee's name	Char(30)		
POSITION	Employee's position	Char(3)		SUP = supervisor; BUY = buyer; OTH = other
EMAIL_ADDRESS*	Employee's email address	Char(30)		

TABLE 4-4

Items Table

Column	Description	Data Type	Key	Valid Values
ITEM_ID	Item id	Char(10)	X	
EFFDT	Effective date	Date	X	
EFF_STATUS	Effective status	Char(1)	X	A = active; I = inactive
DESCR	Item description	Char(30)		

*All of these fields are delivered fields from PeopleSoft.

TABLE 4-5

Locations Table

Column	Description	Data Type	Key	Valid Values
ITEM_ID	Item id	Char(10)	X	
PROCESS_LOC_ID	Location id	Char(10)	X	
EFFDT	Effective date	Date	X	
EFF_STATUS	Effective status	Char(1)	X	A = active; I = inactive
DESCR	Location description	Char(30)		

TABLE 4-6

Vendors Table

Column	Description	Data Type	Key	Valid Values
VENDORID	Vendor id	Char(10)	X	
EFFDT	Effective date	Date	X	
EFF_STATUS	Effective status	Char(1)	X	A = active; I = inactive
VENDOR	Company name	Char(30)		
STREET1	Street	Char(30)		
STREET2	Street	Char(30)		
CITY	City	Char(20)		
STATE	State	Char(2)		

TABLE 4-7

Units of Measure Table

Column	Description	Data Type	Key	Valid Values
UNIT_MEASURE	Unit of measure	Char(4)	X	
DESCR	Unit of measure Description	Char(30)		

If you look at these new table descriptions for our lookup tables, you will notice the new columns EFFDT and EFF_STATUS. These fields enable us to maintain the data as they relate to the current date. For instance, if an employee's position were scheduled to change to *supervisor* at the beginning of the year, you could create a new record with the *position* set to SUPERVISOR, an effective date set to the beginning of the year and an effective status of ACTIVE. When the first of the year arrives, the employee's current record would automatically reflect the new position. This functionality is built into PeopleSoft. All we have to do to implement it is to include the effective date and effective status fields in our tables.

Instead of using the delivered records for these lookup tables, we are going to create our own versions for purely educational purposes.

PART 3

Creating PeopleSoft Data Objects

This part of this book has the reader actually developing the Warehouse Ordering application using PeopleSoft. All of the objects required for the Warehouse Ordering application will be created. The PeopleSoft object types that will be discussed and created in this part of the book are

- Fields
- Records
- Panels
- Panel groups
- Menus
- Menu groups
- Projects

Each chapter covers one of these object types. Each chapter begins with a definition of the object type; then, the reader will be shown how to create an object of this type. Finally, each object in our Warehouse Ordering application will be created step by step. The CD at the back of the book presents Screencam movies of the entire application being created.

We would like to emphasize once again that this book's intention is not to teach inventory solutions. Rather, it is to teach the necessary steps to create PeopleSoft applications. Therefore, the Warehouse Ordering application is not a real-world inventory solution and should not be used as one.

In addition, many of the objects we are creating already exist in PeopleSoft's Purchasing and Inventory Modules, and we are creating simplified versions purely for instructional purposes.

CHAPTER 5

Fields

Now that the Warehouse Ordering requirements have been defined, we are ready to begin developing our application. The first data objects we will explore and create are fields.

Definition of a Field

A *field* is the definition of a single entity. Name, Social Security number (SSN), and phone number can all be defined as fields. Fields are very similar to SQL column definitions. However, it is very important to understand that PeopleSoft field definitions are global objects that can be used in many different record definitions. In this context, *global* means that if you change a field's definition, those changes will effect all the records of which that field is a part. Fields are used in record definitions, where they are given additional attributes that are specific to the record. The field's record attributes are not global. They are intended only for the particular record for which they have been edited. The field record attributes will be discussed in detail in the next chapter.

Types of Fields

A PeopleSoft field can be any of the following types:

- Character*
- Long character
- Number
- Date
- Time
- Date-time
- Image

Steps in Creating Fields with PeopleSoft

This section will discuss the steps required for creating fields. There are several types of field. The initial and last steps for creating all fields are identical regardless of the type. Therefore, this section discusses the initial steps first. Again, these steps are the same for all types, so they are

---

*If a field is a character of 4 or fewer, then it can be added to the Translate Table if desired. Refer to Chapter 1 for a description of a Translate Table.

shown only once. Next, each type of field will be discussed. Finally, the last steps, which are the same for all field types, are shown. These steps are shown only once as well. Steps 1 to 4 are the initial steps regardless of type of field being created; steps 5 to 7 are the next steps for creating fields regardless of the type being created. The following steps will be taken to create our fields in the Application Designer:

1. Select FILE, NEW from the menu bar, or click on the NEW icon (displayed in Fig. 5-1).

2. The New dialog box will then appear with a list of object types (Fig. 5-2). Select FIELD and click on OK.

3. The New Field screen will appear with a list of field types (Fig. 5-3). Select the desired field type and double-click on the OK button.

Figure 5-1
NEW icon.

Figure 5-2
New dialog box with FIELD selected.

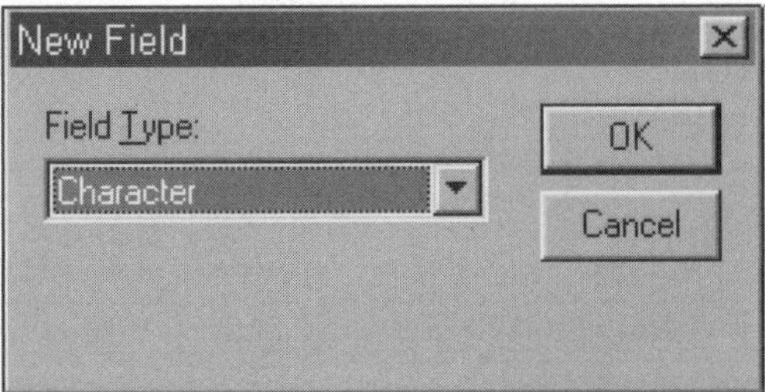

Figure 5-3
New Field dialog box.

4. Once the field type is selected, the Field Definition screen will appear in the Object Workspace (Fig. 5-4). The Field Definition screen requests the entry of such information as field length, long name, and short name. This screen will require different entries based on the field type of the new field. The following sections show the entries for each type of field.

   Character field. Figure 5-4 shows what the entries are for a new field of field type Character. Character fields require field length, long name, short name, format type, family name, display name, and field help context number.

   Long-character field. Figure 5-5 shows what the entries are for a new field of field type Long Character. Long-character fields require maximum length, raw binary, long name, short name, and field help context number.

   Number field. Figure 5-6 shows what the entries are for a new field of field type Number. Number fields allow entry of integer positions, decimal positions, long name, short name, and field help context number. If the number field is to be a signed field, the Signed box must be checked.

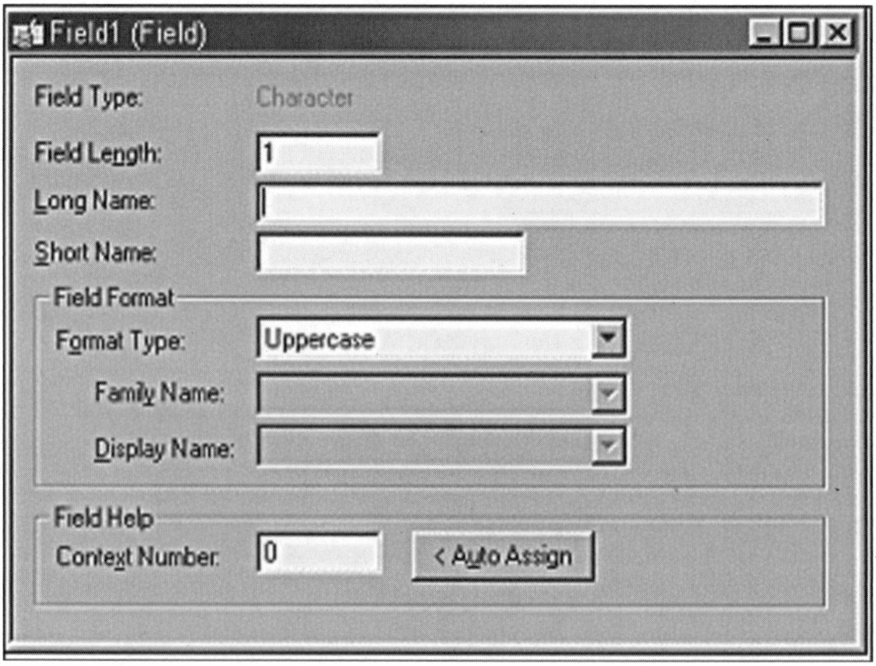

Figure 5-4
Character field definition.

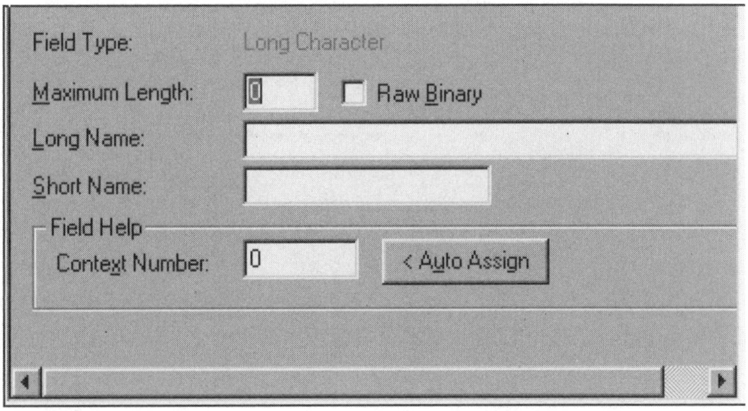

Figure 5-5
Long-character field definition.

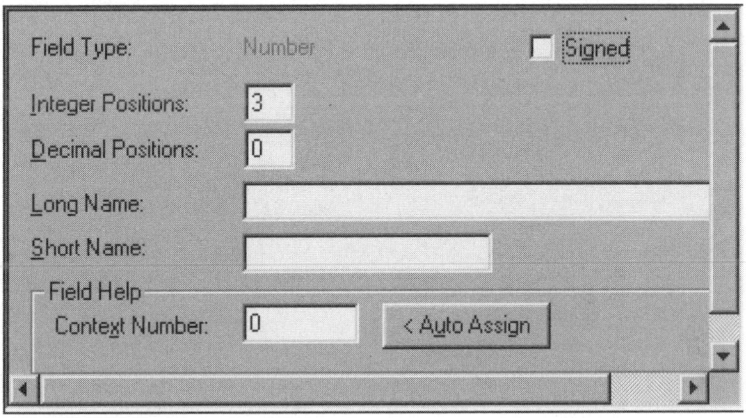

Figure 5-6
Number field definition.

Date field. Figure 5-7 shows what the entries are for a new field of field type Date. Date fields allow entry of long name, short name, default century, and field help context number.

Time field. Figure 5-8 shows what the entries are for a new field of field type Time. Time fields allow entry of long name, short name, time formatting, and field help context number.

Date-time field. Figure 5-9 shows what the entries are for a new field of field type Datetime. Date-time fields allow entry of long name, short name, default century, time formatting, and field help context number.

Figure 5-7
Date field definition.

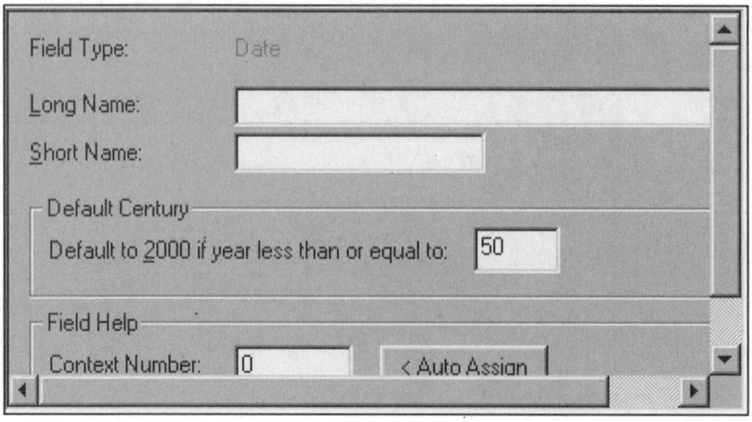

Figure 5-8
Time field definition.

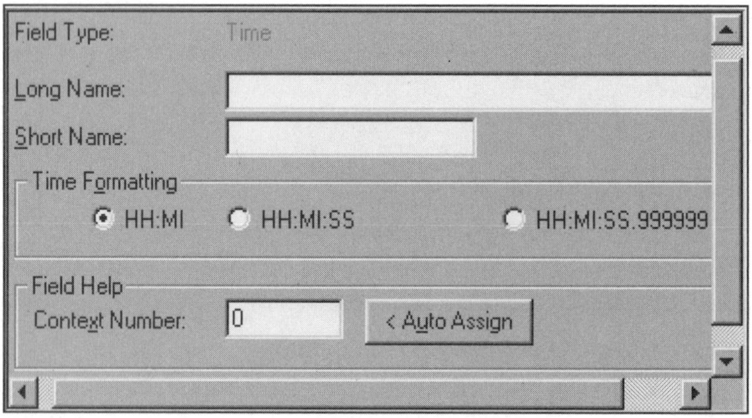

Figure 5-9
Date-time field definition.

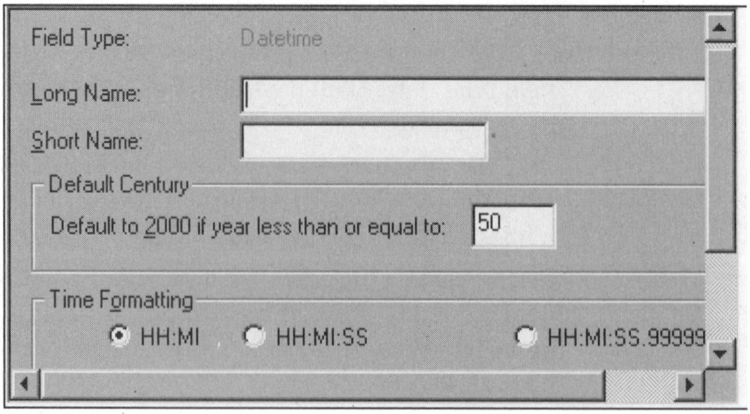

Image field. Figure 5-10 shows what the entries are for a new field of field type Image. Image fields allow entry of maximum length, image format, long name, short name, and field help context number.

5. Regardless of what type of field you selected in step 3 above, the next step is to select FILE, OBJECT PROPERTIES, or you could select the OBJECT PROPERTIES icon (Fig. 5-11) from the toolbar. Once the OBJECT PROPERTIES icon is selected, the GENERAL tab will be displayed to allow you to enter comments (Fig. 5-12).
6. To enter a translate value for character fields which are four characters or fewer, select the TRANSLATE tab of FILE, OBJECT PROPERTIES. Translate values can be added, changed, or deleted (Fig. 5-13)
7. Finally, select FILE, SAVE AS to save the new field. [You could also select the SAVE AS icon (Fig. 5-14) from the toolbar to save only the current object. If you select the SAVE ALL icon (Fig. 5-15), the Application Designer will save all objects that have changes.] If you had made changes and then attempted to exit without saving your changes, you will be prompted with a dialog to indicate whether you want to save your changes (Fig. 5-16).

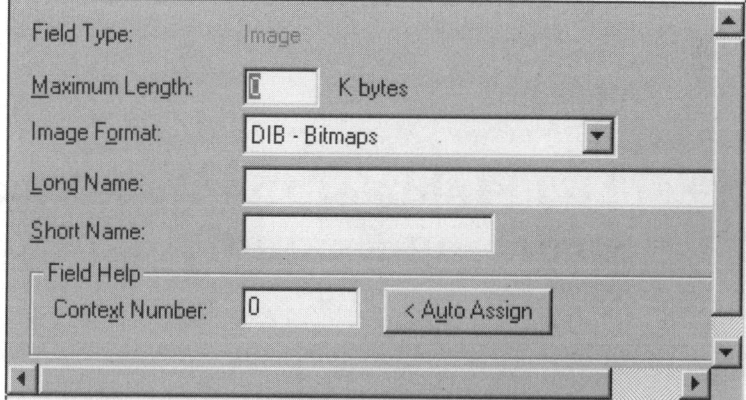

Figure 5-10
Image field definition.

Figure 5-11
OBJECT PROPERTIES icon.

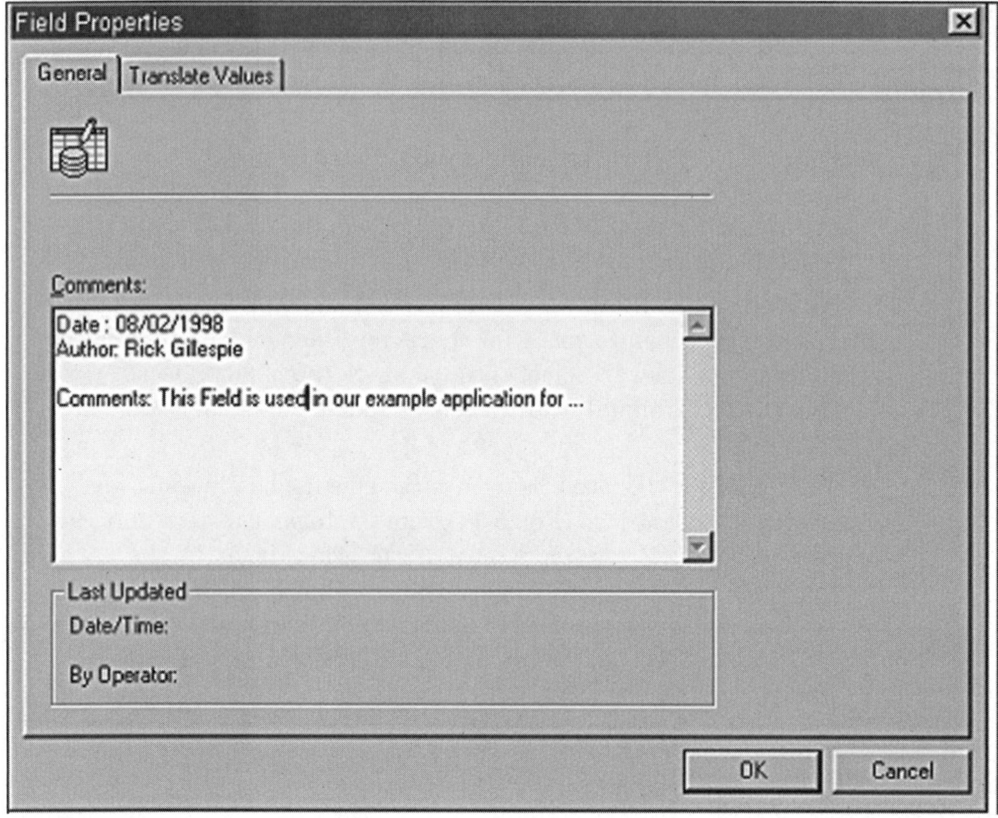

Figure 5-12 GENERAL tab of the Field Properties dialog box.

The Fields of the Warehouse Ordering Example

The rest of this chapter is devoted to the creation of the fields needed to develop our example application. With the use of screen captures, you will be shown the steps required to create the field definitions. When we implement a new feature, a detailed explanation will be given.

The field definitions that we are going to create are

- INT_ORDER_ID
- REQUESTED_DT
- EMP_ID

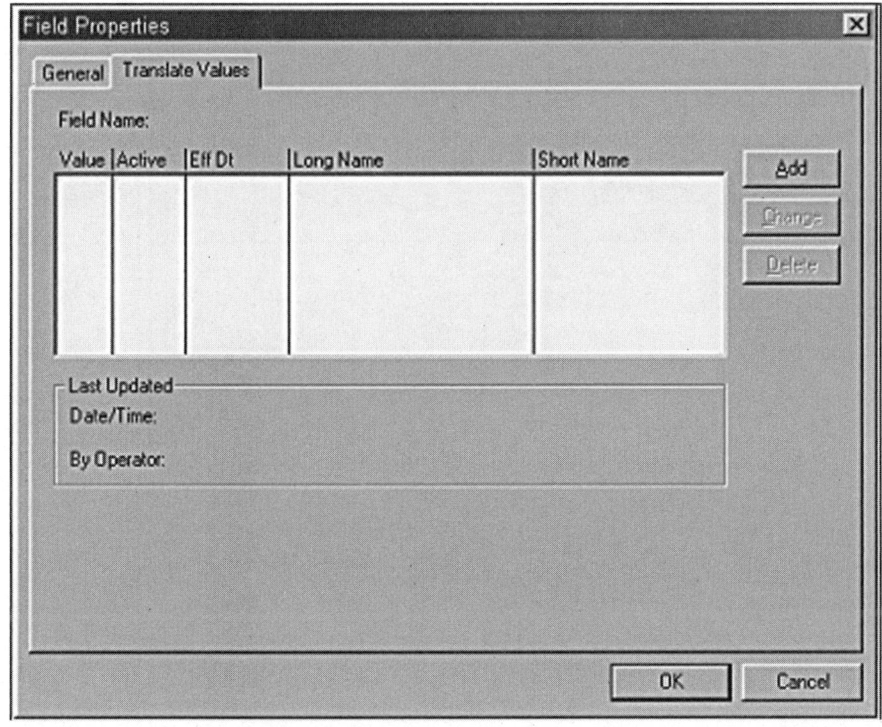

Figure 5-13 TRANSLATE VALUES tab of Field Properties dialog box.

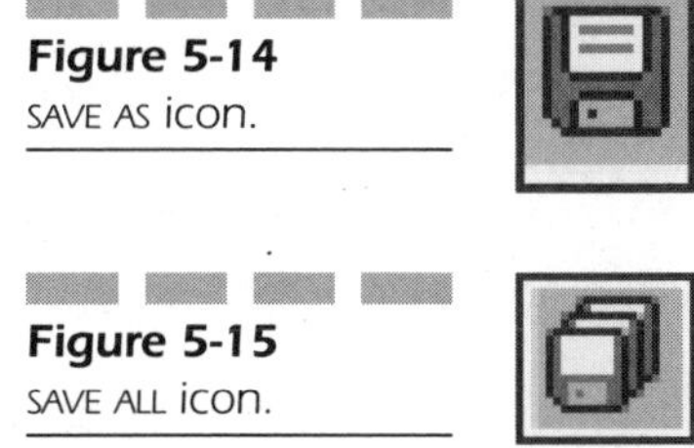

Figure 5-14
SAVE AS icon.

Figure 5-15
SAVE ALL icon.

Figure 5-16
Save Changes dialog box.

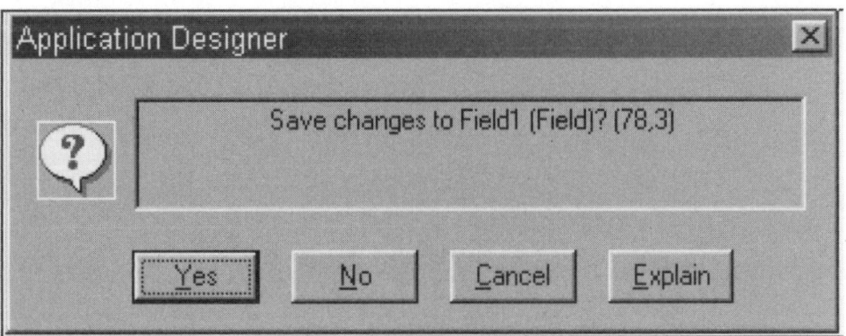

- PROCESS_DT
- PROCESS_LOC_ID
- LINE_NUM
- LINE_STAT
- INT_STAT
- UNIT_MEASURE
- ITEM_ID
- EXT_ORDER
- EXT_STAT
- POSITION
- VENDORID
- VENDOR
- PO_NUM
- PROM_DT

The remaining fields needed in our application will be PeopleSoft delivered fields. The PeopleSoft delivered fields that will be used follow:

- NAME
- EFF_STATUS
- EFFDT
- EMAIL_ADDRESS
- DESCR
- STREET1
- STREET2
- CITY
- STATE
- QTY

Getting Started by Creating a Project

Before we start creating our fields, let's first open a new project and save it as ORDER_EXAMPLE. This project is where we will group all the objects we are going to create or utilize. To create the new project, choose FILE, NEW from the menu or select the NEW icon (Fig. 5-1) from the toolbar. When the new dialog box is displayed, select PROJECT. An empty "untitled" project icon should now be in the Project Workspace as shown in Figure 5-17.

To save the project, select FILE, SAVE PROJECT AS as shown in Figure 5-18.

A Save dialog box will now prompt you for the project's name as shown in Figure 5-19.

Type `ORDER_EXAMPLE`, then press OK. You should now see that the "untitled" project icon now shows `ORDER_EXAMPLE`.

Figure 5-17
PROJECT icon.

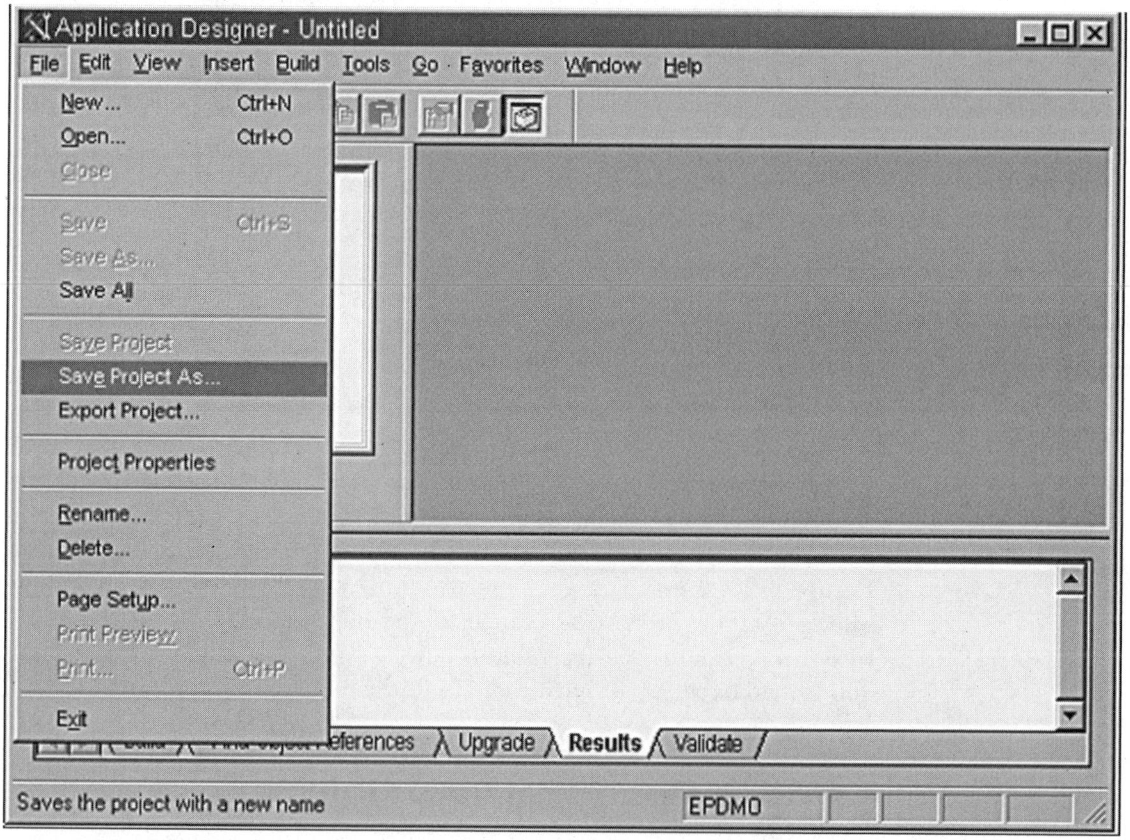

Figure 5-18 Illustration showing how to select FILE, SAVE PROJECT AS.

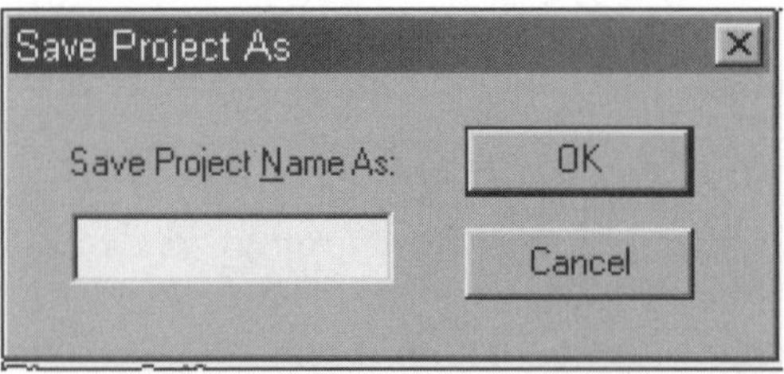

Figure 5-19
Save Project As dialog box.

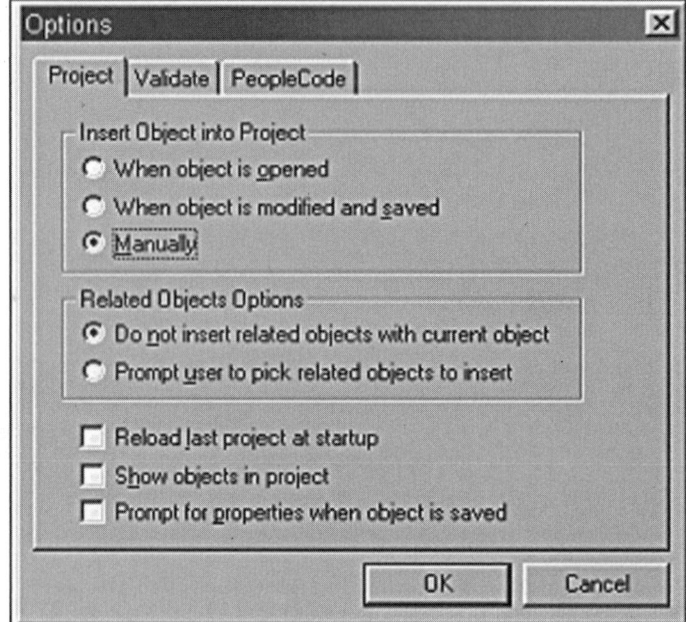

Figure 5-20
Project options.

The last thing we need to do before we start adding objects to our project is to check the Projects setting. Select TOOLS, OPTIONS from the menu bar. This is where we define how objects will be added to the project. Figure 5-20 shows the settings we shall use for this project. I have selected MANUAL INSERTION of objects and have requested that the application not prompt me for related objects. These settings are personal. You should experiment with them to find which options you prefer.

Creating Our Warehouse Objects

Finally, we are ready to start creating the objects needed for the Warehouse Ordering example presented previously.

`INT_ORDER_ID` Follow the steps below in order to create the internal order id field. This field is named INT_ORDER_ID.

1. Select FILE, NEW from the menu bar or select the NEW icon from the toolbar. The New screen will then appear with a list of object types. Select FIELD and click on OK
2. The New Field screen will appear with a list of field types. Select CHARACTER.
3. Set the following information in the Field dialog box as shown in Figure 5-21:
   - Set the field length to 10.
   - Set the long name to INTERNAL ORDER ID.
   - Set the short name to INTERNAL ORD ID.
   - Set the format type to UPPERCASE.
4. Now select FILE, OBJECT PROPERTIES (or the OBJECT PROPERTIES icon from the toolbar). The GENERAL tab will appear. Enter in the comments as shown in Figure 5-22. Click the OK button when finished entering the comments.
5. This is the first object that we are going to save. If you select the SAVE ALL icon (Figure 5-23), the Application Designer will save all

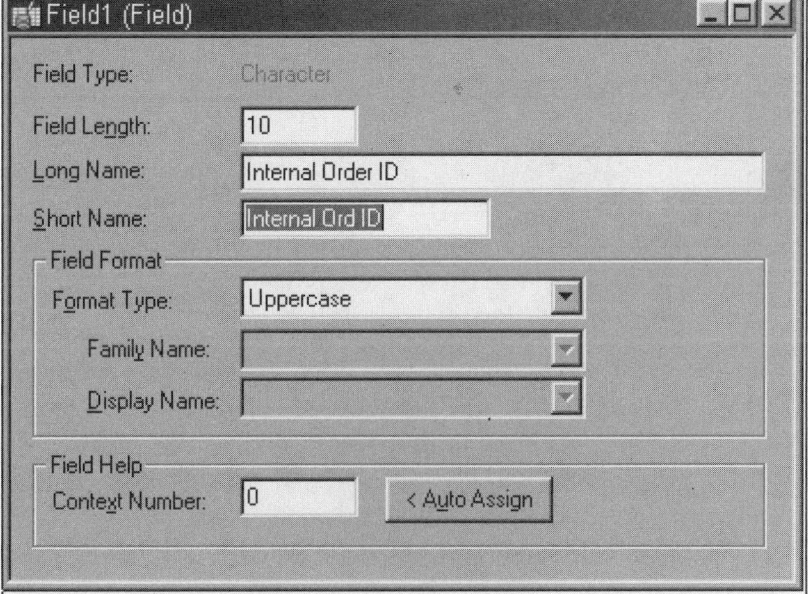

Figure 5-21 Field dialog box for our internal order id field.

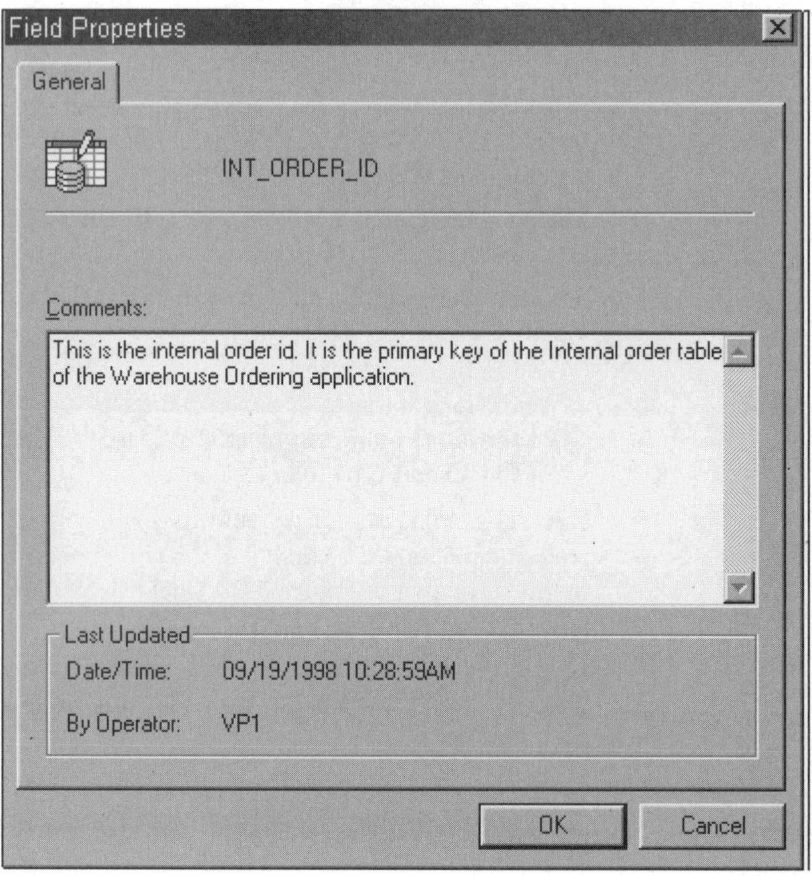

Figure 5-22 Adding comments on the GENERAL tab of the Object Properties dialog box for the new field.

Figure 5-23 SAVE ALL icon.

objects that have changes. It is a good idea to use SAVE ALL just to be on the safe side. Save the field as `INT_ORDER_ID`.

6. Because the Projects options were set to MANUAL INSERTION, we now need to insert the field into the project. Select INSERT, CURRENT OBJECT INTO PROJECT, or push F7. A Fields folder should now be displayed under the PROJECT icon in the Project Workspace. If you expand the folder, the field `INT_ORDER_ID` should be displayed.

REQUESTED_DT To create the initial date of request field (REQUESTED_DT), perform the following steps:

1. Select FILE, NEW from the menu bar, and the New screen will then appear with a list of object types. Select FIELD and click on OK.
2. The New Field screen will appear with a list of field types. Select DATE.
3. Set the following information in the Field dialog box as shown in Figure 5-24.
   - Set the long name to DATE REQUESTED.
   - Set the short name to DATE REQUESTED. (Note that it is okay for the long name and short name to be the same.)
   - Set DEFAULT TO 2000 if year is less than or equal to 50. Enter 50 in the Set Default to 2000 if year less than or an equal to edit box. If a user enters a two-digit year and the value is less than 50 then the century is set to 2000. This value can be changed for fields requiring different logic.
4. Select FILE, OBJECT PROPERTIES (or the OBJECT PROPERTIES icon from the toolbar), and the GENERAL tab of the Object Properties dialog box will appear. Enter the comments shown in Figure 5-25 and click the OK button when finished.
5. Save the field as REQUESTED_DT.
6. Because the Projects options were set to MANUAL INSERTION, we now need to insert the field into the project. Select INSERT, CURRENT OBJECT INTO PROJECT, or push F7.

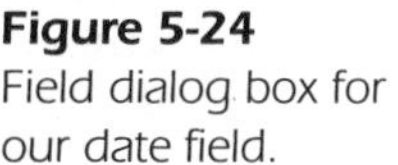

Figure 5-24
Field dialog box for our date field.

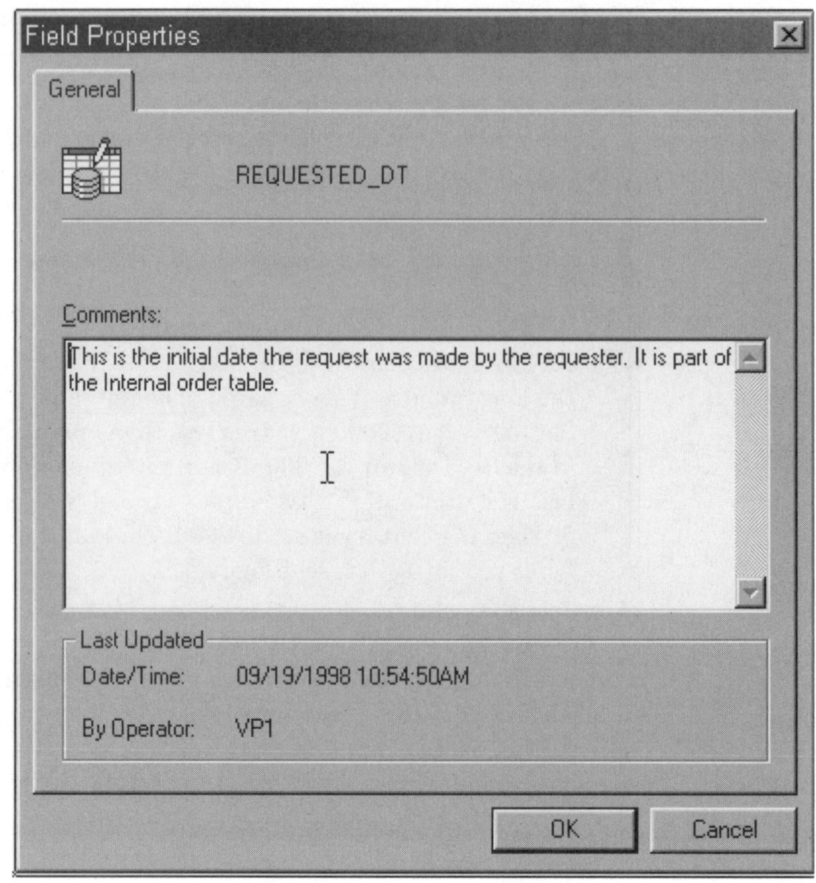

Figure 5-25
Enter comments for the REQUESTED_DT field on the GENERAL tab of the Object Properties dialog box.

EMP_ID To create the employee id field (EMP_ID), perform the following steps:

1. Select FILE, NEW from the menu bar. (You could also select the NEW icon from the toolbar.) The New screen will then appear with a list of object types. Select FIELD and click on OK.
2. The New Field screen will appear with a list of field types. Select CHARACTER.
3. Fill in the information displayed in Figure 5-26.
   - Set the field length to 9.
   - Set the long name to EMPLOYEE ID.
   - Set the short name to EMPLOYEE ID.

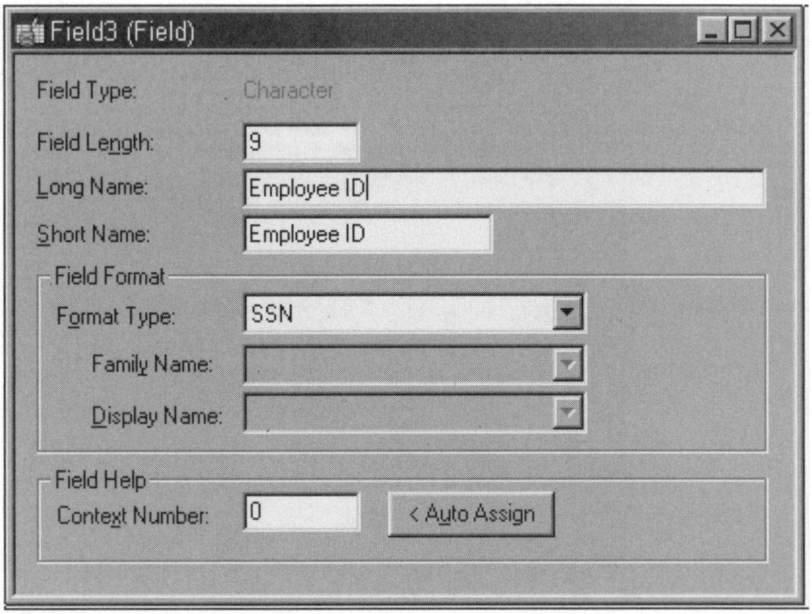

Figure 5-26 Field dialog box for employee id.

- Set format type to SSN.

  We are going to be using the Social Security number as the employee's ID. Please note that in the field definition that we have selected the SSN format. This will force a ###-##-#### format on the employee id field when it is displayed.

4. Select FILE, OBJECT PROPERTIES to get to the GENERAL tab of the Object Properties dialog box. Enter the comments shown in Figure 5-27 and click OK once all comments are entered.
5. Save the field as `EMP_ID`.
6. Manually insert the field into the project. Select INSERT, CURRENT OBJECT INTO PROJECT, or push F7.

PROCESS_DT Follow the steps below in order to create the warehouse delivery date field, named `PROCESS_DT`.

1. Select FILE, NEW from the menu bar. (You could also select the NEW icon from the toolbar.) The New screen will then appear with a list of object types. Select FIELD and click on OK.
2. The New Field screen will appear with a list of field types. Select DATE.

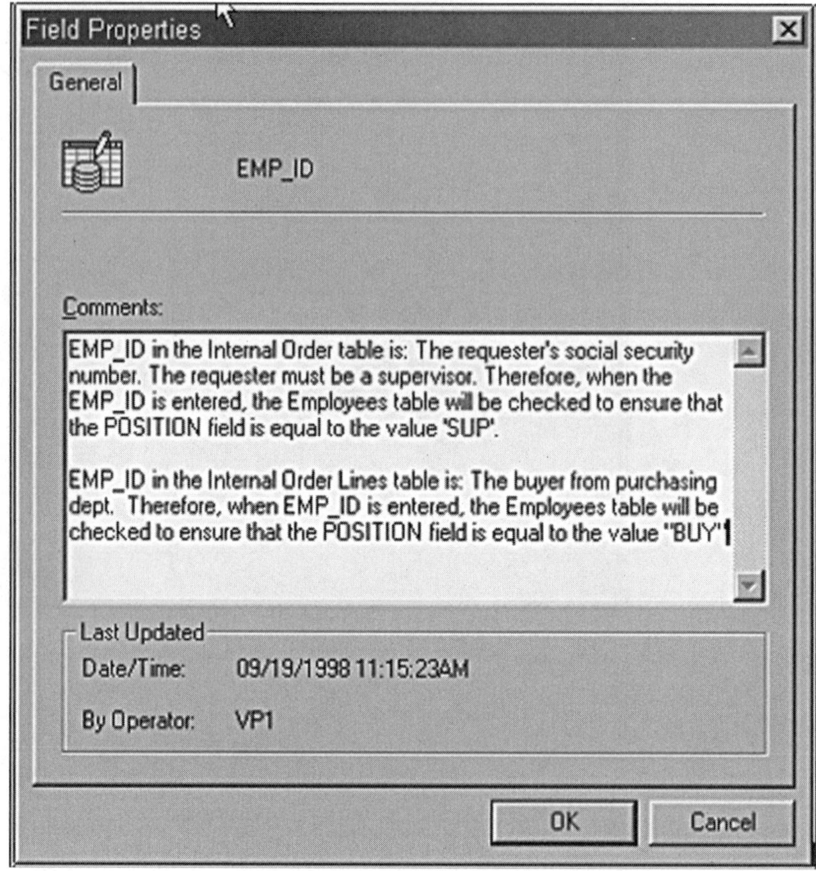

Figure 5-27 Enter comments for the EMP_ID field on the GENERAL tab of the Object Properties dialog box.

3. Set the following information as displayed in Figure 5-28:
   - Set the long name to PROCESS DATE.
   - Set the short name to PROCESS DATE.
   - Set the DEFAULT TO 2000 if year less than or equal to 50.

4. Select FILE, OBJECT PROPERTIES to bring up the GENERAL tab of the Object Properties dialog box. Enter the comments shown in Figure 5-29 and click OK once all comments are entered.
5. Save the field as PROCESS_DT.
6. Because the Projects options were set to MANUAL INSERTION, we now need to insert the field into the project. Select INSERT, CURRENT OBJECT INTO PROJECT, or push F7.

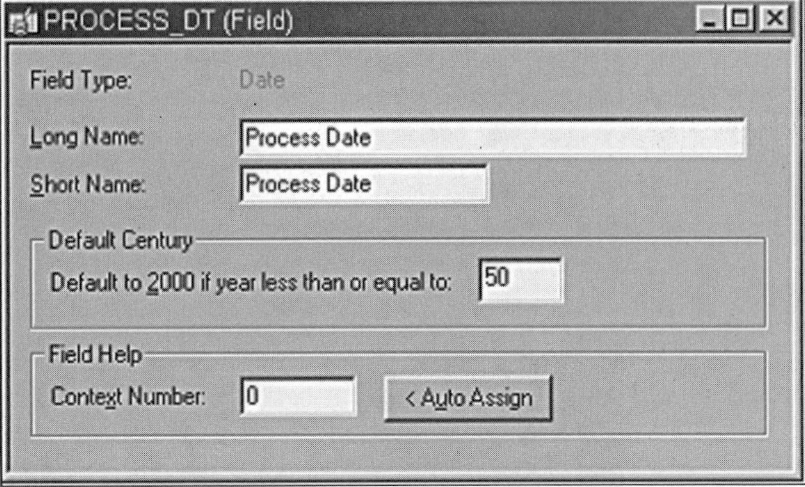

Figure 5-28
Field Dialog box for process date.

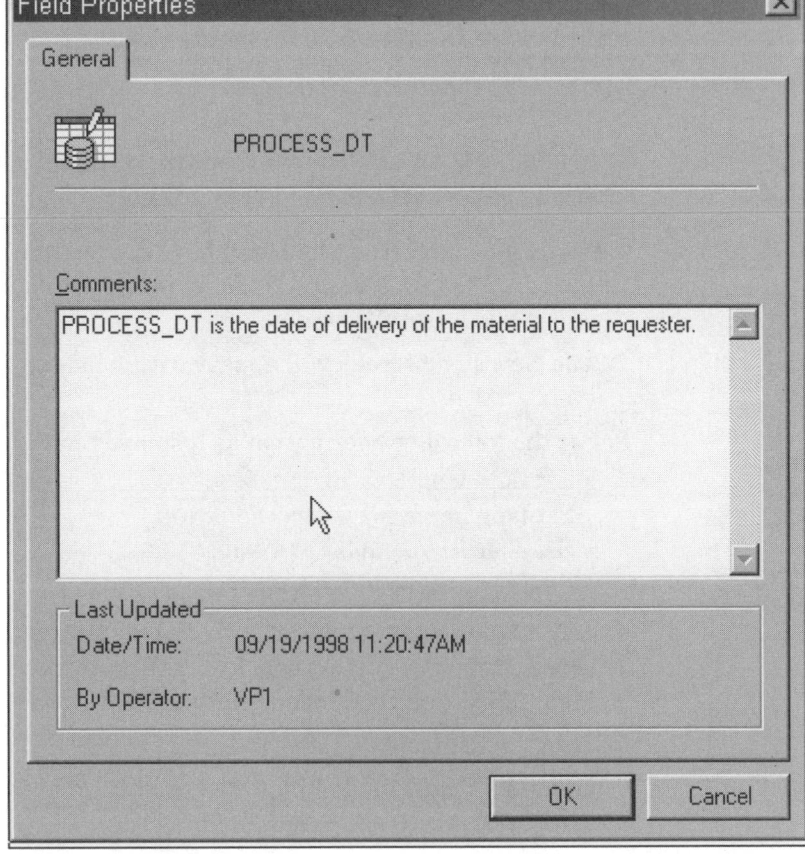

Figure 5-29
Enter comments for the `PROCESS_DT` field on the GENERAL tab of the Object Properties dialog box.

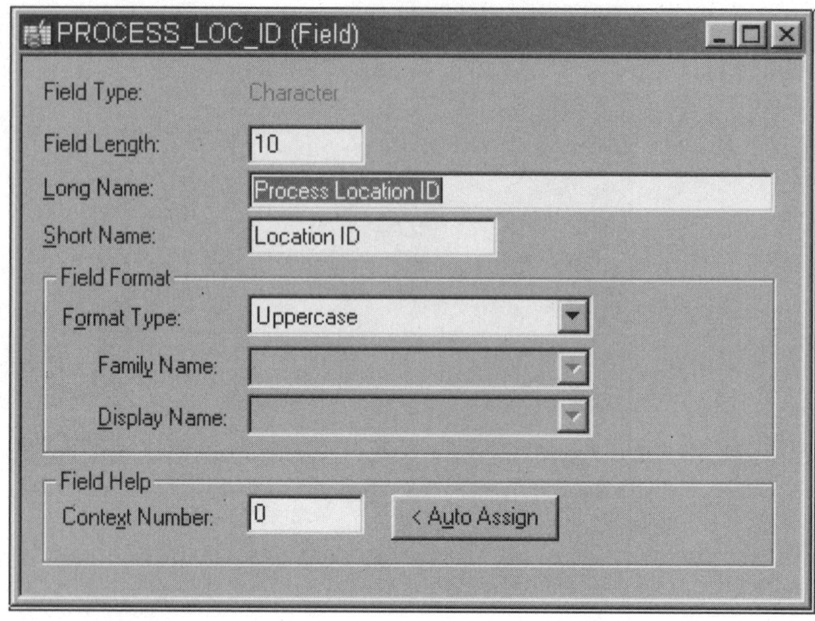

Figure 5-30
Field dialog box for process location id.

PROCESS_LOC_ID Follow the steps below in order to create the process location field, which is named PROCESS_LOC_ID.

1. Select FILE, NEW from the menu bar, or select the NEW icon from the toolbar. The NEW screen will then appear with a list of object types. Select FIELD and click on OK.
2. The New Field screen will appear with a list of field types. Select CHARACTER.
3. Set the following information as displayed in Figure 5-30.
   - Set field length to 10.
   - Set long name to PROCESS LOCATION.
   - Set short name to LOCATION ID.
   - Set format type to UPPERCASE.
4. Select FILE, OBJECT PROPERTIES to display the GENERAL tab of the Object Properties dialog box. Enter the comments shown in Figure 5-31 and click OK once all comments are entered.
5. Save the field as PROCESS_LOC_ID.
6. Manually insert the field into the project by selecting INSERT, CURRENT OBJECT INTO PROJECT or pushing F7.

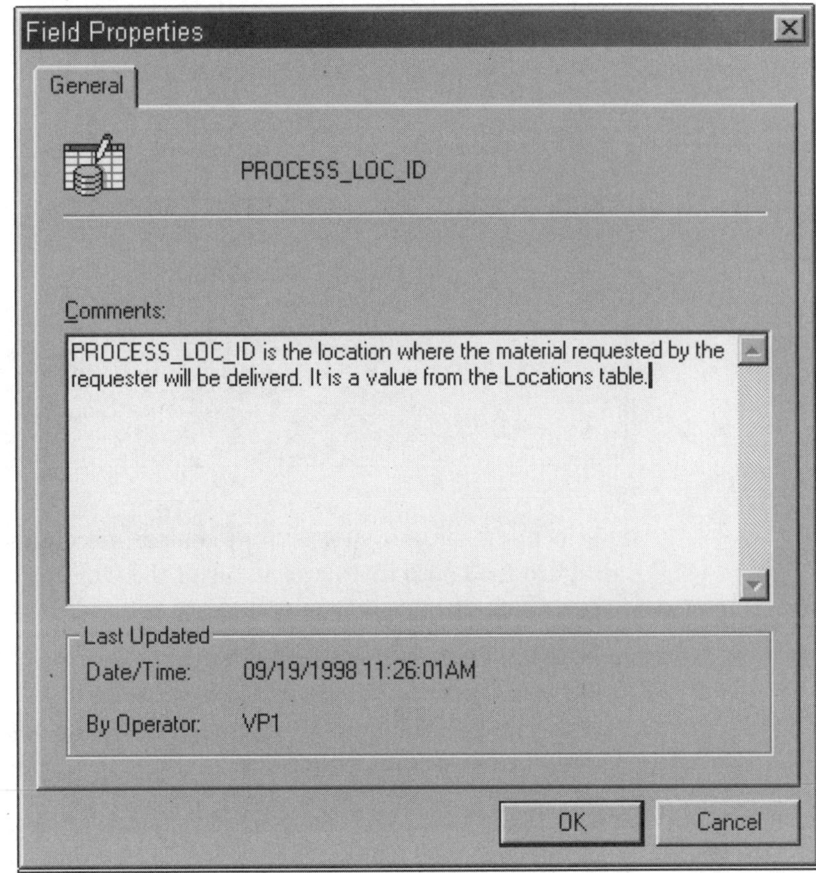

Figure 5-31 Enter comments for the PROCESS_LOC_ID field on the GENERAL tab of the Object Properties dialog box.

LINE_NUM Complete the following steps in order to create the line number field (LINE_NUM):

1. Select FILE, NEW from the menu bar. (You could also select the NEW icon from the toolbar.) The New screen will then appear with a list of object types. Select FIELD and click on OK.
2. The New Field screen will appear with a list of field types. Select NUMBER.
3. Set the following information as displayed in Figure 5-32.
   - Set the integer positions to 3.
   - Set the decimal positions to 0.
   - Set the long name to INTERNAL ORDER LINE NUMBER.
   - Set the short name to LINE #.

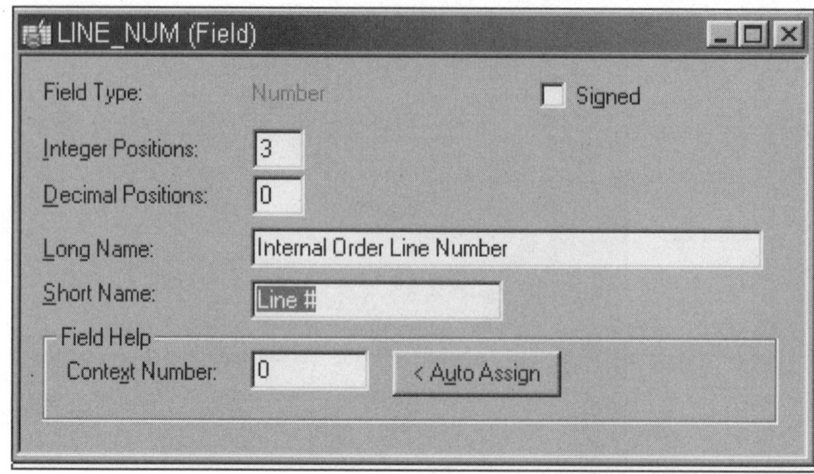

Figure 5-32 Field dialog box for Internal Order Line Number.

4. Select FILE, OBJECT PROPERTIES to enter the comments shown in Figure 5-33 onto the GENERAL tab of the Object Properties dialog box. Click OK once all comments are entered.
5. Save the field as LINE_NUM.
6. Because the Projects options were set to MANUAL INSERTION, we now need to insert the field into the project. Select INSERT, CURRENT OBJECT INTO PROJECT or push F7.

LINE_STAT Complete the following steps in order to create the line status field (LINE_STAT):

1. Select FILE, NEW from the menu bar. (You could also select the NEW icon from the toolbar.) The New screen will then appear with a list of object types. Select FIELD and click on OK.
2. The New Field screen will appear with a list of field types. Select CHARACTER.
3. Set the following information as displayed in Figure 5-34:
   - Set field length to 3.
   - Set long name to INTERNAL ORDER LINE STATUS.
   - Set short name to LINE STATUS.
   - Set format type to UPPERCASE.
4. This is the first field that uses *translate values*. From the requirements, we know that the valid values, for the line status field, are
   - Reserved
   - On order

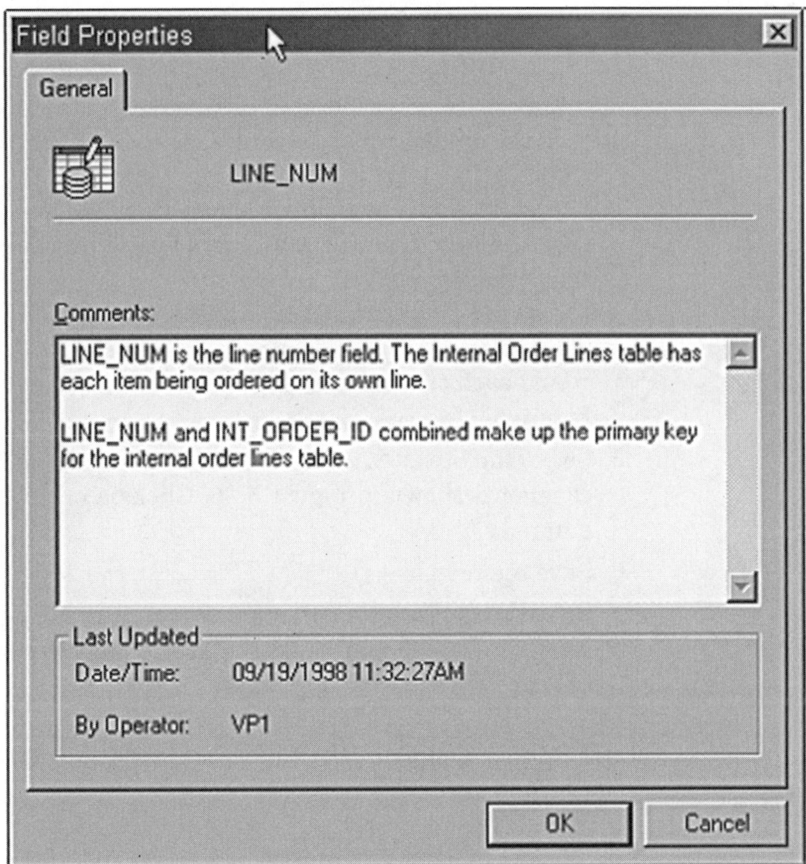

Figure 5-33
Enter comments for the `LINE_NUM` field on the GENERAL tab of the Object Properties dialog box.

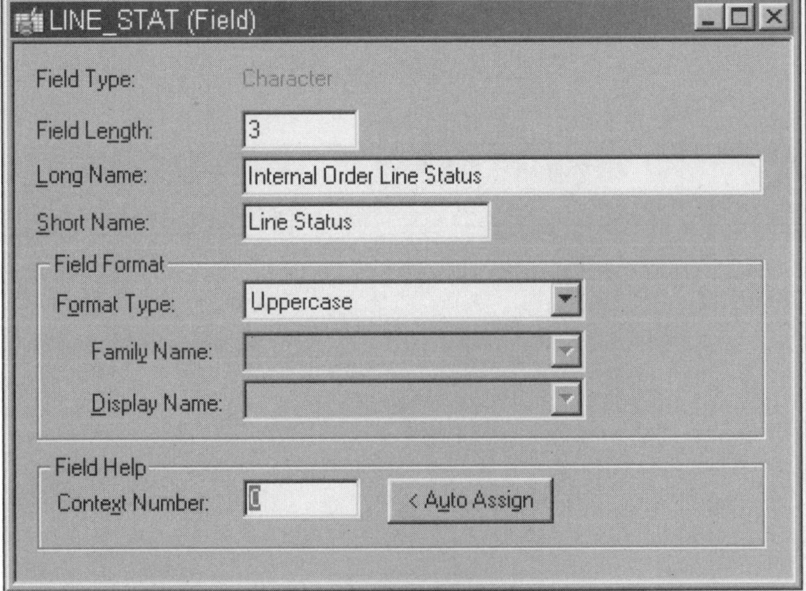

Figure 5-34
Field dialog box for line status.

- Fulfilled

  To set up the translate values, select FILE, OBJECT PROPERTIES, ALT ENTER, or the PROPERTIES icon (Fig. 5-35) from the toolbar. The TRANSLATE tab is available because this field is a character data type and less than five characters long. From the TRANSLATE tab, select the ADD button.

  Figure 5-36 illustrates an example of an Add Translate Table Value dialog box.

  Add each of the `LINE_STAT` translate values illustrated in Figure 5-37.

5. Select the GENERAL tab of the Object Properties dialog and enter all comments shown in Figure 5-38. Click OK once all comments are entered.
6. Save the field as `LINE_STAT`.
7. Because the Projects options were set to MANUAL INSERTION, we now need to insert the field into the project. Select INSERT, CURRENT OBJECT INTO PROJECT, or push F7.

`INT_STAT` Complete the following steps to create the internal order status field (`INT_STAT`):

Figure 5-35
PROPERTIES icon.

Figure 5-36
Add Translate Table Value dialog box.

Add Translate Table Value

Field Name: LINE_STAT

Field Value:

Effective Date: 11/17/1998 Inactive

Long Name:

Short Name:

OK Cancel

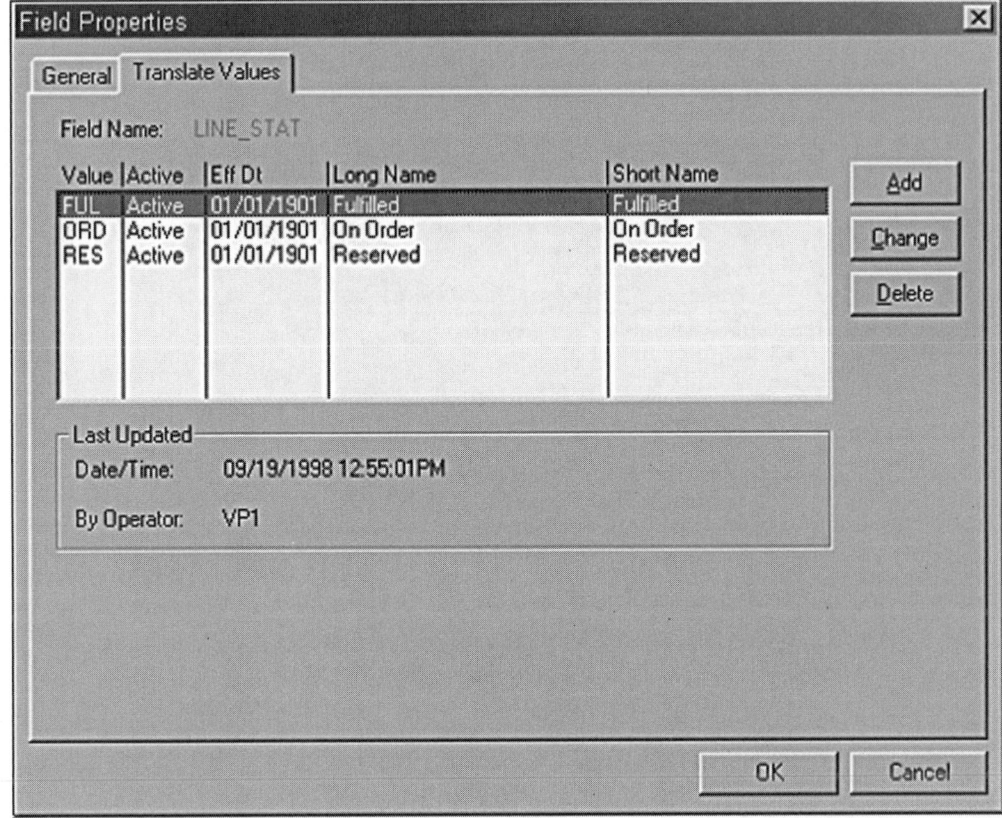

Figure 5-37 FIELD PROPERTIES TRANSLATE VALUES tab.

1. Select FILE, NEW from the menu bar. (You could also select the NEW icon from the tool bar.) The New screen will then appear with a list of object types. Select FIELD and click on OK.
2. The New Field screen will appear with a list of field types. Select CHARACTER.
3. Set the following information as displayed in Figure 5-39.
   - Set the field length to 3.
   - Set the long name to INTERNAL ORDER STATUS.
   - Set the short name to INT ORD STATUS.
   - Set the format type to UPPERCASE.

   From the requirements, we know that the valid values (*translate values*), for this field, are

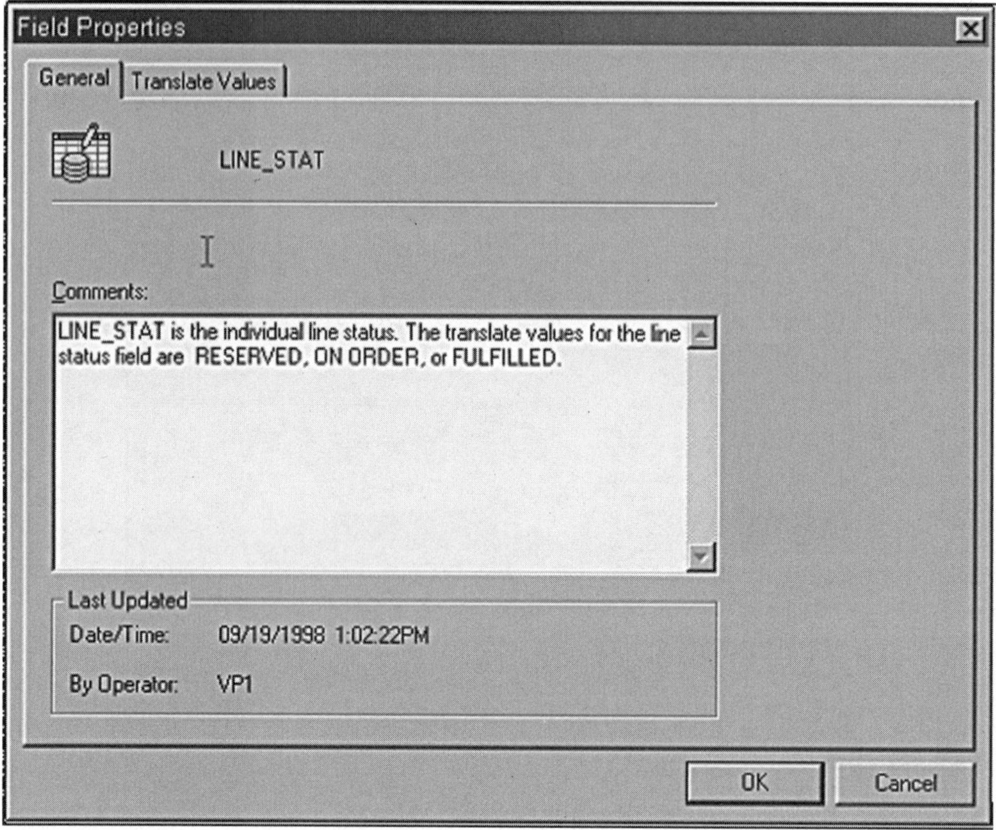

Figure 5-38 Enter comments for the `LINE_STAT` field on the GENERAL tab of the Object Properties dialog box.

- New
- On order
- Canceled
- Ready
- Fulfilled

4. To set up the translate values, select FILE, OBJECT PROPERTIES, ALT ENTER, or the PROPERTIES icon from the toolbar (Fig. 5-40). On the TRANSLATE tab, which is available because this field is a character data type and fewer than five characters long, ADD the translate values that are illustrated in Figure 5-41.

Figure 5-39 Field dialog box for our internal order status field.

Figure 5-40 PROPERTIES icon.

5. Click on the GENERAL tab of the Object Properties dialog and enter comments shown in Figure 5-42. Once all comments are entered, click on OK.
6. Save the field as `INT_STAT`.
7. Because the Projects options were set to MANUAL INSERTION, we now need to insert the field into the project. Select INSERT, CURRENT OBJECT INTO PROJECT, or push F7.

UNIT_MEASURE Complete the following steps in order to create the unit of measure field (`UNIT_MEASURE`):

1. Select FILE, NEW from the menu bar. (You could also select the NEW icon from the toolbar.) The New screen will then appear with a list of object types. Select FIELD and click on OK.

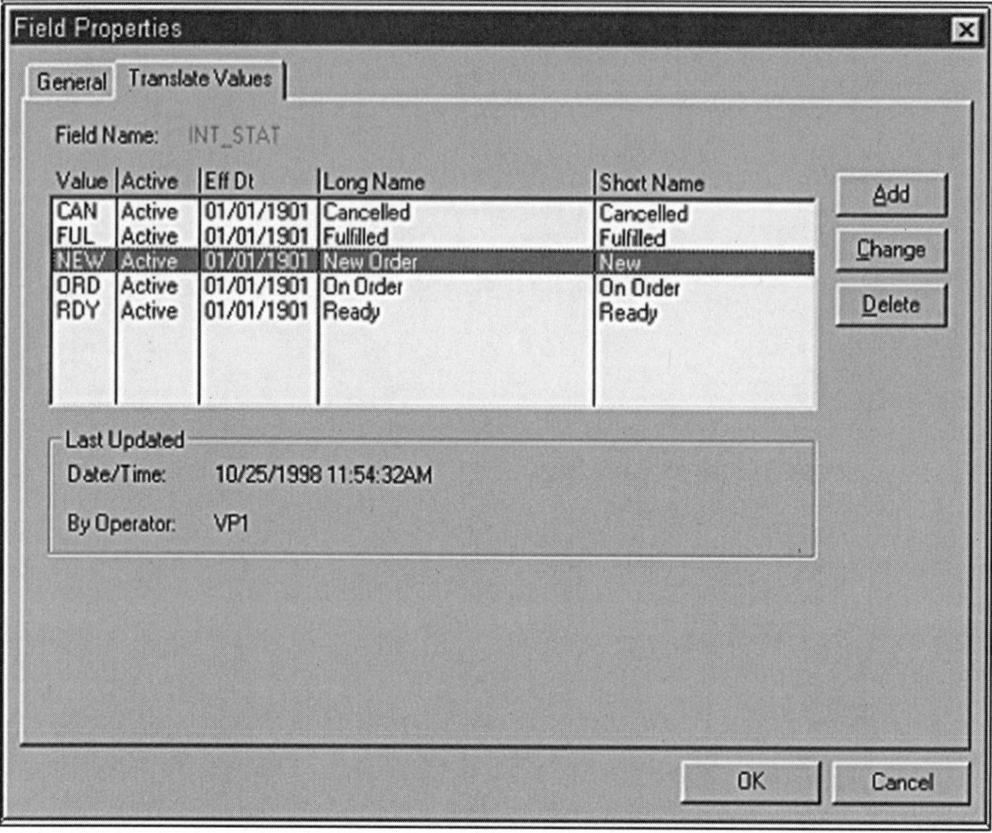

Figure 5-41 Internal order status translate values.

2. The New Field screen will appear with a list of field types. Select CHARACTER.
3. Set the following information as displayed in Figure 5-43:
   - Set the field length to 4.
   - Set the long name to UNIT OF MEASURE.
   - Set the short name to UNIT.
   - Set the format type to UPPERCASE.
4. Select FILE, OBJECT PROPERTIES to get to the GENERAL tab of the Object Properties dialog box. Enter the comments shown in Figure 5-44 and click OK when the comments are complete.
5. Save the field as `UNIT_MEASURE`.

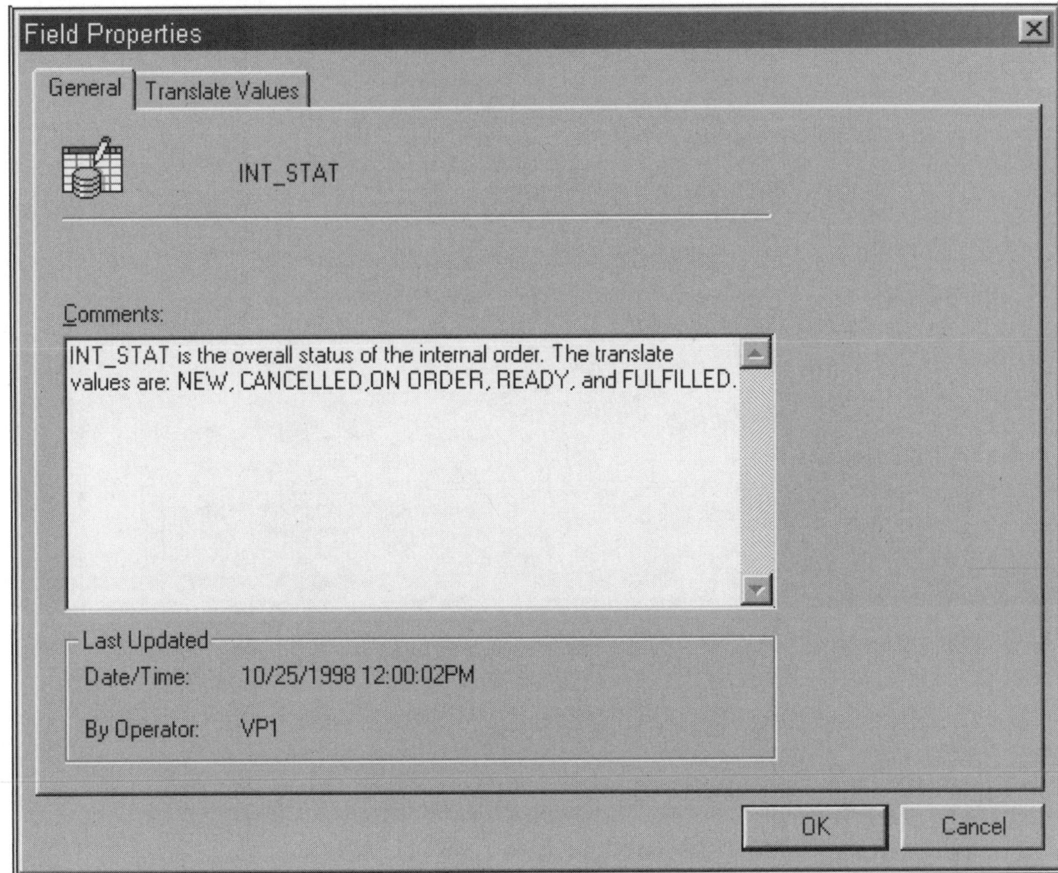

Figure 5-42 Enter comments for the INT_STAT field on the GENERAL tab of the Object Properties dialog box.

6. Manually insert the field into the project by selecting INSERT, CURRENT OBJECT INTO PROJECT or pushing F7.

ITEM_ID Complete the following steps to create the Item id field (ITEM_ID):

1. Select FILE, NEW from the menu bar. (You could also select the NEW icon from the toolbar.) The New screen will then appear with a list of object types. Select FIELD and click on OK.

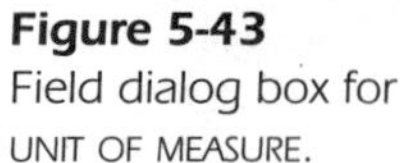

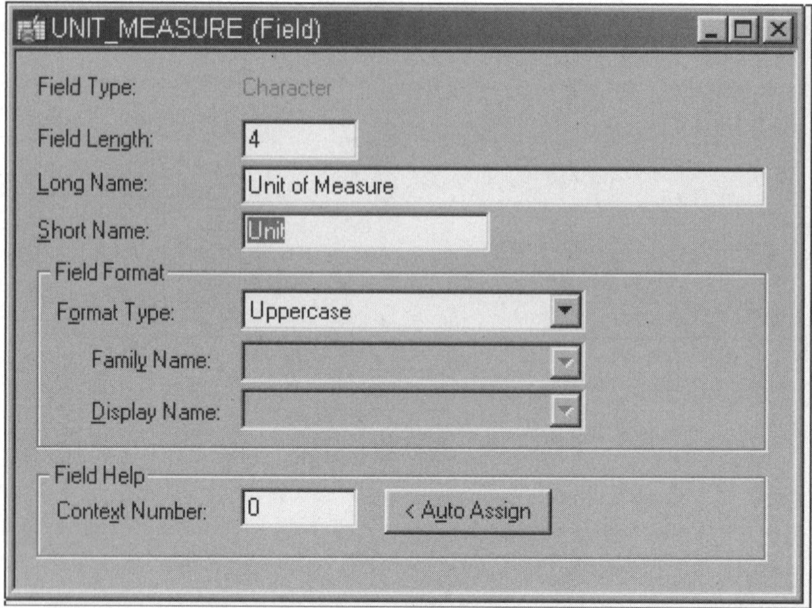

Figure 5-43 Field dialog box for UNIT OF MEASURE.

2. The New Field screen will appear with a list of field types. Select CHARACTER.
3. Set the following information as displayed in Figure 5-45.
   - Set the field length to 10.
   - Set the long name to ITEM ID.
   - Set the short name to ITEM ID.
   - Set the format type to UPPERCASE.
4. Select FILE, OBJECT PROPERTIES and enter the comments shown in Figure 5-46 onto the GENERAL tab. Once all comments are entered, click OK.
5. Save the field as `ITEM_ID`.
6. Because the Projects options were set to MANUAL INSERTION, we now need to insert the field into the project. Select INSERT, CURRENT OBJECT INTO PROJECT, or push F7.

EXT_ORDER Complete the following steps in order to create the external order field (`EXT_ORDER`):

1. Select FILE, NEW from the menu bar, or select the NEW icon from the

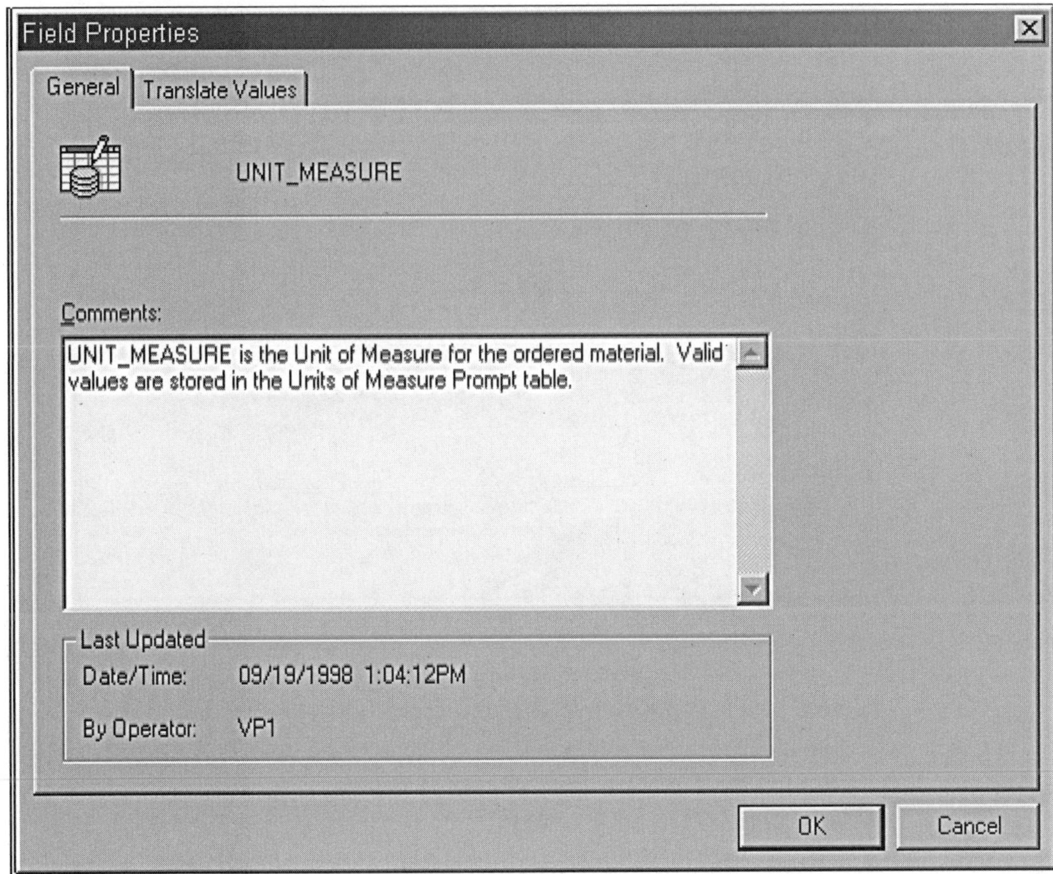

Figure 5-44 Enter comments for the UNIT_MEASURE field on the GENERAL tab of the Object Properties dialog box.

toolbar. The New screen will then appear with a list of object types. Select FIELD and click on OK.

2. The New Field screen will appear with a list of field types. Select CHARACTER.
3. Set the following information as displayed in Figure 5-47:
   - Set the field length to 1.
   - Set the long name to EXTERNAL ORDER.
   - Set the short name to EXTERNAL ORD.
   - Set the format type to UPPERCASE.

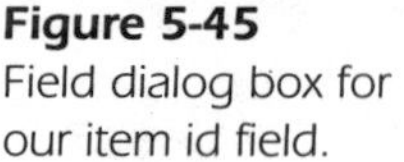

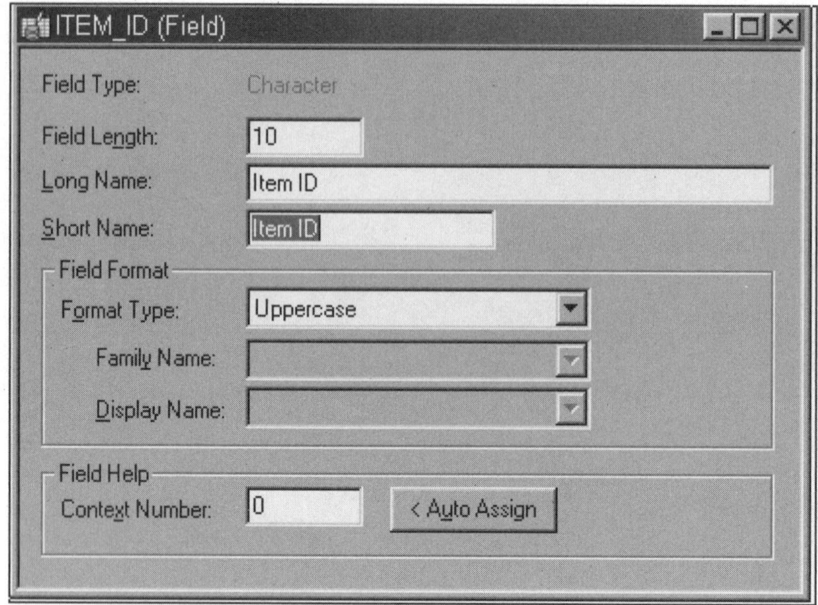

Figure 5-45 Field dialog box for our item id field.

4. Select FILE, OBJECT PROPERTIES to access the GENERAL tab of the Object Properties dialog. Enter all comments shown in Figure 5-48 and press OK when comments are complete.
5. Save the field as `EXT_ORDER`.
6. Because the Projects options were set to MANUAL INSERTION, we now need to insert the field into the project. Select INSERT, CURRENT OBJECT INTO PROJECT, or push F7.

Note that the `EXT_ORDER` field will be used as a yes/no field. Since the only values that will be available are *yes* and *no*, we do not have to set translate values. PeopleSoft uses internal logic to associate an internal `PSYESNO` field for the translate values. Setting this field up as a `Yes\No Translate Edit` will be done when we create the record field definitions in the next chapter.

EXT_STAT Complete the following steps in order to create the external order status (`EXT_STAT`).

1. Select FILE, NEW from the menu bar, or select the NEW icon from the toolbar. The New screen will then appear with a list of object types. Select FIELD and click on OK.

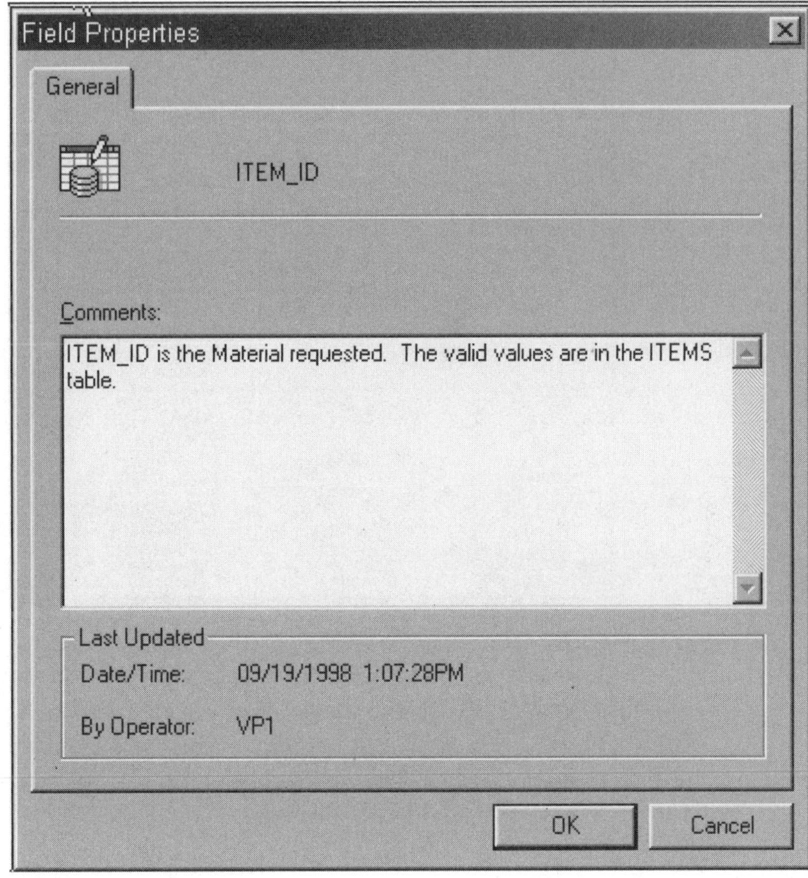

Figure 5-46
Enter comments for the `ITEM_ID` field on the GENERAL tab of the Object Properties dialog box.

2. The New Field screen will appear with a list of field types. Select CHARACTER.
3. Set the following information as displayed in Figure 5-49:
   - Set the field length to 3.
   - Set the long name to EXTERNAL ORDER STATUS.
   - Set the short name to EXT ORD STATUS.
   - Set the format type to UPPERCASE.

   From the requirements, we know that the valid values, for this field, are

   - On order
   - Received

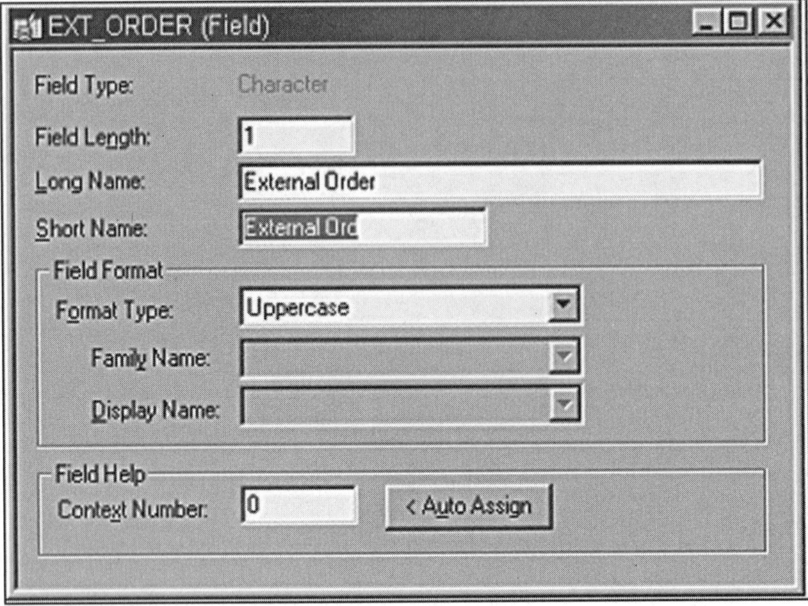

Figure 5-47
Field dialog box for our external order field.

4. To set up the translate values, select FILE, OBJECT PROPERTIES, ALT ENTER, or the PROPERTIES icon from the toolbar. On the TRANSLATE tab, which is available because this field is a character data type and fewer than five characters long, ADD the translate values that are illustrated in Figure 5-50.
5. Select the GENERAL tab of the Object Properties dialog box and enter the comments shown in Figure 5-51. When the comments are complete, click on OK.
6. Save the field as `EXT_STAT`.
7. Because the Projects options were set to MANUAL INSERTION, we now need to insert the field into the project. Select INSERT, CURRENT OBJECT INTO PROJECT, or push F7.

POSITION Complete the following steps to create the employee's position field (`POSITION`).

1. Select FILE, NEW from the menu bar, or select the NEW icon from the toolbar. The New screen will then appear with a list of object types. Select FIELD and click on OK.
2. The New Field screen will appear with a list of field types. Select CHARACTER.

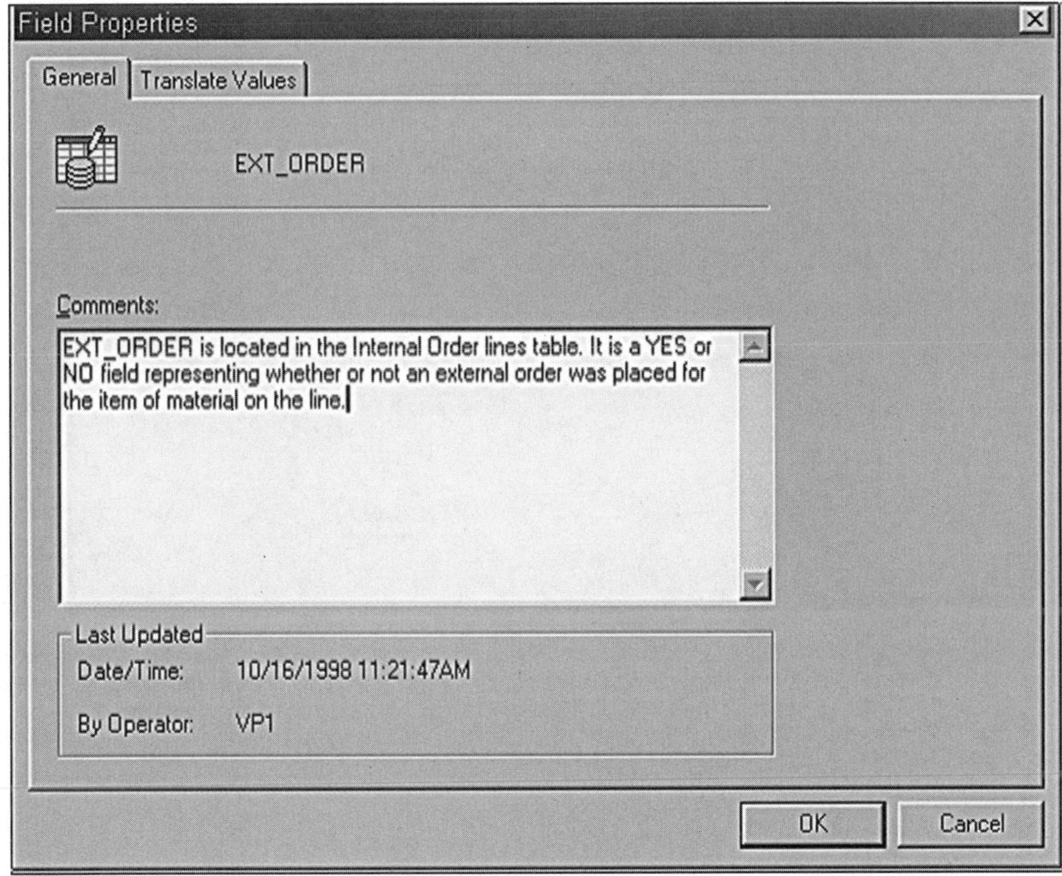

Figure 5-48 Enter comments for the EXT_ORDER field on the GENERAL tab of the Object Properties dialog box.

3. Set the following information as displayed in Figure 5-52:
   - Set the field length to 3.
   - Set long name to EMPLOYEES POSITION.
   - Set short name to EMP POSITION.
   - Set format type to UPPERCASE.

   From the requirements, we know that the valid values, for this field, are

   - Supervisor
   - Buyer
   - Other

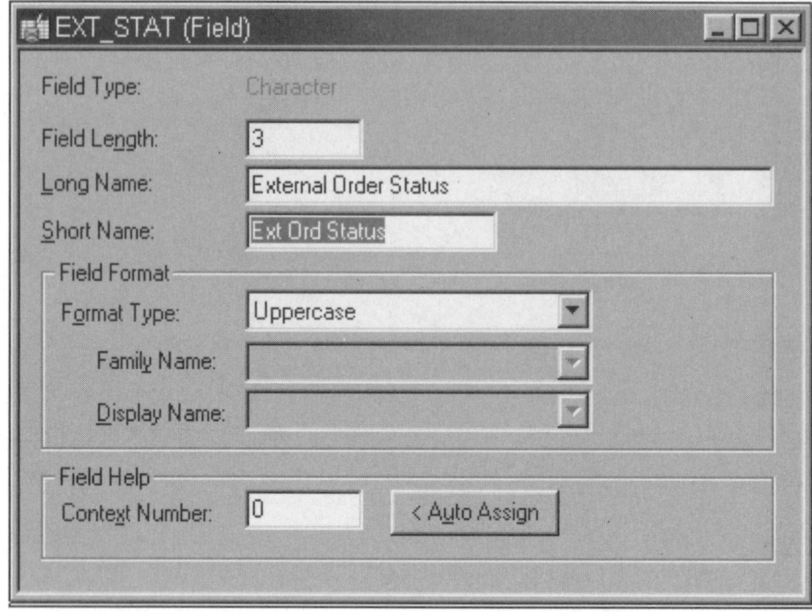

Figure 5-49 Field dialog box for our external order status field.

4. To set up the translate values, select FILE, OBJECT PROPERTIES, ALT ENTER, or the PROPERTIES icon (Fig. 5-53) from the toolbar. On the TRANSLATE tab, which is available because this field is a character data type and fewer than five characters long, ADD the translate values that are illustrated in Figure 5-54.
5. Select the GENERAL tab on the Object Properties dialog box to enter the comments shown in Figure 5-55. Once all the comments are entered, click on OK.
6. Save the field as `POSITION`.
7. Manually insert the field into the project by selecting INSERT, CURRENT OBJECT INTO PROJECT or pushing F7.

VENDORID Complete the following steps in order to create the vendor id field (`VENDORID`).

1. Select FILE, NEW from the menu bar (or you could also select the NEW icon from the toolbar). The New screen will then appear with a list of object types. Select FIELD and click on OK.
2. The New Field screen will appear with a list of field types. Select CHARACTER.

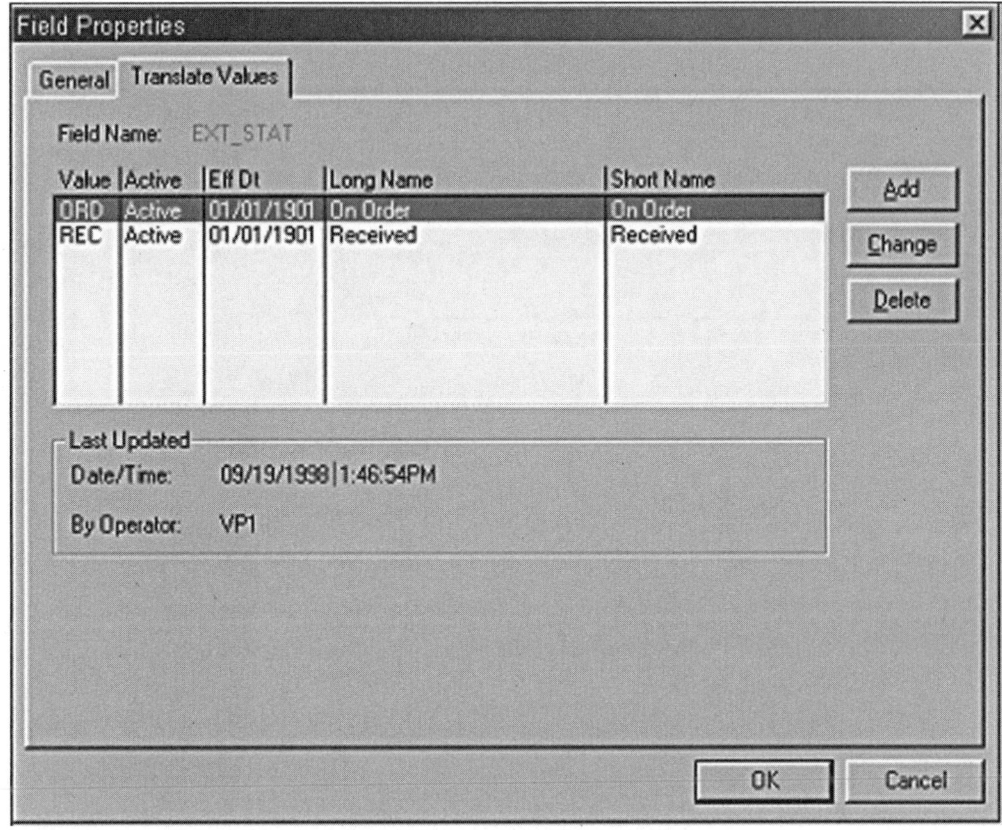

Figure 5-50 Translate values for our external order status field.

3. Set the following information as displayed in Figure 5-56:
   - Set field length to 10.
   - Set the long name to VENDOR ID.
   - Set the short name to VENDOR ID.
   - Set the format type to UPPERCASE.
4. Select FILE, OBJECT PROPERTIES and enter comments on the GENERAL tab of the Object Properties dialog box as shown in Figure 5-57. Click OK once all comments are entered.
5. Save the field as `VENDORID`.
6. Because the Projects options were set to MANUAL INSERTION, we now need to insert the field into the project. Select INSERT, CURRENT OBJECT INTO PROJECT, or push F7.

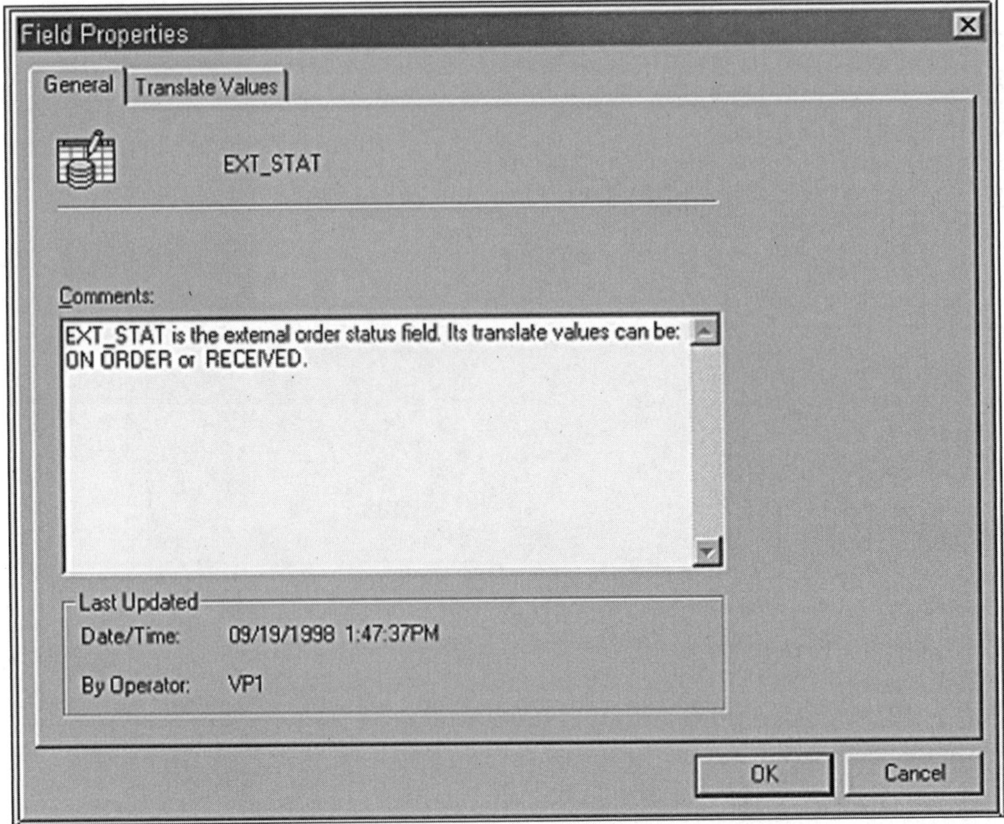

Figure 5-51 Enter comments for the EXT_STAT field on the GENERAL tab of the Object Properties dialog box.

VENDOR Complete the following steps to create the vendor field (VENDOR):

1. Select FILE, NEW from the menu bar (or select the NEW icon from the toolbar). The New screen will then appear with a list of object types. Select FIELD and click on OK.
2. The New Field screen will appear with a list of field types. Select CHARACTER.
3. Set the following information as displayed in Figure 5-58.
   - Set the field length to 30.
   - Set the long name to COMPANY NAME.

Figure 5-52
Field dialog box for our employees position field.

POSITION (Field)

Field Type: Character

Field Length: 3

Long Name: Employees Position

Short Name: Emp Position

Field Format

Format Type: Uppercase

Family Name:

Display Name:

Field Help

Context Number: 0

< Auto Assign

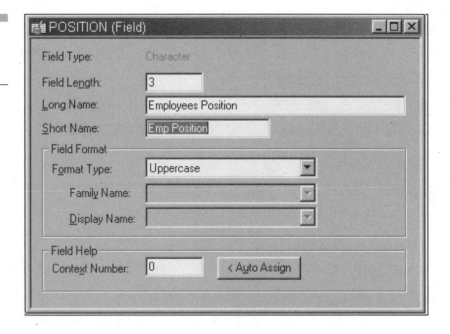

Figure 5-53
PROPERTIES icon.

- Set the short name to COMPANY.
- Set the format type to UPPERCASE.

4. Select FILE, OBJECT PROPERTIES to get to the GENERAL tab and enter all comments. Click OK when finished.
5. Save the field as VENDOR.
6. Because the Projects options were set to MANUAL INSERTION, we now need to insert the field into the project. Select INSERT, CURRENT OBJECT INTO PROJECT, or push F7.

PO_NUM Complete the following steps to create the purchase order field (PO_NUM).

1. Select FILE, NEW from the menu bar (or select the NEW icon from the toolbar). The New screen will then appear with a list of object types. Select FIELD and click on OK.

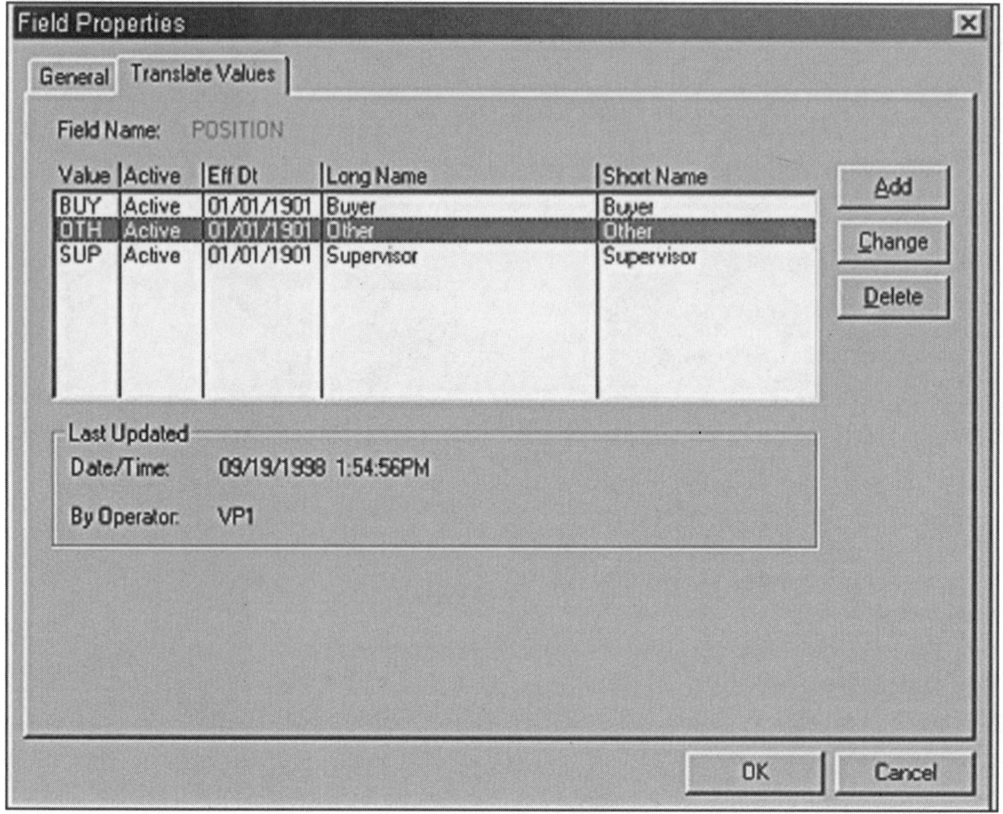

Figure 5-54 Translate values for our position field.

2. The New Field screen will appear with a list of field types. Select CHARACTER.
3. Set the following information as displayed in Figure 5-59:
   - Set the field length to 10.
   - Set the long name to PURCHASE ORDER NUMBER.
   - Set the short name to PO NUMBER.
   - Set the format type to UPPERCASE.
4. Select FILE, OBJECT PROPERTIES to display the GENERAL tab of the Object Properties dialog. Enter the comments shown in Figure 5-60 and click OK once all comments are entered.
5. Save the field as PO_NUM.

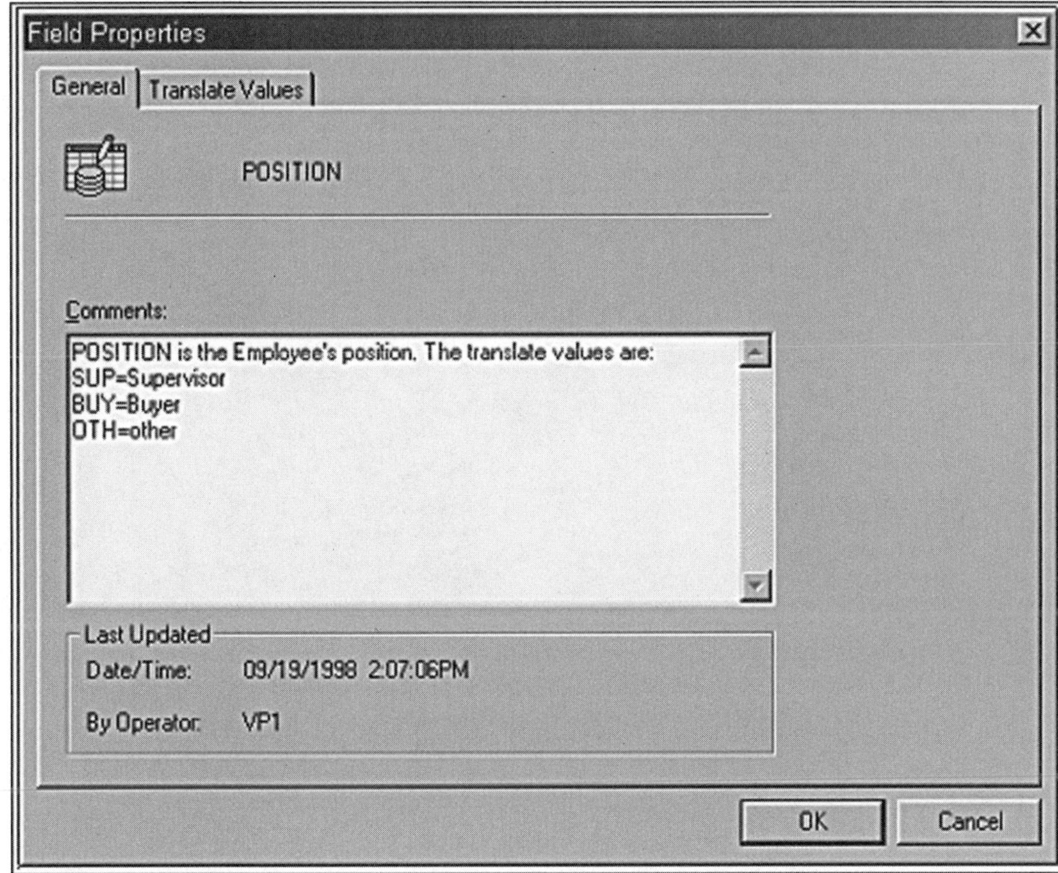

Figure 5-55 Enter comments for the POSITION field on the GENERAL tab of the Object Properties dialog box.

6. Because the Projects options were set to MANUAL INSERTION, we now need to insert the field into the project. Select INSERT, CURRENT OBJECT INTO PROJECT, or push F7.

PROM_DT Complete the following steps in order to create the promise date field (PROM_DT):

1. Select FILE, NEW from the menu bar (or select the NEW icon from the toolbar). The New screen will then appear with a list of object types. Select FIELD and click on OK.

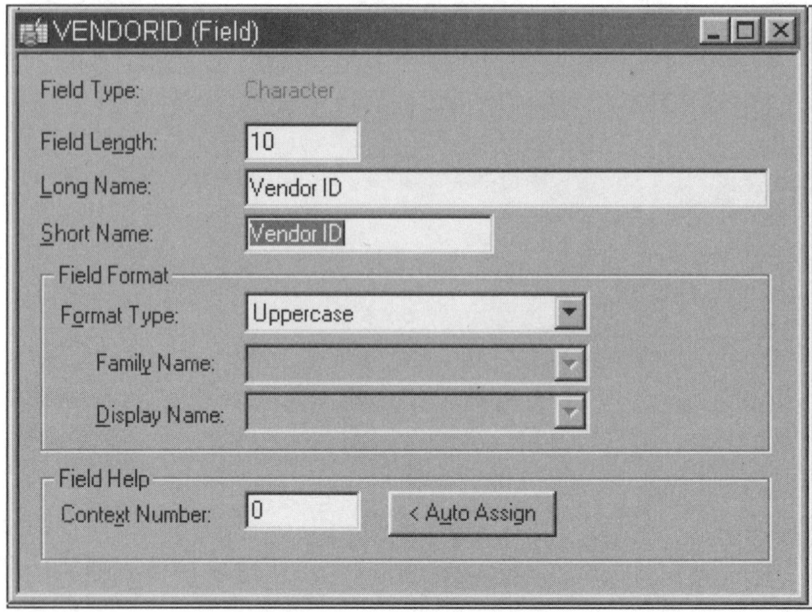

Figure 5-56
Vendor id definition.

2. The New Field screen will appear with a list of field types. Select DATE.
3. Set the following information as displayed in Figure 5-61.
   - Set the long name to PROMISE DATE.
   - Set the short name to PROMISE DATE.
   - Set DEFAULT TO 2000 if year less than or equal to 50.
4. Select FILE, OBJECT PROPERTIES to enter the comments shown in Figure 5-62 onto the GENERAL tab of the Object Properties dialog box. Click OK once all comments are entered.
5. Save the field as `PROM_DT`.
6. Because the Projects options were set to MANUAL INSERTION, we now need to insert the field into the project. Select INSERT, CURRENT OBJECT INTO PROJECT, or push F7.

Using Delivered Fields for Remaining Fields We are going to use delivered fields for the rest of the fields for our example. Before we begin creating our records, we need to open all the fields we are going to use and include them in our project. To do this, open the following records and press the F7 key.

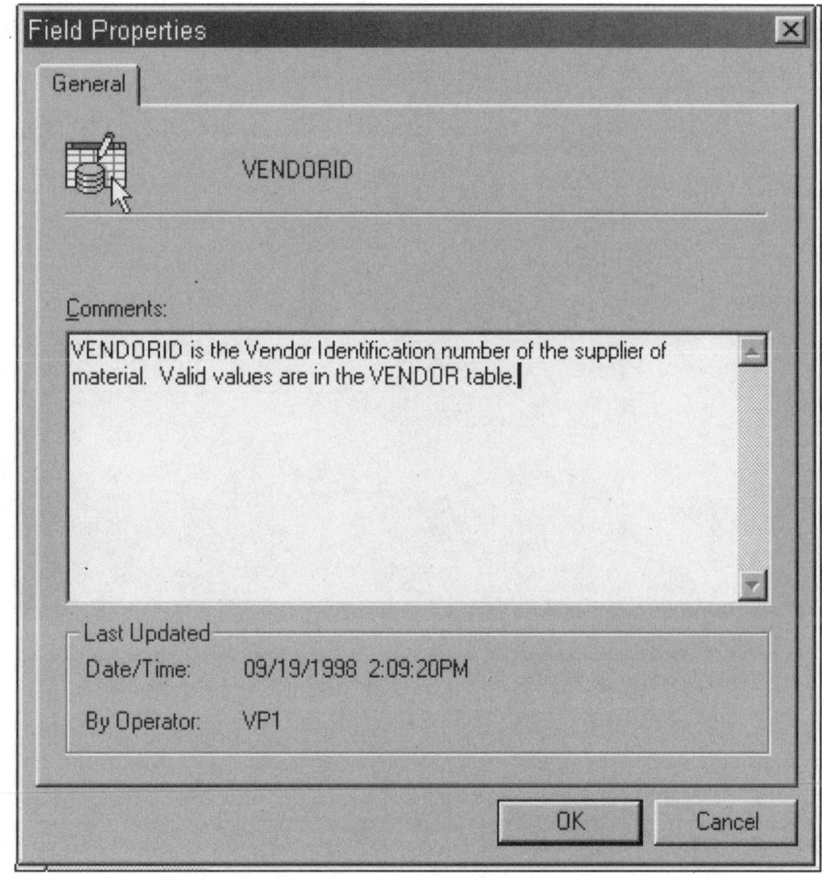

Figure 5-57
Enter comments for the `VENDORID` field on the GENERAL tab of the Object Properties dialog box.

- NAME
- EFF_STATUS
- EFFDT
- EMAIL_ADDRESS
- DESCR
- STREET1
- STREET2
- CITY
- STATE
- QTY

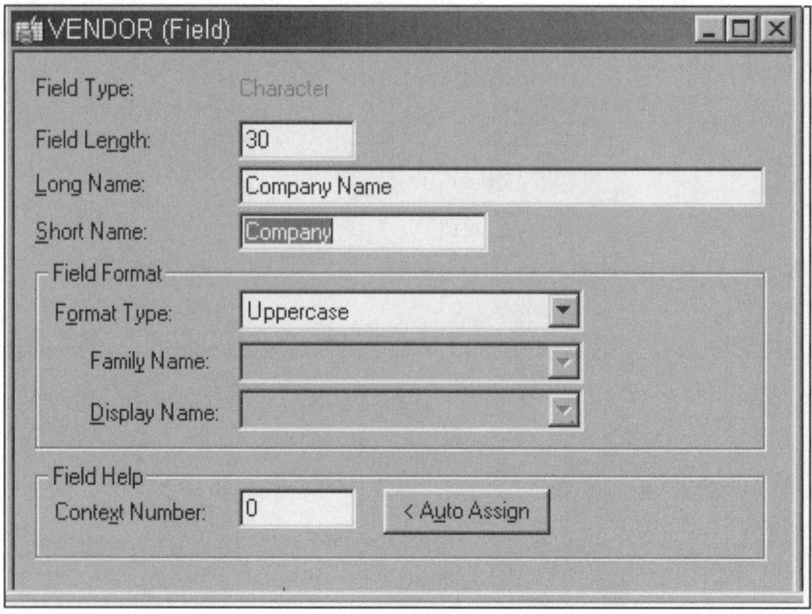

Figure 5-58
Vendor definition.

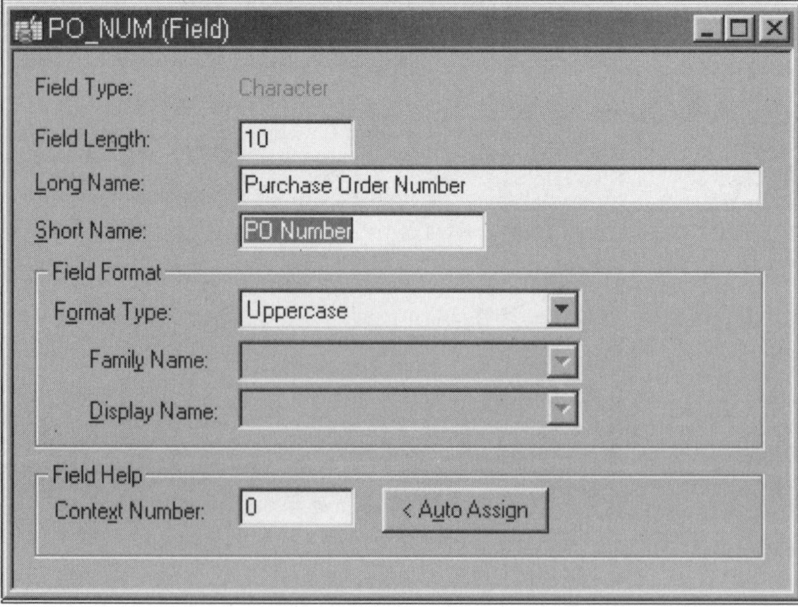

Figure 5-59
`PO_NUM` definition.

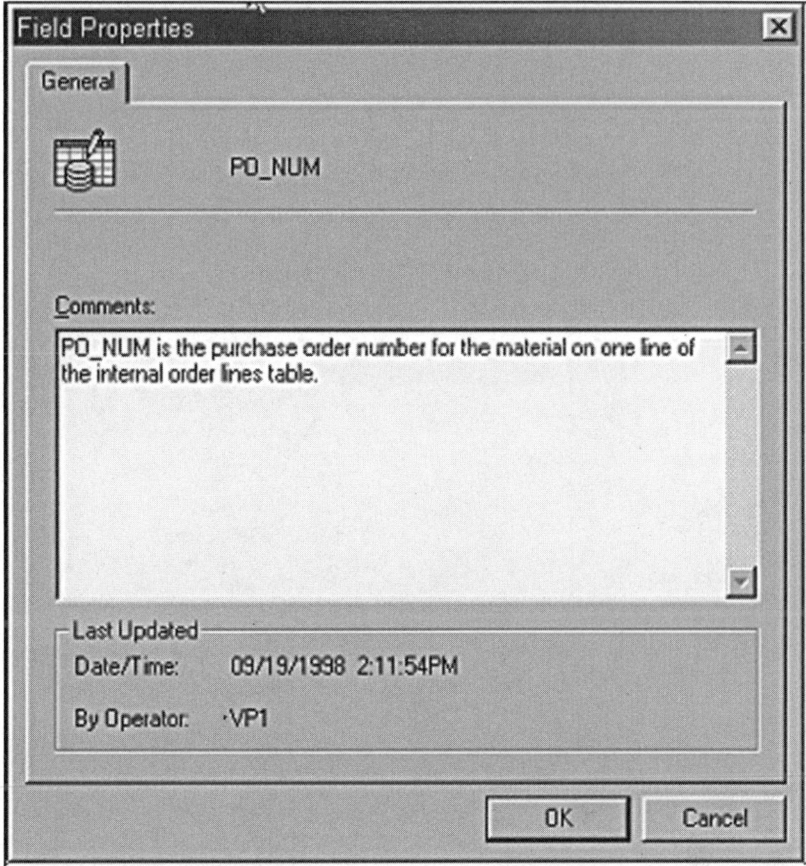

Figure 5-60
Enter comments for the PO_NUM field on the GENERAL tab of the Object Properties dialog box.

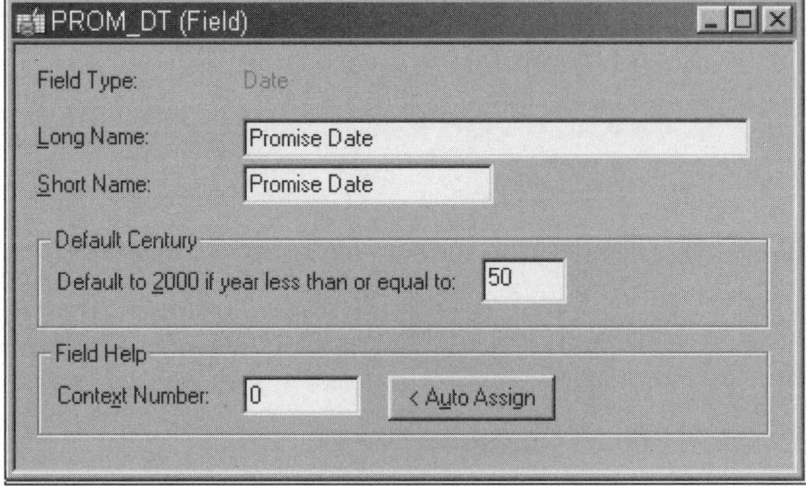

Figure 5-61
Field dialog box for our promise date field.

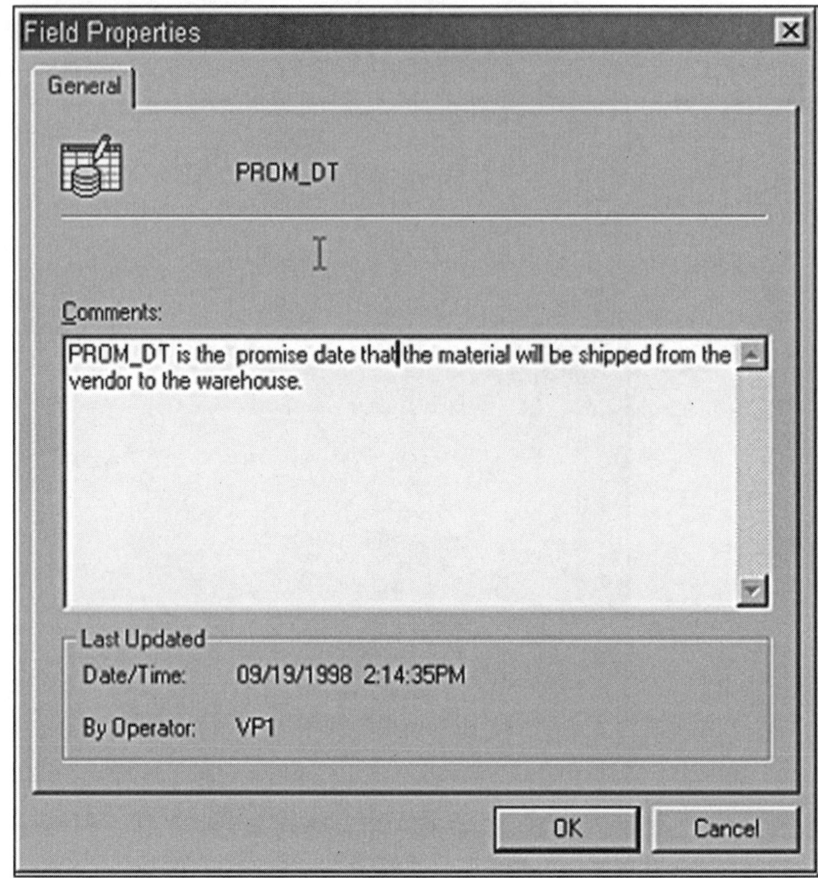

Figure 5-62
Enter comments for the PROM_DT field on the GENERAL tab of the Object Properties dialog box.

Project Workspace with All Fields

When you have completed this, your Project Workspace should look the same as Figure 5-63.

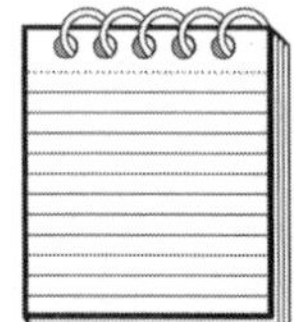

NOTE *When modifying existing fields, it is imperative that the impact of the change on related objects be determined. To do so, select* EDIT, FIND OBJECT REFERENCES. *This will list objects related to the field.*

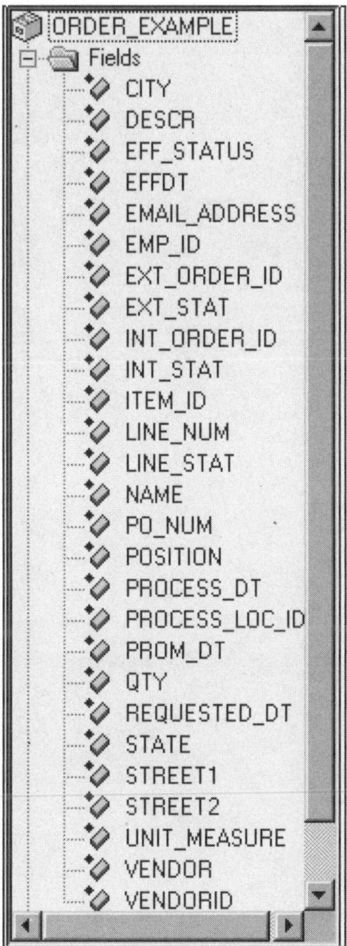

Figure 5-63 Project Workspace with all the example fields.

CHAPTER 6

Records

The next step in developing our Warehouse Ordering application is to create records. In Chapter 5, we created all the fields needed for this application. Now that all the fields are created, we can start organizing the fields and adding them to records. This chapter will give a definition of a record, explain all the types of record, and finally create the records for the Warehouse Ordering application.

Record Definitions

Most PeopleSoft records are at their lowest level equivalent to SQL tables or views. (In fact, when we are done creating the record definitions for our example, we will create SQL tables or views in a build process.) *Records* are a logical grouping of one or more field definitions. For instance, our internal order record contains the following field definitions: INT_ORDER_ID, REQUESTED_DT, EMP_ID, PROCESS_DT, PROCESS_LOC_ID, and STATUS. A record description can be opened and displayed in the Object Workspace of the Application Designer. There are four different options for displaying a record definition:

- Field Display
- Use Display
- Edits Display
- PeopleCode Display

Field Display

To display a record's Field Display, select VIEW, FIELD DISPLAY, or click on the FIELD DISPLAY icon shown in Figure 6-1. Figure 6-2 shows a Field Display of a record definition.

The Field Display of the record definition shows the fields and their data types, length, format, and help context number, as well as the short and long descriptions of each of the fields that make up the record definition. All of these reflect the values that were entered when we created the fields. It is important to note that if you change any of the Field properties that were discussed in the previous chapter, such as short and long name or the translate values, the changes will affect all the records in which the field is used. To open Field Definitions, select the field from the record definition and right-click on your mouse. A popup menu will then be displayed. Select VIEW DEFINITION, and the field's Definition window will be opened.

Figure 6-1
FIELD DISPLAY icon.

ITEM (Record)

Field Name	Type	Len	Format	H	Short Name	Long Name
BUSINESS_UNIT	Char	5	Upper		Unit	Business Unit
CUST_ID	Char	15	Upper		Customer	Customer ID
ITEM	Char	22	Upper		Item ID	Item ID
ITEM_LINE	Nbr	3			Line	Item Line
ITEM_STATUS	Char	1	Upper		Status	Item Status
ENTRY_TYPE	Char	5	Upper		Entry Type	Entry Type
ENTRY_REASON	Char	5	Upper		Reason	Entry Reason
BAL_AMT	Sign	13.2			Balance	Customer Balance
ACCOUNTING_DT	Date	10			Acctg Date	Accounting Date
ASOF_DT	Date	10			As Of	As Of Date
POST_DT	Date	10			Posted	Posted Date
DUE_DT	Date	10			Due	Due Date
CR_ANALYST	Char	8	Upper		Analyst	Credit Analyst
SALES_PERSON	Char	8	Upper		Sales	Sales Person

Figure 6-2 Field display of a record definition.

Use Display

Record definitions are similar to SQL tables in that they have a primary key, an index, and default attributes. Understanding how the keys are used in PeopleSoft is very important. The Use Display option is a means of viewing this information. The Use Display can be viewed by either using the View menu and then selecting USE DISPLAY, or by clicking on the USE DISPLAY icon shown in Figure 6-3. The information displayed on the Use Display can be selected or modified on the USE tab of the Record Field Properties dialog.

Figure 6-4 shows an example Use Dialog. In order to begin editing a Field's Key, Audit, and Default properties, double-click on the desired field, and a Record Field Properties dialog will be displayed. Figure 6-5 shows the USE tab of the Record Field Properties dialog.

The USE tab of the Record Field Properties dialog allows editing of the key structure of the record. A record's keys are used to identify a unique row of fields. They are the same as the primary key terminology used in SQL. As in SQL, there are parent/child relationships with records. In

Figure 6-3
USE DISPLAY icon.

ITEM (Record)

Field Name	Type	Key	Dir	CurC	Srch	List	Sys	Audt	H	Default
BUSINESS_UNIT	Char	Key	Asc		Yes	Yes	No			OPR_DEF_TBL_FS.BU
CUST_ID	Char	Key	Asc		Yes	Yes	No			
ITEM	Char	Key	Asc		Yes	Yes	No			
ITEM_LINE	Nbr	Key	Asc		Yes	Yes	No			
ITEM_STATUS	Char				No	Yes	No			'0'
ENTRY_TYPE	Char				No	No	No			
ENTRY_REASON	Char				No	No	No			
BAL_AMT	Sign			Yes	No	No	No			
ACCOUNTING_DT	Date				No	No	No			
ASOF_DT	Date				No	No	No			ITEM.ACCOUNTING_D
POST_DT	Date				No	No	No			
DUE_DT	Date				No	No	No			ITEM.ACCOUNTING_D
CR_ANALYST	Char	Alt	Asc		No	Yes	No			CUSTOMER.CR_ANAL'
SALES_PERSON	Char				No	No	No			CUSTOMER.SALES_PE

Figure 6-4 Use Display of a record definition.

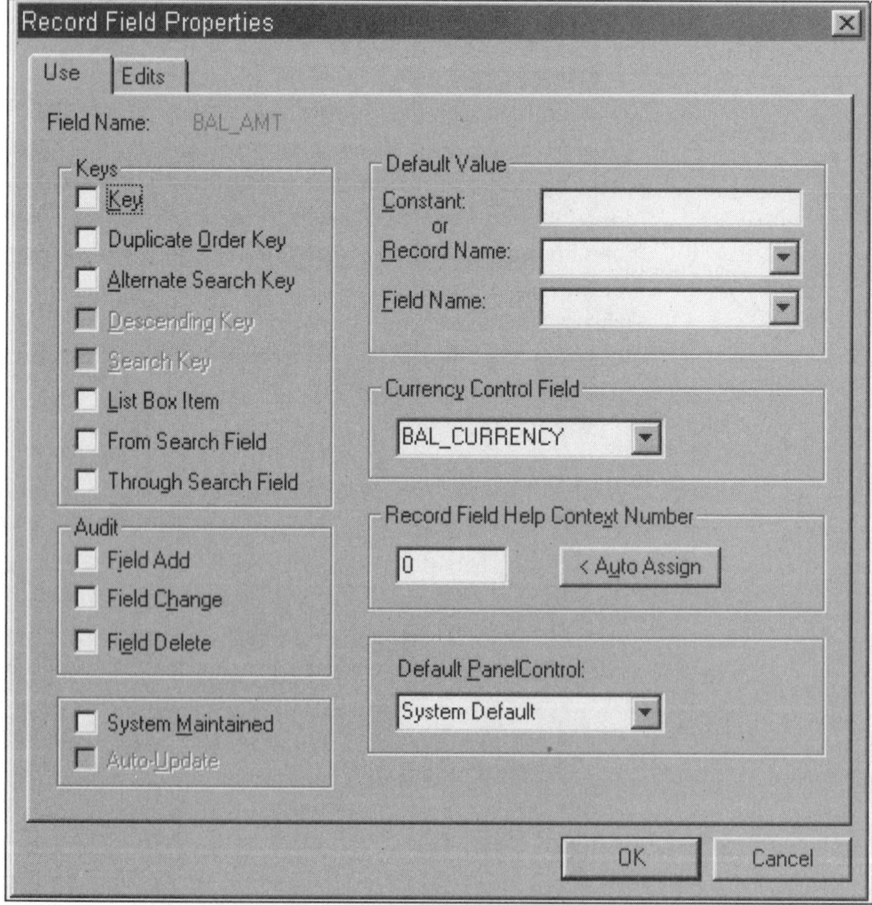

Figure 6-5 USE tab of the Record Field Properties dialog.

order to identify a relationship between a parent and a child record, the child record's keys must include all the keys of the parent and at least one new key. A good example of a parent/child relationship in our example is the internal order record and the internal order lines record. The field that uniquely identifies the internal order record is `INT_ORDER_ID`. In the internal order lines record, `INT_ORDER_ID` and `LINE_NUM` are combined to create a unique identification of the internal order lines record and to relate it to a unique internal order.

The following key selections are available in the USE tab of the Record Field Properties dialog;

- *Key*. This option defines the *field* as or a part of the unique identifier.
- *Duplicate Order Key*. This option is used when the *record* was not defined to have any unique identifying keys. This option is very rare. If you were working with a record that might have multiple nonunique rows of data, you should identify the record with a system-generated nonnatural key to force uniqueness.
- *Alternate Search Key*. This option is very useful. It will create an index on the field when the record is built. Moreover, whenever an Update/Display dialog is displayed for this record, this field will be displayed in the Alternate Search Group Box to allow the user to enter its values to find the desired row.
- *Descending Key*. This option allows you to set the order in which the Field's values will be returned. If it is selected, the retrieval order will be descending. This is very useful for date fields.
- *Search Key*. This option is available only if the Key option was selected. This is used to make the Field available in the Update/Display dialog.
- *List Box Key*. This option is available only if the Key option was selected. This is used to display the Field as a column in the list box that is displayed in the Update/Display dialog. This gives the user a better understanding of what the possible selections are.
- *From Search Field*. You can use this option when you would like to return values in the Update/Display list box that are in a range of values. This is a unique option and can be used only with records that are based on views. An example of this will be shown when we create our record definitions.
- *Through Search Field*. You can use this option when you would like to return values in the Update/Display list box that are in a

range of values. This is a unique option and can be used only with records that are based on views. This is the same as the From Search Field option, but instead of being the beginning value, it is the end value. An example of this will be shown when we create our record definitions.

The next group in the USE tab of the Record Field Properties dialog below the Key group box refers to the field-level auditing features built into PeopleSoft. If you select any of the following options, a row will be inserted into the `PSAUDIT` table:

- Field Add
- Field Change
- Delete

The `PSAUDIT` table stores the operator id of the person making the change as well as the time and the action that occurred. This is a very useful feature for tracking changes made to sensitive data. Later when we go over PeopleSoft's Query tool, we will see an example of how you can access this table for reporting.

The next group box below the Audit group box has a System Maintained option and an Auto Update option. System Maintained is only for documentation purposes. Auto Update is available only for date and time variables. When selected, it will set the value equal to the server's date and/or time. We are going to use this feature to ascertain the date when our internal order was entered.

The Defaults group box has two options that you can choose. You can set the default either to a constant value or to a value stored in a field of a record. After this is set, whenever a new record is created, the default will be set to this value.

The help context number is useful if you are planning to create a context-sensitive help system for your application extensions.

The last option you can select from the USE tab is what type of control you would like this field to default to when you add it to a panel. Your options are

- Edit box
- Drop-down list
- Radio button
- Check box

All of these controls will be used in our example. Do not fear if you do not have this option set properly when you first create your record definition. If it is not what you would like when you are creating your panels, you can simply open the record definition and make the required changes. This can happen for purely aesthetic reasons when you decide that you want to switch from a drop-down list to radio buttons.

Edits Display

The next group of attributes in the record definition is detailed in the Edits Display. It can be viewed by either using the View menu, then selecting EDITS DISPLAY or by clicking on the EDITS DISPLAY icon shown in Figure 6-6. Figure 6-7 shows an example record being displayed in the Edits Display. The information displayed on the Edits Display can be modified in the EDITS tab of the Record Field Definition Properties dialog.

The EDITS tab of the Record Field Properties dialog allows editing of the data validation edits placed on the individual fields. By double clicking on a field in the Edits Display of the record the EDITS tab of the Record Field Definition Properties dialog will be displayed. The first option you can choose is whether the field is required. If the Required check box is selected, a user would not be able to move from the field or

Figure 6-6 EDITS DISPLAY icon.

ITEM (Record)

Field Name	Type	Req	Edit	Prompt Table	Set Control Field	Rs Dt
BUSINESS_UNIT	Char	Yes	Prompt	SP_BUARDS_NONVW		No
CUST_ID	Char	Yes	Prompt	CUST_BI_A2_VW		No
ITEM	Char	Yes				No
ITEM_LINE	Nbr	No				No
ITEM_STATUS	Char	Yes	Xlat			No
ENTRY_TYPE	Char	Yes	Prompt	ENTRY_TYPE_TBL		No
ENTRY_REASON	Char	No	Prompt	ENTRY_REASN_TBL		No
BAL_AMT	Sign	No				No
ACCOUNTING_DT	Date	Yes				No
ASOF_DT	Date	No				No
POST_DT	Date	Yes				No
DUE_DT	Date	No				No
CR_ANALYST	Char	No	Prompt	CR_ANALYST_TBL	BUSINESS_UNIT	No

Figure 6-7 Edits Display of a record definition.

save the record without first entering a value. The next group of options deals with the built-in data validation that PeopleSoft offers. The options that are displayed vary according to the date type of the field that you are editing.

Figure 6-8 shows the options available for a Character data type on the EDITS tab of the Record Properties dialog. If you select the TABLE EDIT radio control, the three drop-down list boxes below it will become enabled. The Type drop-down list box contains the following options:

- Prompt Table Edit
- Prompt Table with No Edit
- Translate Table Edit
- Yes/No Table Edit

Figure 6-9 shows the options available for a Long Character and Image data types on the EDITS tab of the Record Properties dialog. The only option available for these data types is whether they are required.

Figure 6-10 shows the options available for a Numbers, Signed Numbers, and Times data types on the EDITS tab of the Record Properties dialog. These data types edit options are

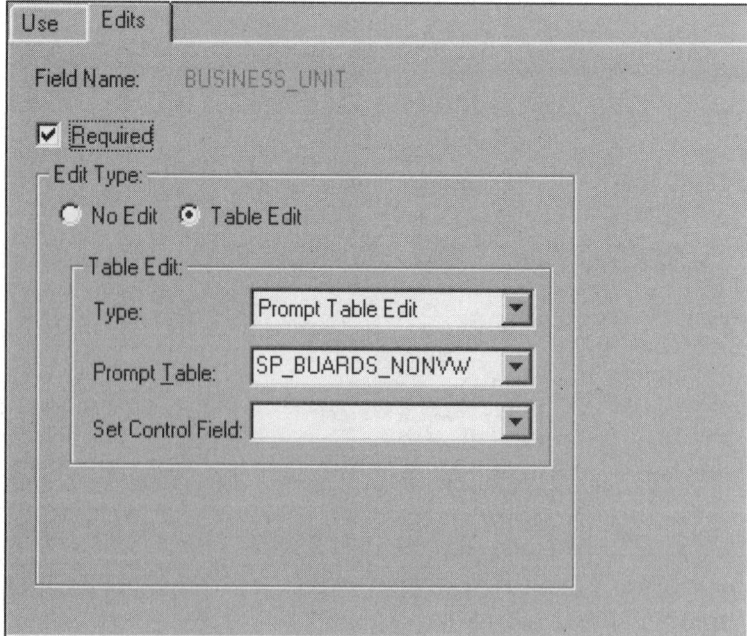

Figure 6-8
Character's EDITS tab of the Record Field Properties dialog.

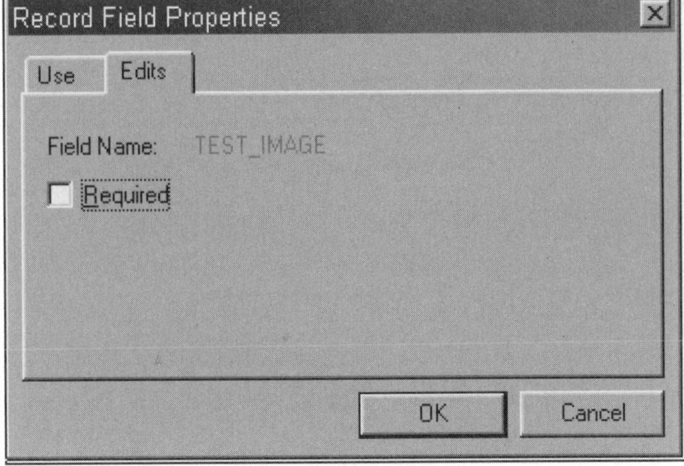

Figure 6-9 Image's and Long Character's EDIT tab of the Record Field Properties dialog.

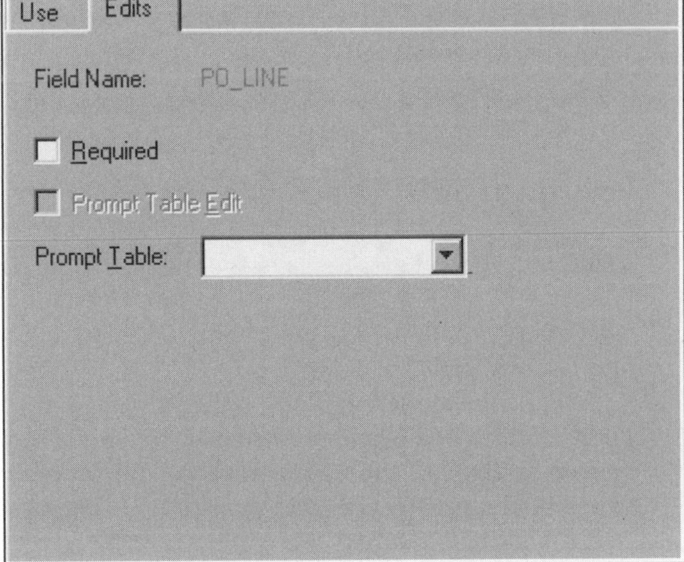

Figure 6-10 Numbers, Signed Numbers, and Times EDITS tab of the Record Field Properties dialog.

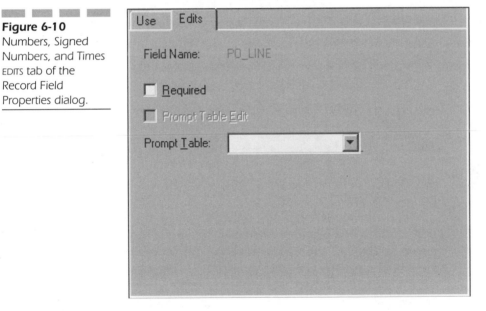

- Required
- Prompt Table

Figure 6-11 shows the options available for the Date data type on the EDITS tab of the Record Properties dialog. These data type edit options are

- Required

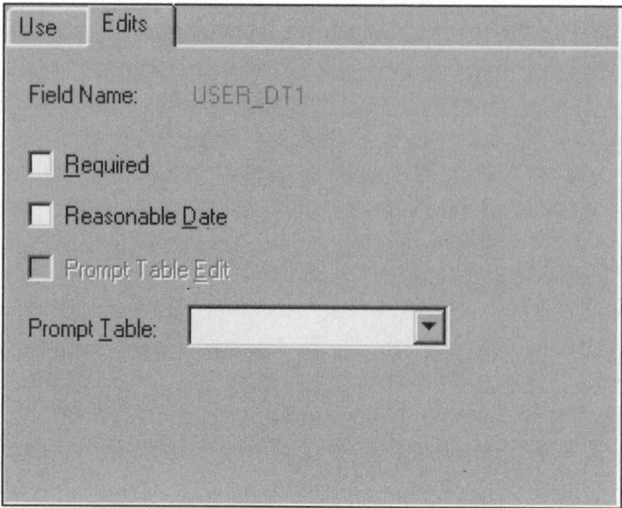

Figure 6-11 Date's EDITS tab of the Record Field Properties dialog.

- Reasonable Date—30-day window of before and after current system date
- Prompt Table

PeopleCode Display

The last group of attributes of the record definition is shown in the PeopleCode Display. It can be viewed either by using the View menu, then selecting "PeopleCode Display," or by clicking on the PEOPLECODE DISPLAY icon shown in Figure 6-12.

Where PeopleSoft records really differ from plain SQL objects are that PeopleSoft's whole-event model was built around them. What this means is that all the events that we can program with extended logic are stored at the record level. Figure 6-13 shows the PeopleCode Display that is available when a record definition is open in the Application Designer. This is the place where you can determine whether there is any PeopleCode associated with the fields or record. PeopleCode is PeopleSoft's own fourth-generation language. All the abbreviated column headings shown in the PeopleCode Display reference a PeopleSoft event.

Figure 6-12 PEOPLECODE DISPLAY icon.

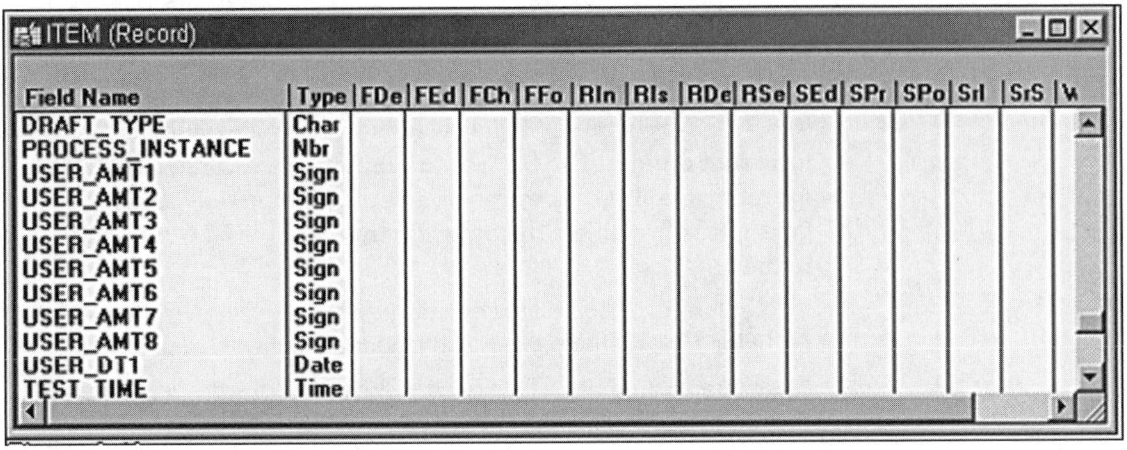

ITEM (Record)

Field Name	Type	FDe	FEd	FCh	FFo	RIn	RIs	RDe	RSe	SEd	SPr	SPo	SrI	SrS	W
DRAFT_TYPE	Char														
PROCESS_INSTANCE	Nbr														
USER_AMT1	Sign														
USER_AMT2	Sign														
USER_AMT3	Sign														
USER_AMT4	Sign														
USER_AMT5	Sign														
USER_AMT6	Sign														
USER_AMT7	Sign														
USER_AMT8	Sign														
USER_DT1	Date														
TEST_TIME	Time														

Figure 6-13 PeopleCode Display of a record definition.

- `FDe` = `FieldDefault`. This event allows you to set default values for fields that have not been assigned a value by the user.
- `FEd` = `FieldEdit`. This event allows you to validate fields after a user has made a change.
- `FCh` = `FieldChange`. This event allows you to execute logic on the basis of the new data that have been entered into a field.
- `FFo` = `FieldFormula`. This event is usually reserved for derived records that contain specific functions that can be called with PeopleCode from other events.
- `RIn` = `RowInit`. This event is fired for each new row of data to be displayed. You would place code here to set the initial properties of the fields that are to be displayed.
- `RIs` = `RowInsert`. This event differs from `RowInit` in that it occurs when you are inserting (F7) a new row into the buffer.
- `RDe` = `RowDelete`. This event allows you to create logic to verify that the data can be deleted (F8).
- `RSe` = `RowSelect`. This event allows you to filter out rows of data as the application reads them from the database.
- `SEd` = `SaveEdit`. This event is where you can verify the data in multiple fields and validate how they relate to each other. It is fired when the panel group is saved.

- `SPr = SavePreChg.` This event allows you to execute last minute logic before the data are saved to the database. It is fired when the panel group is saved.
- `SPo = SavePostChg.` This event is where you would place logic that could utilize SQL Data Manipulation Language (DML) for related tables that were not a part of the current panel group. It is fired after the panel groups data have been updated to the database.
- `SrI = SearchInit.` This event allows you to set default values for fields that will appear in the Update/Display Search dialog.
- `SrS = SearchSave.` This event allows you to work with values that were entered in the Search dialog. It is fired after the user presses the OK or SEARCH button on the Search dialog.
- `Wrk = WorkFlow.` This event is where you place the logic to execute a workflow event. It is executed after the panel group has been saved.
- `PPr = PrePopup.` This is a menu PeopleCode event. It allows you to perform logic immediately before a popup menu is displayed.

Those of you with a Windows programming background will immediately notice that these events do not relate to the Windows event model. In PeopleSoft, 99 percent of the Windows API (application program interface) are taken care of by the application. The only thing that somewhat relates to Windows programming is that there are PeopleCode functions that can gray or hide controls, and they allow you to set some colors. This does not allow for very much creativity on behalf of the programmers, but it does enforce conformity across the entire application.

If there is any code in any of the above-mentioned PeopleCode events, the PeopleCode Display will show a “yes” in the appropriate column. All of the PeopleCode that you can develop will be entered into one of these events in a record definition. If you click on one of the columns in the PeopleCode Display, a PeopleCode Editor will be displayed. Figure 6-14 shows the PeopleCode Editor. The left drop-down list at the top contains the fields that make up the record. The drop-down list on the top right contains all the PeopleCode events that you can enter in PeopleCode.

In Chapter 12 we will delve into more detail about PeopleCode. In that chapter we will go over the key features and functions available with PeopleCode. In addition, we will implement several enhancements to our example to show you some of the possibilities.

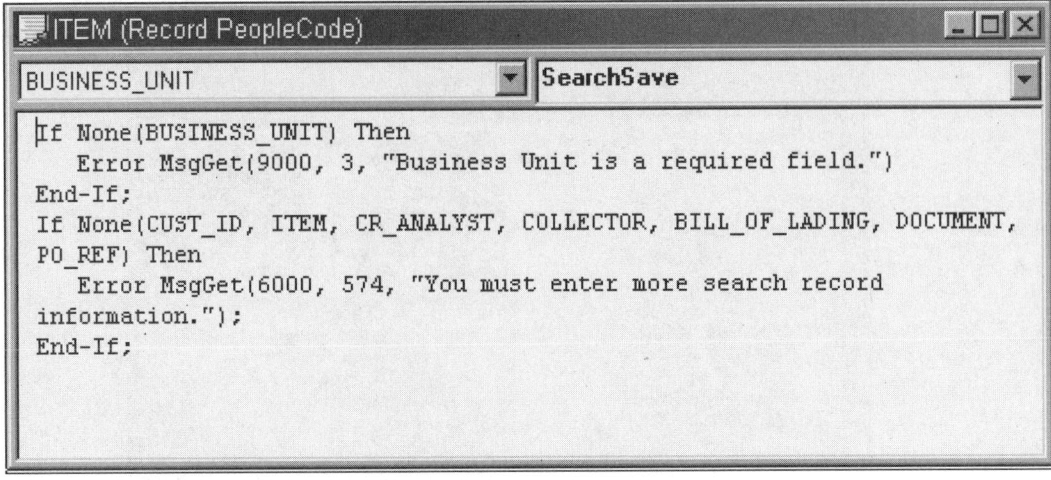
ITEM (Record PeopleCode)
BUSINESS_UNIT
SearchSave
If None(BUSINESS_UNIT) Then
Error MsgGet(9000, 3, "Business Unit is a required field.")
End-If;
If None(CUST_ID, ITEM, CR_ANALYST, COLLECTOR, BILL_OF_LADING, DOCUMENT,
PO_REF) Then
Error MsgGet(6000, 574, "You must enter more search record
information.");
End-If;

Figure 6-14 PeopleCode Editor.

Record Build Options

PeopleSoft Records that are going to be used to store application data must be "built" before they can be used in your application. The build process can be as involved as creating SQL tables in the database to as simple as setting up a SQL Select that will be passed to the database each time the record is referenced. Figure 6-15 shows the icon that can be pressed to initiate the build process. You could also select the Build menu and then select CURRENT OBJECT.

The Build options that you select from the Build dialog will depend on what kind of record you are creating. Figure 6-16 shows the Build dialog. The number of records displayed in this dialog depends on whether you are building all the records in the project or just the current record. Our example is the latter.

If you are creating a new SQL table record, you can select the Create Table and Create Index options. If you are only modifying an existing SQL table record, you would select the Alter Table option. The Create

Figure 6-15 Build option for record definitions.

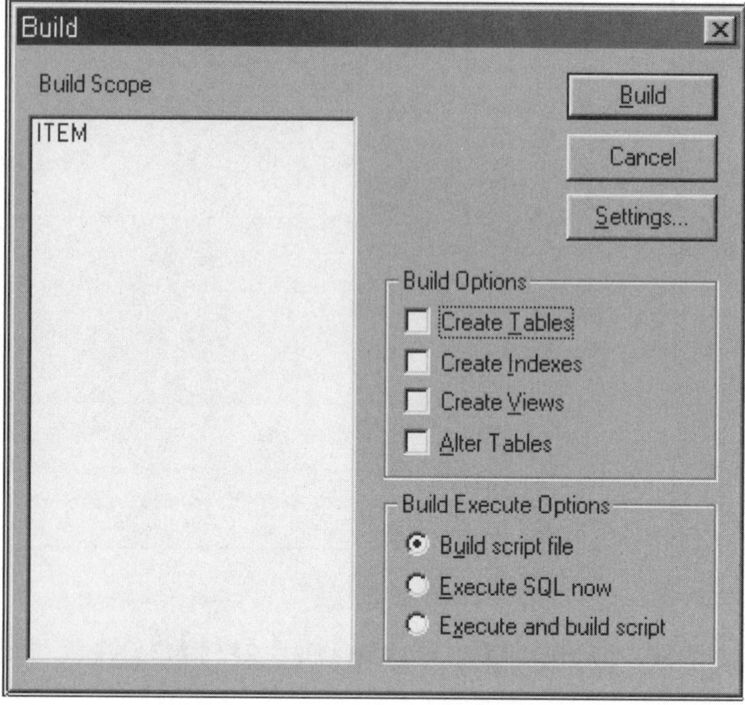

Figure 6-16 Record definition Build dialog.

View option is for SQL view records that are based on previously existing objects in the database.

The Build Execute options that are available to you depend on the database platform you are connected to and what security privileges you are granted in the Security Administrator application for the APPLICATION_DESIGNER menu. (Please refer to Chapter 10 for a more complete overview of the Security Administrator.) If you have access to all three execute options, you would either be able to create a SQL script file, create a SQL script file and execute, or just execute the SQL immediately with no SQL script file generated. The controls for these options are radio buttons and therefore are mutually exclusive.

Before you execute any of these options, it is a good idea to view your current build preferences. To view your current build settings, go to the Build menu and select the Settings menu. Figures 6-17 through 6-20 show your current build preferences.

The CREATE tab of the Build Settings dialog allows the developer to select what should be done to the table or to the view if it already exists during the build process. The choices are to re-create the table if it

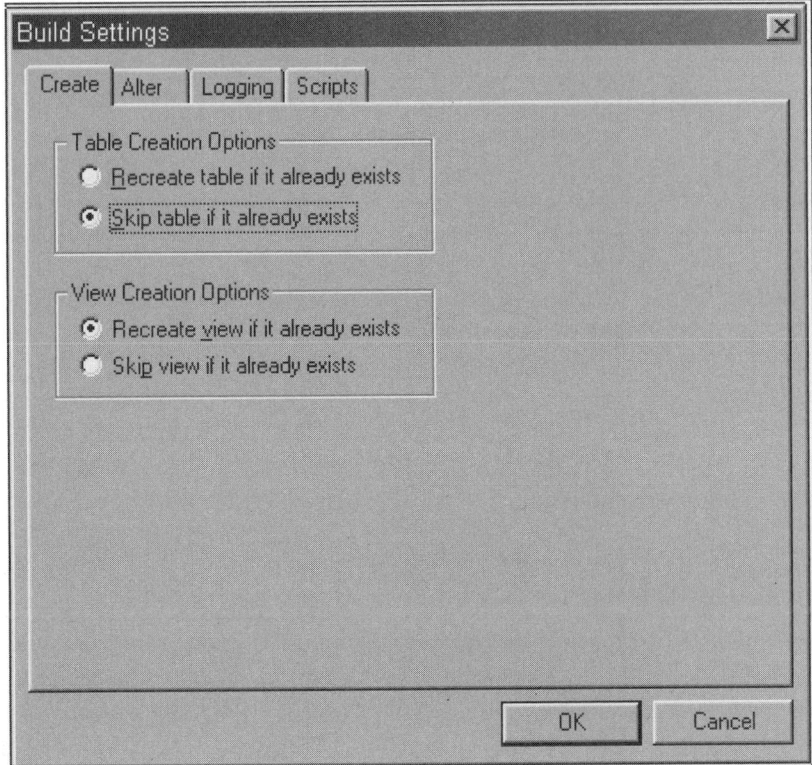

Figure 6-17
CREATE tab of the Build Settings dialog.

already exists or to skip the table if it already exists. The View Creation options are to re-create the view if it already exists or to skip the view if it already exists.

The ALTER tab of the Build Settings dialog allows the developer to select the Drop Column options of "drop column if data present" and "skip record if data present." The Change Column Length options are to "truncate data if field is too short" and "skip the record if field is too short." The Alter Any option allows the developer to select Adds, Changes, Renames, and Deletes.

The LOGGING tab of the Build Setting dialog allows the developer to select the level of errors that will be logged to the log file. The logging level can reflect fatal errors only; fatal errors and warnings; or fatal errors, warnings, and information. The output can be logged to the Output window and/or to a specified log file.

The SCRIPTS tab of the Build Setting dialog allows the developer to select to "write alter comments to the script," select to have the script

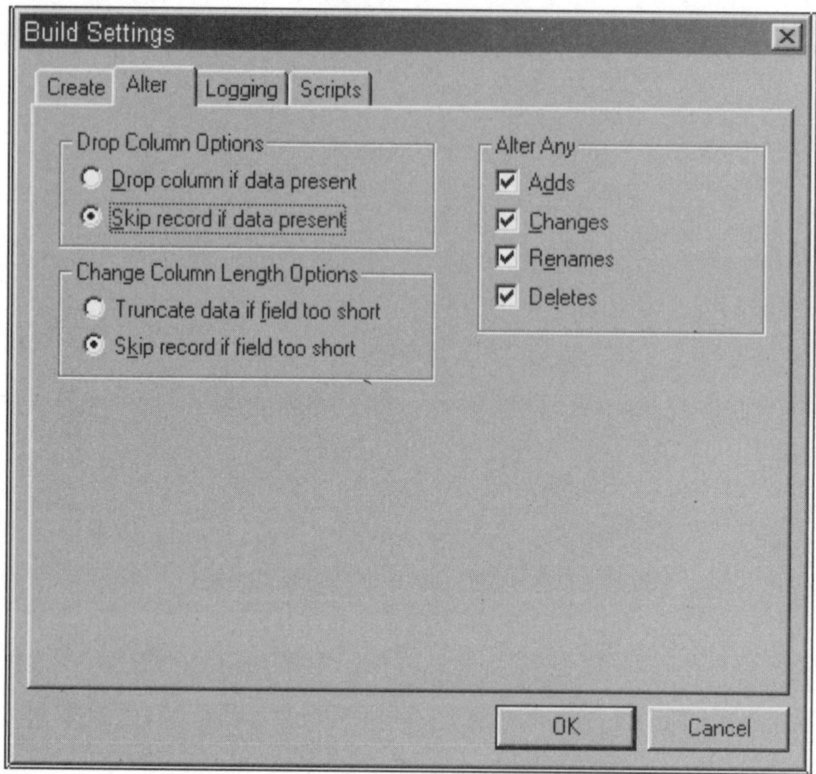

Figure 6-18 ALTER tab of the Build Settings dialog.

file output to a single file or to separate files, or select the file overwrite options. The output filename can also be specified on this tab.

SQL Table Records

SQL Table Records have a one to one link to a table in the database. In PeopleSoft when you build a standard SQL Table Record, a table with the prefix `PS_` is created in the database. From within the Application Designer and PeopleSoft's Query, you will not reference the object with the `PS_` prefix. However, you must remember, when you are accessing the data from either SQR or other SQL tools, that the nonsystem application records that were delivered or the records that you created from the Application Designer will have the `PS_` prefix. For example, when we create our `ITEMS` table, the actual table created in the database will be `PS_ITEMS`.

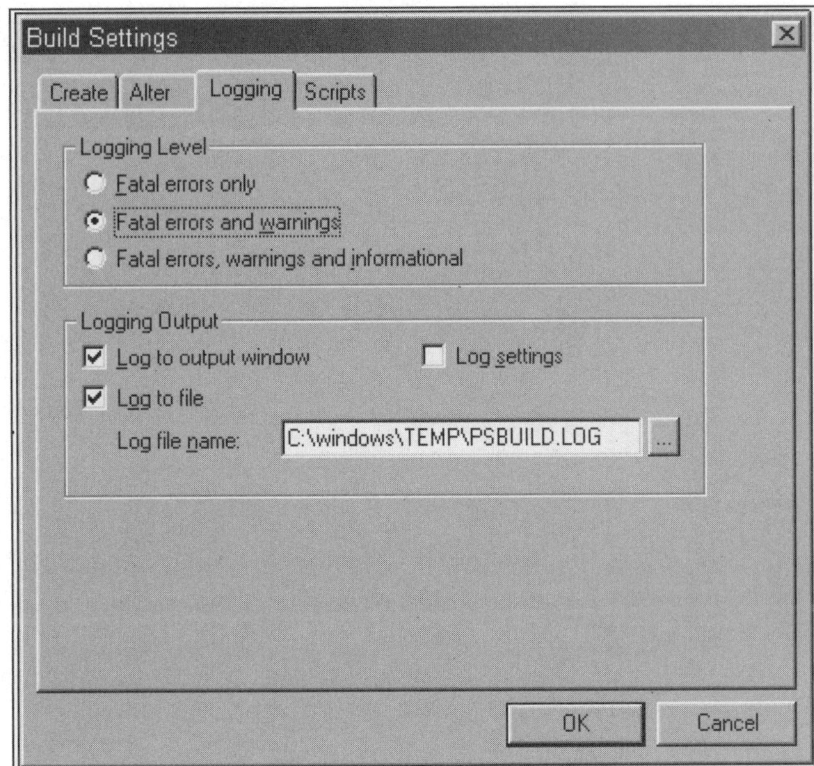

Figure 6-19 LOGGING tab of the Build Settings dialog.

In order to set up your records to be SQL Table Records, you must open the Properties dialog for the record and select the TYPE tab. You can access this dialog when you have a record definition open and selected from within the Application Designer. Your options are to press the PROPERTIES icon (Fig. 6-21) or to go to the File menu and select the Object Properties menu.

In the TYPE tab of the Record Properties dialog (Fig. 6-22) on the bottom left, please note the edit box titled "Non-Standard SQL Table Name." It is enabled only when the Record type is set to either a SQL Table or one of the View options that create database objects. This is where you can override the standard process that sets the prefix PS_. This option is used mainly for when you would like to have a PeopleSoft Record access an external systems data object. For SQL Table Records, there are no other options available from this dialog.

The Data Administrator options are the last area you need to be sure you check before you execute a Build SQL Table Record. This is where

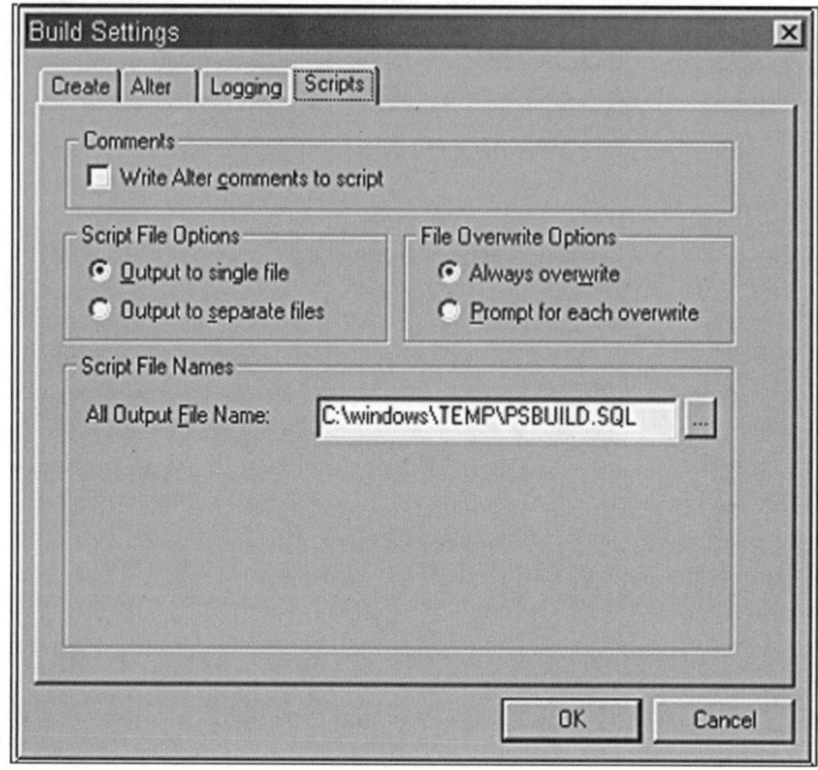

Figure 6-20
SCRIPTS tab of the Build Settings dialog.

Figure 6-21
PROPERTIES icon.

you would set up the Tablespace for the tables you are going to build. These options vary according to the database platform you are using with PeopleSoft. If your database platform utilizes Tablespaces, please contact your Database Administrator for the correct settings. To access the Tablespace DDL dialog, select the Tools menu, Data Administration, then select Tablespace DDL.

View Records

Records can also be associated with SQL select statements. If the SQL select statement is compiled and stored on the database as a View, there will need to be a build process to create the SQL View. PeopleSoft also

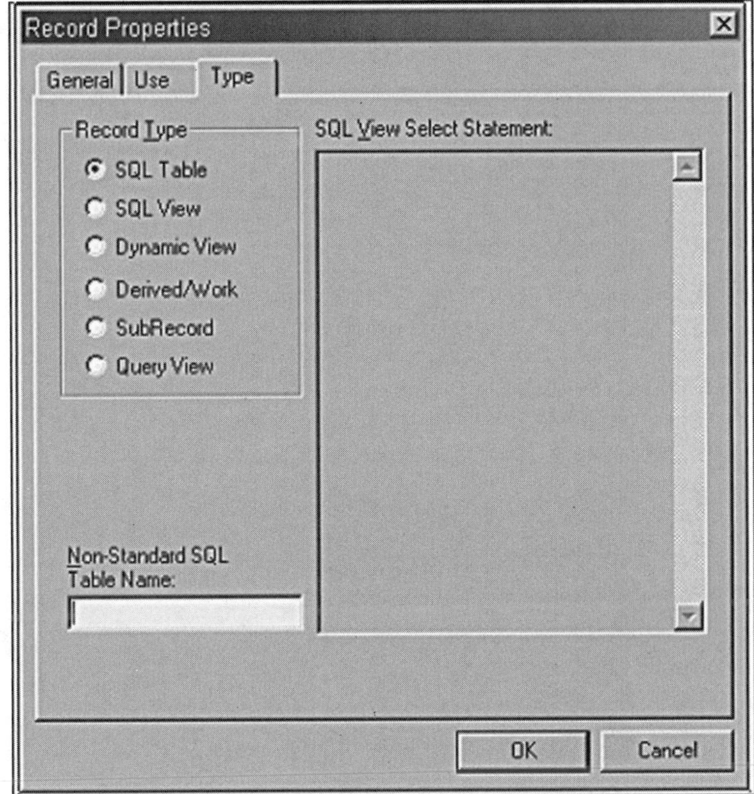

Figure 6-22
TYPE tab of the record definition.

allows you to define the record type to be a Dynamic View. A Dynamic View's select statement is not compiled into a database view. Instead, the SQL is passed to the database each time the record is used.

SQL View Records are very useful. You can use them to filter data for security reasons. They can also join multiple tables to create one easy-to-use object. In addition, you can use them to view and work with data that are external to the PeopleSoft application.

A SQL View Record's and Dynamic View Record's select statement is created in the TYPE tab of the record definition (see Fig. 6-23). When these options are selected, the SQL View Select Statement edit box is enabled, allowing you to enter the select statement. It is very important to note that the order in which you enter the column names in the select statement must match the order in which the fields are placed in the record definition. In addition, the field definitions should match the size and data types of their related columns.

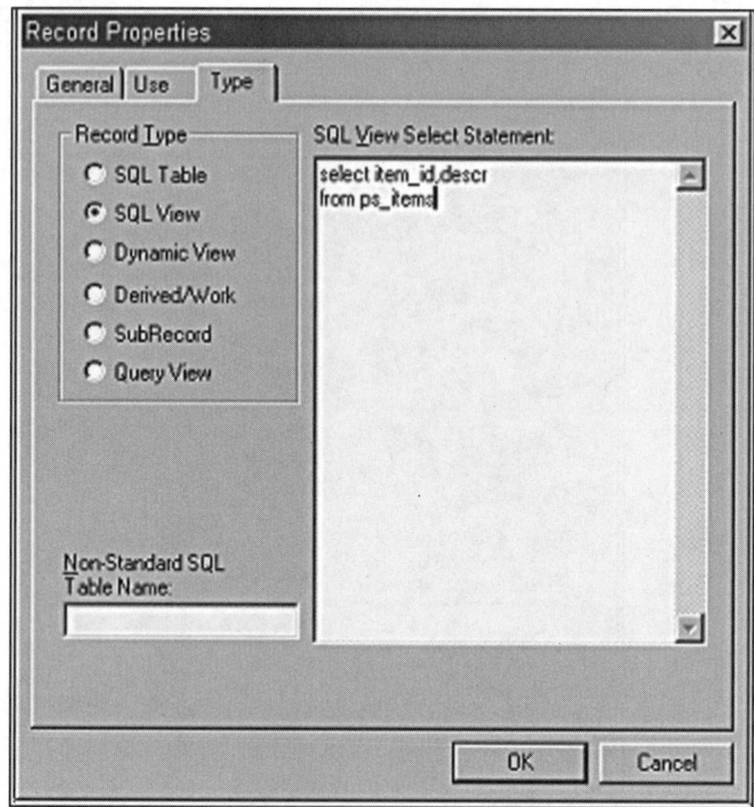

Figure 6-23
TYPE tab for SQL View Record.

When the Query View option is selected, the SQL VIEW SELECT STATEMENT is grayed out and a new CLICK TO LAUNCH QUERY button is displayed below the Record Type group box. Figure 6-24 shows the Query View option selected.

To build the SQL select statement for a Query View Record, click on the QUERY button. Figure 6-25 shows the Query tabbed dialog that will be displayed. The DICTIONARY tab is displayed first. The Database Dictionary tree view control that is found on the left of the tab displays all the PeopleSoft records that can be selected. If you are going to create a joined view, you can select multiple records, and a Join Criteria dialog will automatically be displayed to allow you to select what fields should be used to relate the records to each other (Fig. 6-26).

The next tab on the Query View dialog is where you can select the fields that will be included in your record (Fig. 6-27). A great feature of the Query View records is that you do not have to manually fill the

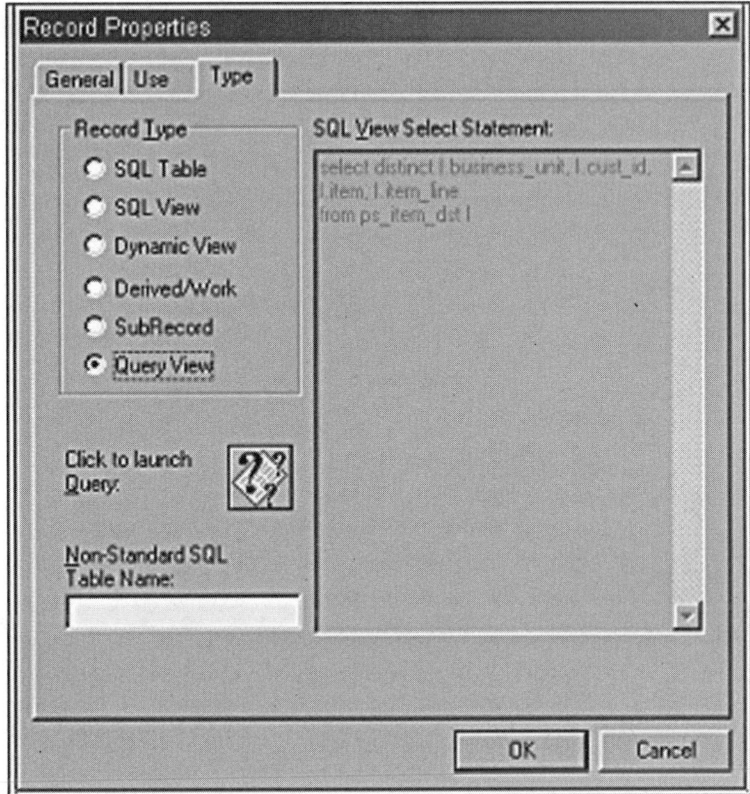

Figure 6-24
TYPE tab for Query View Record.

record definition with the field definitions. Instead, all the fields that you select in the FIELDS tab will automatically be included in the right order on your record definition.

If you double-click on one of the fields that you have selected, a Field Property tabbed dialog will be displayed. Figures 6-28 through 6-33 show Field Property options for Query View. From these dialogs, you can change the defaults for the column number, heading, order by, aggregate, and either the Translate or related Field Properties. Please note the AGGREGATE tab in Figure 6-31. This is where you can set up a min, max, sum, count, or average function on the selected field.

The CRITERIA and the HAVING CRITERIA tabs of the Query View Dialog are very similar (see Figs. 6-34 and 6-35, respectively). The CRITERIA tab is where you will build the Where clause of your select statement. The HAVING CRITERIA tab is where you build the Having clause of the select statement. You can select the fields and/or constants that will be used to

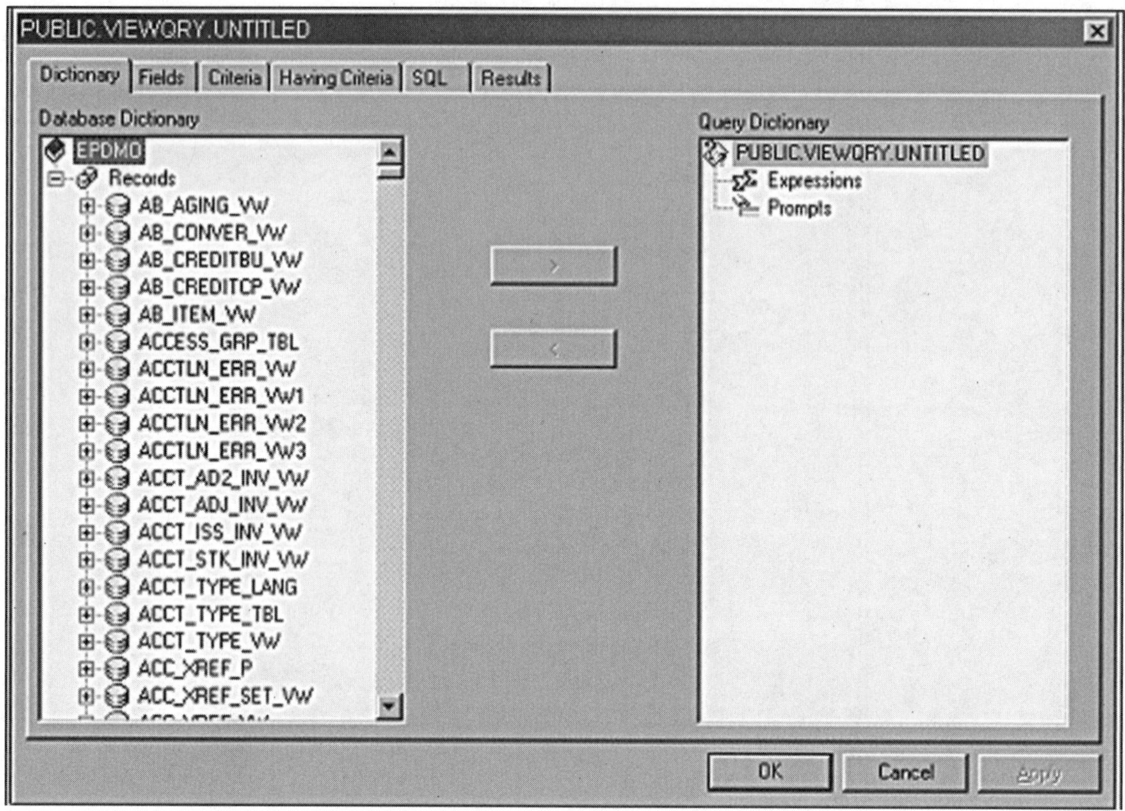

Figure 6-25 DICTIONARY tab for Query View dialog.

filter the rows of data that are returned. You would use the HAVING CRITERIA tab if you were using one of the Aggregate Functions on a field on which you would like to set criteria. An example of this would be if we wanted to find the sum of all the orders that have been requested when the order is less than $100. To accomplish this, you would set an aggregate sum function to the quantity of the orders and in the HAVING CRITERIA tab would include only the orders that were smaller than $100. This criterion needs to be placed in the Having clause because SQL does not allow you to include aggregate columns in the Where clause.

The SQL tab of the Query View dialog is simply a disabled edit box that displays the SQL select statement that you have built using the previous tabs. Figure 6-36 shows the SQL tab.

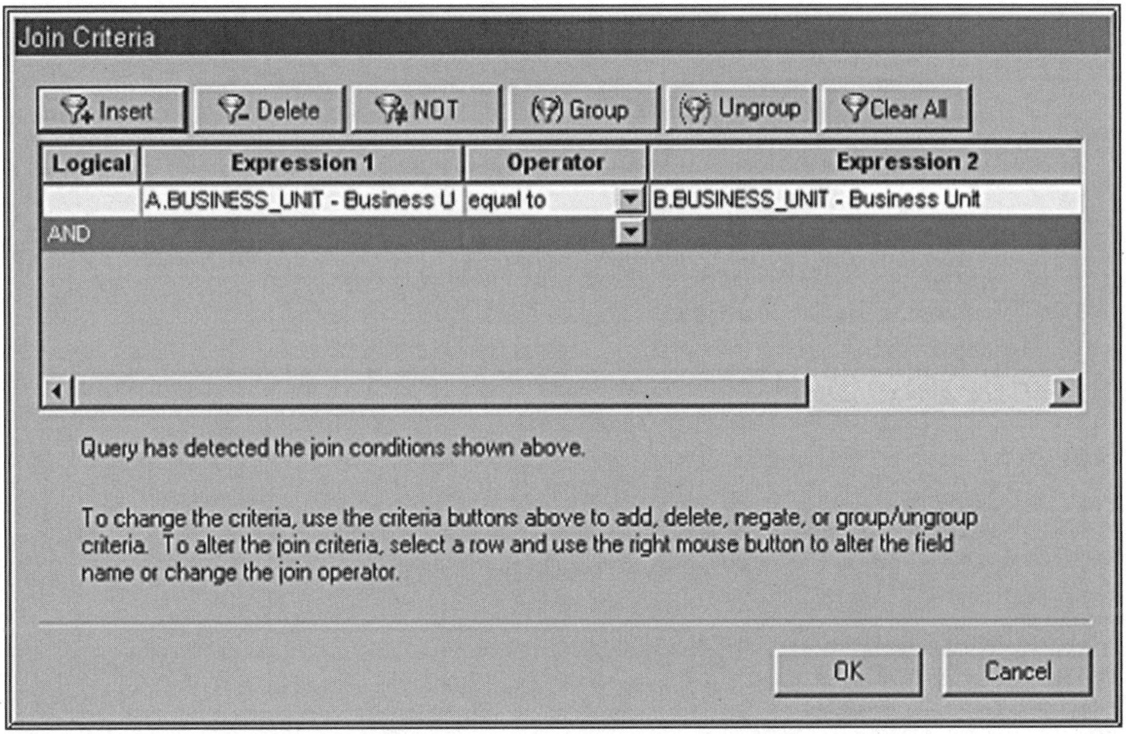

Figure 6-26 Join Criteria dialog from Query View dialog.

The final tab of the Query View dialog is the RESULTS tab (Fig. 6-37). When you select this tab for the first time after you have built your query, the select statement is executed against the database and the resulting rows of data are returned for you to view in a tabular format. This feature allows you to verify your query and make changes where needed. Once you have made any changes and you return to the RESULTS tab, the new query will be executed and its rows will be displayed.

When you are satisfied with the query you have created, press the OK button. This will return you to the TYPE tab of the Record Properties dialog. Press OK here, also. The record definition should now contain all the fields that you selected in the Query dialog.

Before you can use any of these Query records, except the dynamic ones, you must go through the build process that was discussed earlier in the chapter.

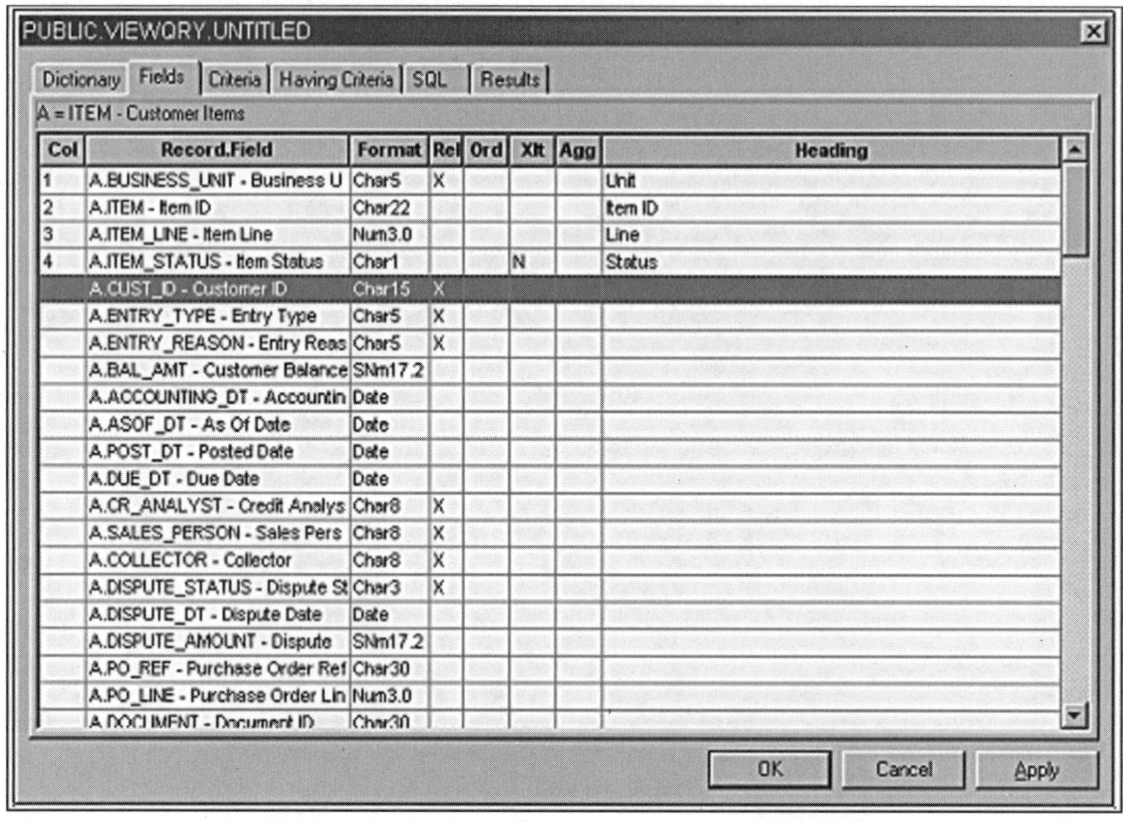

Figure 6-27 FIELDS tab for Query View dialog.

Figure 6-28 COLUMN # tab for Field Properties in the Query View dialog.

Field Properties (ITEM_STATUS - Item Status)

Column# | Heading | Order By | Aggregate | Translate

Column Number: 4

OK Cancel

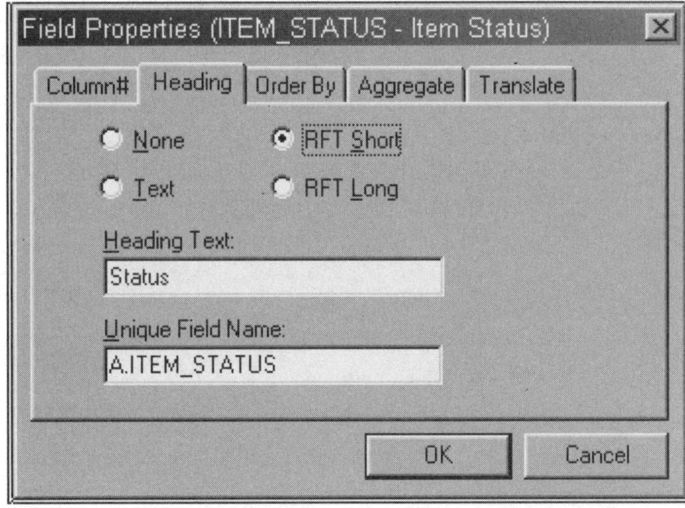

Figure 6-29
HEADING tab for Field Properties in the Query View dialog.

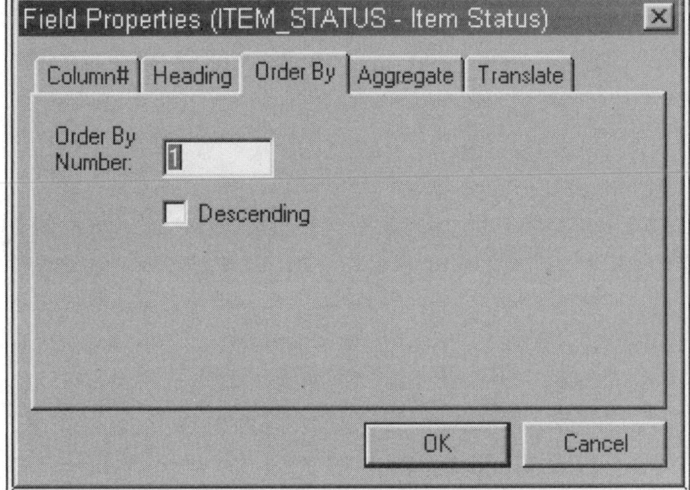

Figure 6-30
ORDER BY tab for Field Properties in the Query View dialog.

Subrecords

Subrecords are used to group related fields that can be used in other Record definitions. An example of this is an address subfield. This subfield can be defined with the following fields for a simplified standard U.S. address:

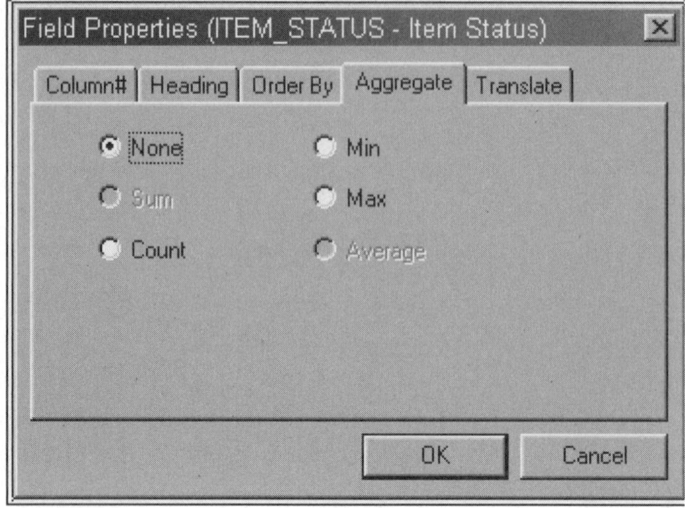

Figure 6-31 AGGREGATE tab for Field Properties in the Query View dialog.

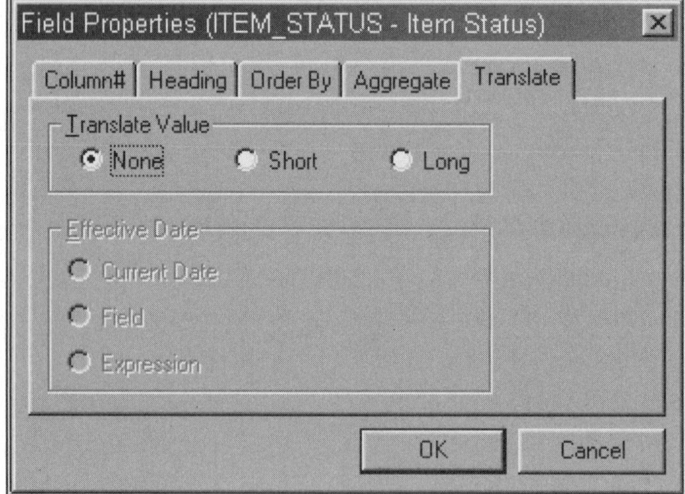

Figure 6-32 TRANSLATE tab for Field Properties in the Query View dialog.

- `Street1`
- `Street2`
- `City`
- `State`
- `Zip`

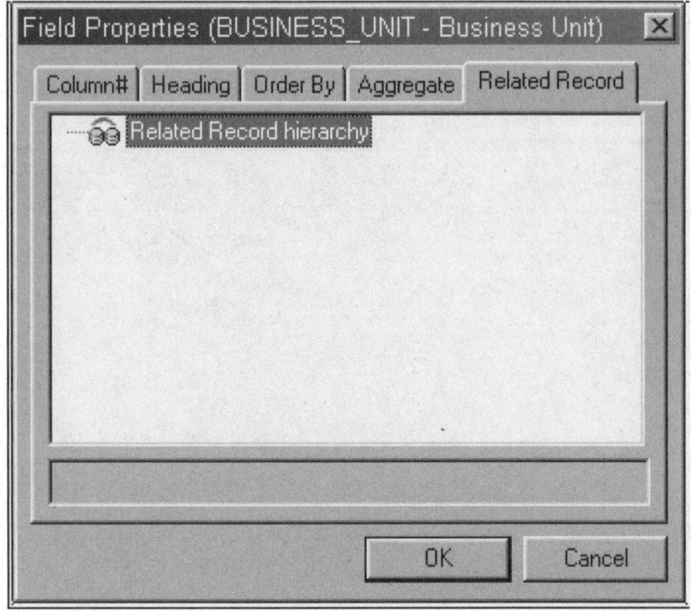

Figure 6-33 Related Record tab for Field Properties in the Query View dialog.

Addresses are required in a large number of records. By setting it up as a subrecord, you are maintaining uniformity throughout your application. All you have to do to include it in a record definition is go to the Insert menu and select the SUBRECORD option. Figure 6-38 shows the insert dialog that will be displayed to allow you to insert the desired subrecord into the record definition.

Figure 6-39 shows a sample record with the address subrecord included. If you need to view the subrecords definition, you can select the VIEW DEFINITIONS from the View menu with the subrecord selected in the record definition.

If any changes are made to a subrecord, it is important that you rebuild all the records that are utilizing it. In order to find all the places the subrecord is being used, you can use the Application Designers Find Object references functionality. Choose the FIND OBJECT REFERENCES option from the Edit menu with the subrecord's definition selected in the object workspace. All the records that the subrecord is used in will be displayed in the Output window. You can then double-click on them from the Output window. Their record definitions will automatically be displayed in the Object Workspace, where you can then rebuild them if necessary.

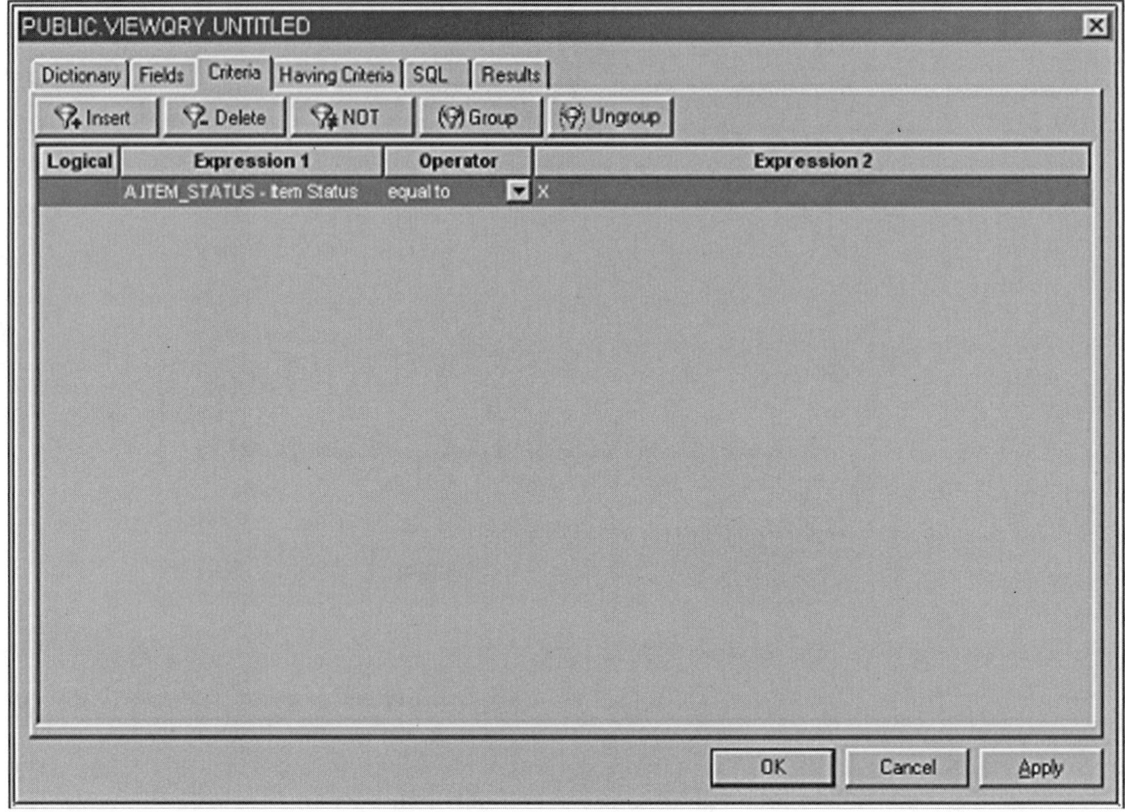

Figure 6-34 CRITERIA tab for Query View dialog.

Derived Records

Derived records are unique. They are not used to store application data. They can be used to hold fields that are used in panels for display data. This is useful when you would like to display a total that would not normally be stored in the database. Derived records are also used to store logic that can be used by other records in their own PeopleCode events. The records that are used to store generic code that can be used from any record in effect become libraries of functionality. PeopleSoft is shipped with many of these libraries. The naming convention for derived records is to start with FUNCLIB_. The functions that create the library

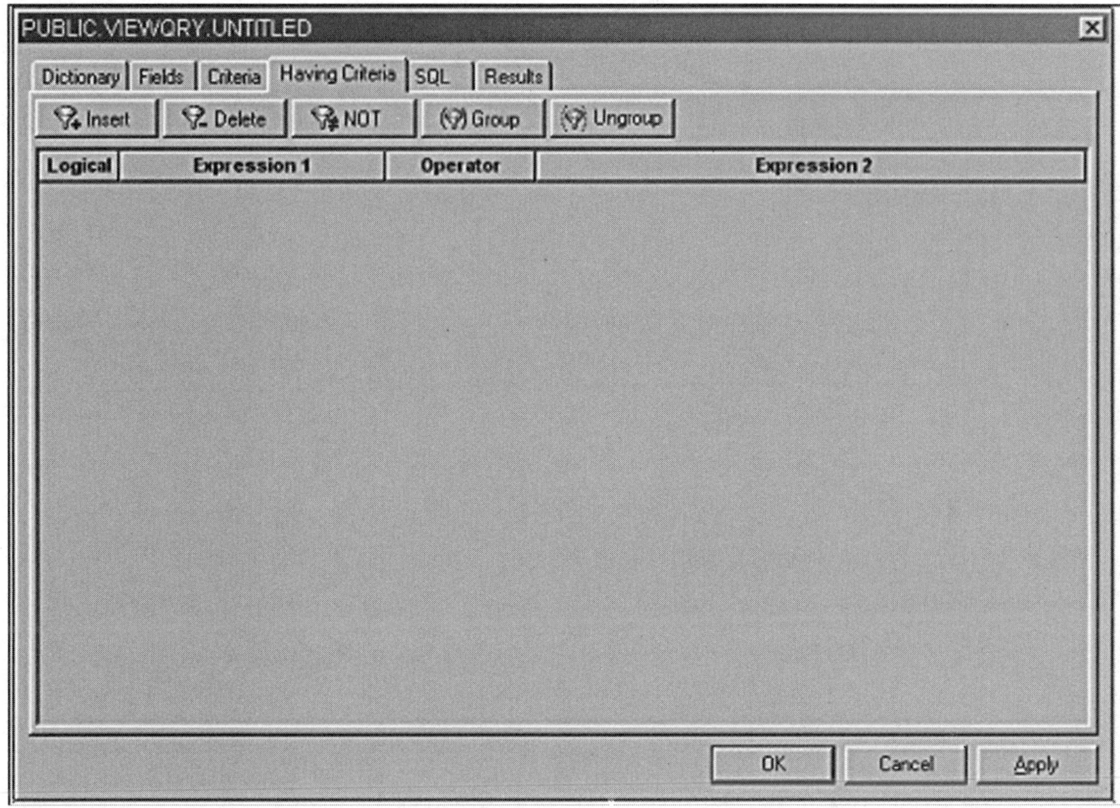

Figure 6-35 HAVING CRITERIA tab for Query View dialog.

are stored in the `FieldFormula` PeopleCode event. The following PeopleCode snippet shows how you would call a function stored in a PeopleSoft functional library:

```
declare function My_Example_Function peoplecode
FUNCLIB_SAMPLE.FIELD_01 FieldFormula;
```

Since derived records are not used to store application data, there is no need to run a build process to create any SQL objects in the database. All PeopleCode, even for nonderived records, is stored in a PeopleSoft system table (`PSPCMPROG`) as binaries. In a later chapter devoted to PeopleCode, we will develop our own derived records.

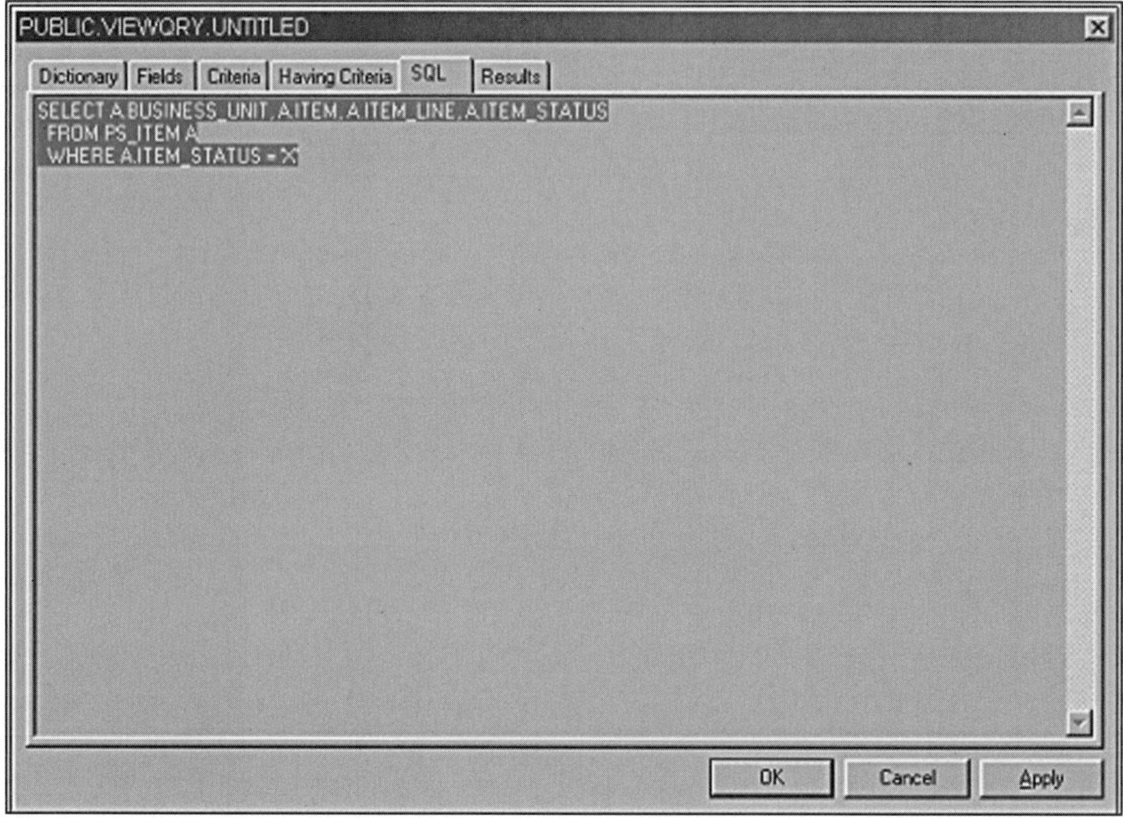

Figure 6-36 SQL tab for Query View dialog.

Example Record Definitions

Now that we have covered the basics of how records are created and what they can be used for, we will create the records we need for the first pass at our example. You may recall that we mapped out the physical data model in Chapter 3. For the rest of this chapter, we will first show a table containing the fields and attributes that we plan to use to create our records. All of these tables are the same as those mentioned in Chapter 3 except for Table 6-8, which shows the fields we will use to create the SQL View table for the External Order Record.

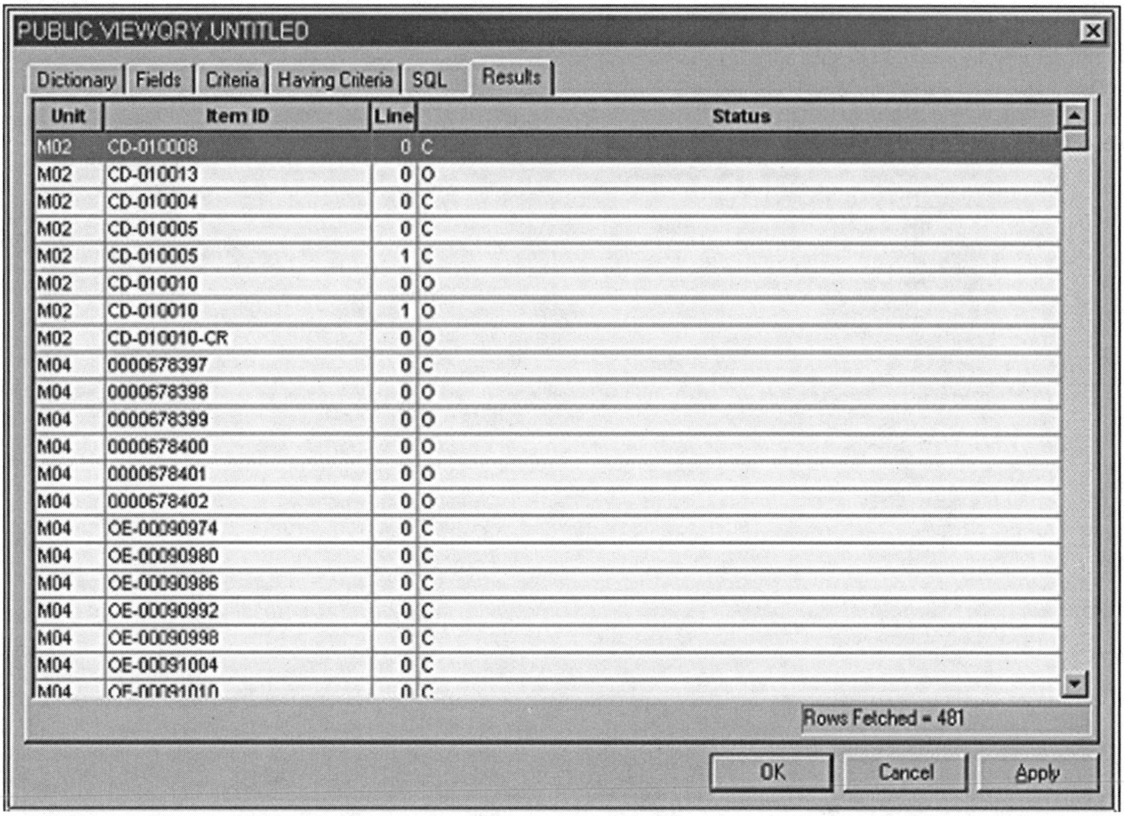

PUBLIC.VIEWQRY.UNTITLED

Dictionary | Fields | Criteria | Having Criteria | SQL | Results

Unit	Item ID	Line	Status
M02	CD-010008	0	C
M02	CD-010013	0	O
M02	CD-010004	0	C
M02	CD-010005	0	C
M02	CD-010005	1	C
M02	CD-010010	0	O
M02	CD-010010	1	O
M02	CD-010010-CR	0	O
M04	0000678397	0	C
M04	0000678398	0	O
M04	0000678399	0	O
M04	0000678400	0	O
M04	0000678401	0	O
M04	0000678402	0	O
M04	OE-00090974	0	C
M04	OE-00090980	0	C
M04	OE-00090986	0	C
M04	OE-00090992	0	C
M04	OE-00090998	0	C
M04	OE-00091004	0	C
M04	OE-00091010	0	C

Rows Fetched = 481

OK Cancel Apply

Figure 6-37 RESULTS tab for Query View dialog.

EMPLOYEES Record

We are going to start by creating all the prompt tables that are to be used for Data Validation. Table 6-1 lists the fields and attributes that will make up our `EMPLOYEES` record.

Before we begin, with the Application Designer open, we must make sure that the current project is the same one we created for our fields. If it is not, we must open the `Order_Example` project. With that done, let's start by selecting either the NEW icon or the FILE then NEW menu options. The New dialog will then be displayed (Fig. 6-40). Now select RECORD and press the OK button.

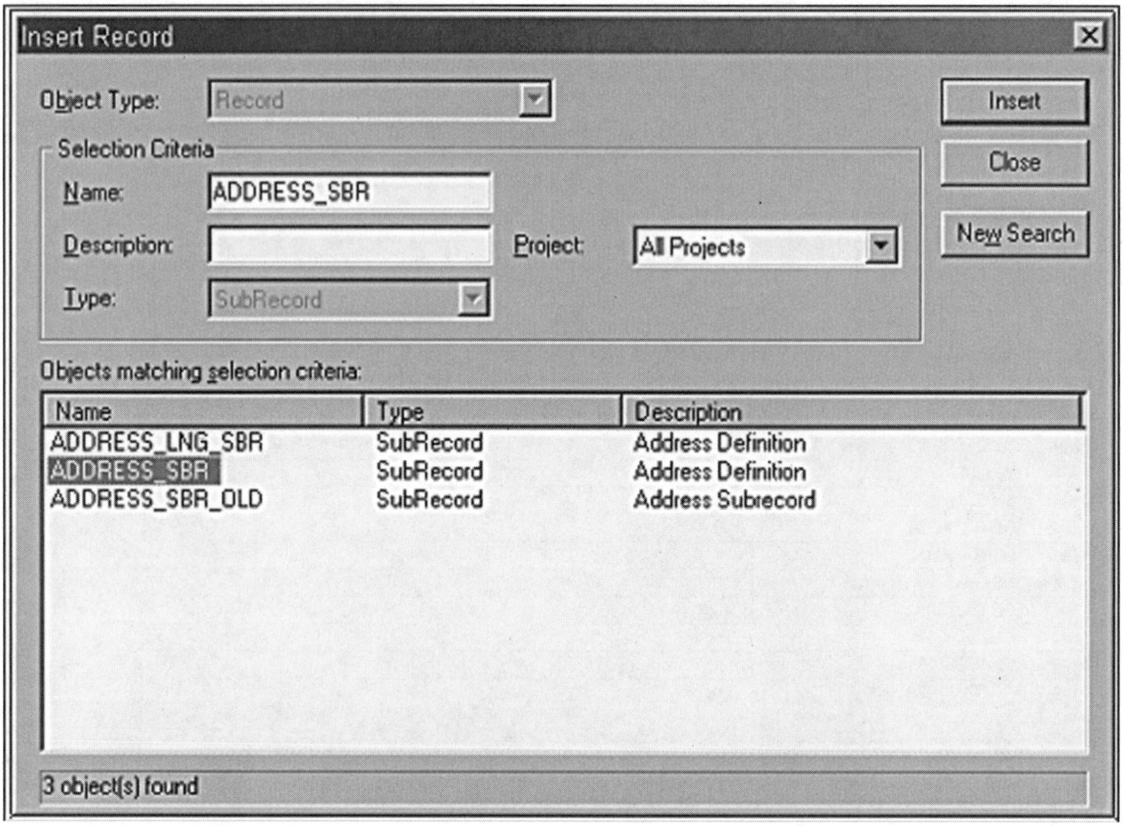

Insert Record

Object Type: Record

Selection Criteria

Name: ADDRESS_SBR

Description:

Project: All Projects

Type: SubRecord

Insert

Close

New Search

Objects matching selection criteria:

Name	Type	Description
ADDRESS_LNG_SBR	SubRecord	Address Definition
ADDRESS_SBR	SubRecord	Address Definition
ADDRESS_SBR_OLD	SubRecord	Address Subrecord

3 object(s) found

Figure 6-38 Insert Subrecord dialog.

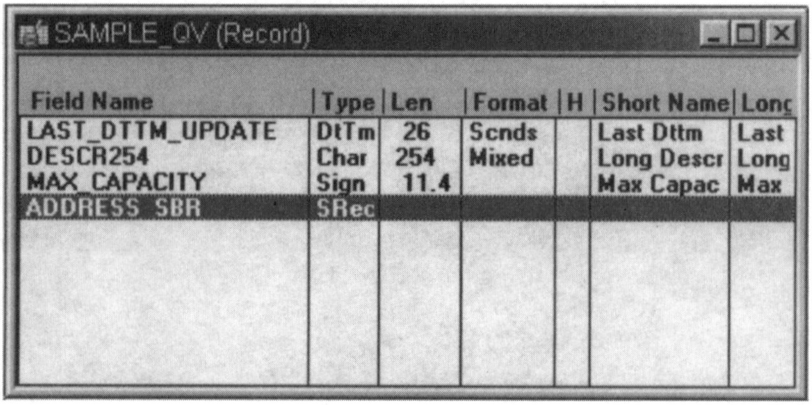

SAMPLE_QV (Record)

Field Name	Type	Len	Format	H	Short Name	Long
LAST_DTTM_UPDATE	DtTm	26	Scnds		Last Dttm	Last
DESCR254	Char	254	Mixed		Long Descr	Long
MAX_CAPACITY	Sign	11.4			Max Capac	Max
ADDRESS_SBR	SRec					

Figure 6-39 Sample Record with subrecord.

TABLE 6-1

EMPLOYEES Record

Column	Description	Data Type	Key	Valid Values
EMP_ID	Employee id	Char(10)	X	
EFFDT	Effective date	Date	X	
EFF_STATUS	Effective status	Char(1)	X	A = active; I = inactive
NAME	Employee's name	Char(30)		
POSITION	Employee's position	Char(3)		SUP = supervisor; BUY = buyer; OTH = other
EMAIL_ADDRESS	Employee's email address	Char(30)		

Figure 6-40
New dialog.

A new empty record definition should now be displayed in the Object Workspace. We are now ready to begin to add the fields to the EMPLOYEES record definition. The easiest way to do this is to use the drag-and-drop method. Expand the Fields Folder in the Project Workspace, and select only the first field that we plan to add. Keep the left mouse button pressed down, and drag the field to the new record definition. Drag and drop the following fields onto the new record definition:

- EMP_ID
- EFFDT
- EFF_STATUS
- NAME
- POSITION
- EMAIL_ADDRESS

If your record definition's field view looks like the one in Figure 6-41, press the SAVE ALL icon, or select the FILE, SAVE ALL menu options. In the Save As dialog, enter `EMPLOYEES` and press OK (Fig. 6-42). If your project's options are set to MANUAL INSERT, please press F7.

The `EMPLOYEES` record is now ready for us to begin setting all the record's field attributes. Let's start with the first field inserted into the record definition. The Use values for the record's field attributes of `EMP_ID` are

- Key
- Search key
- List Box Item

The Search Key option will place this field in all the search dialogs that are used for the internal order record. The List Box Item option will place this field as a column in the resulting list box in the search dialogs.

Record1 (Record)

Field Name	Type	Len	Format	H	Short Name	Long Name
EMP_ID	Char	9	SSN		Employee II	Employee ID
EFFDT	Date	10			Eff Date	Effective Date
EFF_STATUS	Char	1	Upper		Status	Status as of Eff
NAME	Char	50	Name		Name	Name
POSITION	Char	3	Upper		Emp Positio	Employees Posi
EMAIL_ADDRESS	Char	30	Mixed		From	Submitted By

Figure 6-41 EMPLOYEES record definition.

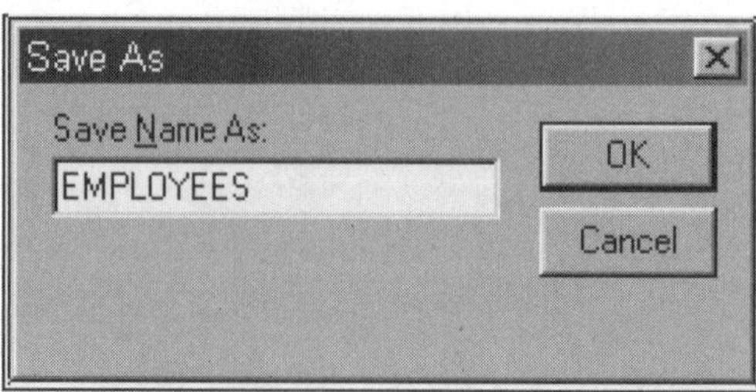

Figure 6-42 EMPLOYEES Save As dialog.

The only Edits property for this field is that it is required. EMP_ID is a key field and is therefore required. Although this is a one-to-one relationship, you still must set the required check box in the EDITS tab of the fields record attributes. Figures 6-43 and 6-44 show the Use and Edit tabbed dialogs for EMP_ID.

The next field we set the record attributes for is EFFDT. The Use values that are associated with the field attributes of EFFDT are

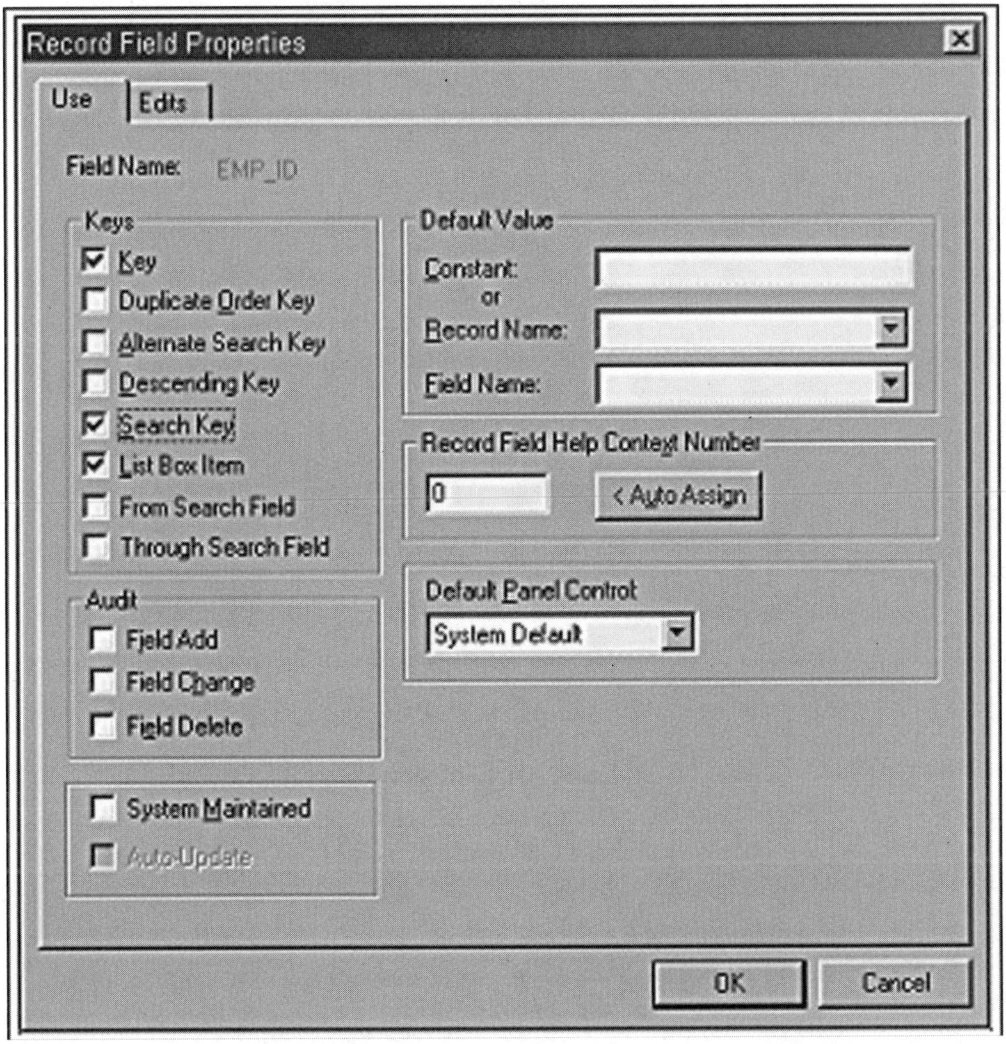

Figure 6-43 EMP_ID Use dialog.

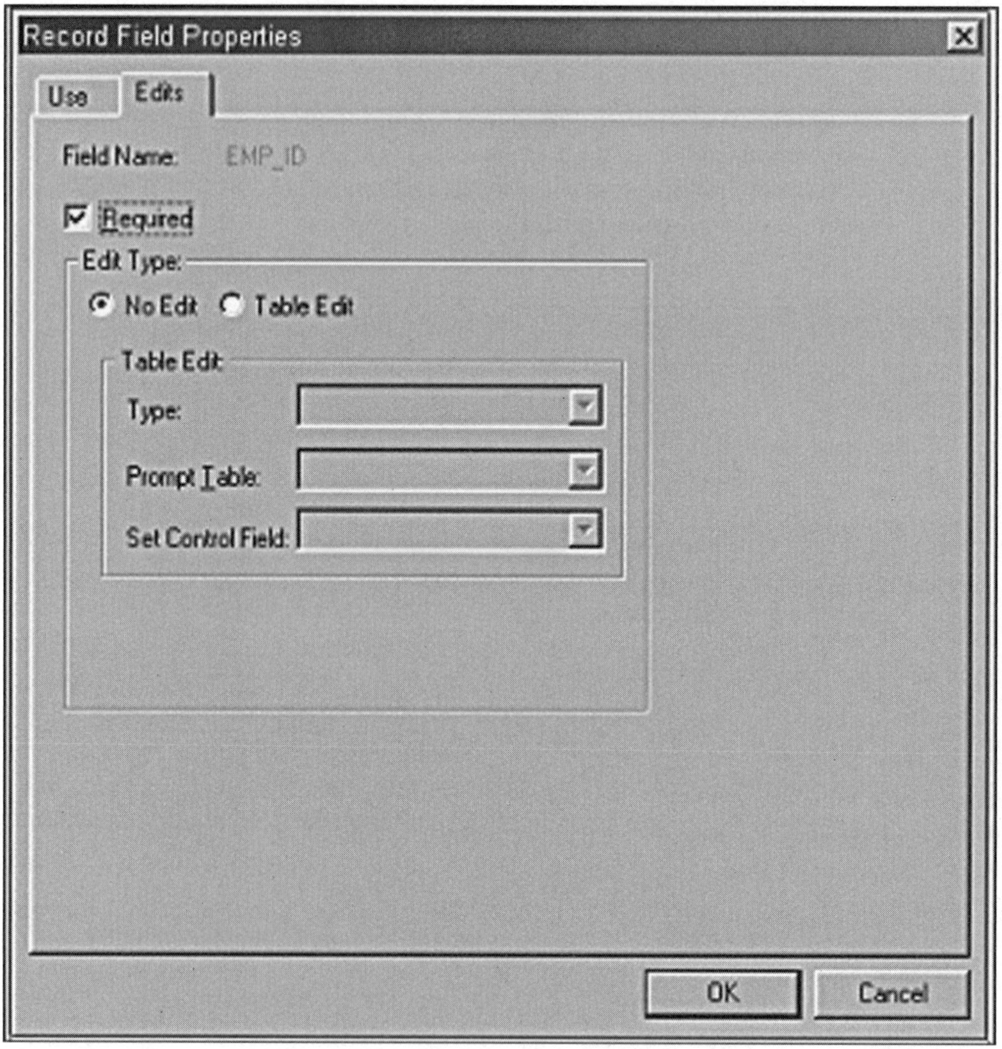

Figure 6-44 `EMP_ID` Edits dialog.

- Key
- Descending Key
- Default constant set to the system date `%date`

The Descending Key option returns the most recent `EFFDT`. The default constant `%date` will automatically place the system date in the `EFFDT` when it is opened for the first time.

The only Edits property that we are going to set for EFFDT is that it is required. Figures 6-45 and 6-46 show the Use and Edit tabbed dialogs for EFFDT.

The next field we set the record attributes for is EFF_STATUS. The Use value that is associated to the field attributes of EFF_STATUS is the default constant set to A. The default constant A will automatically set the initial effective status to ACTIVE when a new record is added.

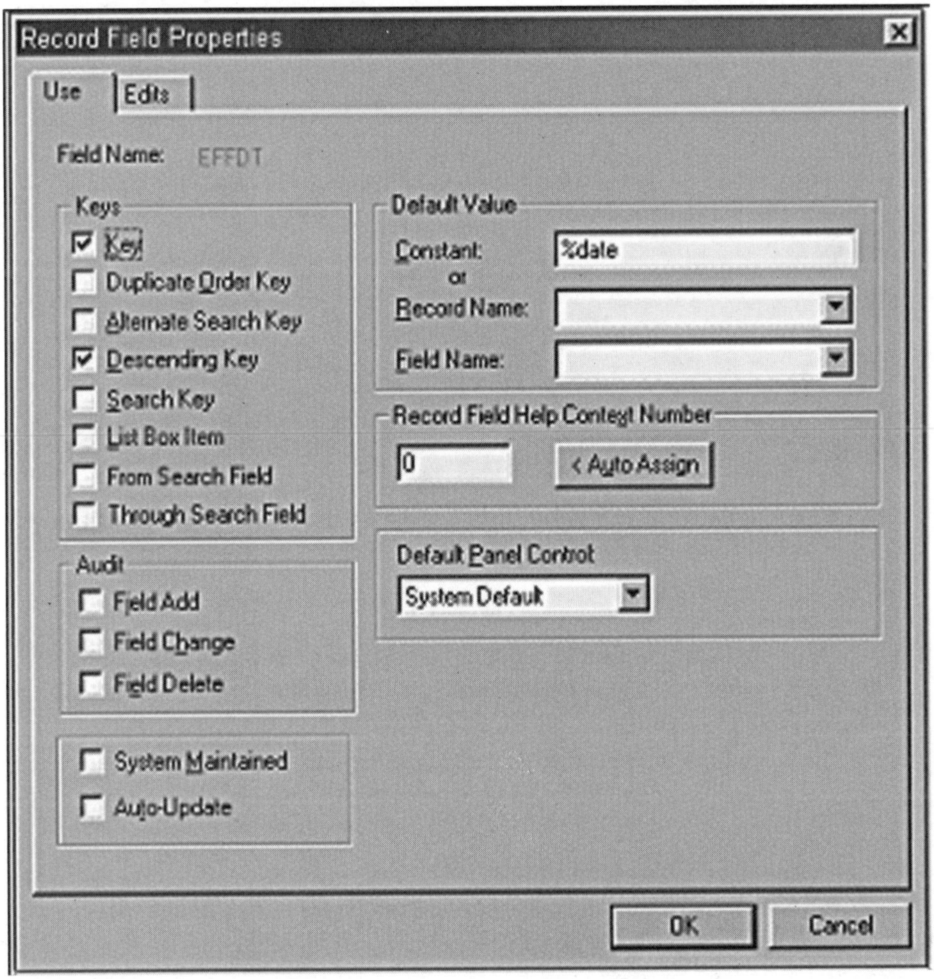

Figure 6-45 EFFDT Use dialog.

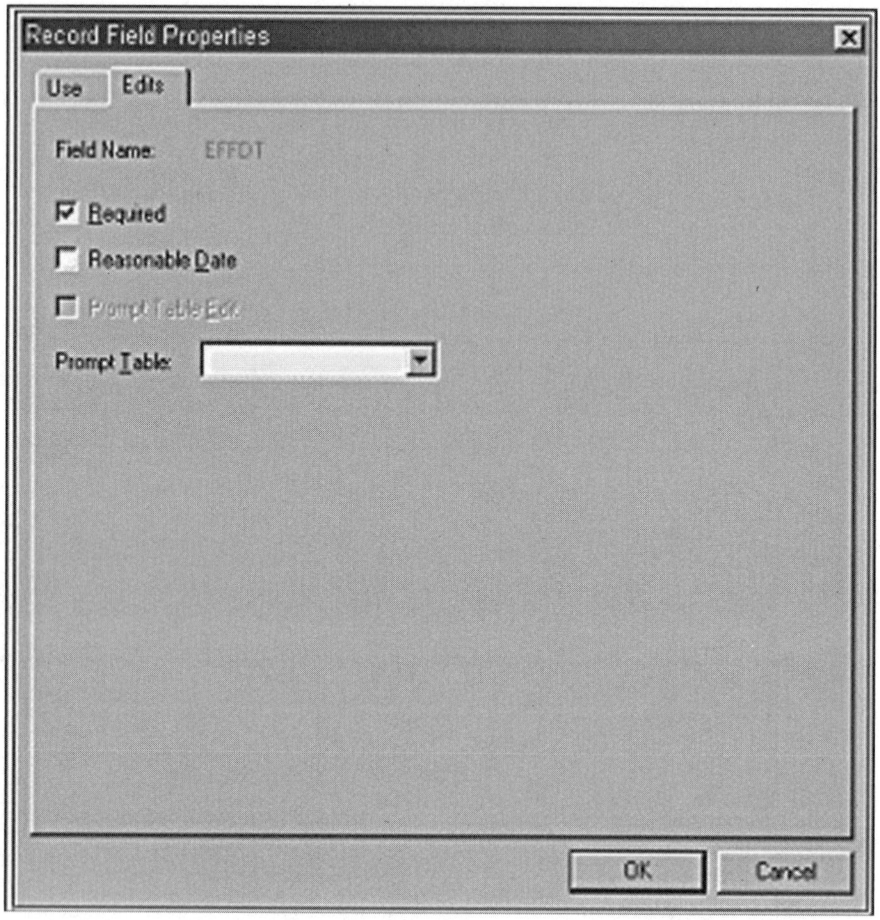

Figure 6-46
EFFDT Edits dialog.

The only Edit property that we are going to set for EFF_STATUS is that it is required. Figures 6-47 and 6-48 show the Use and Edits tabbed dialogs for EFF_STATUS.

The next field we set the record attributes for is NAME. The Use values that are associated with the field attributes of NAME are

- Alt Search Key
- List Box Item

The Alt Search Key option will place this field in all the search dialogs that are used for the internal order record. The Alt Search Key option does not make this field part of the primary key; instead it cre-

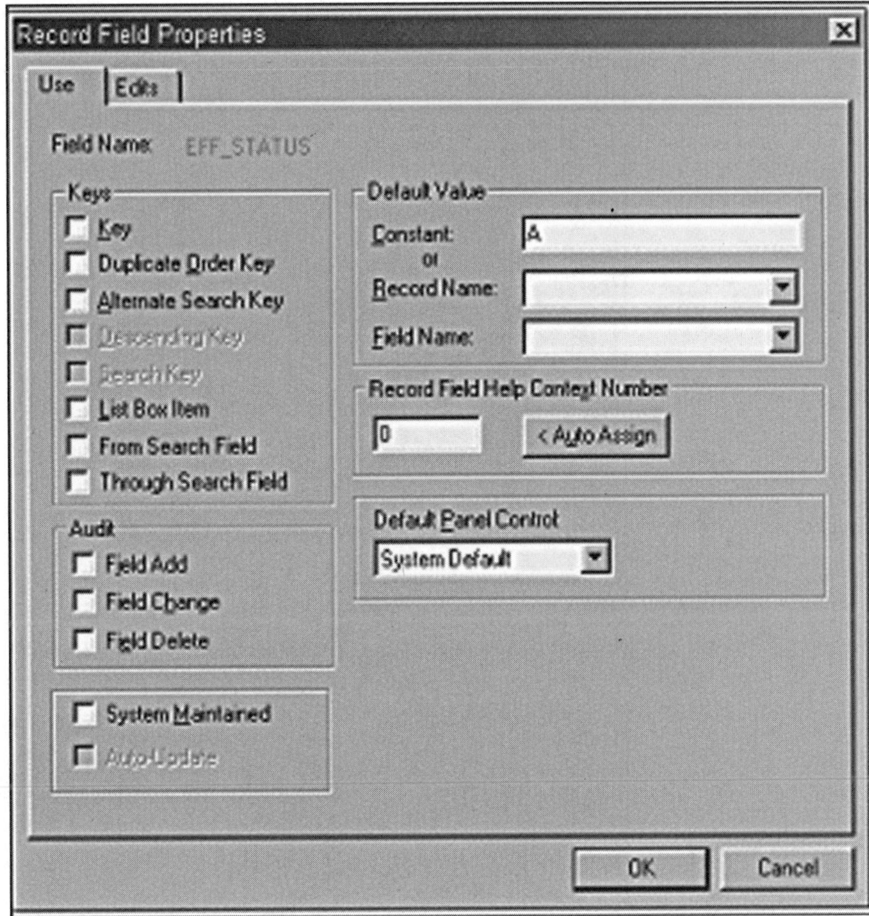

Figure 6-47 EFF_STATUS Use dialog.

ates an index on the field. The List Box Item option will place this field as a column in the resulting list box in the search dialogs.

The only Edit property that we are going to set for NAME is that it is required. Figures 6-49 and 6-50 show the Use and Edit tabbed dialogs for NAME.

The next field we set the record attributes for is POSITION. The Use values that are associated with the field attributes of POSITION are

- Alt Search Key
- List Box Item

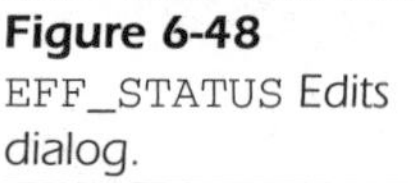

Figure 6-48
EFF_STATUS Edits dialog.

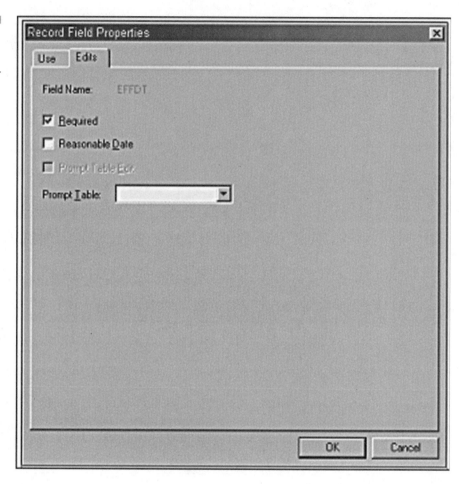

The Alt Search Key option will place this field in all of the search dialogs that are used for the internal order record. The Alt Search Key option does not make this field part of the primary key; instead it creates an index on the field. The list box item option will place this field as a column in the resulting list box in the search dialogs.

The POSITION is not only required but also has a table edit type of Translate Table Edit. Figures 6-51 and 6-52 show the Use and Edits tabbed dialogs for POSITION.

The last field of the EMPLOYEES record definition is EMAIL_ADDRESS. We are not going set any Use or Edits attributes for this field. The Use Display of your EMPLOYEES record should look like the one shown in Figure 6-53.

The final step we must execute before we can use the EMPLOYEES

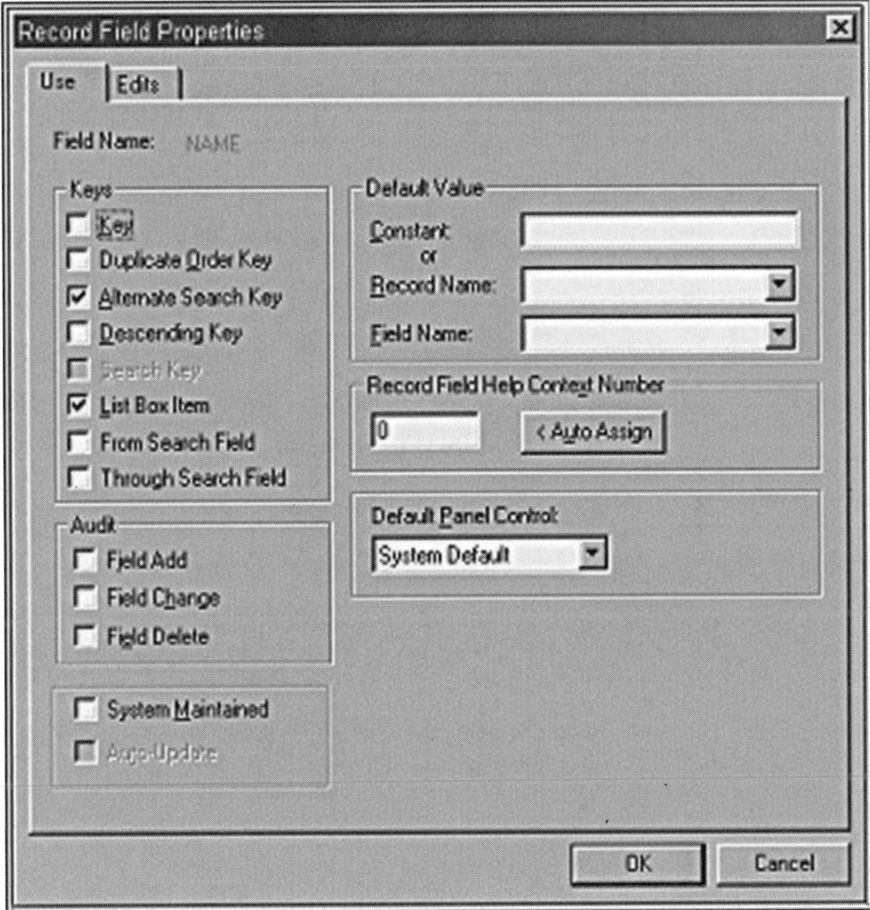

Figure 6-49
NAME Use dialog.

record is to initiate the build process. Select BUILD, CURRENT OBJECT..., or press the BUILD icon from the toolbar. With the build dialog displayed, select the Create Table check box. The Create Indexes check box will automatically be selected and grayed out. Next, select the EXECUTE AND BUILD SCRIPT radio button. (Fig. 6-54). When you have completed this, press the BUILD button at the top right of the dialog.

The results of the build will be displayed in the Output window of the Application Designer. Figure 6-55 shows the output for the build process for the EMPLOYEES record. If the build process did not complete successfully, the output would tell you that there were errors. In order to debug the problem, you are able to double-click on the log file or the script file, and those files will automatically be displayed for you.

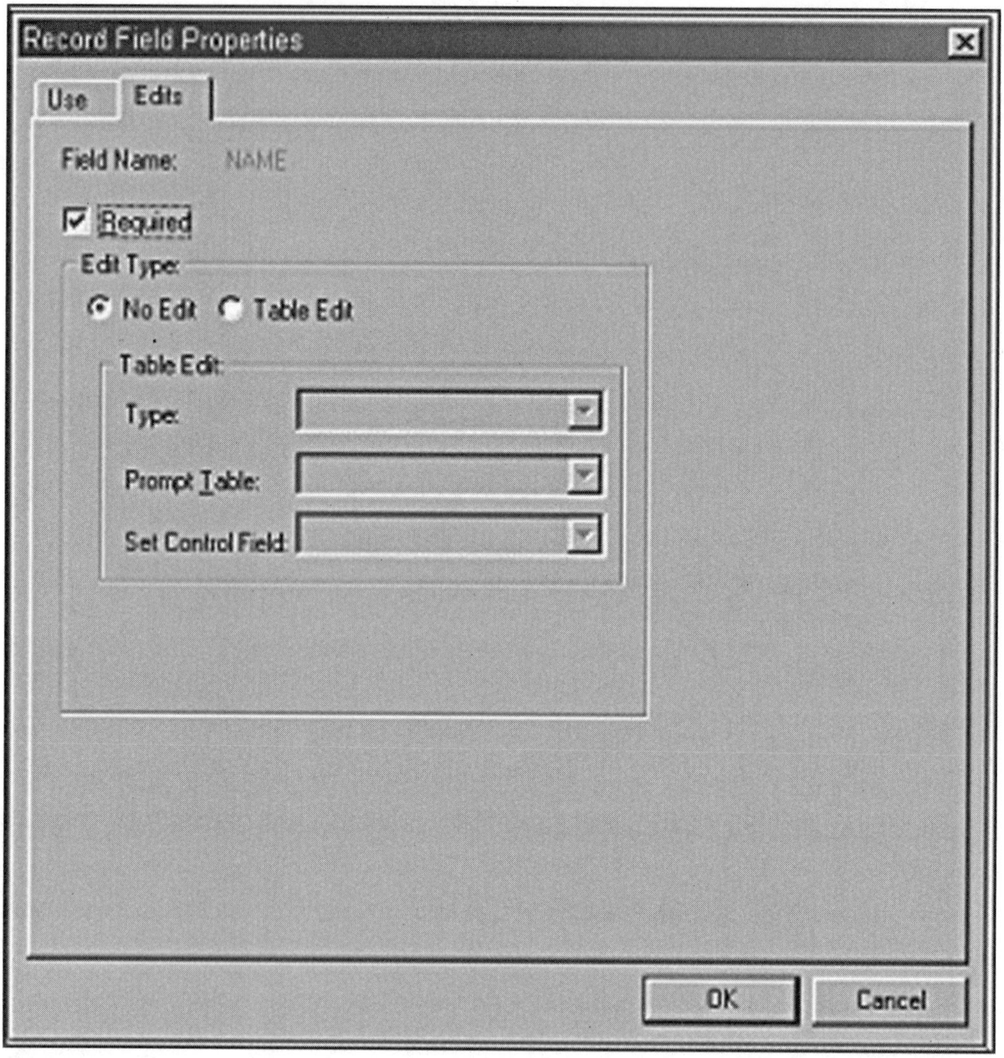

Figure 6-50 NAME Edits dialog.

BUYER_VW Record

The next record we are going to create is based on the record we just created. The BUYER_VW record is a Query View record that will contain only the employees who have the position of *Buyer*. To create a Query View record, press the NEW toolbar icon, or select FILE, NEW menu options.

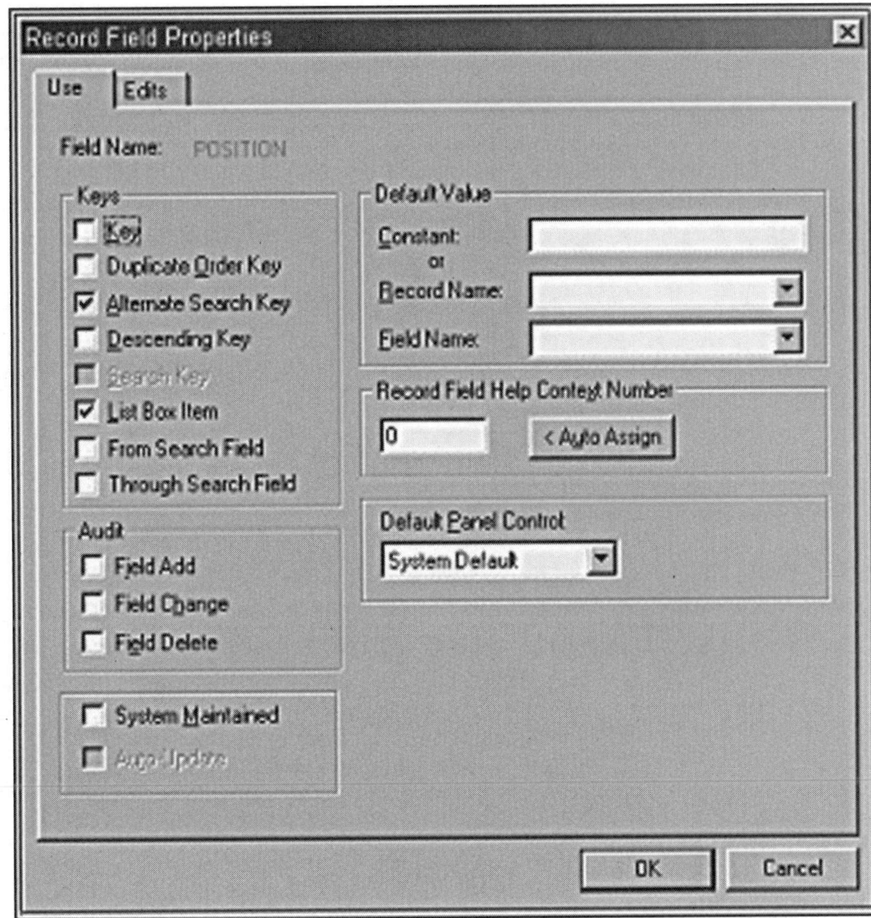

Figure 6-51 POSITION Use dialog.

From the new dialog, select RECORD and press OK. A new empty record definition should now be displayed in the Object Workspace. Before we create the Query View record, we need to save the empty record definition. Press the SAVE icon and enter BUYER_VW in the save dialog and press OK. Now select the RECORDS PROPERTY icon and select the TYPE tab from the Record Properties dialog. Figure 6-56 shows the empty TYPE tab for the BUYER_VW record.

From the TYPE tab, press the CLICK TO LAUNCH QUERY button. The Query dialog should now be displayed (Fig. 6-57).

With the Query View dialog open, double-click on the EMPLOYEES record. A New dialog should be displayed prompting you to select which

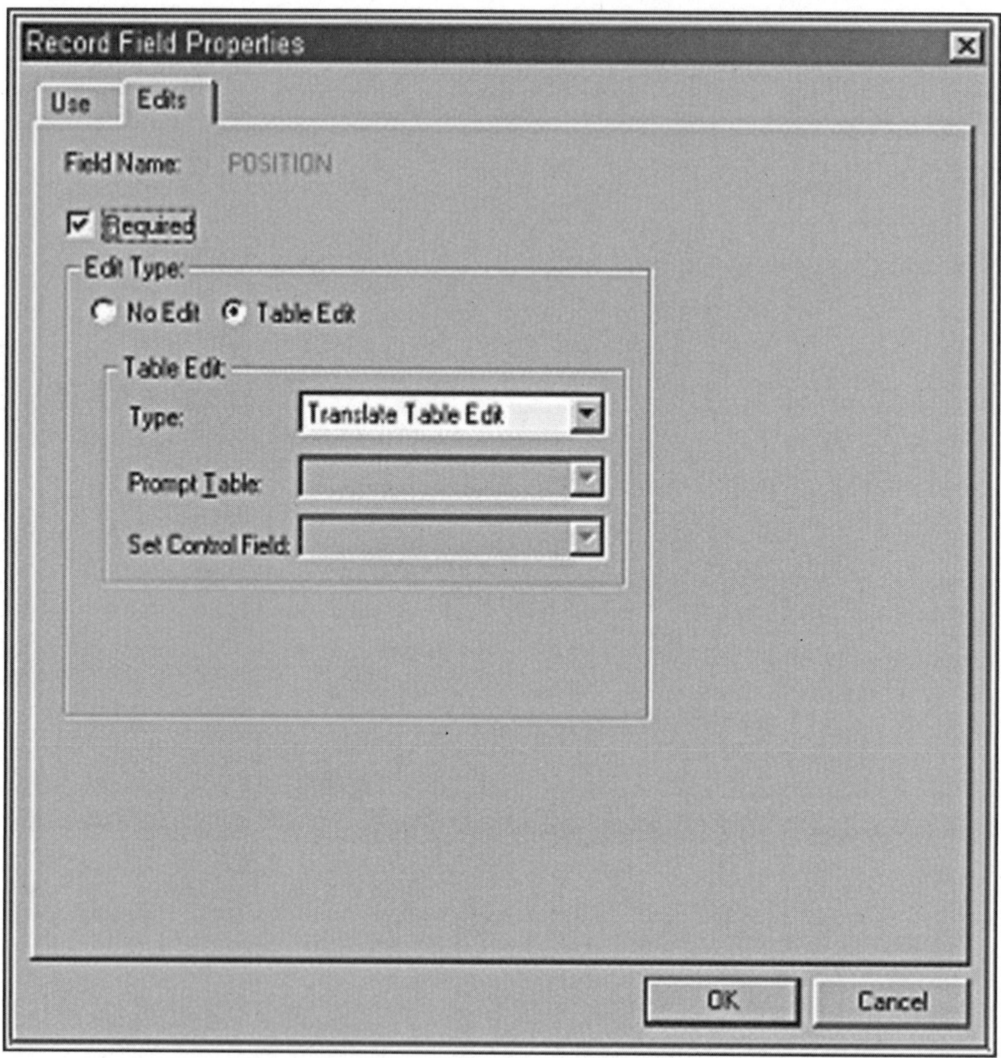

Figure 6-52 POSITION Edits dialog.

effective dated rows you want to include in the New view (Fig. 6-58). Select the radio buttons that represent the rows that are less than or equal to the current date and press OK. Figure 6-58 shows the correct selections.

Figure 6-59 shows the FIELDS tab of the Query View dialog. Select

EMPLOYEES (Record)

Field Name	Type	Key	Dir	CurC	Srch	List	Sys	Audt	H	Default
EMP_ID	Char				No	No	No			
EFFDT	Date	Key	Desc		No	No	No			%date
EFF_STATUS	Char				No	No	No			'A'
NAME	Char	Alt	Asc		No	Yes	No			
POSITION	Char	Alt	Asc		No	Yes	No			
EMAIL_ADDRESS	Char				No	No	No			

Figure 6-53 EMPLOYEES Record Edits display.

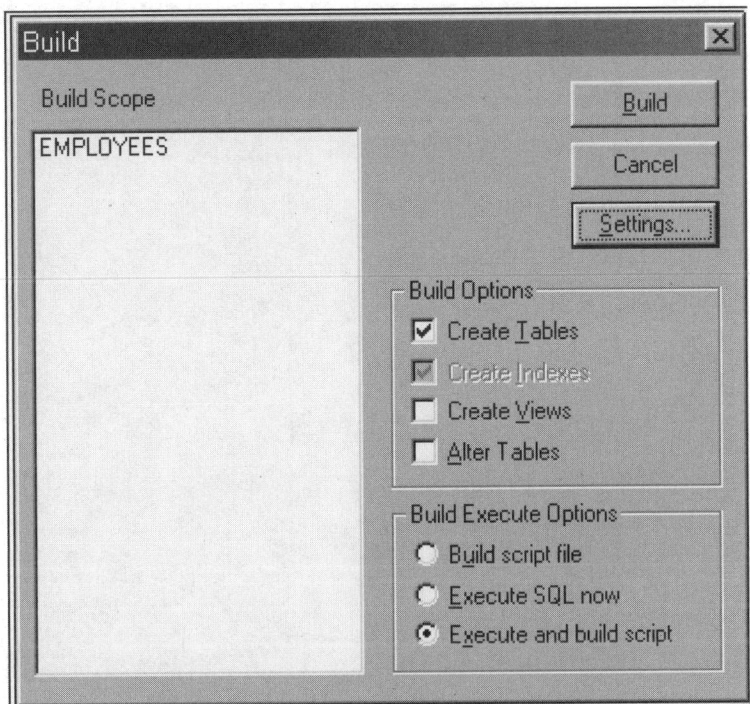

Figure 6-54 Build dialog for EMPLOYEES record.

EMP_ID, EFFDT, EFF_STATUS, NAME, EMAIL_ADDRESS in that order. Items 1 through 5 should be displayed in the "Col" column.

We are now ready to set the criteria to limit the rows to only the employees who are buyers. To do this, go to the CRITERIA tab. There

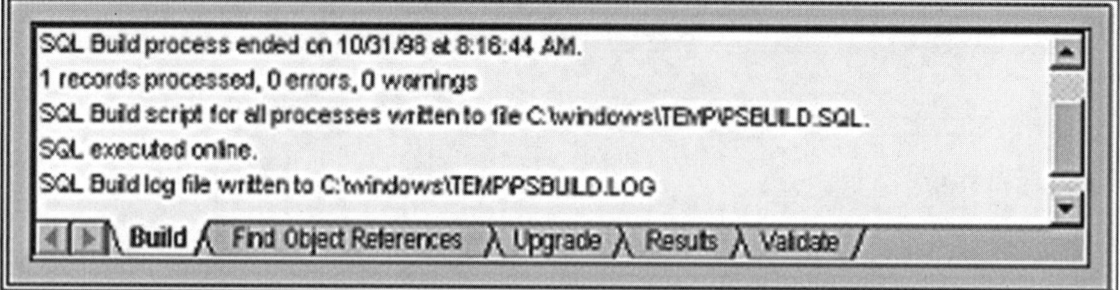

Figure 6-55 Output window after build process.

Figure 6-56 BUYER_VW TYPE tab.

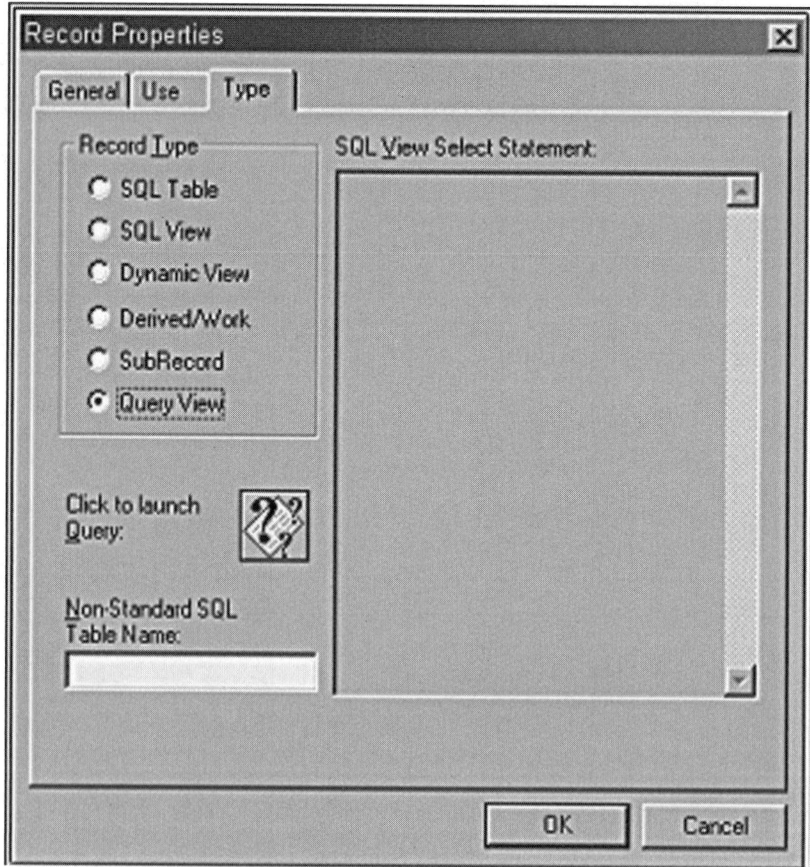

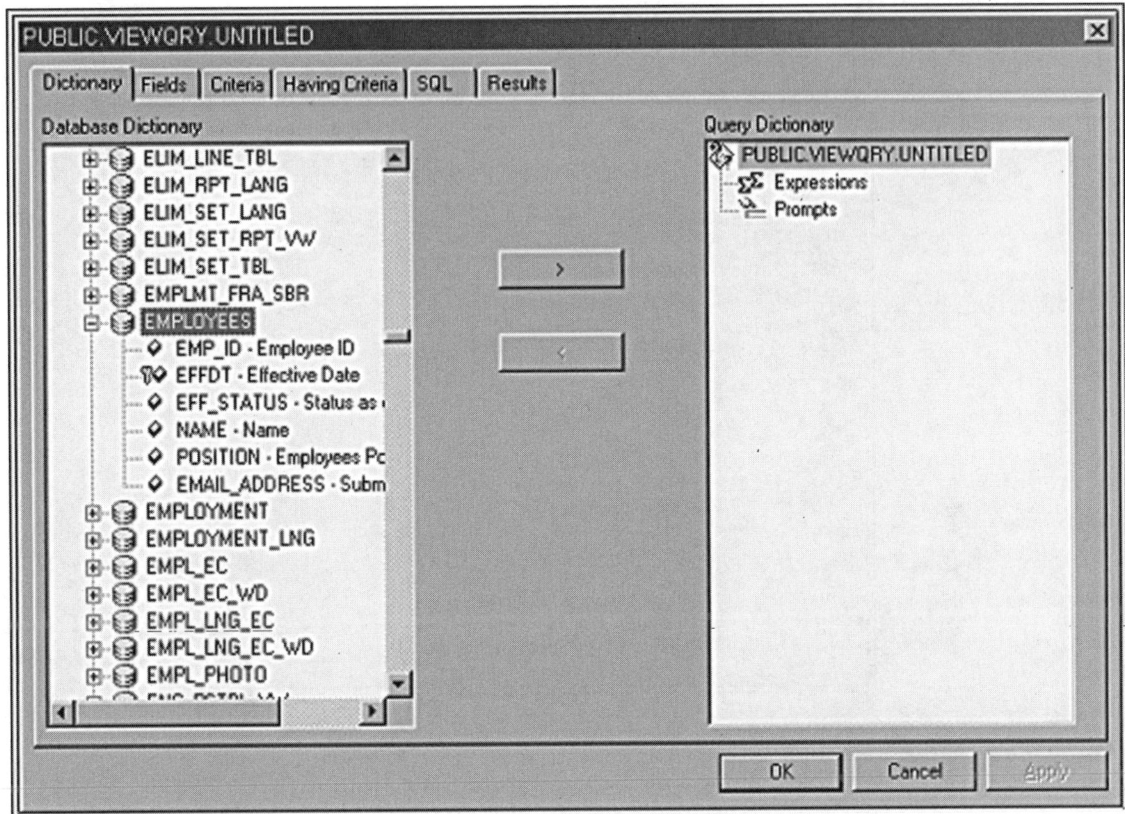

Figure 6-57 Query View.

should already be one criterion displayed for the effective date. To add ours, we must press the INSERT button at the top left of the tab. An empty line should be displayed below the effective date criteria. Leave the boolean connector of AND. Double-click on the box to the immediate left of the AND. A field dialog should now be displayed for you to select the desired field. Select the `POSITION` field and press OK. Figure 6-60 shows the Field dialog. To complete our criteria, we need to place the constant `BUY` in the empty rightmost box of our new line. Use your right mouse button to show the popup menu displayed in Figure 6-61. Select CONSTANT in the dialog that is then displayed, then enter `BUY` and press OK (Fig. 6-62). Figure 6-63 shows the completed CRITERIA tab.

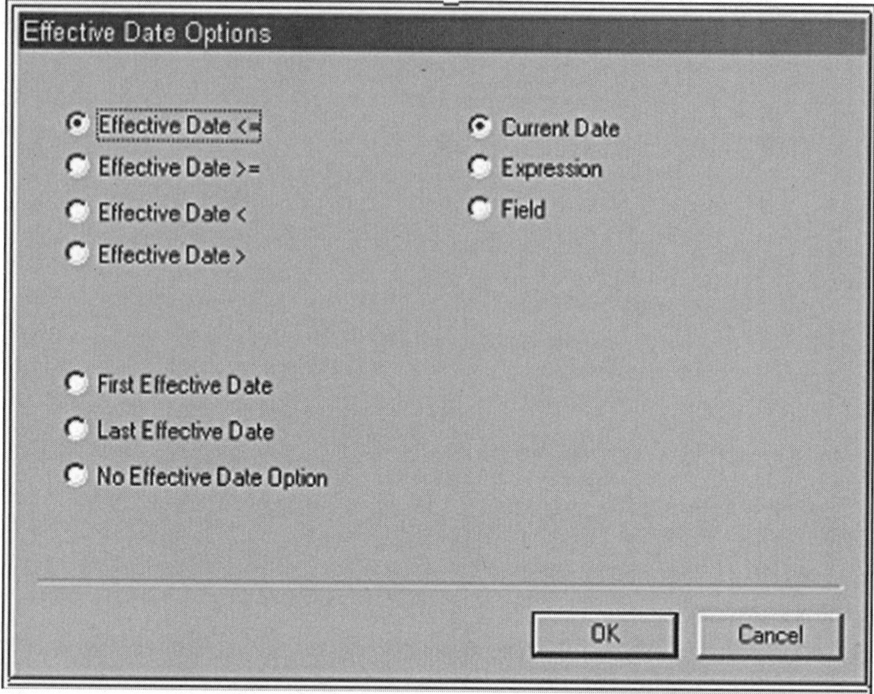

Figure 6-58 Effective Date options.

To verify that we have built our select statement correctly, select the SQL tab. The following select statement should be displayed. If all is correct, press the OK button.

```
SELECT A.EMP_ID, A.EFFDT, A.EFF_STATUS, A.NAME, A.EMAIL_ADDRESS
 FROM PS_EMPLOYEES A
 WHERE A.EFFDT =
   (SELECT MAX(EFFDT) FROM PS_EMPLOYEES
   WHERE EFFDT <= CURRENT DATE)
 AND A.POSITION = 'BUY'
```

The TYPE tab should now contain our SQL select that we just created. Figure 6-64 displays the finished TYPE tab. Now press OK. When the record definition is displayed, it should have all of the fields that we selected from the Query View dialog. Figure 6-65 shows the BUYER_VW record's definition with its fields now present. This feature is only for Query View records. If you had built your own SQL select statement, you would have to enter the fields into the record definition in the same order that they were entered in the select statement.

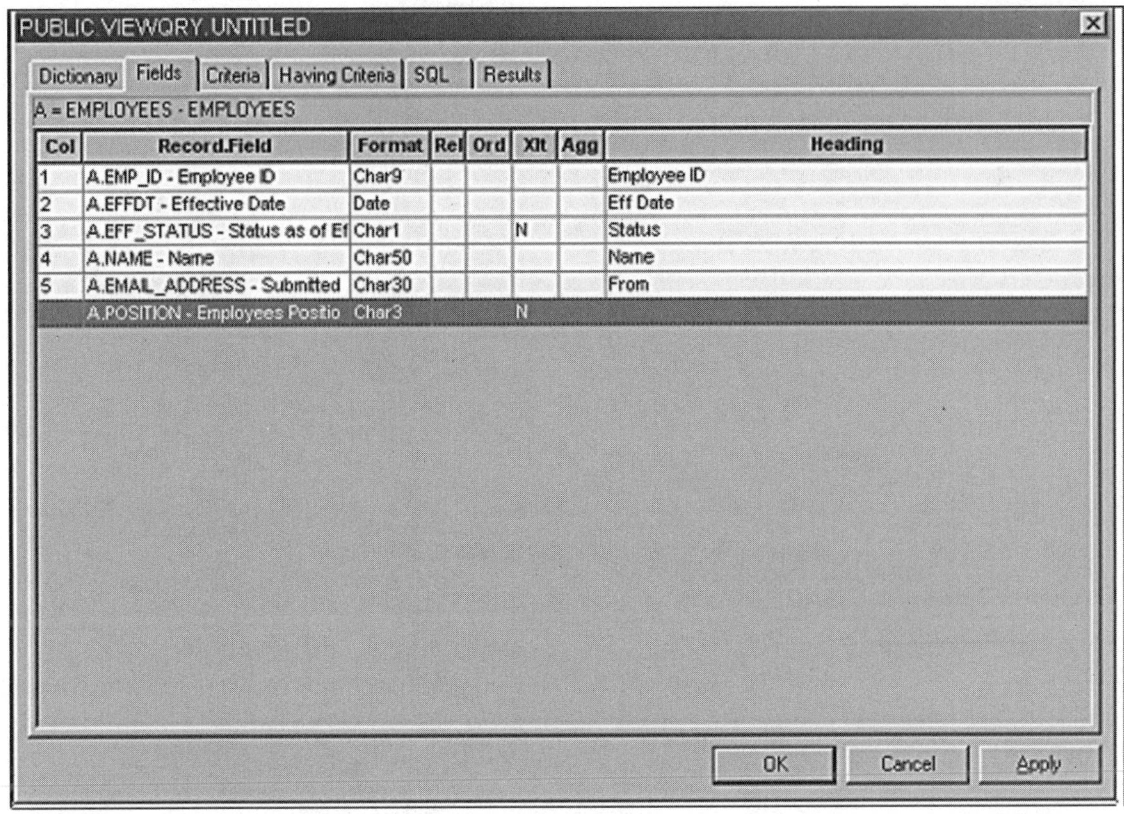

Figure 6-59 FIELDS tab of Query View dialog for BUYER_VW.

Since this record is based on a simple filter query, all the Use and Edits record field attributes were carried forward from the EMPLOYEES record. We do not need to make any changes. To be sure, check both of the Use and Edits displays before you build the object. If they match those of the EMPLOYEES record, then all you have to do is Select BUILD, CURRENT OBJECT, or press the BUILD icon from the toolbar. With the Build dialog displayed, select the Create Views and Create Indexes check boxes. Next, select the EXECUTE AND BUILD SCRIPT radio button. The Output window should then display a successful status message.

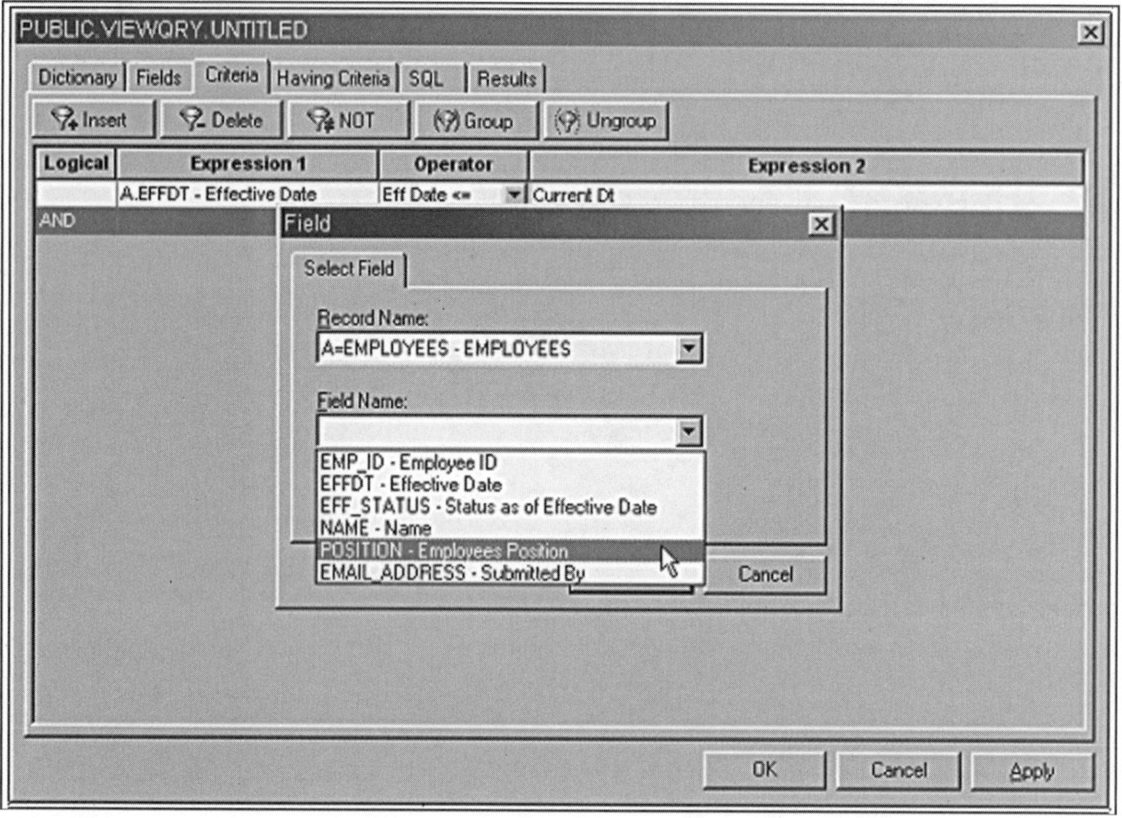

Figure 6-60 Field dialog.

ITEMS Record

Table 6-2 lists the fields and attributes that are going to make up our ITEMS record.

We are now going to create the ITEMS record. Press the NEW toolbar icon, or select FILE, NEW menu options. From the new dialog select RECORD and press OK. A new empty record definition should now be displayed in the Object Workspace. In the Project Workspace with the fields folder expanded, drag and drop the following fields onto the new record definition.

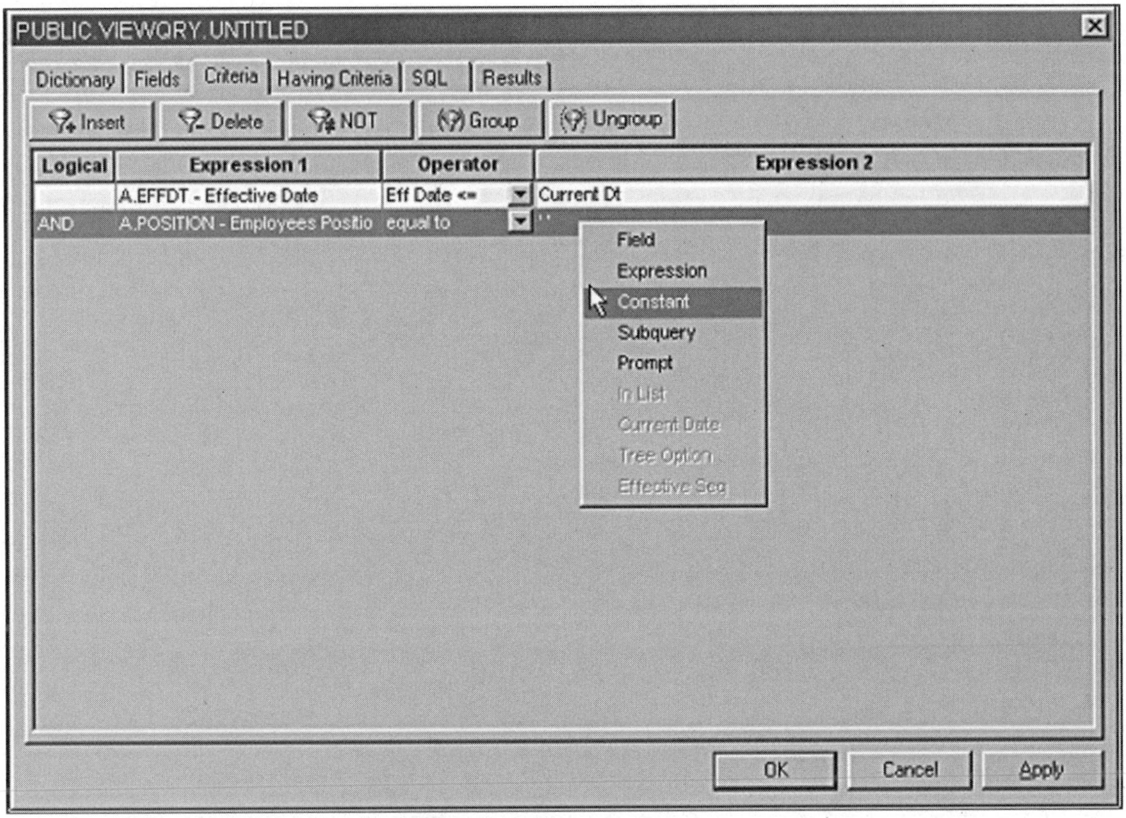

Figure 6-61 Popup menu to allow the user to select the expression type.

Figure 6-62
Constant dialog.

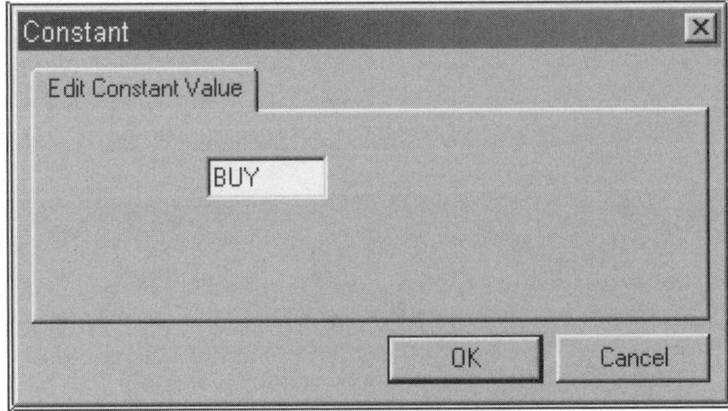

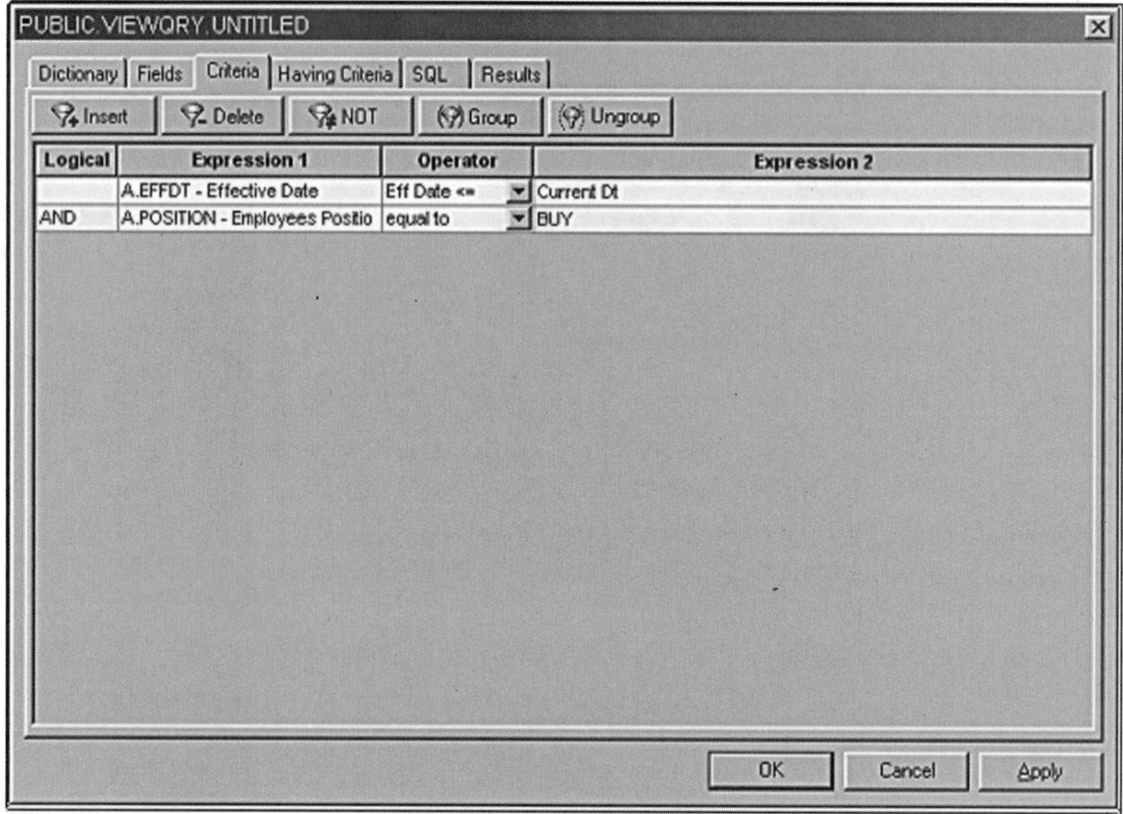

Figure 6-63 Finished CRITERIA tab of the Query View dialog for BUYER_VW.

- ITEM_ID
- EFFDT
- EFF_STATUS
- DESCR

If your record definition's field view looks like the one in Figure 6-66, please press the SAVE ALL icon or select the FILE, SAVE ALL menu options. In the Save As dialog, enter ITEMS and press OK. If your project's options are set to MANUAL INSERT, please press F7.

The ITEMS record is now ready for us to begin setting all the record's field attributes. Let's start with the first field inserted into the record definition. The Use values for the record's field attributes of ITEM_ID are

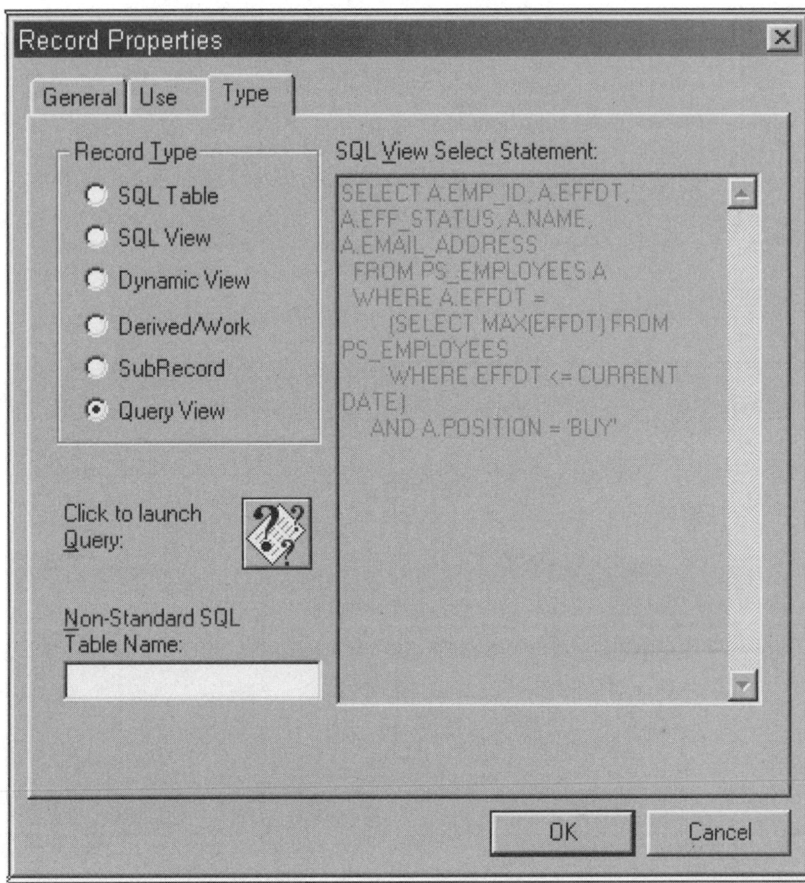

Figure 6-64 TYPE Tab of the Query View dialog for BUYER_VW.

BUYER_VW (Record)

Field Name	Type	Len	Format	H	Short Name	Long Name
EMP_ID	Char	9	SSN		Employee I	Employee ID
EFFDT	Date	10			Eff Date	Effective Date
EFF_STATUS	Char	1	Upper		Status	Status as of Effective Date
NAME	Char	50	Name		Name	Name
EMAIL_ADDRESS	Char	30	Mixed		From	Submitted By

Figure 6-65 BUYER_VW record definition.

TABLE 6-2

ITEMS Record

Column	Description	Data Type	Key	Valid Values
ITEM_ID	Item id	Char(10)	X	
EFFDT	Effective date	Date	X	
EFF_STATUS	Effective status	Char(1)	X	A = active; I = inactive
DESCR	Item description	Char(30)		

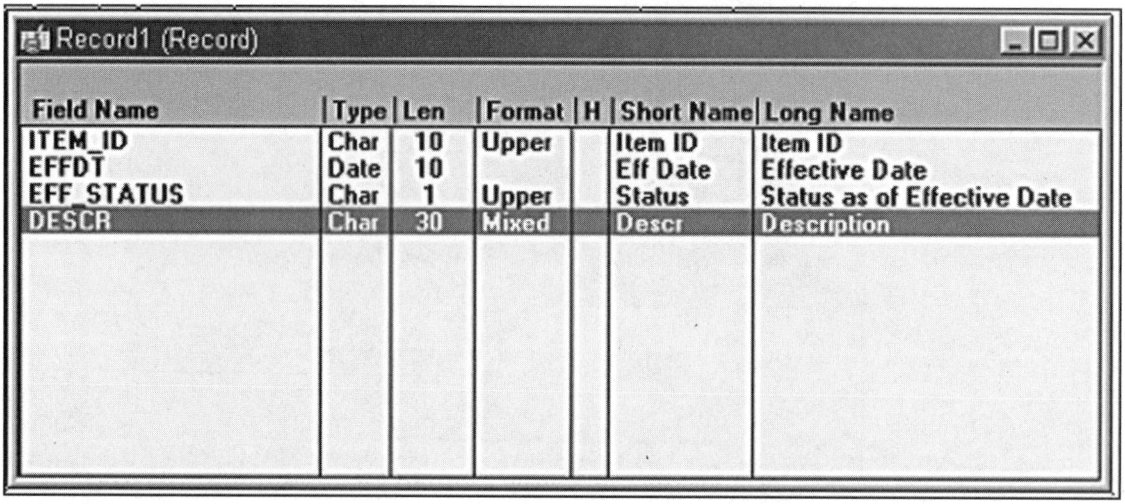

Record1 (Record)

Field Name	Type	Len	Format	H	Short Name	Long Name
ITEM_ID	Char	10	Upper		Item ID	Item ID
EFFDT	Date	10			Eff Date	Effective Date
EFF_STATUS	Char	1	Upper		Status	Status as of Effective Date
DESCR	Char	30	Mixed		Descr	Description

Figure 6-66 ITEMS Record Edits display.

- Key
- Search Key
- List Box Item

The Search Key option will place this field in all the search dialogs that are used for the internal order record. The List Box Item option will place this field as a column in the resulting list box in the search dialogs.

The only Edits property for this field is that it is required. ITEM_ID is a key field and is therefore required. Figures 6-67 and 6-68 show the Use and Edit tabbed dialogs for ITEM_ID.

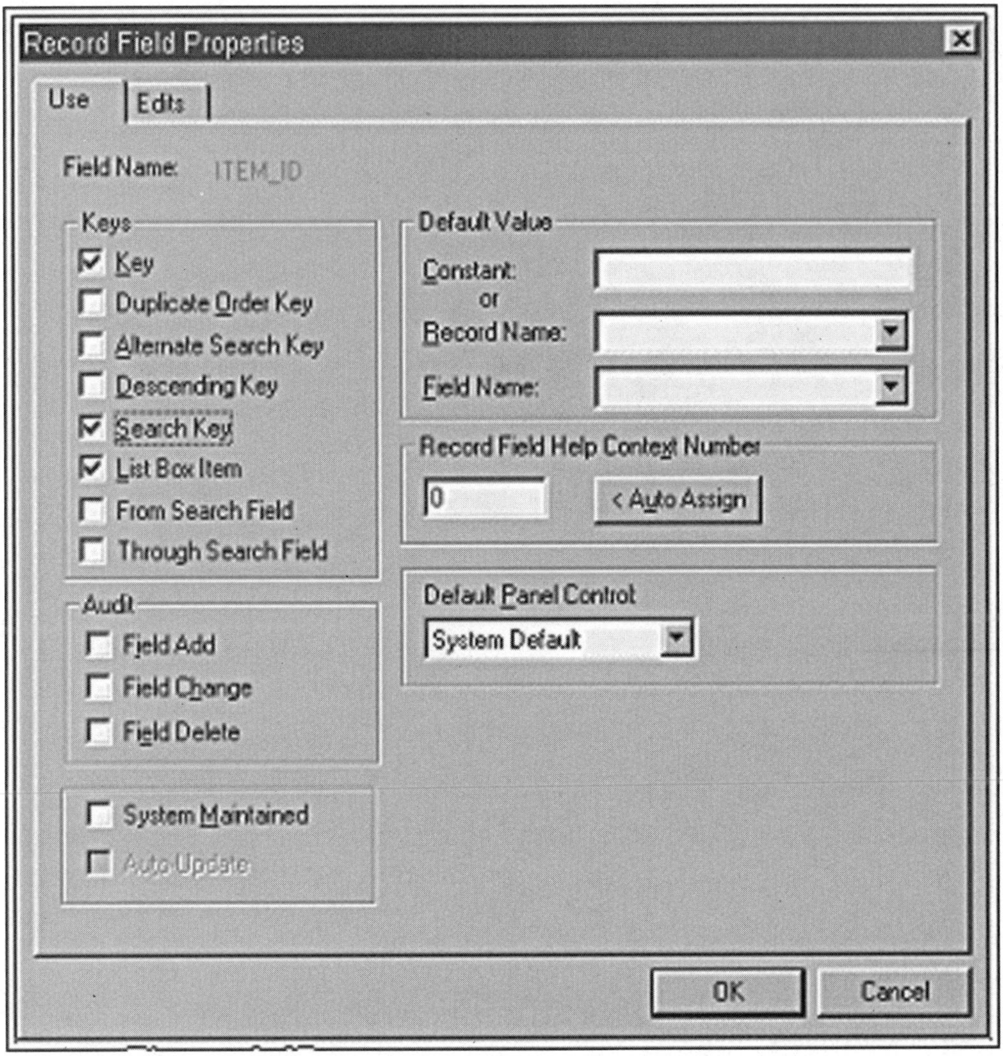

Figure 6-67 ITEM_ID Use dialog.

The next field we set the record attributes for is EFFDT (effective dated table). The Use values that are associated with the field attributes of EFFDT are

- Key
- Descending Key

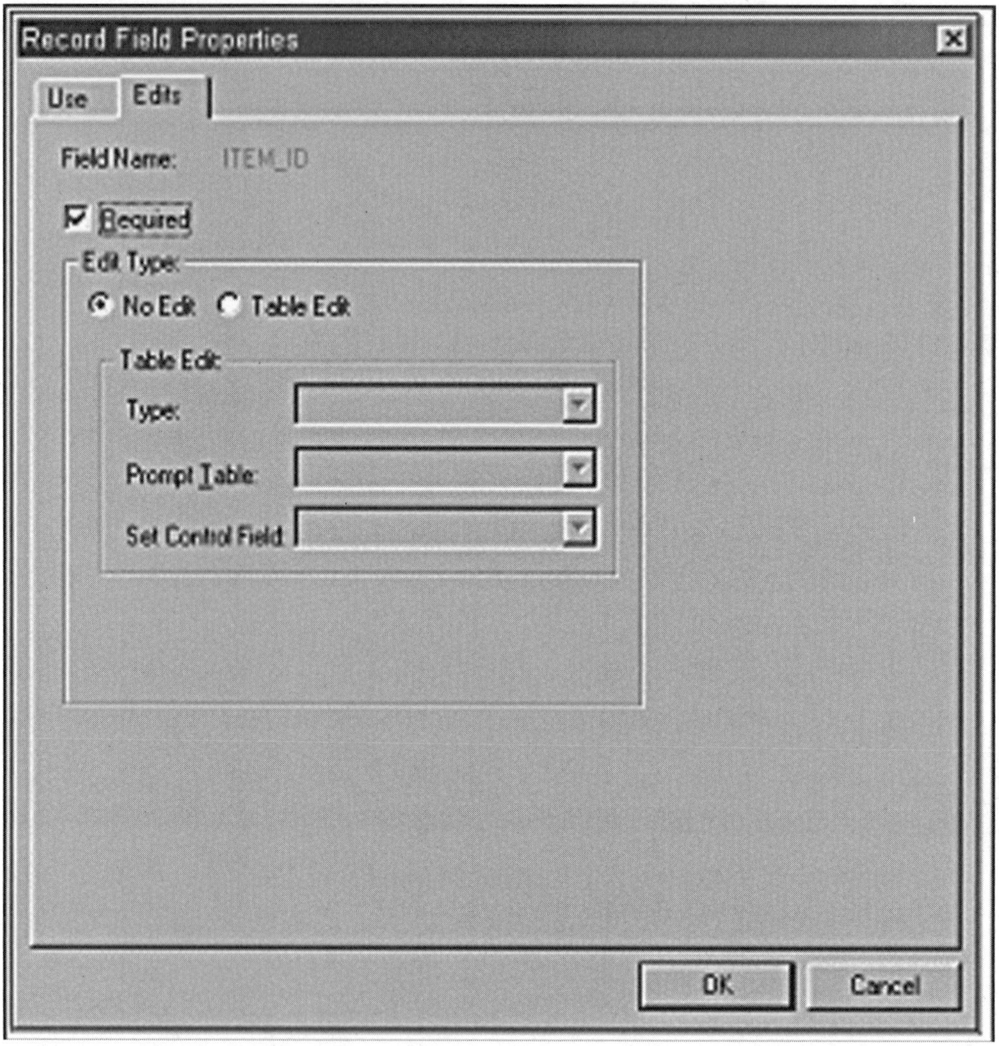

Figure 6-68 ITEM_ID Edits dialog.

- Default constant set to the system date %date

The Descending Key option returns the most recent EFFDT. The default constant %date will automatically place the system date in the EFFDT when it is opened for the first time.

The only Edits property that we are going to set for EFFDT is that it is

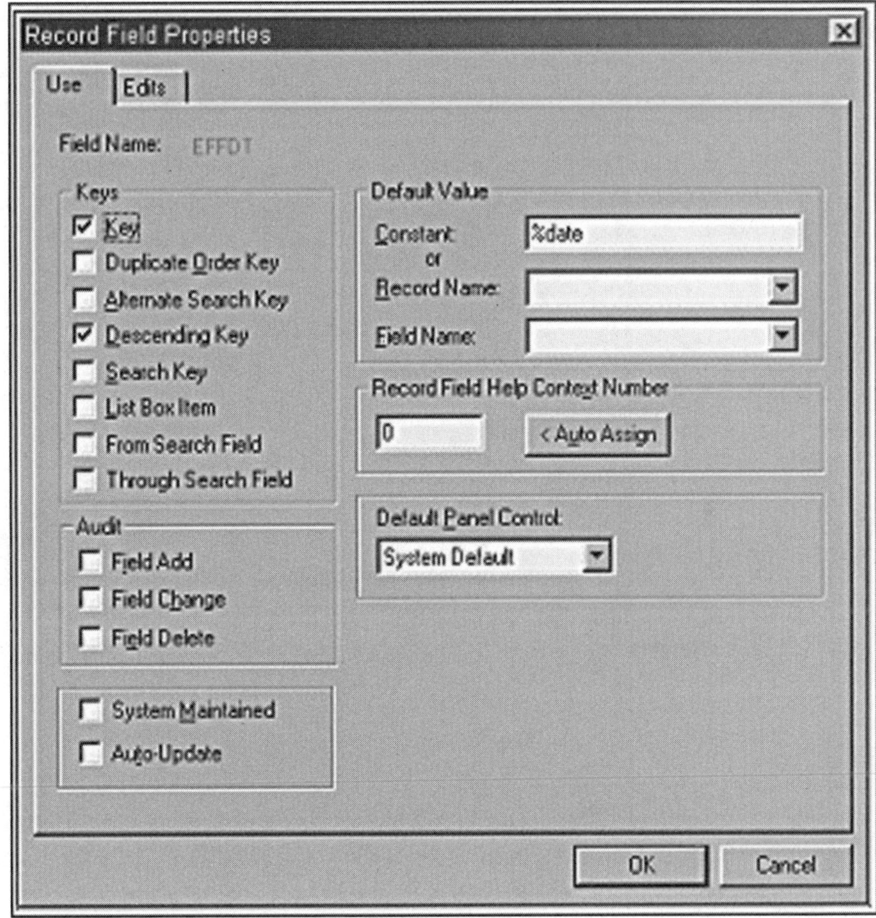

Figure 6-69
EFFDT use dialog.

required. Figures 6-69 and 6-70 show the Use and Edit tabbed dialogs for EFFDT.

The next field we set the record attributes for is EFF_STATUS. The Use value that is associated with the field attributes of EFF_STATUS is the default constant set to A. The default constant A will automatically set the initial effective status to ACTIVE when a new record is added.

The only Edits property that we are going to set for EFF_STATUS is that it is required. Figures 6-71 and 6-72 show the Use and Edit tabbed dialogs for EFF_STATUS.

The next field we set the record attributes for is DESCR. The Use values that are associated to the field attributes of DESCR are

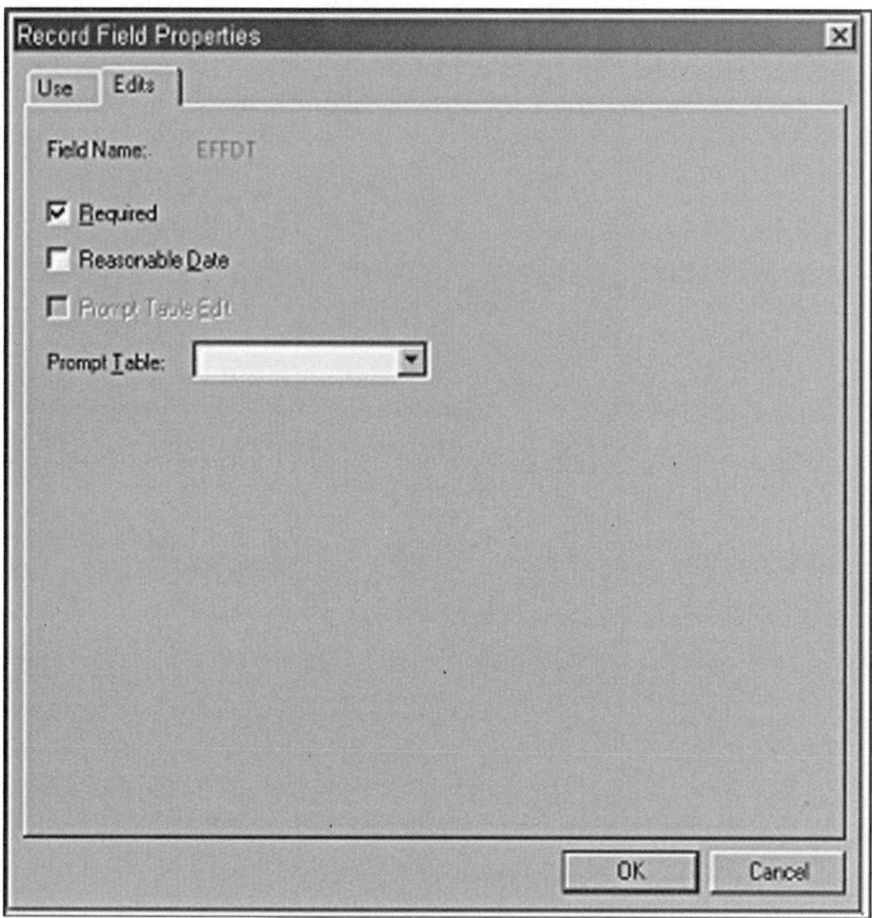

Figure 6-70
EFFDT Edits dialog.

- Alt Search Key
- List Box Item

The Alt Search Key option will place this field in all the search dialogs that are used for the internal order record. The Alt Search Key option does not make this field part of the primary key; instead it creates an index on the field. The List Box Item option will place this field as a column in the resulting list box in the search dialogs.

The only Edits property that we are going to set for DESCR is that it is required. Figures 6-73 and 6-74 show the Use and Edits tabbed dialogs for DESCR.

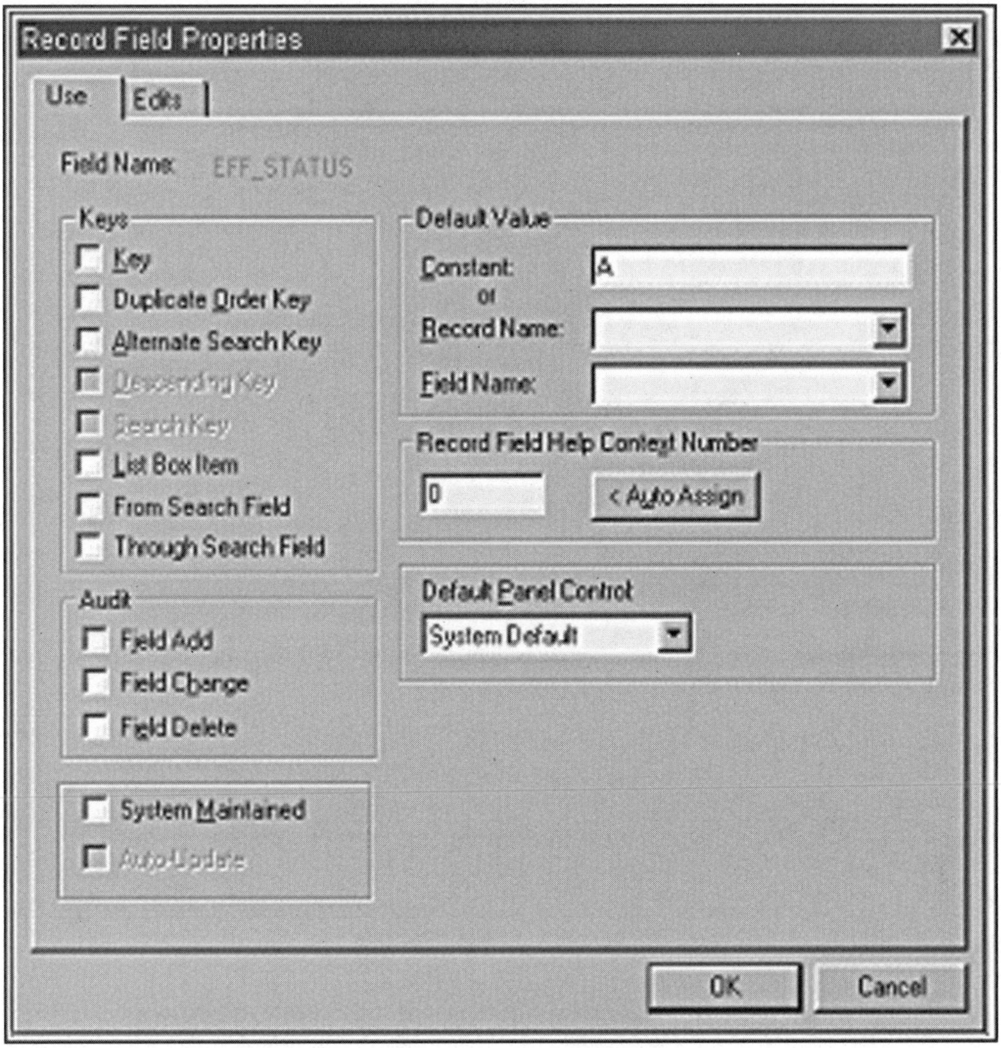

Figure 6-71 EFF_STATUS Use dialog.

The Use Display of your ITEMS record should look like the one shown in Figure 6-75.

To build ITEMS, select BUILD, CURRENT OBJECT, or press the BUILD icon from the toolbar. With the build dialog displayed, select the Create Table check box. The Create Indexes check box will automatically be selected

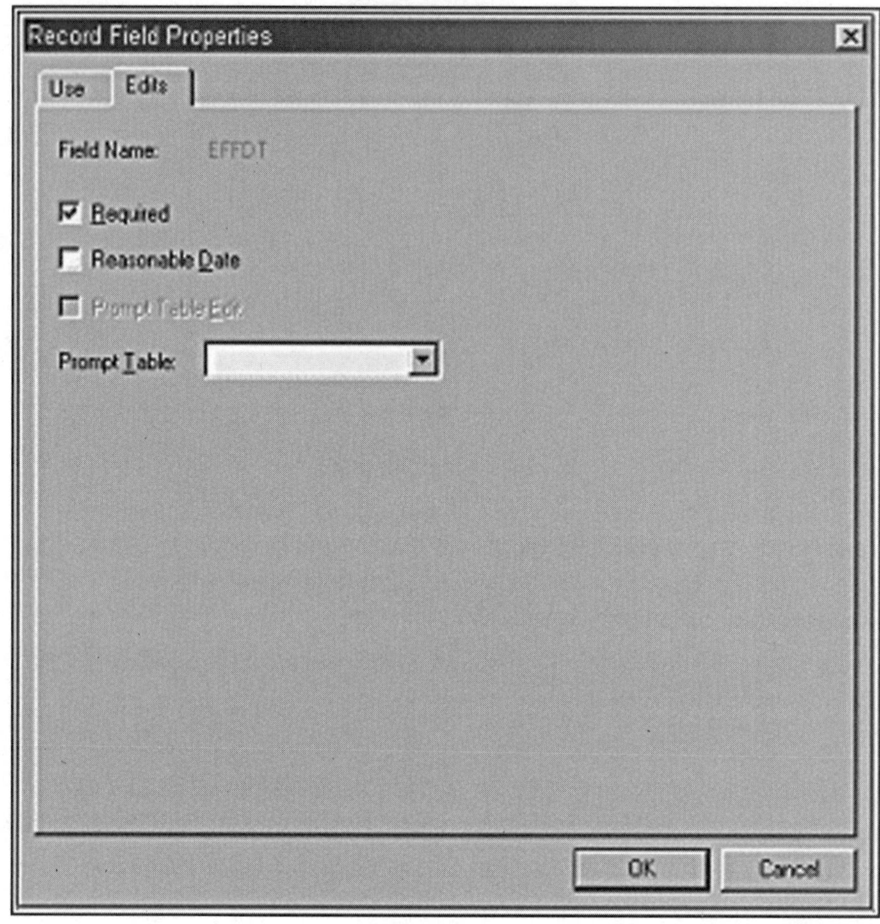

Figure 6-72 EFF_STATUS Edits dialog.

and grayed out. Next, select the EXECUTE AND BUILD SCRIPT radio button. When you have completed this, press the BUILD button at the top right of the dialog. On completion, a status of "1 records processed, 0 errors and 0 warnings" will be displayed in the Output window.

LOCATIONS Record

Table 6-3 lists the fields and attributes making up our Locations record.

We are now going to create the LOCATIONS record. Press the NEW toolbar icon, or select FILE, NEW menu options. From the New dialog select RECORD and press OK. A new empty record definition should now

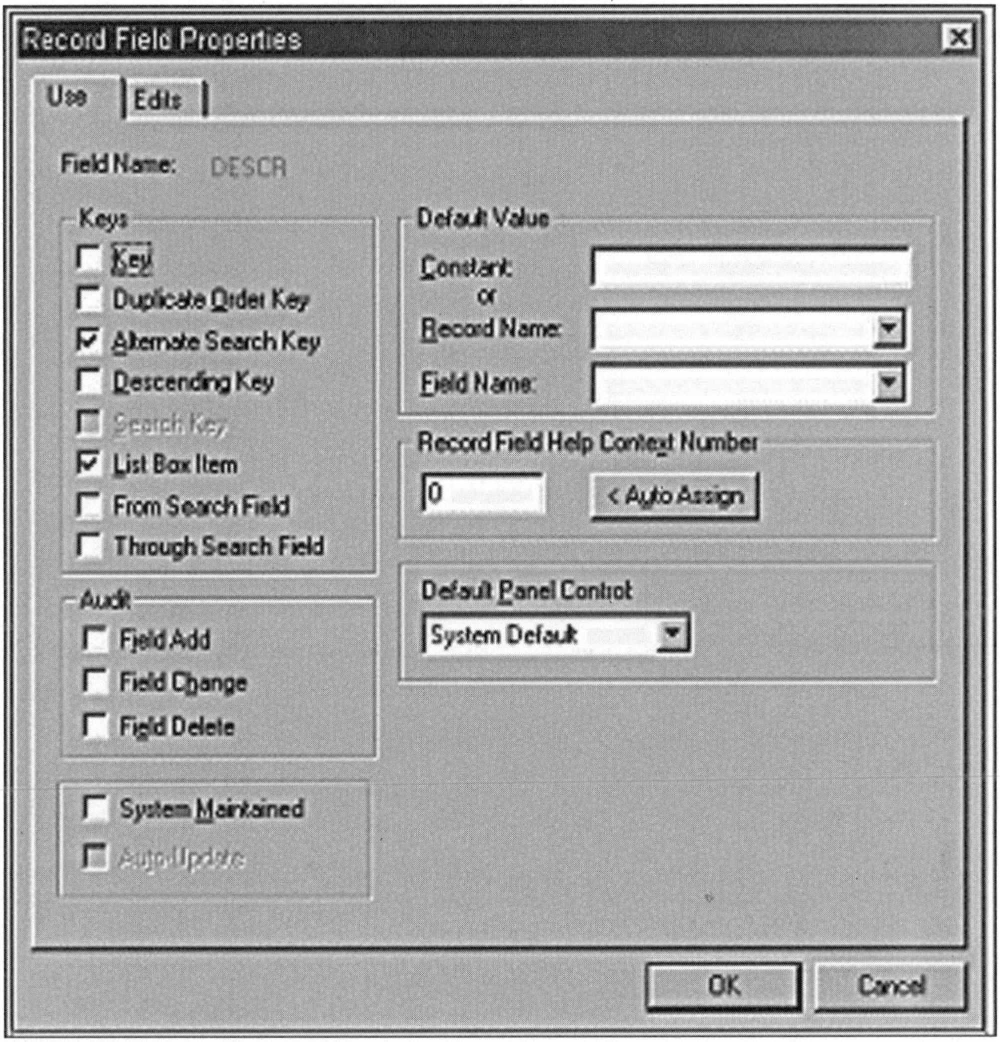

Figure 6-73 DESCR Use dialog.

be displayed in the Object Workspace. In the Project Workspace with the fields folder expanded, drag and drop the following fields onto the new record definition:

- PROCESS_LOC_ID
- EFFDT

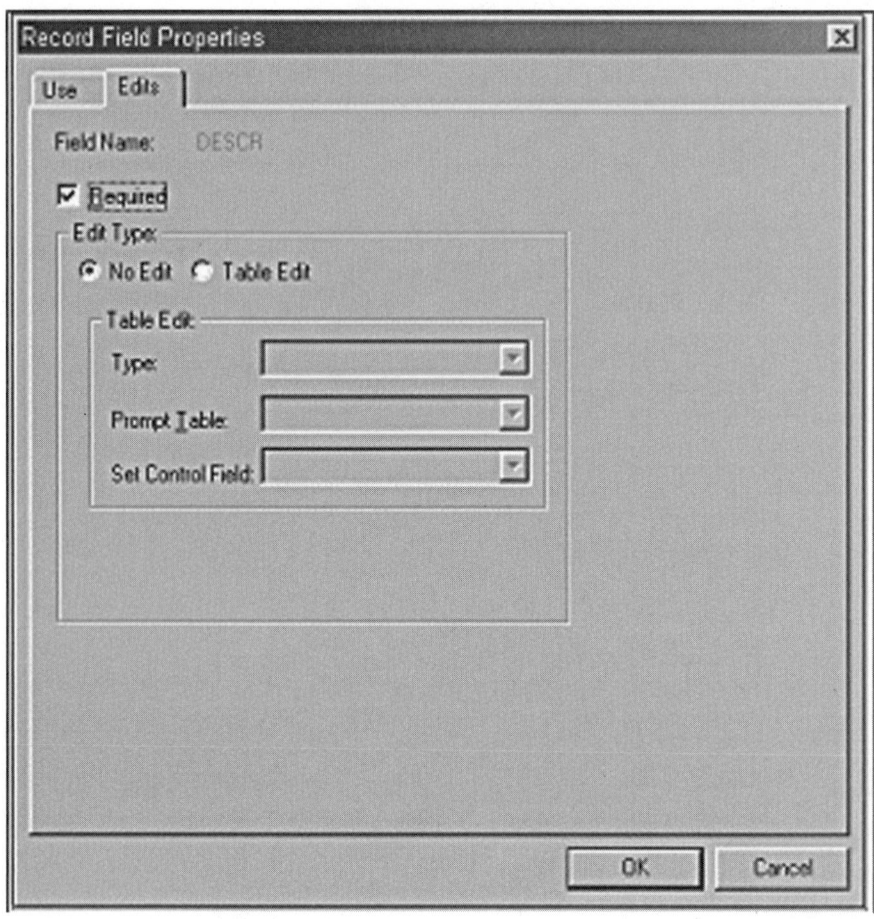

Figure 6-74
DESCR Edits dialog.

- EFF_STATUS
- DESCR

If your record definition's field view looks like the one in Figure 6-76, please press the SAVE ALL icon, or select the FILE, SAVE ALL menu options. In the Save As dialog, enter ITEMS and press OK. If your project's options are set to manual insert, please press F7.

The LOCATIONS record is now ready for us to begin setting all of the record's field attributes. Let's start with the first field inserted into the record definition. The Use values for the record's field attributes of PROCESS_LOC_ID are

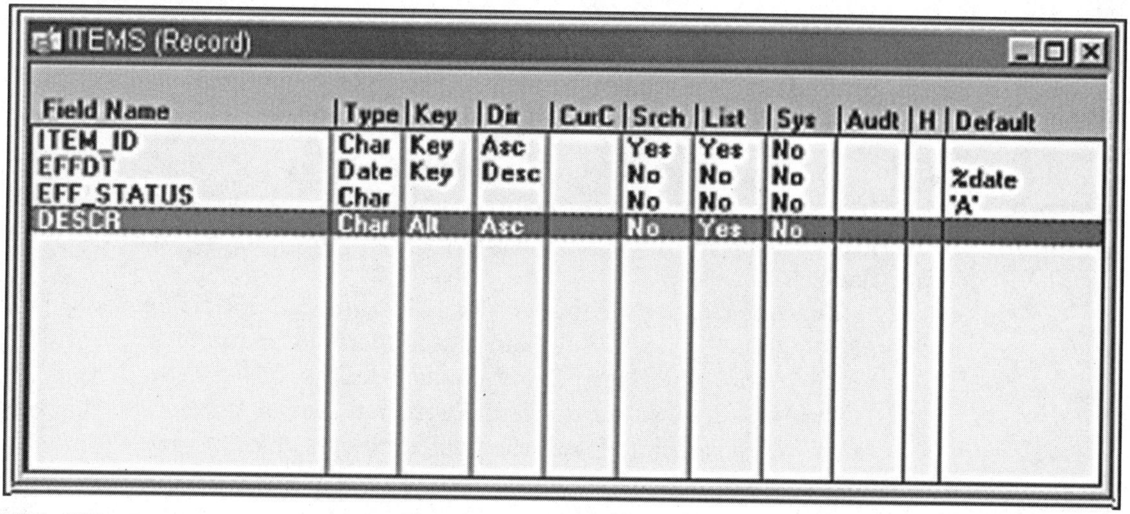

ITEMS (Record)

Field Name	Type	Key	Dir	CurC	Srch	List	Sys	Audt	H	Default
ITEM_ID	Char	Key	Asc		Yes	Yes	No			
EFFDT	Date	Key	Desc		No	No	No			%date
EFF_STATUS	Char				No	No	No			'A'
DESCR	Char	Alt	Asc		No	Yes	No			

Figure 6-75 ITEMS Record Use display.

TABLE 6-3

LOCATIONS Record

Column	Description	Data Type	Key	Valid Values
PROCESS_LOC_ID	Location id	Char(10)	X	
EFFDT	Effective date	Date]	X	
EFF_STATUS	Effective status	Char(1)	X	A = active; I = inactive
DESCR	Location description	Char(30)		

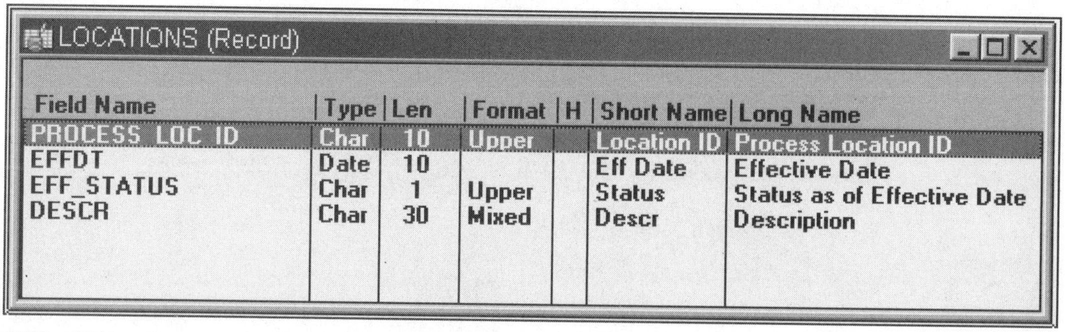

LOCATIONS (Record)

Field Name	Type	Len	Format	H	Short Name	Long Name
PROCESS_LOC_ID	Char	10	Upper		Location ID	Process Location ID
EFFDT	Date	10			Eff Date	Effective Date
EFF_STATUS	Char	1	Upper		Status	Status as of Effective Date
DESCR	Char	30	Mixed		Descr	Description

Figure 6-76 LOCATIONS Record Fields display.

- Key
- Search Key
- List Box Item

The Search Key option will place this field in all of the search dialogs that are used for the internal order record. The List Box Item option will place this field as a column in the resulting list box in the search dialogs.

The only Edits property for this field is that it is required. PROCESS_LOC_ID is a key field and is therefore required. Figures 6-77 and 6-78 show the Use and Edits tabbed dialogs for PROCESS_LOC_ID.

The next field we set the record attributes for is EFFDT. The Use values that are associated with the field attributes of EFFDT are

- Key
- Descending Key
- Default constant set to the system date %date

The Descending Key option returns the most recent EFFDT. The default constant %date will automatically place the system date in the EFFDT when it is opened for the first time.

The only Edit property that we will set for EFFDT is that it is required. Figures 6-79 and 6-80 show the Use and Edit tabbed dialogs for EFFDT.

The next field we set the record attributes for is EFF_STATUS. The Use value that is associated with the field attributes of EFF_STATUS is the default constant set to A. The default constant A will automatically set the initial effective status to active when a new record is added.

The only Edits property that we are going to set for EFF_STATUS is that it is required. Figures 6-81 and 6-82 show the Use and Edits tabbed dialogs for EFF_STATUS.

The next field we set the record attributes for is DESCR. The Use values that are associated with the field attributes of DESCR are

- Alt Search Key
- List Box Item

The Alt Search Key option will place this field in all the search dialogs that are used for the internal order record. The Alt Search Key option does not make this field part of the primary key; instead it cre-

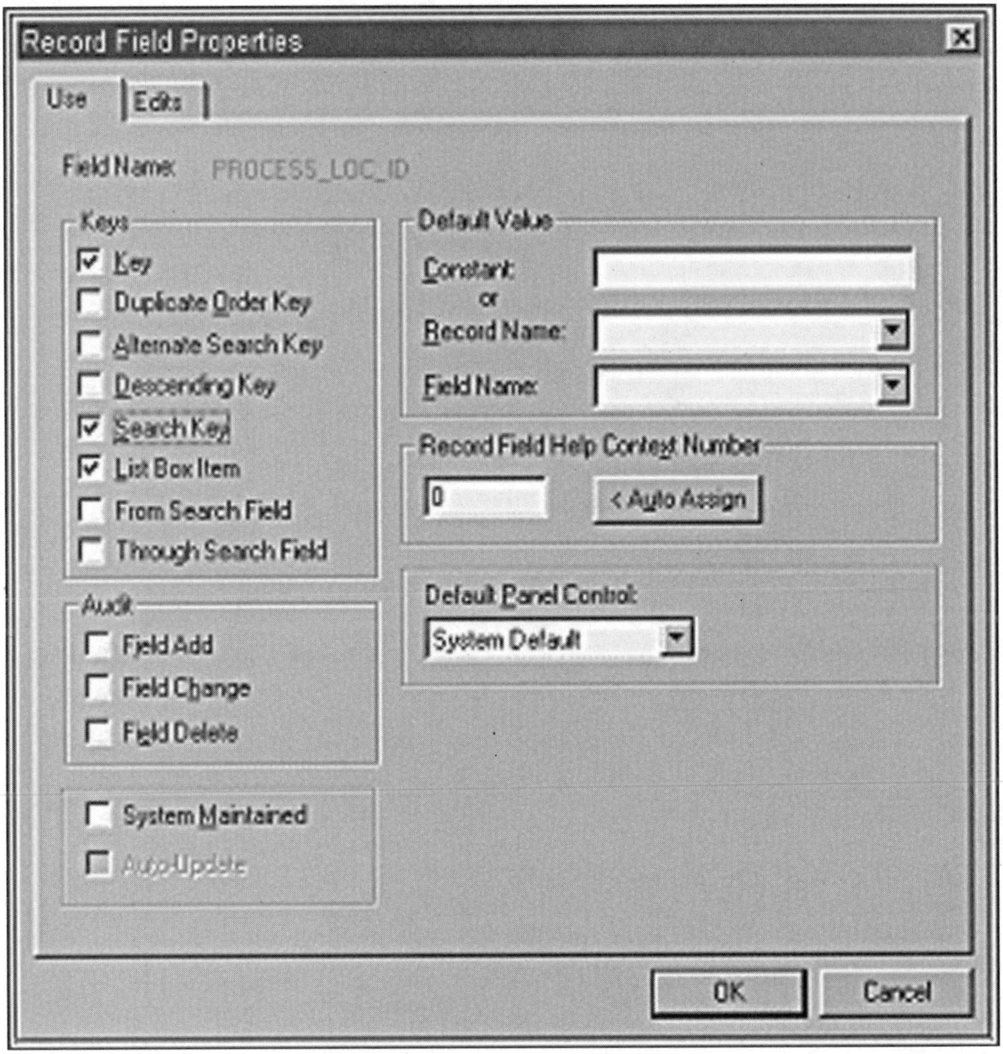

Figure 6-77 PROCESS_LOC_ID Use dialog.

ates an index on the field. The List Box Item option will place this field as a column in the resulting list box in the search dialogs.

The only Edits property that we will set for DESCR is that it is required. Figures 6-83 and 6-84 show the Use and Edits tabbed dialogs for DESCR.

The Use Display of your LOCATIONS record should look like the one in Figure 6-85.

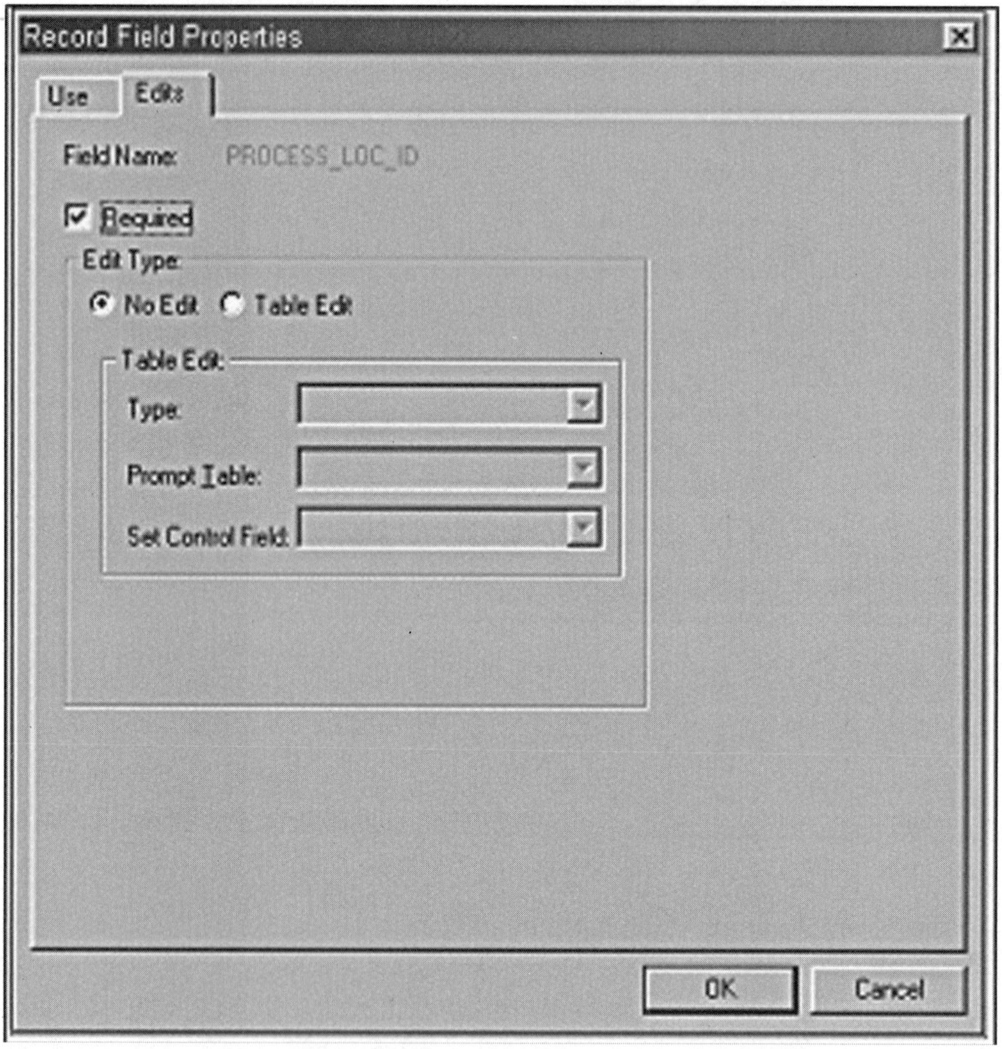

Figure 6-78 PROCESS_LOC_ID Edits dialog.

To build LOCATIONS, select BUILD, CURRENT OBJECT, or press the BUILD icon from the toolbar. With the build dialog displayed, select the Create Table check box. The Create Indexes check box will automatically be selected and grayed out. Next, select the EXECUTE AND BUILD SCRIPT radio button. When you have completed this, press the BUILD button at the top right of the dialog. On completion, a status of "1 records processed, 0 errors and 0 warnings" will be displayed in the Output window.

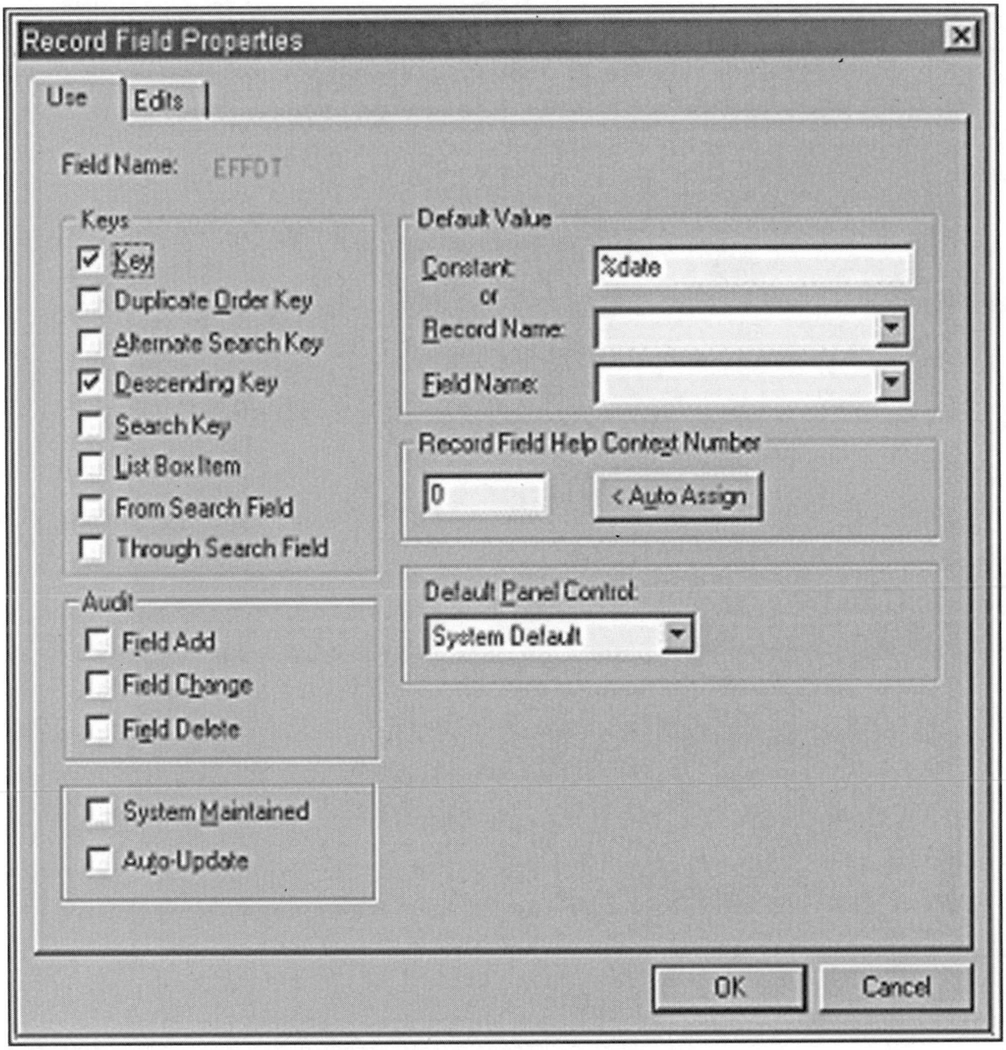

Figure 6-79 EFFDT Use dialog.

VENDORS Record

Table 6-4 lists all the fields and attributes making up our VENDORS record.

We will now create the VENDORS record. This record will give us an opportunity to explore subrecords. In the beginning of this chapter we

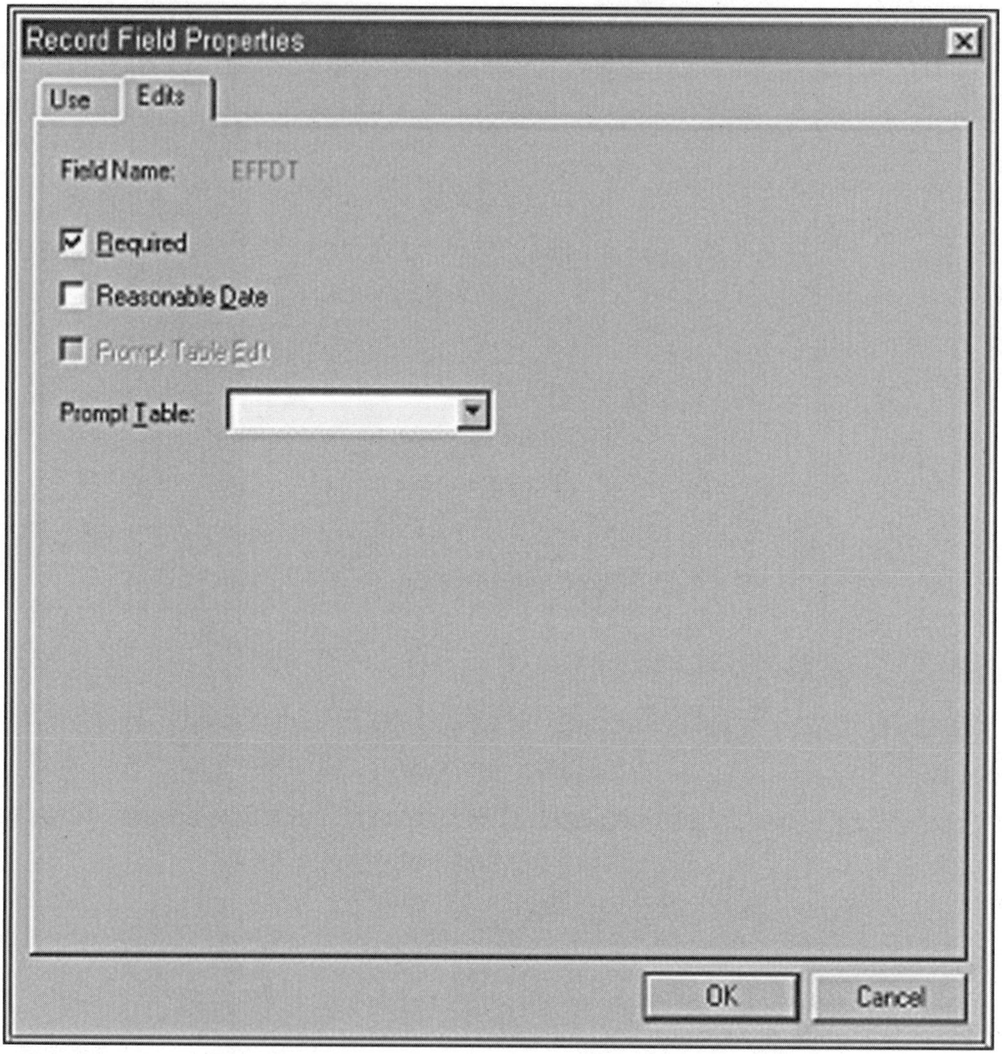

Figure 6-80 EFFDT Edits dialog.

discussed how you could use subrecords, and mentioned that a great place to use them is with addresses. PeopleSoft is shipped with an address subrecord (ADDRESS_SBR), but instead of using it, we are going to create our own. Press the NEW toolbar icon or select FILE, NEW menu options. From the New dialog, select RECORD and press OK. A new empty record definition should now be displayed in the Object Workspace. In

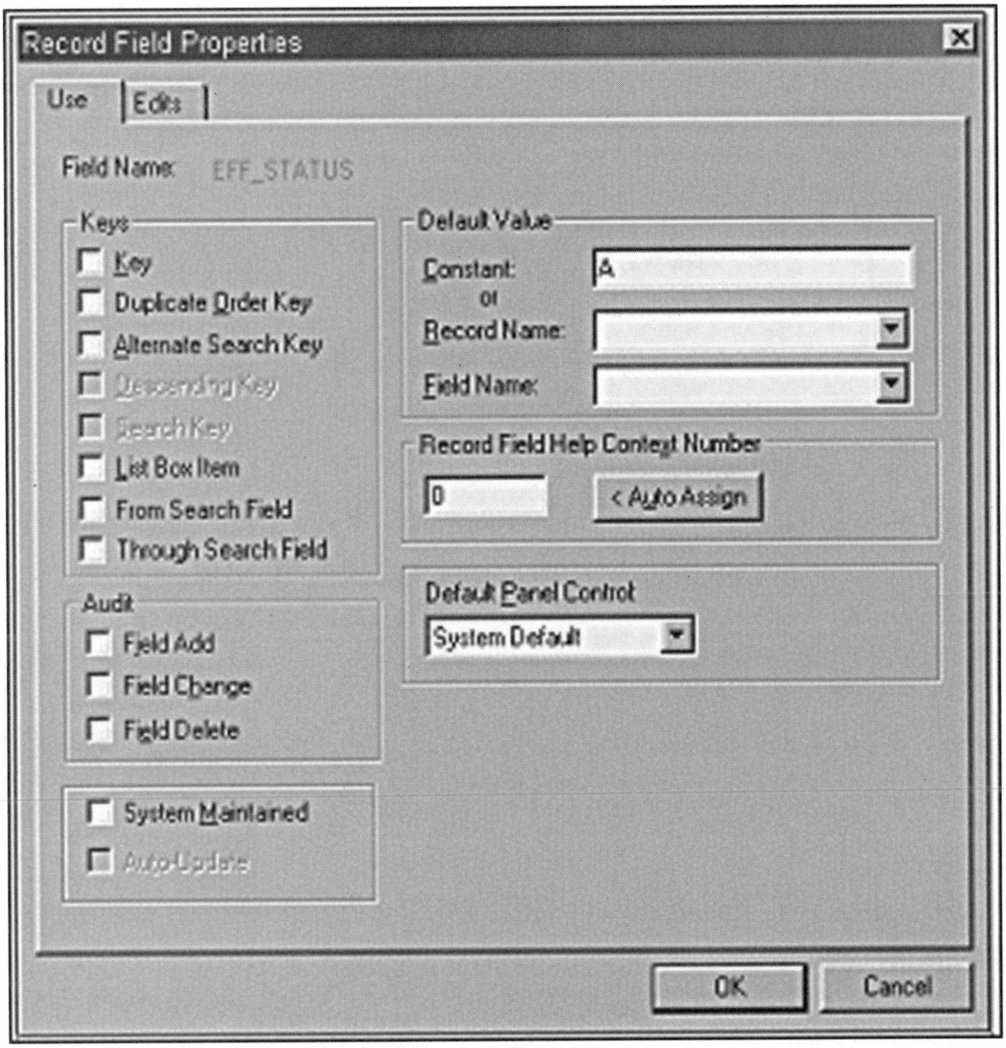

Figure 6-81 EFF_STATUS Use dialog.

the Project Workspace with the fields folder expanded, drag and drop the following fields onto the new record definition:

- STREET1
- STREET2
- CITY

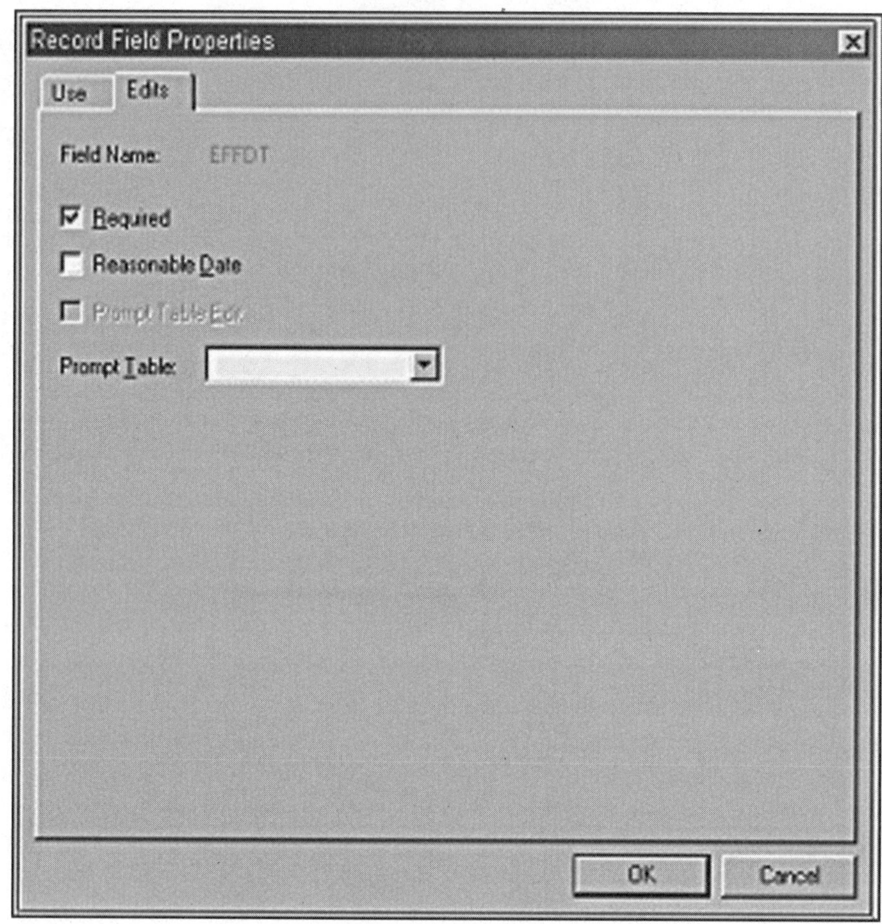

Figure 6-82 EFF_STATUS Edits dialog.

TABLE 6-4 VENDORS Record

Column	Description	Data Type	Key	Valid Values
VENDORID	Vendor id	Char(10)	X	
EFFDT	Effective date	Date	X	
EFF_STATUS	Effective status	Char(1)	X	A = active; I = inactive
VENDOR	Company name	Char(30)		
STREET1	Street	Char(30)		ADD_SBR
STREET2	Street	Char(30)		ADD_SBR
CITY	City	Char(20)		ADD_SBR
STATE	State	Char(2)		ADD_SBR

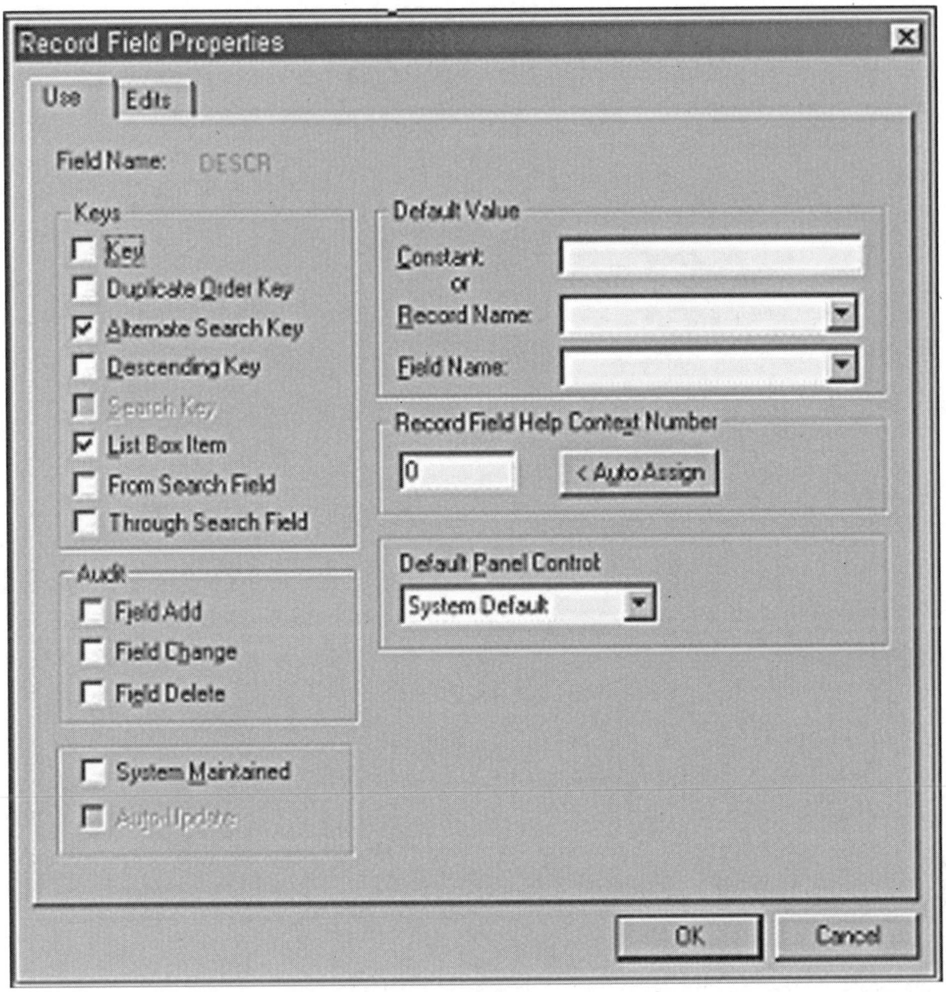

Figure 6-83 DESCR Use dialog.

■ STATE

If your record definition's field view looks like the one in Figure 6-86, press the SAVE ALL icon or select the FILE, SAVE ALL menu options. In the Save As dialog, enter ADD_SBR and press OK. The naming convention for subrecords is to add _SBR to the end of the name. If your project's options are set to MANUAL INSERT, please press F7.

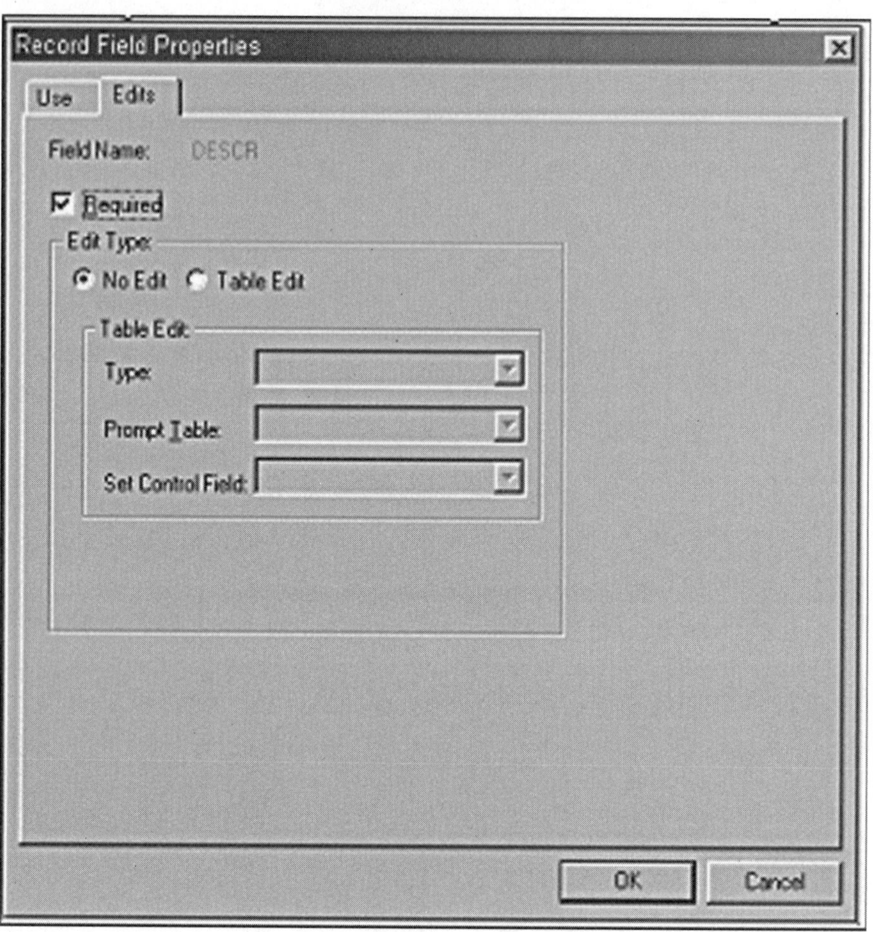

Figure 6-84
DESCR Edits dialog.

LOCATIONS (Record)

Field Name	Type	Key	Dir	CurC	Srch	List	Sys	Audt	H	Default
PROCESS_LOC_ID	Char	Key	Asc		Yes	Yes	No			
EFFDT	Date	Key	Desc		No	No	No			%date
EFF_STATUS	Char				No	No	No			'A'
DESCR	Char	Alt	Asc		No	Yes	No			

Figure 6-85 LOCATIONS Record Use display.

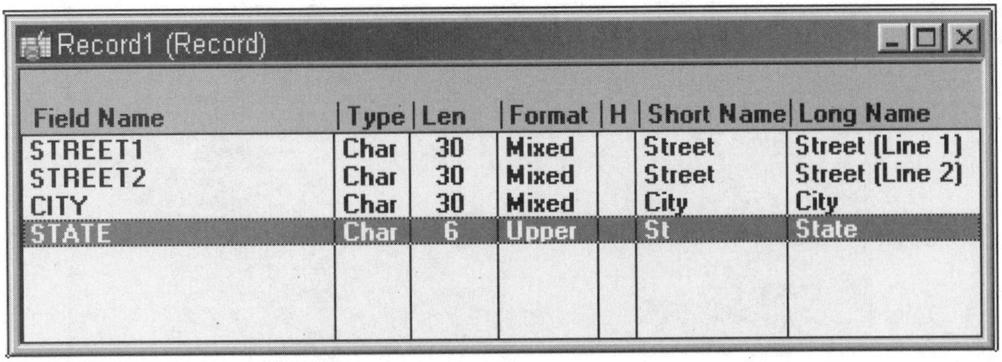

Field Name	Type	Len	Format	H	Short Name	Long Name
STREET1	Char	30	Mixed		Street	Street (Line 1)
STREET2	Char	30	Mixed		Street	Street (Line 2)
CITY	Char	30	Mixed		City	City
STATE	Char	6	Upper		St	State

Figure 6-86 ADD_SBR Record Use display.

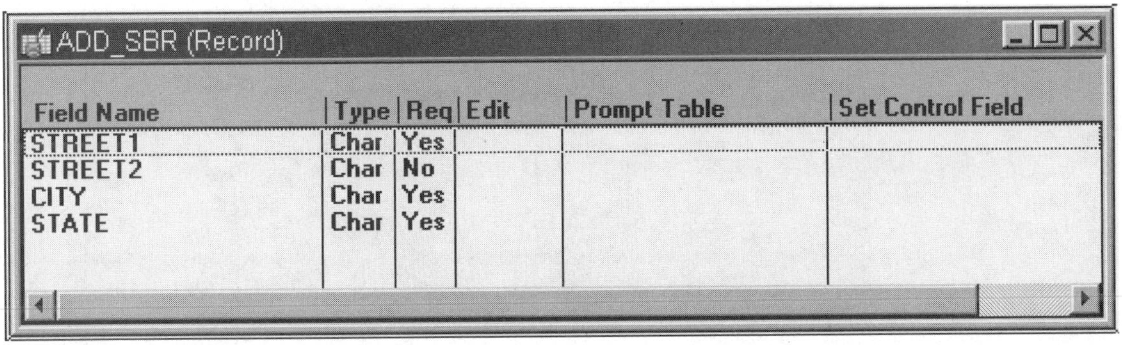

Field Name	Type	Req	Edit	Prompt Table	Set Control Field
STREET1	Char	Yes			
STREET2	Char	No			
CITY	Char	Yes			
STATE	Char	Yes			

Figure 6-87 Edits Display for ADD_SBR.

The only Edits options we are going to set for this record are that STREET1, CITY, and STATE are going to be required. Figure 6-87 is a screen capture of the Edits display of ADD_SBR.

The only thing left to do for the ADD_SBR is to set the record type to subrecord and resave the record. To do this, press the PROPERTIES icon, or select FILE, OBJECT PROPERTIES or ALT-ENTER. Select the TYPE tab and then set the record type to SUBRECORD and press OK. Figure 6-88 is a screen capture of the TYPE tab for the object properties of the ADD_SBR subrecord.

We are now ready to create our VENDORS record. Press the NEW toolbar icon, or select FILE, NEW menu options. From the NEW dialog select RECORD and press OK. A new empty record definition should now be dis-

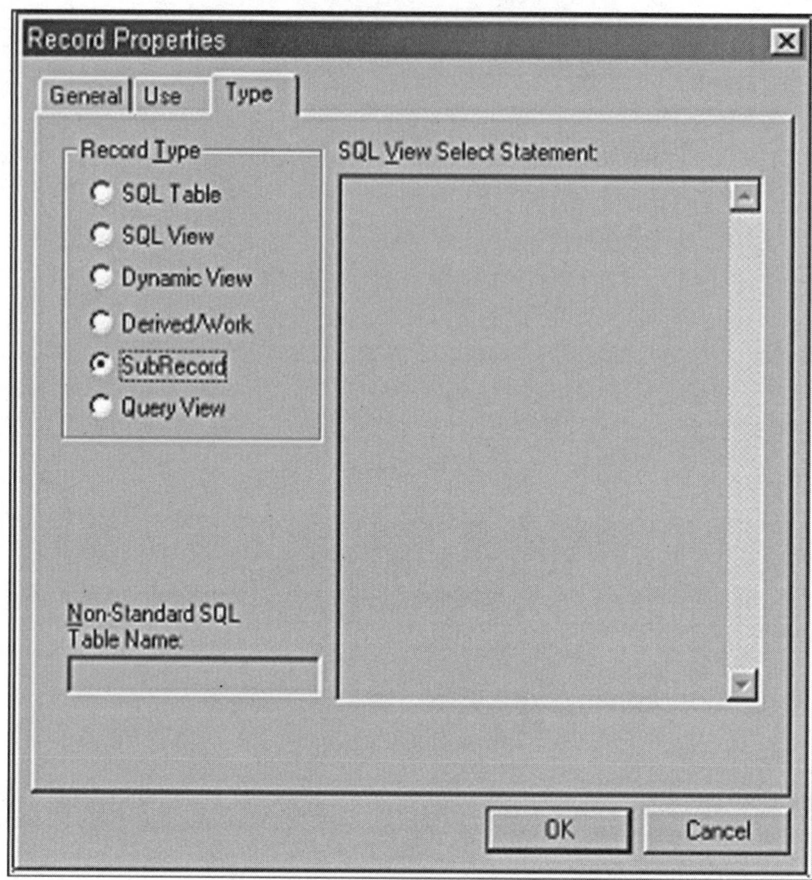

Figure 6-88 TYPE tab of the Properties Dialog for ADD_SBR.

played in the Object Workspace. In the Project Workspace with the fields folder expanded, drag and drop the following fields onto the new record definition:

- VENDORID
- EFFDT
- EFF_STATUS
- VENDOR

Now we are going to insert the subrecord ADD_SBR to include the address fields we require for this record. With the VENDORS record definition selected in the Object Workspace, select INSERT, SUBRECORD. The insert record dialog will then be displayed (Fig. 6-89). Enter ADD_SBR

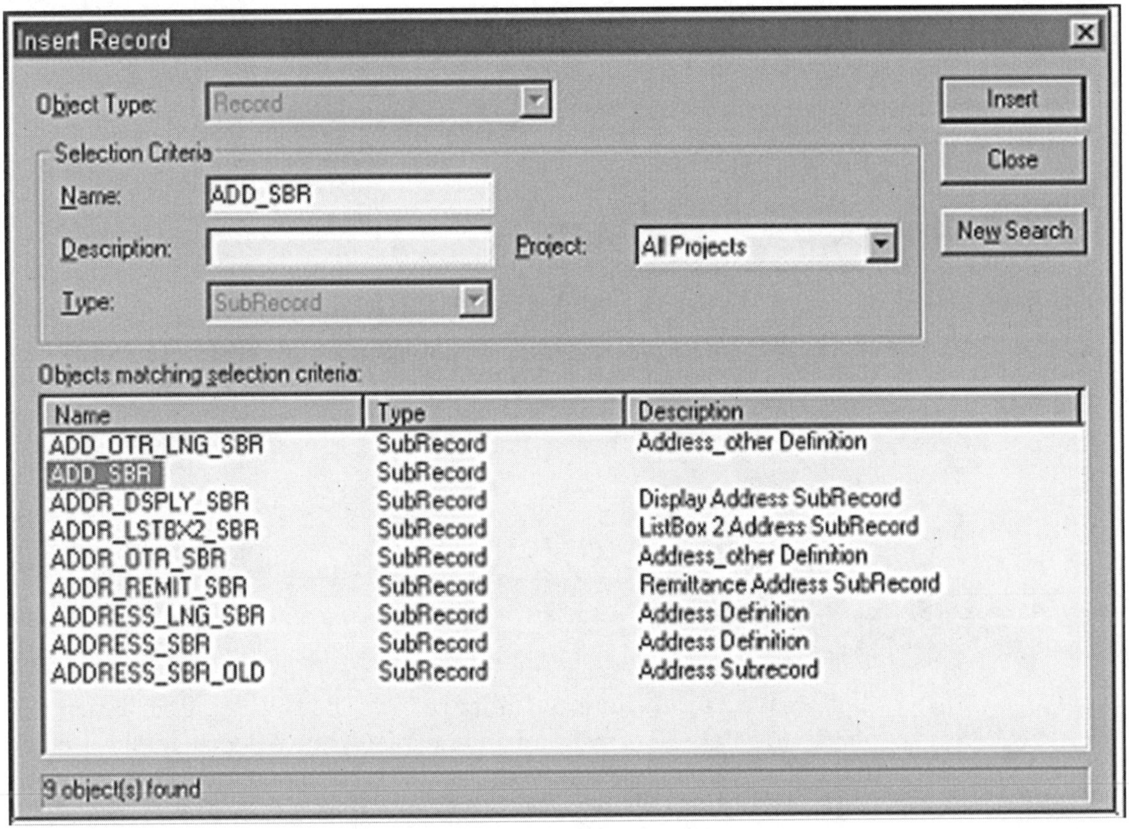

Figure 6-89 Insert Record dialog for ADD_SBR.

and press the INSERT button. If you type the whole name, the subrecord will automatically be inserted into the VENDORS record. Otherwise, you will need to select the desired subrecord from the list of objects that match the selection criteria.

If your record definition's field view looks like the one in Figure 6-90, please press the SAVE ALL icon or select the FILE, SAVE ALL menu options. In the Save As dialog, enter VENDORS and press OK. If your project's options are set to MANUAL INSERT, please press F7.

The VENDORS record is now ready for us to begin setting all the record's field attributes. Let's start with the first field inserted into the record definition. The Use values for the record's field attributes of VENDORID are

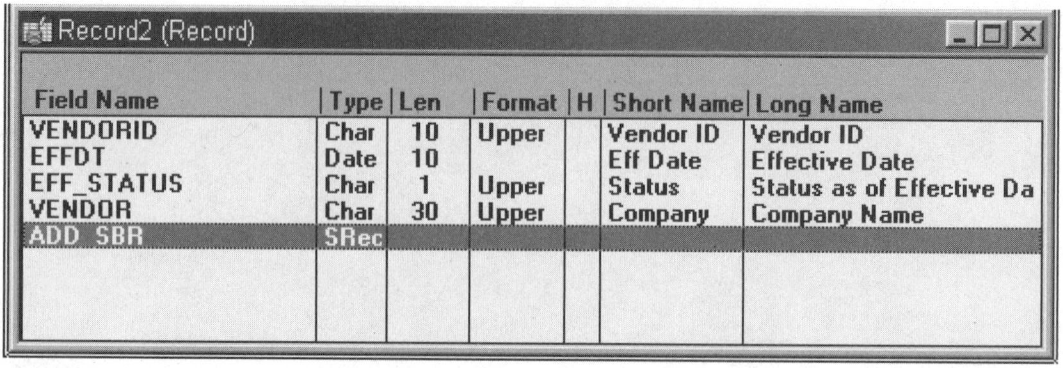

Record2 (Record)

Field Name	Type	Len	Format	H	Short Name	Long Name
VENDORID	Char	10	Upper		Vendor ID	Vendor ID
EFFDT	Date	10			Eff Date	Effective Date
EFF_STATUS	Char	1	Upper		Status	Status as of Effective Da
VENDOR	Char	30	Upper		Company	Company Name
ADD_SBR	SRec					

Figure 6-90 VENDORS Record Fields display.

- Key
- Search Key
- List Box Item

The Search Key option will place this field in all the search dialogs that are used for the internal order record. The List Box Item option will place this field as a column in the resulting list box in the search dialogs.

The only Edit property for this field is that it is required. VENDORID is a key field and is therefore required. Figures 6-91 and 6-92 show the Use and Edit tabbed dialogs for VENDORID.

The next field we set the record attributes for is EFFDT. The Use values that are associated with the field attributes of EFFDT are

- Key
- Descending Key
- Default constant set to the system date %date

The Descending Key option returns the most recent EFFDT. The default constant %date will automatically place the system date in the EFFDT when it is opened for the first time.

The only Edits property that we are going to set for EFFDT is that it is required. Figures 6-93 and 6-94 show the Use and Edits tabbed dialogs for EFFDT.

The next field we set the record attributes for is EFF_STATUS. The Use value that is associated with the field attributes of EFF_STATUS is

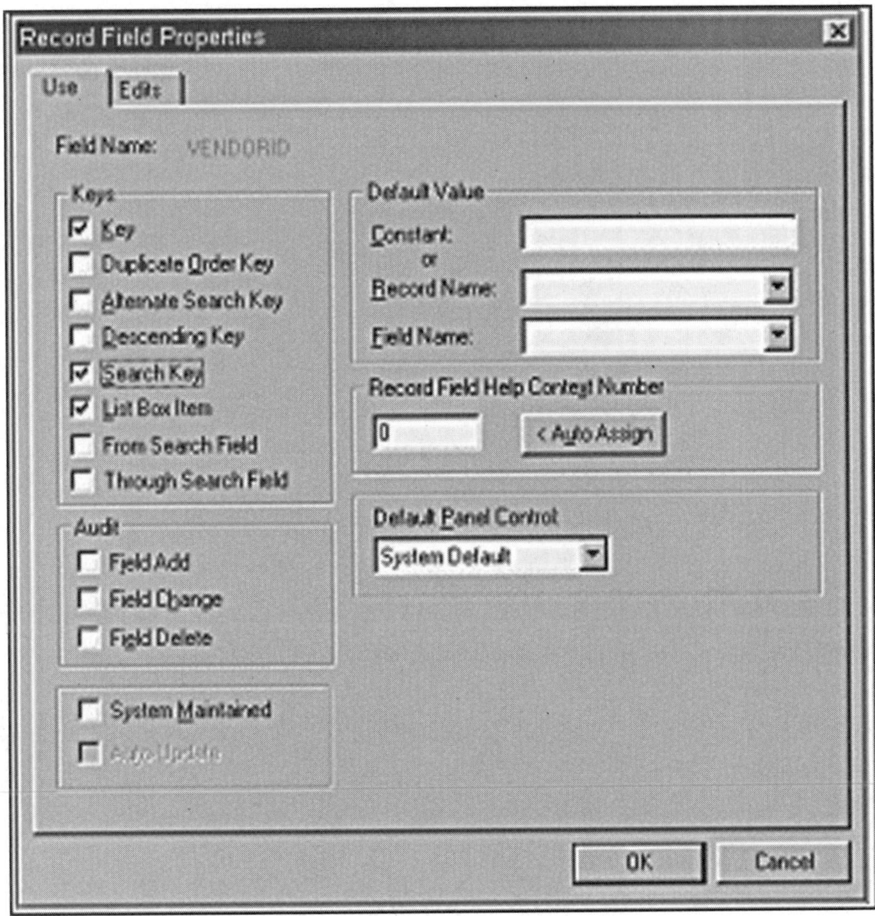

Figure 6-91 VENDORID Use dialog.

the default constant set to A. The default constant A will automatically set the initial effective status to ACTIVE when a new record is added.

The only Edits property that we are going to set for EFF_STATUS is that it is required. Figures 6-95 and 6-96 show the Use and Edits tabbed dialogs for EFF_STATUS.

The next field we set the record attributes for is VENDOR. The Use values that are associated with the field attributes of VENDOR are

- Alt Search Key
- List Box Item

The Alt Search Key option will place this field in all the search dialogs that are used for the internal order record. The Alt Search Key

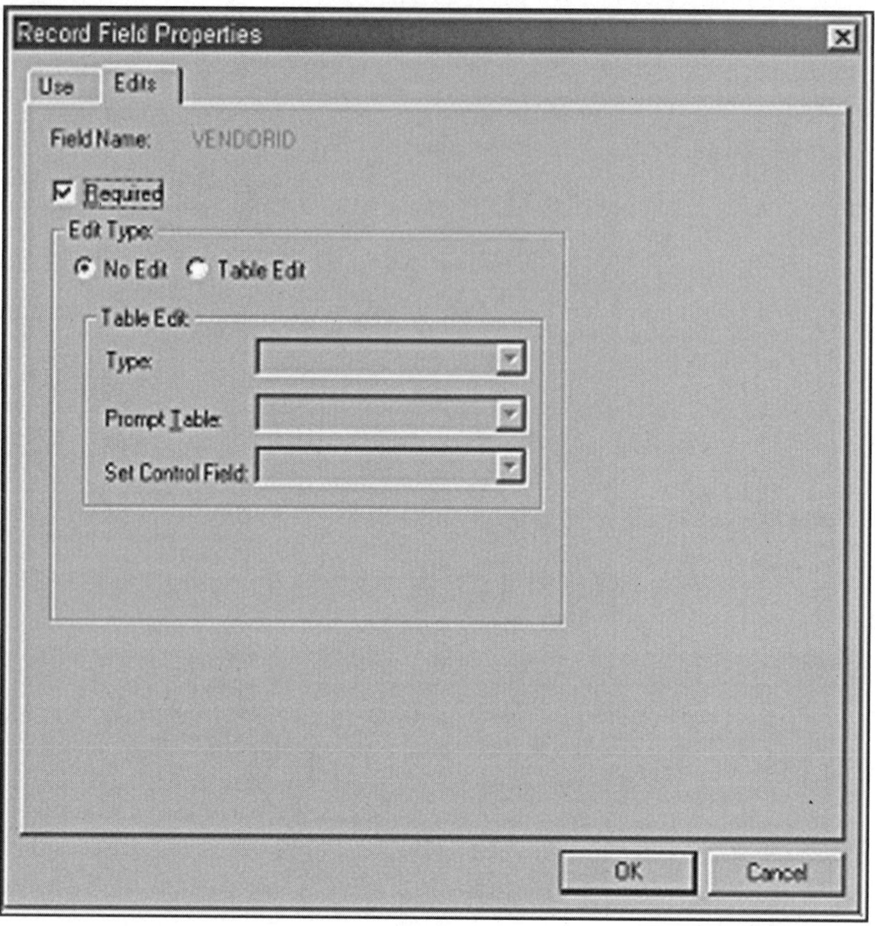

Figure 6-92
VENDORID Edits dialog.

option does not make this field part of the primary key; instead it creates an index on the field. The List Box Item option will place this field as a column in the resulting list box in the search dialogs.

The only Edits property that we will set for VENDOR is that it is required. Figures 6-97 and 6-98 show the Use and Edit tabbed dialogs for VENDOR.

The Use Display of your VENDORS record should look like the one in Figure 6-99.

To build VENDORS, select BUILD, CURRENT OBJECT, or press the BUILD icon from the toolbar. With the build dialog displayed, select the Create Table check box. The Create Indexes check box will automatically be selected and grayed out. Next, select the EXECUTE AND BUILD SCRIPT radio

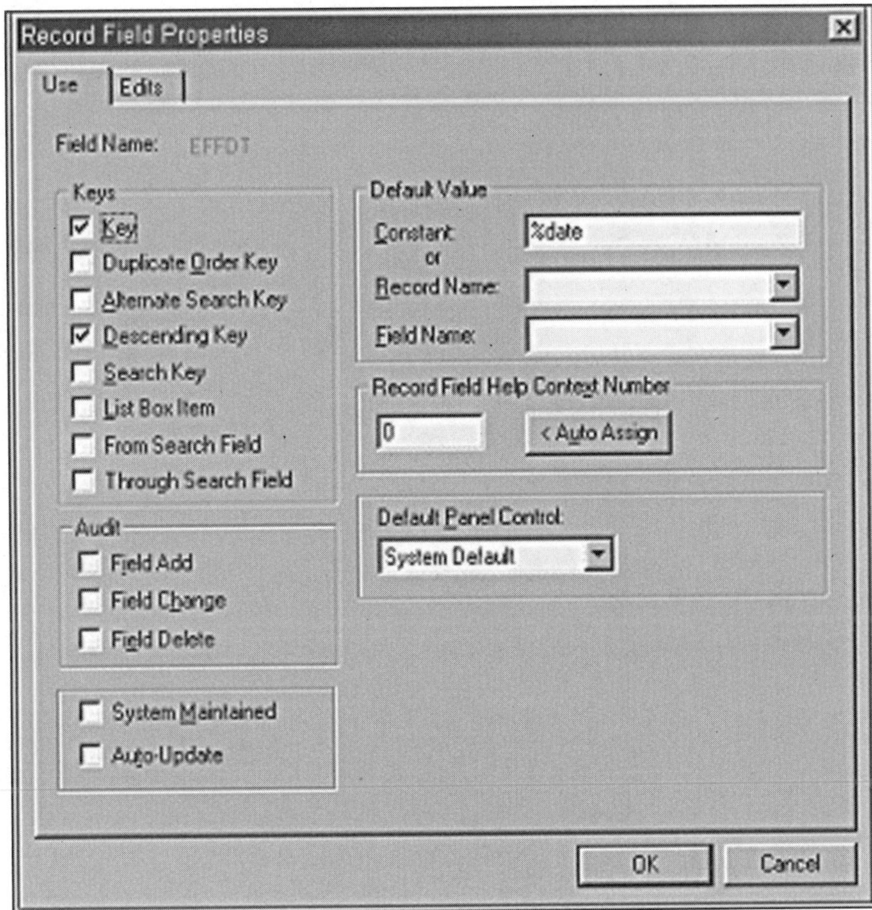

Figure 6-93
EFFDT Use dialog.

button. When you have completed this, press the BUILD button at the top right of the dialog. On completion, a status of "1 records processed, 0 errors and 0 warnings" will be displayed in the Output window.

UNITS_MEASURE Record

Table 6-5 contains all the fields and attributes making up our UNITS_MEASURE record.

We are now going to create the UNITS_MEASURE record. Press the NEW toolbar icon or select FILE, NEW menu options. From the New dialog, select RECORD and press OK. A new empty record definition should now be displayed in the Object Workspace. In the Project Workspace with the

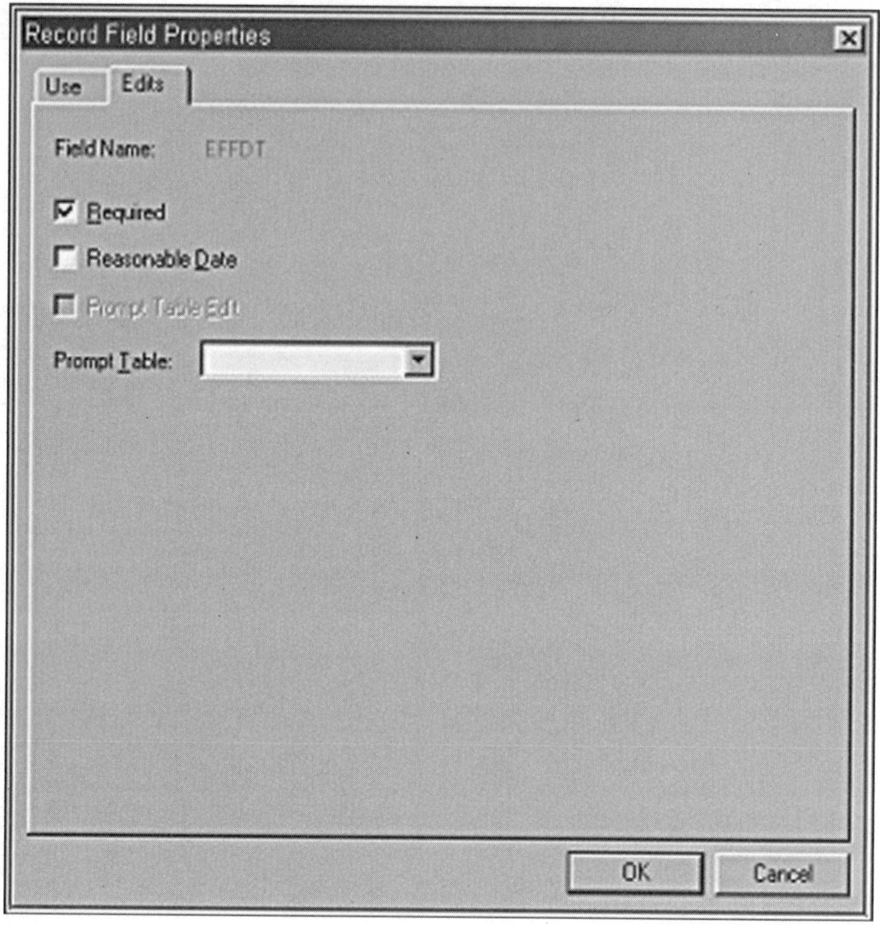

Figure 6-94
EFFDT Edits dialog.

Fields folder expanded, drag and drop the following fields onto the new record definition:

- UNIT_MEASURE
- DESCR

If your record definition's field view looks like the one in Figure 6-100, press the SAVE ALL icon or select the FILE, SAVE ALL menu options. In the Save As dialog, enter UNIT_MEASURE and press OK. If your project's options are set to MANUAL INSERT, please press F7.

The UNIT_MEASURE record is now ready for us to begin setting all the record's field attributes. Let's start with the first field inserted into the

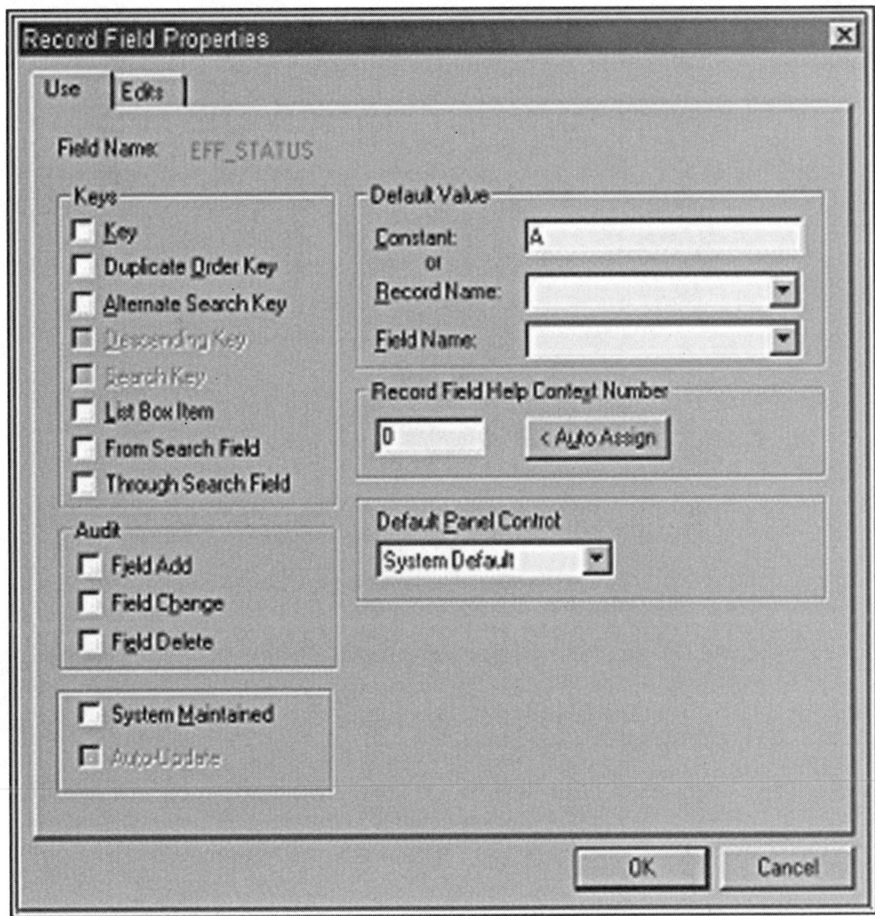

Figure 6-95 EFF_STATUS Use dialog.

record definition. The Use values for the record's field attributes of UNIT_MEASURE are

- Key
- Search Key
- List Box Item

The Search Key option will place this field in all the search dialogs that are used for the internal order record. The List Box Item option will place this field as a column in the resulting list box in the search dialogs.

The only Edits property for this field is that it is required.

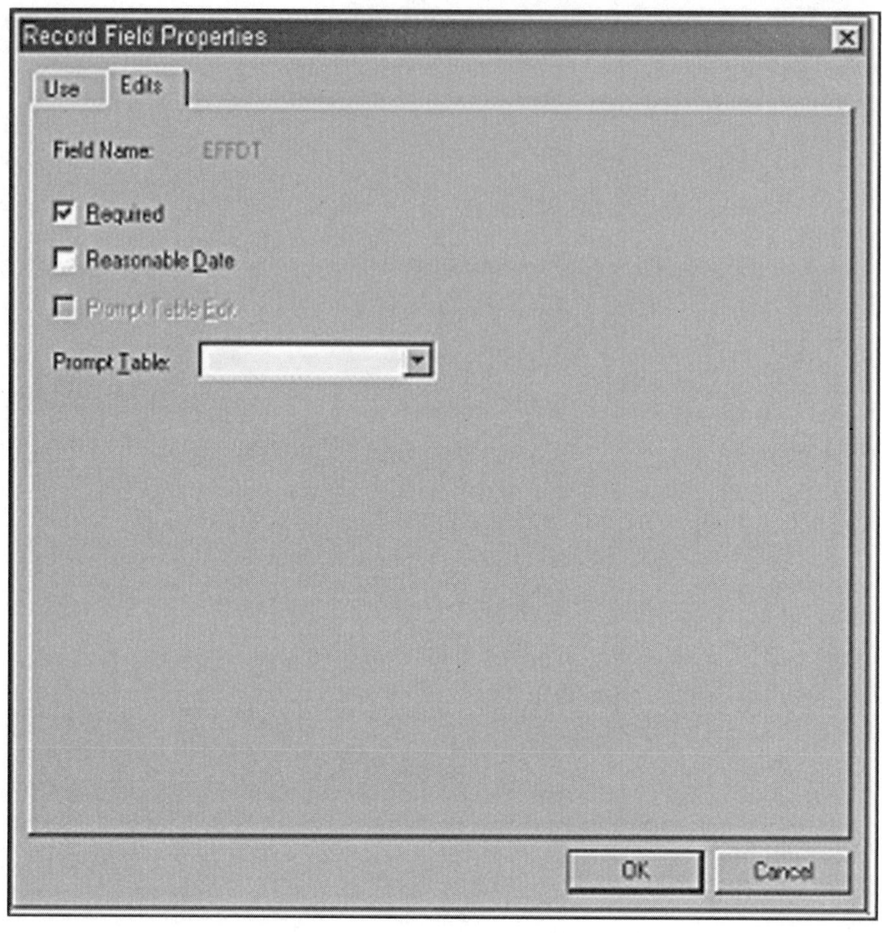

Figure 6-96 EFF_STATUS Edits dialog.

UNIT_MEASURE is a key field and is therefore required. Figures 6-101 and 6-102 show the Use and Edits tabbed dialogs for UNIT_MEASURE.

The next field we set the record attributes for is DESCR. The Use values that are associated with the field attributes of DESCR are

- Alt Search Key
- List Box Item

The Alt Search Key option will place this field in all the search dialogs that are used for the internal order record. The Alt Search Key option does not make this field part of the primary key; instead it creates an index on the field. The List Box Item option will place this field as a column in the resulting list box in the search dialogs.

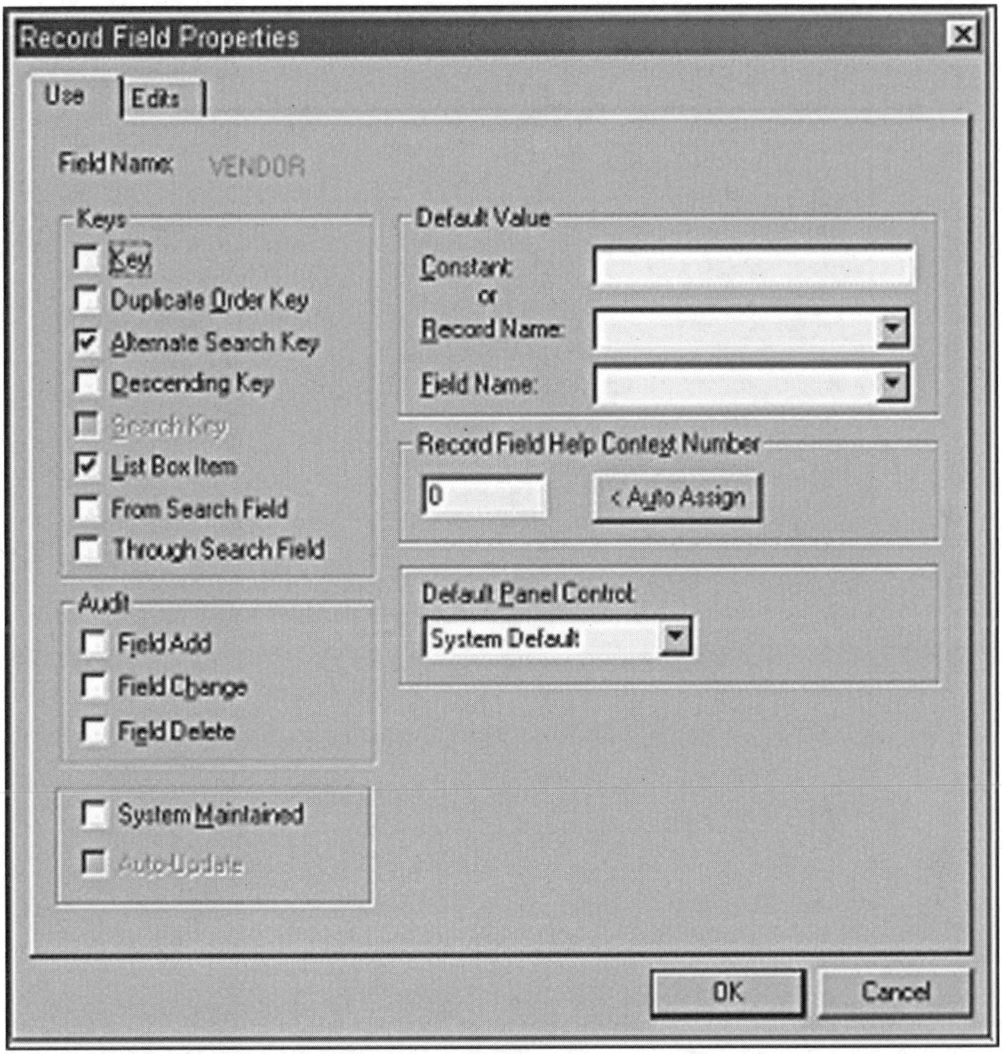

Figure 6-97 VENDOR Use dialog.

The only Edits property that we will set for DESCR is that it is required. Figures 6-103 and 6-104 show the Use and Edit tabbed dialogs for DESCR.

The Use Display of your UNIT_MEASURE record should look like the one in Figure 6-105.

To build UNIT_MEASURE, select BUILD, CURRENT OBJECT, or press the

Figure 6-98
VENDOR Edits dialog.

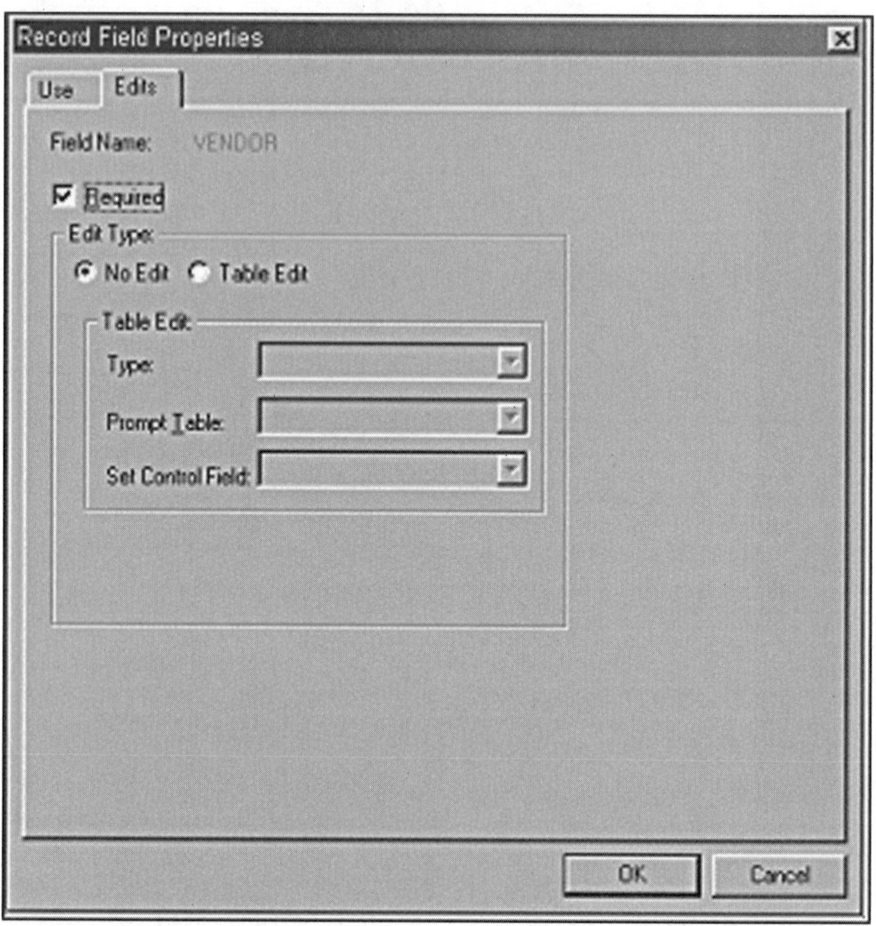

VENDORS (Record)

Field Name	Type	Key	Dir	CurC	Srch	List	Sys	Audt	H	Default
VENDORID	Char	Key	Asc		Yes	Yes	No			
EFFDT	Date	Key	Desc		No	No	No			%date
EFF_STATUS	Char				No	No	No			'A'
VENDOR	Char	Alt	Asc		No	Yes	No			
ADD_SBR	SRec				No	No	No			

Figure 6-99 VENDORS Record Use display.

TABLE 6-5

UNITS_MEASURE Record

Column	Description	Data Type	Key	Valid Values
UNIT_MEASURE	Unit of measure	Char(4)	X	
DESCR	Unit of measure description	Char(30)		

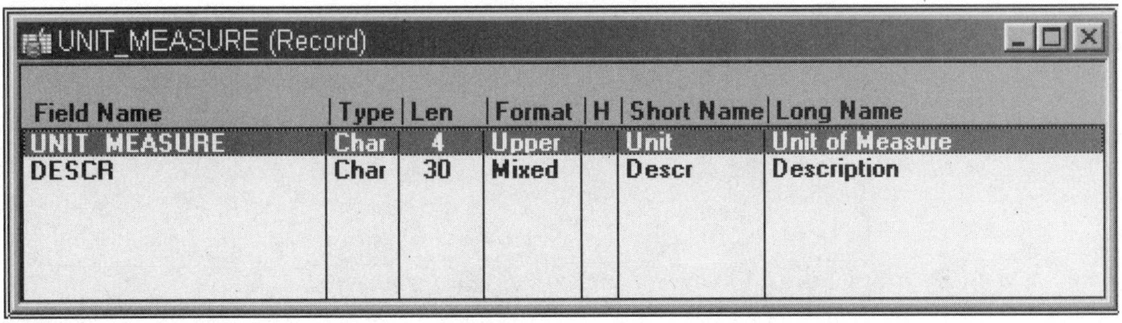

Field Name	Type	Len	Format	H	Short Name	Long Name
UNIT_MEASURE	Char	4	Upper		Unit	Unit of Measure
DESCR	Char	30	Mixed		Descr	Description

Figure 6-100 UNIT_MEASURE Record Fields display.

BUILD icon from the toolbar. With the build dialog displayed, select the Create Table check box. The Create Indexes check box will automatically be selected and grayed out. Next, select the EXECUTE AND BUILD SCRIPT radio button. When you have completed this, press the BUILD button at the top right of the dialog. On completion, a status of "1 records processed, 0 errors and 0 warnings" will be displayed in the Output window.

INT_ORDER Record

Table 6-6 lists the fields and attributes that will make up our internal order INT_ORDER, record.

After all the prompt tables have been created, we can begin to create the main records of our application. The first of these records that we will create will be a SQL Table record for the Internal Order entity.

Press the NEW toolbar icon, or select FILE, NEW menu options. From the New dialog select RECORD and press OK. A new empty record definition should now be displayed in the Object Workspace.

The following fields, which should already be in our project's Fields folder, will be used to create our record:

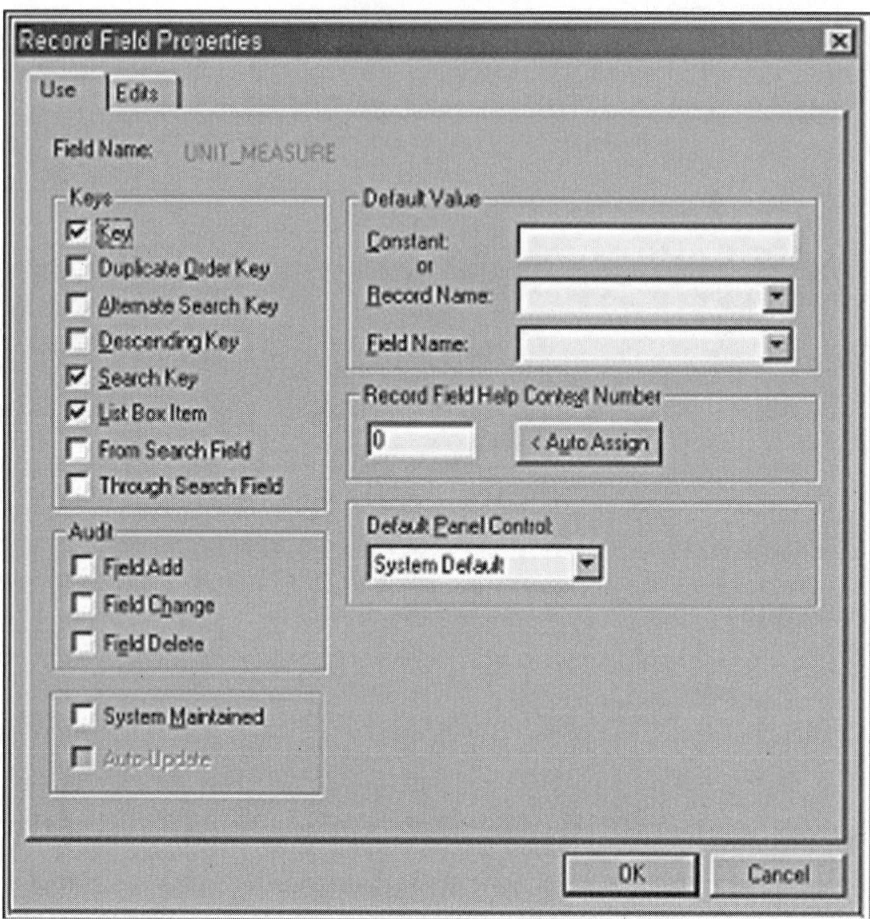

Figure 6-101 UNIT_MEASURE Use dialog.

- INT_ORDER_ID
- REQUESTED_DT
- EMP_ID
- PROCESS_DT
- PROCESS_LOC_ID
- INT_STAT

Drag and drop these fields in the same order as they are displayed into the new record definition. If your record definition's field view looks like the one in Figure 6-106, press the SAVE ALL icon or select the FILE, SAVE ALL menu options. In the Save As dialog, enter INT_ORDER and press OK.

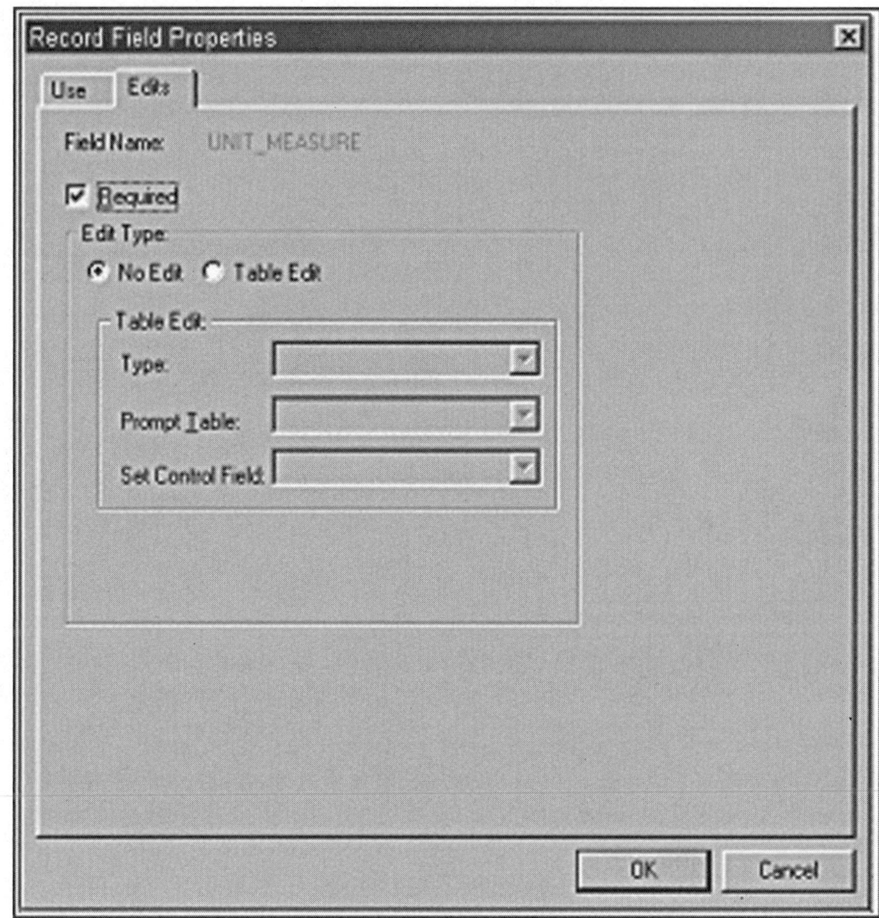

Figure 6-102
UNIT_MEASURE
Edits dialog.

The internal order record is now ready for us to begin setting all the record's field attributes. Let's start with the first field inserted into the record definition. The Use values that are associated with the field attributes of `INT_ORDER_ID` are

- Key
- Search Key
- List Box Item

The Search Key option will place this field in all the search dialogs that are used for the internal order record. The List Box Item option will

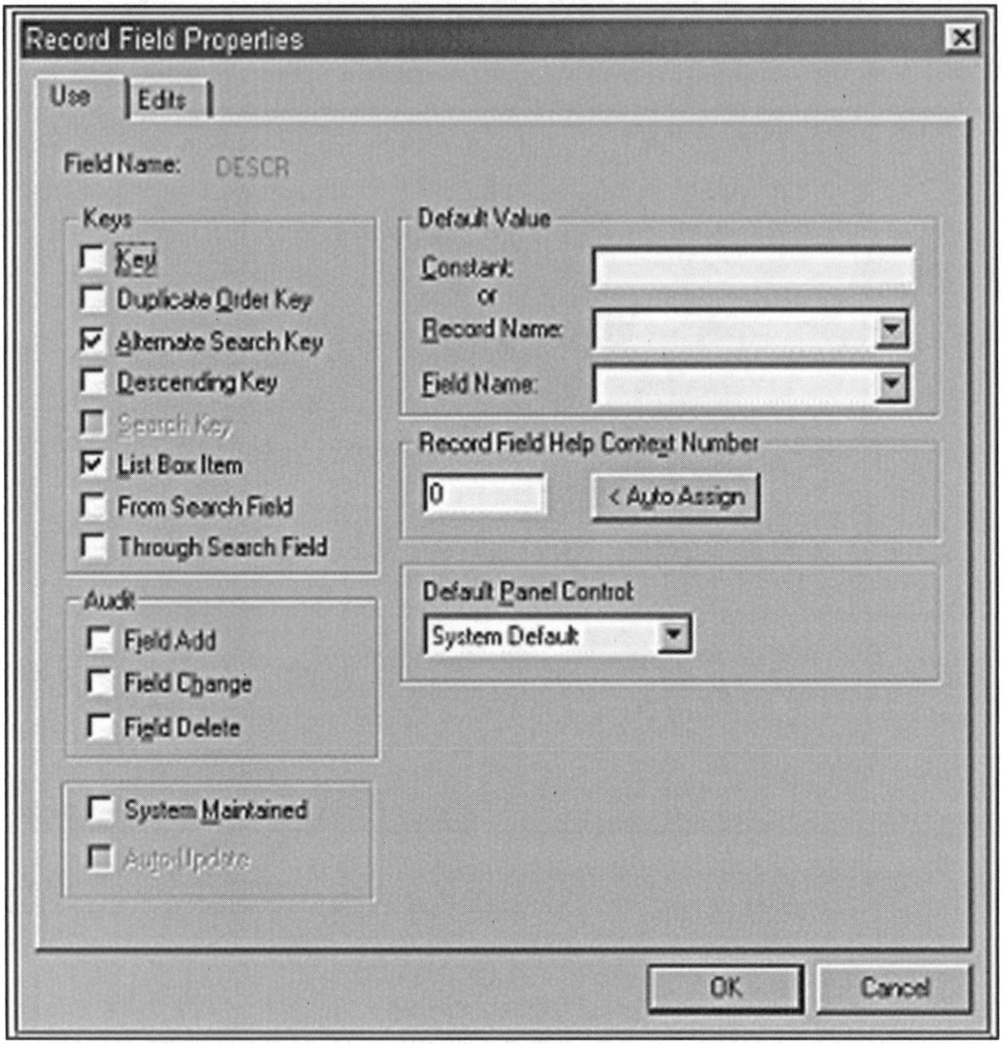

Figure 6-103 DESCR Use dialog.

place this field as a column in the resulting list box in the search dialogs.

The only Edits property for this field is that it is required. INT_ORDER_ID is a key field and is therefore required. Figures 6-107 and 6-108 show the Use and Edits tabbed dialogs for INT_ORDER_ID.

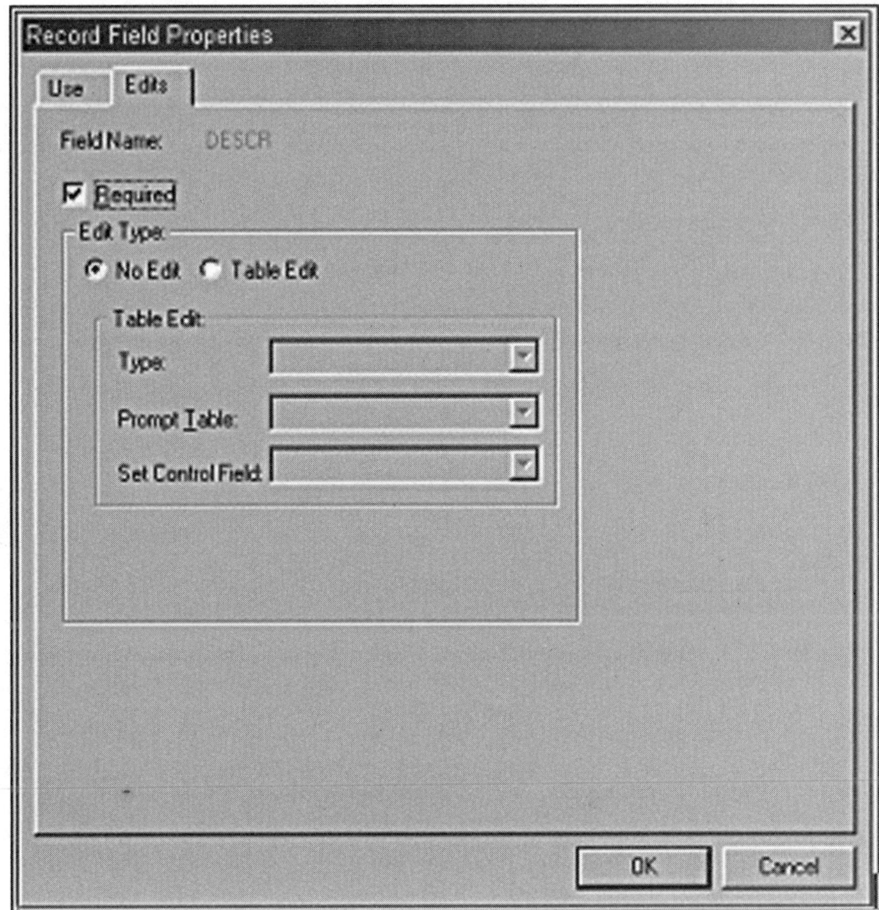

Figure 6-104
DESCR Edits dialog.

The next field we set the record attributes for is REQUESTED_DT. The Use values that are associated to the field attributes of REQUESTED_DT are

- Alt Search Key
- List Box Item
- Default to system date

The Alt Search Key option will place this field in all the search dialogs that are used for the internal order record. The Alt Search Key option does not make this field part of the primary key; instead it cre-

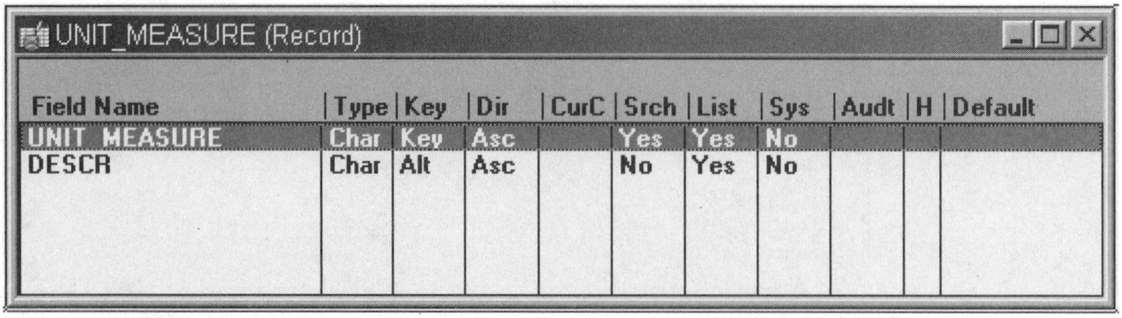

UNIT_MEASURE (Record)

Field Name	Type	Key	Dir	CurC	Srch	List	Sys	Audt	H	Default
UNIT_MEASURE	Char	Key	Asc		Yes	Yes	No			
DESCR	Char	Alt	Asc		No	Yes	No			

Figure 6-105 UNIT_MEASURE Record Use display.

TABLE 6-6

INT_ORDER Record

Column	Description	Data Type	Key	Valid Values
INT_ORDER_ID	Internal order id	Char(10)	X	
REQUESTED_DT	Initial date of the request	Date		=> Today
EMP_ID	Requester	Char(10)		Supervisor from the employee TBL
PROCESS_DT	Warehouse delivery date	Date		=> Today
PROCESS_LOC_ID	Delivery location	Char(10)		Location TBL
INT_STAT	Overall status	Char(3)		New Canceled On order Ready Fulfilled

ates an index on the field. The List Box Item option will place this field as a column in the resulting list box in the search dialogs. To set the default value to the current system date we will place `%date` in the Default Value Constant edit box.

REQUESTED_DT Edits properties include required and reasonable date. The reasonable date functionality will force a 30-day plus or minus constraint from the current system date. This will mean that only dates

INT_ORDER (Record)

Field Name	Type	Len	Format	H	Short Name	Long Name
INT_ORDER_ID	Char	10	Upper		Internal Ord	Internal Order ID
REQUESTED_DT	Date	10			Date Reque	Date Requested
EMP_ID	Char	9	SSN		Employee II	Employee ID
PROCESS_DT	Date	10			Process Da	Process Date
PROCESS_LOC_ID	Char	10	Upper		Location ID	Process Location ID
INT_STAT	Char	3	Upper		Int Ord Stat	Internal Order Status

Figure 6-106 `INT_ORDER` record definition.

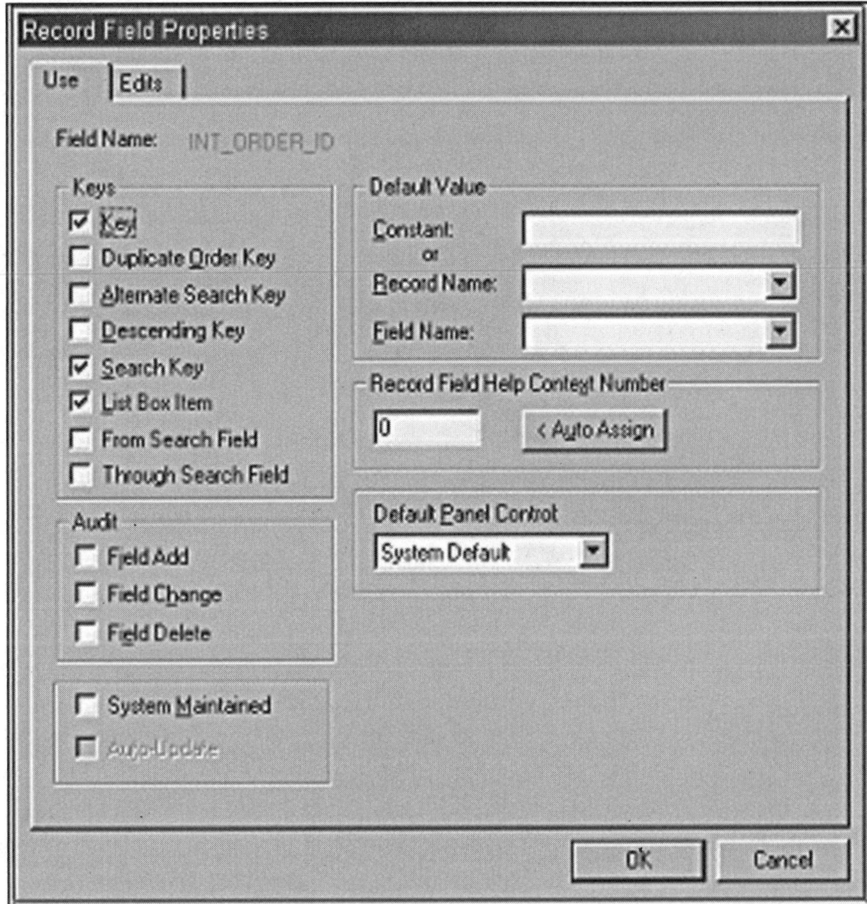

Figure 6-107 `INT_ORDER_ID` Use dialog.

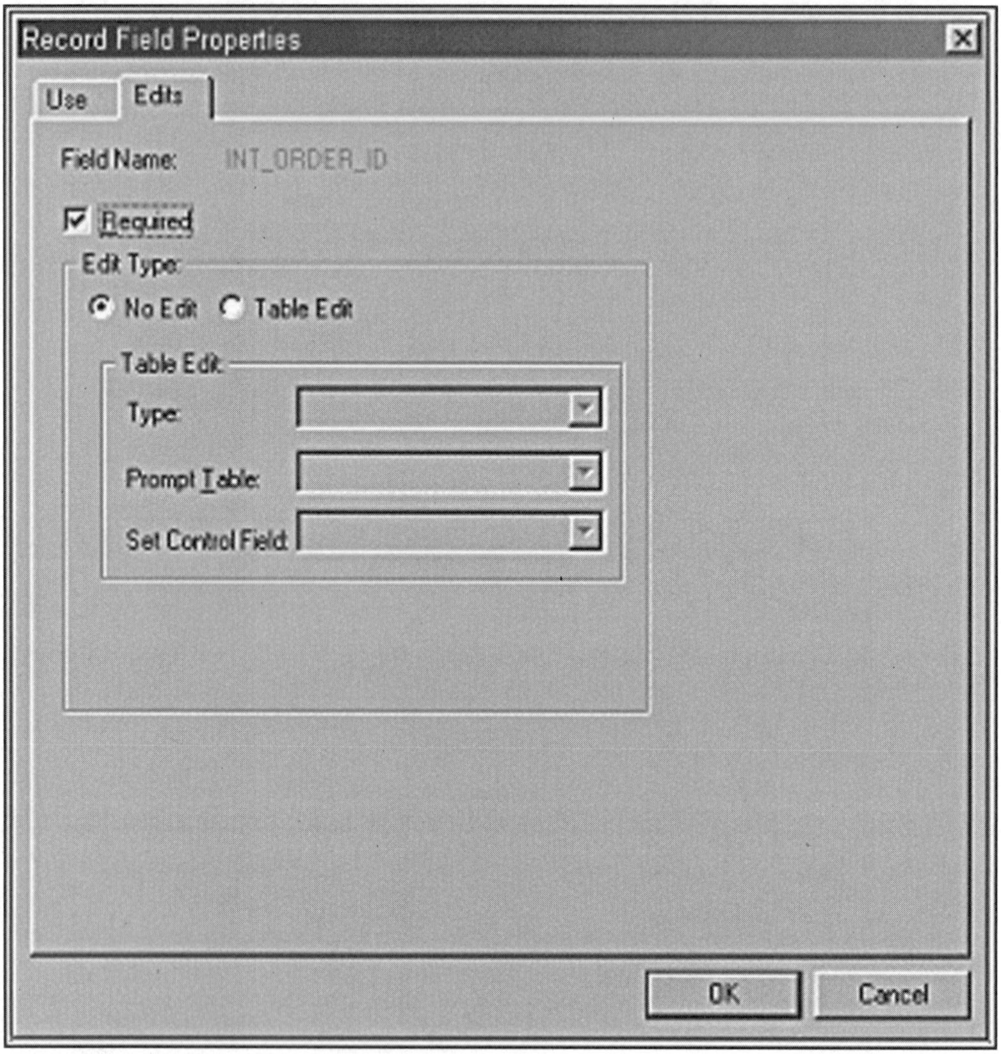

Figure 6-108 INT_ORDER_ID Edits dialog.

that are either within 30 days before or after today will be allowed. Figures 6-109 and 6-110 show the Use and Edits tabbed dialogs for REQUESTED_DT.

The next field for which we are going to set up record attributes for the INT_ORDER record is the EMP_ID field. The EMP_ID field's key attributes are

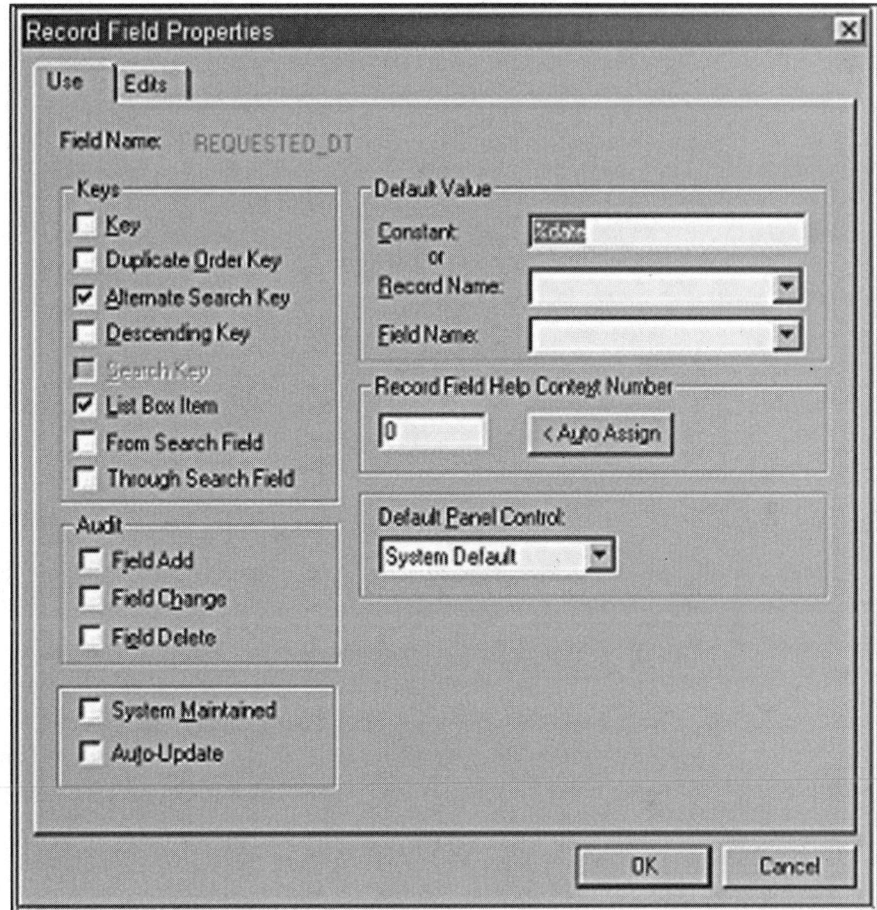

Figure 6-109 REQUESTED_DT Use dialog.

- Alt Search Key
- List Box Item

The Alternate Search Key option will create an index on the EMP_ID field. The EMP_ID field will also be displayed in the Alternate Search Keys section of all the search dialogs. The List Box Item option will place this field as a column in the resulting list box in the search dialogs.

Not only is this field required in the internal order record; we are going to set up a prompt table edit. For Data Validation, we will require that the valid entries exist in our EMPLOYEES record that we have already created. To do this, we select the TABLE EDIT radio button from

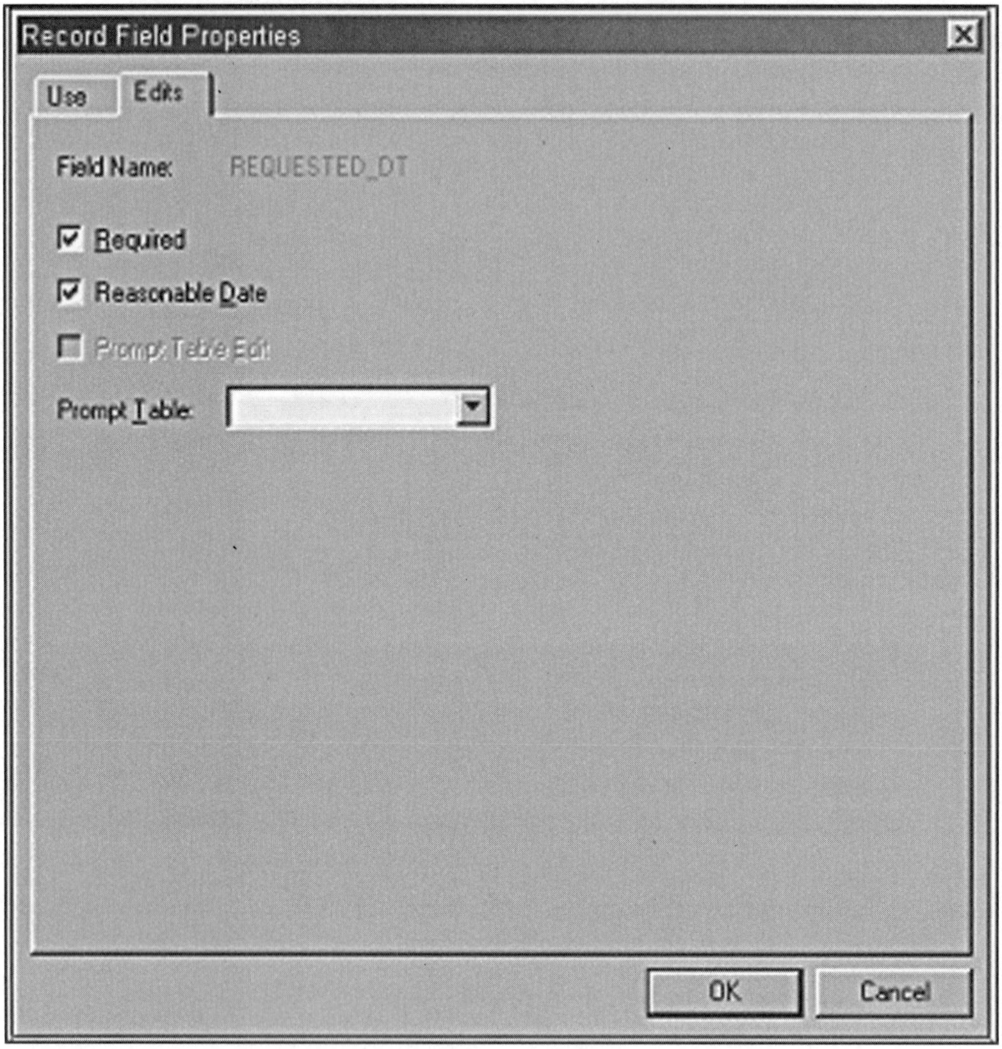

Figure 6-110 REQUESTED_DT Edits dialog.

the Edits Tab dialog for the EMP_ID fields record attributes. The drop-down list boxes will then be enabled. Select the Prompt Table options from the Type drop-down and then select the EMPLOYEES record from the Prompt Table drop-down. Figures 6-111 and 6-112 show the Use and Edit tabbed dialogs for EMP_ID.

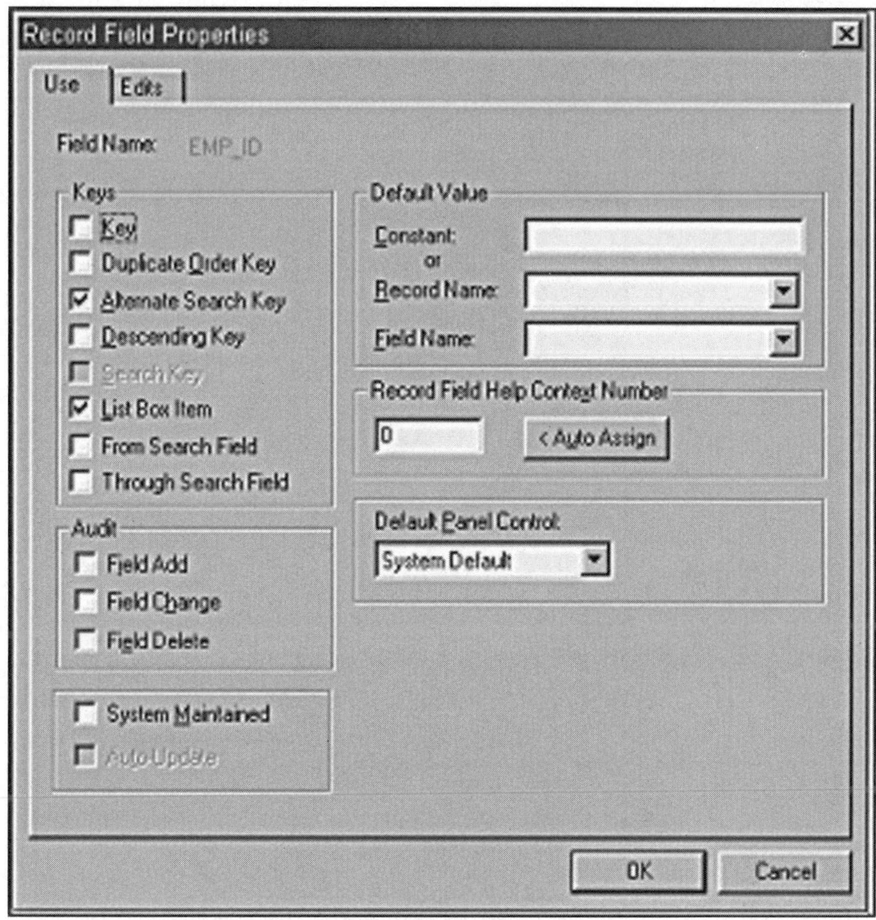

Figure 6-111
EMP_ID Use dialog.

The next field we set the record attributes for is PROCESS_DT. The Use values that are associated with the field attributes of PROCESS_DT are

- Alt Search Key
- List Box Item

The only edits property for PROCESS_DT is that it is required. Figures 6-113 and 6-114 show the Use and Edits tabbed dialogs for PROCESS_DT.

The next field for which we are going to set up record attributes for the INT_ORDER record is the PROCESS_LOC_ID field. PROCESS_LOC_ID field's key attributes are

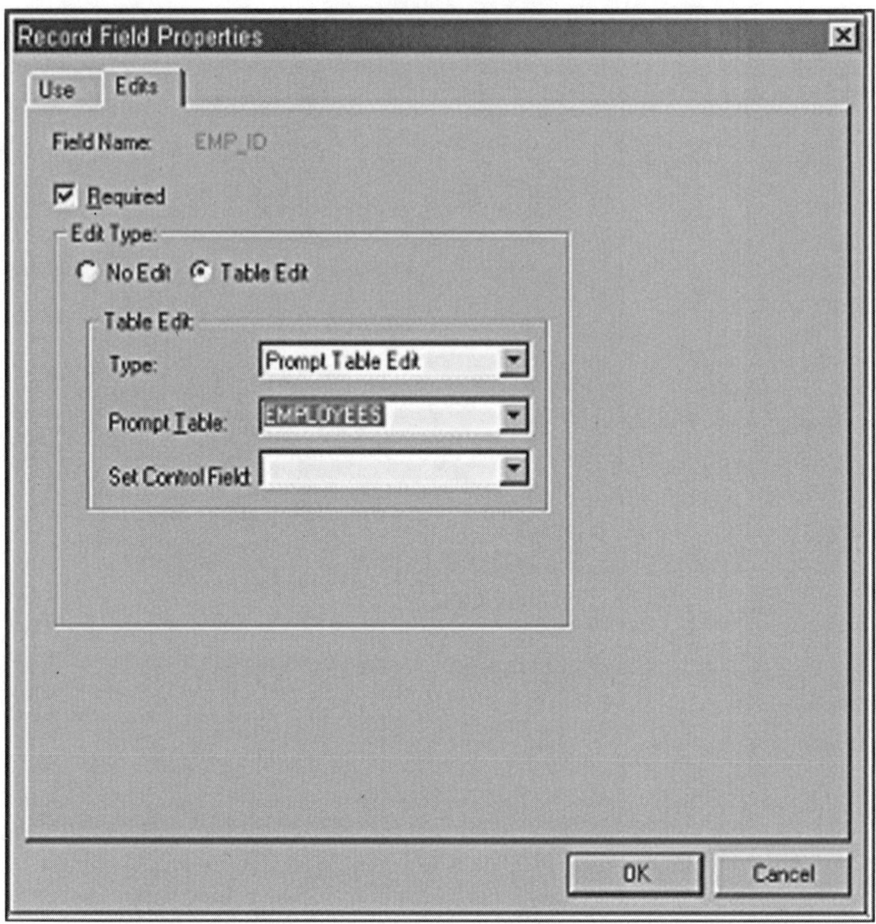

Figure 6-112 EMP_ID Edits dialog.

- Alt Search Key
- List Box Item

The Alternate Search Key option will create an index on the PROCESS_LOC_ID field. The PROCESS_LOC_ID field will also be displayed in the Alternate Search Keys section of all the search dialogs. The List Box Item option will place this field as a column in the resulting list box in the search dialogs.

Not only will this field be required in the Internal Order record; we are going to set up a prompt table edit. For Data Validation, we will require that the valid entries exist in our PROCESS_LOC_ID record that

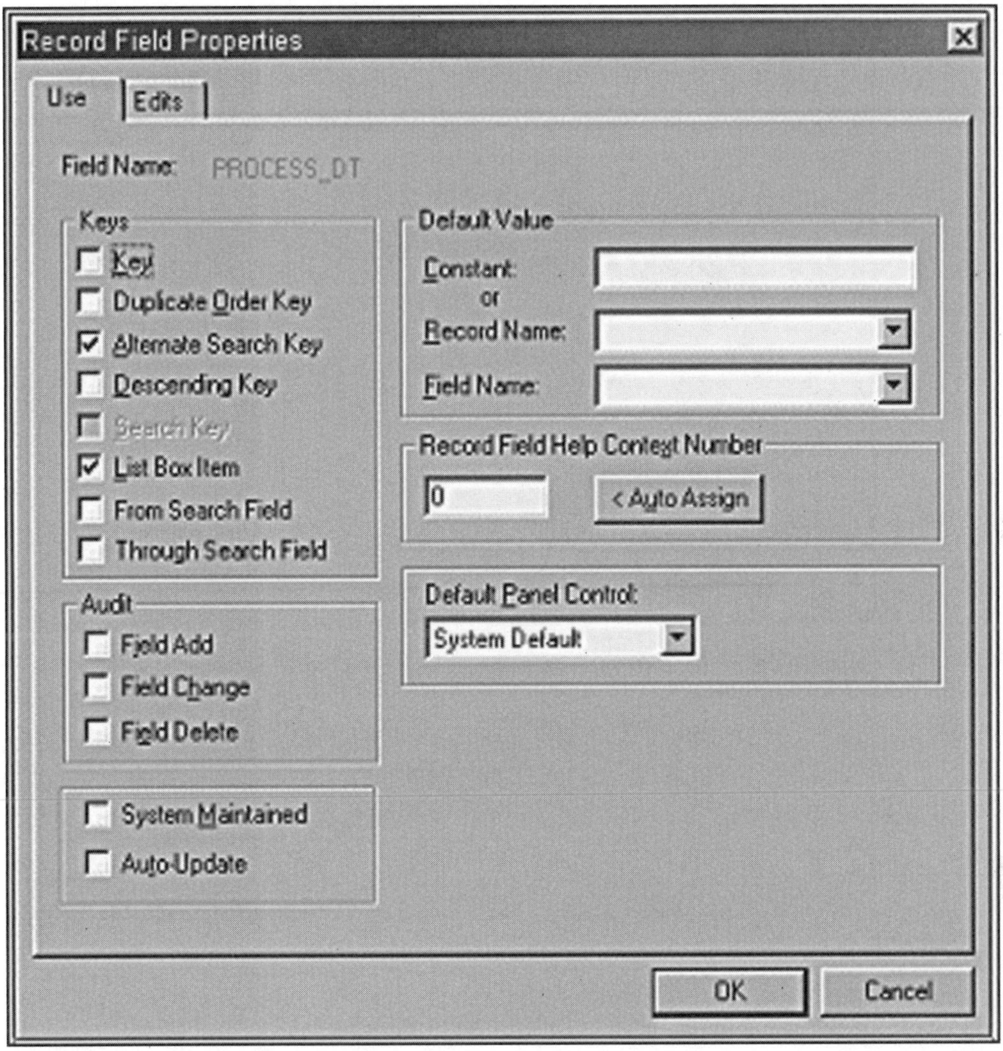

Figure 6-113 PROCESS_DT Use dialog.

we have already created. To do this, we select the TABLE EDIT radio button from the Edits Tab dialog for the PROCESS_LOC_ID fields record attributes. The drop-down list boxes will then be enabled. Select the Prompt Table options from the Type drop-down and then select the PROCESS_LOC_ID record from the Prompt Table drop-down. Figures 6-115 and 6-116 show the Use and Edit tabbed dialogs for PROCESS_LOC_ID.

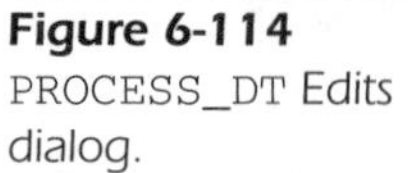

Figure 6-114 PROCESS_DT Edits dialog.

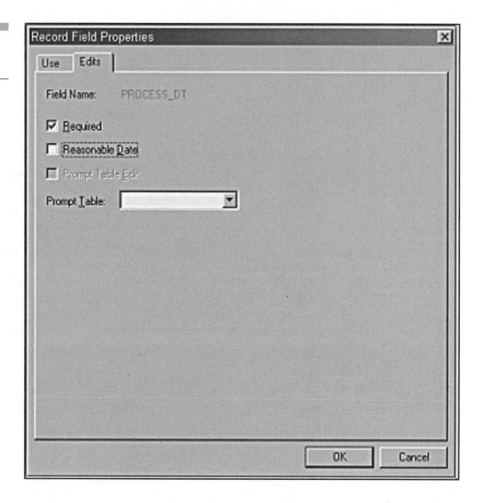

The next field we set the record attributes for is INT_STAT. The Use values that are associated to the field attributes of INT_STAT are

- Default constant values NEW
- Default panel control RADIO BUTTON

We are going to set the default panel control to RADIO BUTTON, which will allow us to place five separate INT_STAT controls on our panel. Each one will be set to represent one of the five translate values we set up for INT_STAT. The default constant value of NEW will set the radio button that is set to NEW on as a default value. This will be shown in more detail when we create our internal order panels.

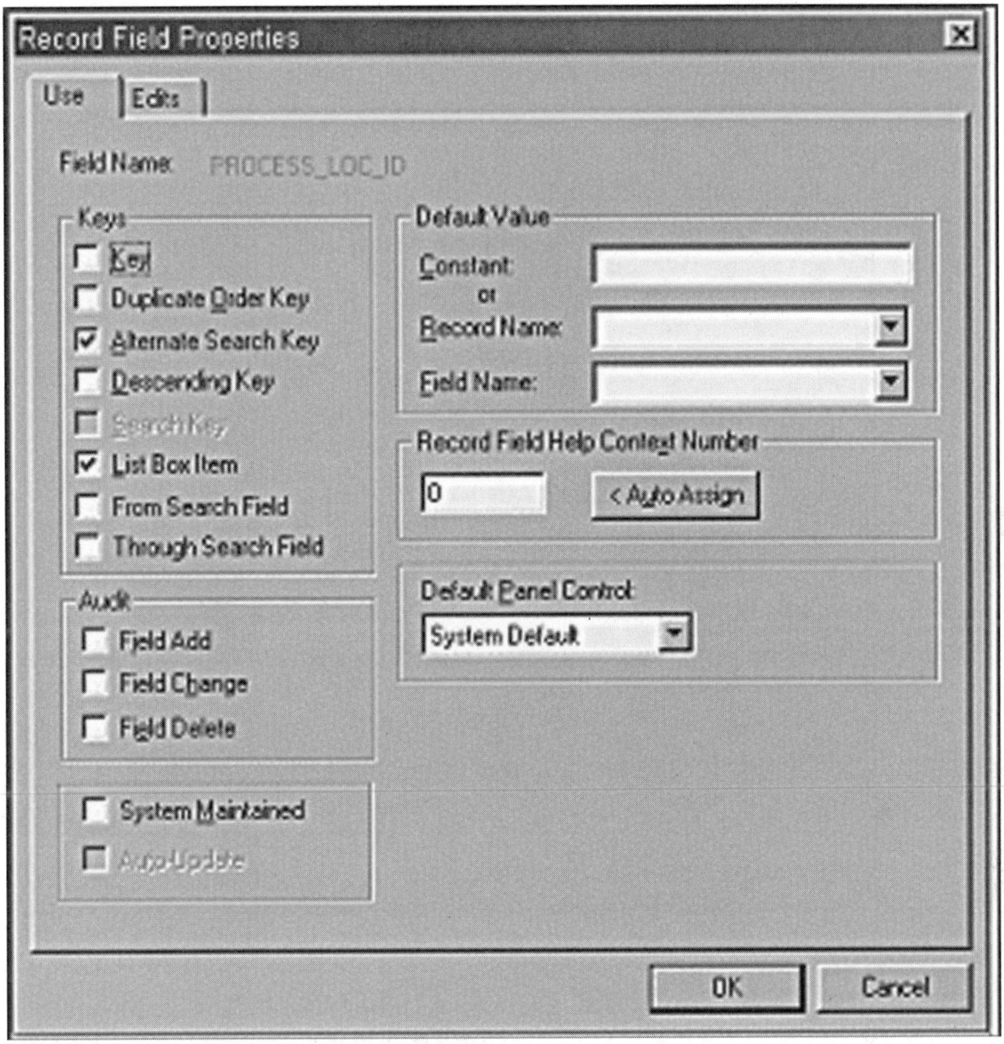

Figure 6-115 PROCESS_LOC_ID Use dialog.

INT_STAT Edits properties include required and a Translate Table Edit. Figures 6-117 and 6-118 show the Use and Edit tabbed dialogs for INT_STAT.

The Use Display of your INT_ORDER record should be like the one in Figure 6-118*a*. If so, the INT_ORDER record is now ready to be built. Follow the same instructions as for the previous SQL Table records. Select

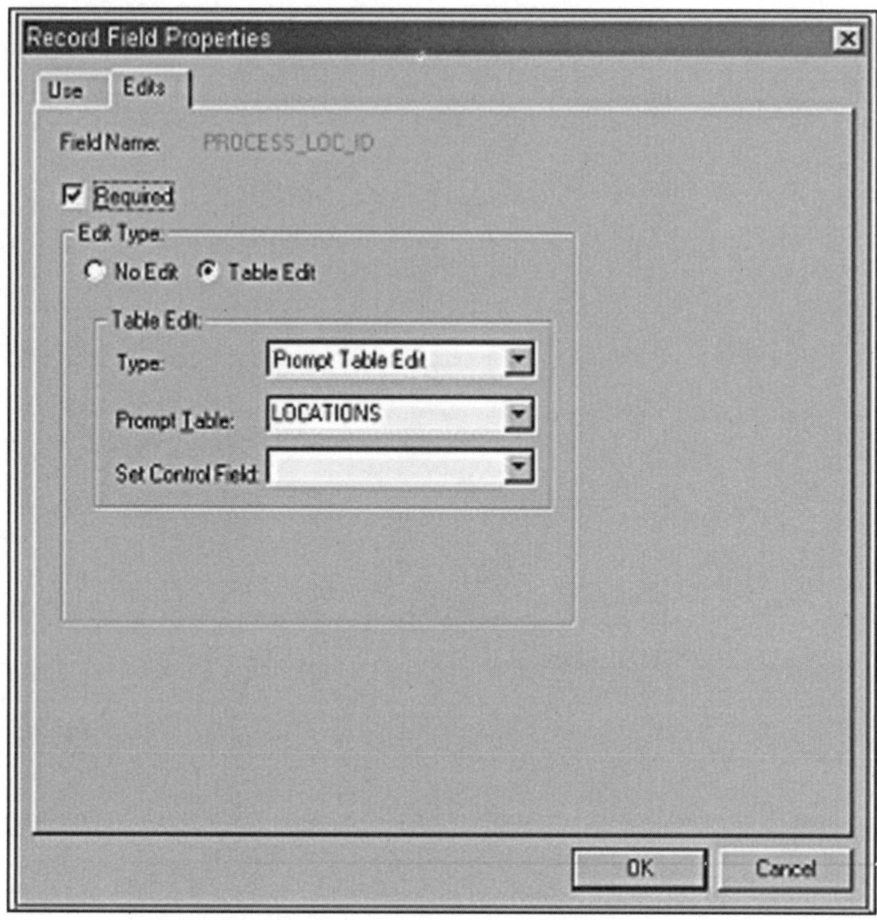

Figure 6-116 PROCESS_LOC_ID Edits dialog.

from the menu BUILD, CURRENT OBJECT, or press the BUILD icon. From the build dialog, select CREATE TABLES and BUILD AND EXECUTE SCRIPT. After you press the BUILD button, a successful status should be displayed in the Output window.

INT_ORDER_LINES Record

Table 6-7 lists the fields and attributes that will make up our internal order (INT_ORDER_LINES) record.

The next record is INT_ORDER_LINES, and it is a child record of the INT_ORDER record that we just created. The relationship is created by

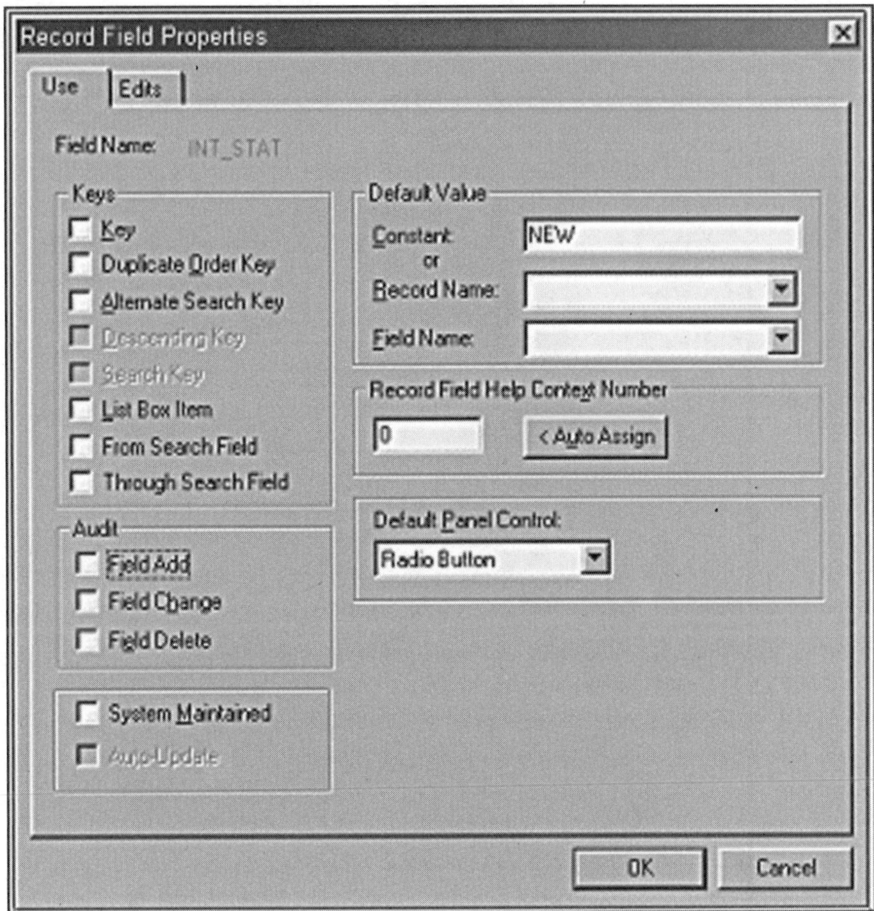

Figure 6-117 INT_STAT Use dialog.

including the key field of INT_ORDER and another unique identifier. We are going to use the LINE_NUM and the INT_ORDER_ID as the key fields for this record. Many of the fields that we are going to create as a part of the INT_ORDER_LINES record will be used primarily for the external order record view that we will create next. Please follow the following instructions to create your INT_ORDER_LINES record.

Press the NEW toolbar icon, or select FILE, NEW menu options. From the New dialog select RECORD and press OK. A new empty record definition should now be displayed in the Object Workspace.

The following fields, which should already be in our project's fields folder, will be used to create our record.

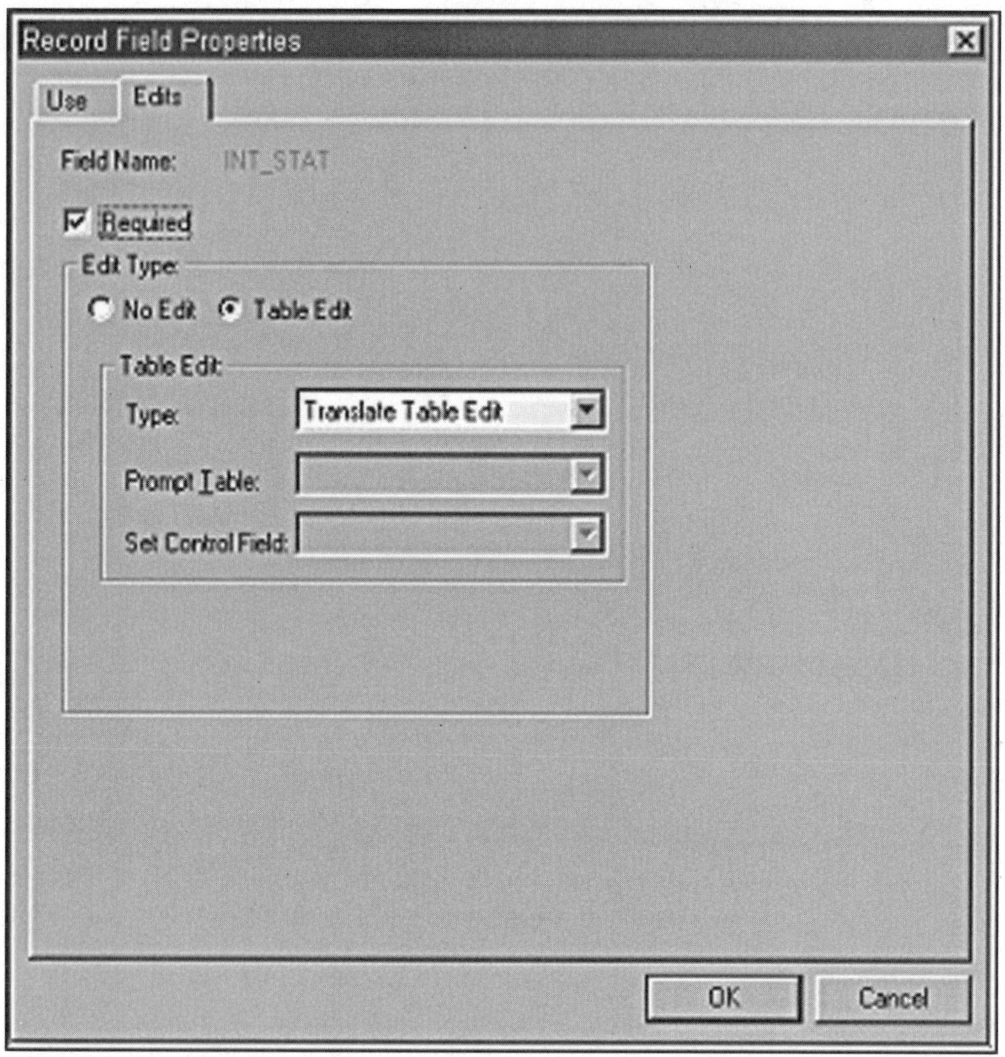

Figure 6-118 INT_STAT Edits dialog.

- INT_ORDER_ID
- LINE_NUM
- ITEM_ID
- QTY
- UNIT_MEASURE

INT_ORDER (Record)

Field Name	Type	Key	Dir	CurC	Srch	List	Sys	Audt	H	Default
INT_ORDER_ID	Char	Key	Asc		Yes	Yes	No			
REQUESTED_DT	Date	Alt	Asc		No	Yes	No			%date
EMP_ID	Char	Alt	Asc		No	Yes	No			
PROCESS_DT	Date	Alt	Asc		No	Yes	No			
PROCESS_LOC_ID	Char	Alt	Asc		No	Yes	No			
INT_STAT	Char				No	No	No			'NEW'

Figure 6-118a Use Display of the `INT_ORDER` record.

- `LINE_STAT`
- `EXT_ORDER`
- `EMP_ID`
- `REQUESTED_DT`
- `VENDORID`
- `PO_NUM`
- `PROM_DT`
- `EXT_STAT`

Drag and drop these fields in the same order as they are displayed into the new record definition. If your record definition's field view looks like the one in Figure 6-119, please press the SAVE ALL icon or select the FILE, SAVE ALL menu options. In the Save As dialog, enter `INT_ORDER` and press OK.

The internal order lines record is now ready for us to set the record's field attributes. The first field for which we are going to set the record's field attributes is `INT_ORDER_ID`. The only Use value for the

TABLE 6-7

INT_ORDER_LINES Record

Column	Description	Data Type	Key	Valid Values
INT_ORDER_ID	Internal order id	Char(10)	x	Internal order TBL
LINE_NUM	Line number	Number	x	
ITEM_ID	Material requested	Char(10)		Item TBL
QTY	Amount requested	Number		
UNIT_MEASURE	Unit of measure	Char(4)		Unit TBL
LINE_STAT	Line status	Char(3)		Reserved
				On order
				Fulfilled
EXT_ORDER	External order	Char(1)		Yes or no
EMP_ID	Buyer from purchasing	Char(10)		Buyer from employee TBL
REQUESTED_DT	Initial date of the request	Date		=> Today
VENDORID	Vendor id for supplier	Char(10)		Vendor TBL
PO_NUM	Purchase order reference	Char(10)		
PROM_DT	Promised date			=> Today
EXT_STAT	External order status	Char(3)		On order
				Received

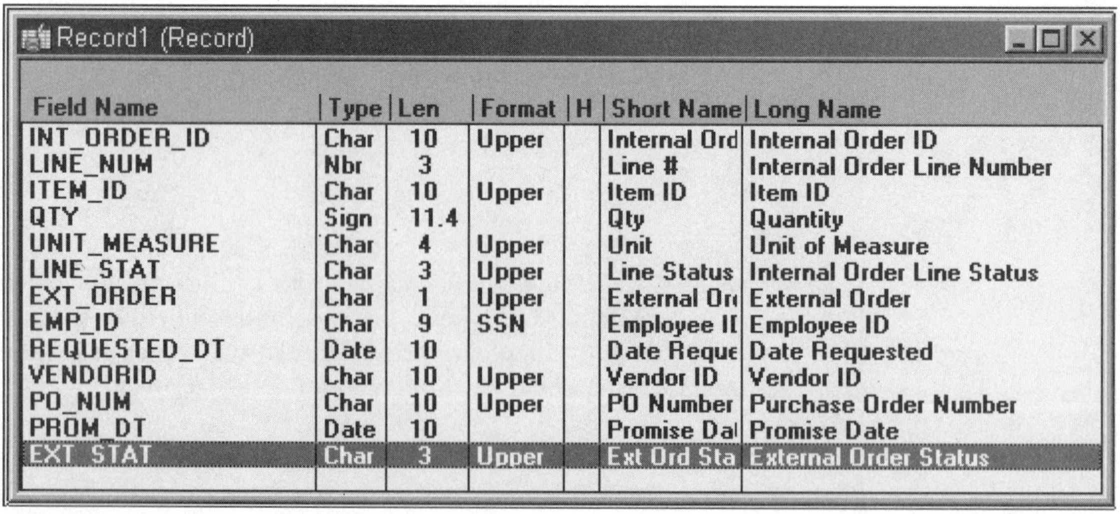

Record1 (Record)

Field Name	Type	Len	Format	H	Short Name	Long Name
INT_ORDER_ID	Char	10	Upper		Internal Ord	Internal Order ID
LINE_NUM	Nbr	3			Line #	Internal Order Line Number
ITEM_ID	Char	10	Upper		Item ID	Item ID
QTY	Sign	11.4			Qty	Quantity
UNIT_MEASURE	Char	4	Upper		Unit	Unit of Measure
LINE_STAT	Char	3	Upper		Line Status	Internal Order Line Status
EXT_ORDER	Char	1	Upper		External Or	External Order
EMP_ID	Char	9	SSN		Employee II	Employee ID
REQUESTED_DT	Date	10			Date Reque	Date Requested
VENDORID	Char	10	Upper		Vendor ID	Vendor ID
PO_NUM	Char	10	Upper		PO Number	Purchase Order Number
PROM_DT	Date	10			Promise Dal	Promise Date
EXT_STAT	Char	3	Upper		Ext Ord Sta	External Order Status

Figure 6-119 INT_ORDER_LINES record definition.

INT_ORDER_ID field is that it is a key. We do not need to make it a Search Key or a List Box Item because it will not be searched for directly. This record's values will be returned from a search to INT_ORDER_LINES parent record INT_ORDER.

The only Edits property for this field is that it is required. INT_ORDER_ID is a key field and is therefore required. Figures 6-120 and 6-121 show the Use and Edits tabbed dialogs for INT_ORDER_ID.

The next field for which we are going to set the record's field attributes is LINE_NUM. The only Use value for the LINE_NUM field is that it is a key. Just as the with LINE_NUM, we do not need to make it a Search Key or a List Box Item because it will not be searched for directly. This record's values will be returned from a search to INT_ORDER_LINES parent record INT_ORDER.

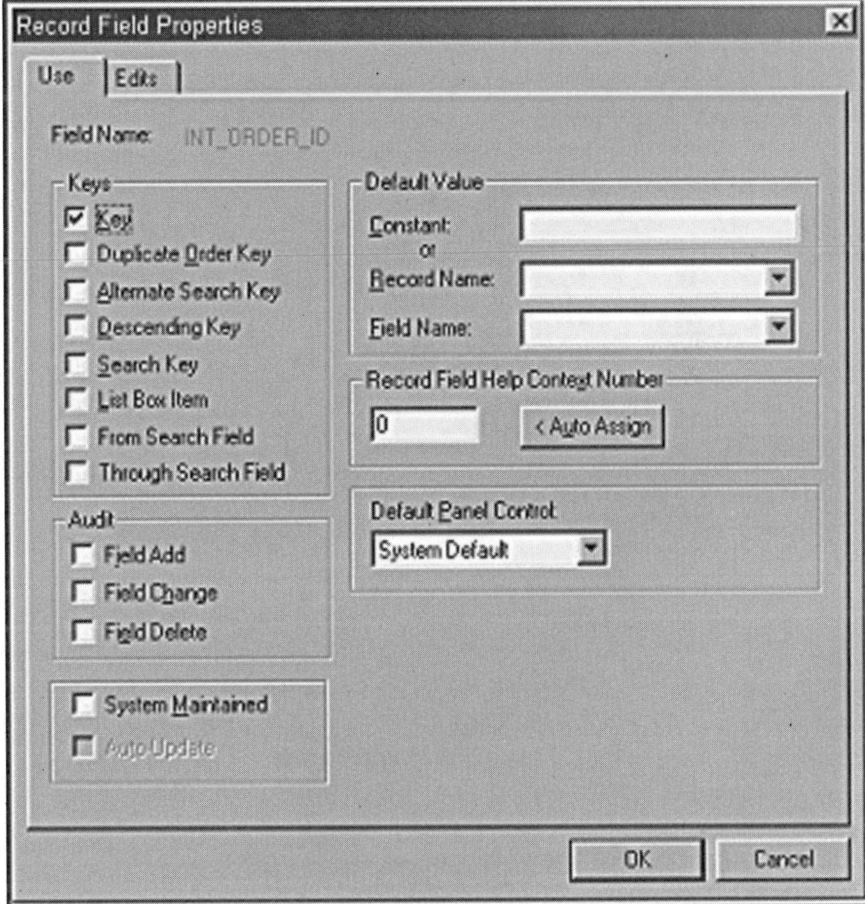

Figure 6-120 INT_ORDER_ID Use dialog.

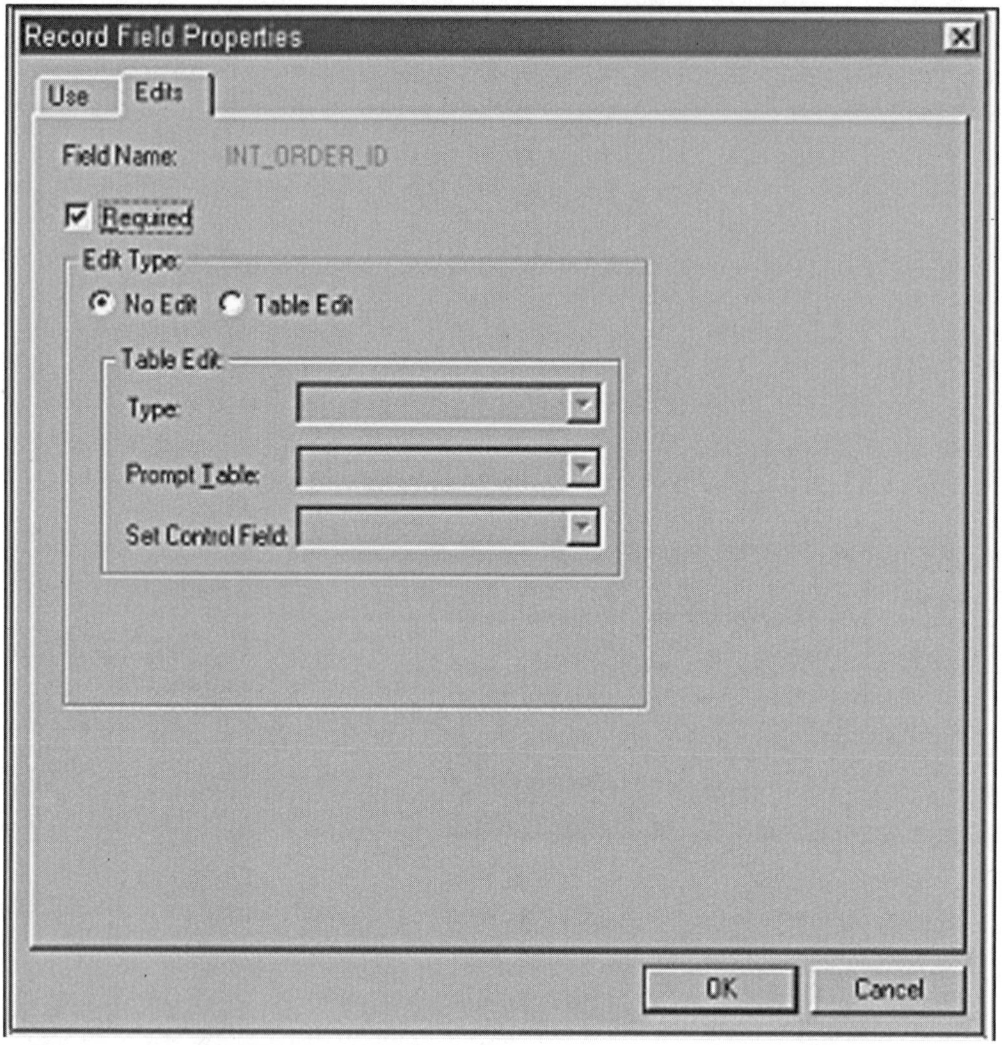

Figure 6-121 INT_ORDER_ID Edits dialog.

The only Edits property for this field is that it is required. LINE_NUM is a key field and is therefore required. Figures 6-122 and 6-123 show the Use and Edits tabbed dialogs for LINE_NUM.

The next field for which we are going to set up record attributes for the INT_ORDER_LINES record is the ITEM_ID field. There are no Use attributes for the ITEM_ID field.

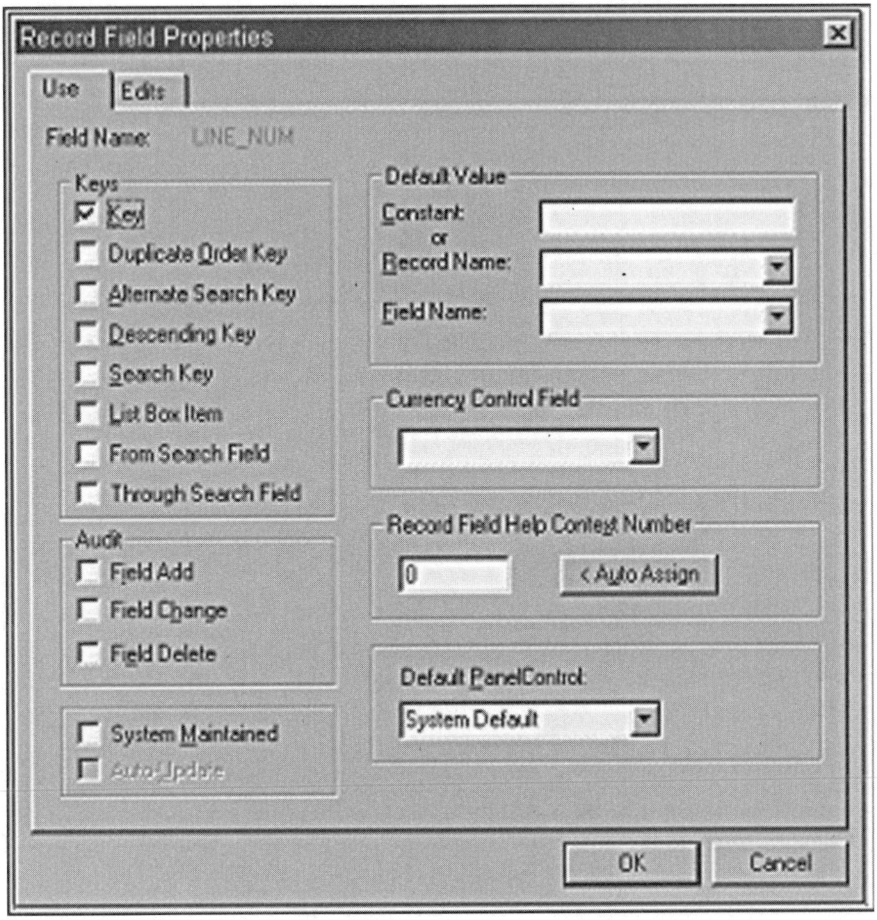

Figure 6-122 LINE_NUM Use dialog.

The Edits attributes for ITEM_ID are that it is required and it uses a prompt table edit. The prompt table edit uses the ITEMS table we already created. Follow the same procedure we used in the INT_ORDER record. Select the TABLE EDIT radio button from the Edits Tab dialog for the ITEM_ID fields record attributes. The drop-down list boxes will be enabled. Select the prompt table options from the type drop-down and then select the ITEMS record from the prompt table drop-down. Figure 6-124 shows the EDITS tab of the Record Fields Property dialog for ITEM_ID.

The next field for which we are going to set up record attributes for the INT_ORDER_LINES record is the QTY field. There are no Use attributes for the QTY field.

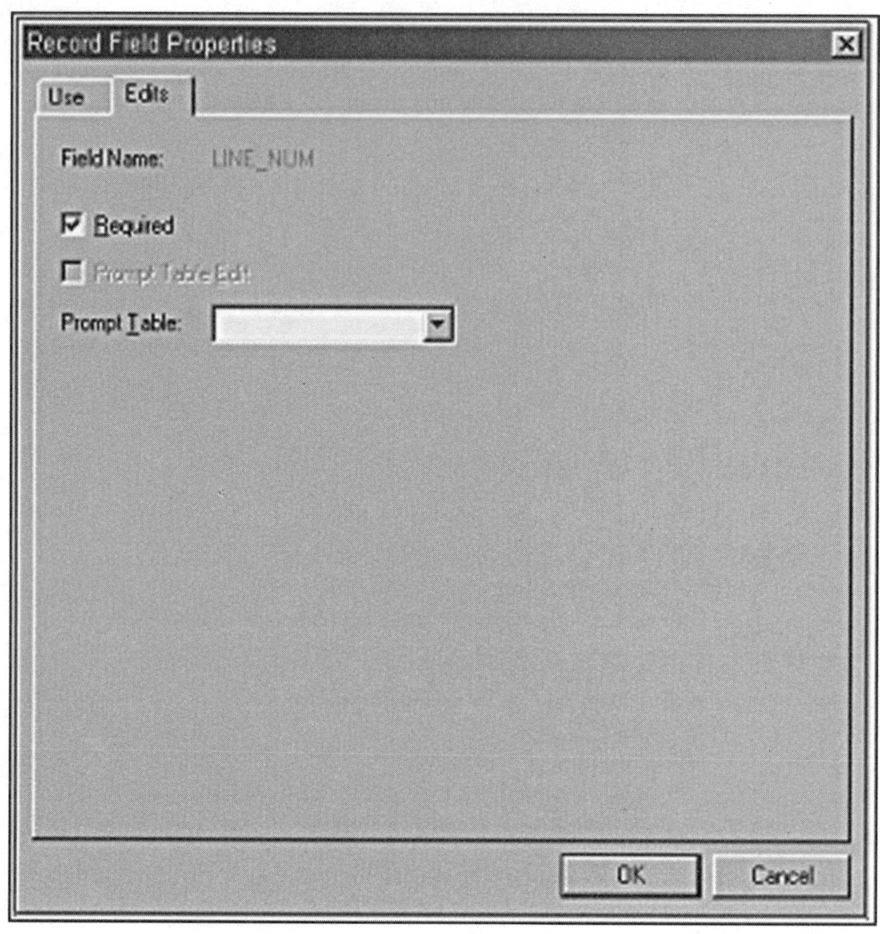

Figure 6-123 LINE_NUM Edits dialog.

In the Edits Tab option we will make QTY a required field. Figure 6-125 shows the EDITS tab of the Record Fields Property dialog for QTY.

The next field for which we are going to set up record attributes for the INT_ORDER_LINES record is the UNIT_MEASURE field. There are no Use attributes for the UNIT_MEASURE field.

The edits attributes for UNIT_MEASURE are that it is required and it uses a prompt table edit. The prompt table edit uses the UNIT_MEASURE table we already created. Follow the same procedure we used in the INT_ORDER record. Select the TABLE EDIT radio button from the Edits Tab dialog for the UNIT_MEASURE fields record attributes. The drop-down list boxes will then be enabled. Select the Prompt Table option

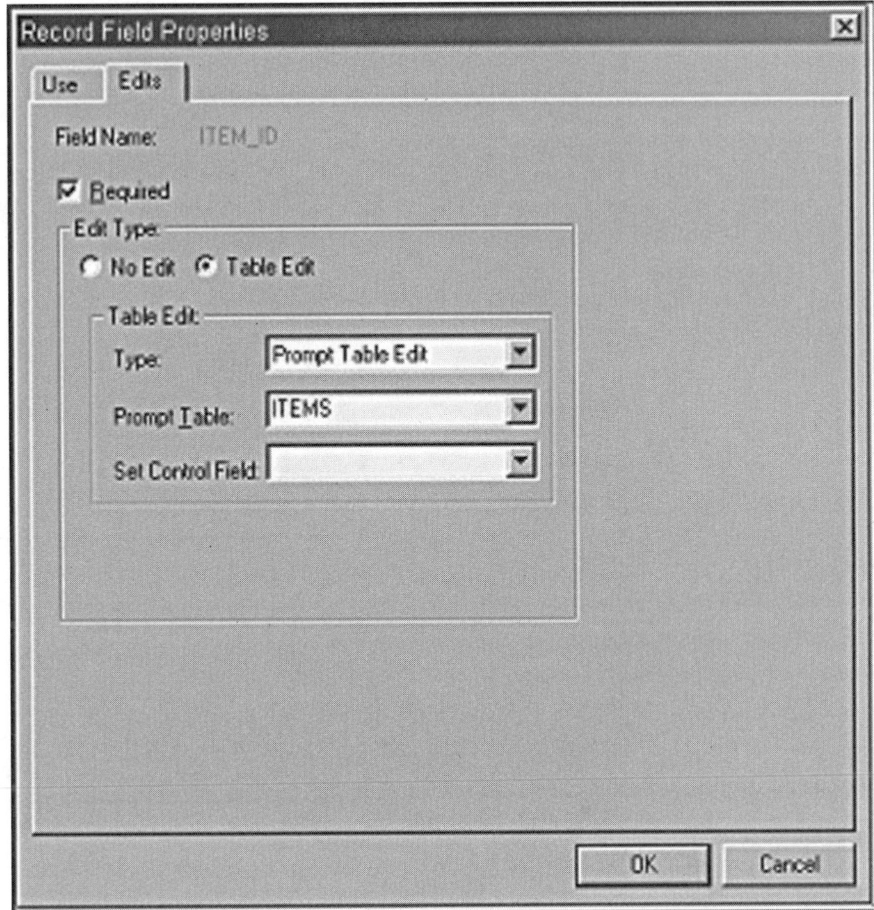

Figure 6-124 ITEM_ID Edits dialog.

from the Type drop-down and then select the UNIT_MEASURE record from the Prompt Table drop-down. Figure 6-126 shows the EDITS tab of the Record Fields Property dialog for UNIT_MEASURE.

The next field we set the record attributes for is LINE_STAT. The only attribute we need to set up for LINE_STAT is an Edits attribute for a Translate Table edit. Figures 6-127 shows the EDITS tab of the Record Fields Property dialog for LINE_STAT.

The next field we set the record attributes for is EXT_ORDER. The Use values that are associated with the field attributes of EXT_ORDER are

- Default constant values N
- Default panel control CHECK BOX

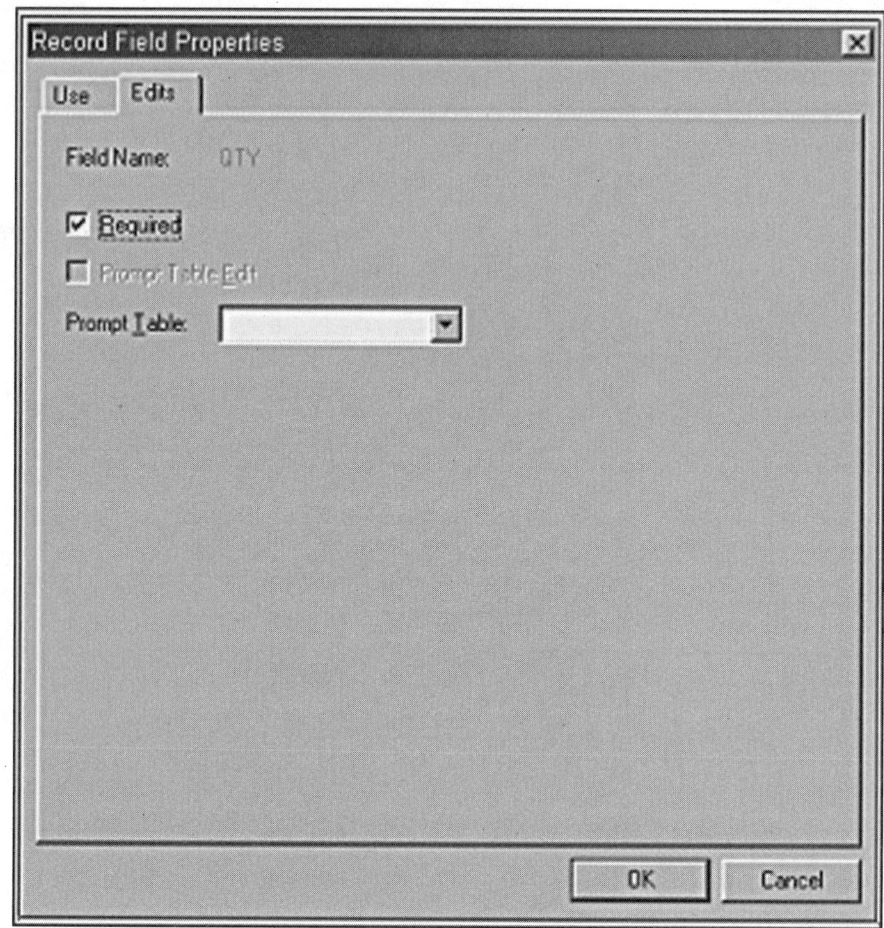

Figure 6-125
QTY Edits dialog.

We are going to set the default panel control to CHECK BOX. The default value for the check box will be N, which means that the check box will be OFF. We will set this up when we create our panels. This field will be used to determine whether there will be an external order for this line.

The only EXT_ORDER Edits properties is a Yes/No Table Edit. Figures 6-128 and 6-129 show the Use and Edits tabbed dialogs for EXT_ORDER.

The next field of the INT_ORDER_LINES record is the EMP_ID field. There are no Use or Edits record attributes required for the EMP_ID field.

- Alt Search Key

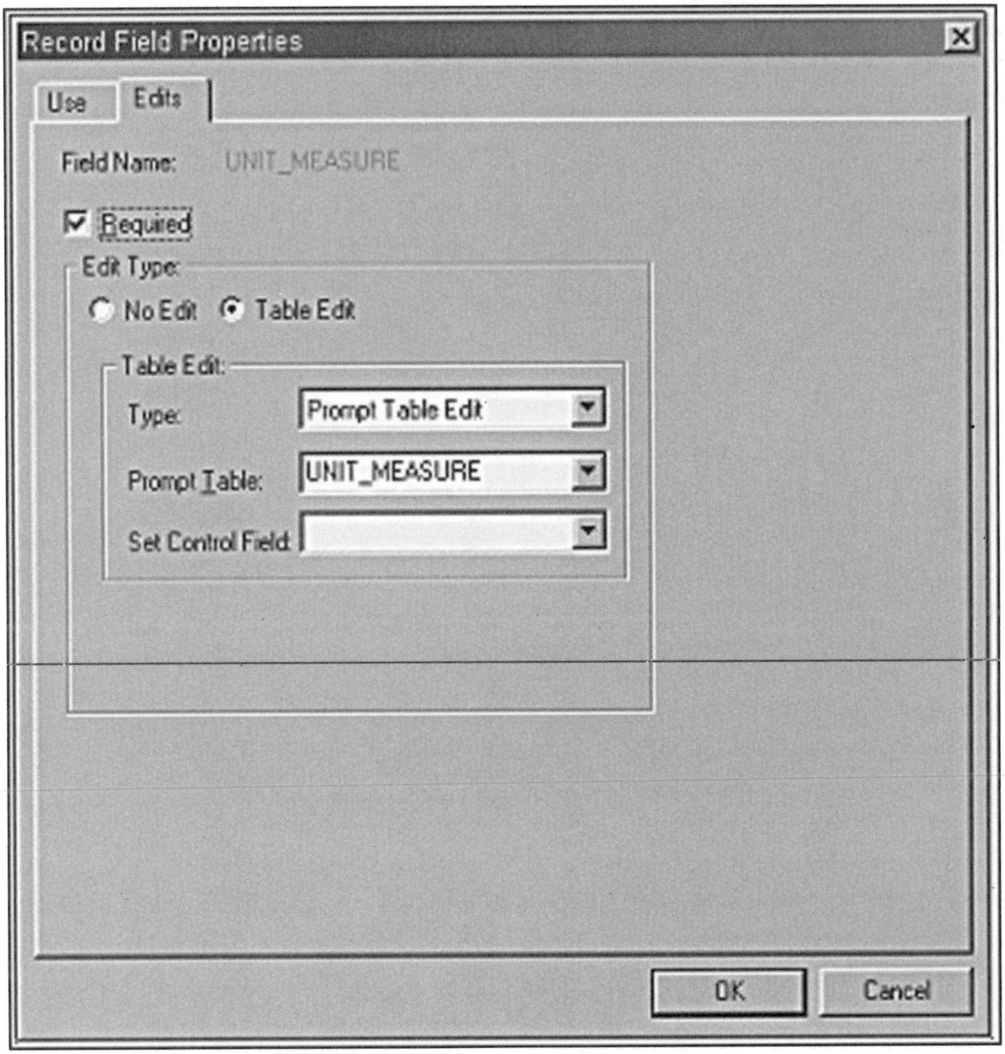

Record Field Properties

Use | Edits

Field Name: UNIT_MEASURE

Required

Edit Type:

No Edit | Table Edit

Table Edit:

Type:	Prompt Table Edit
Prompt Table:	UNIT_MEASURE
Set Control Field:	

OK | Cancel

Figure 6-126 `UNIT_MEASURE` Edits dialog.

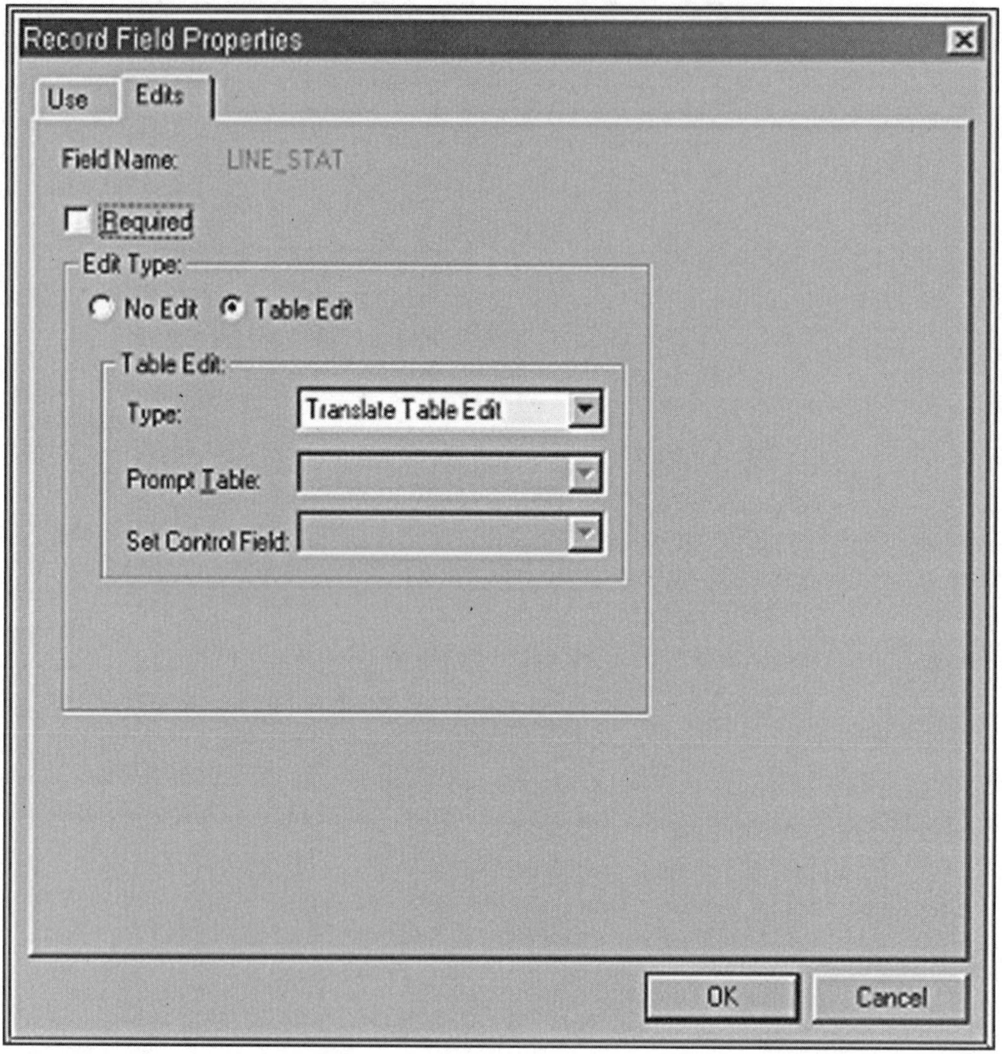

Figure 6-127 `LINE_STAT` Edits dialog.

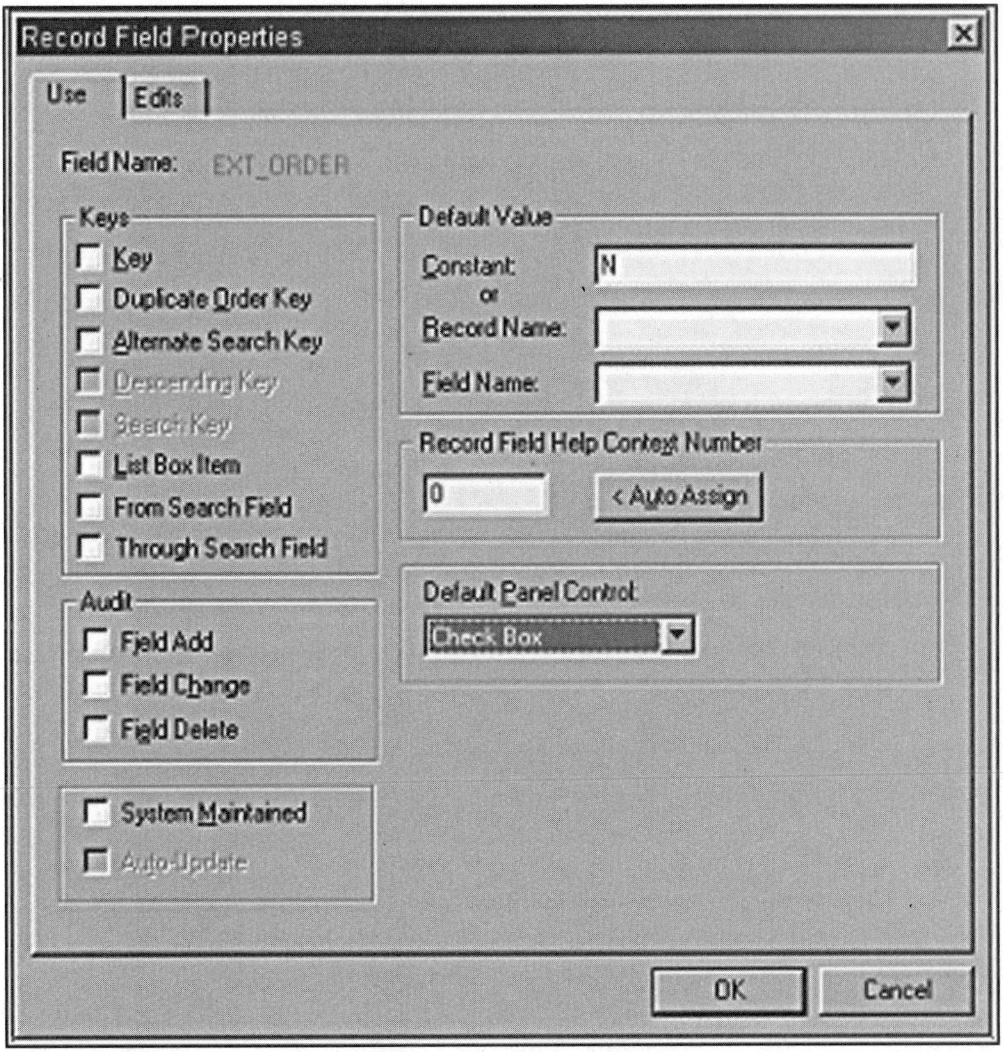

Figure 6-128 EXT_ORDER Use dialog.

Figures 6-130 and 6-131 show the Use and Edit tabbed dialogs for EMP_ID.

The next field of the INT_ORDER_LINES record is REQUESTED_DT. There are no Use or Edits record attributes required for this field. Figures 6-132 and 6-133 show the Use and Edits tabbed dialogs for REQUESTED_DT. We do not need to set any record attributes for VENDOR ID or PO_NUM either

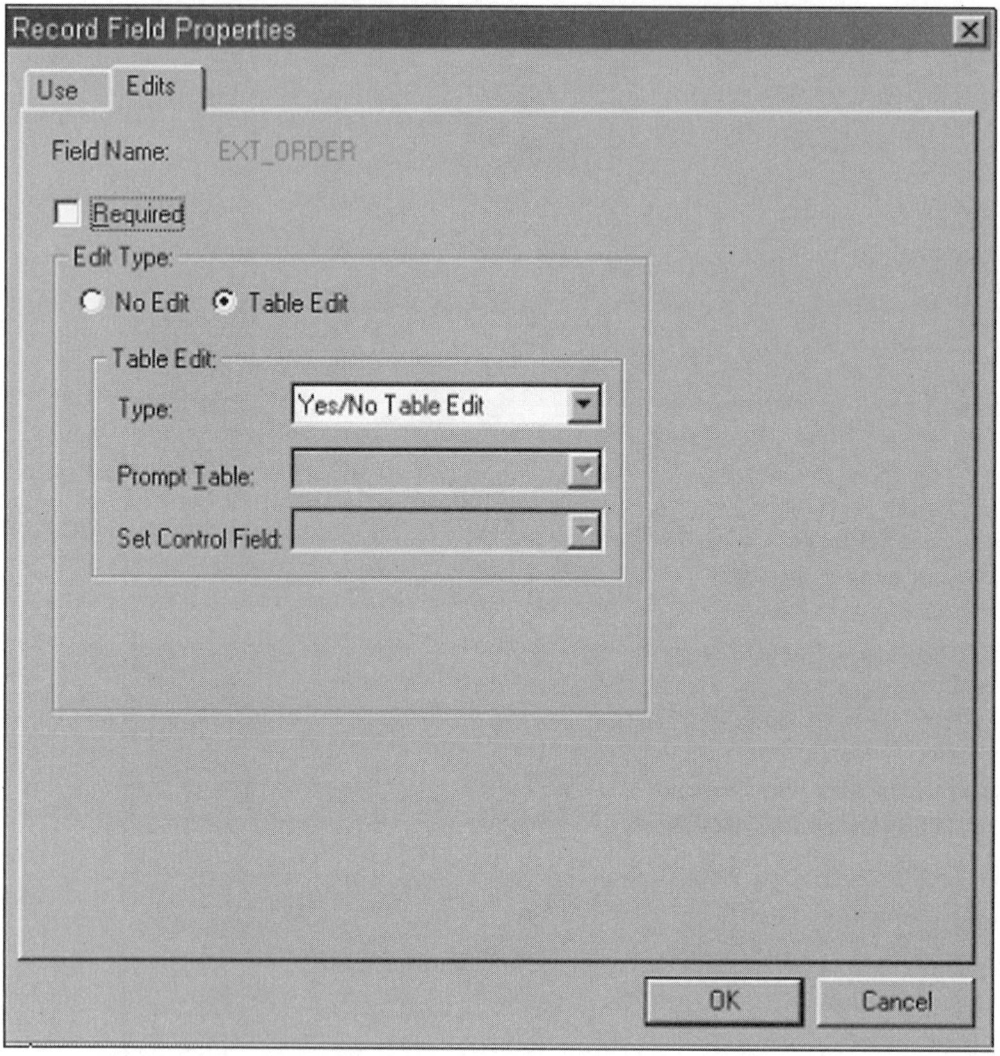

Figure 6-129 EXT_ORDER Edits dialog.

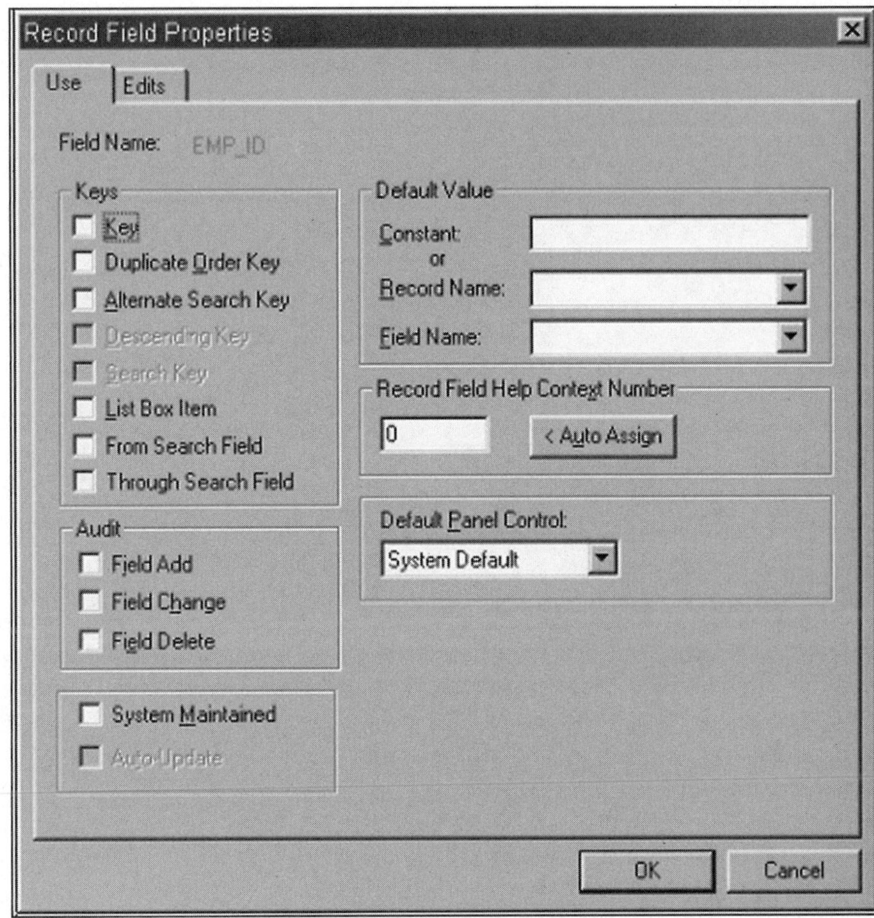

Figure 6-130
`EMP_ID` Use dialog.

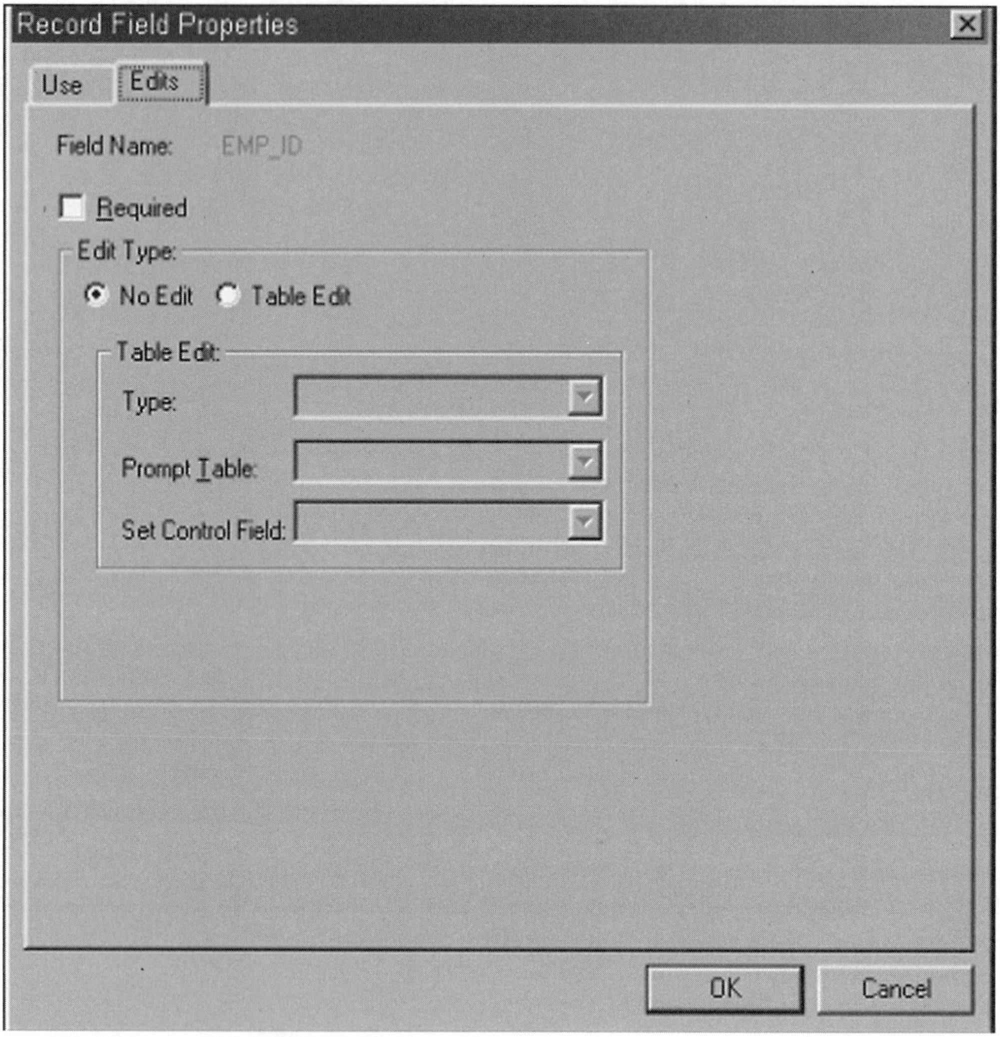

Record Field Properties

Use | Edits

Field Name: EMP_ID

Required

Edit Type:

No Edit | Table Edit

Table Edit:

Type:

Prompt Table:

Set Control Field:

OK | Cancel

Figure 6-131 `EMP_ID` Edits dialog.

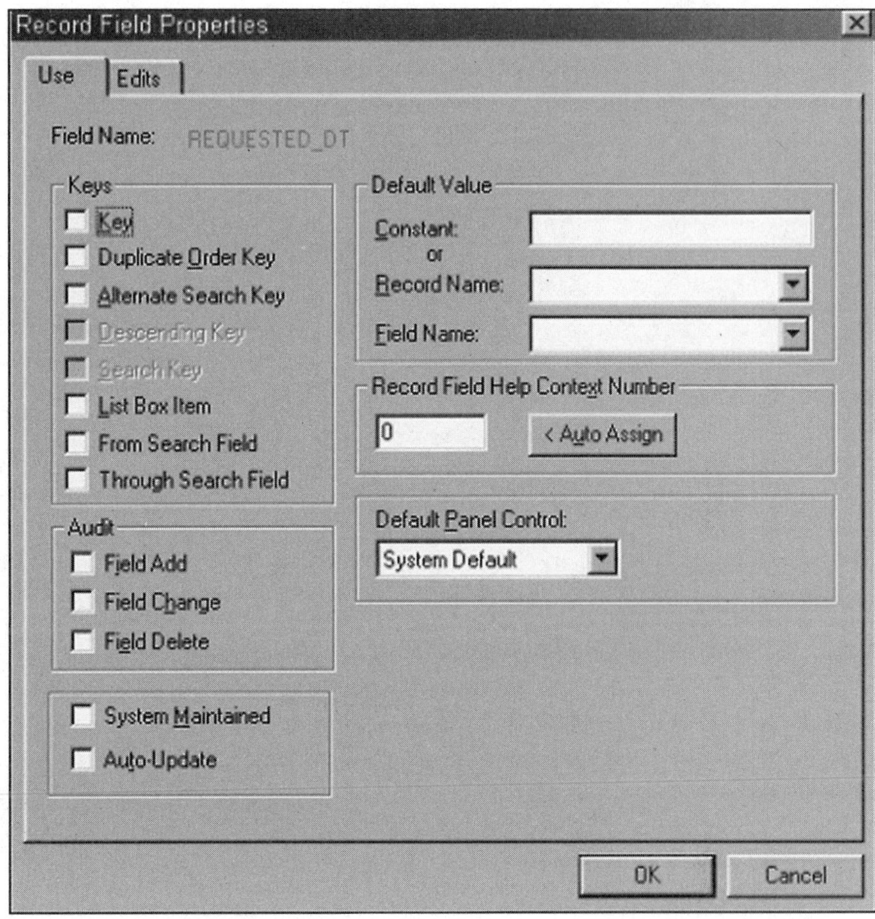

Figure 6-132 REQUESTED_DT Use dialog.

There are no record Properties to be set for field PROM_DT. Figures 6-134 and 6-135 show the blank Use and Edits tabbed dialogs for PROM_DT.

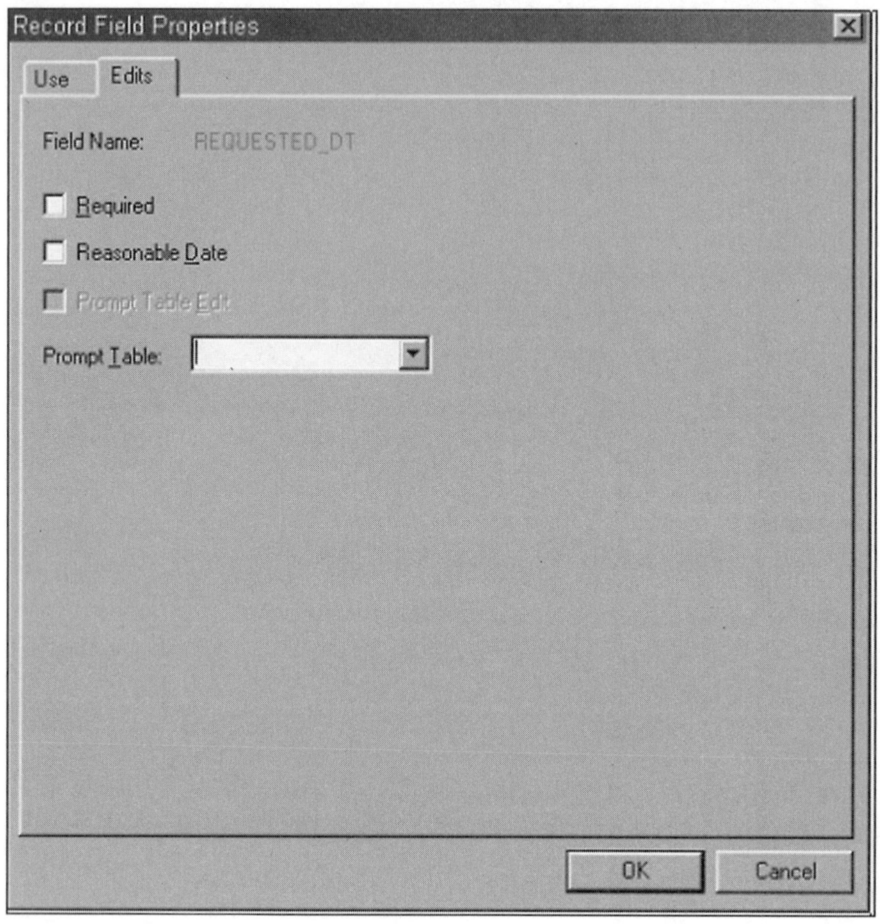

Figure 6-133 REQUESTED_DT Edits dialog.

The next field in the INT_ORDER_LINES record is EXT_STAT. The only record attribute is that it is a Translate Table Edit. Figures 6-136 and 6-137 show the Use and Edit tabbed dialogs for EXT_STAT.

The INT_ORDER_LINES record should look like the one in Figure 6-137*a*. If yours matches Figure 6-137*a*, the INT_ORDER_LINES record is now ready to be built. Follow the same instructions as for the previous

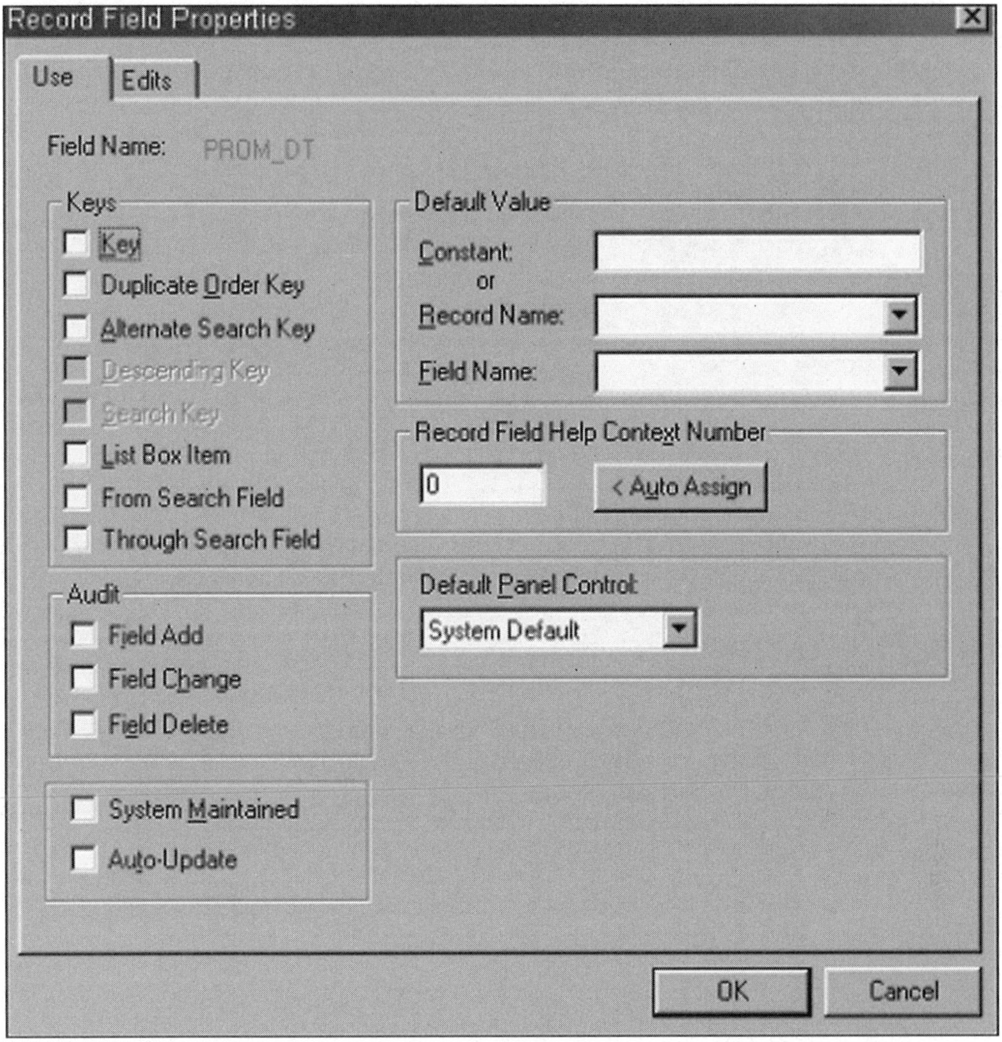

Record Field Properties

Use | Edits

Field Name: PROM_DT

Keys
- Key
- Duplicate Order Key
- Alternate Search Key
- Descending Key
- Search Key
- List Box Item
- From Search Field
- Through Search Field

Audit
- Field Add
- Field Change
- Field Delete

- System Maintained
- Auto-Update

Default Value
Constant:
or
Record Name:
Field Name:

Record Field Help Context Number
0
< Auto Assign

Default Panel Control:
System Default

OK | Cancel

Figure 6-134 PROCESS_DT Use dialog.

SQL Table records. Select from the menu BUILD, CURRENT OBJECT, or press the BUILD icon. From the Build dialog, select CREATE TABLES and BUILD AND EXECUTE SCRIPT. After you press the BUILD button, a successful status should be displayed in the Output window.

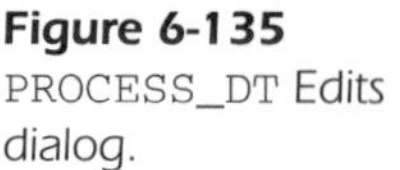

Figure 6-135 PROCESS_DT Edits dialog.

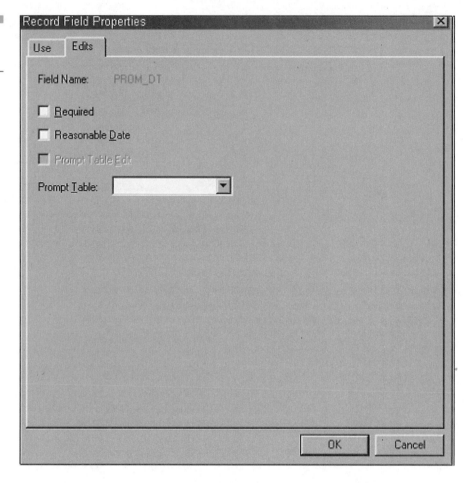

EXT_ORDER_VW Record

Table 6-8 lists all the fields and attributes that make up our external order view record (EXT_ORDER_VW).

The last record that we will create for our example is the EXT_ORDER_VW. This record is a Query View record. To create EXT_ORDER_VW, we are going to select columns from the INT_ORDER_LINES record, taking only the rows that have the EXT_ORDER field of the INT_ORDER_LINES record set to Y or "yes." The best way to fully explain this is to simply begin creating the record.

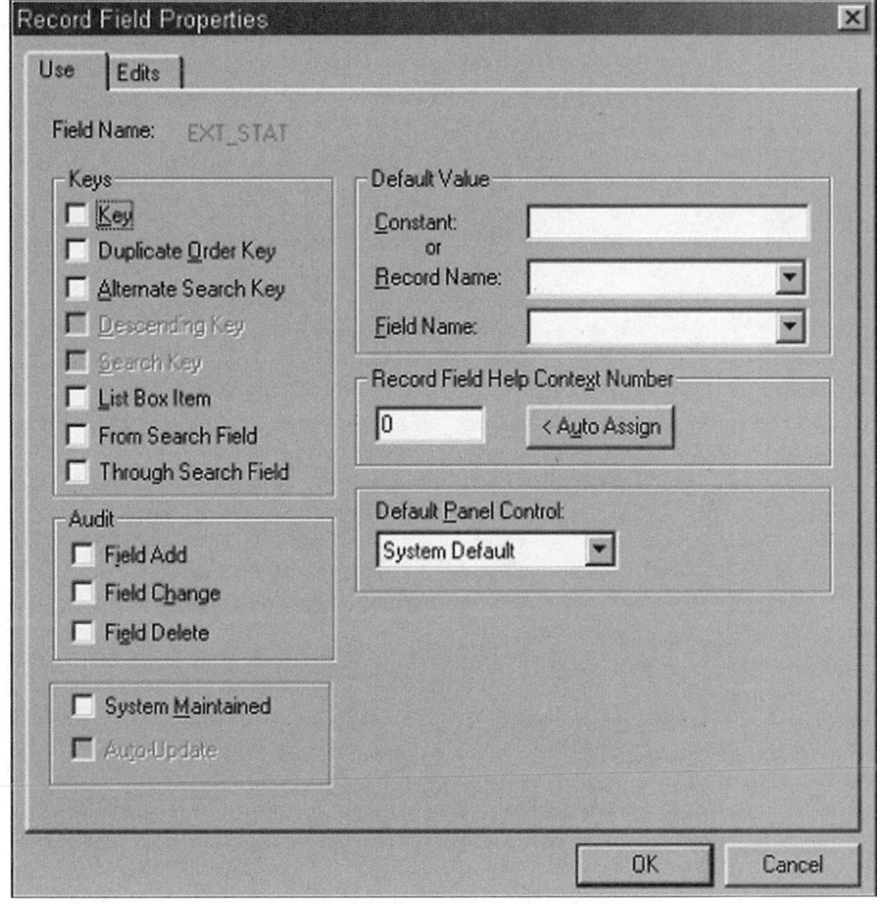

Figure 6-136 EXT_STAT Use dialog.

The first step in creating Query View records is to open a new record and save it. Let's save our new record as EXT_ORDER_VW. The next step is to open the properties dialog and select the TYPE tab. With the TYPE tab now active, select the QUERY VIEW radio button. Figure 6-138 shows the TYPE tab selected with the QUERY VIEW radio button selected. You should now see the CLICK TO LAUNCH QUERY button displayed toward the bottom left of the dialog.

We are now ready to begin creating the Query View. Press the CLICK TO LAUNCH QUERY button. When the Query dialog is displayed, select the INT_ORDER record from the Database Dictionary tree view control and

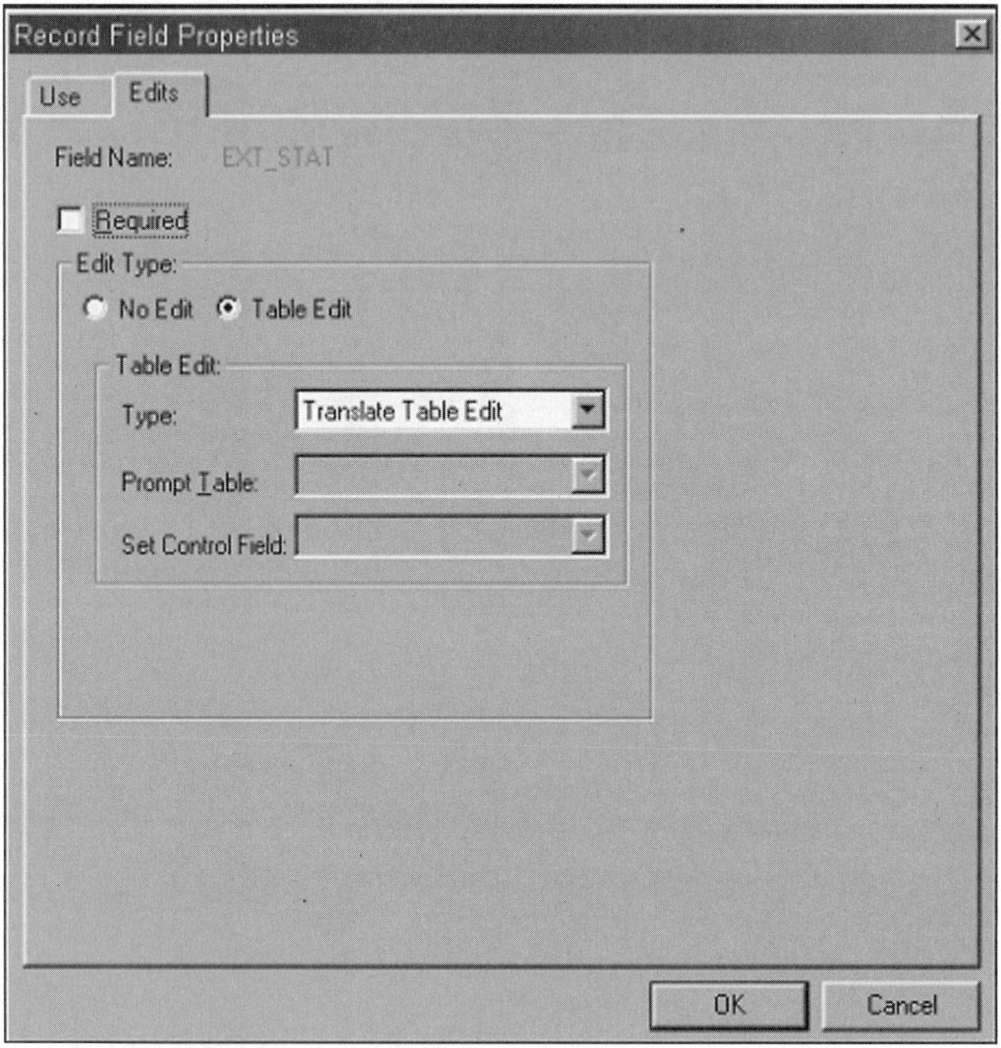

Figure 6-137 EXT_STAT Edits dialog.

then press the right arrow button on the middle of the dialog. Figure 6-139 shows the dialog after the right arrow button has been pressed with the INT_ORDER_LINES record selected. The Query Dictionary tree view control displayed on the DICTIONARY tab should now contain the INT_ORDER_LINES record.

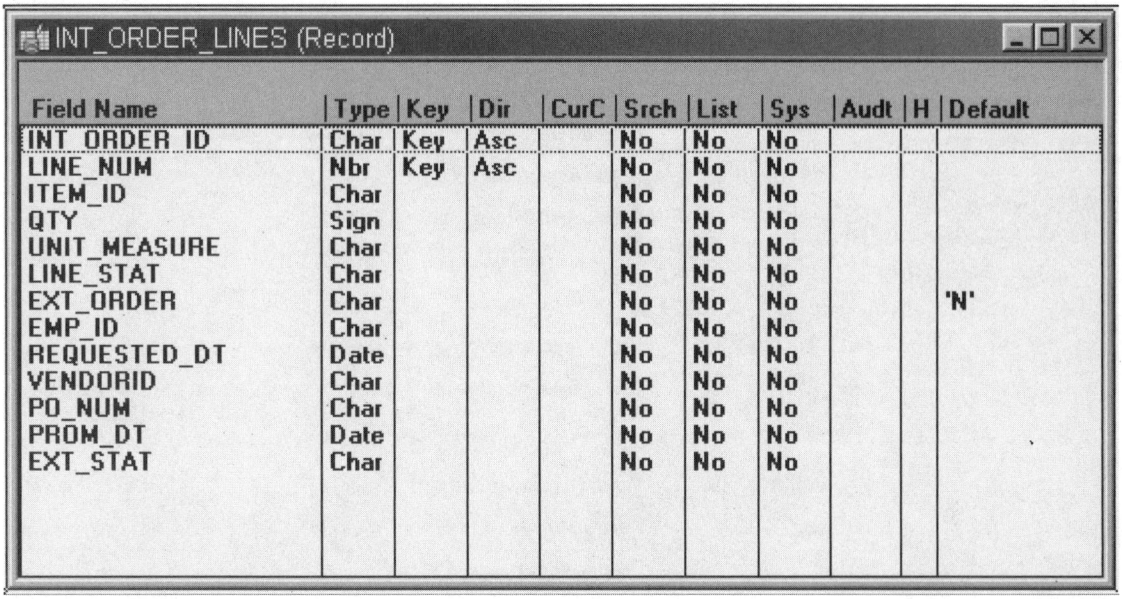

INT_ORDER_LINES (Record)

Field Name	Type	Key	Dir	CurC	Srch	List	Sys	Audt	H	Default
INT_ORDER_ID	Char	Key	Asc		No	No	No			
LINE_NUM	Nbr	Key	Asc		No	No	No			
ITEM_ID	Char				No	No	No			
QTY	Sign				No	No	No			
UNIT_MEASURE	Char				No	No	No			
LINE_STAT	Char				No	No	No			
EXT_ORDER	Char				No	No	No			'N'
EMP_ID	Char				No	No	No			
REQUESTED_DT	Date				No	No	No			
VENDORID	Char				No	No	No			
PO_NUM	Char				No	No	No			
PROM_DT	Date				No	No	No			
EXT_STAT	Char				No	No	No			

Figure 6-137*a* `INT_ORDER_LINES` record.

The next step we need to complete is to select all the fields that will make up the `EXT_ORDER_VW`. Single-click on the FIELDS tab. Select the following fields from the available fields:

- INT_ORDER_ID
- LINE_NUM
- REQUESTED_DT
- PROCESS_DT
- ITEM_ID
- QTY
- UNIT_MEASURE
- EMP_ID
- VENDORID
- PO_NUM
- PROM_DT

TABLE 6-8

EXT_ORDER_VW Record

Column	Description	Data Type	Key	Valid Values
INT_ORDER_ID	Internal order id	Char(10)	X	
LINE_NUM	Line number	Number	X	
REQUESTED_DT	Initial date of the request	Date		=> Today
PROCESS_DT	Warehouse delivery date	Date		=> Today
ITEM_ID	Material requested	Char(10)		Item TBL
QTY	Amount requested	Number		
UNIT_MEASURE	Unit of measure	Char(4)		Unit TBL
EMP_ID	Buyer from purchasing	Char(10)		Buyer from employee TBL
VENDORID	Vendor ID for supplier	Char(10)		Vendor TBL
PO_NUM	Purchase order reference	Char(10)		
PROM_DT	Promised date			=> Today
EXT_STAT	External order status	Char(3)		On order
				Received
LINE_STAT	Line status	Char(3)		Reserved
				On order
				Fulfilled

- EXT_STAT
- LINE_STAT

A 1 through 12 should now be displayed beside the record field name in the "Col" column. Figure 6-140 shows the FIELDS tab with the INT_ORDER_LINES fields selected.

Query View records automatically fill the blank record definition with the fields that we have selected in the order of their column numbers.

All that is left to do in the Query dialog is to set the criteria we will use to filter out any INT_ORDER_LINES that are not external orders. Select the CRITERIA tab by single-clicking on it. With the CRITERIA tab displayed, press the INSERT button. A new blank line with a default logical AND will be displayed under the join criteria that we already selected. Double-click on the "Expression 1" column in the new blank line. A Field

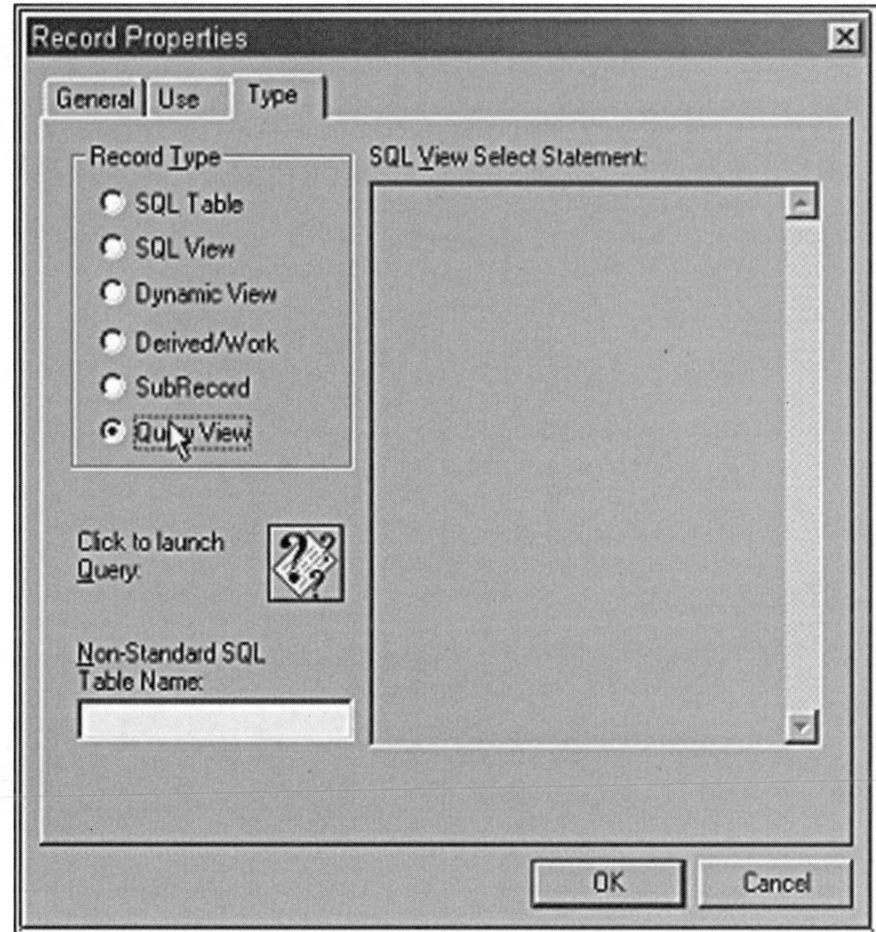

Figure 6-138 Record Properties Type dialog.

dialog will then be displayed allowing you to select the desired field. Select the `INT_ORDER_LINES` record and then the `EXT_ORDER` field. Figure 6-141 shows the Field dialog with the correct selections.

The only thing left to do in this tab is to set the constant value of `Y` in the "Expression 2" column. Double-click on the empty "Expression 2" column. In the Edit Constant dialog, enter a `Y` in the edit box and then press OK. Figure 6-142 shows the Constant dialog with the correct values entered.

If the SQL select statement in the SQL tab matches the following select statement, you are now all cleared to press the OK button of the Query Dialog.

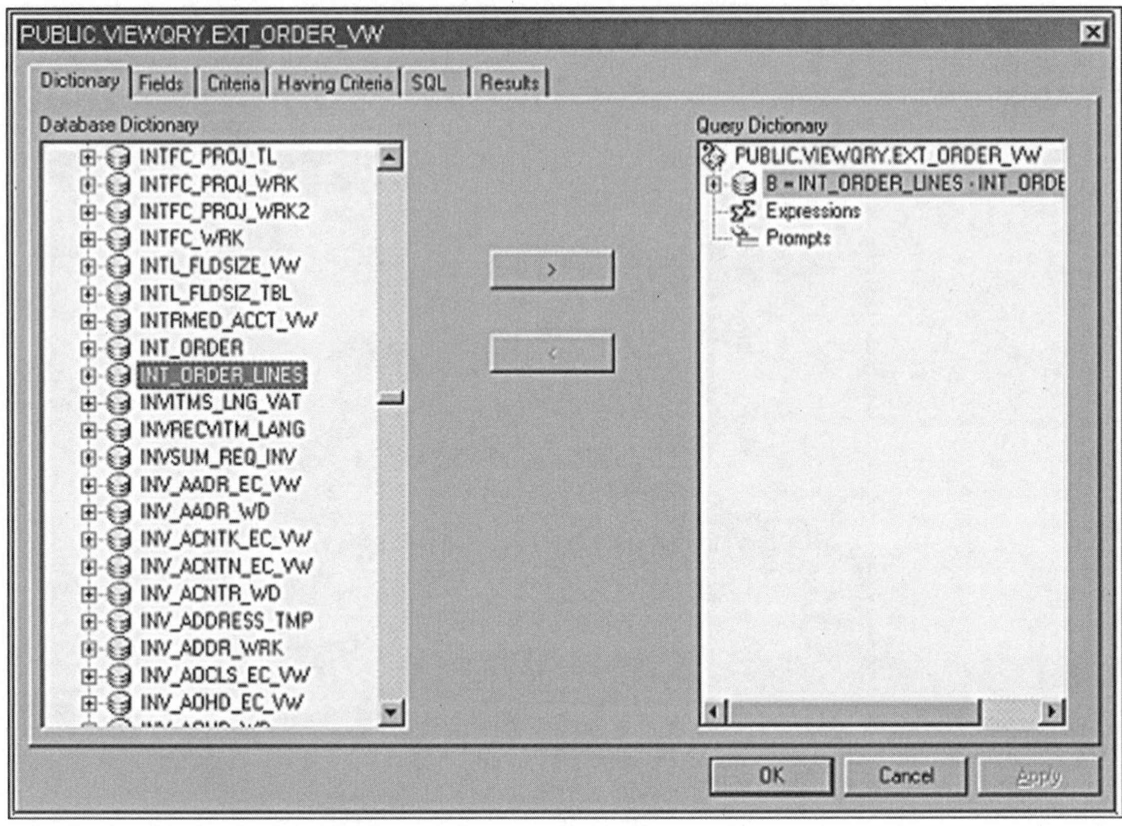

Figure 6-139 Query Dictionary tree view.

```
SELECT INT_ORDER_ID, LINE_NUM, ITEM_ID, QTY, UNIT_MEASURE,
LINE_STAT, EMP_ID, REQUESTED_DT, VENDORID, PO_NUM, PROM_DT,
EXT_STAT
 FROM PS_INT_ORDER_LINES
 WHERE EXT_ORDER = 'Y'
```

The Record Properties dialog should now be displayed with the TYPE tab exposed, and the select statement we just built should be displayed in the grayed-out SQL View select statement edit box. Figure 6-143 shows the Record Properties TYPE tab with the our SQL select statement.

After you press OK, the record definition will be displayed with all the

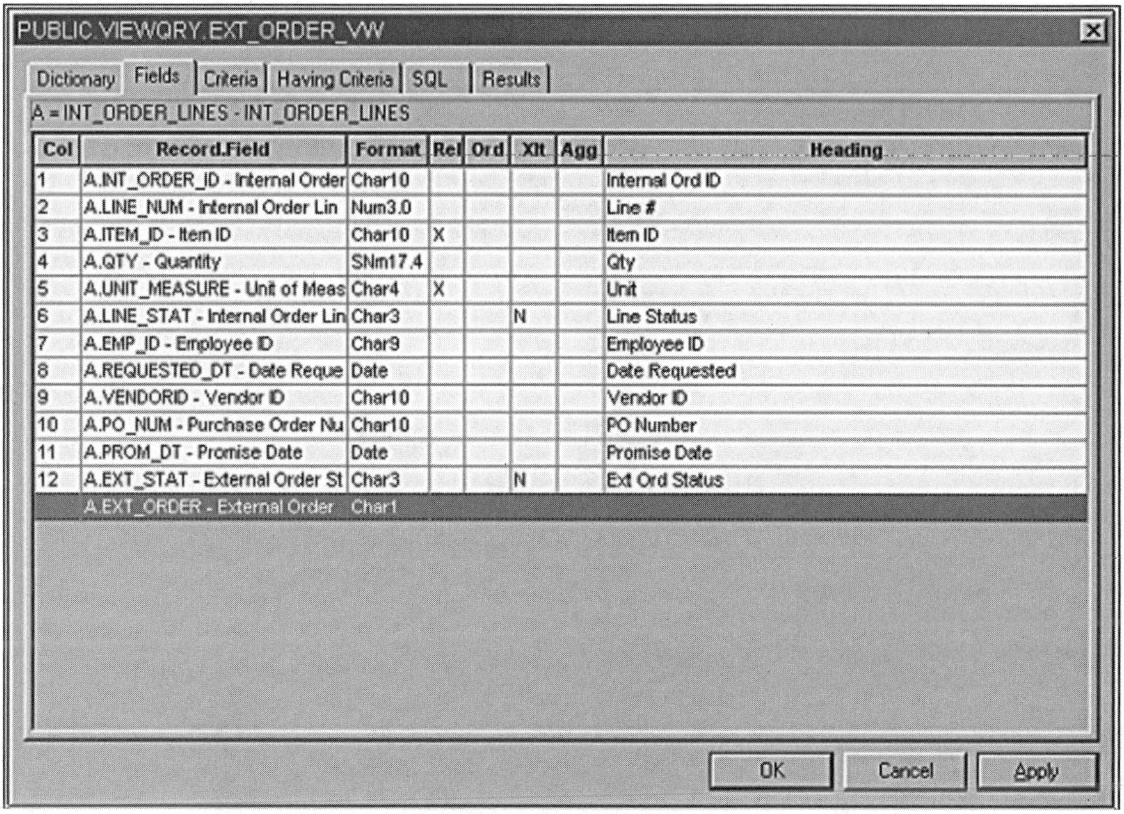

PUBLIC.VIEWQRY.EXT_ORDER_VW

Dictionary | Fields | Criteria | Having Criteria | SQL | Results

A = INT_ORDER_LINES - INT_ORDER_LINES

Col	Record.Field	Format	Rel	Ord	Xlt	Agg	Heading
1	A.INT_ORDER_ID - Internal Order	Char10					Internal Ord ID
2	A.LINE_NUM - Internal Order Lin	Num3.0					Line #
3	A.ITEM_ID - Item ID	Char10	X				Item ID
4	A.QTY - Quantity	SNm17.4					Qty
5	A.UNIT_MEASURE - Unit of Meas	Char4	X				Unit
6	A.LINE_STAT - Internal Order Lin	Char3			N		Line Status
7	A.EMP_ID - Employee ID	Char9					Employee ID
8	A.REQUESTED_DT - Date Reque	Date					Date Requested
9	A.VENDORID - Vendor ID	Char10					Vendor ID
10	A.PO_NUM - Purchase Order Nu	Char10					PO Number
11	A.PROM_DT - Promise Date	Date					Promise Date
12	A.EXT_STAT - External Order St	Char3			N		Ext Ord Status
	A.EXT_ORDER - External Order	Char1					

OK | Cancel | Apply

Figure 6-140 QUERY VIEW FIELD tab for `INT_ORDER_LINES` fields.

fields that we selected in the order we set with column numbers as shown in Figure 6-144. This is the same order in which they are displayed in the SQL select statement.

The external order record is now ready for us to set its record's field attributes. It is very possible that when creating a Query View record most of or all the record field attributes will be carried forward from the records from which they have been selected. Nevertheless, it is always a good idea to go through joined records to be sure that the Use and Edits record field attributes are correct.

The first field for which we are going to set the record's field attributes is `INT_ORDER_ID`. The Use values for the record's field attributes of `INT_ORDER_ID` are

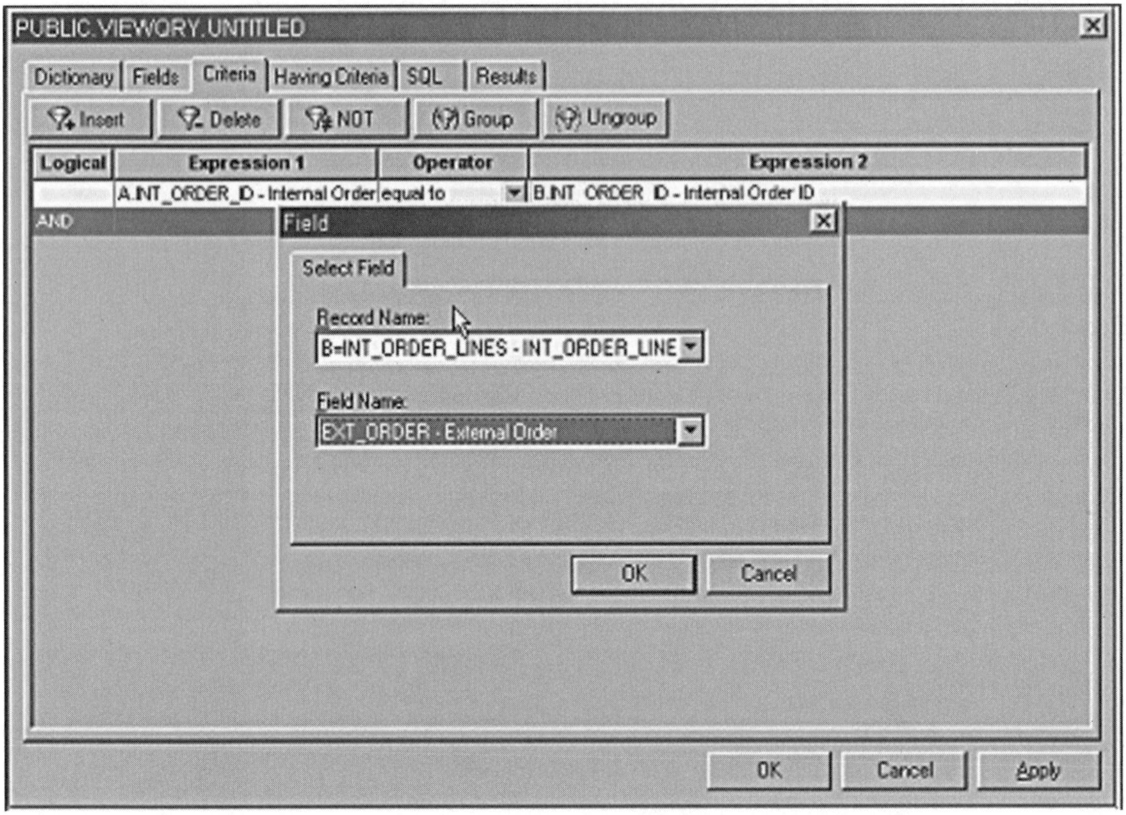

Figure 6-141 Field dialog from the CRITERIA tab of the Query dialog.

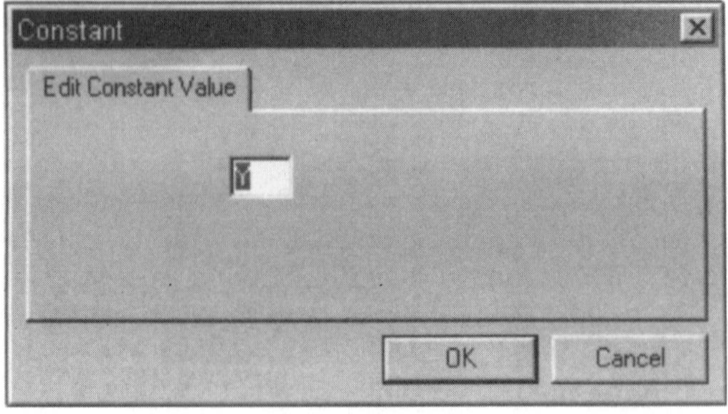

Figure 6-142 Constant dialog from the CRITERIA tab of the Query dialog.

Figure 6-143 Complete EXT_ORDER_VW Record Properties TYPE tab.

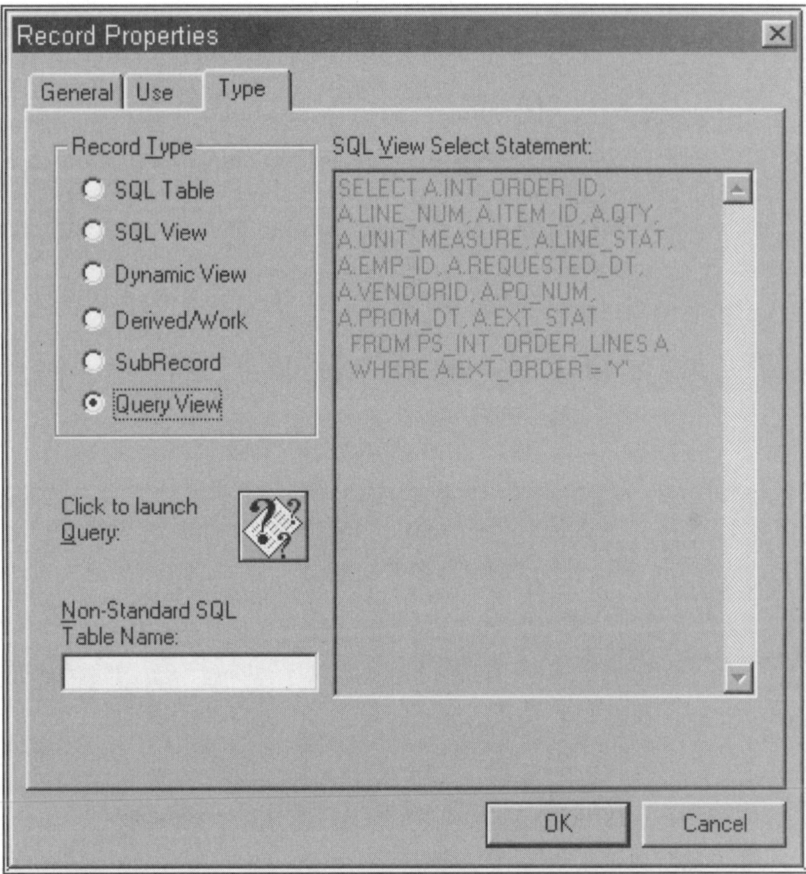

EXT_ORDER_VW (Record)

Field Name	Type	Key	Dir	CurC	Srch	List	Sys	Audt	H	Default
INT_ORDER_ID	Char	Key	Asc		Yes	Yes	No			
LINE_NUM	Nbr	Key	Asc		Yes	Yes	No			
ITEM_ID	Char				No	No	No			
QTY	Sign				No	No	No			
UNIT_MEASURE	Char				No	No	No			
LINE_STAT	Char				No	No	No			
EMP_ID	Char				No	No	No			
REQUESTED_DT	Date				No	No	No			
VENDORID	Char				No	No	No			
PO_NUM	Char				No	No	No			
PROM_DT	Date				No	No	No			
EXT_STAT	Char				No	No	No			

Figure 6-144 External Order View record definition.

- Key
- Search Key
- List Box Item

The Search Key option will place this field in all the search dialogs that are used for the internal order record. The List Box Item option will place this field as a column in the resulting list box in the search dialogs.

The only Edits property for this field is that it is required. INT_ORDER_ID is a key field and is therefore required. Figures 6-145 and 6-146 show the Use and Edits tabbed dialogs for INT_ORDER_ID.

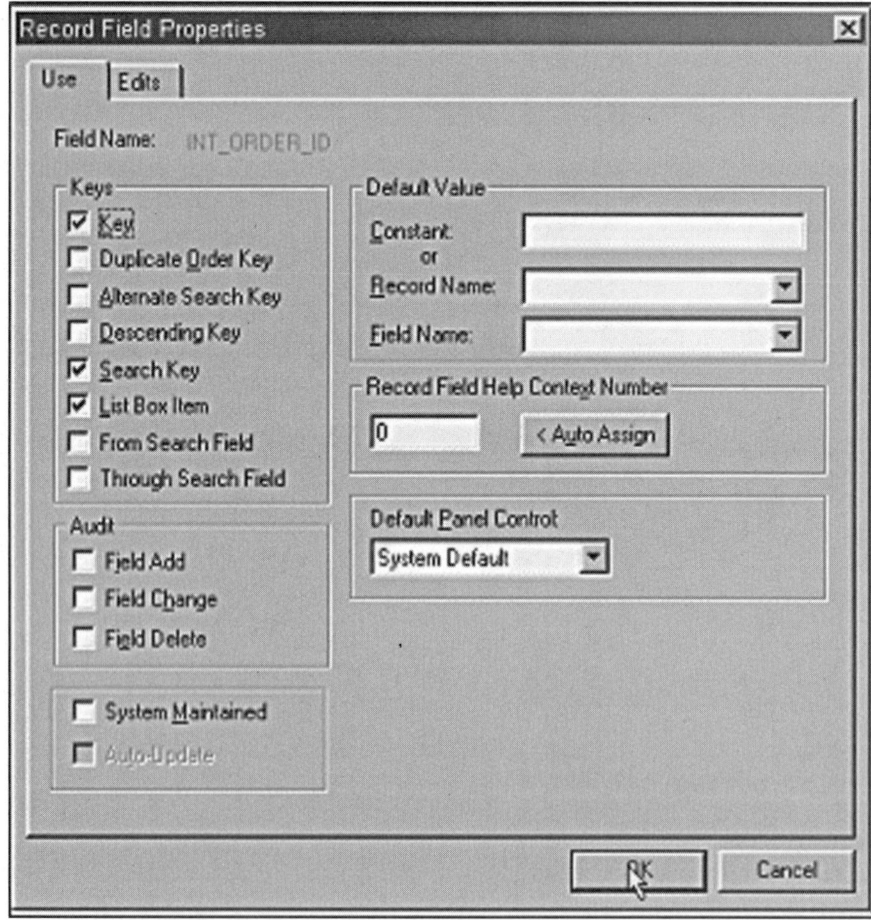

Figure 6-145 INT_ORDER_ID Use dialog.

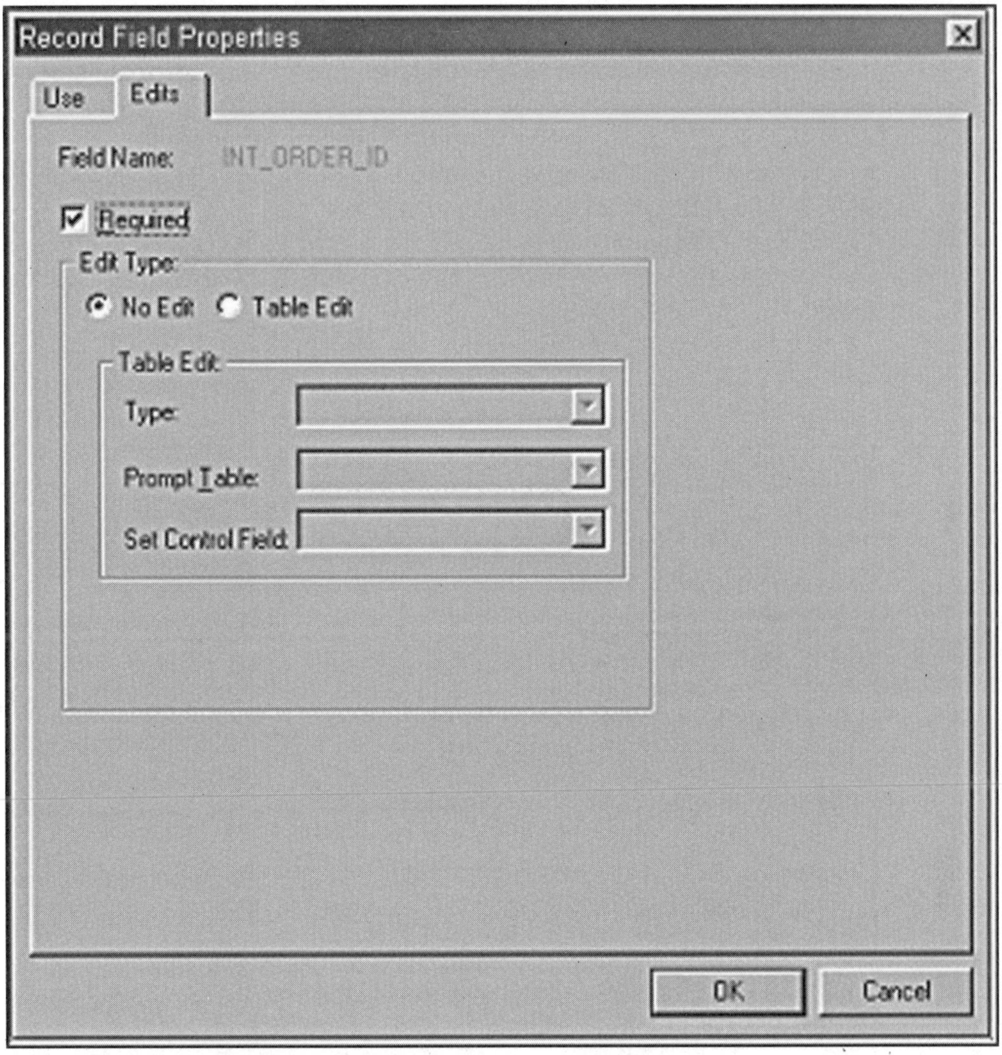

Figure 6-146 INT_ORDER_ID Edits dialog.

The next field for which we are going to set the record's field attributes is LINE_NUM. The Use values for the record's field attributes of LINE_NUM are

- Key
- Search Key

- List Box Item

The combination of the INT_ORDER_ID and LINE_NUM will make up the primary search keys for the EXT_ORDER_VW record.

The only Edits property for this field is that it is required. LINE_NUM is a key field and is therefore required. Figures 6-147 and 6-148 show the Use and Edit tabbed dialogs for LINE_NUM.

The next field for which we are going to set up record attributes for the EXT_ORDER_VW record is the ITEM_ID field. There are no Use attributes for the ITEM_ID field.

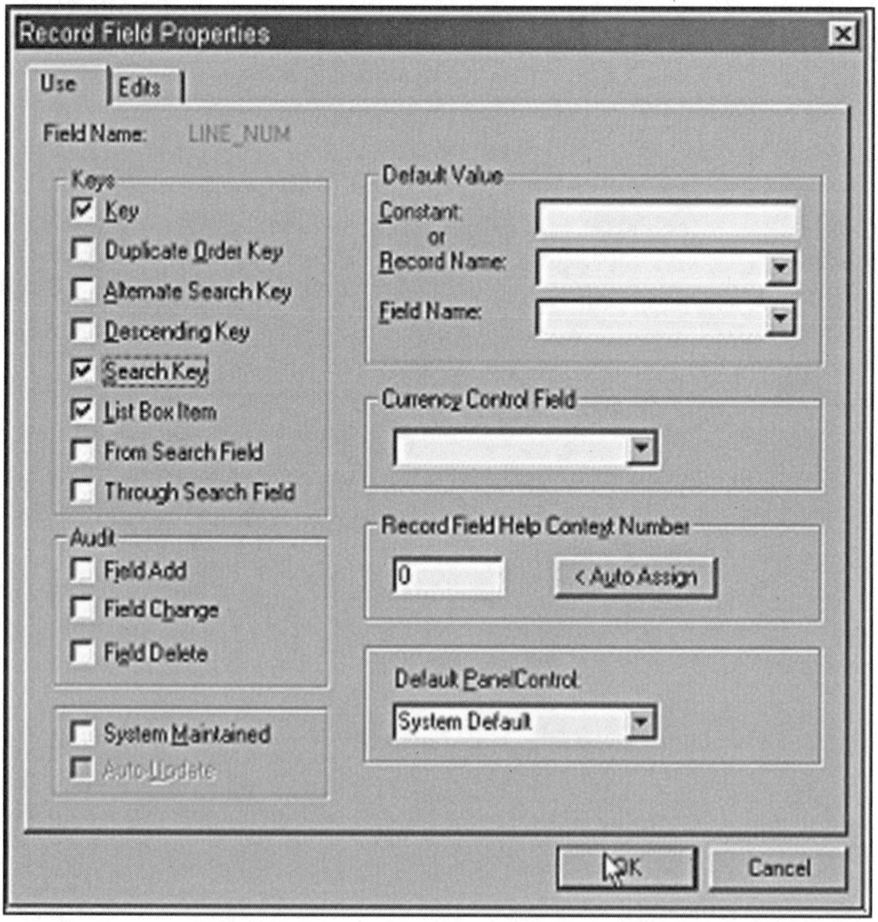

Figure 6-147 LINE_NUM Use dialog.

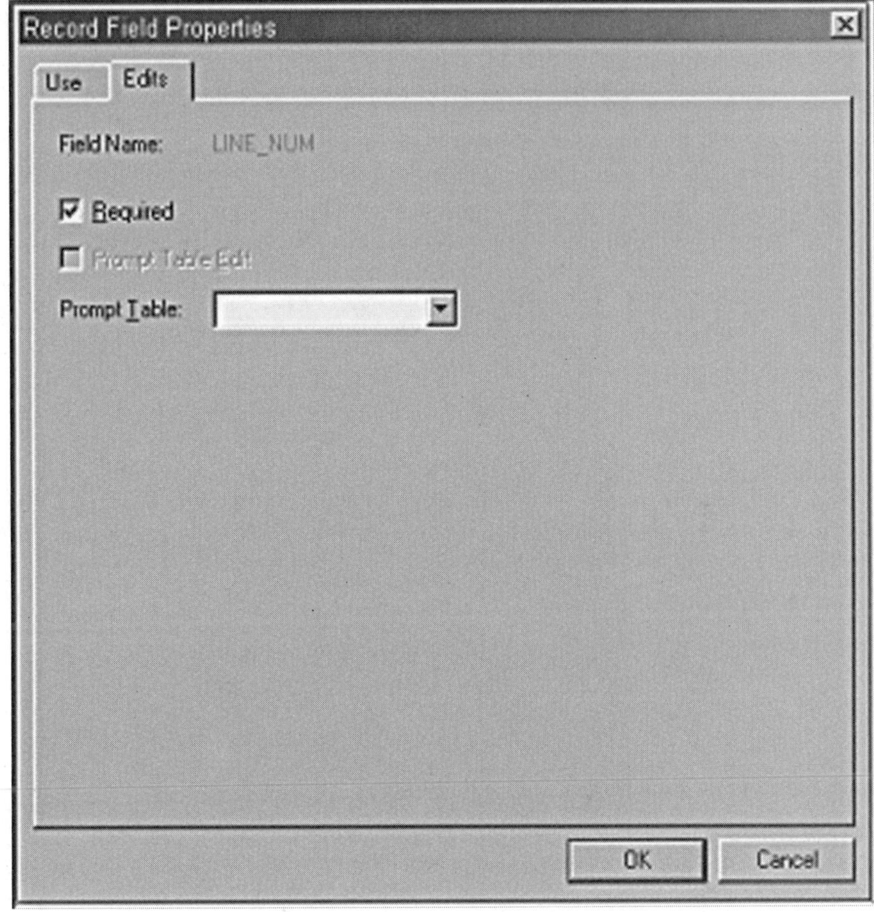

Figure 6-148
LINE_NUM Edits dialog.

The Edits attributes for ITEM_ID are that it is required and it uses a prompt table edit. The prompt table edit uses the ITEMS table we already created. Follow the same procedure we used in the INT_ORDER and INT_ORDER_LINES record. Select the TABLE EDIT radio button from the Edits Tab dialog for the ITEM_ID fields record attributes. The drop-down list boxes will then be enabled. Select the Prompt Table options from the Type drop-down and then select the ITEMS record from the Prompt Table drop-down. Figures 6-149 shows the Edits tab of the Record Field Properties dialog for ITEM_ID.

The next field for which we are going to set up record attributes for

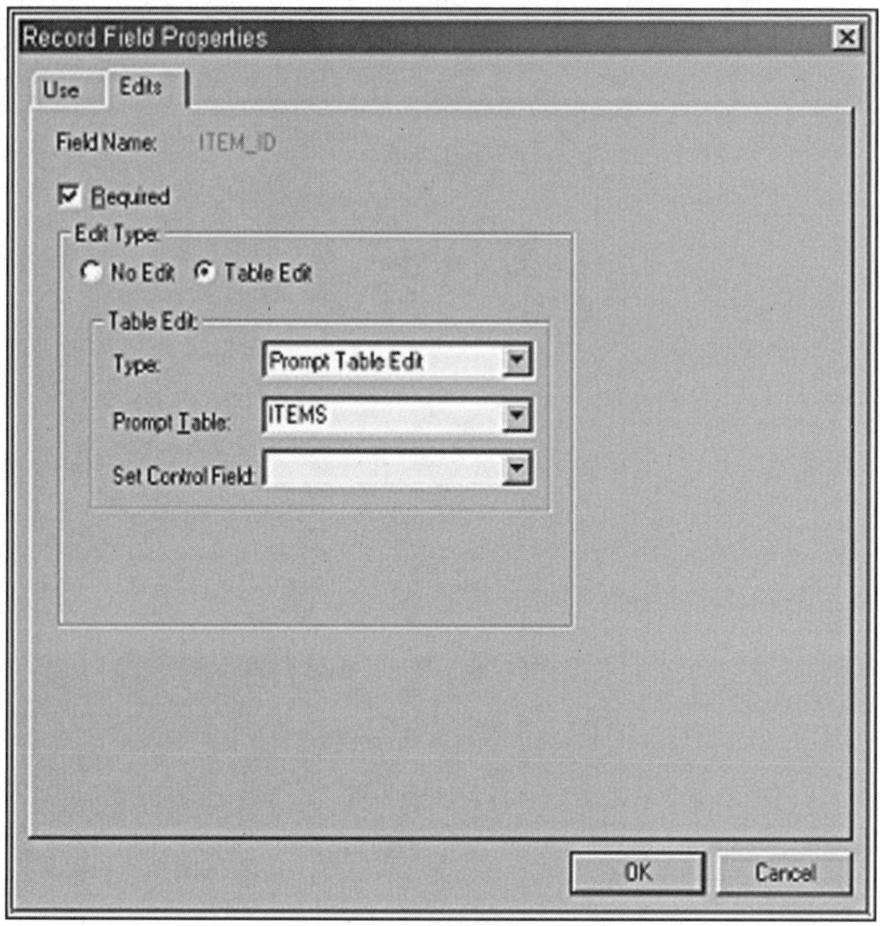

Figure 6-149 ITEM_ID Edits dialog.

the EXT_ORDER_VW record is the QTY field. There are no Use attributes for the QTY field.

In the EDITS tab we will make QTY a required field. Figure 6-150 shows the EDITS tab of the Record Field Properties dialog for QTY.

The next field for which we are going to set up record attributes for the EXT_ORDER_VW record is the UNIT_MEASURE field. There are no Use attributes for the UNIT_MEASURE field.

The Edits attributes for UNIT_MEASURE are that it is required and it uses a prompt table edit. The prompt table edit uses the UNIT_MEASURE table we already created. Select the TABLE EDIT radio button from the Edits Tab dialog for the UNIT_MEASURE fields record attributes. The

Figure 6-150
QTY Edits dialog.

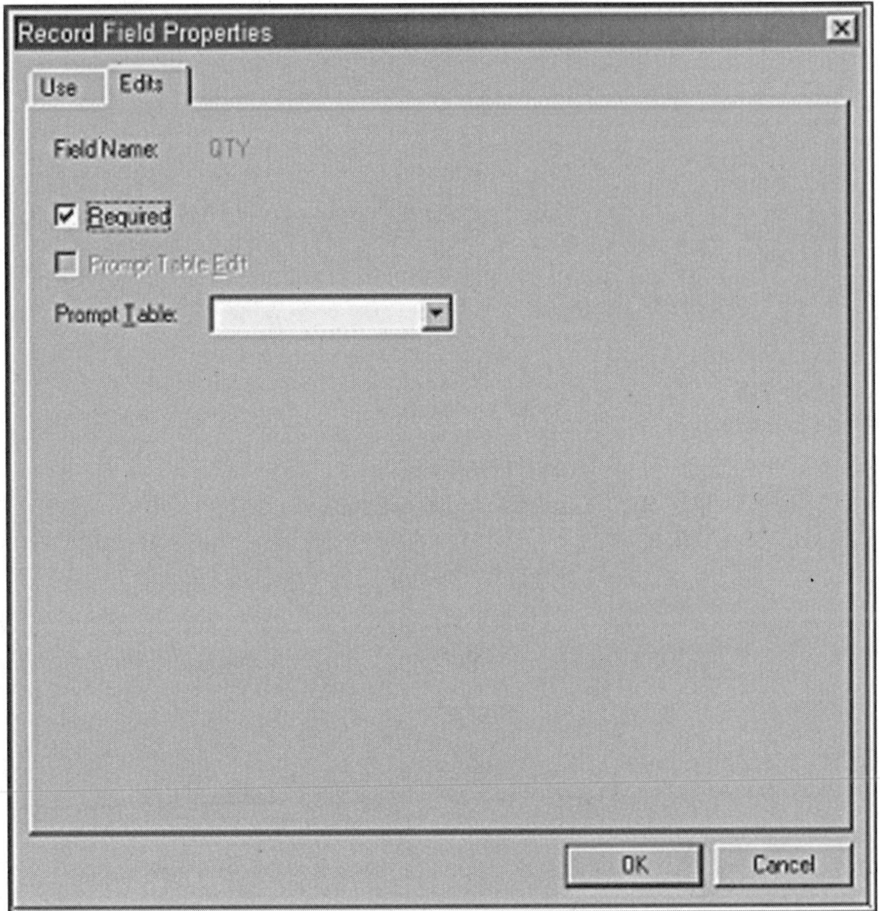

drop-down list boxes will then be enabled. Select the Prompt Table options from the Type drop-down and then select the UNIT_MEASURE record from the Prompt Table drop-down. Figure 6-151 shows the EDITS tab of the Record Field Properties dialog for UNIT_MEASURE. The next field in the EXT_ORDER_VW record is LINE_STAT. We do not need to set any record attributes for this field.

The next field for which we are going to set up record attributes for the EXT_ORDER_VW record is the EMP_ID field. The EMP_ID field's key attributes are

- Alt Search Key
- List Box Item

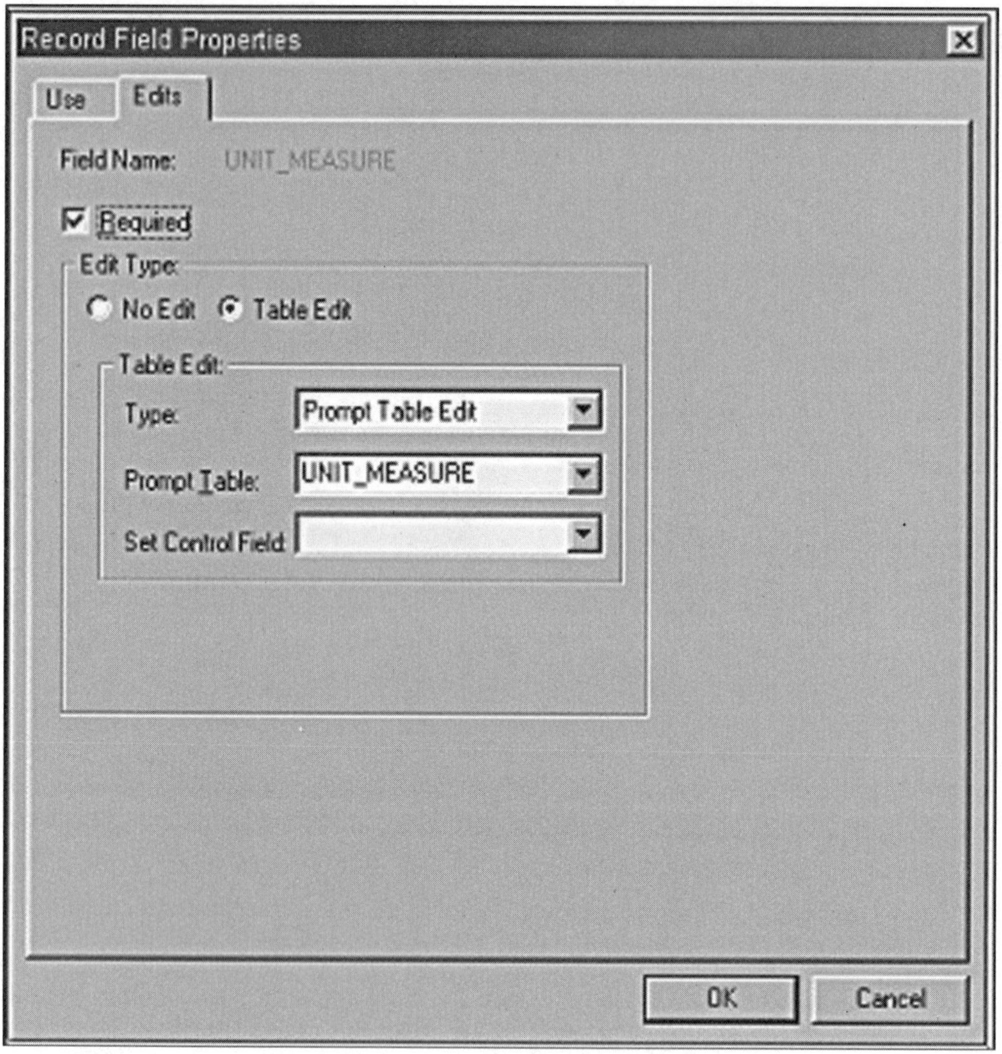

Figure 6-151 UNIT_MEASURE Edits dialog.

The Alternate Search Key will create an index on the EMP_ID field. The EMP_ID field will also be displayed in the Alternate Search Keys section of all the search dialogs. The List Box Item option will place this field as a column in the resulting list box in the search dialogs.

In addition to this field being required in the Internal Order record, we are going to set up a prompt table edit. For Data Validation we will require that the valid entries exist in our BUYER_VW record that we have already created. To do this we select the TABLE EDIT radio button from the Edits Tab dialog for the EMP_ID fields record attributes. The drop-down list boxes will then be enabled. Select the Prompt Table options from the Type drop-down and then select the BUYER_VW record from the Prompt Table drop-down. Figures 6-152 and 6-153 show the Use and Edit tabbed dialogs for EMP_ID.

The next field we set the record attributes for is REQUESTED_DT. The Use values that are associated with the field attributes of REQUESTED_DT are

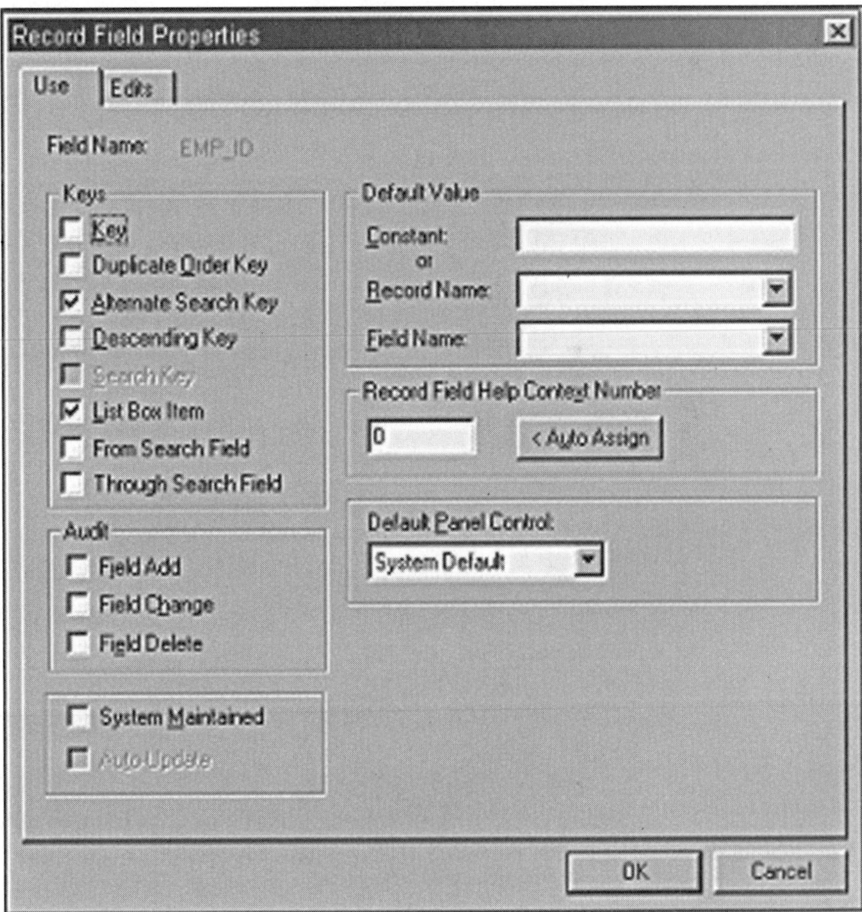

Figure 6-152
EMP_ID Use dialog.

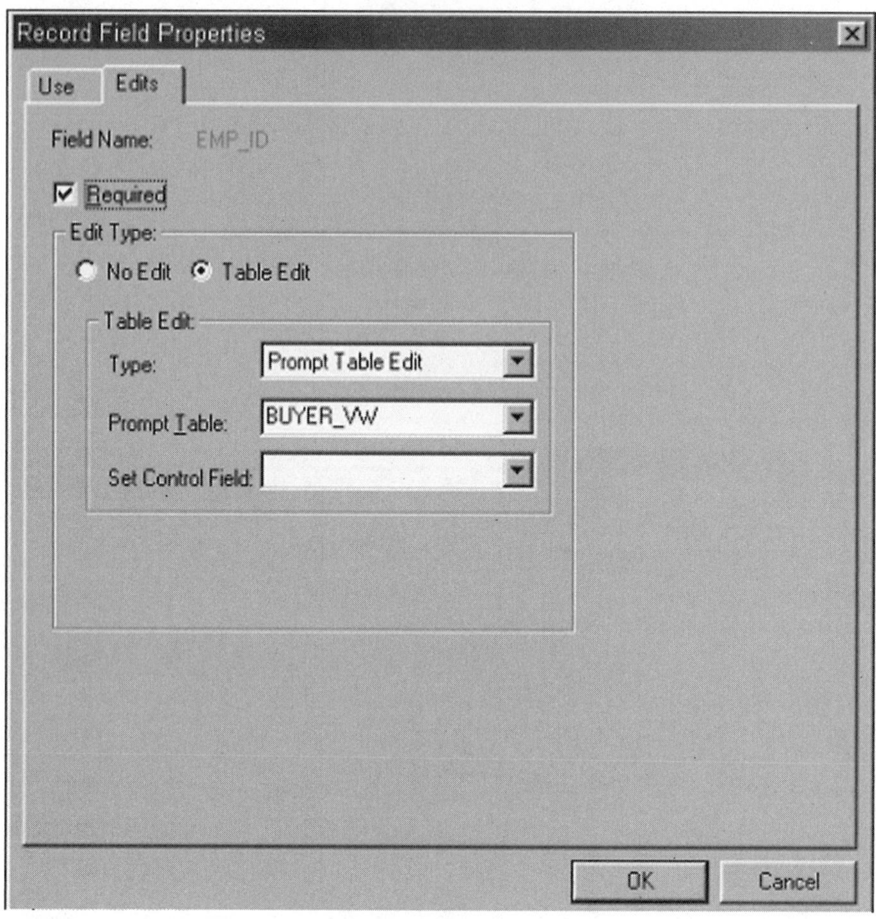

Figure 6-153
EMP_ID Edits dialog.

- Alt Search Key
- List Box Item
- Default to system date

Figures 6-154 and 6-155 show the Use and Edits tabbed dialogs for REQUESTED_DT.

The next field we set the record attributes for is VENDORID. The Use values that are associated to the field attributes of VENDORID are

- Alt Search Key
- List Box Item

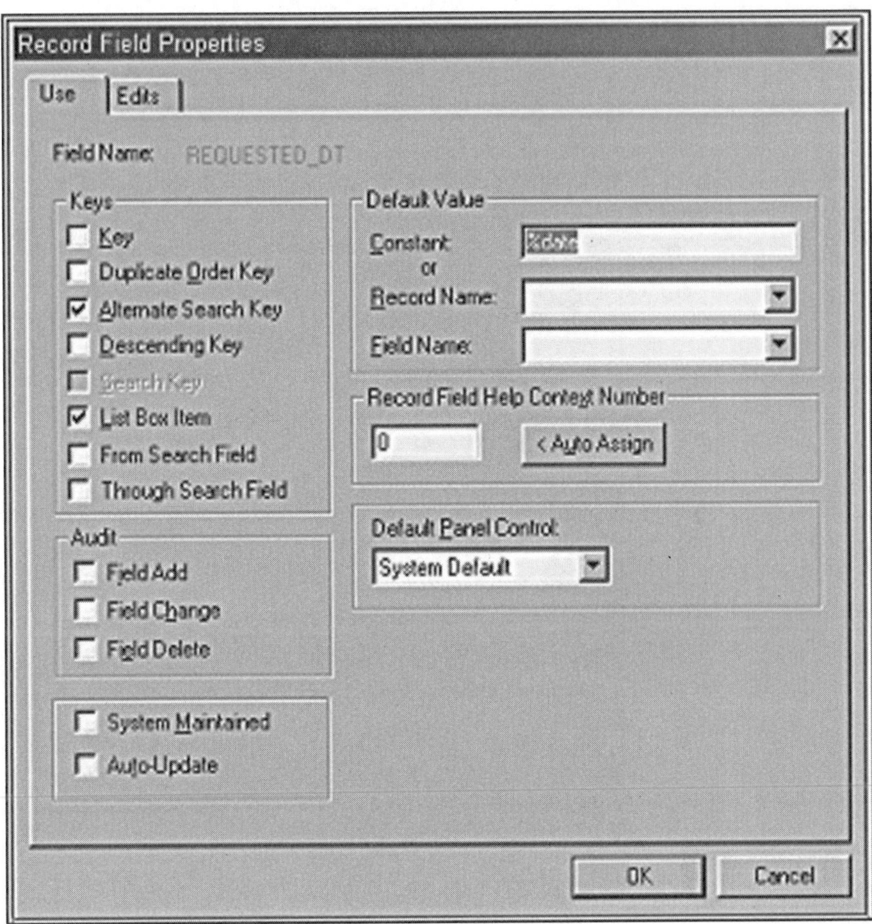

Figure 6-154 REQUESTED_DT Use dialog.

The Edits properties for VENDORID are that it has a prompt table edit utilizing our VENDORS record. Figures 6-156 and 6-157 show the Use and Edits tabbed dialogs for VENDORID.

The next field we set the record attributes for is PO_NUM. The Use values that are associated with the field attributes of PO_NUM are

- Alt Search Key
- List Box Item

Figures 6-158 and 6-159 show the Use and Edits tabbed dialogs for PO_NUM.

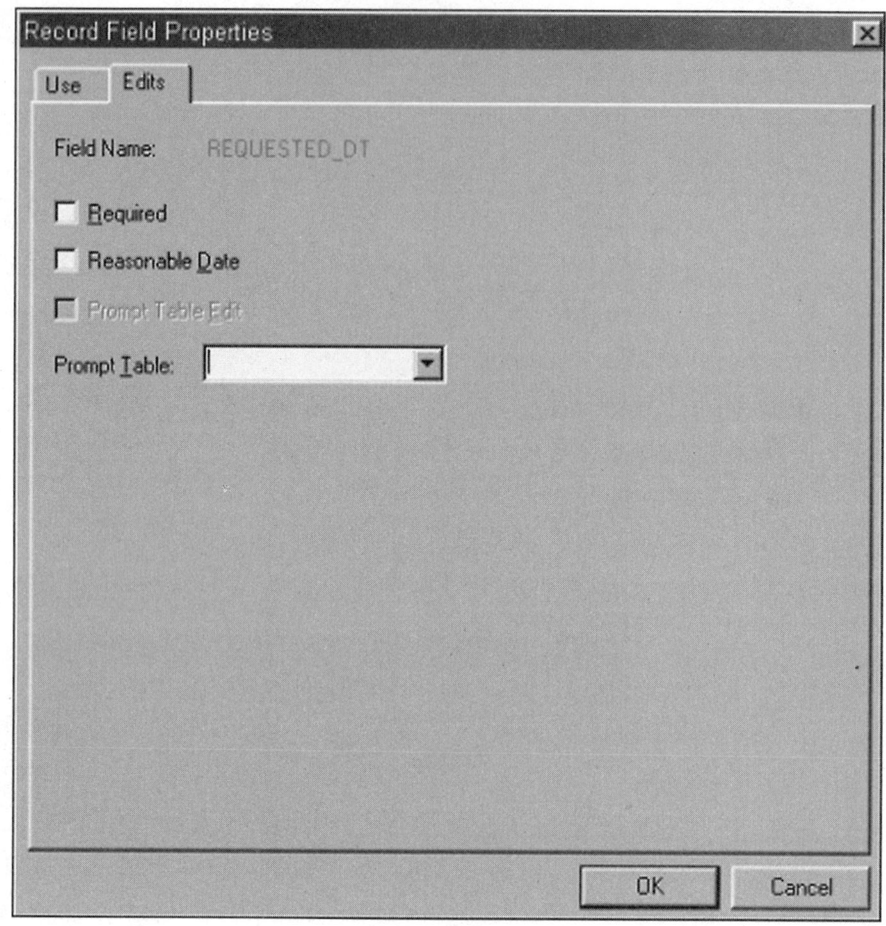

Figure 6-155 REQUESTED_DT Edits dialog.

The next field we set the record attributes for is PROM_DT. The Use values that are associated with the field attributes of PROM_DT are

- Alt Search Key
- List Box item

Figures 6-160 and 6-161 show the Use and Edits tabbed dialogs for PROM_DT.

The next field we set the record attributes for is EXT_STAT. The Use value that we are going to associate with the field attributes of EXT_STAT is the default panel control set to RADIO BUTTON. Setting the

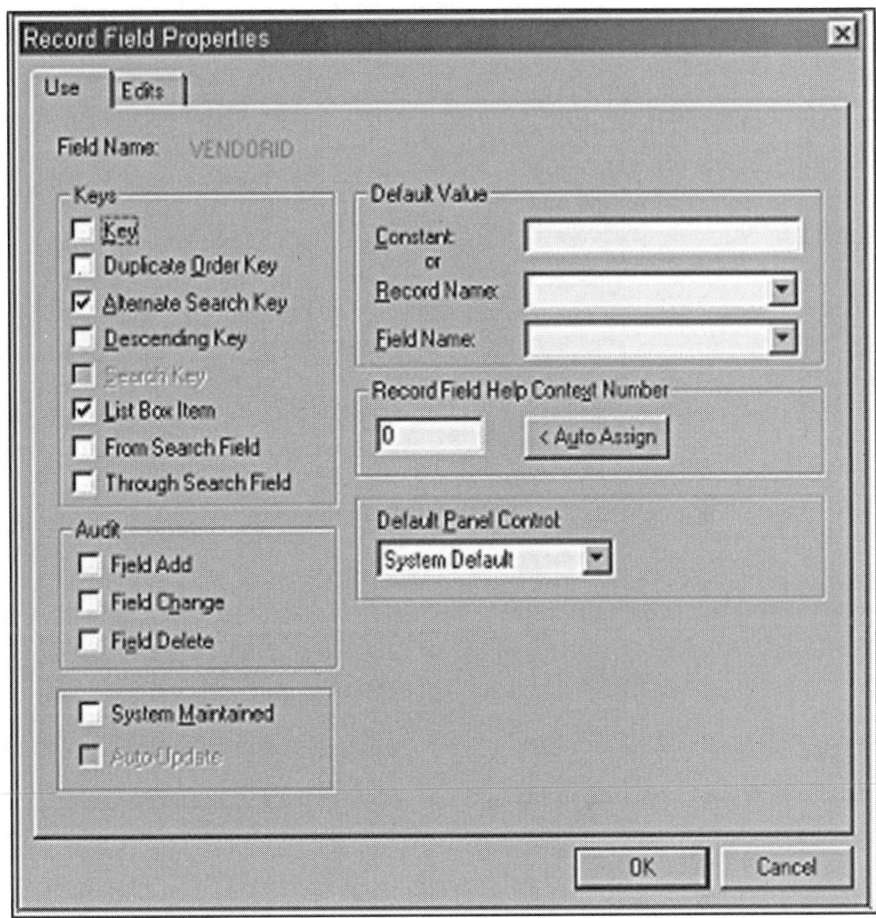

Figure 6-156 VENDORID Use dialog.

default panel control to RADIO BUTTON will allow us to place five separate EXT_STAT controls on our panel. Each one will be set to represent one of the five translate values we set up for EXT_STAT. The default constant value of NEW will set the radio button that is set to NEW on as a default value. This will be shown in more detail when we create our internal order panels.

EXT_STAT Edits properties include required and a translate table edit. Figures 6-162 and 6-163 show the Use and Edits tabbed dialogs for EXT_STAT.

The next field we set the record attributes for is LINE_STAT. The only attribute we need to set up for LINE_STAT is an edits attribute for a

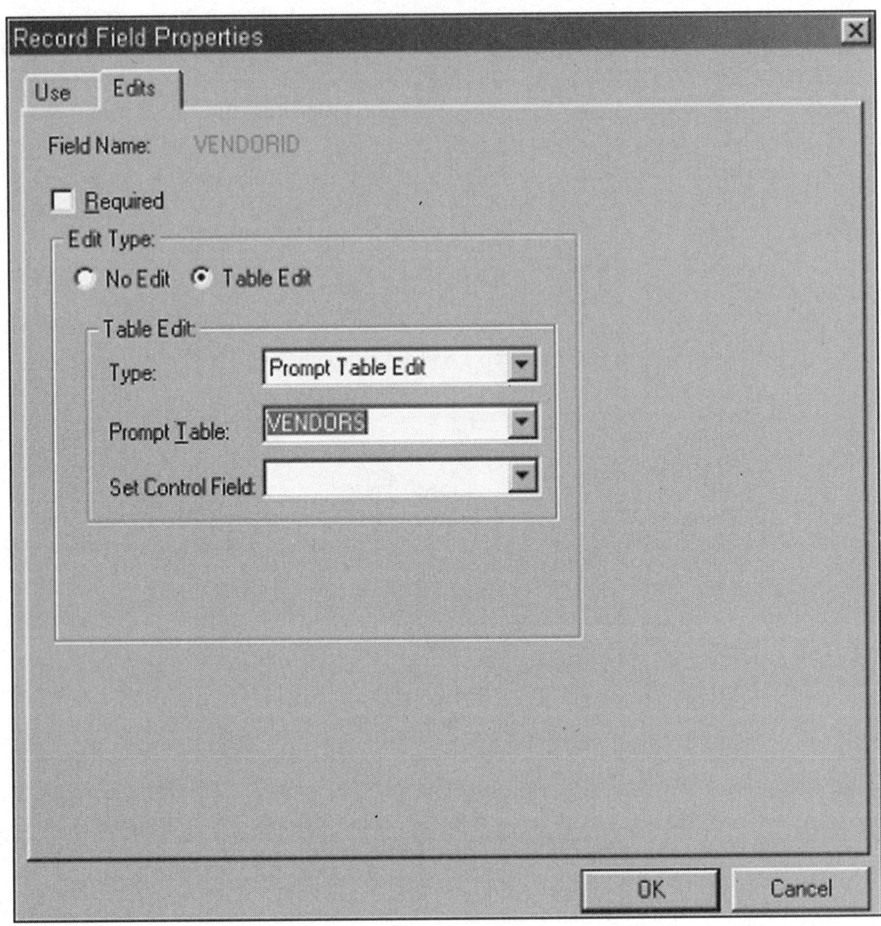

Figure 6-157 VENDORID Edits dialog.

translate table edit. Figures 6-164 shows the EDITS tab of the Record Field Properties dialog for LINE_STAT.

The EXT_ORDER_VW record is ready to be built if yours matches the one shown in Figure 6-165. Follow the same instructions as for the previous SQL Table records. Instead of selecting CREATE TABLES, you are going to select CREATE VIEWS and CREATE INDEXES. Select from the menu BUILD, CURRENT OBJECT, or press the BUILD icon. From the Build dialog select CREATE VIEWS, CREATE INDEXES, and BUILD AND EXECUTE SCRIPT. After you press the BUILD button, a successful status should be displayed in the Output window.

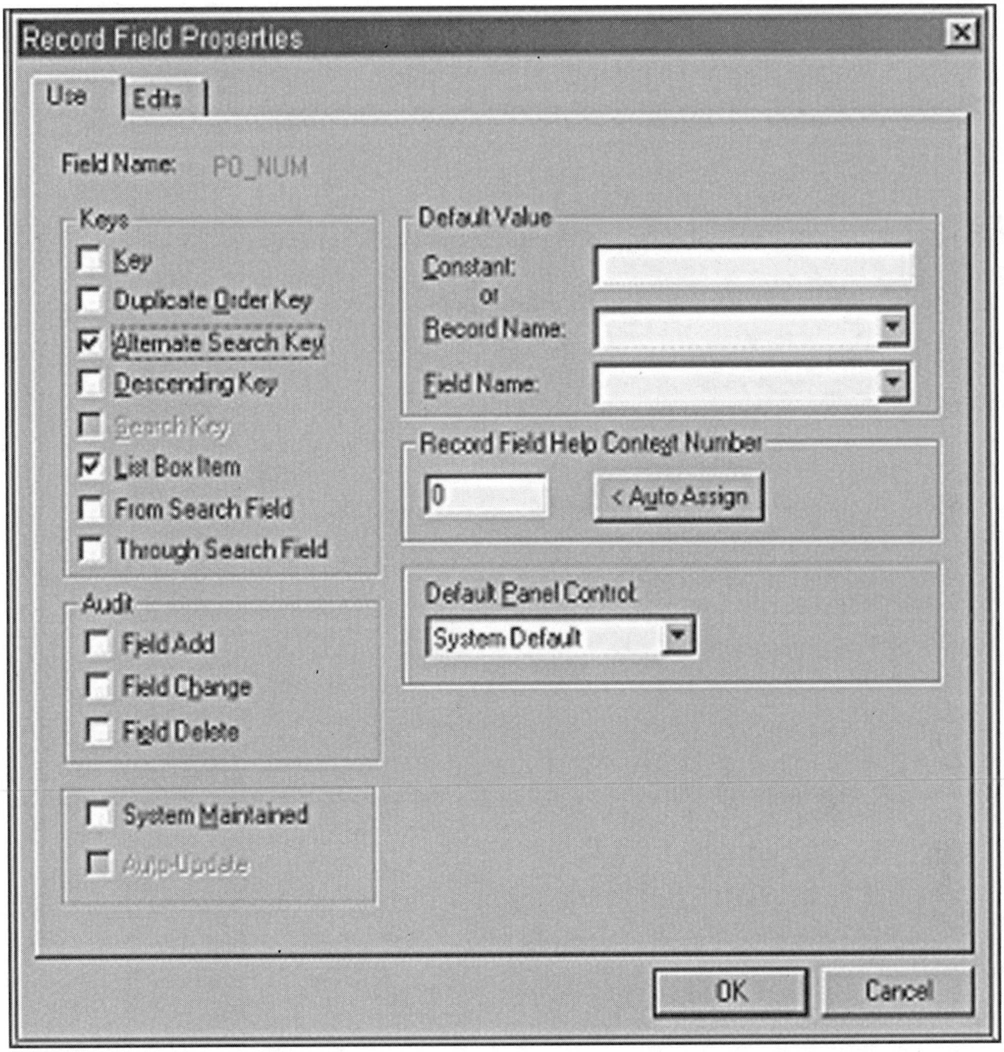

Figure 6-158 PO_NUM Use dialog.

All of our example records should now be built and included into our project. Figure 6-166 displays the Project view with the Records folder open.

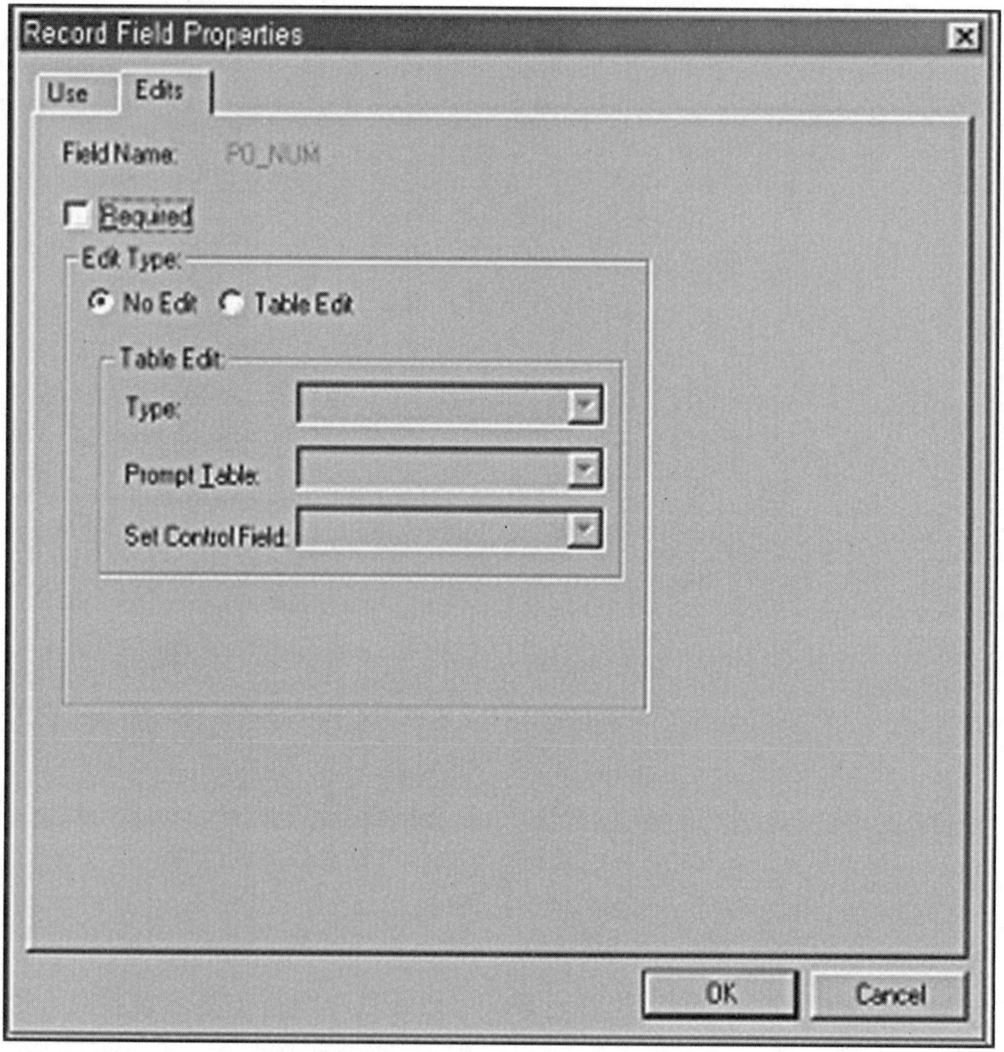

Figure 6-159 PO_NUM Edits dialog.

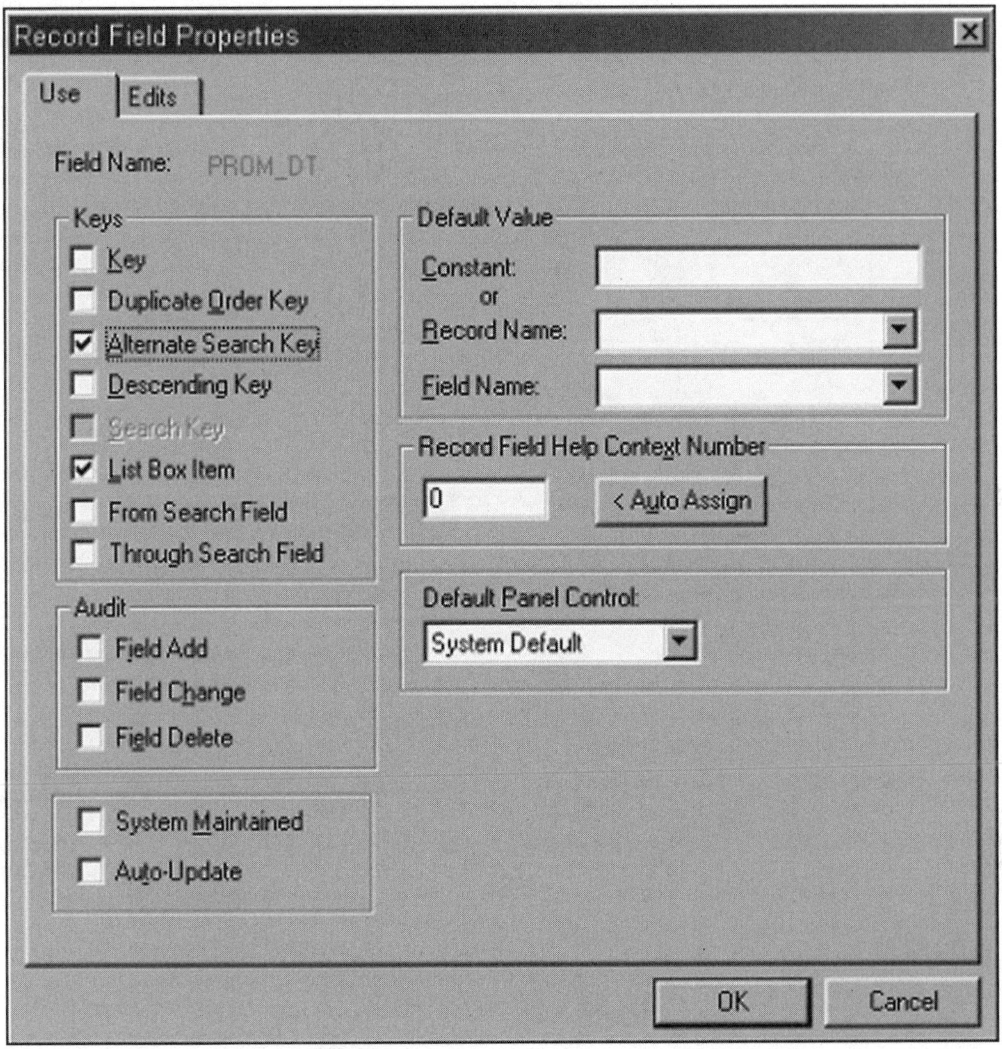

Figure 6-160 PROM_DT Use dialog.

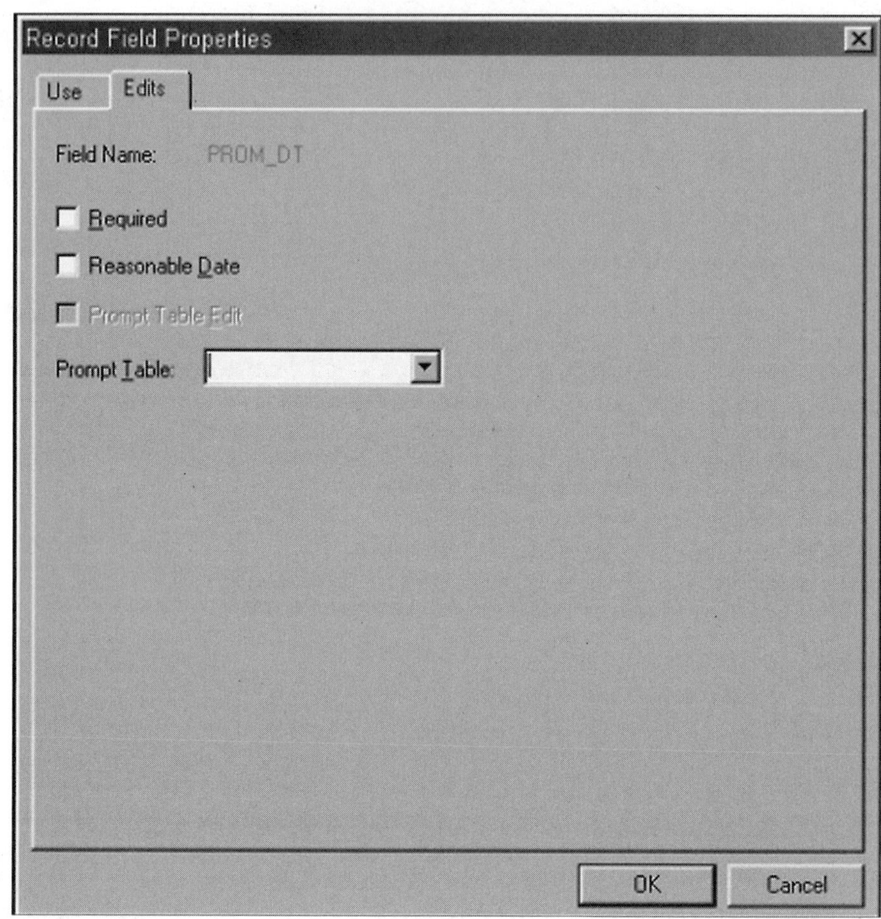

Figure 6-161 PROM_DT Edits dialog.

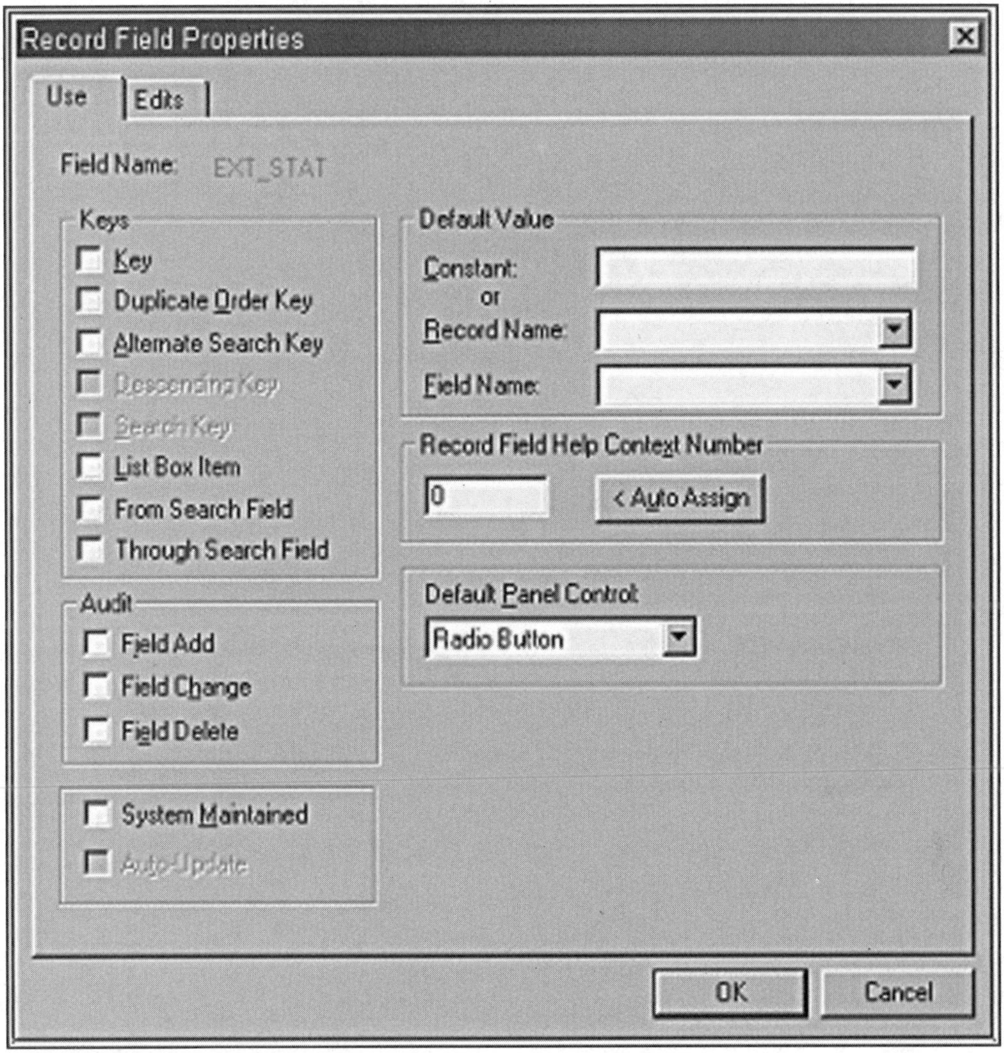

Figure 6-162 EXT_STAT Use dialog.

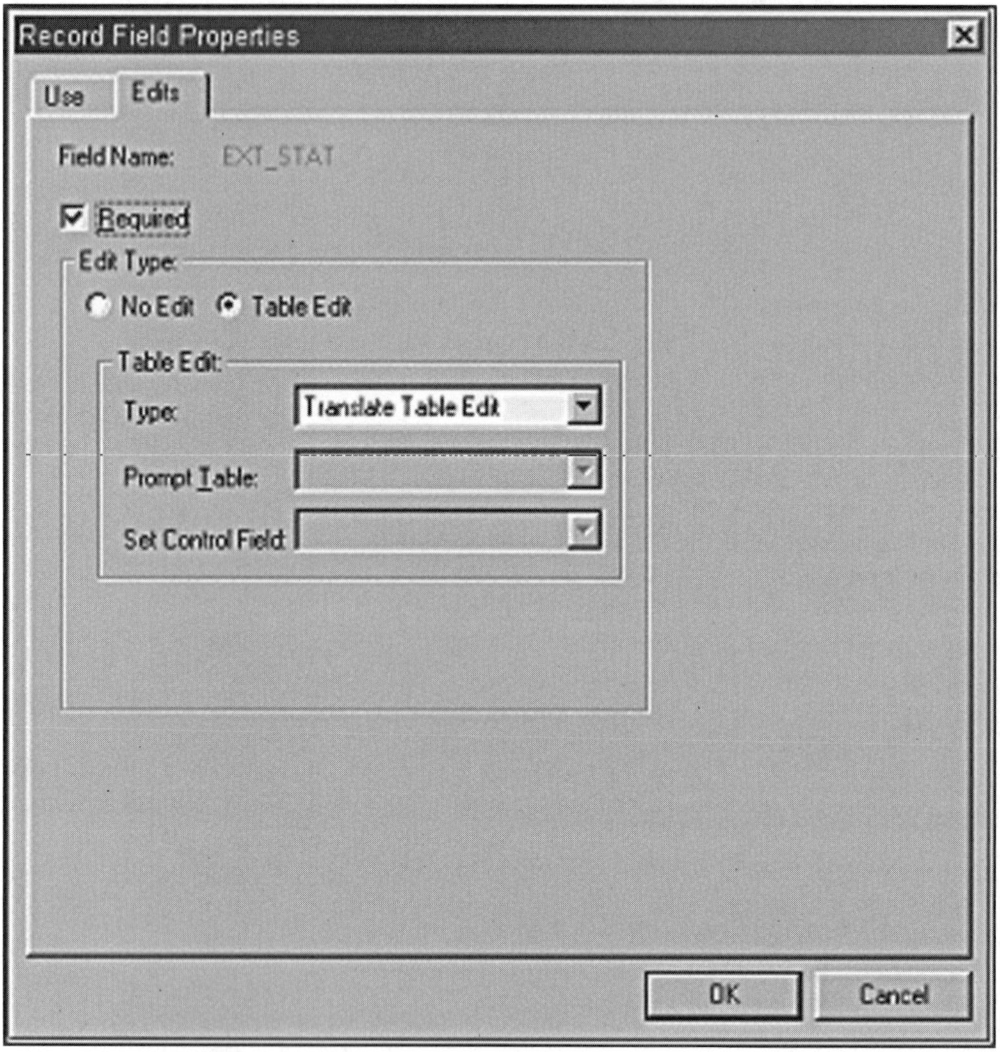

Figure 6-163 EXT_STAT Edits dialog.

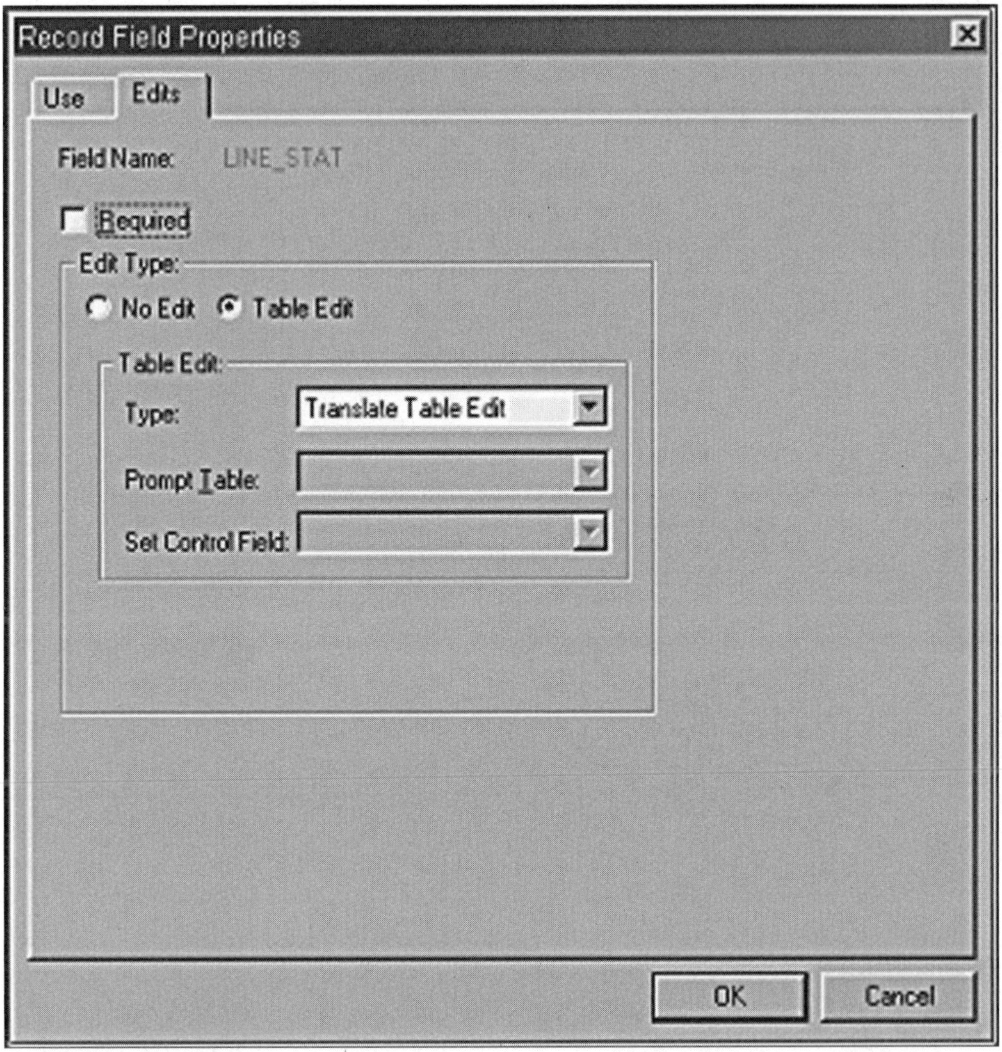

Record Field Properties

Use | Edits

Field Name: LINE_STAT

Required

Edit Type:

No Edit | Table Edit

Table Edit:

Type: Translate Table Edit

Prompt Table:

Set Control Field:

OK | Cancel

Figure 6-164 LINE_STAT Edits dialog.

EXT_ORDER_VW (Record)

Field Name	Type	Key	Dir	CurC	Srch	List	Sys	Audt	H	Default
INT_ORDER_ID	Char	Key	Asc		Yes	Yes	No			
LINE_NUM	Nbr	Key	Asc		Yes	Yes	No			
ITEM_ID	Char				No	No	No			
QTY	Sign				No	No	No			
UNIT_MEASURE	Char				No	No	No			
LINE_STAT	Char				No	No	No			
EMP_ID	Char	Alt	Asc		No	Yes	No			
REQUESTED_DT	Date	Alt	Asc		No	Yes	No			
VENDORID	Char	Alt	Asc		No	Yes	No			
PO_NUM	Char	Alt	Asc		No	Yes	No			
PROM_DT	Date	Alt	Asc		No	Yes	No			
EXT_STAT	Char				No	No	No			

Figure 6-165 EXT_ORDER_VW record.

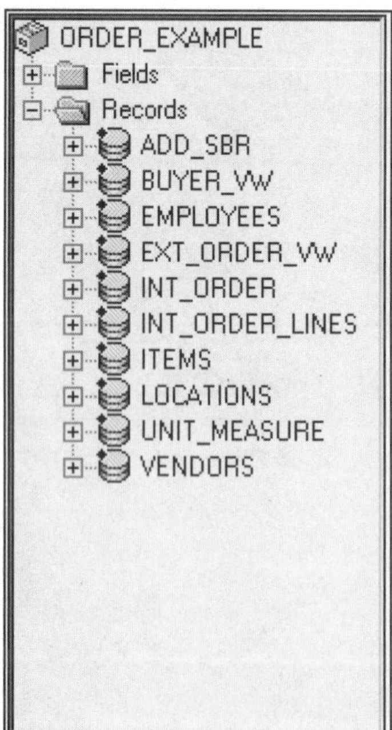

Figure 6-166 Project view with the Records folder open.

CHAPTER 7

Panels

Definition of a Panel

A *panel* in PeopleSoft is a graphical user interface (GUI) screen created by the developer that allows the user(s) to have access to the data in the database without having to perform SQL commands on the data. When designing a panel, the developer decides what data will be on the panel, how they are organized, and what graphical controls will be used to display the data.

Types of Graphical Control on a Panel

The developer can select from the following graphical controls when creating the panel:

- *Frame.* A frame control is a display only box around a group of controls.
- *Group box.* A group box control is similar to a frame in that it is a display-only box around a group of controls. However, a group box differs from a frame because it has a text label to help describe what the group of controls represents.
- *Static text.* A static text control is display-only text with a maximum length of 30 alphanumeric characters that cannot be modified.
- *Static image.* A static image control allows the developer to place an image on the panel. This image is a static image and therefore cannot be modified.
- *Check box.* A check-box control is a box that when checked indicates "yes" and when not checked, "no."
- *Drop-down box.* A drop-down box contains a list of valid values from which the user may select.
- *Edit box.* An edit box allows the user to enter data in the field. The length is usually a fixed value based on the length of the object.
- *Image.* An image control allows displaying of an image from an image record in the database.
- *Long edit box.* A long edit box control allows the user to enter variable-length data in the field.
- *Push button.* A push-button control when clicked causes some action to occur or process to run.
- *Radio buttons.* A radio button is a round button. Radio buttons are always in groups and can be selected only one at a time. When the information next to the radio button is selected (by clicking on it with the left mouse button), the round button is shaded in. Otherwise, the radio button is a non-shaded round symbol.
- *Tree.* A tree control is used for searching.
- *Grid.* A grid control is similar to a spreadsheet.
- *Scroll bar.* A scroll bar allows the user to scroll through rows on a panel.

- *Secondary panel.* A control is added to the panel that cannot be seen. It is used to associate a secondary panel to the main or primary panel. The secondary panel is displayed later via a popup menu or via a push-button control.
- *Subpanel.* A subpanel allows the user to create a group of controls and then insert them all on several panels simply by inserting the subpanel.

Steps in Creating a New Panel with PeopleSoft

There are two ways of creating a panel with PeopleSoft:

- Open an existing panel and save it as a different name. Then make changes to it. This works well when the panel you want to create is similar in style to an existing panel already created.
- Create a totally *new* panel.

This section discusses the steps required in creating a totally new panel:

1. Select FILE, NEW and when the New dialog box appears, select PANEL from the list of items and click on the OK push button (Fig. 7-1). A blank panel will then be displayed as shown in Figure 7-2.
2. Once the blank panel is displayed, the next step is to add controls to the panel as required by the developer's design for the new panel.

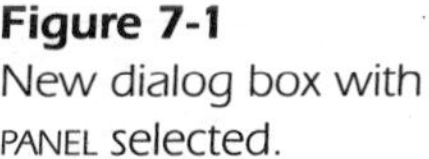

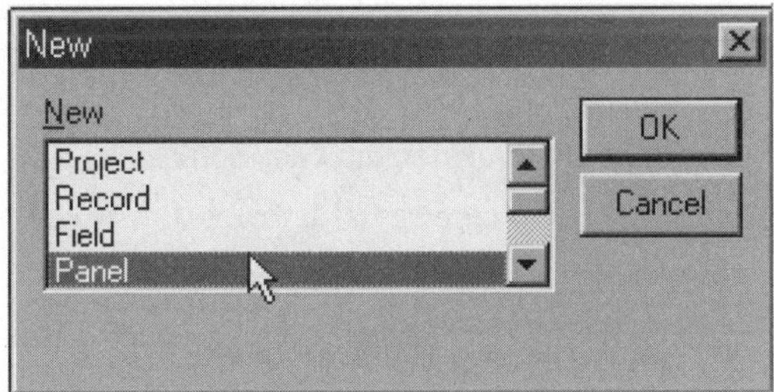

Figure 7-1
New dialog box with PANEL selected.

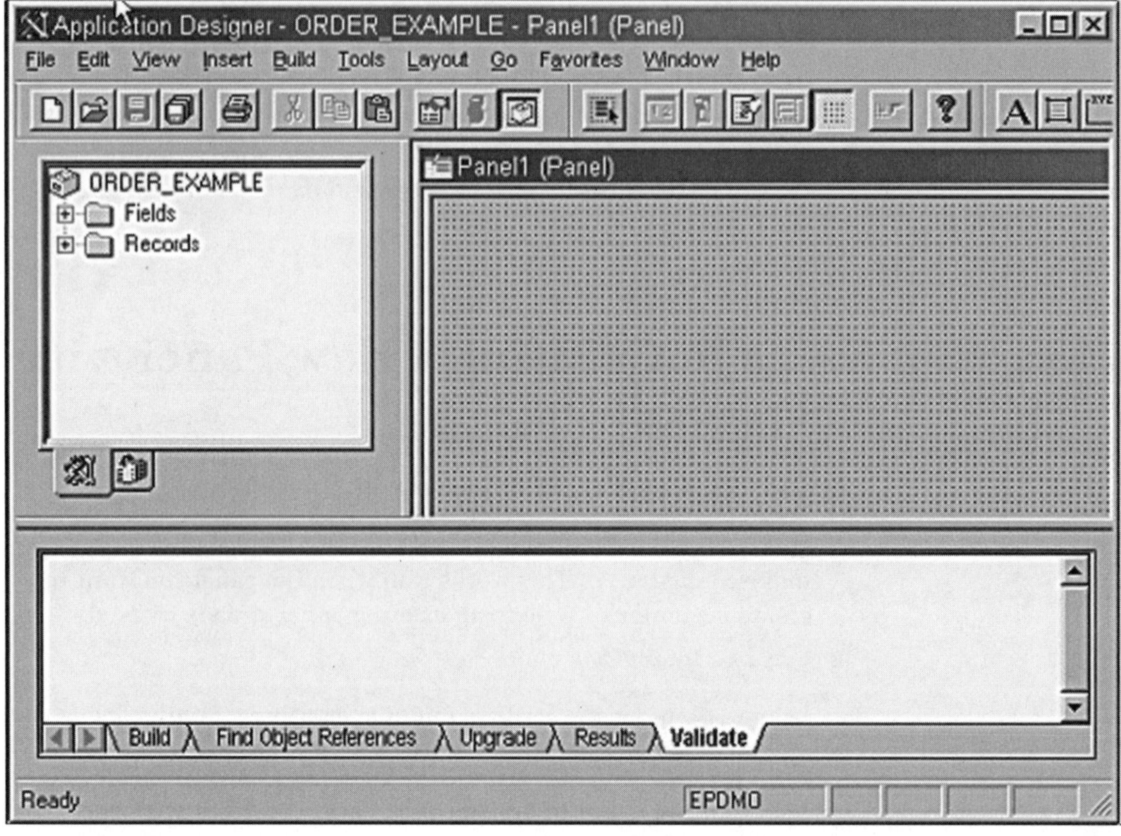

Figure 7-2 Blank panel.

Three Ways to Insert Controls onto a Panel

There are three ways of inserting controls onto a panel:

- Selecting FILE, INSERT from the toolbar
- Dragging and dropping fields from the record to the panel
- Using the Panel Definition toolbar

Selecting FILE, INSERT from the Toolbar

One way to insert controls on a panel is to click on INSERT (Fig. 7-3) from the toolbar and select the desired control from a list of all the controls that can be added to a panel. When the desired control is selected, an icon appears representing that type of control. The developer should then move the icon to the desired location on the panel and click the mouse.

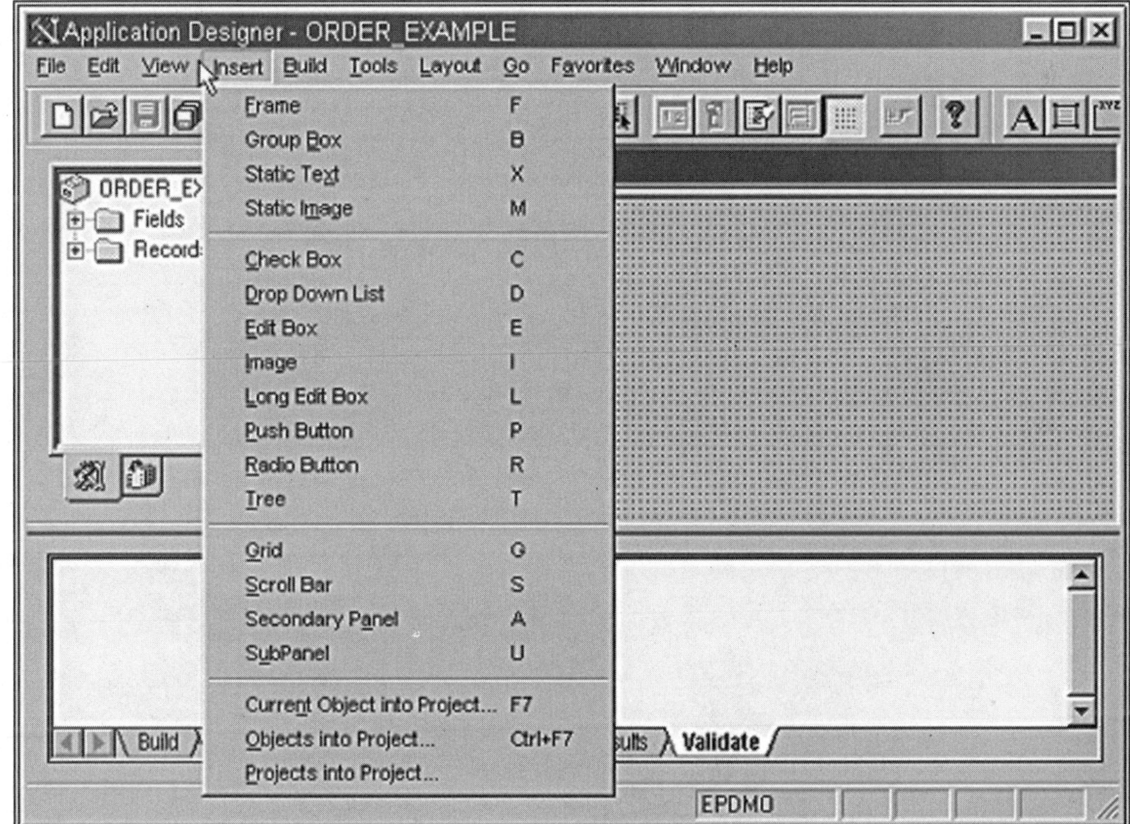

Figure 7-3 Menu that appears when inserting a control onto a panel.

Inserting Controls by the Drag-and-Drop Method

Another way of inserting controls onto a panel is via dragging and dropping fields from the record to the panel. To do this, simply open the record that contains the fields to be inserted onto the new panel. Select a field and drag it over to the new panel that is already opened. Depending on the type of field selected, a specific type of control will be inserted onto the new panel. In other words, each type of field has a default control type that is created when that type of field is dragged onto a panel. Once the field is dropped on the panel, some of the information on the Panel Field Properties dialog is automatically filled in for the developer.

Figure 7-4 Name field from an existing open record was dragged and dropped onto a new panel.

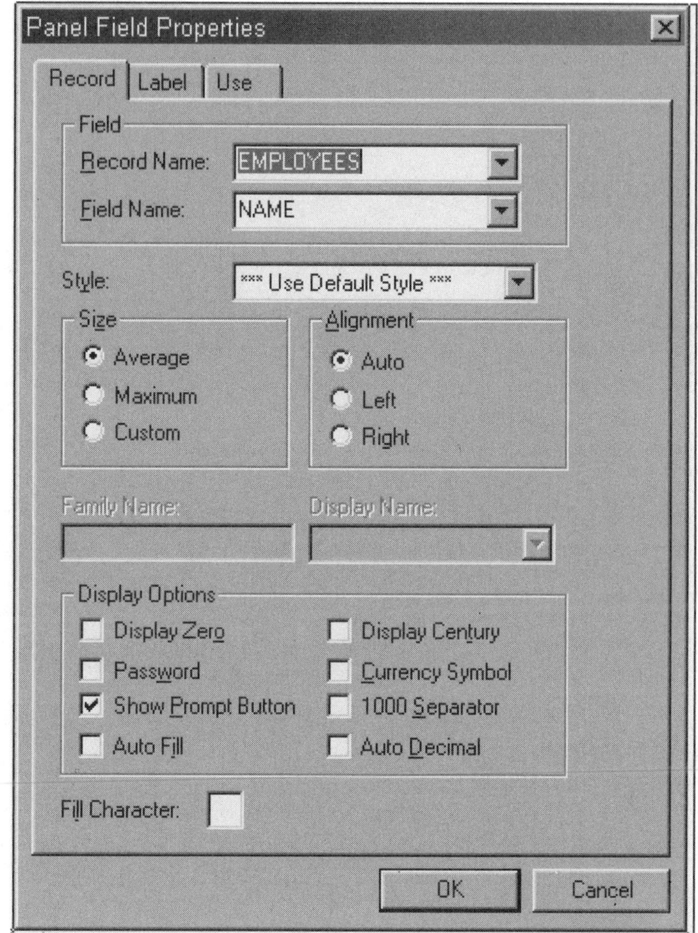

Figure 7-4a
Record Tab of the Panel Field Properties dialog box as it appears after the name field is dropped onto the new panel.

For example, Figure 7-4 shows the name field from the employee record being dropped onto the new panel. Figures 7-4*a* and 7-4*b* illustrate what the Record Tab looks like immediately after the developer dropped that field on the panel.

A field from the Project Workspace can be dragged and dropped onto the panel as well. Again, the default control type will be created on the panel. Figure 7-5 shows what the panel looks like after the position field of the employee record was dragged and dropped from the Project Workspace area of the screen to the new panel.

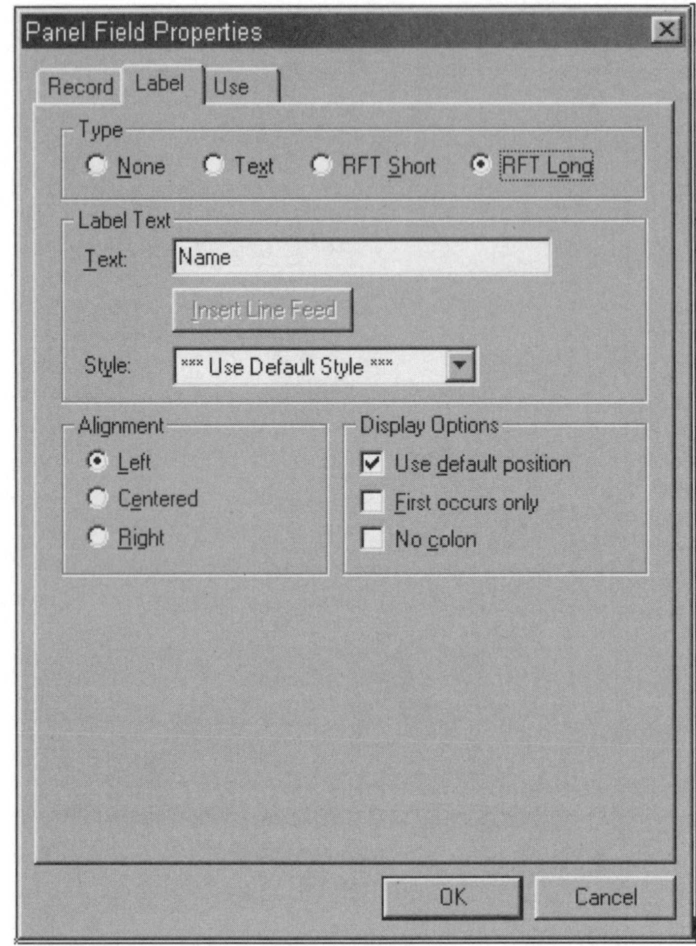

Figure 7-4b Label Tab of the Panel Field Properties dialog box as it appears after the name field is dropped onto the new panel.

Inserting Controls Using the Panel Definition Toolbar

It is possible to insert controls onto a panel using the Panel Definition toolbar, shown in Figure 7-6. As you can see, it consists of small buttons that represent each type of control that can be added to a panel. To insert using a toolbar button, simply click on the one representing the desired control type, and an icon will appear. With each control type, a different icon appears when the toolbar button is selected. This helps

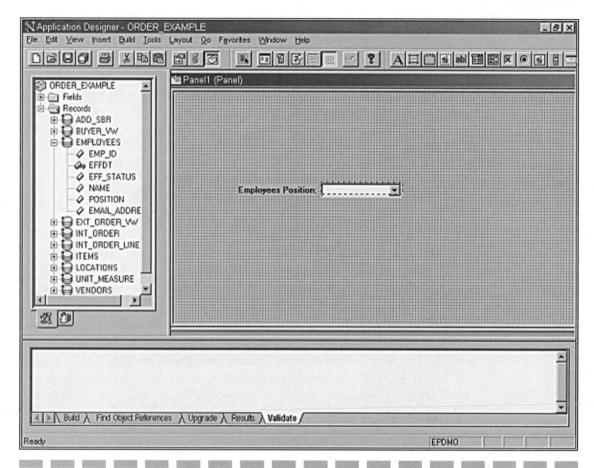

Figure 7-5 Position field was dragged from the project workspace onto the new panel.

Figure 7-6 Panel Definition toolbar.

the developer ensure that the correct button was selected. The developer should place the icon onto the panel in the desired location and click the mouse. At this point, the control is on the panel with default text. The developer would have to associate the control to a record and field and modify the text. Further information on how to do this is presented in the following sections when each control type is discussed in detail.

Steps for Inserting Each Type of Control onto the Panel

The following sections discuss the details associated with inserting each type of control onto a panel.

Edit Box

To insert an edit box on a panel, perform the following steps:

1. Select INSERT, EDIT BOX from the menu or click on the EDIT BOX button on the toolbar (Fig. 7-7). Once the edit box is selected, an EDIT BOX icon appears. The developer must place the icon in the desired position on the panel and click the mouse. Figure 7-8 shows the icon on the panel before the developer clicks on the mouse to place it in the desired position; Figure 7-9, after.
2. Once the edit box is in the desired location on the panel, the next step is to associate it with a field from the record. To do this, double-click on the EDIT BOX icon to bring up the Panel Field Properties dialog box. You could also right-click on the edit box to bring up the popup menu (Fig. 7-10) and then select Panel Field Properties. The Panel Field Properties dialog box is shown in Figure 7-11. Note that there are three tabs on this dialog box. There is a RECORD tab, a LABEL tab, and a USE tab. The default tab that is displayed is the RECORD tab. The RECORD tab allows the developer to enter the following information:
   - *Record name.* The developer selects the record name from the drop-down list of records where the field that is to be associated with the edit box is located.
   - *Field name.* The developer selects the name of the field to be associated with the edit box. Once a record is selected, only the fields belonging to that record are displayed and therefore may be selected. If the developer attempts to enter a field that is not in the record, an error message is displayed as shown in Figure 7-12.

Figure 7-7
EDIT BOX button on the toolbar.

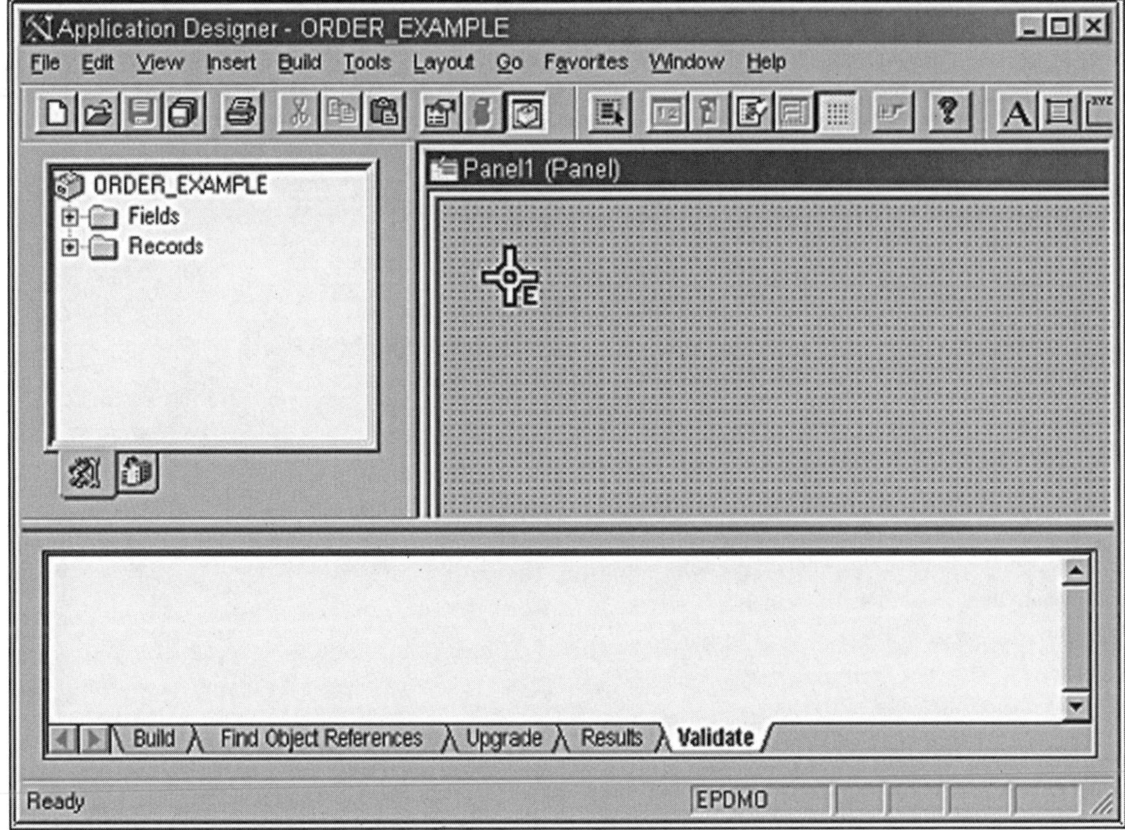

Figure 7-8 EDIT BOX icon as it appears on the panel while the developer inserts it into the desired position on the panel.

- *Style*. The developer can change the color and font of the contents of the edit box by selecting from a list of different styles.
- *Size*. The developer can set the size of the edit box to average size, maximum size, or custom size.
- *Alignment*. The developer can set the alignment of the contents of the field to automatic alignment (autoalignment), left alignment, or right alignment. Autoalignment will left-justify character fields and right-justify number fields.
- *Display options*. The developer can modify the display options of the edit box. Display options that can be modified by the developer include the following options:

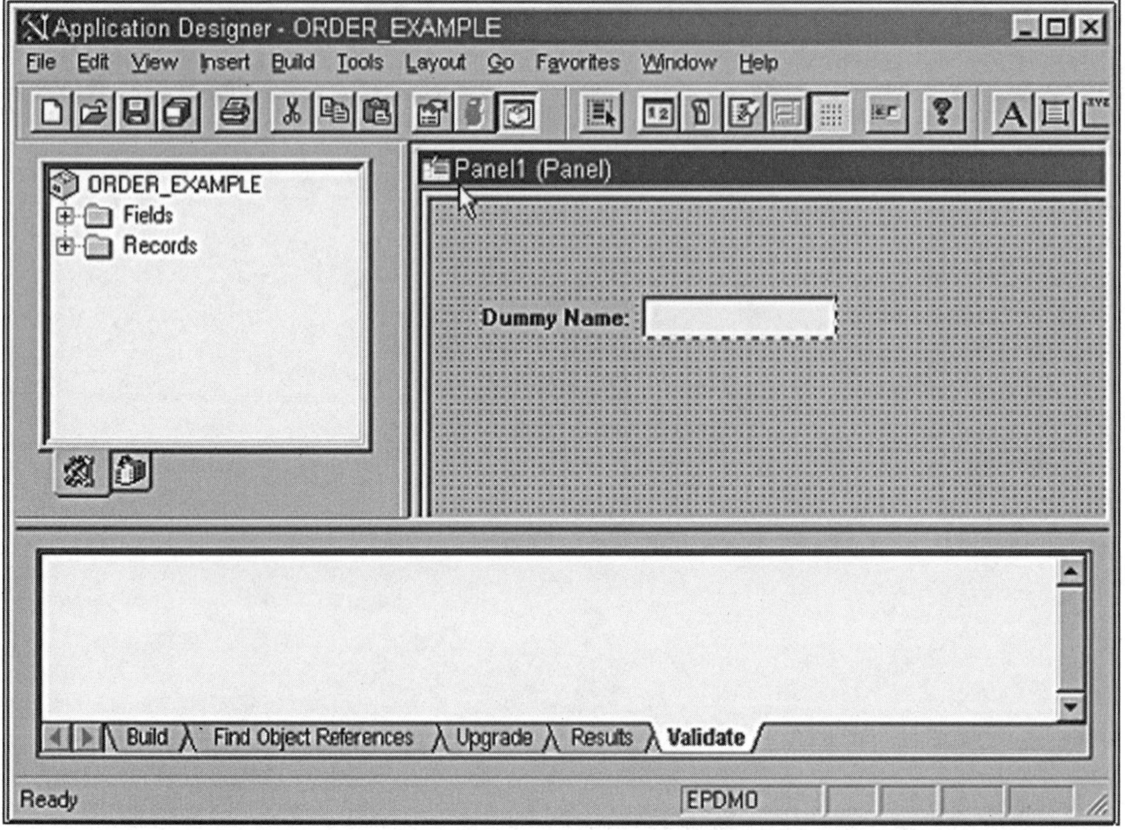

Figure 7-9 Appearance of the panel after the location of the EDIT BOX icon is selected.

Display zero. This display option will display a zero instead of a blank in the edit box.

Password. When the password display option is selected, the actual data value in the edit box will be displayed as asterisks.

Show prompt button. This display option displays a *prompt* button next to the edit box. This means that the edit box is associated with a prompt table. When the user clicks on the prompt button, the values from the *prompt* table for this field will be displayed.

Autofill. This display option automatically fills any blank portion of the edit box with the fill character entered in the fill character

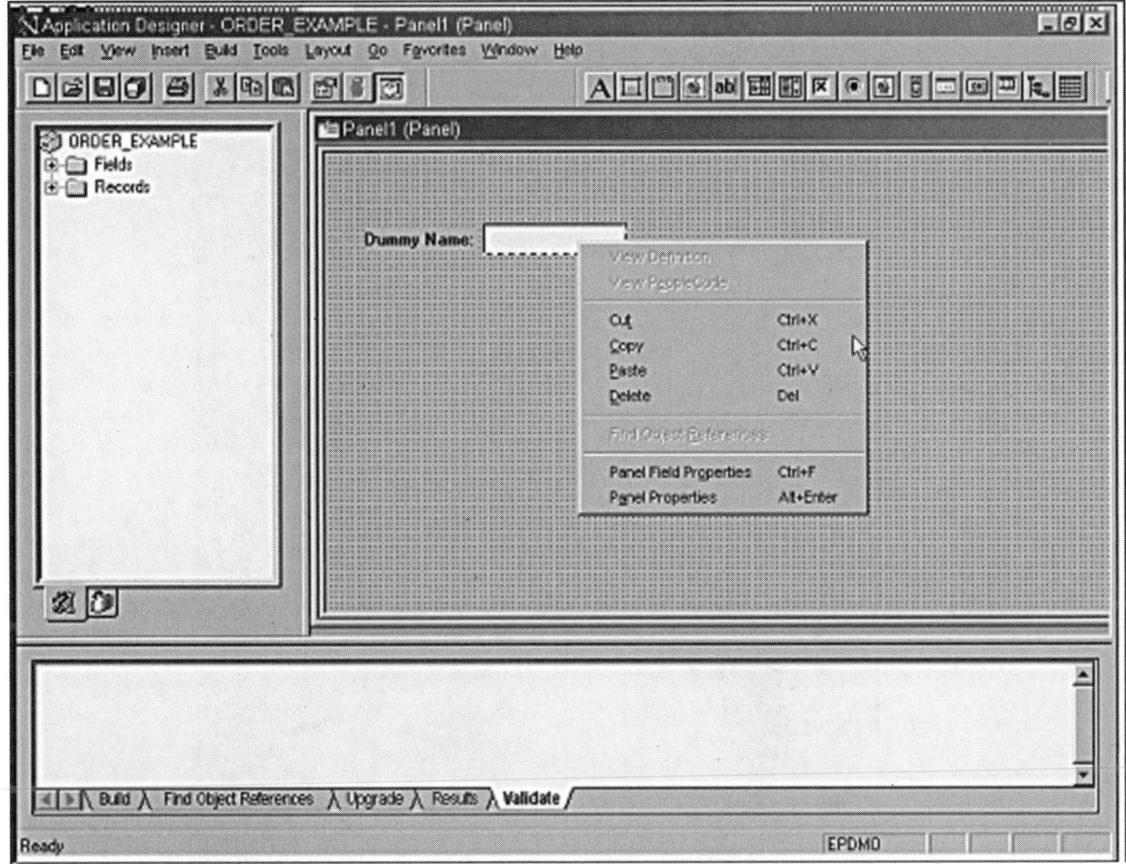

Figure 7-10 Popup menu appears when right-clicking a control on a panel.

box on the RECORD tab. This autofill feature affects the actual data as well as the display of the data.

Display century. This display option when selected allows the year to be entered with four digits. Otherwise the default century is 19.

Currency symbol. When this display option is selected, a currency symbol will be displayed in the edit box.

1000 separator. When this display option is selected, the data in the edit box will have 1000 separators to make the number easier to read.

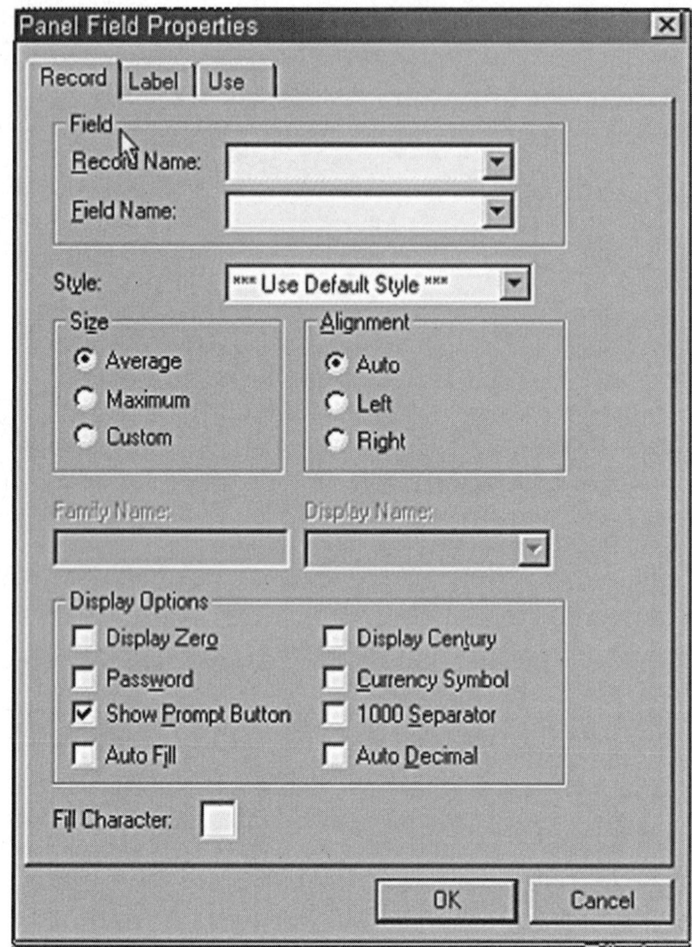

Figure 7-11 RECORD tab of the Panel Field Properties dialog box as it appears when inserting an edit box on a panel.

Autodecimal. When this display option is selected, the numeric value will automatically have a decimal point inserted in it. The location is based on how the number was defined when creating the field.

- *Fill character*. The developer can enter the value of the fill character. This means that where blanks would normally be displayed, the fill character will be displayed instead.

Once all the selections are made and are satisfactory to the developer, the developer should click on the OK button.

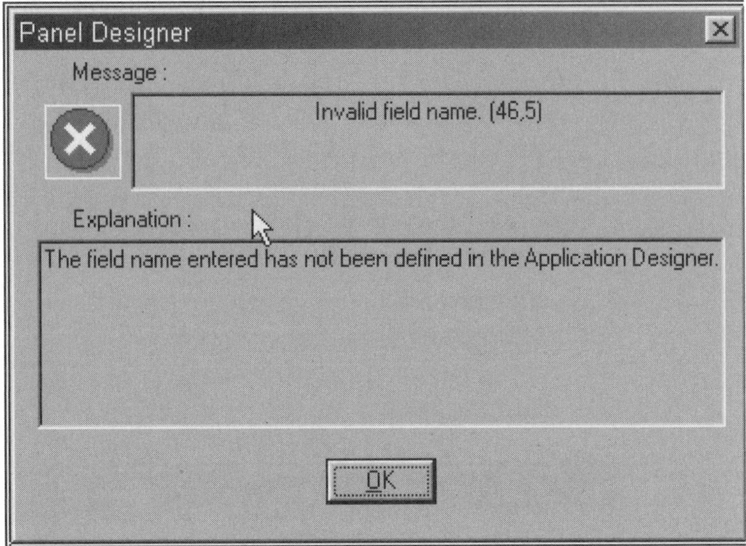

Figure 7-12 Error message displayed when entering invalid field name.

3. The next step is to enter the label that will appear next to the edit box. In order to do so, go to the LABEL tab of the Panel Field Properties dialog box. The LABEL tab allows the developer to enter the following:
   - *Type of Label*. There are four types of label from which the developer can choose:

     NONE. The label is not displayed on the panel.

     TEXT. The text that the developer enters in the text field of this tab is displayed next to the edit box.

     RFT SHORT. The field's short name that was entered when creating the field is displayed next to the edit box.

     RFT LONG. The field's long name that was entered when creating the field is displayed next to the edit box.
   - *Label text*. If the type of label is set to TEXT, then the text entered here is displayed next to the edit box. If the type of label is set to NONE, then the text entered here is just the name of the control and will not be displayed next to the edit box. If RFT SHORT or RFT LONG is selected for the label type, the label text is not applicable.
   - *Style*. The developer can change the color and font of the label by selecting from a list of different styles.

- *Alignment.* The developer can choose left alignment, centered alignment, or right alignment for the label of the edit box.
- *Display options.* The developer can choose "Use default position," "First occurs only," or "No colon."

Figure 7-13 displays the LABEL tab of the Panel Field Properties dialog box.

Once all the selections have been made on the LABEL tab, click on the OK button.

4. Finally, the developer may want to modify some options on the USE tab of the Panel Field Properties dialog box. For example, the edit

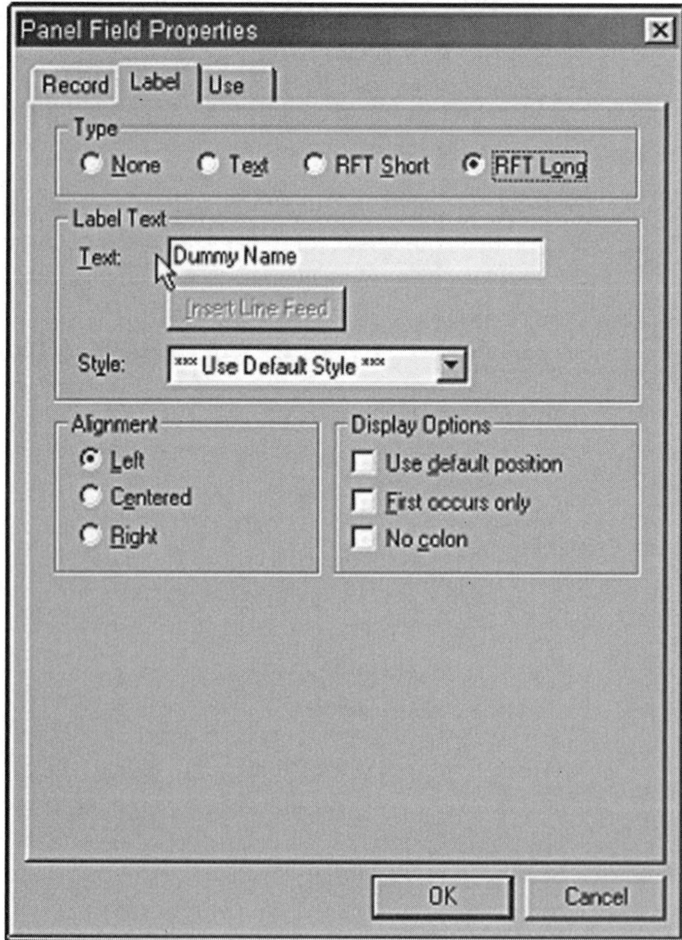

Figure 7-13 LABEL tab of the Panel Field Properties dialog box.

box can be a display-only field, an invisible field, a multicurrency field, a display control field, or a related display field.

- *Display only* means that the user can't change the value displayed in the edit box.
- *Invisible* means the control is invisible to users. When the control is invisible, the label can be displayed if show label is checked.
- A *multicurrency field* means that the field is displayed only if a multicurrency switch in the PeopleTools option panel was selected.
- A *display control field* means this field controls what is displayed in the related display field on the same panel. For example, the display control field could be employee id and the related display field could be employee name.
- A *related display field* means the contents displayed are controlled by the display field contents.

The field can also be associated with a popup menu. If this is the case, when that field on the panel is right-clicked on by the user, the popup menu selected on the USE tab will appear. When all selections are made on the USE tab, click on the OK button. Figure 7-14 shows the USE tab of the Panel Field Properties screen.

5. To save the panel at this point, if desired, the developer would select FILE, SAVE.

Long Edit Box

To insert a long edit box on a panel, perform the following steps:

1. Select INSERT, LONG EDIT BOX from the menu or click on the LONG EDIT BOX button on the toolbar (Fig. 7-15). Once the long edit box is selected, the LONG EDIT BOX icon appears. This icon is shaped like a hand with the index finger pointing. The developer must position the finger of the icon where he wants the top left corner of the long edit box to go. Then, the developer should press the left button on the mouse and hold it down while dragging the icon down and to the right. This action creates a rectangle that represents the long edit box. The developer should not release the button on the mouse until the long edit box is of the desired size and in the desired location on the panel. Figure 7-16 shows the panel after the developer clicks on the mouse to place it in the desired position.

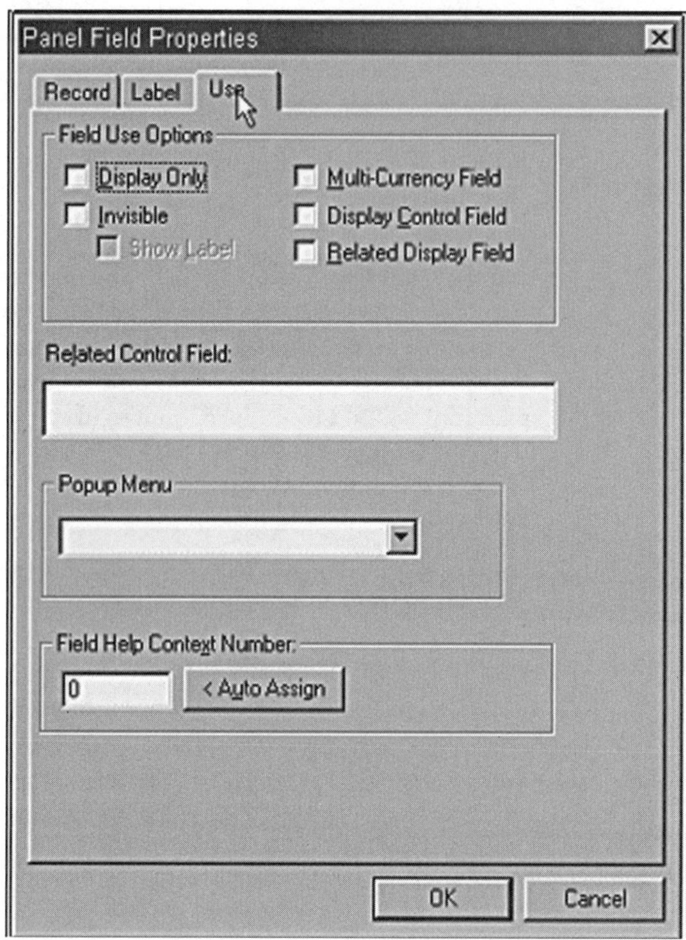

Figure 7-14
USE tab of the Panel Field Properties dialog box.

Figure 7-15
LONG EDIT BOX button from toolbar.

2. Once the long edit box is in the desired location on the panel, the next step is to associate the long edit box with a field from the record. To do this, double-click on the long edit box to bring up the Panel Field Properties dialog box. You could also right-click on the edit box to bring up the popup menu (Fig. 7-10) and then select Panel Field Properties. The Panel Field Properties dialog box is

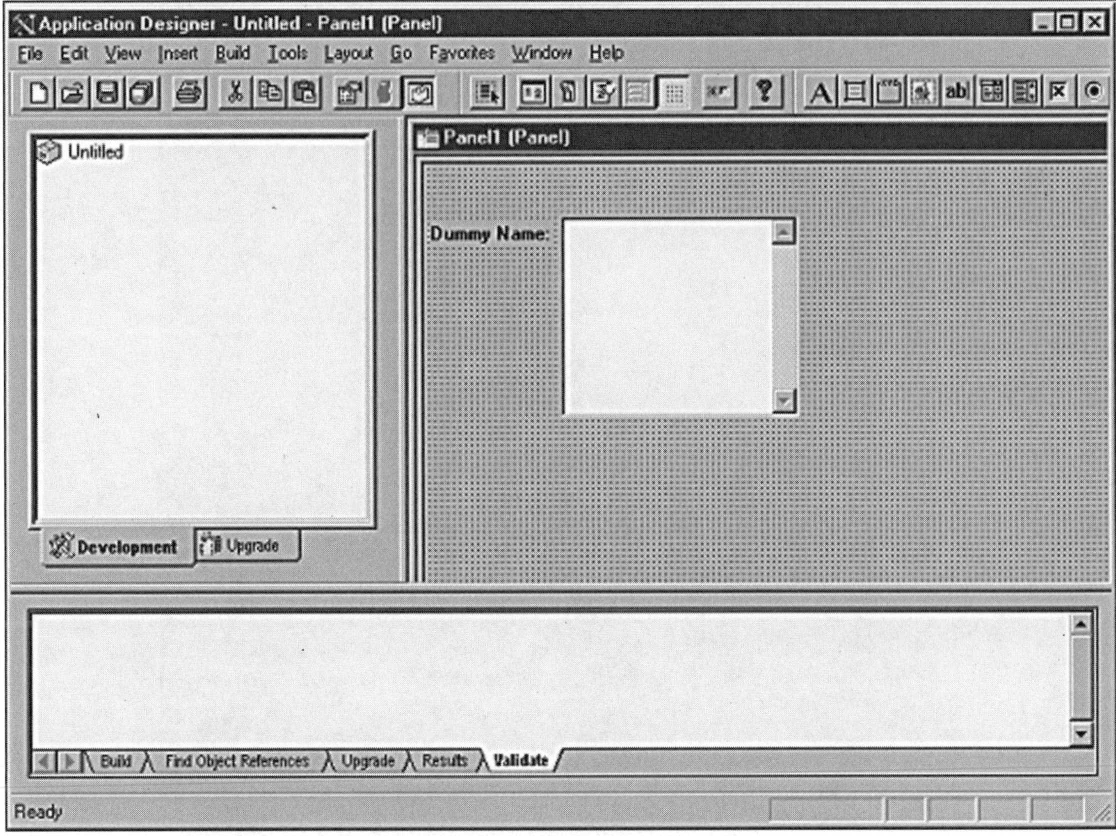

Figure 7-16 Long edit box as it appears on the new panel.

shown in Figure 7-17. Note that there are three tabs on this dialog box: a RECORD tab, a LABEL tab, and a USE tab. The default tab that is displayed is the RECORD tab. The RECORD tab allows the developer to enter the following information for the long edit box:

- *Record name.* The developer selects the record name from the drop-down list of records where the field that is to be associated with the long edit box is located.
- *Field name.* The developer selects the name of the field to be associated with the long edit box. Once a record is selected, only the fields belonging to that record are displayed and therefore may be selected. If the developer attempts to enter a field that is not in the record, an error message is displayed.

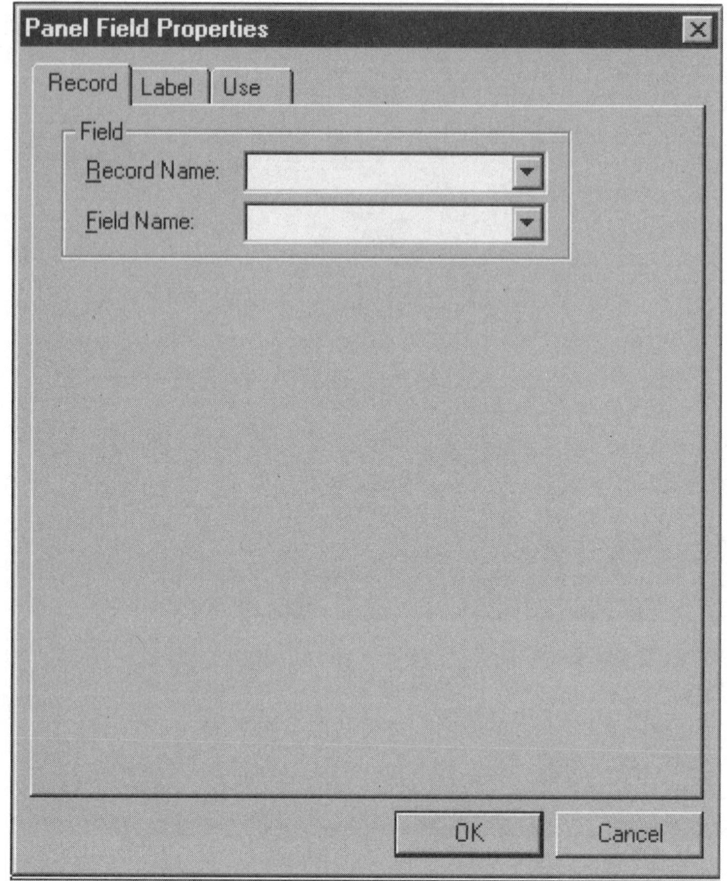

Figure 7-17 RECORD tab of the Panel Field Properties dialog box as it appears when inserting a long edit box on a panel.

3. The next step is to enter the label that will appear next to the long edit box. In order to do so, go to the LABEL tab of the Panel Field Properties dialog box. The LABEL tab of the Panel Field Properties dialog box for the long edit box is the same as the one for the edit box. The LABEL tab allows the developer to enter the following:
   - *Type of label.* NONE, TEXT, RFT SHORT, or RFT LONG.
   - *Label text.* If the type of label is set to TEXT, then the text entered here is displayed next to the long edit box. If the type of label is set to NONE, then the text entered here is just the name of the control and will not be displayed next to the long edit box. If

RFT SHORT or RFT LONG is selected for the label type, the label text is not applicable.

- *Style.* The developer can change the color and font of the label by selecting from a list of different styles.
- *Alignment.* The developer can choose left alignment, centered alignment, or right alignment for the label of the long edit box.
- *Display options.* The developer can choose "Use default position," "First occurs only," or "No colon."

3. Finally, bring up the USE tab of the Panel Field Properties dialog box and make the desired selections. The USE TAB as it appears for the long edit box is shown in Figure 7-18.
4. Save the panel by selecting FILE, SAVE.

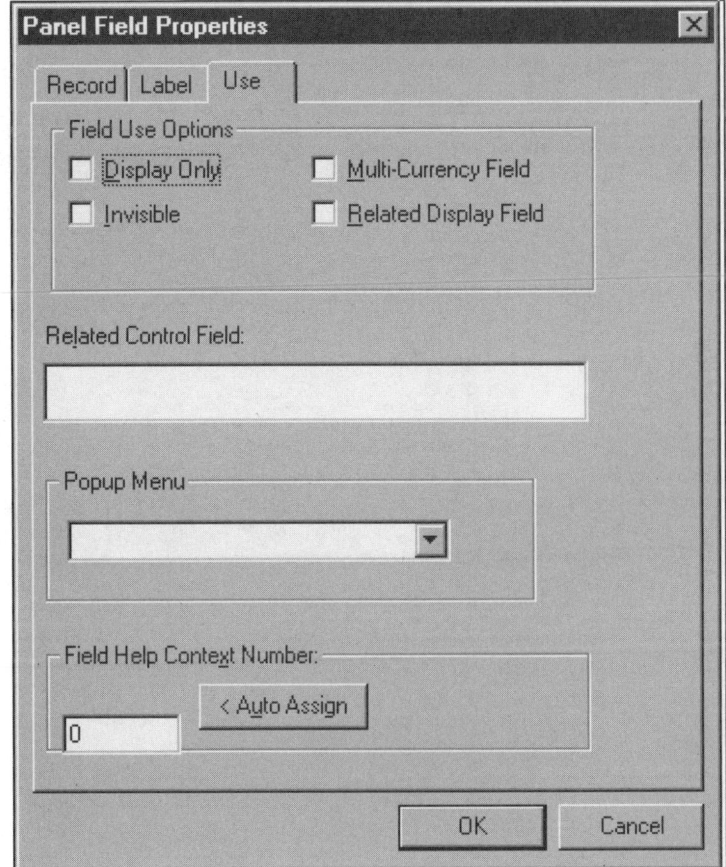

Figure 7-18
USE tab of the Panel Field Properties dialog box as it appears when inserting a long edit box.

Drop-Down List

To insert a drop-down list on a panel, perform the following steps:

1. Select INSERT, DROP DOWN LIST from the menu or click on the DROP-DOWN LIST button on the toolbar (Fig. 7-19). Once the drop-down list is selected, a DROP-DOWN LIST icon appears. The developer must place the icon in the desired position on the panel and click the mouse. Figure 7-20 shows the panel after the developer clicks on the mouse to place the drop-down list in the desired position.

Figure 7-19 DROP-DOWN LIST button from the toolbar.

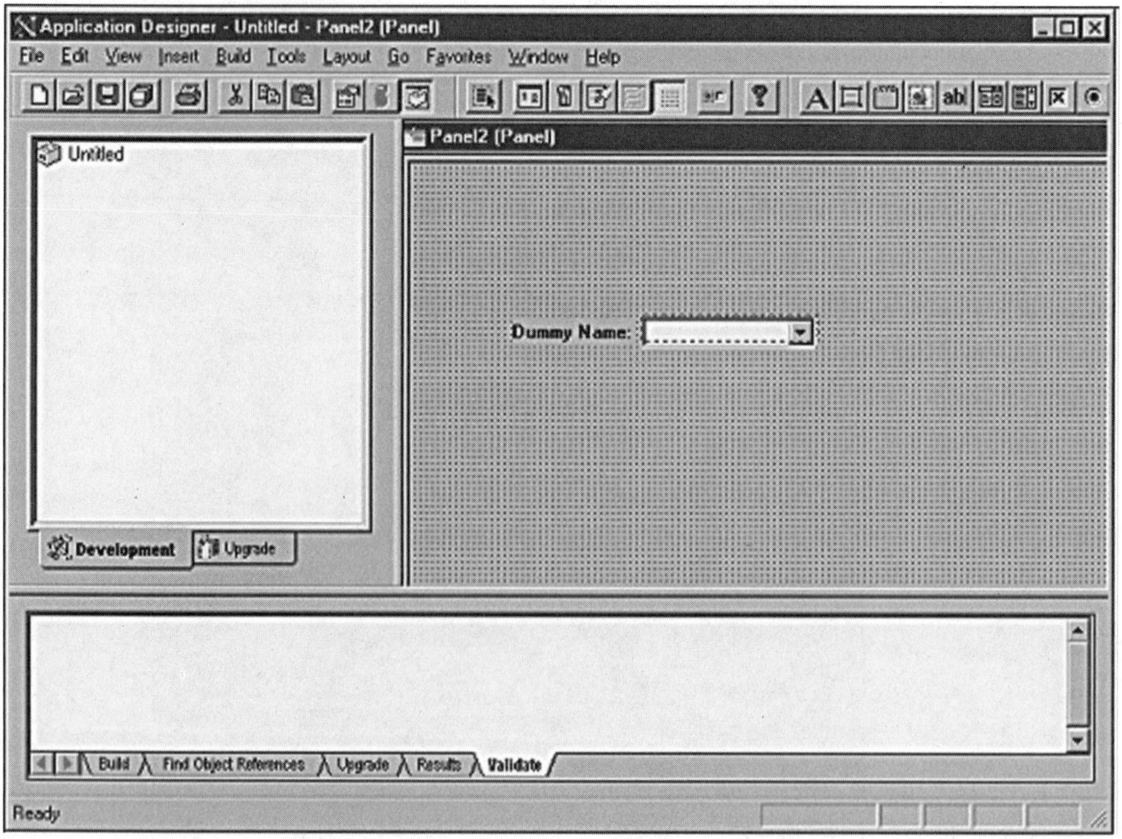

Figure 7-20 The drop-down list just inserted onto the new panel.

2. Once the drop-down list is in the desired location on the panel, the next step is to associate it with a field from the record. To do this, double-click on the drop-down list to bring up the Panel Field Properties dialog box. You could also right-click on the drop-down list to bring up the popup menu (Fig. 7-10) and then select Panel Field Properties. The Panel Field Properties dialog box is shown in Figure 7-21. Note that there are three tabs on this dialog box: a RECORD tab, a LABEL tab, and a USE tab. The default tab that is displayed is the RECORD tab, which allows the developer to enter the following information:
   - *Record name.* The developer selects the record name from the drop-down list of records where the field that is to be associated with the drop-down list is located.

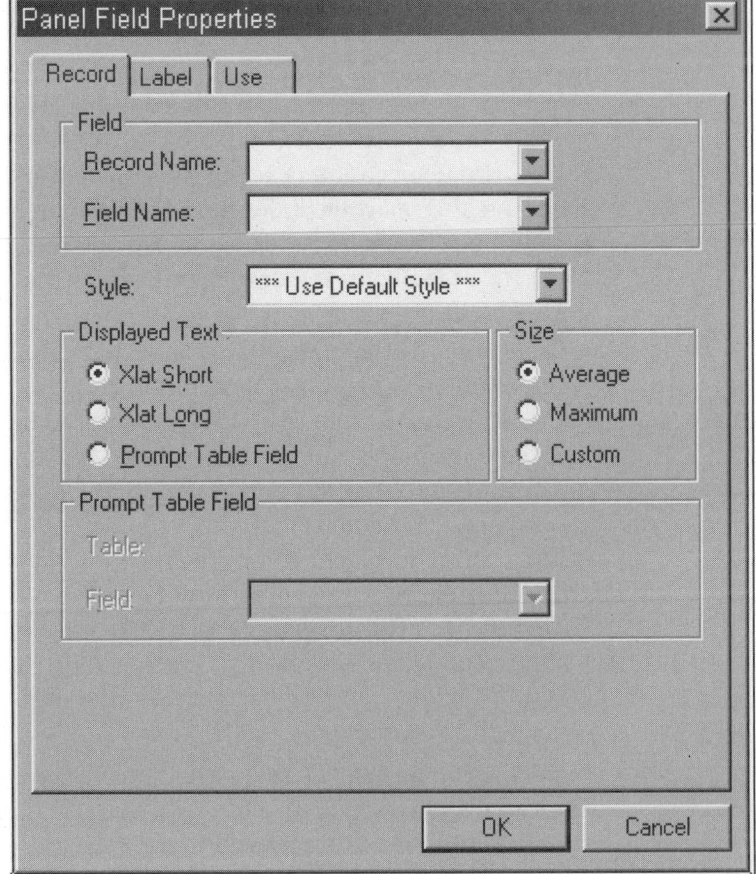

Figure 7-21 Record tab of the Panel Field Properties dialog box as it appears when inserting a drop down list control on to the panel.

- *Field name.* The developer selects the name of the field to be associated with the drop-down list. Once a record is selected, only the fields belonging to that record are displayed and therefore may be selected. If the developer attempts to enter a field that is not in the record an error message is displayed as shown in Figure 7-12.
- *Style.* The developer can change the color and font of the contents of the drop-down list by selecting from a list of different styles.
- *Size.* The developer can set the size of the drop-down list to average size, maximum size, or custom size.
- *Displayed text.* The developer selects whether the text displayed is the short translate name, the long translate name, or a field from a prompt table.

Once all the selections are made and are satisfactory to the developer, the developer should click on the OK button.

3. The LABEL tab of the Panel Field Properties dialog box allows the developer to modify the label text that appears next to the drop-down list control. As mentioned in step 2, the developer must select one of the three radio buttons for display text (XLAT SHORT, XLAT LONG, or PROMPT TABLE FIELD). If XLAT SHORT is selected, then the short name is automatically filled in on the LABEL tab of the Panel Field Properties dialog box. Therefore, to change this text, the developer must go to the LABEL tab and modify it accordingly. The LABEL tab allows the developer to enter the following:
   - *Type of label.* NONE, TEXT, RFT SHORT, or RFT LONG.
   - *Label text.* If the type of label is set to TEXT, then the text entered here is displayed next to the drop-down list. If the type of label is set to NONE, then the text entered here is just the name of the control and will not be displayed next to the drop-down list. If RFT SHORT or RFT LONG is selected for the label type, the label text is not applicable.
   - *Style.* The developer can change the color and font of the label by selecting from a list of different styles.
   - *Alignment.* The developer can choose left alignment, centered alignment, or right alignment for the label of the drop-down list.
   - *Display options.* The developer can choose "Use default position," "First occurs only," or "No colon."
4. Finally, bring up the USE tab of the Panel Field Properties dialog box and make the desired selections. The USE tab as it appears for the drop-down list is shown in Figure 7-22.

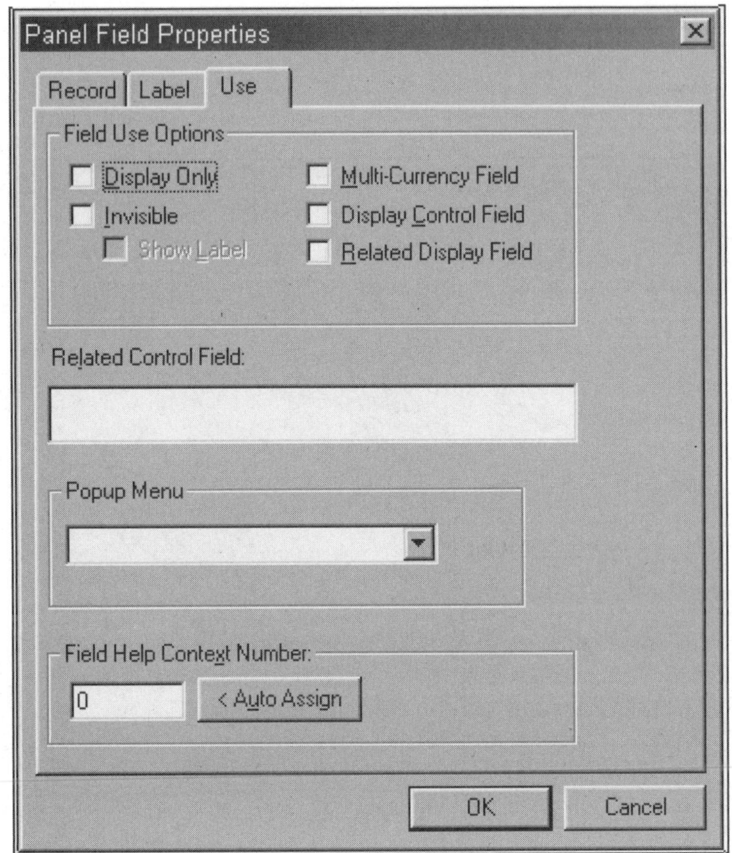

Figure 7-22
USE tab of Panel Field Properties dialog box as it appears for drop-down lists.

Check Box

To insert a check box on a panel, perform the following steps:

1. Select INSERT, CHECK BOX from the menu or click on the CHECK BOX button on the toolbar (Fig. 7-23). Once the check box is selected, a CHECK BOX icon appears. The developer must place the icon in the desired position on the panel and click the mouse. Figure 7-24 shows the panel after the developer clicks on the mouse to place the check box in the desired position.
2. Once the check box is in the desired location on the panel, the next step is to associate the checkbox with a field from the record. To do this, double-click on the check box to bring up the Panel Field

Figure 7-23
CHECK-BOX button.

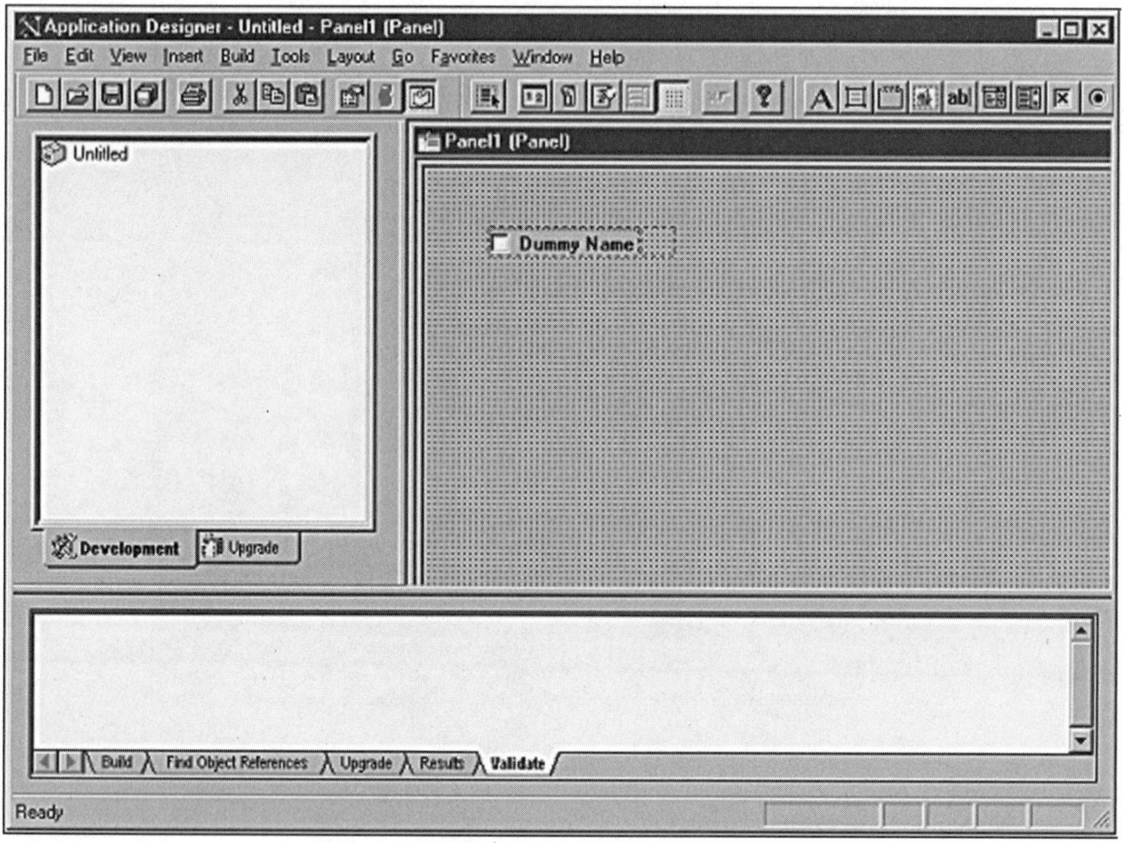

Figure 7-24 The check-box control immediately following insertion onto a new panel.

Properties dialog box. You could also right-click on the check box to bring up the popup menu (Fig. 7-10) and then select Panel Field Properties. The RECORD tab for check-box controls (Fig. 7-25) allows the developer to enter the following information:

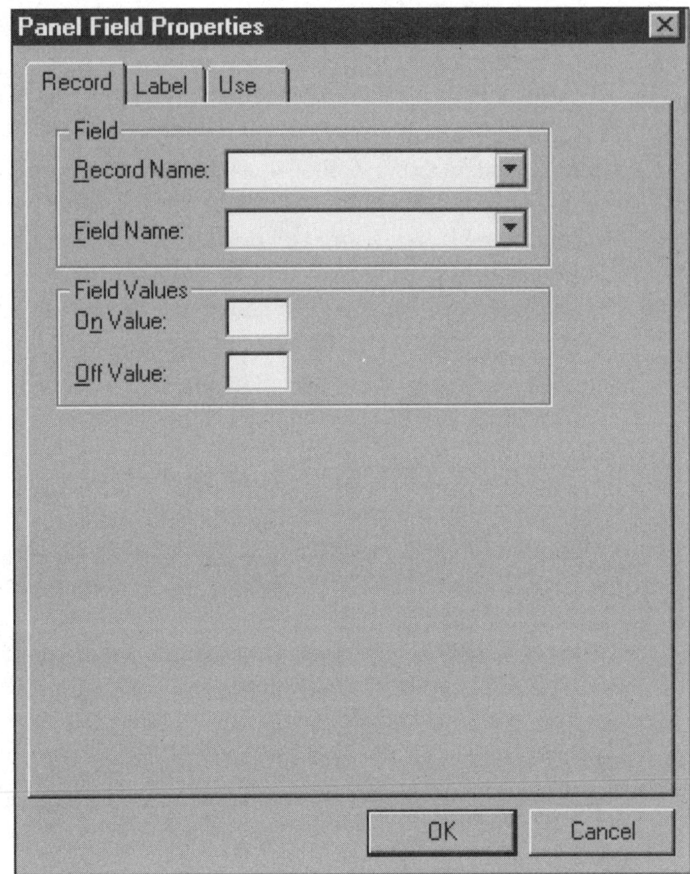

Figure 7-25
RECORD tab as it appears for check-box controls.

- *Record name.* The developer selects the record name from the drop-down list of records where the field that is to be associated with the check box is located.
- *Field name.* The developer selects the name of the field to be associated with the check box. Once a record is selected, only the fields belonging to that record are displayed and therefore may be selected. If the developer attempts to enter a field that is not in the record, an error message is displayed as shown in Figure 7-12.
- *Field values.* The developer must enter the ON value for the checkbox and the OFF value for the checkbox. The ON value is the value to be written to the database when the check box is

checked. The OFF value is the value to be written to the database when the check box is not checked.

Once all the selections are made and are satisfactory to the developer, the developer should click on the OK button.

3. Bring up the LABEL tab of the Panel Field Properties dialog box to make any modifications to the check box label type, label text, or alignment. In addition, the developer can choose to place the label to the left of the check box or to the right of the check box via the Location field. Figure 7-26 shows the LABEL tab of the Panel Field Properties dialog box for check boxes.
4. Finally, bring up the USE tab of the Panel Field Properties dialog box and make the desired selections.

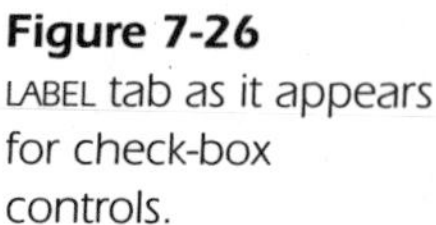

Figure 7-26 LABEL tab as it appears for check-box controls.

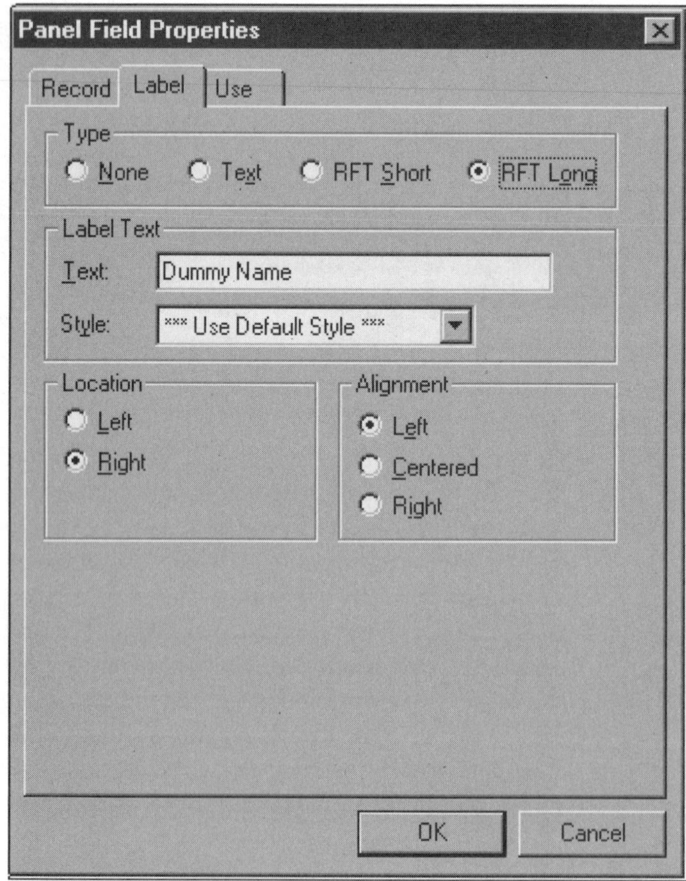

Radio Button

To insert a radio button on a panel, perform the following steps:

1. Select INSERT, RADIO BUTTON from the menu or click on the RADIO BUTTON button on the toolbar (Fig. 7-27). Once the radio button is selected, a RADIO BUTTON icon appears. The developer must place the icon in the desired position on the panel and click the mouse. Figure 7-28 shows the panel after the developer clicks on the mouse to place the radio button in the desired position.

Figure 7-27
RADIO BUTTON button.

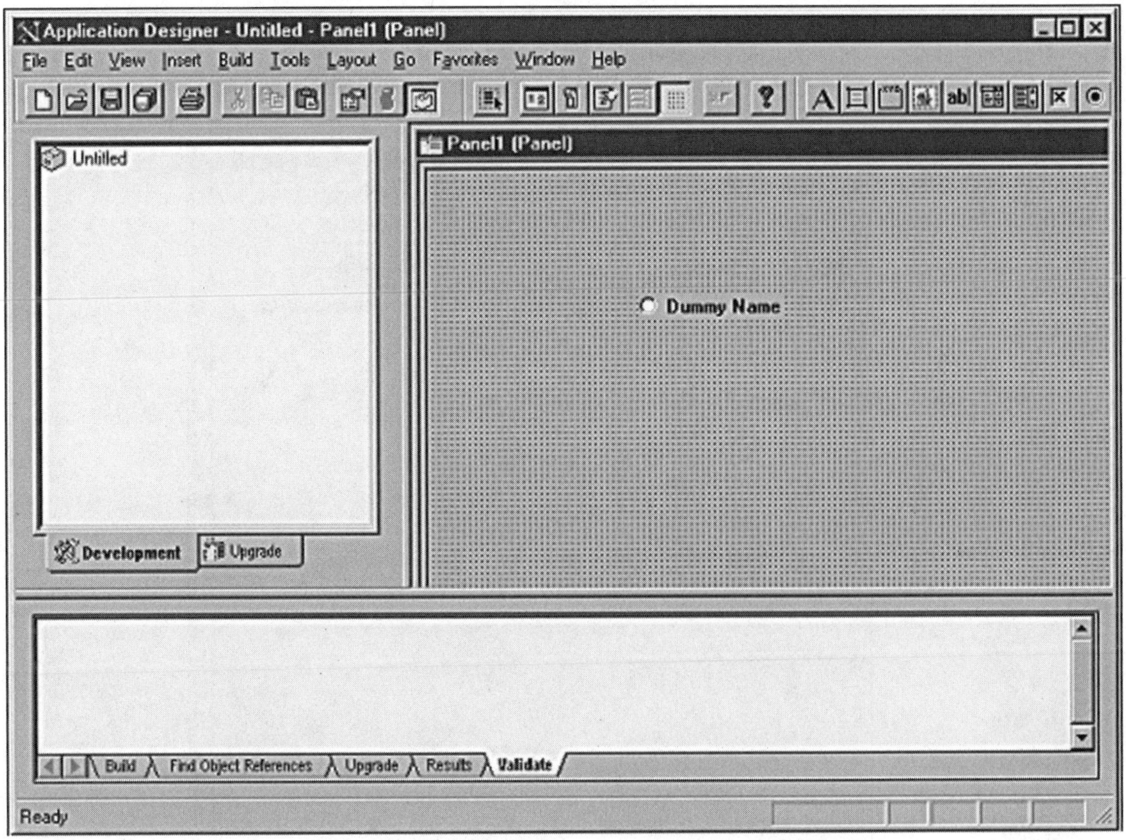

Figure 7-28 The radio button control immediately after insertion onto a new panel.

2. Once the radio button is in the desired location on the panel, the next step is to associate it with a field from the record. To do this, double-click on the radio button to bring up the Panel Field Properties dialog box. You could also right-click on the radio button to bring up the popup menu (Fig. 7-10) and then select Panel Field Properties. The RECORD tab of the Panel Field Properties dialog box is shown in Figure 7-29. The record tab for radio button controls allows the developer to enter the following information:
   - *Record name.* The developer selects the record name from the drop-down list of records where the field that is to be associated with the radio button is located.
   - *Field name.* The developer selects the name of the field to be associated with the radio button. Once a record is selected, only the fields belonging to that record are displayed and therefore may

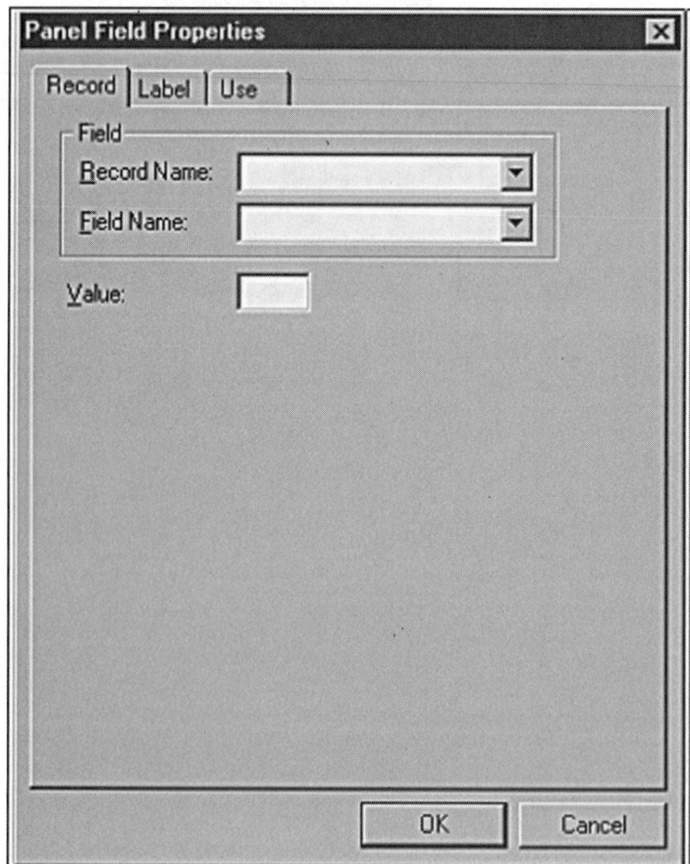

Figure 7-29 RECORD tab as it appears for radio button controls.

be selected. If the developer attempt to enter a field that is not in the record, an error message is displayed as shown in Figure 7-12.

- *Value*. The developer must enter the value that will be written to the database when this radio button is selected.

Once all the selections are made and are satisfactory to the developer, the developer should click on the OK button.

3. Bring up the LABEL tab of the Panel Field Properties dialog box to make any modifications to the radio button label type, label text, or location. Refer to Figure 7-30 to view the LABEL tab of the Panel Field Properties dialog box as it appears for radio buttons.
4. Finally, bring up the USE tab of the Panel Field Properties dialog box and make the desired selections.

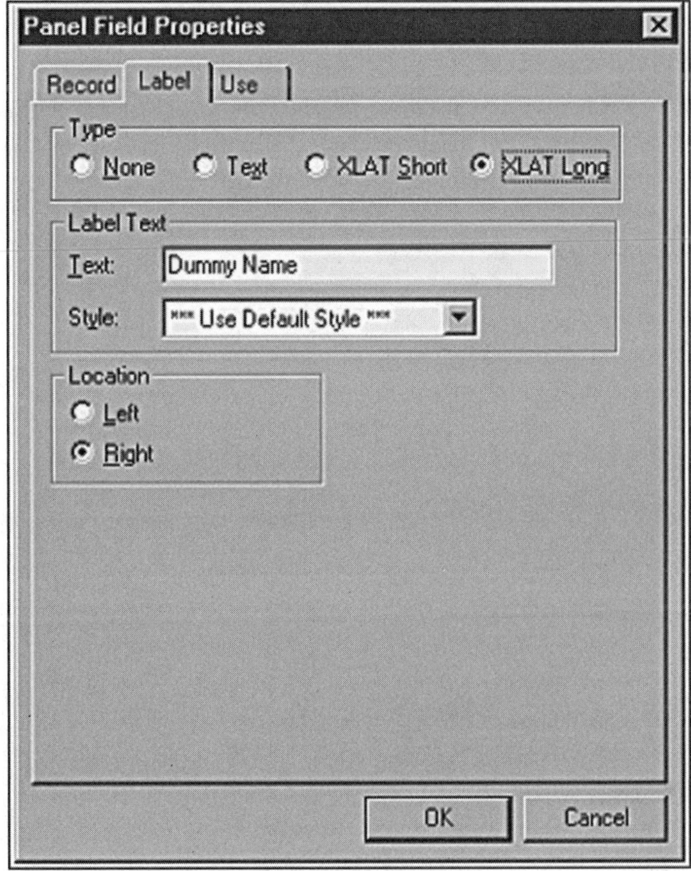

Figure 7-30
LABEL tab of the Panel Field Properties dialog box as it appears for radio buttons.

Push Button

To insert a push-button control on a panel, perform the following steps:

1. Select INSERT, PUSH BUTTON from the menu or click on the PUSH BUTTON button on the toolbar (Fig. 7-31). Once the push button is selected, a PUSH BUTTON icon appears. The developer must place the icon in the desired position on the panel and click the mouse. Figure 7-32 shows the panel after the developer clicks on the mouse to place the push button in the desired position.

Figure 7-31 PUSH BUTTON button.

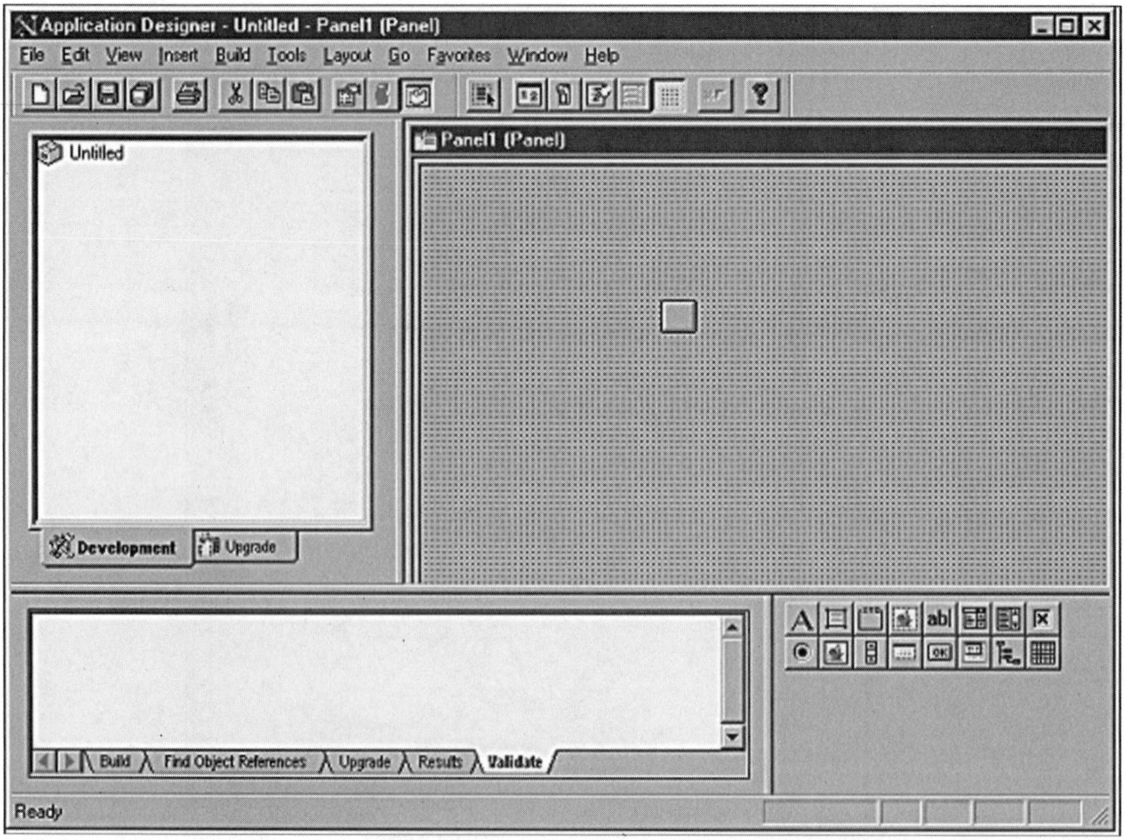

Figure 7-32 The push-button control just inserted onto a new panel.

2. Once the push button is in the desired location on the panel, the next step is to associate it with a field on a panel. To do this, double-click on the push button to bring up the Panel Field Properties dialog box.

   The RECORD tab for push-button controls allows the developer to select the push-button type. Based on the push-button type, PeopleCode, a process defined in the Process Scheduler, or a secondary panel will be run when the push button is pressed at run time. The push button can be one of the following types:

   - *Command.* When a push button is set up as a command push button, the developer must enter a record name and a field name. The field that is entered in on the record tab will be modified when the push button is pressed on the basis of the PeopleCode that is associated with the push button. This field must have PeopleCode in the Field Change event. The RECORD tab with a push-button-type command is shown in Figure 7-33.
   - *Process.* When a push button is set up as a process push button, the developer must enter the process type and name. Then, when

Figure 7-33
RECORD tab of the Panel Field Properties dialog box as it appears for push-button controls when the type is set to command.

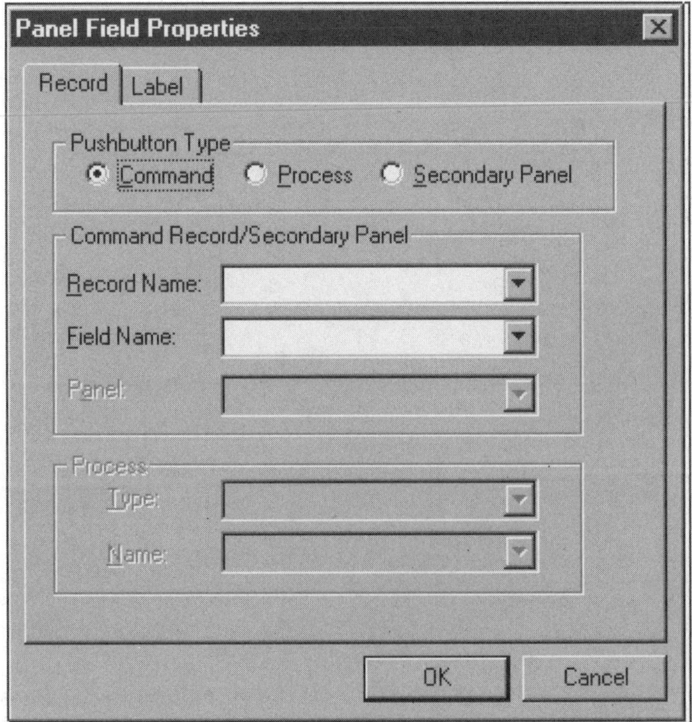

the push button is pressed, the process will be run. The process entered is a process that was setup in the Process Scheduler. Figure 7-34 shows the RECORD tab of the Panel Field Properties dialog box with a push-button-type process.

- *Secondary panel.* When a push button is set up as a secondary panel push button, the developer must enter the associated record and field name and the name of the secondary panel. When the push button is pressed, the secondary panel will be displayed on the screen. The RECORD tab with a push-button-type secondary panel is shown in Figure 7-35.

3. The next step is to bring up the LABEL tab of the Panel Field Properties dialog box and modify the desired options. The LABEL tab for push buttons allows the developer to modify the following:
   - *Type of label.* There are four types of label to choose from:
     IMAGE. When the developer selects type of image, an image will be displayed inside the push button.

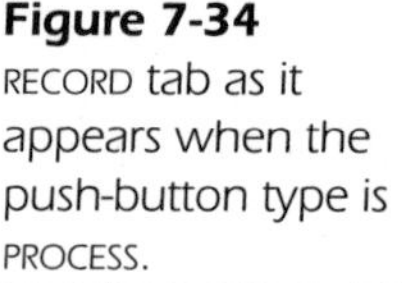

Figure 7-34
RECORD tab as it appears when the push-button type is PROCESS.

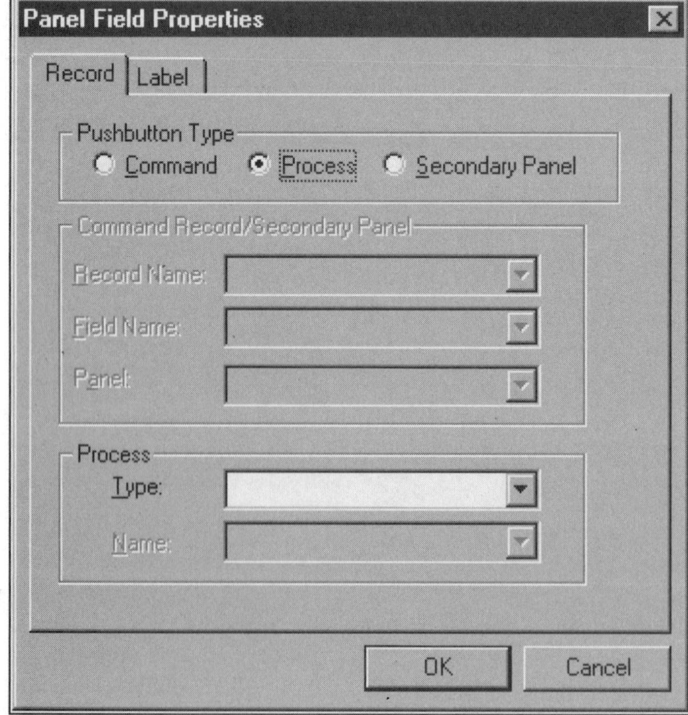

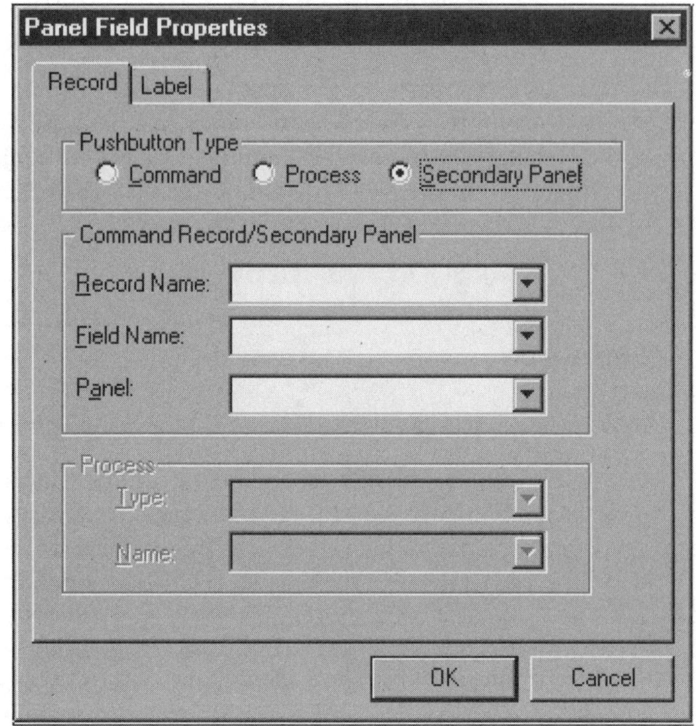

Figure 7-35
Record Tab as it appears when the push-button type is SECONDARY PANEL.

TEXT. The text that the developer enters in the Label Text field of this tab is displayed on the push button.

RFT SHORT. The field's short name that was entered when creating the field is displayed inside the push button.

RFT LONG. The field's long name that was entered when creating the field is displayed inside the push button.

- *Label text.* If the type of label is set to TEXT, then the text entered here is displayed inside the push button. Otherwise, the label text will just be informational and will not be displayed inside the push button.
- *Style.* The developer can change the color and font of the label by selecting from a list of different styles.
- *Size.* The developer can set the size of the push button to SMALL IMAGE, LARGE IMAGE, or STANDARD TEXT. If none of these sizes is desired, the developer can select CUSTOM and then resize the push button to the desired size.

- *Image*. If the type is set to IMAGE, then the developer can *browse* through the directories of images, *paste* an image, or *clear* the image.

  Once all the selections are made and are satisfactory to the developer, the developer should click on the OK button. Refer to Figure 7-36 to view the LABEL tab of the Panel Field Properties dialog as it appears for push buttons.

4. Save the panel by selecting FILE, SAVE.

Images

To insert an image control on a panel, perform the following steps:

1. Select INSERT, IMAGE from the menu or click on the IMAGE button on the toolbar (Fig. 7-37). Once the image is selected, the IMAGE icon (a hand with the index finger pointing outward with the letter I inside the hand) appears. The developer must position the finger of the icon where he wants the top left corner of the image control to go.

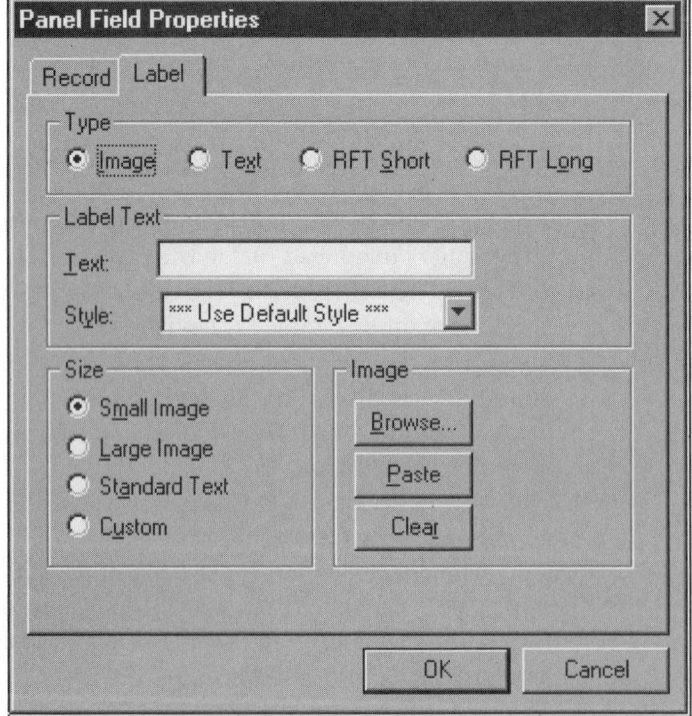

Figure 7-36 LABEL tab of the Panel Field Properties dialog box as it appears for push buttons.

Figure 7-37
IMAGE button.

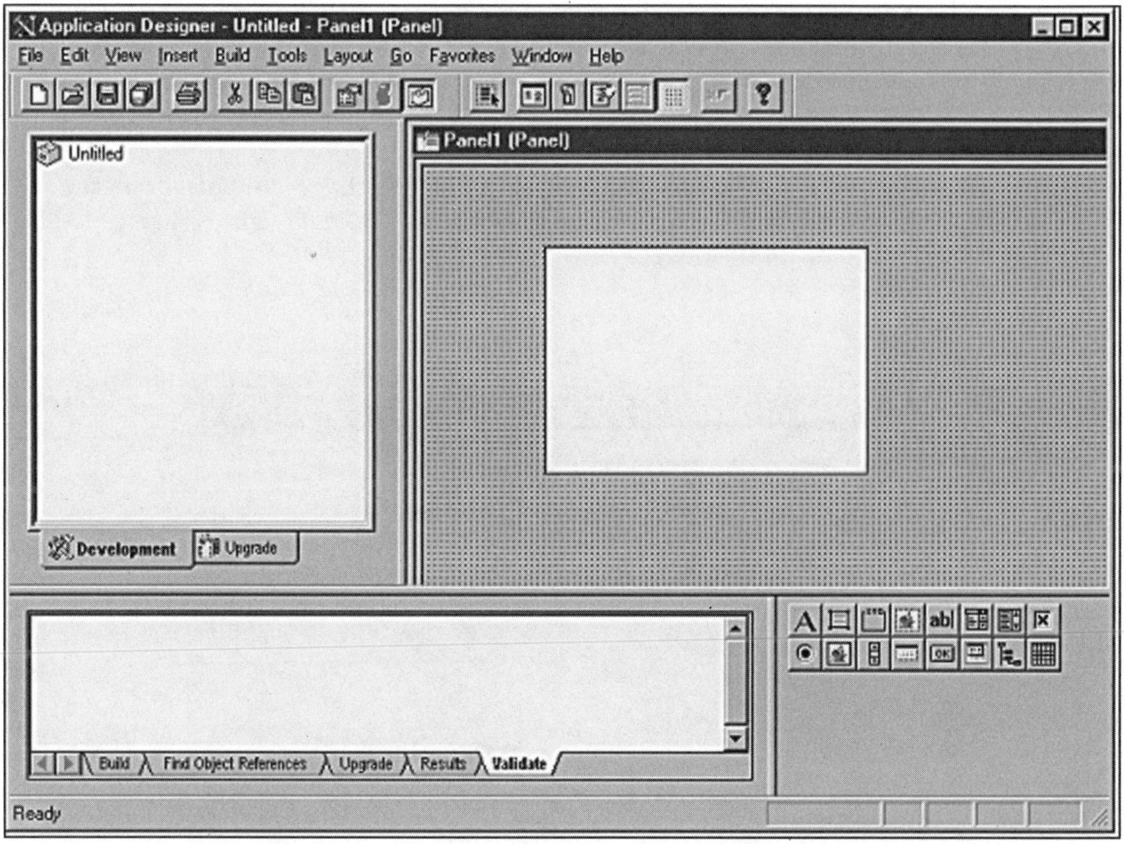

Figure 7-38 The image control immediately after it has been inserted onto the new panel.

Then, the developer should press the left button on the mouse and hold it down while dragging the icon down and to the right. This action creates a rectangle that represents the outline of the image control. The developer should not release the button on the mouse until the image control is of the desired size and in the desired location on the panel. Note that once the image control is on the panel, it can be selected and then can be resized by pulling the handles with the mouse. Figure 7-38 shows the panel after the developer clicks on the mouse to place it in the desired position.

2. Once the image control is in the desired location on the panel, the next step is to associate it with a field from the record. To do this, double-click on the image control to bring up the Panel Field Properties dialog box. You could also right-click on the check box to bring up the popup menu (Fig. 7-10) and then select Panel Field Properties. The Record Tab of the Panel Field Properties dialog box as it appears for image controls is shown in Figure 7-39. The RECORD tab for image controls allows the developer to enter the following information:
   - *Record name.* The developer selects the record name from the drop-down list of records where the field that is to be associated with the image control is located.

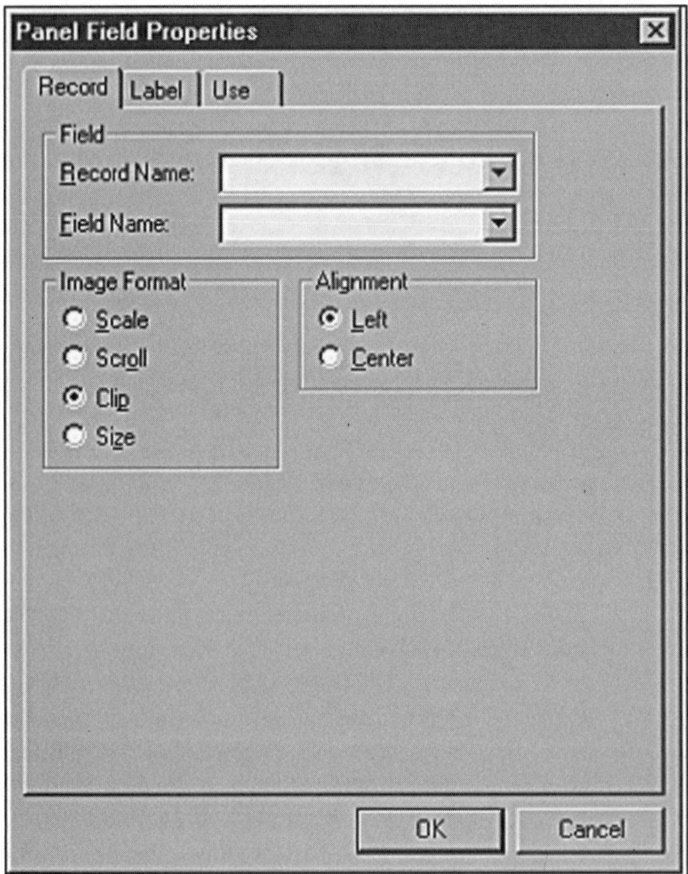

Figure 7-39 RECORD tab as it appears for image controls.

- *Field name.* The developer selects the name of the field to be associated with the image control.
- *Image format.* The developer chooses to have the image displayed in the scale format, scroll format, clip format, or size format.
- *Alignment.* The developer selects whether the image alignment inside the image control is left or center.

Once all the selections are made and are satisfactory to the developer, the developer should click on the OK button.

3. Bring up the LABEL tab of the Panel Field Properties dialog box to enter a brief description of the image control. Figure 7-40 shows

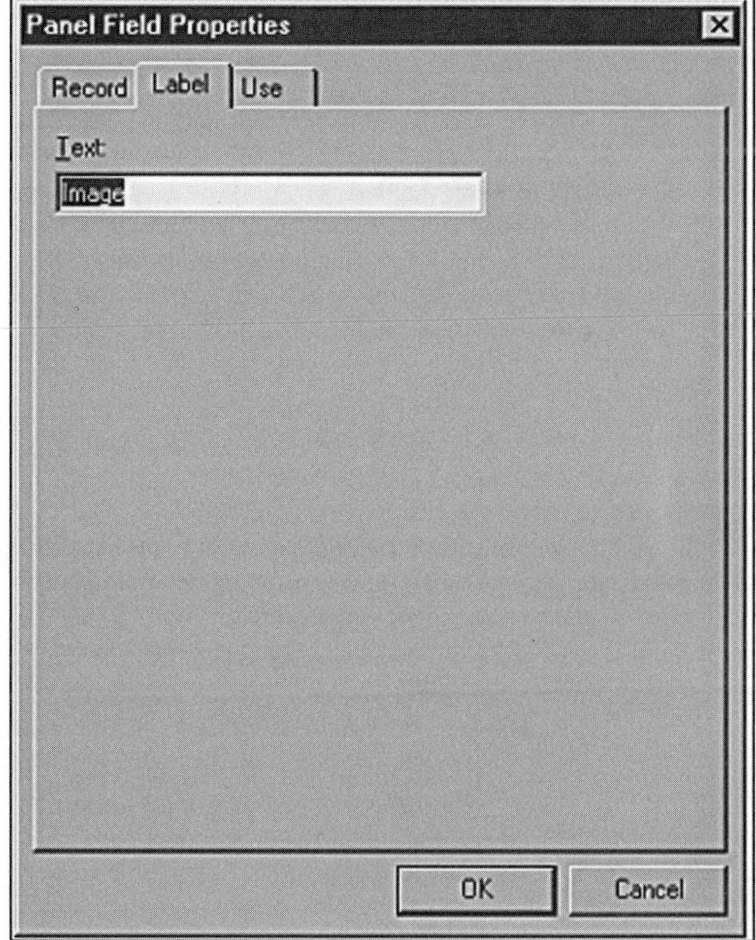

Figure 7-40
LABEL tab as it appears for image controls.

the LABEL tab of the Panel Field Properties dialog box for image controls.

4. Finally, bring up the USE tab of the Panel Field Properties dialog box and make the desired selections.

Text Controls

To insert a text control on a panel, perform the following steps:

1. Select INSERT, TEXT from the menu or click on the TEXT button on the toolbar (Fig. 7-41). Once the text control is selected, a TEXT icon appears. The developer must place the icon in the desired position on the panel and click the mouse. Figure 7-42 shows the panel after the developer clicks on the mouse to place the text control in the desired position.
2. The next step is to bring up the LABEL tab of the Panel Field Properties dialog box. To do so, double-click on the text control. The LABEL tab allows the developer to enter the text that will be displayed on the text control. If desired, the developer can place line feeds in the text so that the text will be displayed on more than one line by simply placing the cursor in the desired position and clicking on the INSERT LINE FEED button. Also, the developer must choose the style and the alignment desired for the text. Figure 7-43 shows what the LABEL tab looks like for text controls. This figure illustrates an example of what the text field looks like when line feeds are inserted. Figure 7-44 shows the text control on the panel. Note that the text is on multiple lines. Once the label settings are as desired, click on OK.
3. Bring up the USE tab of the Panel Field Properties dialog box only if the text control is a multicurrency field, as this is the only option on the USE tab for text controls.
4. Save the panel by selecting FILE, SAVE. Note that it is not necessary to save the panel after each control is inserted. However, it is mentioned here for completeness if this were the last control being added. In addition, it is a good idea to save your work often.

Figure 7-41
TEXT button.

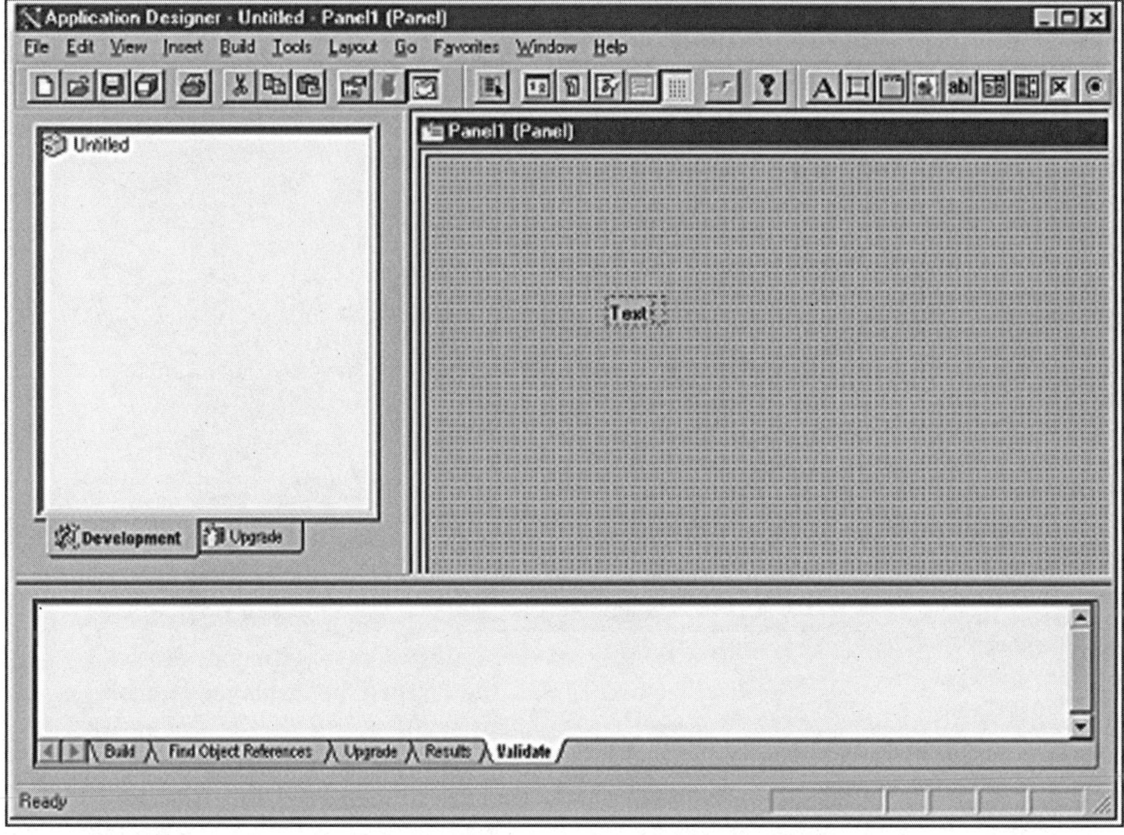

Figure 7-42 Text control immediately following insertion onto the new panel.

Frames

To insert a frame on a panel, perform the following steps:

1. Select INSERT, FRAME from the menu or click on the FRAME button on the toolbar (Fig. 7-45). Once the frame is selected, the frame icon (a hand with the index finger pointing out with the letter F inside the hand) appears. The developer must position the finger of the icon where he wants the top left corner of the frame to go. Then, the developer should press the left button on the mouse and hold it down while dragging the icon down and to the right. This

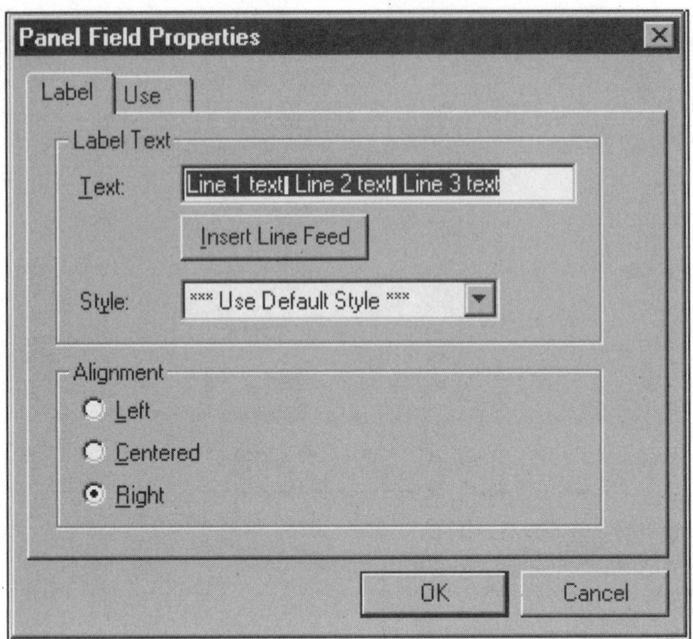

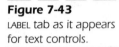

Figure 7-43
LABEL tab as it appears for text controls.

action creates a rectangle that represents the frame. The developer should not release the mouse button until the frame is of the desired size and in the desired location on the panel. Note that once the frame is on the panel, it can be selected and then can be resized by pulling the handles with the mouse. Figure 7-46 shows the panel after the developer clicks on the mouse to place the frame in the desired position.

2. There are no fields to associate with a frame since a frame is simply a box used to organize data on a panel. Therefore, the next step is to bring up the LABEL tab of the Panel Field Properties dialog box. The only purpose of this tab for frames is to allow the developer to enter text that describes what type of data the frame is surrounding. This text will not be displayed on the panel; it is merely for documentation purposes. Figure 7-47 shows the LABEL tab as it appears for frame controls. Click OK when satisfied with the description of the frame.
3. Bring up the USE tab of the Panel Field Properties dialog box only

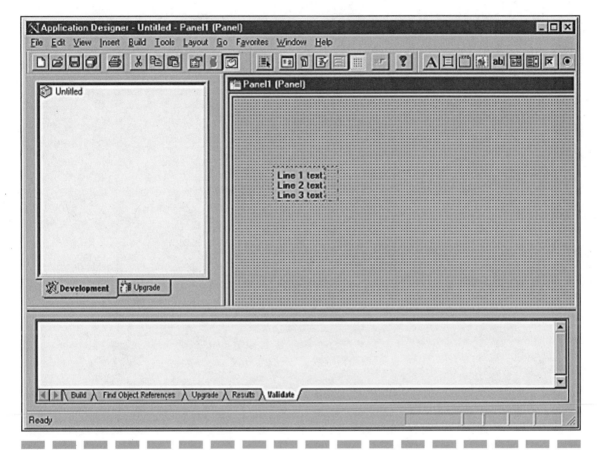

Figure 7-44 Text control created as a result of the label setup shown in Figure 7-43.

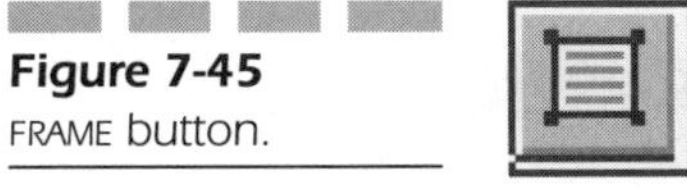

Figure 7-45
FRAME button.

if the frame control is a multicurrency field, as this is the only option on the USE tab for frames.

4. Save the panel by selecting FILE, SAVE if desired.

Note that the frame control can be used to create horizontal or vertical lines on the panel also.

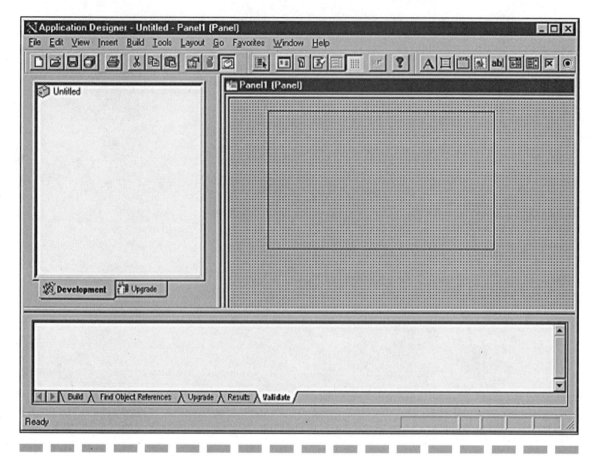

Figure 7-46 Frame control immediately after it has been inserted onto a new panel.

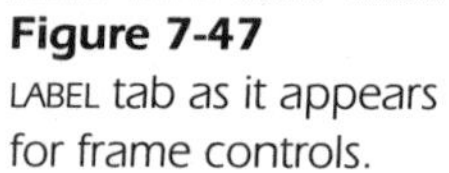

Figure 7-47 LABEL tab as it appears for frame controls.

Group Box Controls

To insert a group box control on a panel, perform the following steps:

1. Select INSERT, GROUP BOX from the menu or click on the GROUP BOX button on the toolbar (Fig. 7-48). Once the group box is selected, the group box icon (a hand with the index finger pointing out with the letter B inside the hand) appears. The finger of the icon must be positioned to indicate where the top left corner of the group box should go. Then, the developer should press the left button on the mouse and hold it down while dragging the icon down and to the right. This action creates a rectangle that represents the group box. The developer should not release the button on the mouse until the group box is of the desired size and in the desired location on the panel. Note that once the group box is on the panel, it can be selected and then can be resized by pulling the handles with the mouse. Figure 7-49 shows the panel after the developer clicks on the mouse to place the group box in the desired position.
2. Bring up the RECORD tab of the Panel Field Properties dialog box to associate the group box with a record name and a field name, if desired. The RECORD tab does not have to be utilized for all group boxes, however; that is, it is not necessary to associate the group box with a record name and field name. The RECORD tab is available if it is desired to do so. One example of when this would make sense is when grouping radio buttons together. The field associated with the group box can be only one value: one of the radio button values. If it is not desired to associate the group box with a record's field, skip this step when creating the group box. Figure 7-50 shows the RECORD tab as it appears for group box controls.
3. The next step is to go to the LABEL tab and enter the Label Type, Label Text, and Label Text Style. When satisfied, click OK. Figure 7-51 shows the LABEL tab with the Label Type set to TEXT and with the Text set to OUR GROUP BOX TEXT. Figure 7-52 shows what the group box setup shown in Figure 7-51 would look like.

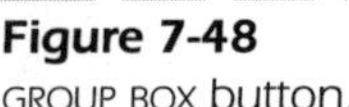

Figure 7-48
GROUP BOX button.

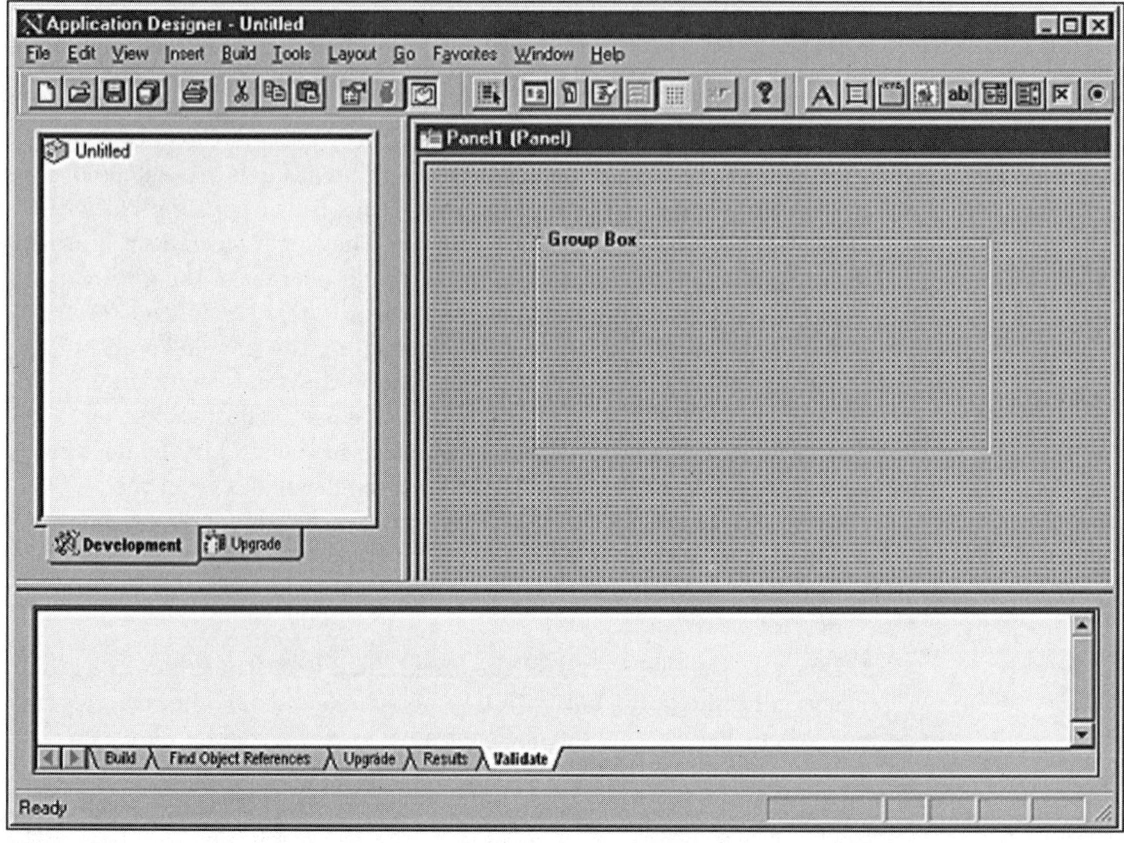

Figure 7-49 Group box immediately following insertion on the new panel.

Figure 7-50 RECORD tab as it appears for group box controls.

Figure 7-51
The LABEL tab as it appears for group boxes. The type is set to TEXT, and our label text is set to *our group box text.*

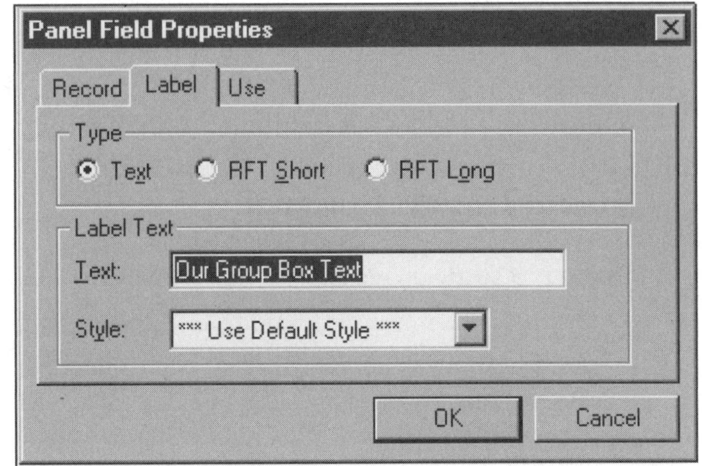

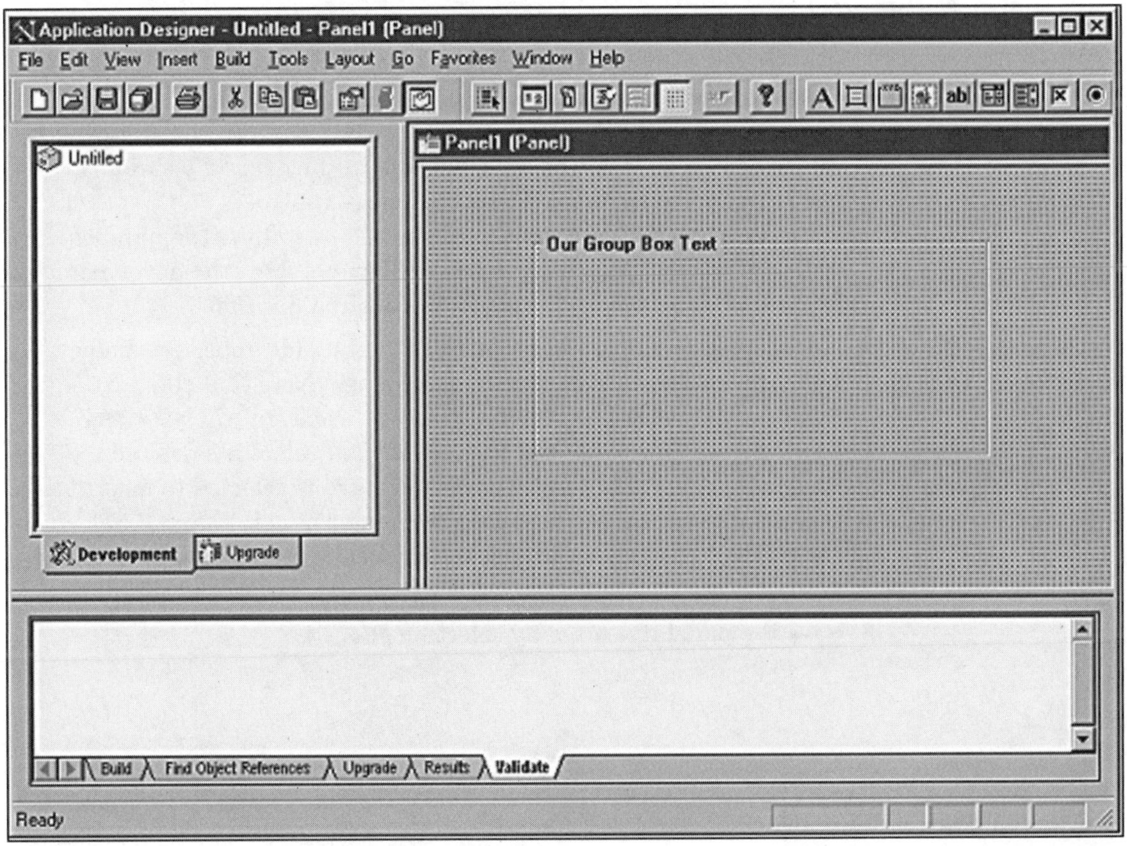

Figure 7-52 The group box created by using the LABEL tab shown in Figure 7-51.

4. Bring up the USE tab of the Panel Field Properties dialog box only if the group box control is a multicurrency field, as this is the only option on the USE tab for group boxes.
5. Save the panel by selecting FILE, SAVE if desired.

Static Image Control

To insert a static image control on a panel, perform the following steps:

1. Select INSERT, STATIC IMAGE from the menu or click on the STATIC IMAGE button on the toolbar (Fig. 7-53). Once the static image is selected, the STATIC IMAGE icon (a hand with the index finger pointing out with the letter M inside the hand) appears. The developer's finger on the icon must be positioned to indicate where the top left corner of the static image control should go. Then, the developer should press the left button on the mouse and hold it down while dragging the icon down and to the right. This action creates a rectangle that represents the outline of the static image control. The developer should not release the mouse button until the static image control is of the desired size and in the desired location on the panel. Note that once the static image control is on the panel, it can be selected and then can be resized by pulling the handles with the mouse. Figure 7-54 shows the panel after the developer clicks on the mouse to place it in the desired position.
2. Next, bring up the LABEL tab of the Panel Field Properties dialog box. Enter some text to identify this image. Note that this text label will not be displayed on the screen. Next, hit the BROWSE button to browse through your image files and select the desired image. Hit the PASTE button once the image is selected to insert the image into the static image control on your panel. Figure 7-55 shows the LABEL tab as it appears for static images. Select OK when ready.
3. Save the panel if desired by selecting FILE, SAVE.

Figure 7-53
STATIC IMAGE button.

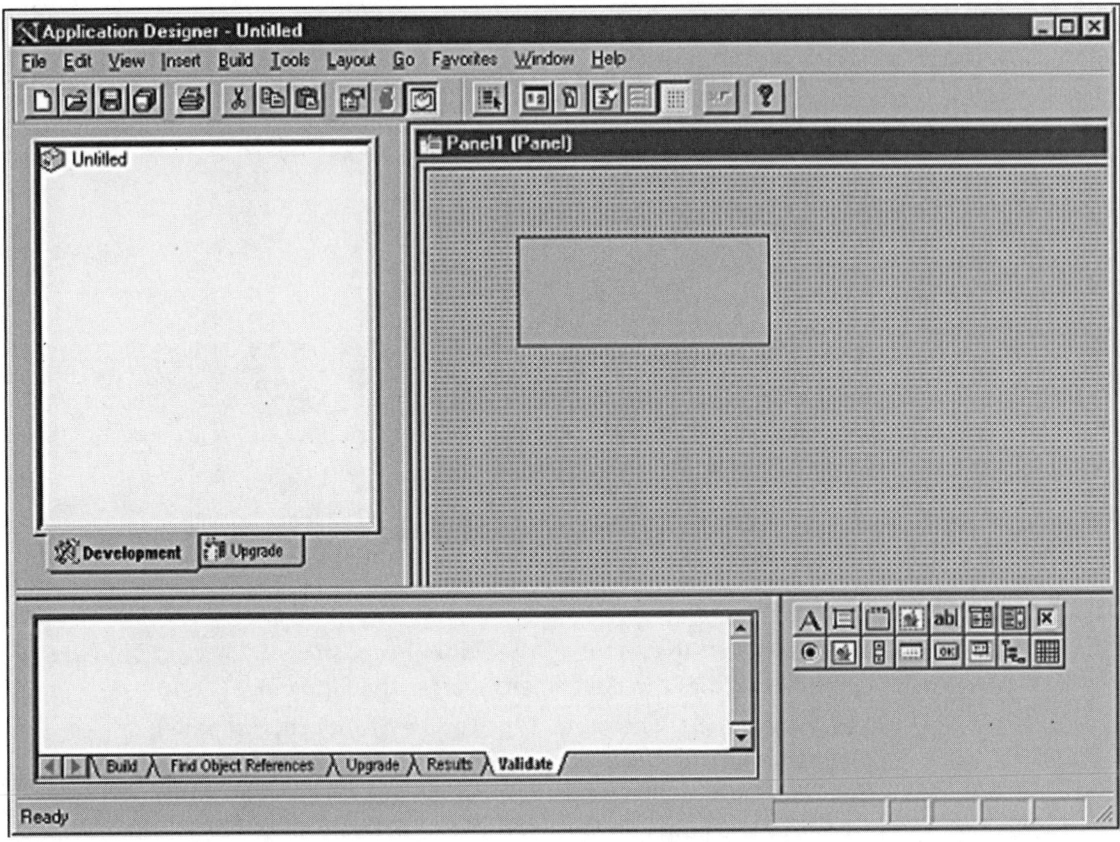

Figure 7-54 Static image control immediately after insertion onto the new panel.

Subpanel Controls

Before a subpanel can be inserted onto a panel, it must first be created. To create a subpanel, perform the following steps:

1. Select FILE, OBJECT PROPERTIES to display the Panel Properties dialog box. There are two tabs on this dialog box: the GENERAL tab (see Fig. 7-56) and the USE tab (Fig. 7-57). The purpose of the GENERAL tab is to allow the developer to enter a description of the panel and any desired comments. It also shows the last time the panel was modified and by whom. Enter the desired description and comments and then click on OK when ready.

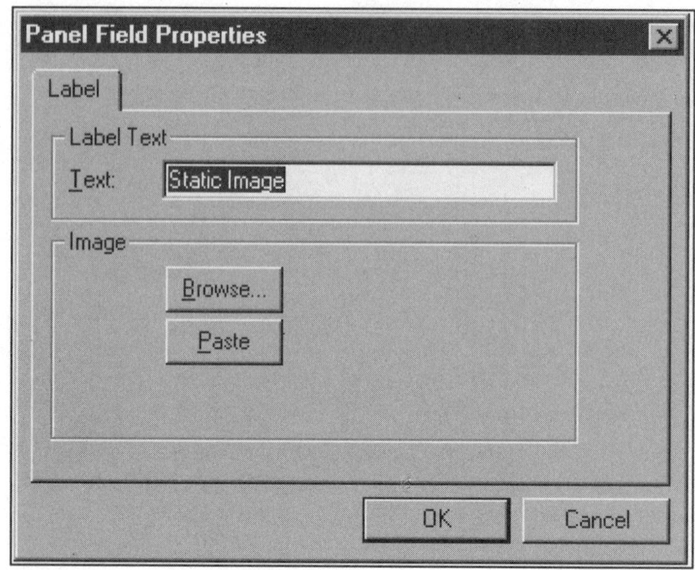

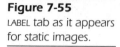

Figure 7-55
LABEL tab as it appears for static images.

2. Next, go to the USE tab of the Panel Properties dialog box. This dialog box allows the developer to enter the following:
   - *Panel type*. The panel type can be Standard, Subpanel, or Secondary Panel. To create a subpanel, select Subpanel for the type.
   - *Panel size*. The panel size can be *autosize*, which automatically sizes the panel on the basis of the fields that will be on the panel, or *custom size*, which allows the developer to modify the panel by dragging the corner of the panel with the mouse.
   - *Panel style*. The developer can change the color and font by selecting from a list of different styles.

   Click OK to save the selections on the USE tab.
3. Save the subpanel by selecting FILE, SAVE.

Now that the subpanel is created, perform the following steps in order to insert the subpanel onto a panel:

1. Open the panel onto which the new subpanel will be going and then select INSERT, SUBPANEL from the menu or click on the SUBPANEL button on the toolbar (Fig. 7-58). The Subpanel dialog box will appear as shown in Figure 7-59.
2. Enter the name of the subpanel to be inserted and the name of the

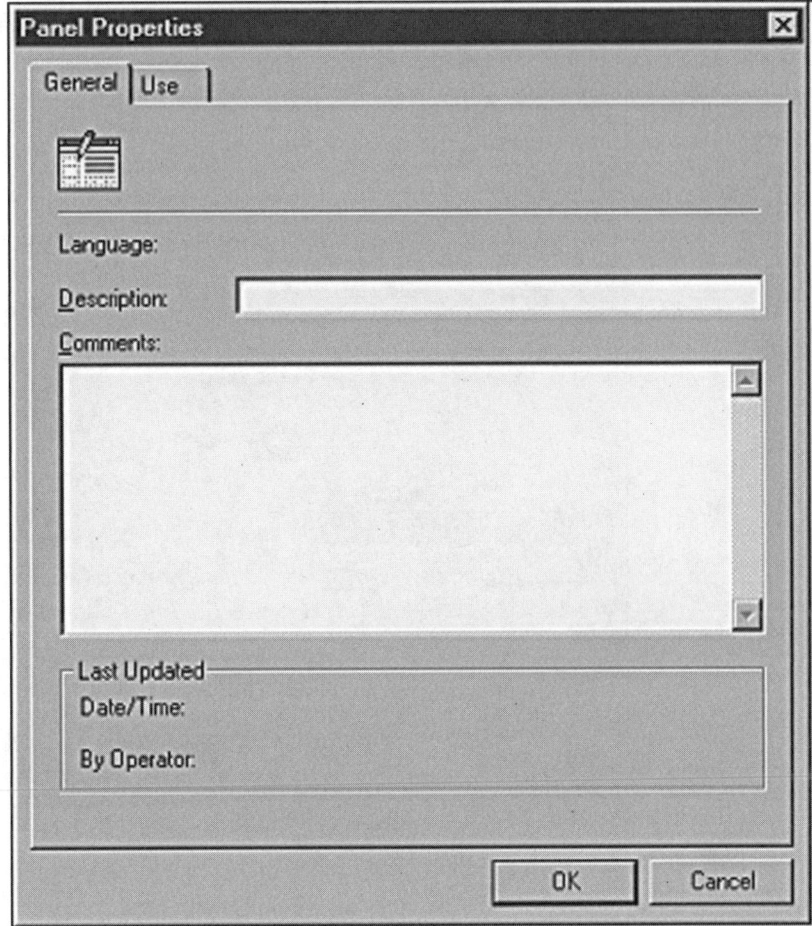

Figure 7-56 GENERAL tab of the Panel Properties dialog box.

record where the subpanel data will be written. Click OK when ready. Once OK is selected, the subpanel is displayed in the panel with the subpanel name. In order to view the actual fields on the subpanel, the TEST panel button must be clicked on or LAYOUT, TEST MODE must be selected.

3. Double-click on the subpanel control of the panel to bring up the Panel Field Properties dialog box. Enter the desired text in the text field of the LABEL tab. This text is for documentation purposes only. Click OK when ready.
4. Save the panel by selecting FILE, SAVE if desired.

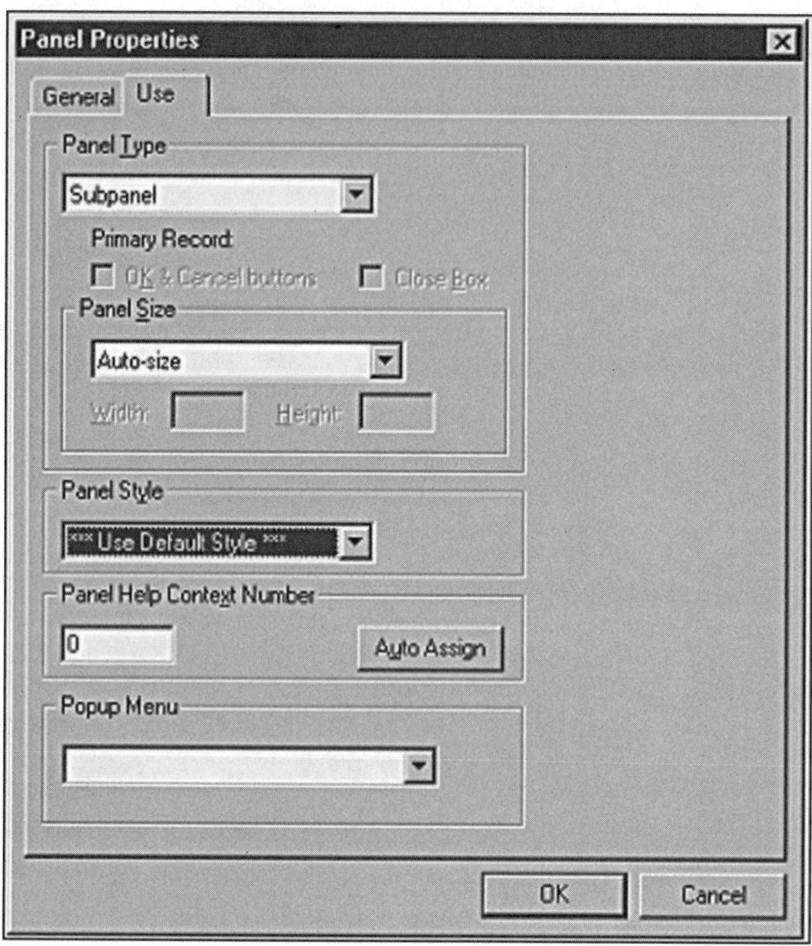

Figure 7-57
USE tab of the Panel Properties dialog box.

Figure 7-58
SUBPANEL button.

Scroll-Bar Controls

To insert a scroll bar on a panel, perform the following steps:

1. Select INSERT, SCROLL BAR from the menu or click on the SCROLL BAR button on the toolbar (Fig. 7-60). Once the scroll bar is selected, the SCROLL BAR icon (a hand with the index finger pointing out with

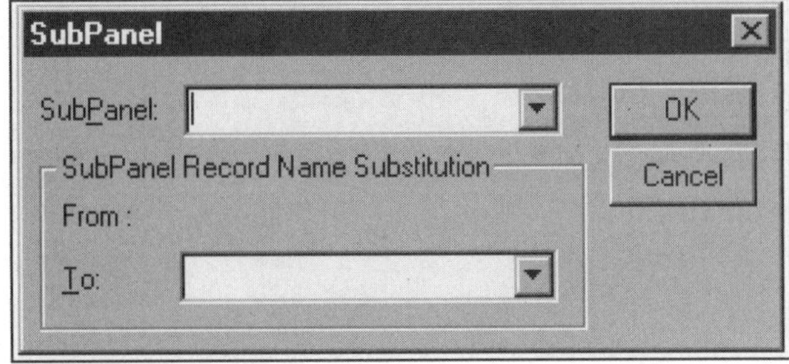

Figure 7-59 Subpanel dialog box appears when inserting a subpanel onto another subpanel.

Figure 7-60 SCROLL BAR button.

the letter S inside the hand) appears. The finger on the icon must be positioned to indicate where the top left corner of the scroll-bar control should go. Then, the developer should press the left button on the mouse and hold it down while dragging the icon down and to the right. The developer should not release the mouse button until the control is of the desired length and in the desired location on the panel. Figure 7-61 shows the panel after the developer clicks on the mouse to place it in the desired position.

2. Bring up the LABEL tab of the Panel Field Properties dialog box to enter text describing the scroll bar. This text is not displayed on the panel. It is for documentation purposes only. Figure 7-62 shows the LABEL Tab of the Panel Field Properties dialog box as it appears for scroll bars.
3. The next step in inserting a scroll bar onto a new panel is to change the scroll-bar use by bringing up the USE tab of the Panel Field Properties dialog box. To do so, double-click on the scroll bar and select the USE tab. The USE tab allows the developer to select the following:
   - *Occurs level.* Each scroll bar must be assigned an occurs level between 1 and 3. If all scroll bars on the panel are independent of each other, all the occurs levels should be set to 1. If, however, there is a parent/child relationship between the scroll bars, then the parent scroll bar should have an occurs level of 1 and the child relationship should have an occurs level of 2.

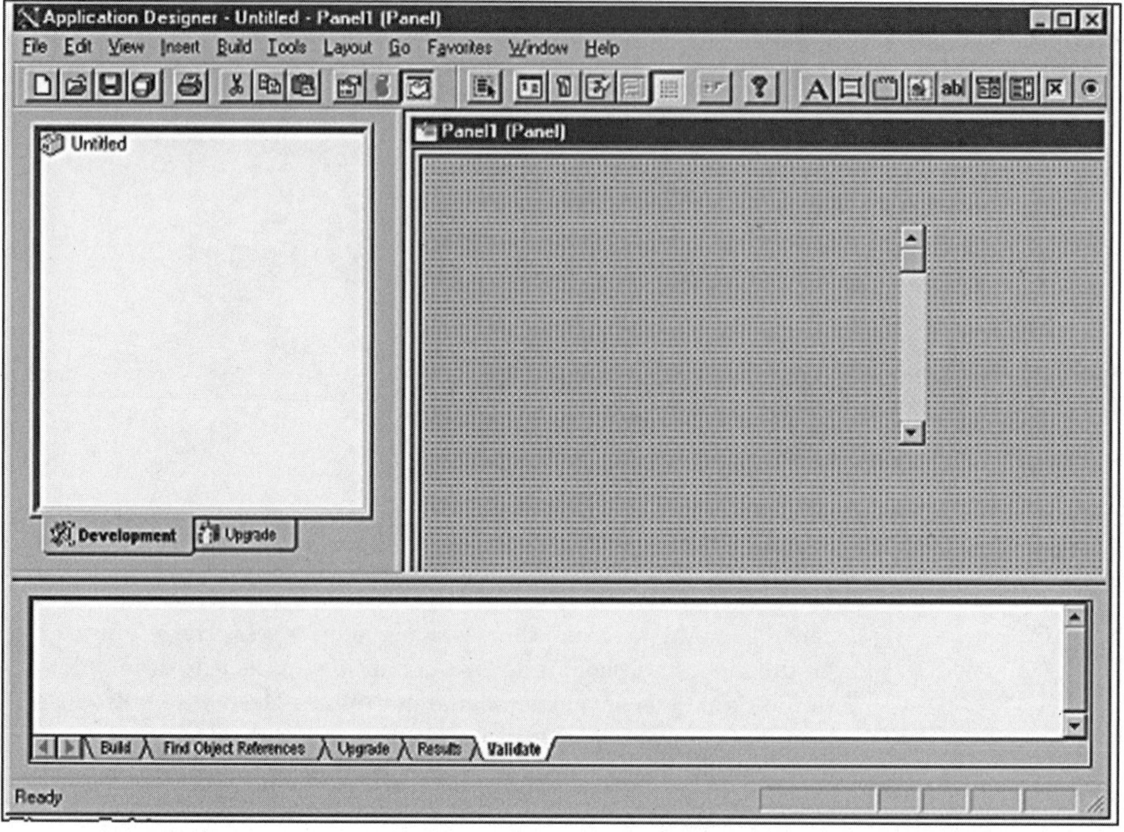

Figure 7-61 Scroll-bar control just after being inserted onto the new panel.

- *Occurs count.* This is the number of rows of data that will be displayed on the panel for the scroll bar.
- *Field use options.* The developer can select options that will affect the scroll bar.

  If INVISIBLE is selected, the scroll bar will be invisible.

  If NO AUTO SELECT is selected, no data will be retrieved from the database automatically.

  If NO AUTO UPDATE is selected, then the database will not be updated automatically.

  If DEFAULT WIDTH is selected, the scroll bar will be returned to the default width size of 17 pixels.

  If NO ROW INSERT is selected, then users can't insert rows.

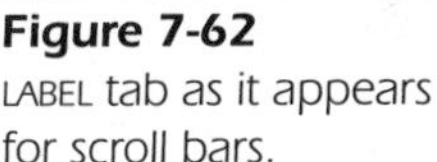

Figure 7-62
LABEL tab as it appears for scroll bars.

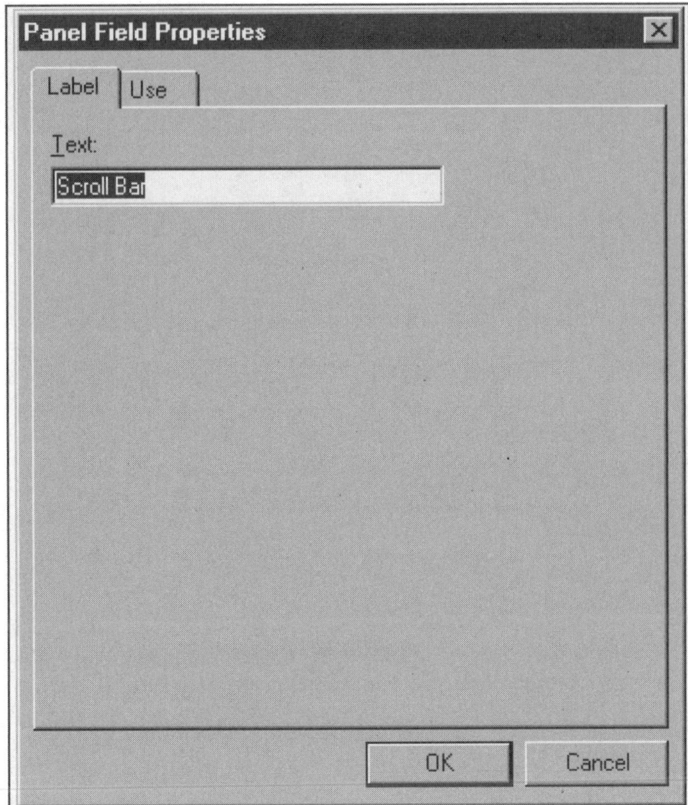

If NO ROW DELETE is selected, then users can't delete rows in this scroll.

- *Field help context number.* The developer can enter a value in here if using Windows online help.

Figure 7-63 shows the USE tab as it appears for scroll bars.

4. Click on OK when all selections on the USE tab are satisfactory. Save the panel by selecting FILE, SAVE if it is desired to save the panel at this time.

Secondary Panels

Before a secondary panel can be inserted onto a panel, it must first be created. To create a secondary panel, perform the following steps:

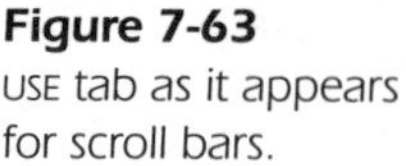

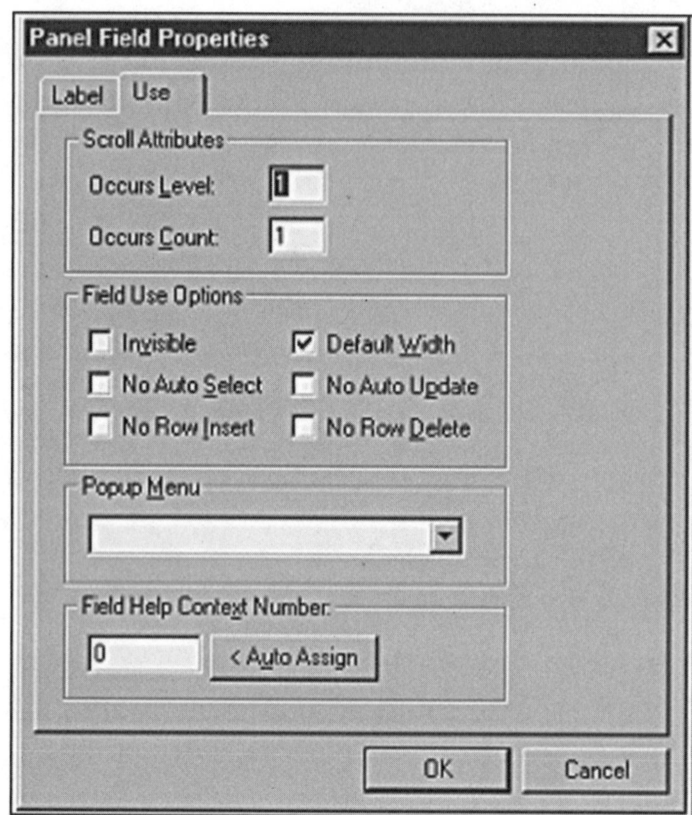

Figure 7-63 USE tab as it appears for scroll bars.

1. Create a new panel by selecting FILE, NEW.
2. Select FILE, OBJECT PROPERTIES to display the Panel Properties dialog box. There are two tabs on this dialog box: the GENERAL tab and the USE tab. The first tab is the GENERAL tab. The purpose of the GENERAL TAB is to allow the developer to enter a description of the panel and any desired comments. It also shows the last time the panel was modified and by whom. Enter the desired description and comments and then click on OK when ready.
3. Next, go to the USE tab of the Panel Properties dialog box (Fig. 7-64). This dialog box allows the developer to enter the following:
   - *Panel type.* The panel type can be Standard, Subpanel, or Secondary Panel. To create a secondary panel, select Secondary Panel for the type.
   - *Panel size.* The panel size can be *autosize*, which automatically sizes the panel according to the fields that will be on the panel,

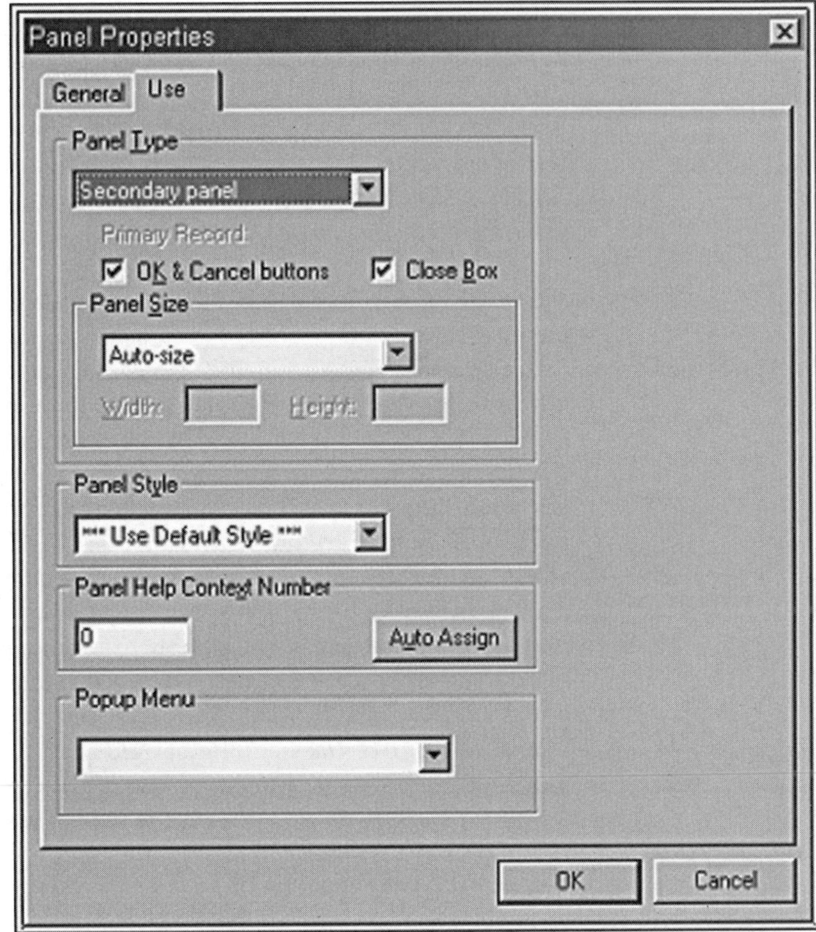

Figure 7-64
USE tab of the Panel Properties dialog box as it appears for secondary panels.

or *custom size*, which allows the developer to modify the panel size by dragging the corner of the panel with the mouse.

- *Panel style.* The developer can change the color and font by selecting from a list of different styles.
- *OK and CANCEL buttons*. The developer can decide whether to include OK and CANCEL buttons on the secondary panel. The default is to include them. When this box is checked, the OK and CANCEL buttons will be displayed on the secondary panel.
- *Close box.* The developer can decide whether the close box is displayed at the top right of the panel. The default is to include the close box. When the close box is checked on the USE tab, the Close box will be displayed on the secondary panel.

Click OK to save the selections on the USE tab.

3. Save the secondary panel by selecting FILE, SAVE.

Associating Secondary Panels with Primary Panels. Once the secondary panel is created, it must be associated with a primary panel. There are two ways to do this: via secondary panel push buttons and/or via secondary panel controls.

SECONDARY PANEL PUSH BUTTONS. The first way of associating a secondary panel with a primary panel is via secondary panel push buttons. When using secondary panel push buttons, the developer must insert a push button onto the primary panel and double-click on it to bring up the Panel Field Properties dialog box for push buttons. As stated earlier in the push-button control section of this chapter, the developer can select the push-button type. The choices for pushbutton type are Command, Process, or Secondary panel. In this case, the developer would, of course, select secondary panel as the type. Then, when the push button is clicked on by the user during run time, the secondary panel will be displayed. This method is the option to use when there is not a requirement to do any processing before the secondary panel is displayed.

SECONDARY PANEL CONTROLS. The second way of associating a secondary panel with a primary panel is to insert a secondary panel control on the primary panel. To do so, perform the following steps:

1. Open the panel on which the new secondary panel control will be going and then select INSERT, SECONDARY PANEL from the menu or click on the SECONDARY PANEL button on the toolbar (Fig. 7-65). Position the secondary panel control in the desired location of the panel. Figure 7-66 shows a new panel with a secondary panel control on it.
2. Double-click on the secondary panel control on the panel to bring up the SECONDARY PANEL tab of the Panel Field Properties dialog box. Enter the name of the associated secondary panel. Figure 7-67 shows the SECONDARY PANEL tab of the Panel Field Properties dialog box.

Figure 7-65 SECONDARY PANEL button.

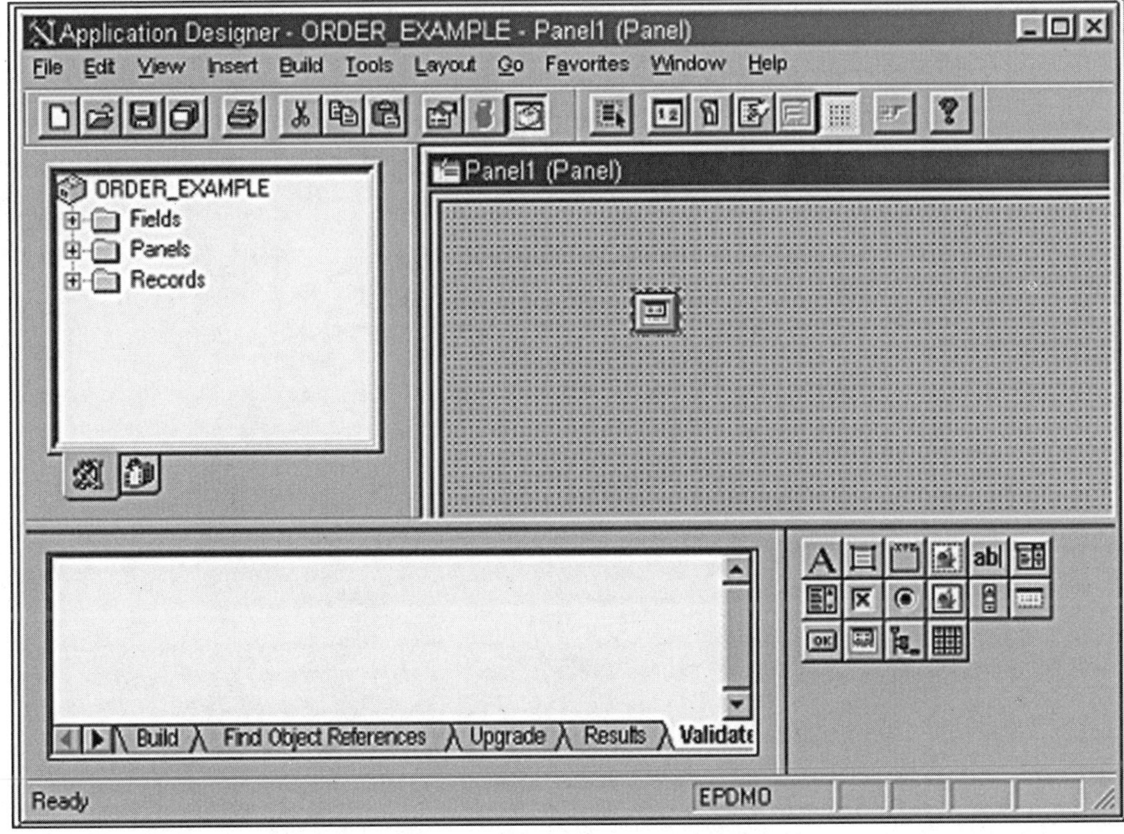

Figure 7-66 New panel with a secondary panel control recently inserted on it.

Figure 7-67 SECONDARY PANEL tab of the Panel Field Properties dialog box.

3. Enter the desired text in the text field of the LABEL tab (Fig. 7-68). This text is for documentation purposes only. Click OK when ready.
4. Go to the Order Panel dialog box by selecting LAYOUT, ORDER. Place the secondary panel in the desired order. This order is the order of the controls when the tab key is pressed. Figure 7-69 shows the Order Panel dialog box.

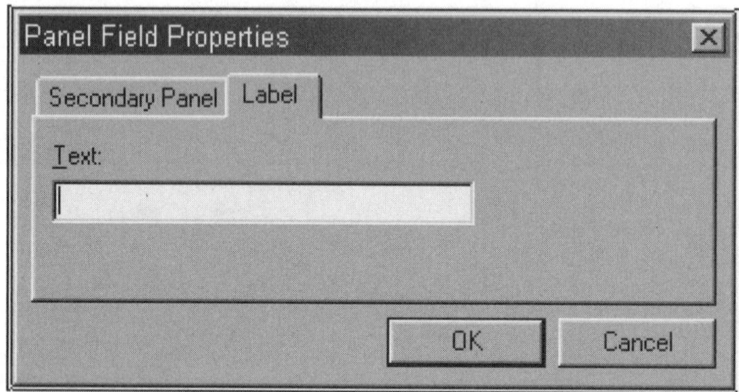

Figure 7-68 LABEL tab of the Panel Field Properties dialog box.

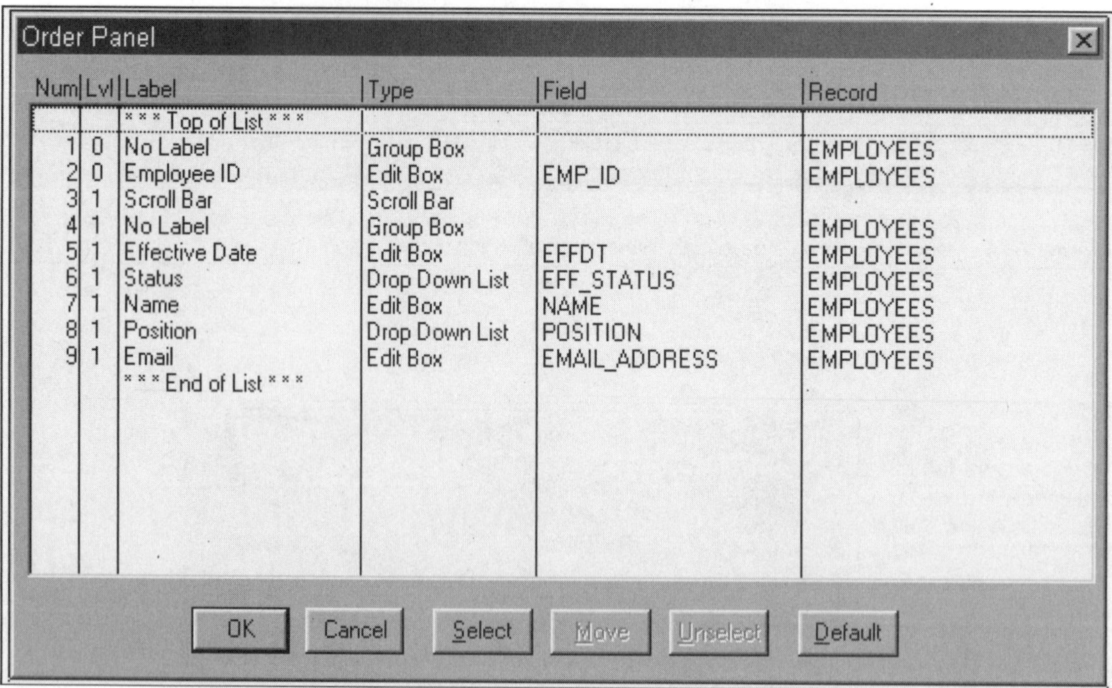

Figure 7-69 Order panel DIALOG BOX.

5. Place a push button of type Command on the panel.
6. Right-click on the push button, and the popup menu shown in Figure 7-69*a* will be displayed. Select "View PeopleCode," and the Field Change Event code will be displayed. Modify this code to call the DoModal PeopleCode function to display the secondary panel.
7. Save the panel by selecting FILE, SAVE.

Grid Controls

HINT *Be careful when using grid controls. As of this writing, grid controls are not supported in the Web deployment. If your panels must be deployed via Tuxedo's Jolt, you should use a scroll bar with a multiple occurs count.*

To insert a grid control on a panel, perform the following steps:

1. Select INSERT, GRID CONTROL from the menu or click on the GRID CONTROL button on the toolbar (Fig. 7-70). Once the grid control is selected, the GRID CONTROL icon (a hand with the index finger pointing out with the letter G inside the hand) appears. The finger of the icon must be positioned to indicate where the top left corner of the grid control should go. Then, the developer should press the

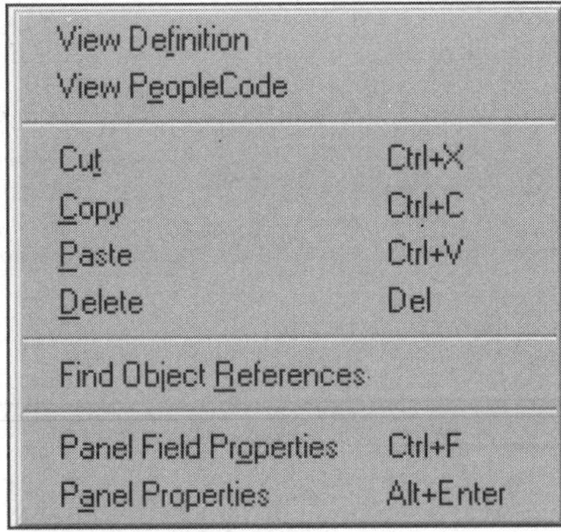

Figure 7-69(a) Popup menu that appears when right mouse button clicks on the COMMAND push button.

Figure 7-70 GRID CONTROL button.

left button on the mouse and hold it down while dragging the icon down and to the right. This action creates a rectangle that represents the outline of the grid control. The developer should not release the button on the mouse until the grid control is the desired size and in the desired location on the panel. Note that once the grid control is on the panel, it can be selected and then can be resized by pulling the handles with the mouse. Figure 7-71 shows the panel after the developer clicks on the mouse to place it in the desired position.

2. The next step is to set the grid properties. Double-click on the grid, and the Grid Properties dialog box will be displayed. There are four tabs on the Grid Properties dialog box: the GENERAL tab, the COLUMNS tab, the LABEL tab, and the USE tab.

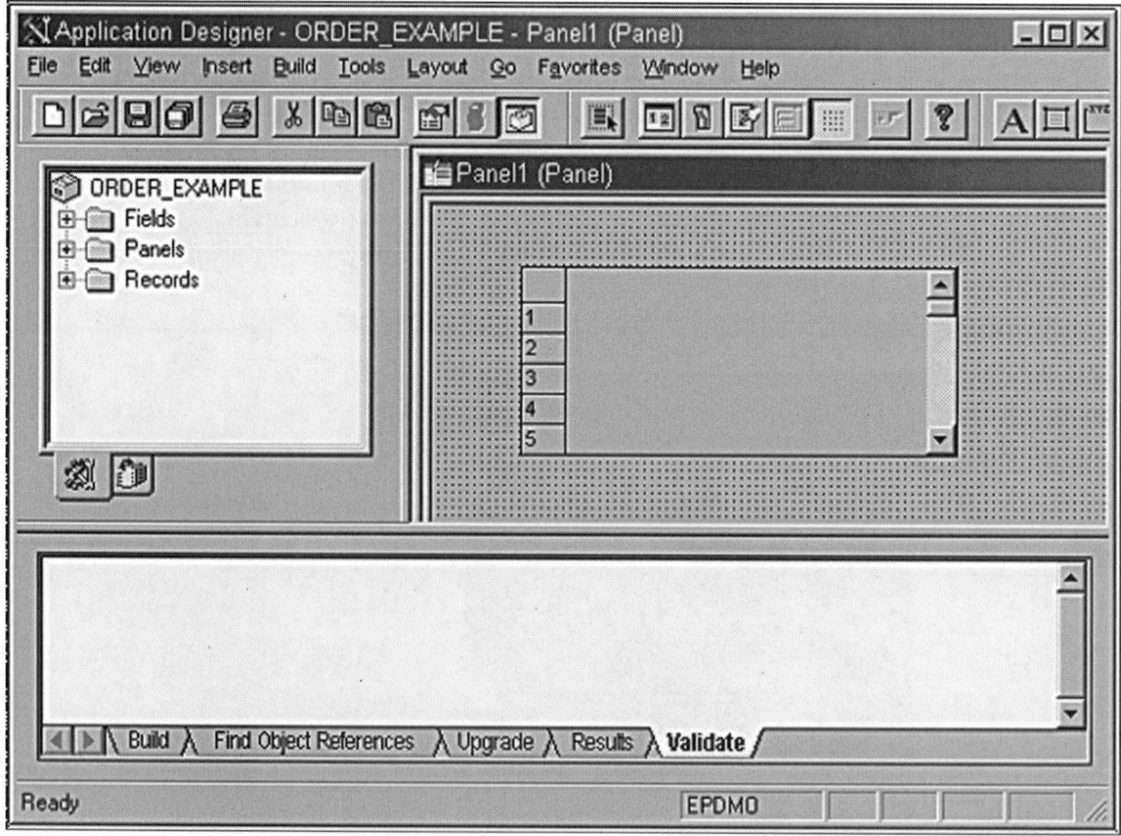

Figure 7-71 Grid control recently inserted on a new panel.

- The GENERAL tab allows the developer to enter the main record and the occurs level. The MAIN RECORD is the name of the record that the majority of the fields in the grid come from. Figure 7-72 shows the GENERAL tab.
- The COLUMNS tab allows the developer to add columns to the grid, remove columns from the grid, move columns around on the grid via the MOVE UP and MOVE DOWN buttons, or modify the field properties. Figure 7-73 shows the COLUMNS tab.

  To add a column to the grid, click on the ADD button and the Add Column Dialog box will appear as shown in Figure 7-74. This dialog box allows the developer to specify the column type. Once the type is selected and OK is clicked, the Panel Field Properties dialog box for that control type will be displayed as discussed earlier in this chapter. Figure 7-75 shows an example of the Panel Field Properties dialog box. This means that the RECORD tab, the LABEL tab, and the USE tab will be available for the

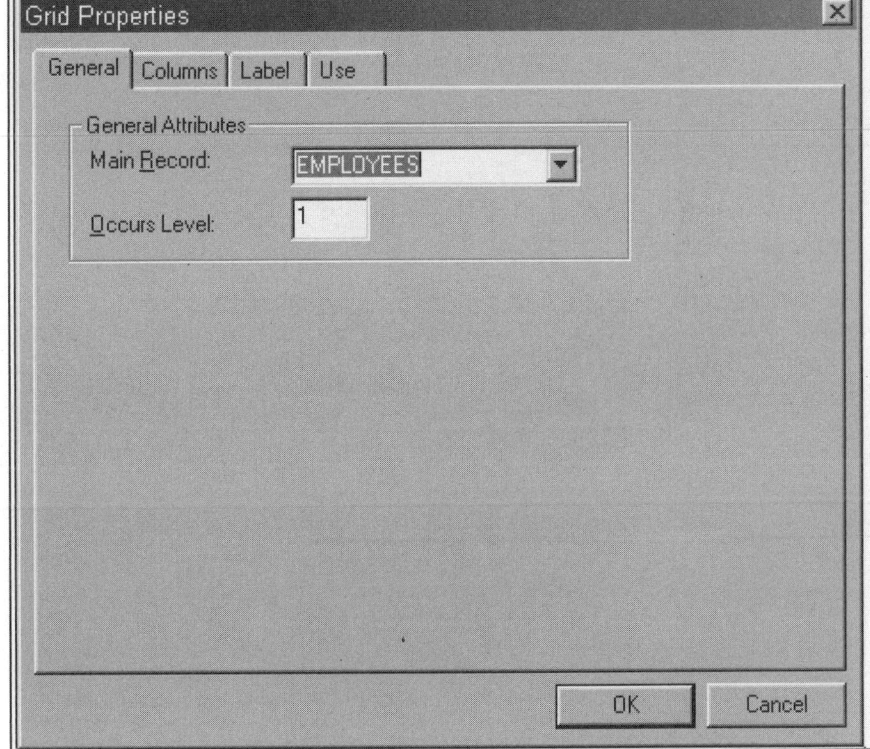

Figure 7-72 The GENERAL tab of the Grid Properties dialog box.

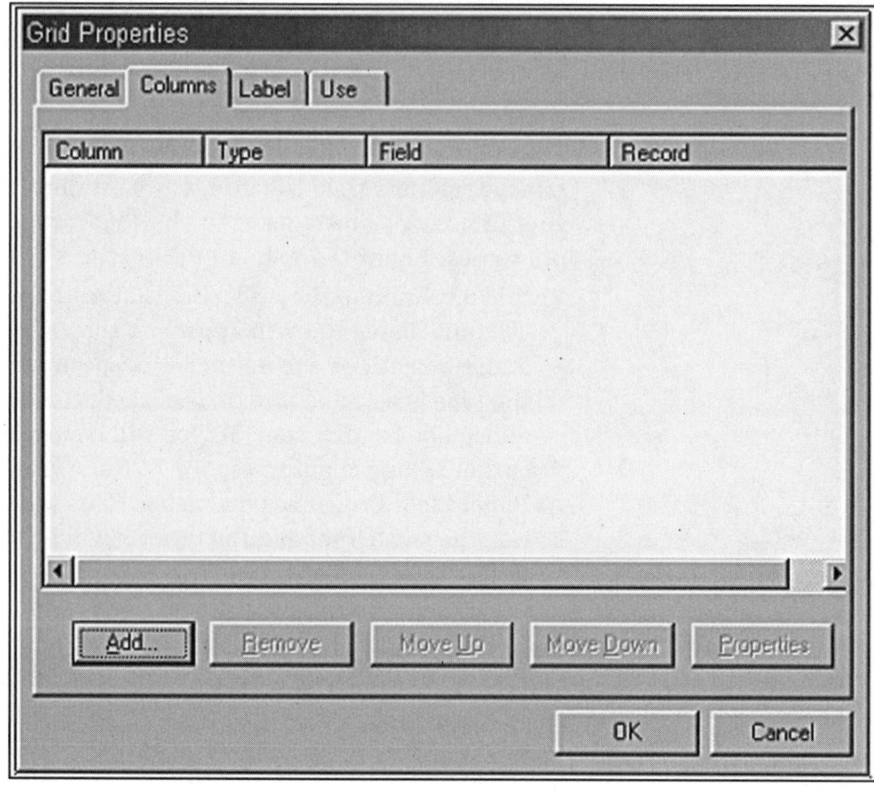

Figure 7-73
The COLUMNS tab of the Grid Properties dialog box when no columns have been added yet.

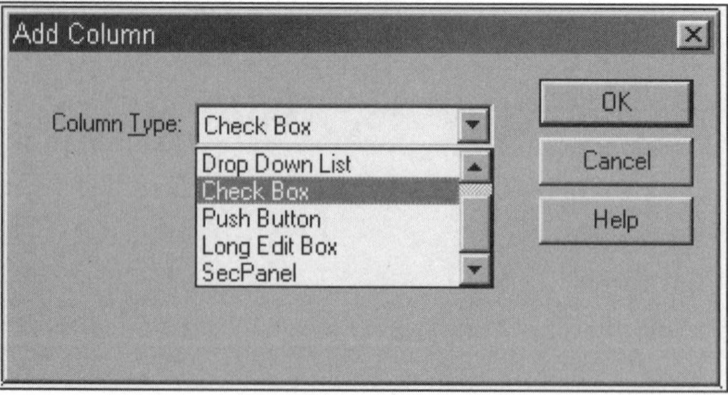

Figure 7-74
The Add Column dialog box.

Figure 7-75 A Panel Field Properties dialog box that appears when adding a column to a grid.

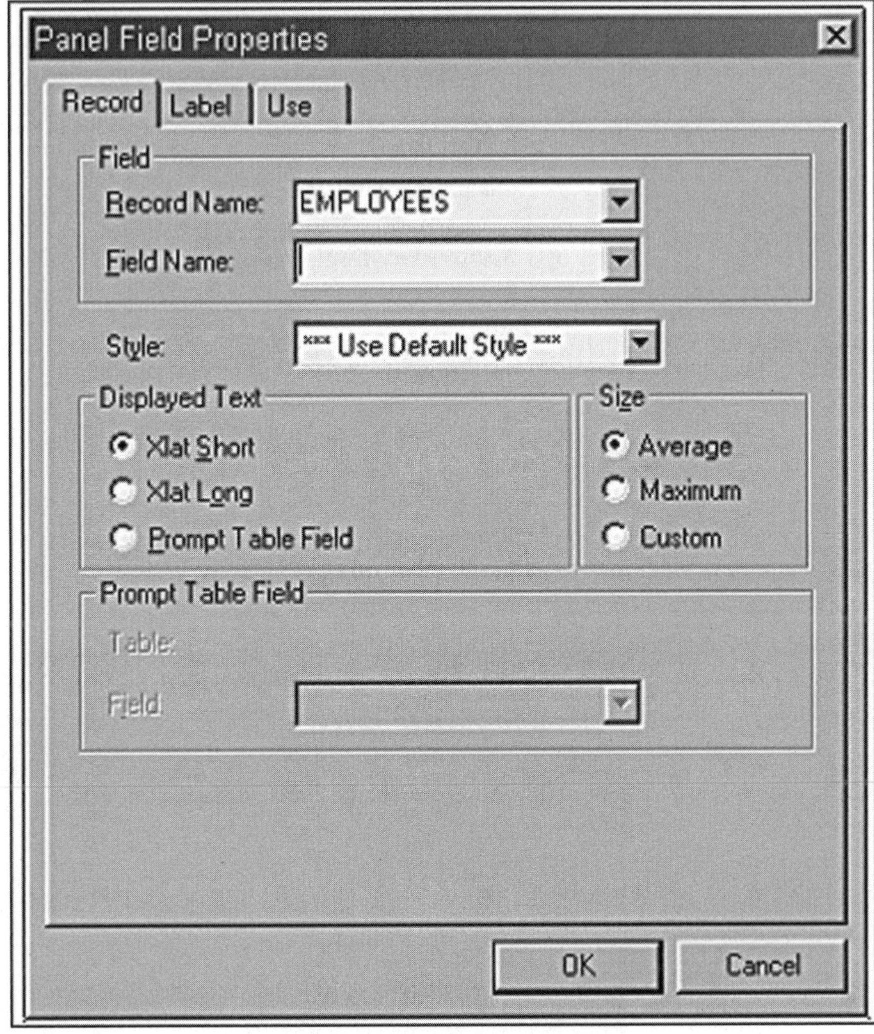

developer to associate the control to a field and a record, choose the size or labels, and so on.

To remove a column from the grid, place the cursor on the column to be deleted while on the COLUMNS tab of the Grid Properties dialog box and then click on the REMOVE button.

The MOVE UP button moves the selected column up one field. The MOVE DOWN button moves the selected column down one field.

The PROPERTIES button on the COLUMNS tab of the Grid Properties dialog box brings up the Panel Field Properties dialog box for the specific control type of the column selected.

- The LABEL tab of the Grid Properties dialog box (Fig. 7-76) allows the developer to
  - *a*. Select the label type. The label type can be NONE, TEXT, or MESSAGE CATALOG.
  - *b*. If MESSAGE CATALOG is selected as the label type, the developer can enter the message set and message number.
  - *c*. Enter the desired label text. (Figure 7-77 shows the grid without any label text; Fig. 7-78 shows the grid with the label text of "Sample grid" centered above the grid.)
  - *d*. Select the alignment of the label. The alignment can be left, center, or right.
  - *e*. Decide whether to show the column headings at the top of each column on the grid. (Figure 7-78 shows the grid with the column headings displayed.)

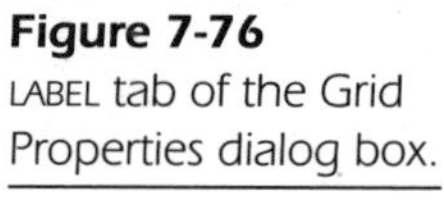

Figure 7-76
LABEL tab of the Grid Properties dialog box.

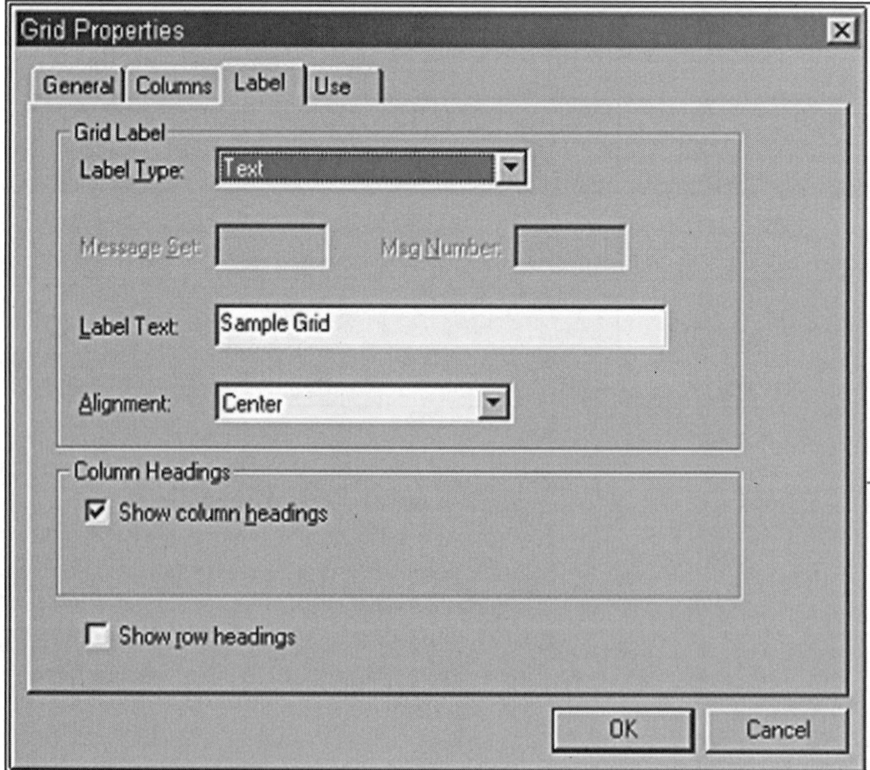

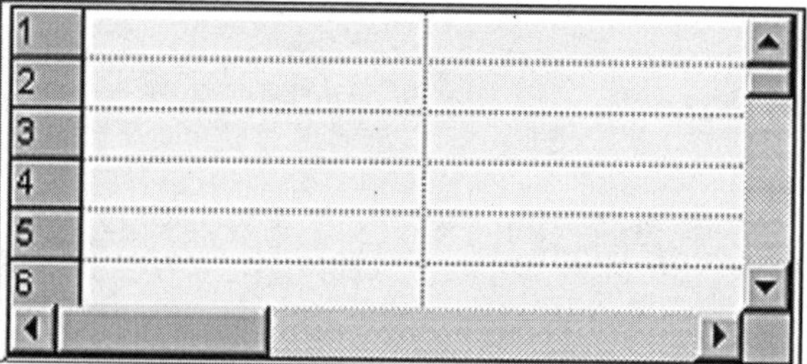

Figure 7-77 Appearance of the grid when the row headings are displayed but the column headings are not displayed.

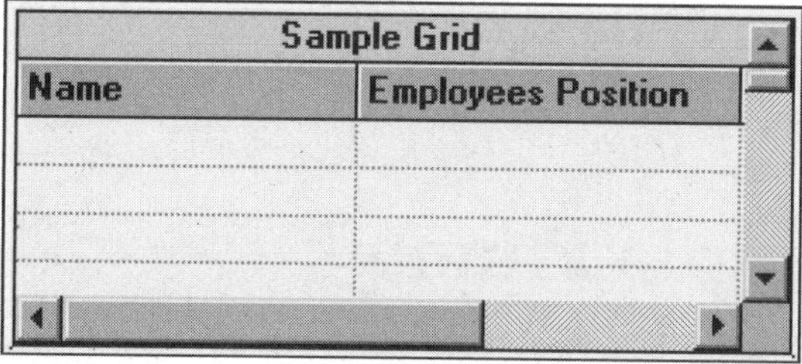

Figure 7-78 Appearance of the grid when the row headings are not displayed but the column headings are displayed.

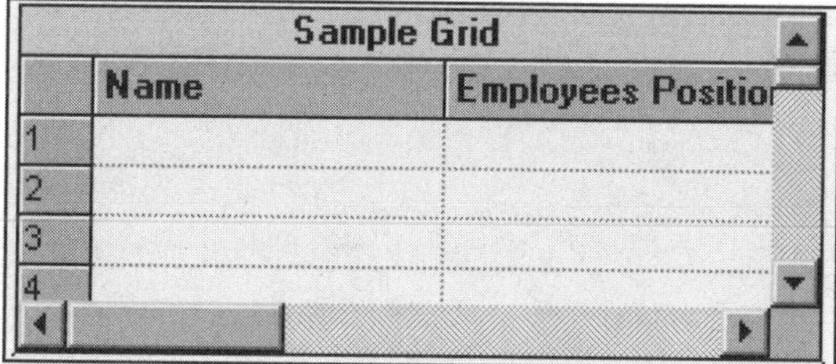

Figure 7-79 Appearance of the grid when the row and column headings are both displayed.

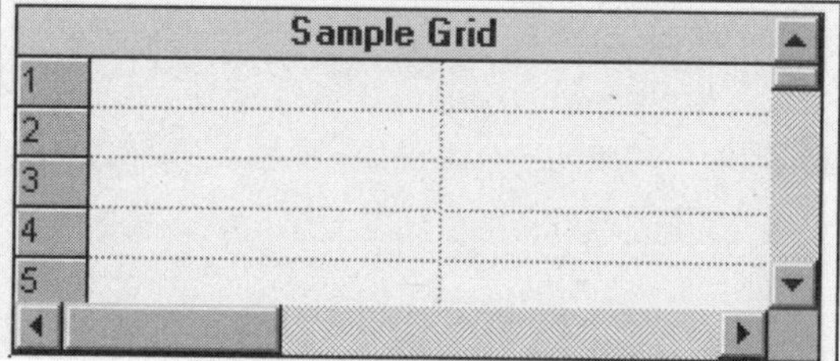

Figure 7-80 Appearance of the grid when the column heading is not displayed but the row heading is displayed.

f. Decide whether to show the row headings in front of each row on the grid. (Figure 7-80 shows the grid when the row headings are not displayed, while Fig. 7-79 shows the grid when the row headings are displayed.)

NOTE *Figure 7-76 is the* LABEL *tab of the Grid Properties dialog box that produces the grid shown in Figure 7-78.*

As can be seen from Figures 7-77 to 7-80, a panel grid can acquire several different appearances. Figure 7-81 shows an example of the Columns Tab after a few columns have been added to the grid.

- The USE tab of the Grid Properties dialog box allows the developer to set data options, display options, and enter the name of a popup menu. Figure 7-82 shows the USE tab of the Grid Properties dialog box. These options are all similar to the scroll bar's use options discussed earlier in this chapter.

Example Panels

Now that you have been exposed to the key concepts of panels, we are going to create our own panels for our example application. The first

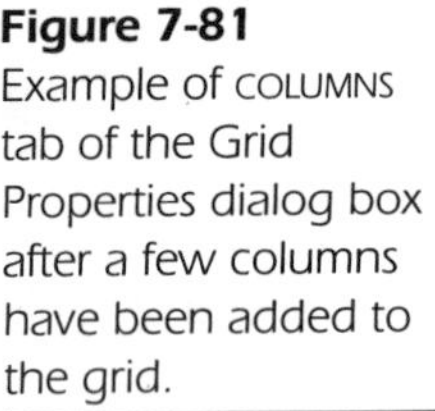

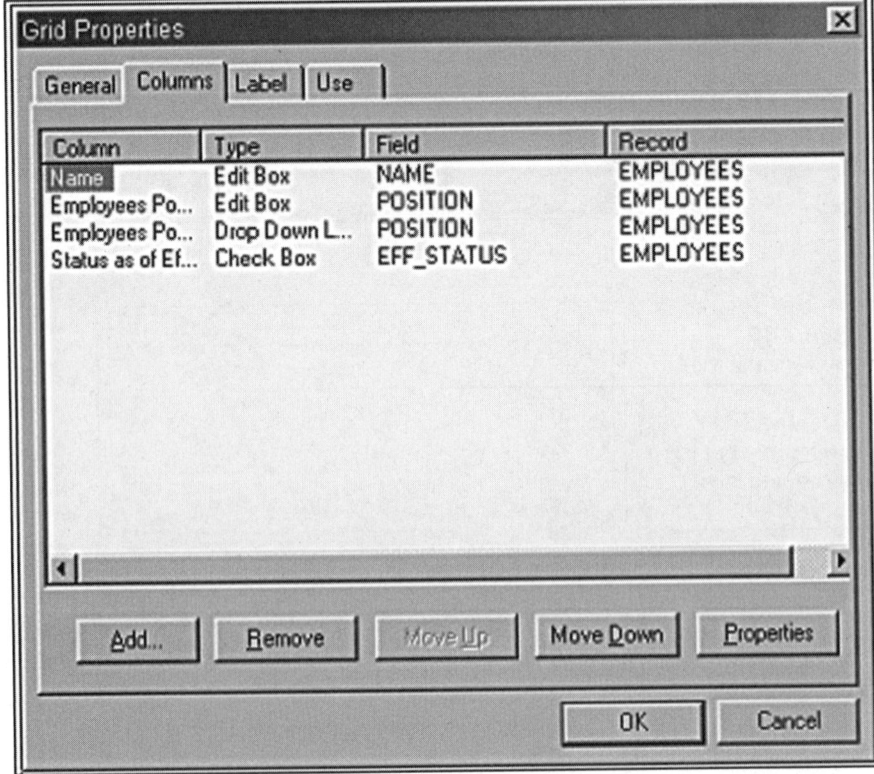

Figure 7-81 Example of COLUMNS tab of the Grid Properties dialog box after a few columns have been added to the grid.

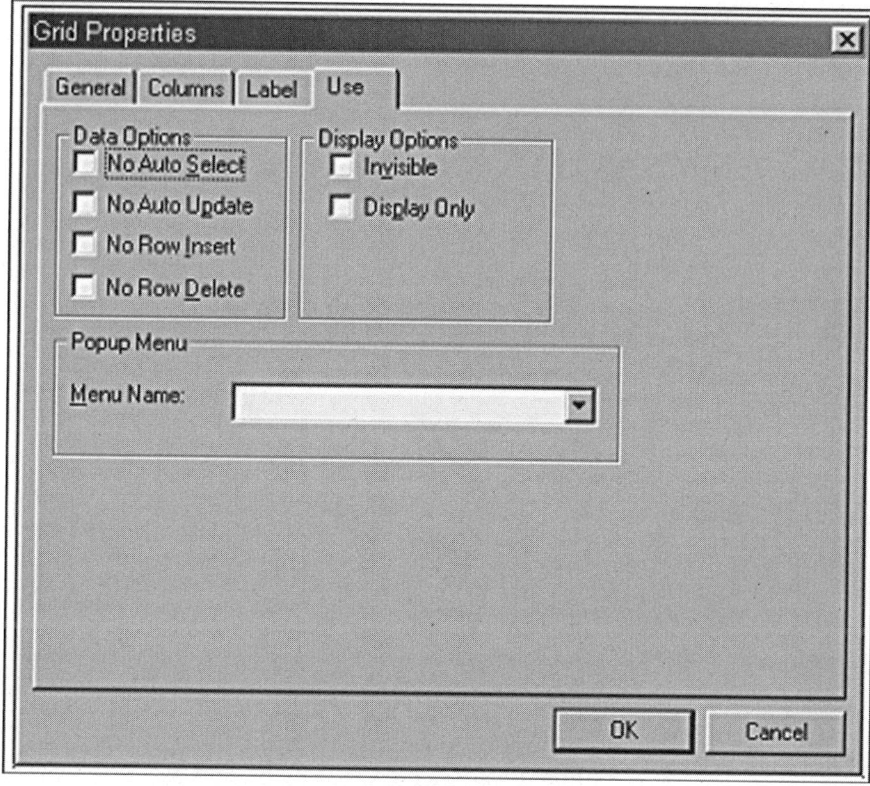

Figure 7-82 The USE tab of the Grid Properties dialog box.

group of panels we will develop will be used for our lookup records. We will create one panel for each of our lookup records. The following records that we created in the previous section are lookup records:

- `EMPLOYEES`
- `BUYER_VW`
- `ITEMS`
- `LOCATIONS`
- `UNIT_MEASURE`
- `VENDORS`

The final group of panels we will develop will consist of panels that will allow the creation and management of both the internal and external orders.

- New Internal Order panel—this panel is for the initial request.

- Internal Order panel—this panel is updated by the warehouse personnel.
- External Order panel—this panel is updated by the buyers.

Employees Panel (`EMPLOYEES_PNL`)

Before we start creating the Employees panel, let's quickly list the fields that are part of the Employees record for quick reference:

- `EMP_ID`
- `EFF_DT`
- `EFF_STATUS`
- `NAME`
- `POSITION`
- `EMAIL_ADDRESS`

The Employees Panel shall have a panel control for each field in the Employees record. The Employee id is part of the key, so it will be a display-only edit box control. There will be a scroll bar on this panel. The scroll bar will allow the user to scroll through the records associated with the Employee id displayed. The effective date, status, and position will be drop-down list controls, and the name and email address will be edit boxes.

To begin creating the Employees panel, press the NEW icon or select FILE, NEW. When the New dialog is displayed, select PANEL and press OK. A new blank panel will be displayed in the Object Workspace of the Application Designer. The first thing we are going to do for this panel is to set up the display-only key field section.

NOTE *Normally you would place all of your key fields at the top of the panel with their Use Panel Field Properties set to display only. An exception to this practice is when you are working with effective dated records. Although the effective date field is a part of the records key structure, you should place the* `EFFDT` *in the editable section of the panel. In addition, you need to include it in the occurs level associated with a scroll bar that should always be present with effective dated record panels.*

We want to insert an edit box that will be associated with the `EMP_ID` field onto the panel. To do so, the `EMPLOYEES` record folder must be expanded in the Project Workspace. Select the EMP_ID field and drag and drop it onto the top left of the panel. Now double-click on the EMP_ID that was placed onto the panel. When the Panel Field Properties dialog is displayed, select the USE tab and set the Display Only check box on. Once you have done this, you can press OK. Figure 7-83 shows the USE tab of the Panel Field Properties for EMP_ID with its correct options. The EMP_ID edit box that was placed onto the panel should now be grayed out, indicating that it is a display-only edit box.

For aesthetic purposes throughout our example we will use group box controls to graphically group related controls. You could use the frame control, but it does not have the beveled three-dimensional look. Therefore, my preference is to use a group box control with no label. Insert the group

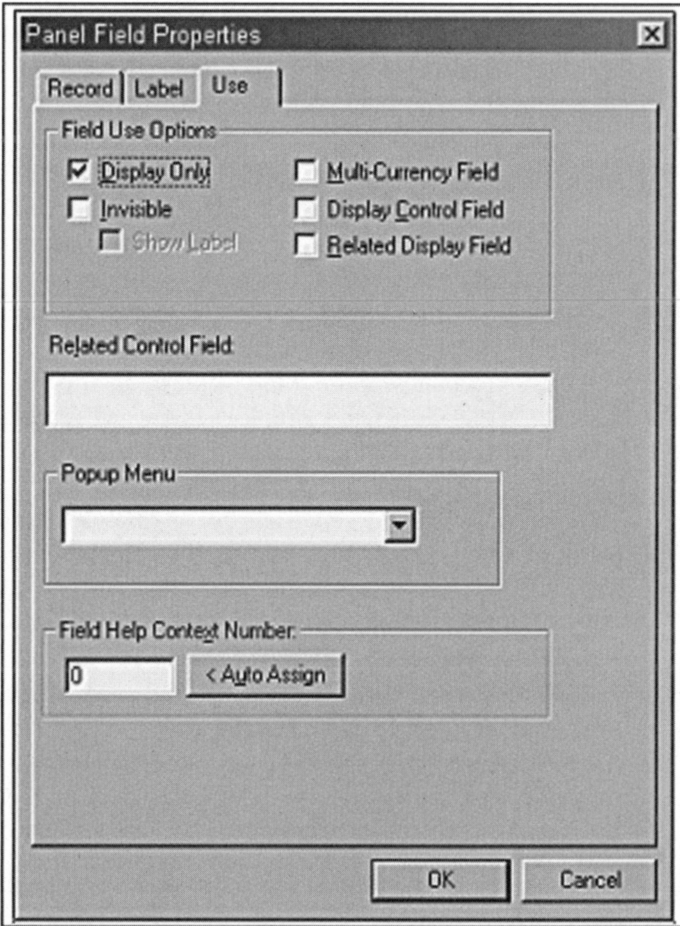

Figure 7-83
USE tab of the Panel Field Properties for EMP_ID.

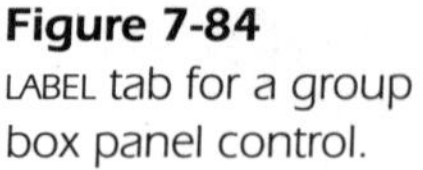

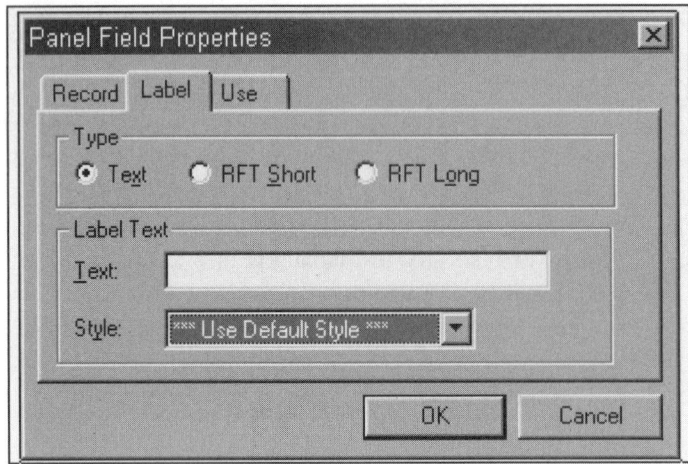

Figure 7-84
LABEL tab for a group box panel control.

box and then double click on it to bring up the Panel Field Properties dialog Box. Figure 7-84 shows the LABEL tab of the Panel Field Properties dialog for the group box control with a blank label.

Before we place the rest of the editable fields on the panel, we are going to put the scroll bar along the right side of the panel. The default values for the Use properties of the scroll bar will be fine. Figure 7-85 shows the default values for the scroll bar. Please note that the occurs level and count are both set to 1. The base occurs level of zero will be set for the `EMP_ID` field, while all of the rest of the fields will have an occurs level of 1, which is controlled by the scroll bar.

The next fields we are going to place on the panel are `EFFDT` and the `EFF_STATUS`. Go to the Employees record folder of the project workspace and select `EFFDT`. Drag and drop it to the panel. Do the same for `EFF_STATUS`. By doing this, the Panel Field Properties are set to default values. The only change we are going to make to these default values is on the LABEL tab of the `EFF_STATUS` field. Change the label type to `RFT_SHORT`. This will use the short description that was set up for the status field in its field definition. Figure 7-86 shows the LABEL tab of the Panel Field Properties dialog for the status field.

Now select the remaining Employee record fields one at a time and drag and drop each one onto the panel. There are a few changes that need to be made to the default field properties. First, the remaining fields of Name, Position, and Email need to have their size attribute of the RECORD tab set to CUSTOM. This will enable us to modify their lengths and to align them symmetrically. Figure 7-87 shows the size attribute set to CUSTOM. In addition, the label text on the LABEL tab for fields Posi-

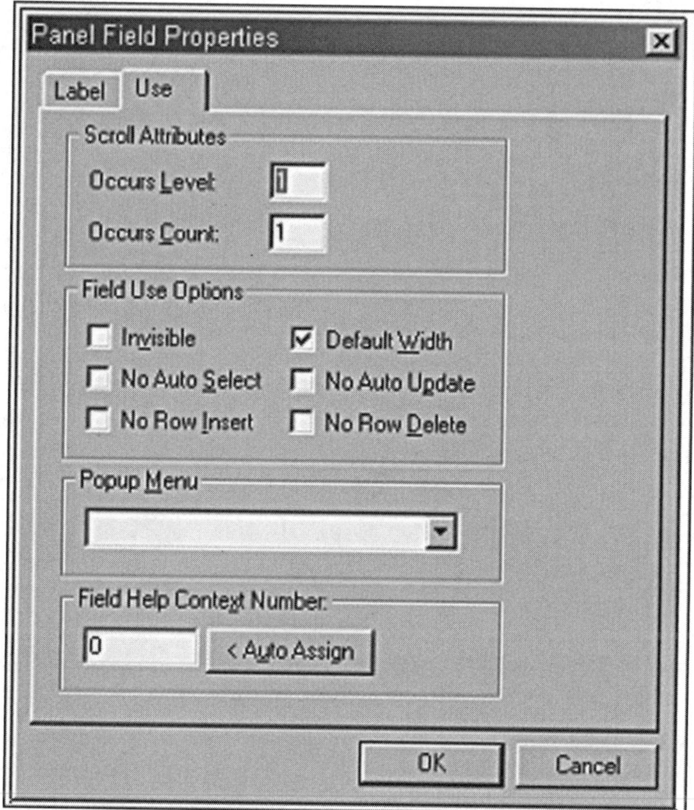

Figure 7-85 Scroll-bar default panel field properties.

tion and Email need to be modified as shown in Figures 7-88 and 7-89. The label type is set to text for each of these fields, so the label text entered for each field will appear on the panel next to the edit boxes. The labels for these fields are going to be overridden with text that we are placing in the Label Text edit box.

The last thing we need to do after we have aligned our controls the way we want them and before we save the panel is to verify that the fields are in a correct tab order. In addition, we need to check that each field is in its correct occurs level. To accomplish this, with the current panel in focus, select the Layout Menu and then the ORDER option. Figure 7-90 shows the Order Panel for our Employees panel. Note that the LVL column indicates the occurs level and the NUM column indicates the order the controls on the panel will be tabbed through. If yours is not the same as the one in Figure 7-90, you can select any columns that are in error and move them where they should be. In the Items panel,

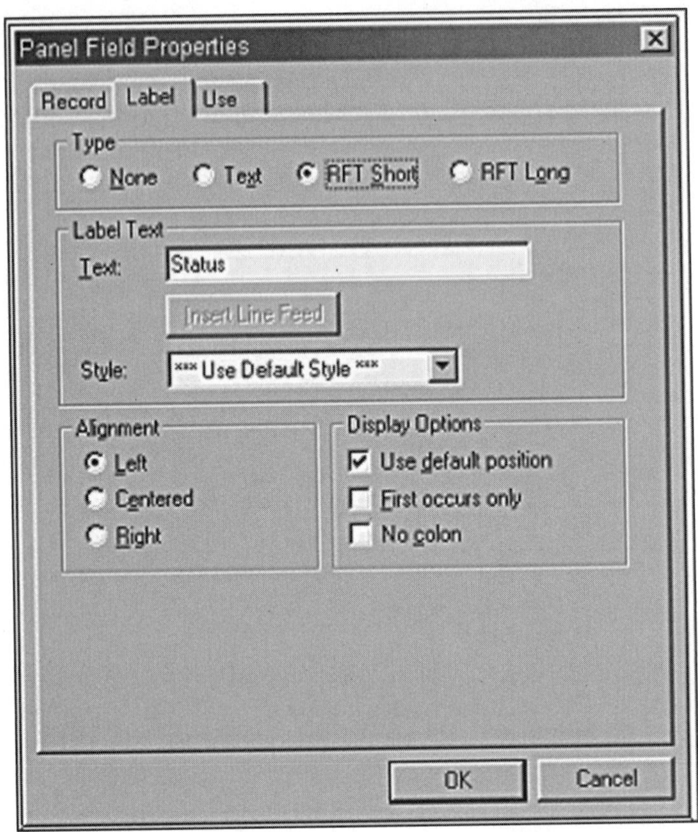

Figure 7-86
LABEL tab of the Status fields Panel Field Properties dialog.

we will go over exactly how you would move your controls in more detail.

When you are done, your panel should look similar to the one in Figure 7-91. If all is correct, please save your panel as EMPLOYEES_PNL and include the panel in the Project by selecting INSERT, OBJECT INTO PROJECT, or hit F7.

Buyer Panel (BUYER_PNL)

For quick reference, the BUYER_VW record contains the following fields:

- EMP_ID
- EFF_DT

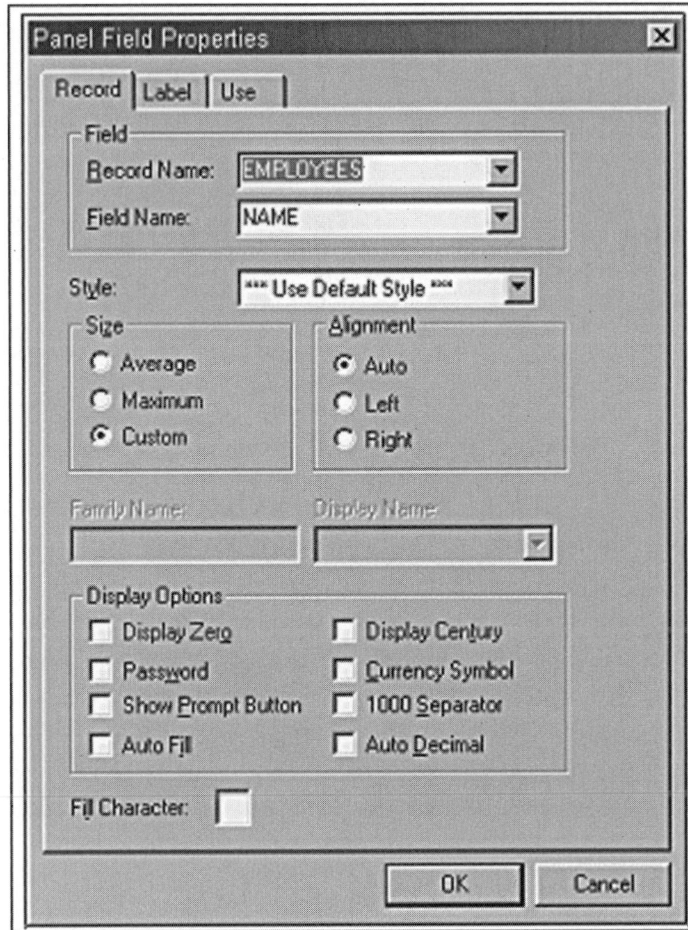

Figure 7-87 RECORD tab for Employees Name field.

- EFF_STATUS
- NAME
- EMAIL_ADDRESS

As discussed in Chapter 6 (Records), the BUYER_VW record is a Query View record that contains only employees who have the position of *buyer*. This means that it is very similar to the Employees record. Therefore, the panel will be very similar to the Employees panel just created. As a result, an easy shortcut to create the panel for the BUYER_VW record is to start with the Employees panel. All we have to do is save a copy of the EMPLOYEES_PNL as BUYER_PNL via FILE, SAVE AS

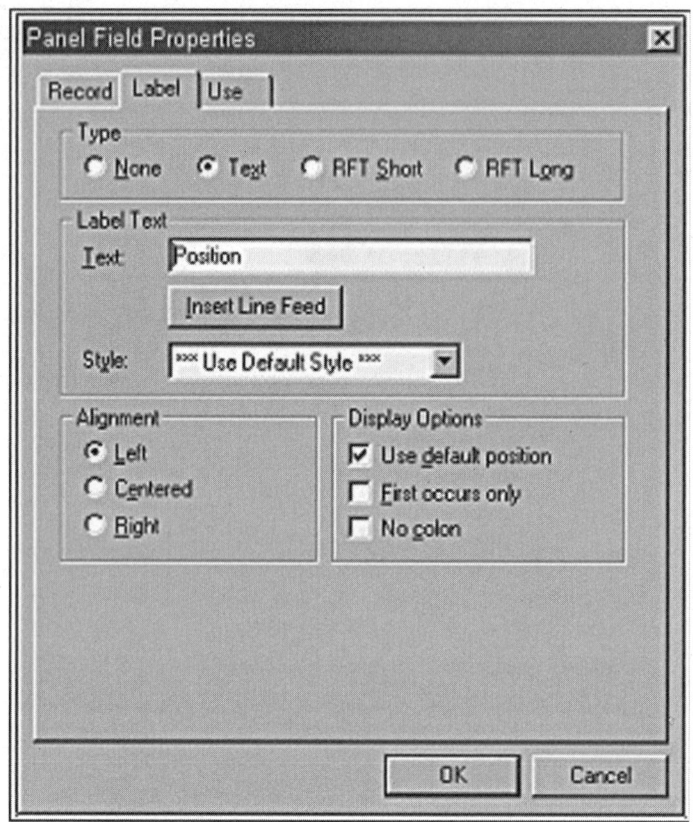

Figure 7-88 LABEL tab for Position with type overridden to Text.

when EMPLOYEES_PNL is open. Then all that is left to do is open the Panel Field Properties dialog for all the fields that are also in the BUYER_VW and change the record name to BUYER_VW. To display the Panel Field Properties dialog, double-click on each of the panel controls. Figure 7-92 shows the RECORD tab of the Panel Field Properties for the EMP_ID field with the change made to the record name. Make this change for all the fields. Since Position is not a field in the BUYER_VW record, simply delete it from the panel. When that is complete, you can align and change labels to make your panel look similar to the panel in Figure 7-93. Do not forget to save your completed panel, and make sure that it is included in your project.

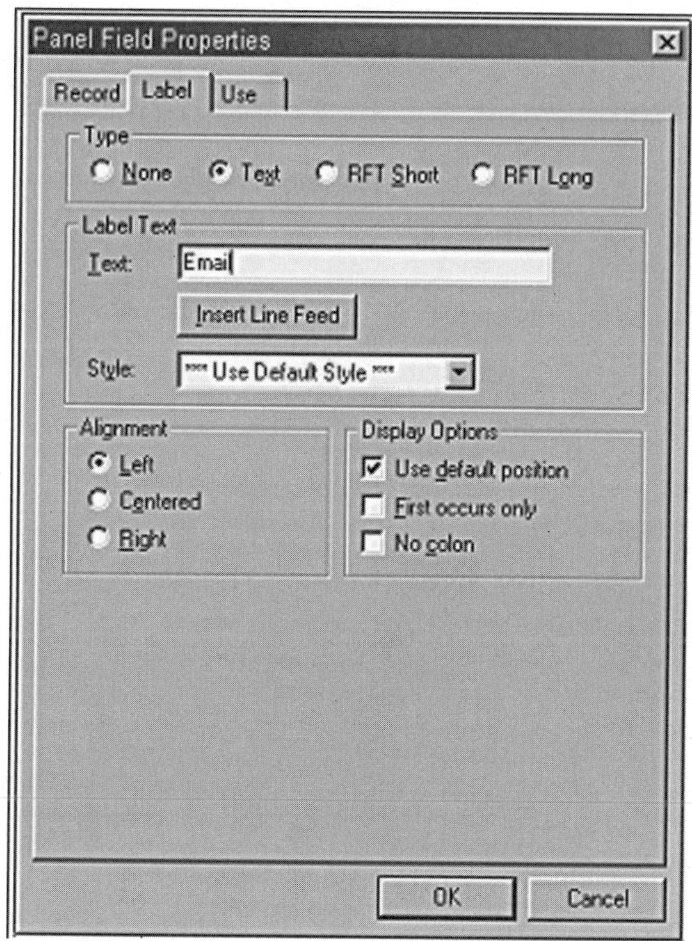

Figure 7-89 LABEL tab for Email with Type overridden to Text.

Items Panel (ITEMS_PNL)

The next panel we are going to create is the Items panel. It will include all the fields of the ITEMS record. ITEMS fields are ITEM_ID, EFFDT, EFF_STATUS, and DESCR. To begin creating the Items panel, press the NEW icon or select FILE, NEW. When the New dialog is displayed, select PANEL and press OK. A new blank panel will be displayed

Order Panel

Num	Lvl	Label	Type	Field	Record
		*** Top of List ***			
1	0	No Label	Group Box		EMPLOYEES
2	0	Employee ID	Edit Box	EMP_ID	EMPLOYEES
3	1	Scroll Bar	Scroll Bar		
4	1	No Label	Group Box		EMPLOYEES
5	1	Effective Date	Edit Box	EFFDT	EMPLOYEES
6	1	Status	Drop Down List	EFF_STATUS	EMPLOYEES
7	1	Name	Edit Box	NAME	EMPLOYEES
8	1	Position	Drop Down List	POSITION	EMPLOYEES
9	1	Email	Edit Box	EMAIL_ADDRESS	EMPLOYEES
		*** End of List ***			

OK Cancel Select Move Unselect Default

Figure 7-90 Order Panel for Employees panel.

in the Object Workspace of the Application Designer. With the ITEMS record folder expanded in the Project Workspace, select the ITEM_ID field and drag and drop it onto the top left of the panel. Now double-click on the ITEM_ID that was placed onto the panel. When the Panel Field Properties dialog is displayed, select the USE tab and set the Display Only check box on. Once you have done this, you can press OK. The ITEM_ID edit box that was placed onto the panel should now be grayed out. Next place a group box control around ITEM_ID and remove the labels text.

For the description and effective date fields, drag and drop them onto the panel from the ITEMS record panel. Do not forget the scroll bar and the no-label group box. When you have completed this procedure, your panel should resemble the one in Figure 7-94.

If you were not careful with the order in which you placed your controls on the panel, your Order panel could resemble the one displayed in

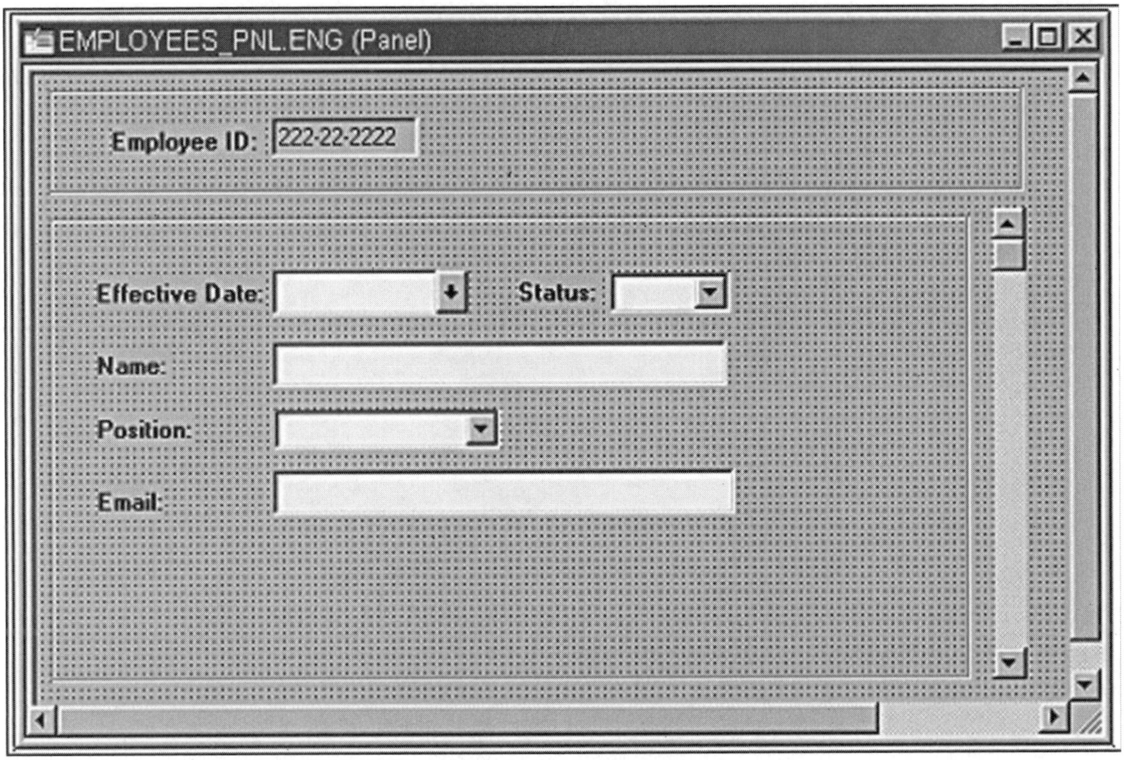

Figure 7-91 Completed Employees panel.

Figure 7-95. Figures 7-96 through 7-99 show in order the steps you would follow to move a field to change its order and occurs level. Our Effective Date field was placed on our panel before the scroll bar was. This sets the wrong occurs level for the Effective Date field. To fix this problem, we need to place the effective date below the scroll bar. To accomplish this, select the Effective Date field with your mouse and then press the SELECT button that will now be enabled. Once the SELECT button has been entered, the Effective Date field will disappear and the MOVE button will be enabled. We now need to select the location in which we want to place our field. Use your mouse to select the field that you want the Effective Date field to be placed after. We selected the group box that was below the scroll bar and then pressed the MOVE button.

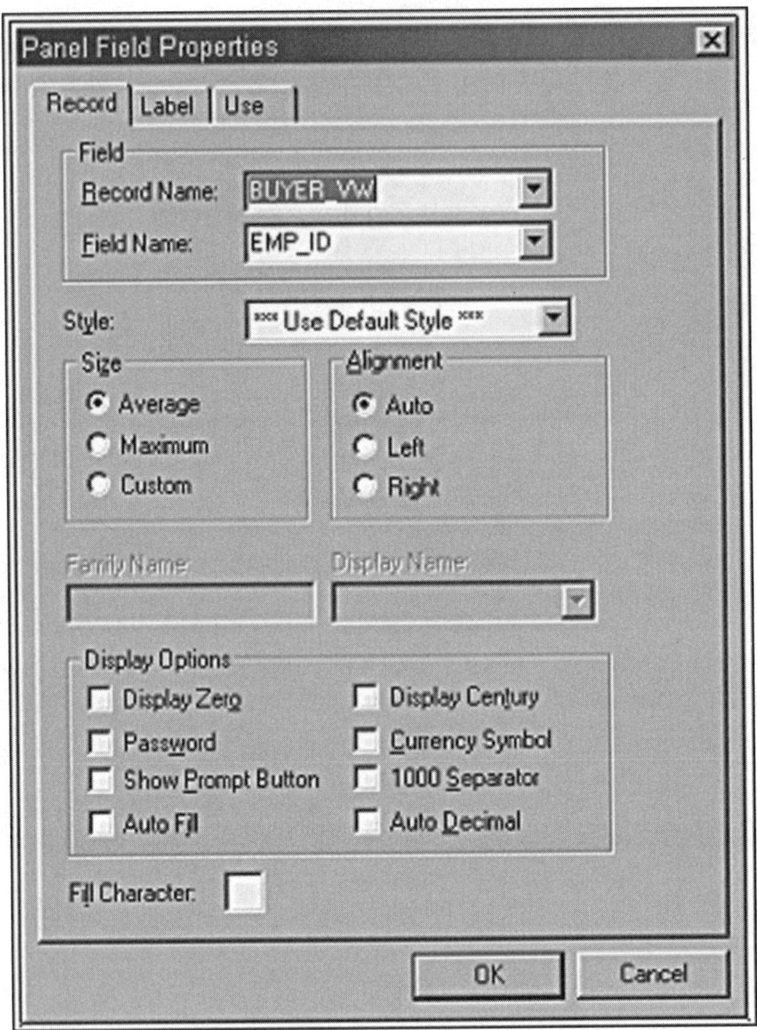

Figure 7-92 EMP_ID control for the Buyer panel.

Figure 7-99 shows the final Order Panel dialog with the Effective Date field in its correct occurs level of 1 and a column number of 5.

Locations Panel (LOCATIONS_PNL)

The next panel we are going to create is the Locations panel. Please follow the same steps as used in our previous examples. The Process Location id should be disabled by selecting Display Only on the USE tab, and

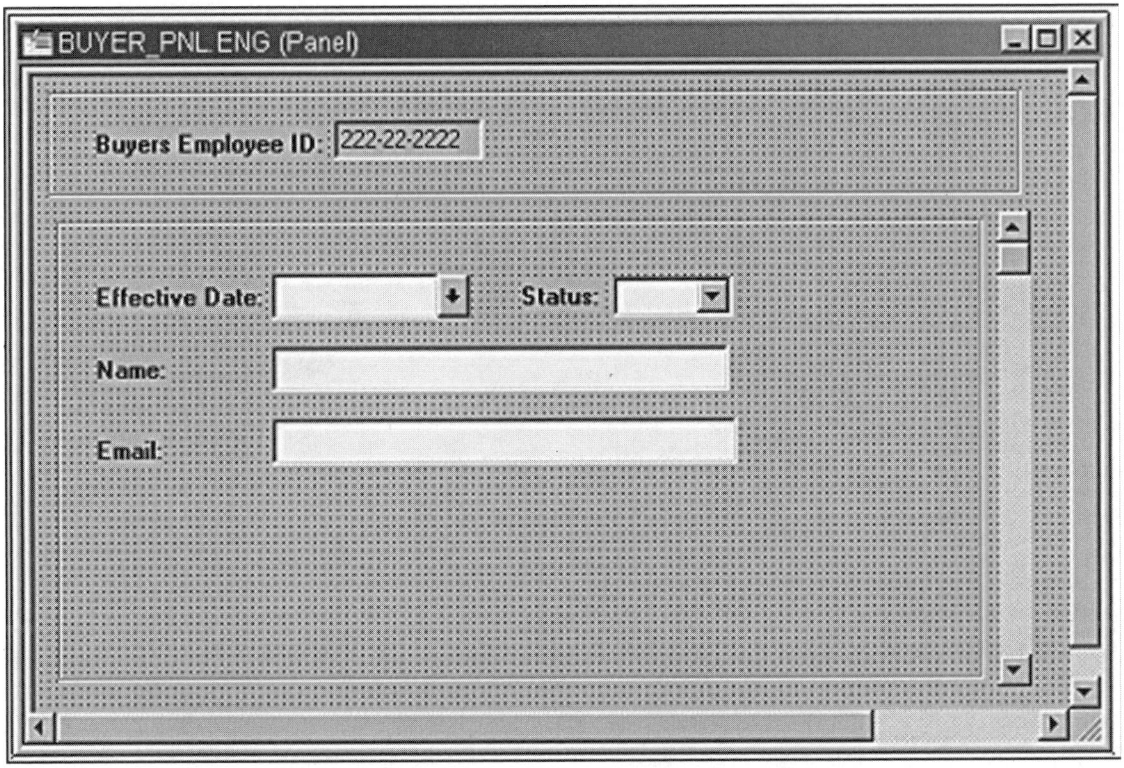

Figure 7-93 Completed Buyer panel.

it should be placed in occurs level 0. Effective Date, Effective Status, and Description should all be placed in occurs level 1, which is controlled by its own scroll bar. You can either create your panel by scratch or simply save the Items panel as your new Locations panel and then change the record name in the RECORD tab of each of the fields' Panel Field Properties dialogs. When you have finished and the order of your fields has checked out, your panel should look similar to the panel in Figure 7-100. Please remember to save your panel and to include it in your project.

Units of Measure Panel (`UNIT_MEASURE_PNL`)

The next panel we will create is the Units of Measure panel. This is one of the easiest panels we are going to create. There are no Effective Date fields; therefore we do not need to use a scroll bar or multiple occurs lev-

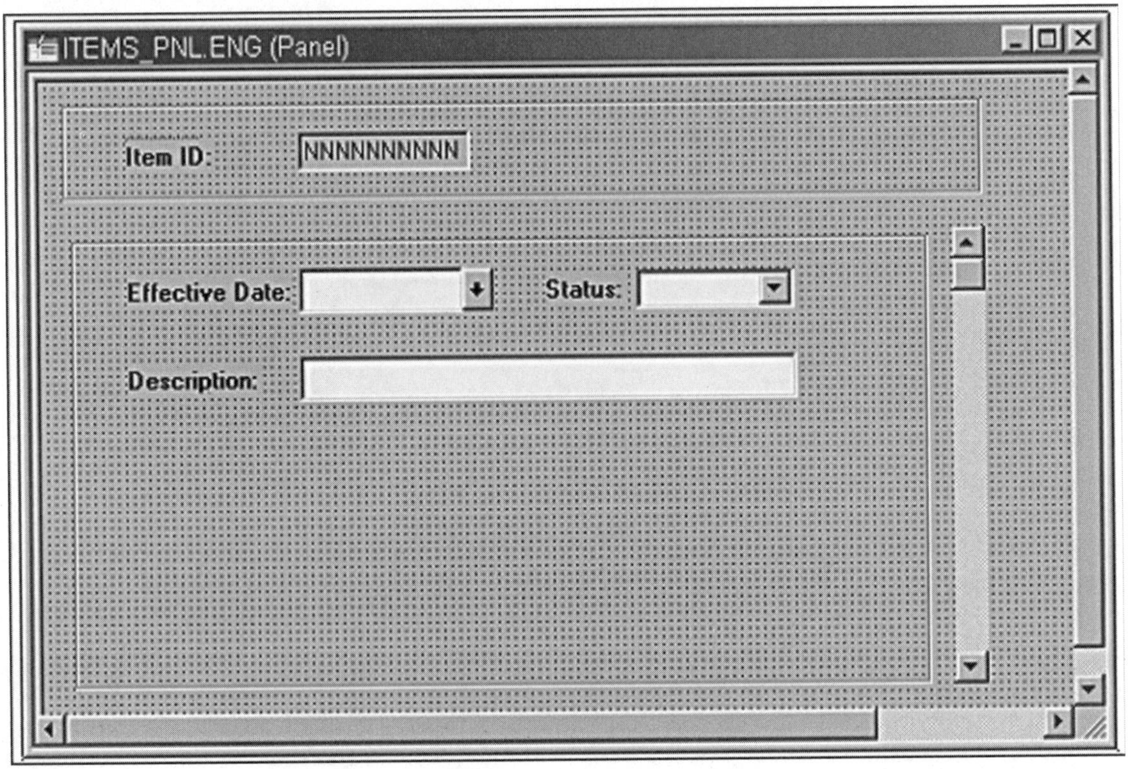

Figure 7-94 Completed Items panel.

els. All we require is that the UNIT_MEASURE field be disabled and placed at the top in our key area and that the Description field be placed below it in the editable nonkey area. When you have finished, your panel should resemble the panel in Figure 7-101. Please remember to save your panel and to include it in your project.

Address Subpanel (ADD_SBR_PNL)

The next panel will create introduces a new topic to our example. If you recall, when we created our Vendor record, we used a subrecord for addresses in its definition. The same logic that would lead you to create a subrecord could lead you toward the creation of a subpanel. Throughout our entire application example, addresses can be used on several dif-

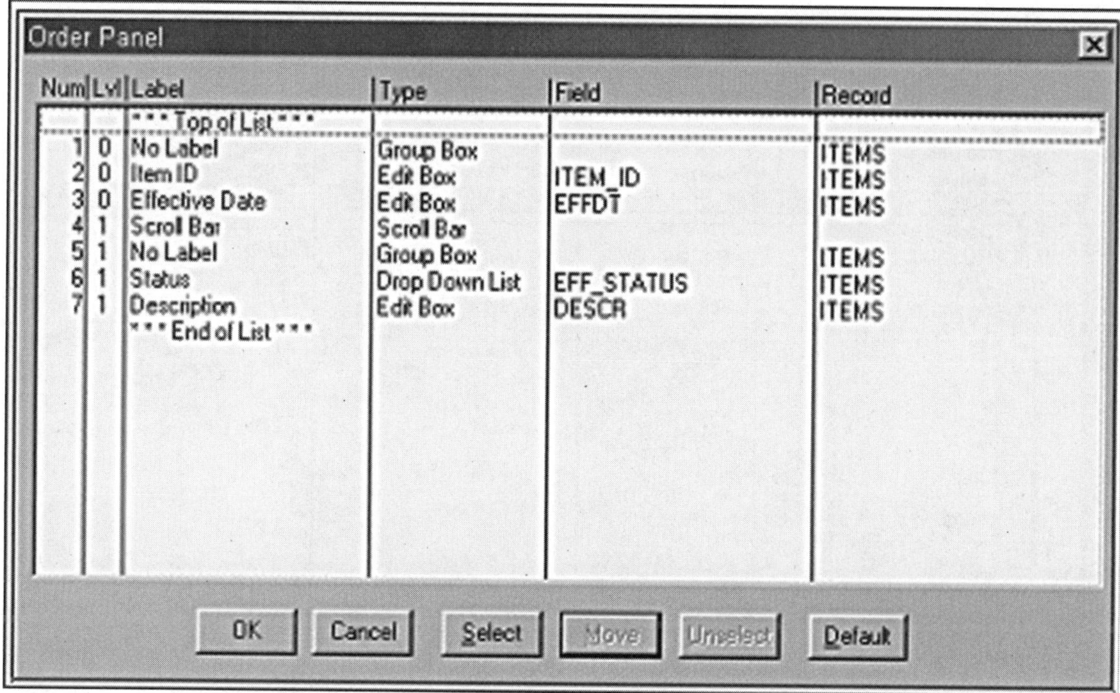

Figure 7-95 Order Panel dialog Effective Date in the wrong order and occurs level.

ferent panels. By using a subpanel for them, we are able to standardize the look and feel of an address. PeopleSoft is delivered with far more substantial address subrecords and subpanels than we are creating. *We are using this only as a tool for you to see and understand the utility of subrecords and subpanels.*

To create our address subpanel, create a new empty panel. Once the empty panel is displayed in the Object Workspace, double-click on it to display the Panel Properties dialog. Select the USE tab and change the panel type to Subpanel. Figure 7-102 shows the USE tab of the Panel Properties dialog, with the panel type changed to Subpanel. When that is complete, press OK to return to the new empty subpanel. Now you are ready to add the fields from the Address subrecord to our subpanel. With the Address subpanel expanded in our Project Workspace, drag and drop `STREET1`, `STREET2`, `CITY`, and `STATE` onto our panel. In addition to checking that the order is correct for our subpanel, we can also adjust

Num	Lvl	Label	Type	Field	Record
		*** Top of List ***			
1	0	No Label	Group Box		ITEMS
2	0	Item ID	Edit Box	ITEM_ID	ITEMS
3	0	Effective Date	Edit Box	EFFDT	ITEMS
4	1	Scroll Bar	Scroll Bar		
5	1	No Label	Group Box		ITEMS
6	1	Status	Drop Down List	EFF_STATUS	ITEMS
7	1	Description	Edit Box	DESCR	ITEMS
		*** End of List ***			

Figure 7-96 Order Panel dialog prior to SELECT operation.

the size of the subpanel to make it only as large as it needs to be. To do this, simply use your mouse to select the panel frame, and with your mouse still pressed down, move the cursor to decrease the size of the panel. When you have completed this, your panel should look similar to the panel in Figure 7-103.

Vendors Panel (VENDORS_PNL)

The last of our lookup panels is the Vendors panel. The Vendors panel will use the fields from the Vendors record. For quick reference purposes, the Vendors record contains the following fields:

- VENDOR_ID
- EFFDT
- EFF_STATUS

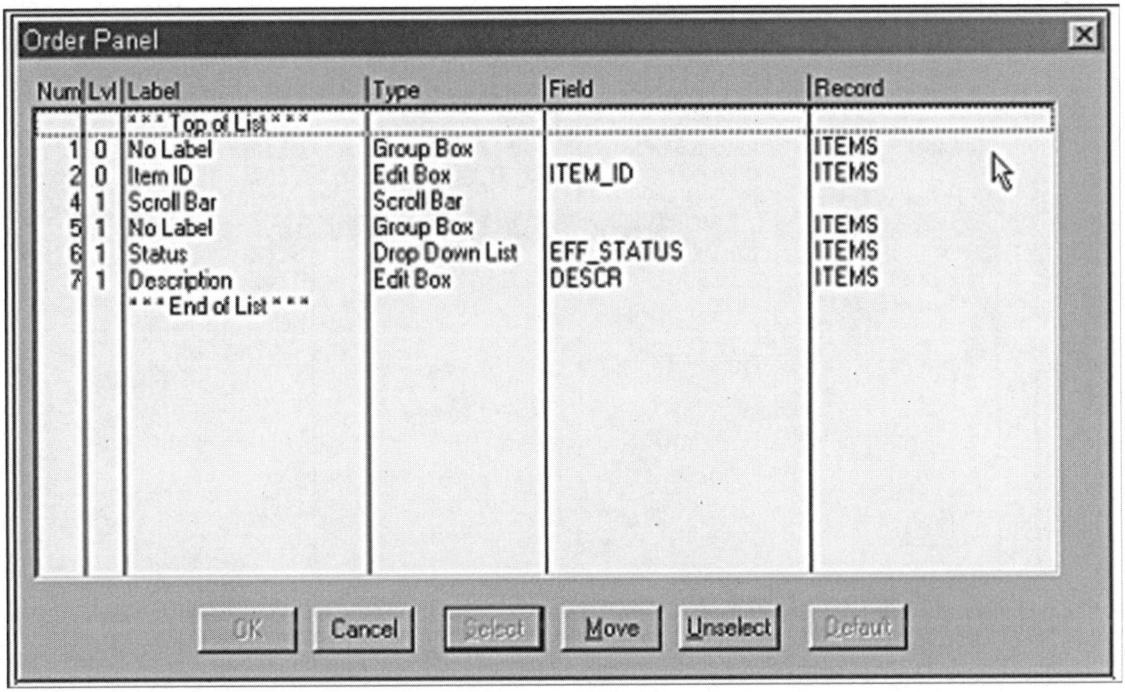

Order Panel

Num	Lvl	Label	Type	Field	Record
		*** Top of List ***			
1	0	No Label	Group Box		ITEMS
2	0	Item ID	Edit Box	ITEM_ID	ITEMS
4	1	Scroll Bar	Scroll Bar		
5	1	No Label	Group Box		ITEMS
6	1	Status	Drop Down List	EFF_STATUS	ITEMS
7	1	Description	Edit Box	DESCR	ITEMS
		*** End of List ***			

OK | Cancel | Select | Move | Unselect | Default

Figure 7-97 Order Panel dialog after SELECT operation.

- VENDOR
- STREET1
- STREET2
- CITY
- STATE

This panel is very similar to the previous panels that we have created, except that it will utilize the Address subpanel that we just created. After you have placed all the nonsubrecord fields from the Vendors record onto the panel in their correct positions and order, you can insert a subpanel control. To insert a subpanel, go to the Insert menu and select SUBPANEL. When the Subpanel dialog is displayed, select the subpanel we just created and set the Record substitution to the Vendors record. Figure 7-104 shows the Subpanel dialog with its correct options selected. Figure 7-105 shows the finished Vendors panel. Before you

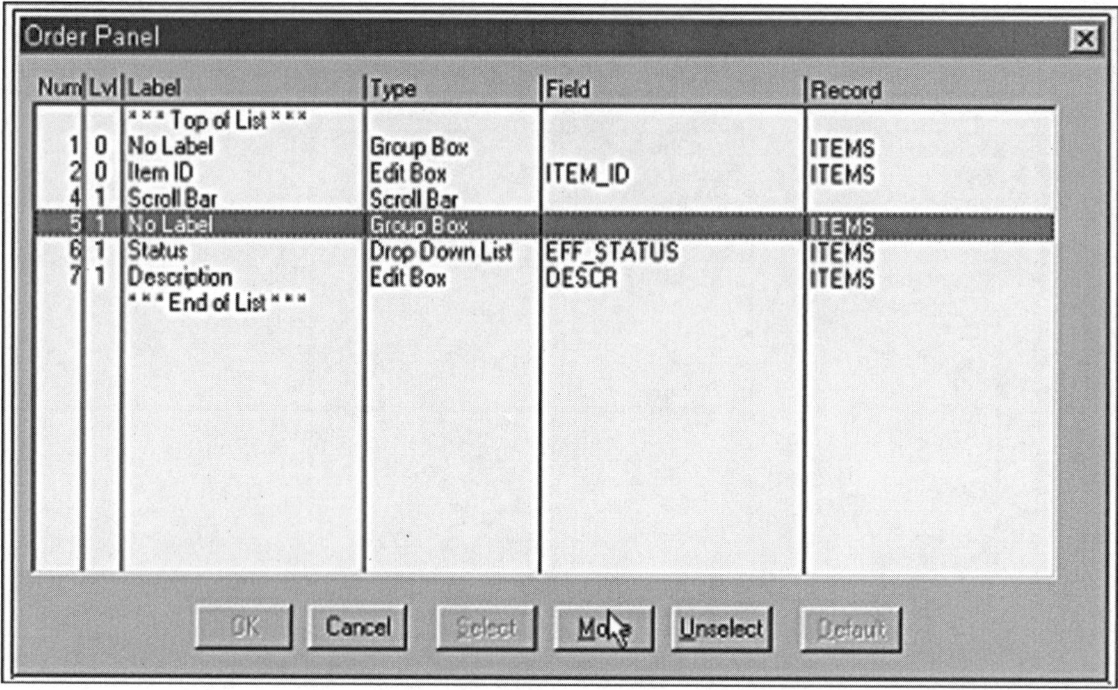

Figure 7-98 Order Panel dialog prior to MOVE operation.

save the panel, make sure that the subpanel is last in the Order panel. If the order is correct, save the panel and include it in your project.

New Internal Order Panel (INT_NEW_ORD_PNL)

We are now ready to start building our main panels. The first one that we are going to create is the New Internal Order panel. The fields that will be placed on this panel will come from several records. The fields from the INT_ORDER record are INT_ORDER_ID, REQUESTED_DT, EMP_ID, PROCESS_DT, and PROCESS_LOC_ID. The fields from INT_ORDER_LINES are LINE_NUM, ITEM_ID, QTY, and UNIT_MEASURE. Also the NAME field of the EMPLOYEES record, the DESCR field of the LOCATIONS record, and the DESCR field of the ITEMS record will be on this panel. This will be the panel that will be filled out initially to let the warehouse personnel know what, where, and when material will be

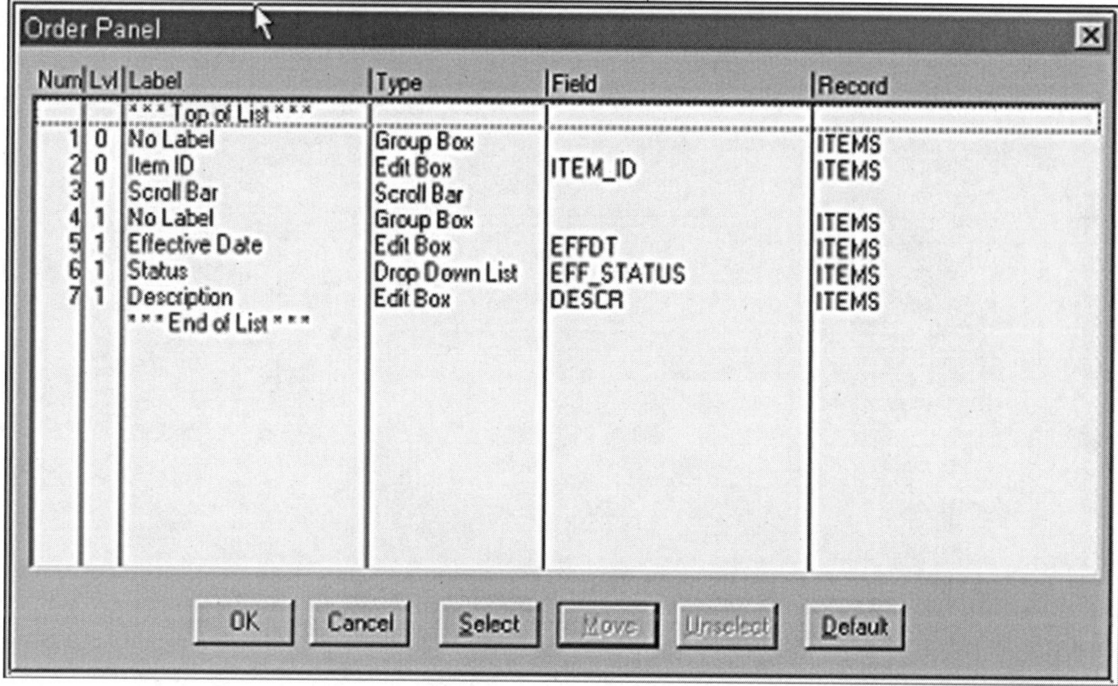

Figure 7-99 Order Panel dialog after MOVE operation.

needed. This panel will be used only for the new internal orders. The people who placed the order will use a read-only version of the internal order panel to view the status of the internal order that they placed.

Please begin creating our New Internal Order panel by adding the following fields from the `INT_ORDER` record to a new blank panel:

- `INT_ORDER_ID`
- `REQUESTED_DT`
- `EMP_ID`
- `PROCESS_DT`
- `PROCESS_LOC_ID`

The `INT_ORDER_ID` field is the key field, so it should be grayed out and placed toward the top of our panel within either a no-label group box or a frame. The rest of these fields should be placed in order in an enabled state below the key section.

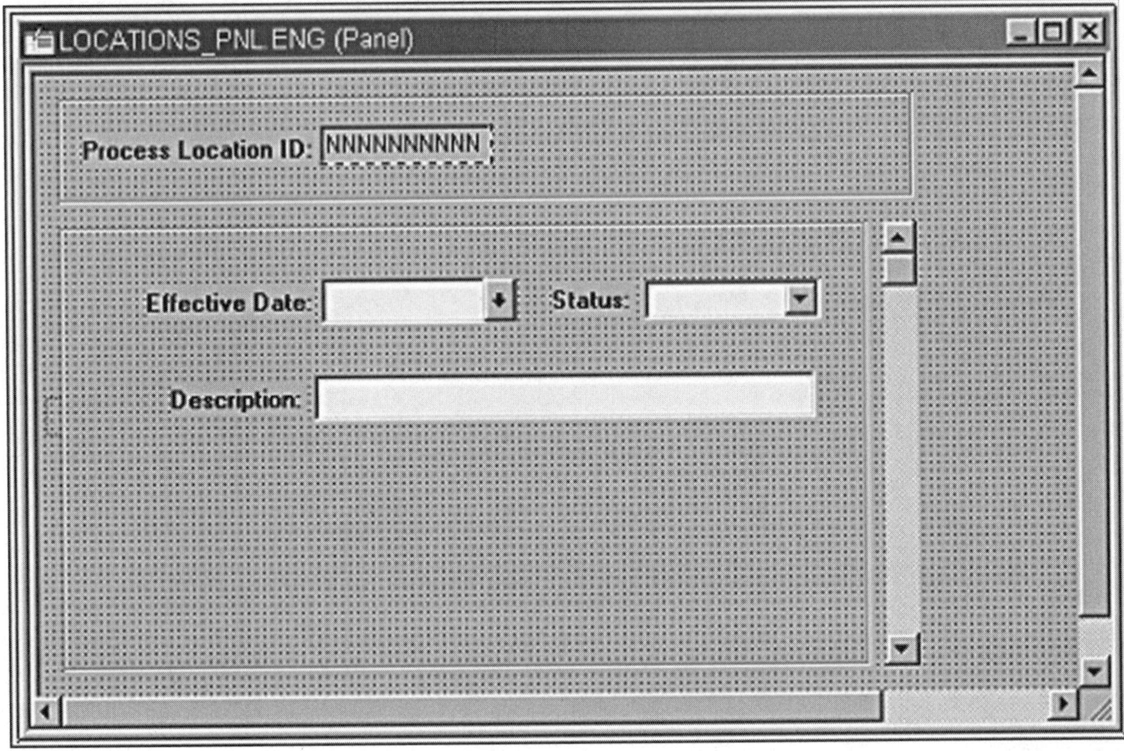

Figure 7-100 Locations panel.

We are now ready to introduce a very important new concept to our panels. This topic is display control and related display fields. All the lookup records that we created early are linked to our main records by system-generated keys that in themselves are not descriptive enough to allow end users to know what they are. PeopleSoft allows us to overcome this by adding a more descriptive read-only field to our panels that will help clarify what our lookup values represent. We are going to use display control and related fields for the Employee id, Process Location id, and Item id, for our New Internal Order panel.

The first step is to bring up the USE tab for the `EMP_ID` and `PROCESS_LOC_ID` fields. The field use option Display Control Field must be selected for these fields. Figure 7-106 shows the Employee id USE tab that will set these fields to Display Control fields. The `PROCESS_LOC_ID` and `ITEM_ID` USE tabs will be identical to this.

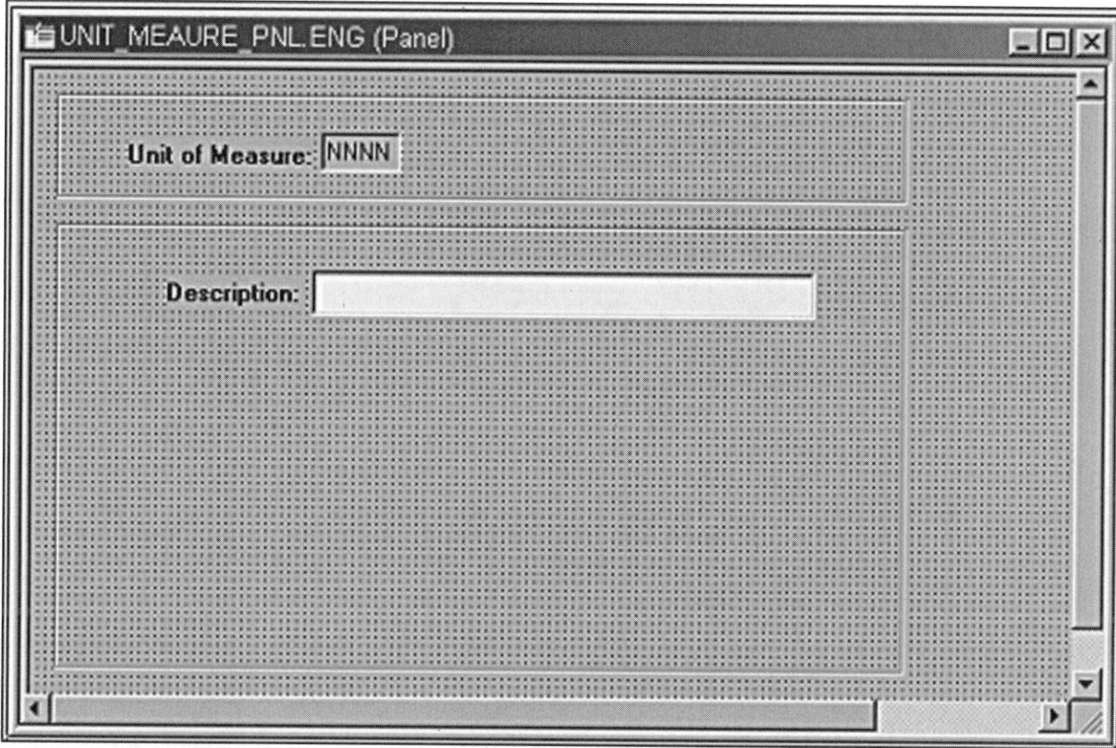

Figure 7-101 Units of Measure panel.

Figures 7-107 through 7-109 show the Panel Field Properties for the Name field. The Name field of the EMPLOYEES record is the related display field for Employee ID. The DESCR field of the LOCATIONS record is the related display field for the Location ID. The related display fields will be set to DISPLAY ONLY with no label, and for each one you must select the proper related control field in the Panel Field Properties dialog USE tab.

Therefore, on the USE tab of the Name field (Fig. 7-109), the DISPLAY ONLY and RELATED DISPLAY FIELD options are selected. In addition, the Related Control Field is set to EMP_ID. The RECORD tab (Fig. 7-107) has the size set to CUSTOM, the record name set to EMPLOYEES, and the field name set to NAME. The LABEL tab type is set to NONE, so no label will be displayed (Fig. 7-108).

On the USE tab of the DESCR field, the Display Only and Related Display Field options are also selected. The Related Control Field is set to

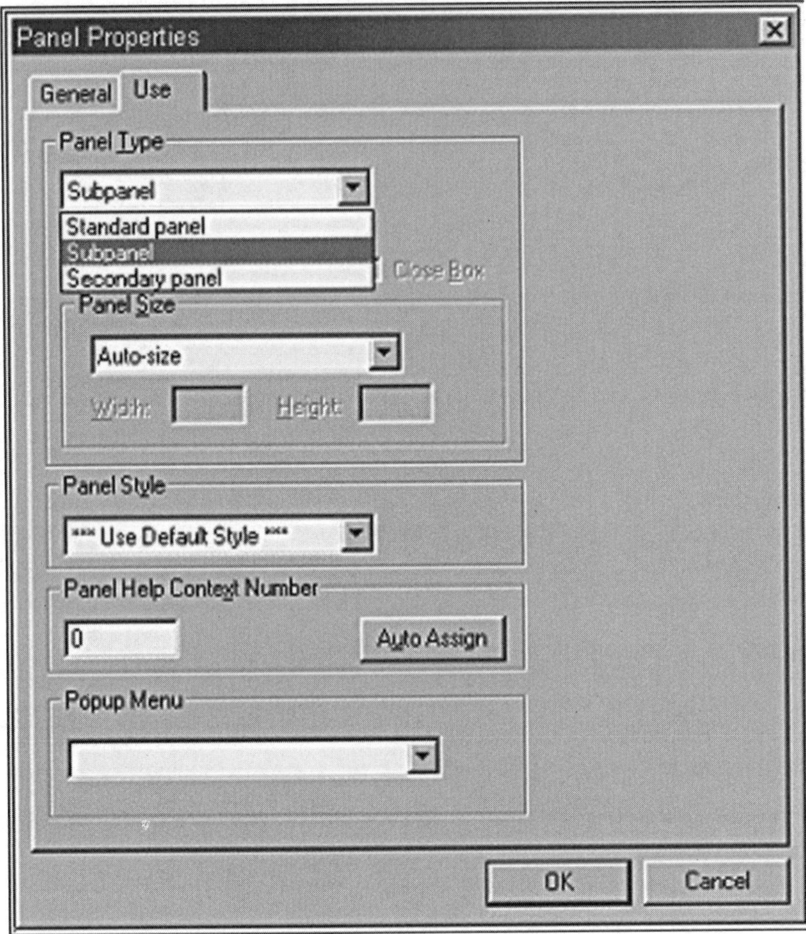

Figure 7-102 Address subpanel Panel Properties dialog.

PROCESS_LOC_ID. The RECORD tab has the record name set to LOCATIONS and the field is DESCR. The LABEL tab has the label type set to NONE.

The Item field will be discussed a little later in this chapter.

Figure 7-110 shows what the panel should look like before we begin adding the fields of the INT_ORDER_LINES record. We have already added the scroll bar that is going to control the INT_ORDER_LINES records. Please add the following fields from the INT_ORDER_LINES record (place them horizontally across the panel at the same height as the top of our new scroll bar):

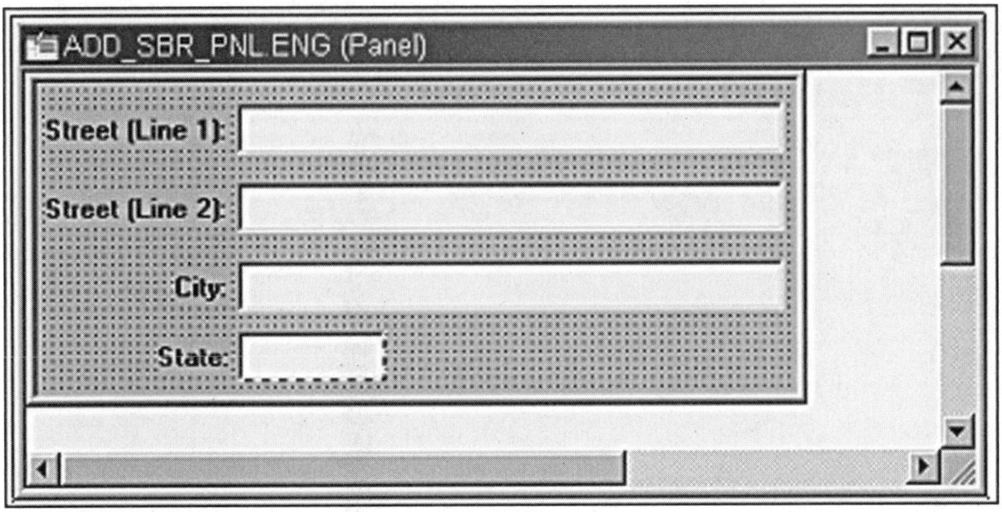

Figure 7-103 Address subpanel.

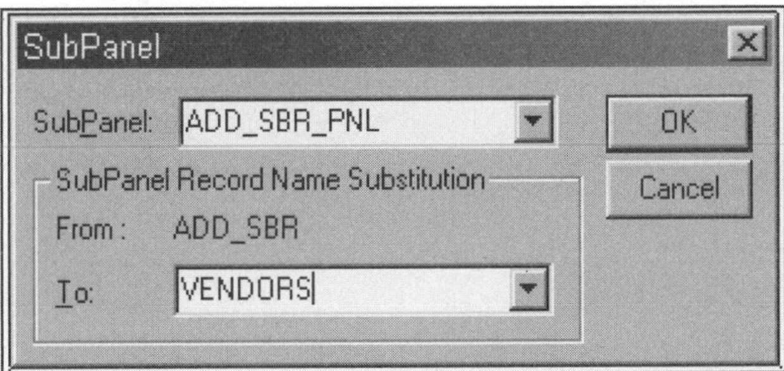

Figure 7-104 Address subpanel.

- LINE_NUM
- ITEM_ID
- QTY
- UNIT_MEASURE

In addition to these fields, we are going to add the description of the Item id as a related display field. We will also add labels above all the fields from the INT_ORDER_LINES record. To do so, go to the LABEL tab of each field and set the label type to RFT SHORT and select the FIRST OCCURS ONLY and the NO COLON display options. This will cause the short

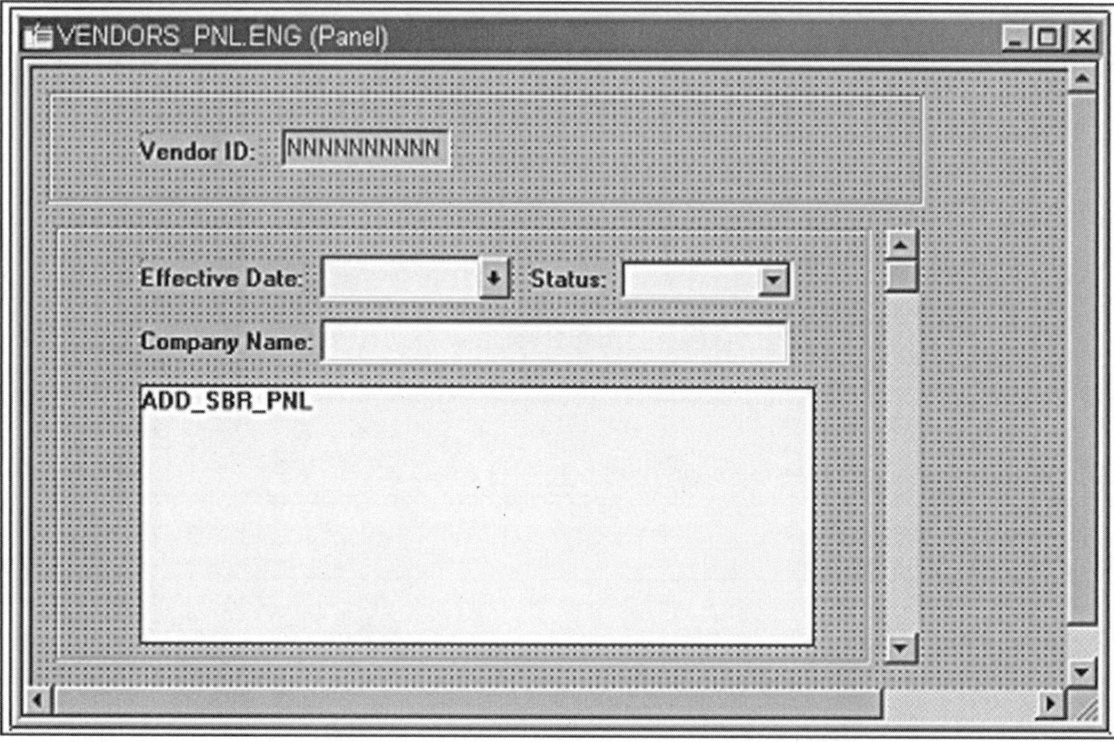

Figure 7-105 Vendors panel.

labels to be displayed with no colon. The labels will exist only the first time the field occurs within the scroll bar. Figure 7-111 shows the LABEL tab of the Panel Field Properties dialog as it appears for all the INT_ORDER_LINES fields.

The DESCR field of the ITEMS record will be used as a related display to the Item id field we have already placed on the panel. We already mentioned that the ITEM_ID USE tab must have the DISPLAY CONTROL FIELD field use option selected as shown in Figure 7-106. Now, place the DESCR field of the ITEMS record next to the ITEM_ID field. Double-click on the DESCR field to bring up the Panel Field dialog box. Set the size to CUSTOM on the RECORD tab. On the LABEL tab, set the label type to NONE. On the USE tab, select RELATED DISPLAY FIELD and select ITEM_ID as the related control field.

The only thing left to do before we check the order of our controls is to

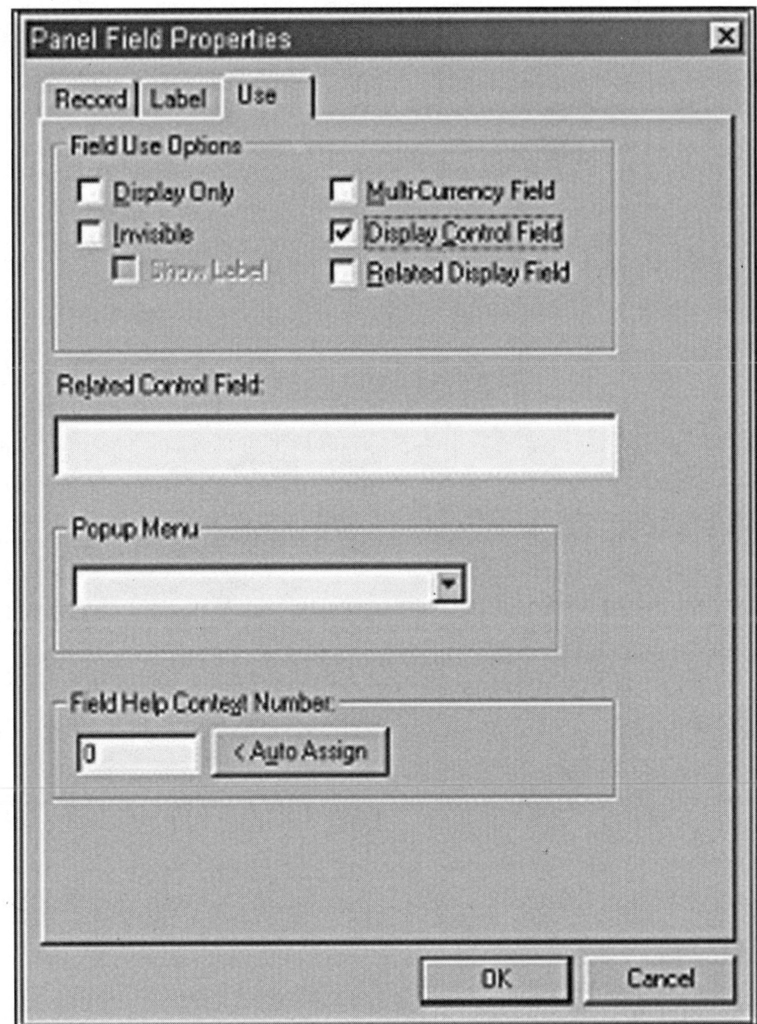

Figure 7-106 Employee id, Process id and Item id USE tab.

open the scroll bar Panel Field Properties dialog and to set the USE scroll attributes (see Fig.7-112). We want this scroll bar to have an occurs level of 1 and an occurs count of 5. Immediately after you set the occurs count and press OK, the panel should resemble the one in Figure 7-113. Note how the new fields that we just added now show up 5 times.

Now check and make modifications to the Order panel (Fig. 7-114). When you are satisfied, save your New Internal Order panel and include it in your project.

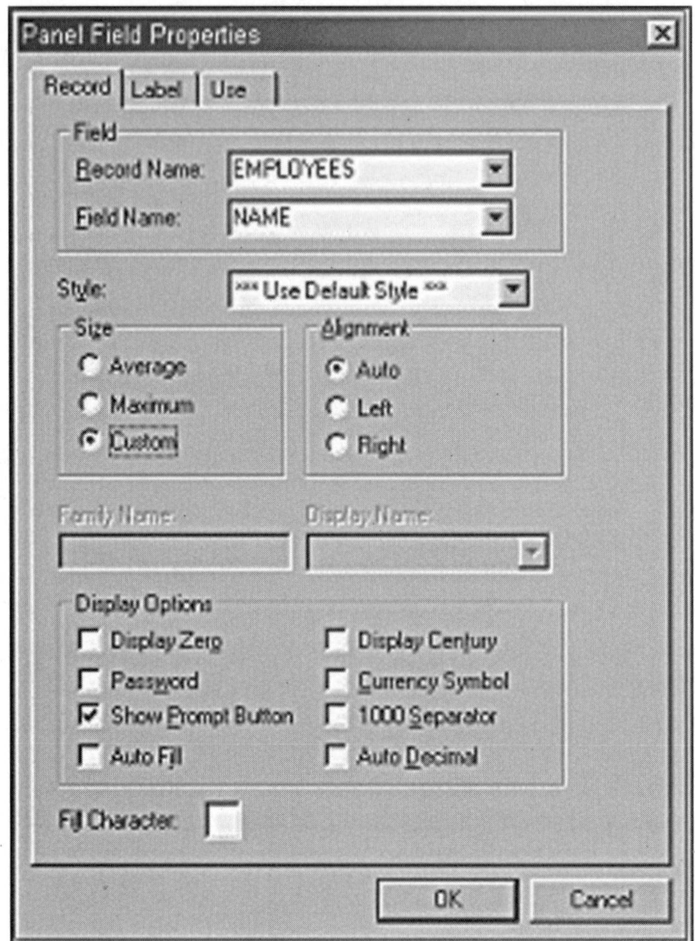

Figure 7-107
NAME RECORD tab.

Internal Order Panel (`INT_ORDER_PNL`)

The Internal Order panel will be used by the warehouse personnel in update mode and by requesters in a read-only mode. It differs from the New Internal Order panel in that it has status fields and other addition fields that allow the internal order to include information about external orders.

To simplify this procedure, we can save our previous New Internal Order panel as Internal Order. To begin, delete the scroll bar and all the fields associated with it. Your panel should look very similar to the one in Figure 7-110, but there should not be a scroll bar. Now we are ready

Figure 7-108
NAME LABEL tab.

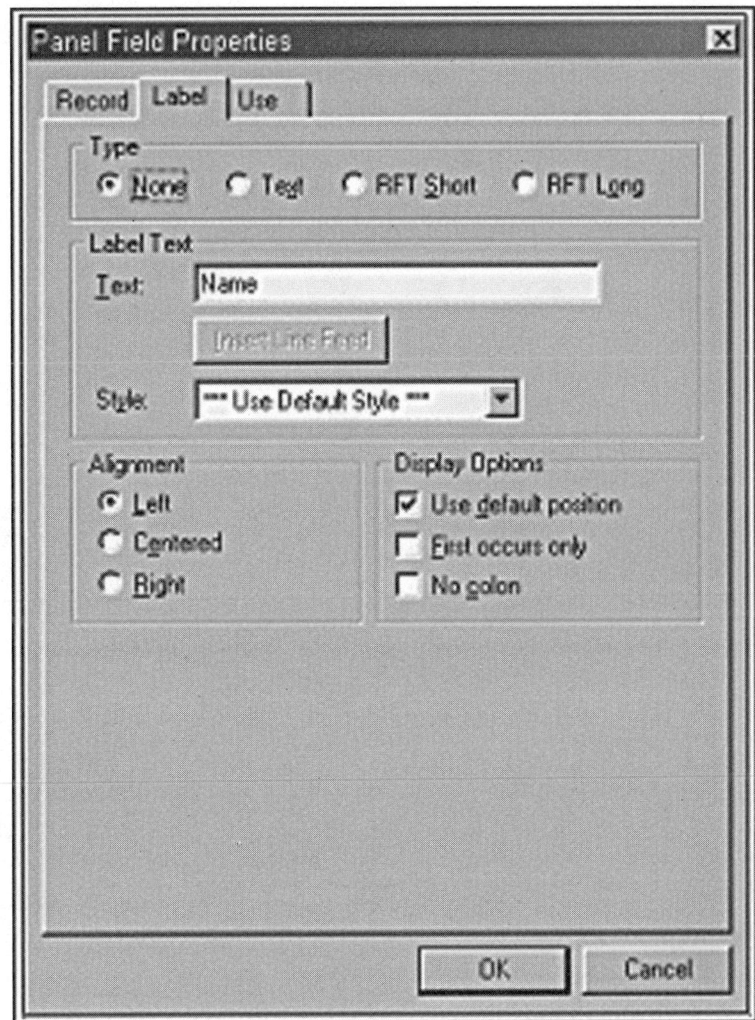

to add the status for the internal order to our Panel. The INT_STAT field from the INT_ORDER record will be used. When we set up this field, we set the default panel control to radio button for this field. Therefore, when we drag and drop it onto our panel from the INT_ORDER record definition, we should see a radio button control with a label of DUMMY NAME. Figure 7-115 shows the default radio control when initially placed on the panel.

We are going to want to have a radio control for each of the following possible statuses that we set up in the translate table:

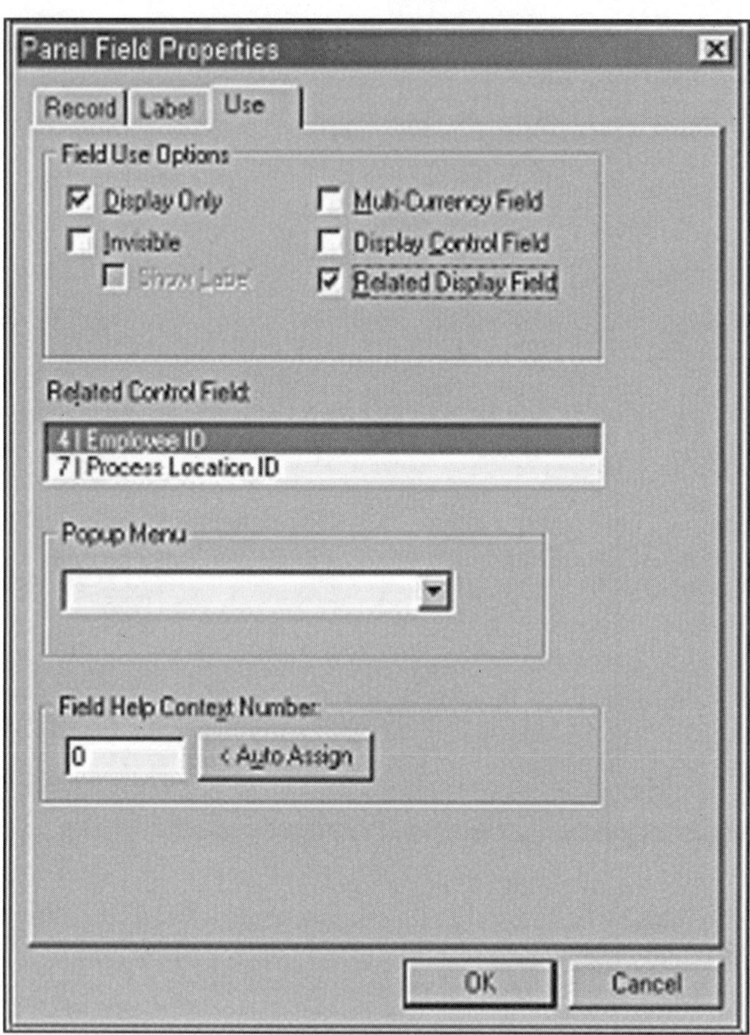

Figure 7-109 NAME use tab.

Text	Value
Canceled	CAN
Fulfilled	FUL
New order	NEW
On order	ORD
Ready	RDY

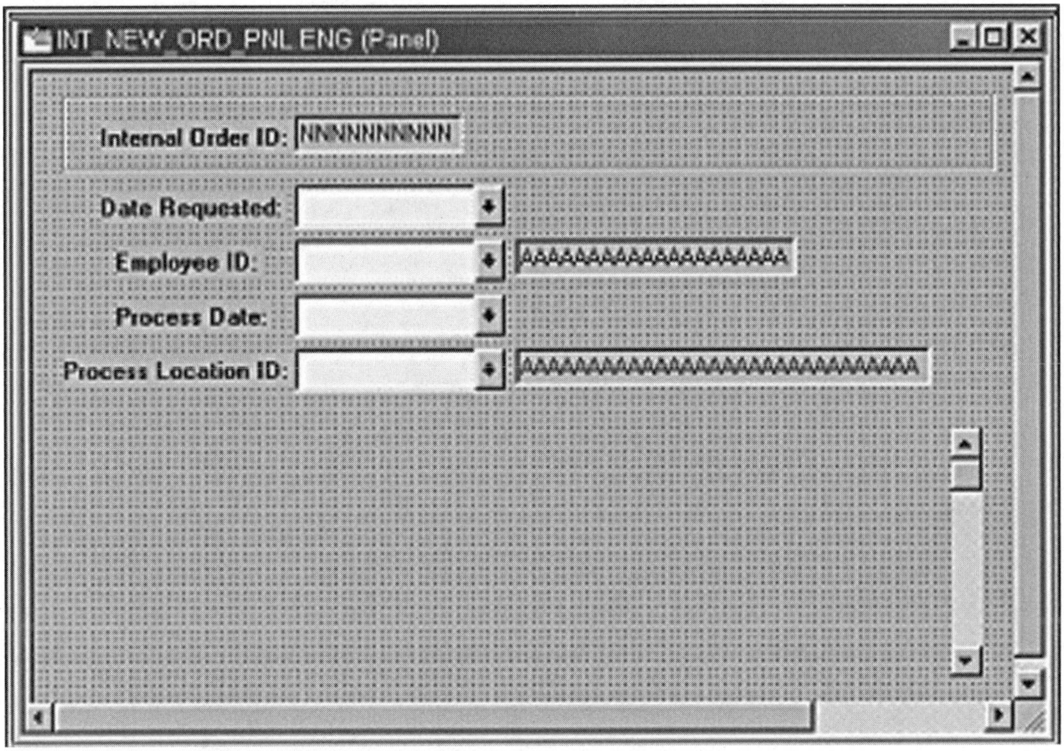

Figure 7-110 Internal Order panel with header fields.

Once you have placed the five radio controls on the panel, you can double-click on them to set the appropriate labels and values. Figures 7-116 and 7-117 show the value and label being set for the NEW radio button. On the RECORD tab, the record name is set to `INT_ORDER`, the field is set to `INT_STAT`, and the value is set to NEW. On the Label tab, the label text is set to NEW ORDER. Repeat this for all five statuses, entering in the correct values and text for each status. When you are done, add a group box control around all of them. This time the group box will get its label from a field. Figures 7-118 and 7-119 show the record being set for the group box and the label settings.

When that has been completed, your panel should resemble the one in Figure 7-120. All that needs to be done to complete the panel is to add a grid control with the following fields from the `INT_ORDER_LINES` record:

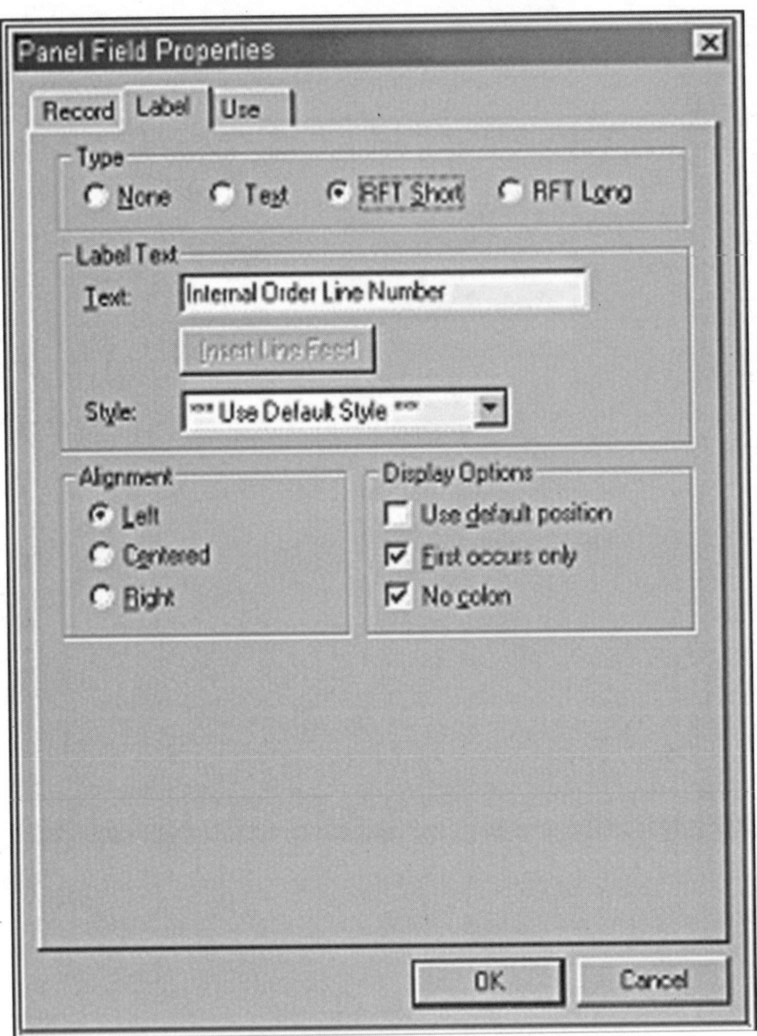

Figure 7-111 LABEL tab for all the INT_ORDER_LINES fields on the New Internal Order panel.

- LINE_NUM
- ITEM_ID
- QTY
- UNIT_MEASURE
- REQUESTED_DT
- EXT_ORDER
- EXT_STAT

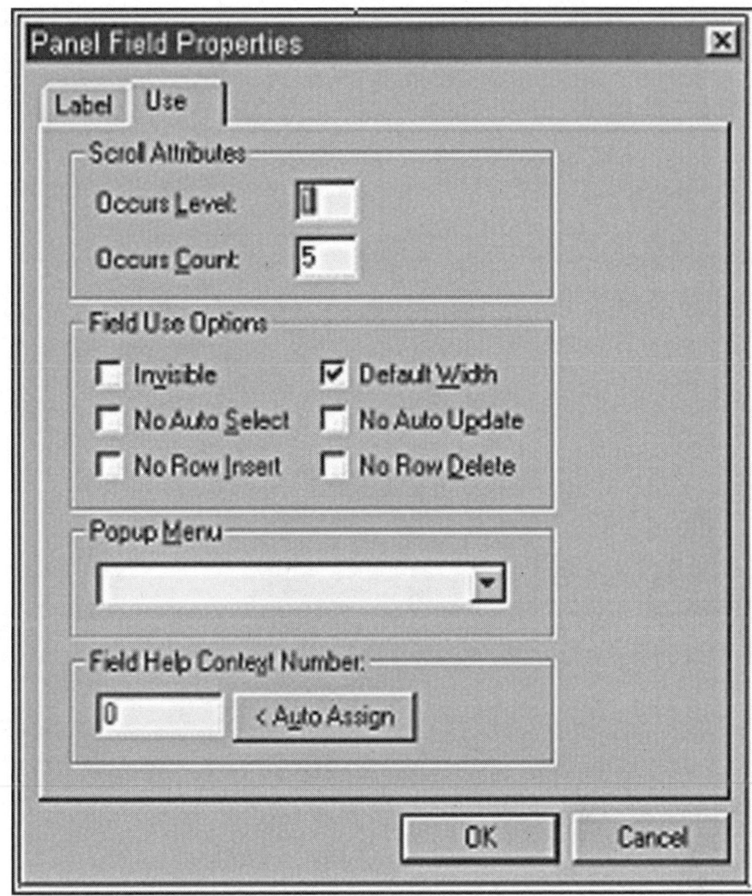

Figure 7-112 Internal Order scroll bar with occurs level.

- PO_NUM
- PROM_DT
- VENDORID

To insert the grid into the panel, either use the GRID toolbar icon or go to the Insert menu and select GRID. Place the grid control below the internal order status group box. The grid will be used much the same way the scroll bar was in our previous panel. The fields contained in the grid are detail records from the INT_ORDER_LINES record. To set up our grid, we are going to have to set the main record, occurs level, and fields to be displayed. The main record is the master record or INT_ORDER for our example. Figure 7-121 shows the correct attributes for main record and occurs level.

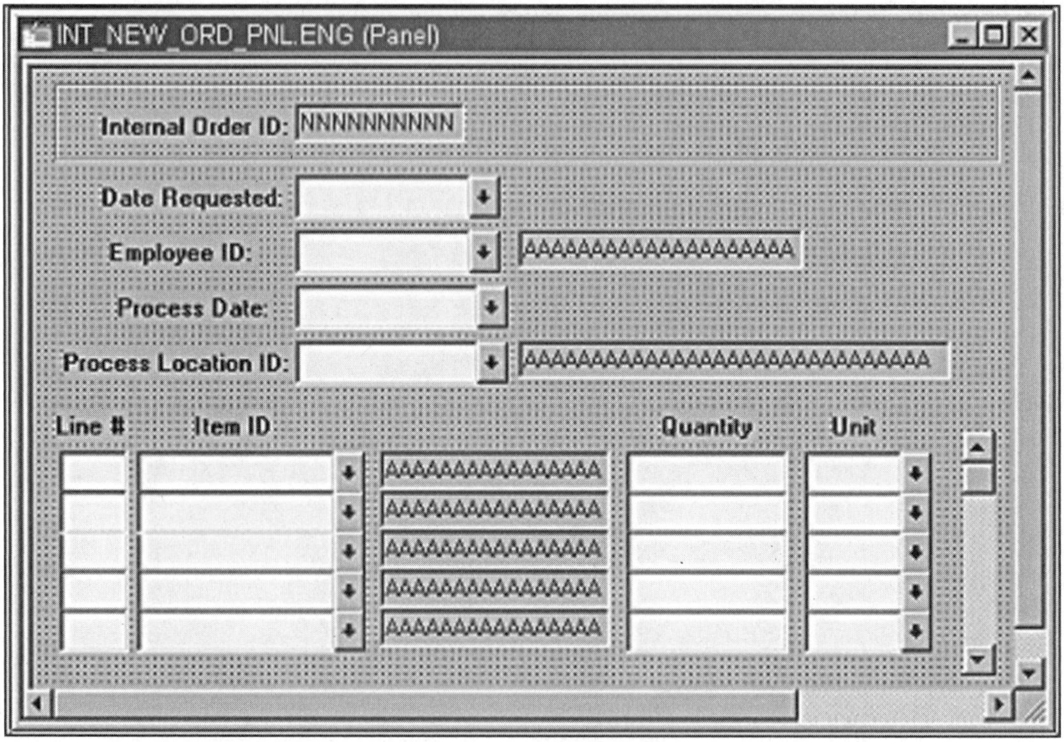

Figure 7-113 Complete Internal Order panel.

Figures 7-122 through 7-124 show the steps taken to add our first field. After you press the ADD button, an Add Column dialog will be displayed to allow you to select the display control style for the field that you are inserting. After you press OK, a Panel Field Properties dialog will be displayed to allow you to choose what field you want and to also set its panel attributes. Select the `INT_ORDER_LINES` record and the `LINE_NUM` field. The last thing you need to do for this field is to set the label to RFT SHORT. This is shown in Figure 7-124.

Repeat this for all the remaining fields that will be included in the grid. The only fields that you might want to insert differently are `EXT_ORDER` and `EXT_STAT`. `EXT_ORDER` can be set up as a check box, and `EXT_STAT` should be set up as a drop-down list. Figure 7-125 shows the Panel Field Properties dialog setting the ON/OFF values for the

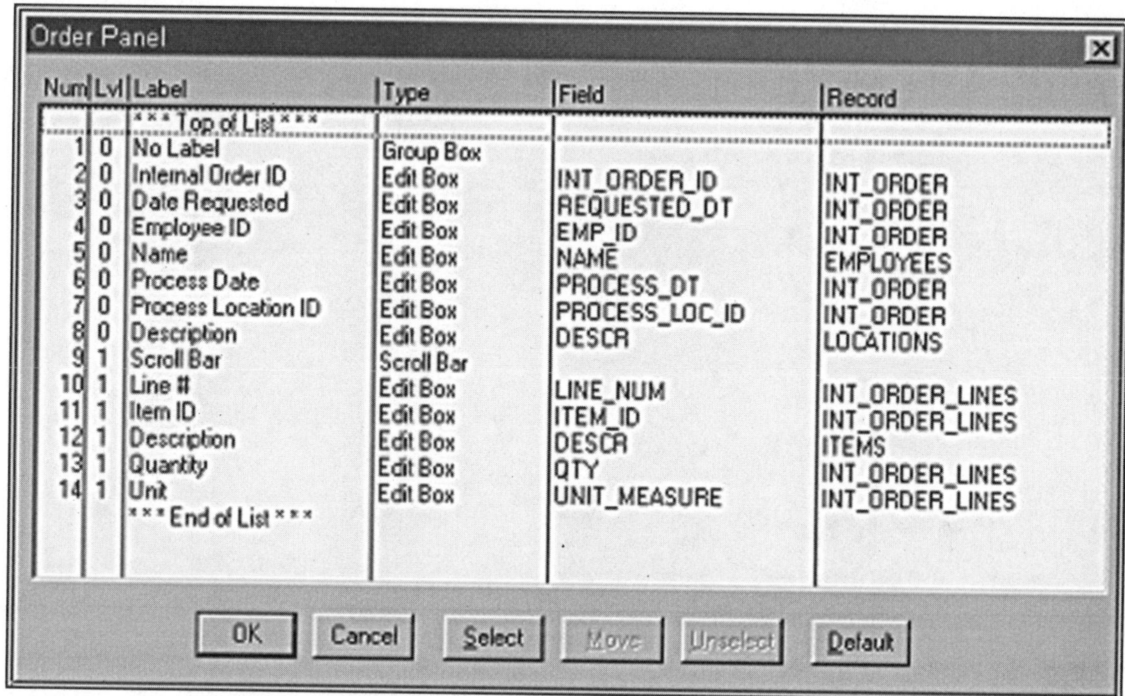

Order Panel

Num	Lvl	Label	Type	Field	Record
		*** Top of List ***			
1	0	No Label	Group Box		
2	0	Internal Order ID	Edit Box	INT_ORDER_ID	INT_ORDER
3	0	Date Requested	Edit Box	REQUESTED_DT	INT_ORDER
4	0	Employee ID	Edit Box	EMP_ID	INT_ORDER
5	0	Name	Edit Box	NAME	EMPLOYEES
6	0	Process Date	Edit Box	PROCESS_DT	INT_ORDER
7	0	Process Location ID	Edit Box	PROCESS_LOC_ID	INT_ORDER
8	0	Description	Edit Box	DESCR	LOCATIONS
9	1	Scroll Bar	Scroll Bar		
10	1	Line #	Edit Box	LINE_NUM	INT_ORDER_LINES
11	1	Item ID	Edit Box	ITEM_ID	INT_ORDER_LINES
12	1	Description	Edit Box	DESCR	ITEMS
13	1	Quantity	Edit Box	QTY	INT_ORDER_LINES
14	1	Unit	Edit Box	UNIT_MEASURE	INT_ORDER_LINES
		*** End of List ***			

Figure 7-114 Order Panel of the Internal Order panel.

Figure 7-115 Radio button control field.

EXT_ORDER check box. Figure 7-126 shows the Panel Field Properties dialog for EXT_STAT, which is set to display the XLAT short variable in the drop-down list box.

After you have entered all the fields into the grid, the COLUMN tab of the Grid Properties dialog should resemble the one in Figure 7-127. If all is satisfactory, hit the OK button. The only thing left to do for this panel is to check the order and then to save and include it in your project. Figure 7-128 shows the Order Panel dialog. Figure 7-129 shows the complete panel.

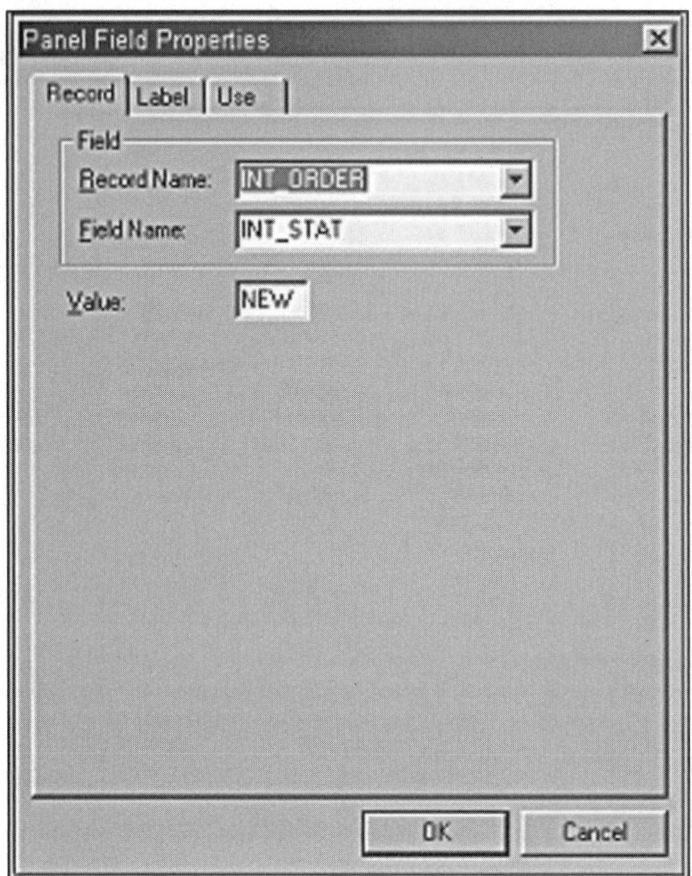

Figure 7-116 Panel Field Properties RECORD tab for radio control field `INT_STAT`.

External Order Panel (EXT_ORDER_PNL)

The last panel we are going to create is the External Order panel. There are no new topics introduced for this panel. I hope that by now all the basic concepts of building PeopleSoft panels are beginning to become second nature to you. Scroll bars, display control and related fields, and grids should all be understood before you continue.

The External Orders panel will contain the fields from the Query View record we created in the record section (`EXT_ORDER_VW`). The key values for our new panel will consist of the `INT_ORDER_ID` and

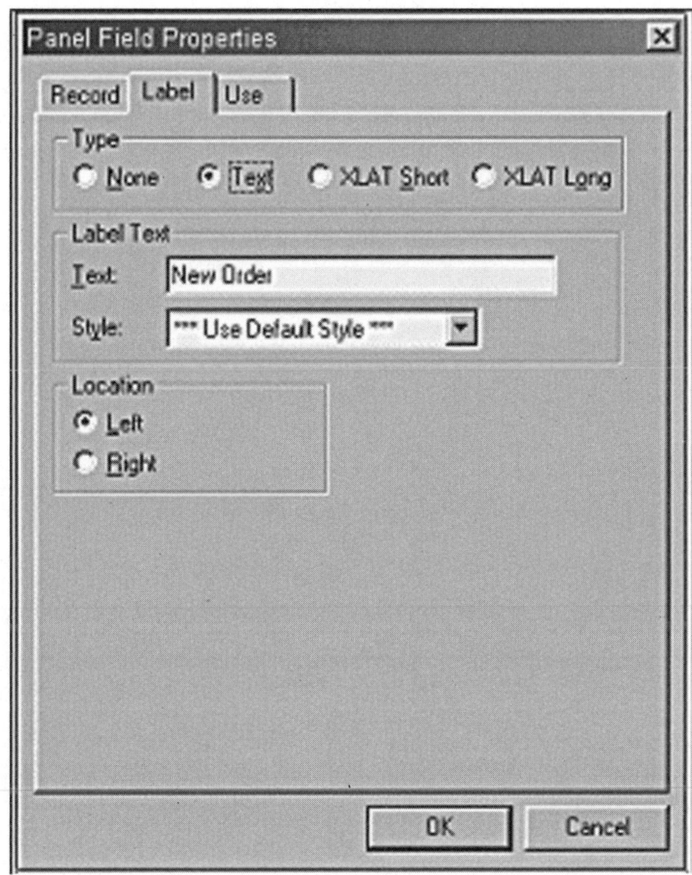

Figure 7-117 Panel Field Properties LABEL tab for radio control field `INT_STAT`.

Figure 7-118 Panel Field Properties RECORD tab for group box internal status.

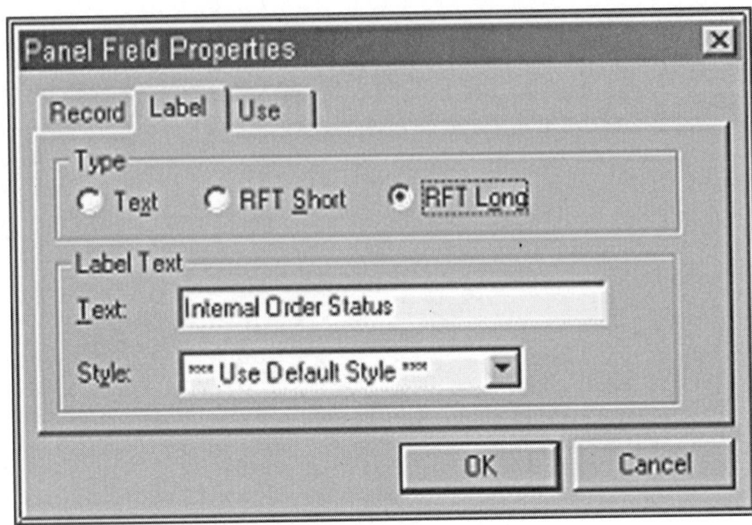

Figure 7-119 Panel Field Properties LABEL tab for group box internal status.

Figure 7-120 Internal Order panel with header fields.

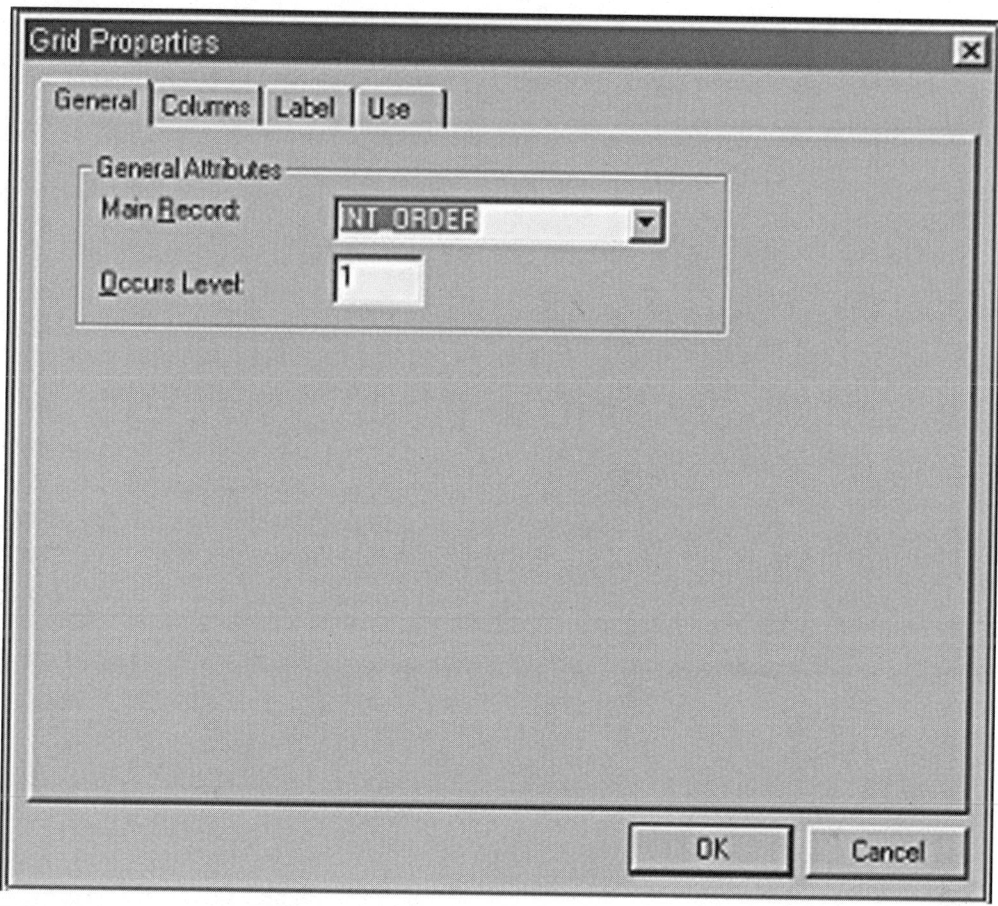

Figure 7-121 GENERAL tab for grid on Internal Order panel.

LINE_NUM. The rest of the fields from the EXT_ORDER_VW record should be placed onto your panel to make it resemble the one in Figure 7-130. If you have any problems with this panel, please refer to the CD that was included with this book. The screen movies go over the entire creation process.

When you have added all your panels, your Project Workspace should look the same as the one in Figure 7-131.

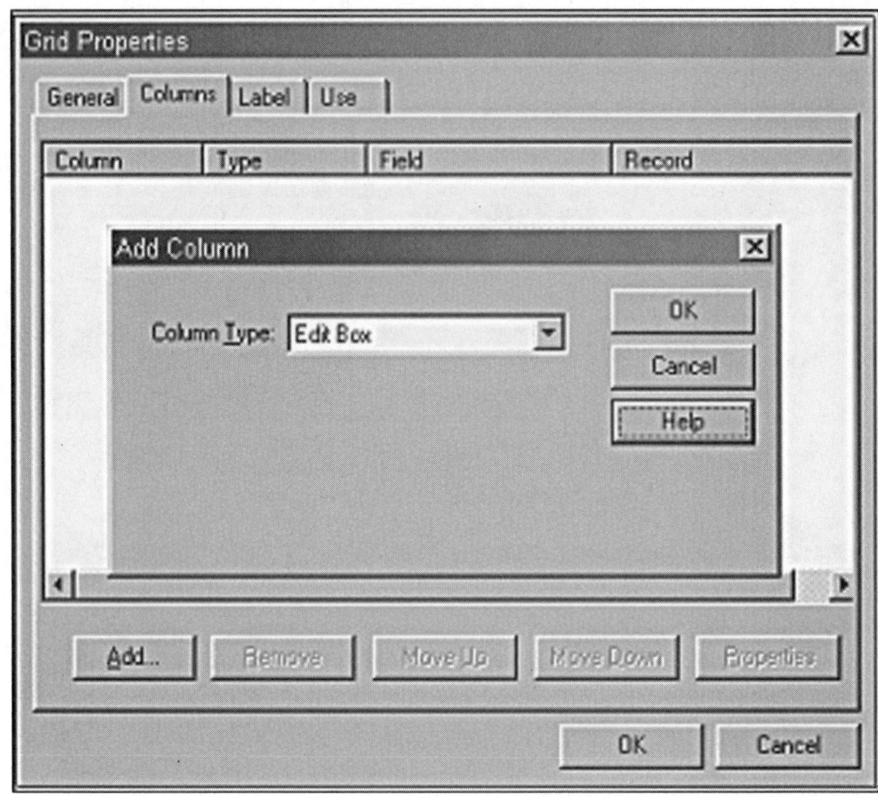

Figure 7-122 COLUMNS tab for grid on Internal Order panel with Add Column dialog.

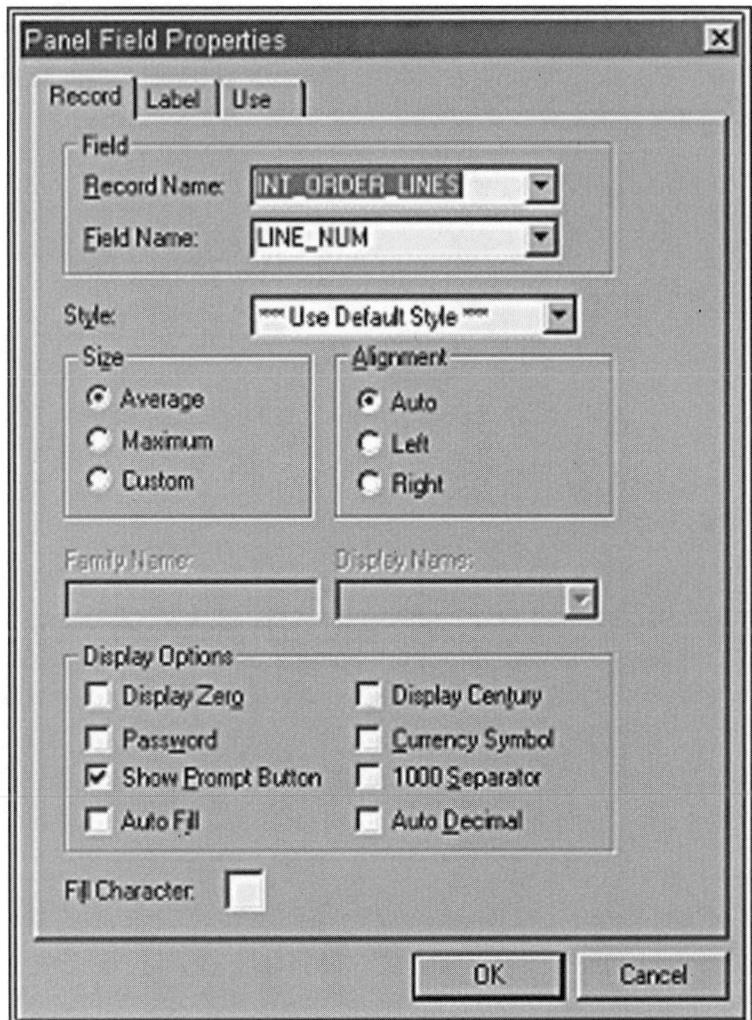

Figure 7-123 Panel Field Properties Dialog Record Tab allowing us to choose field for grid.

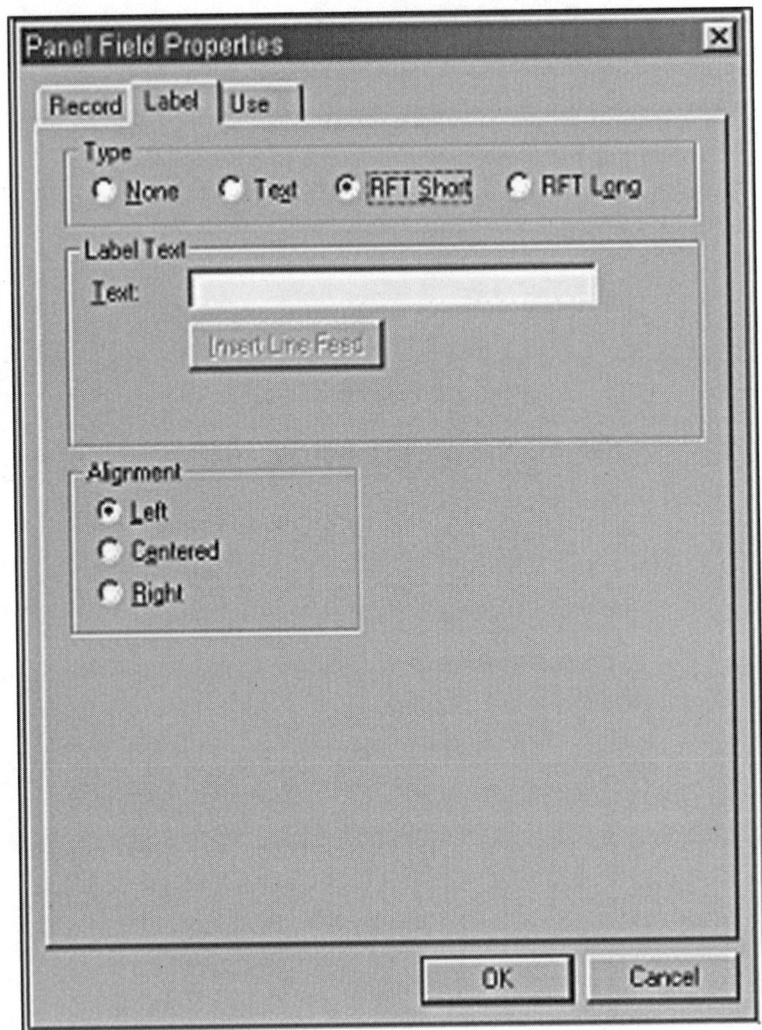

Figure 7-124 Panel Field Properties dialog LABEL tab setting the label to RFT SHORT.

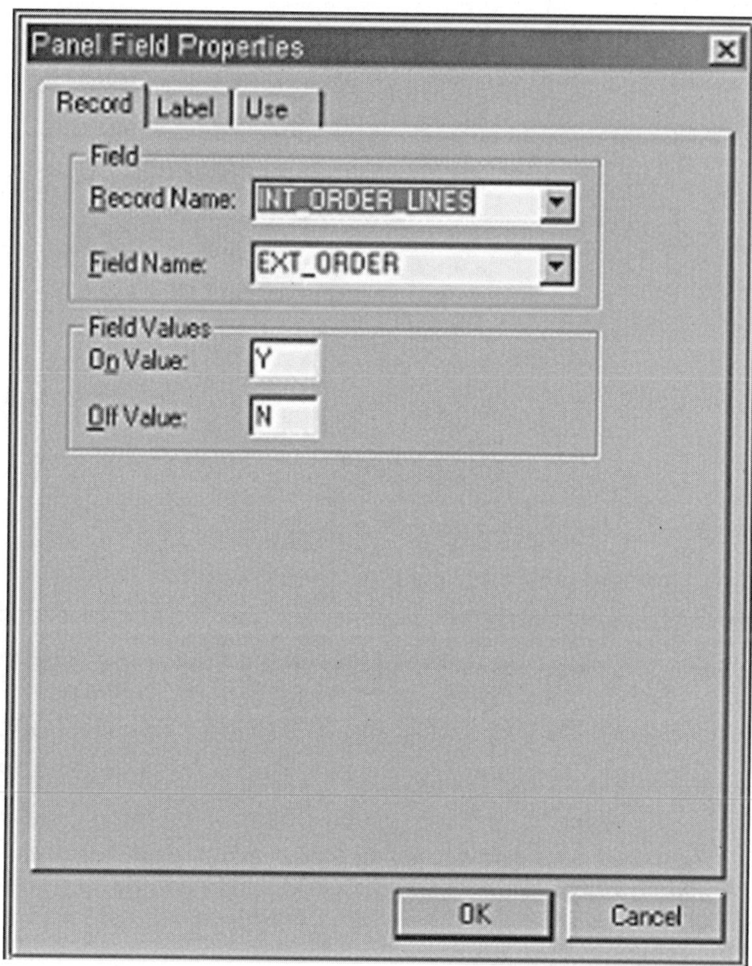

Figure 7-125
Panel Field Properties dialog RECORD tab for EXT_ORDER.

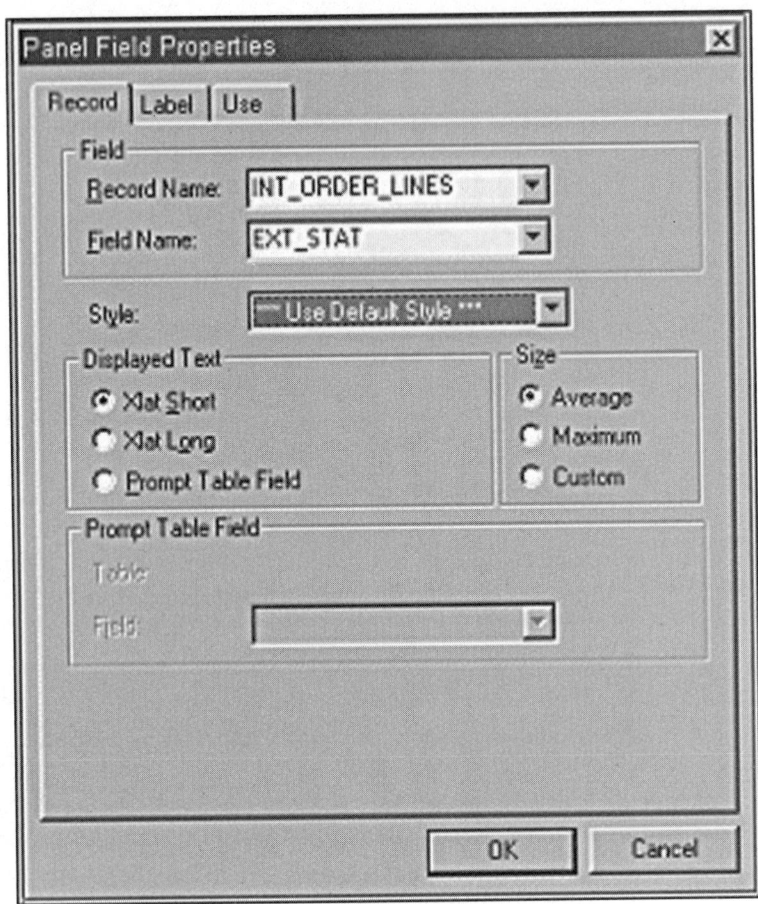

Figure 7-126
Panel Field Properties Record Tab for a Translate table field.

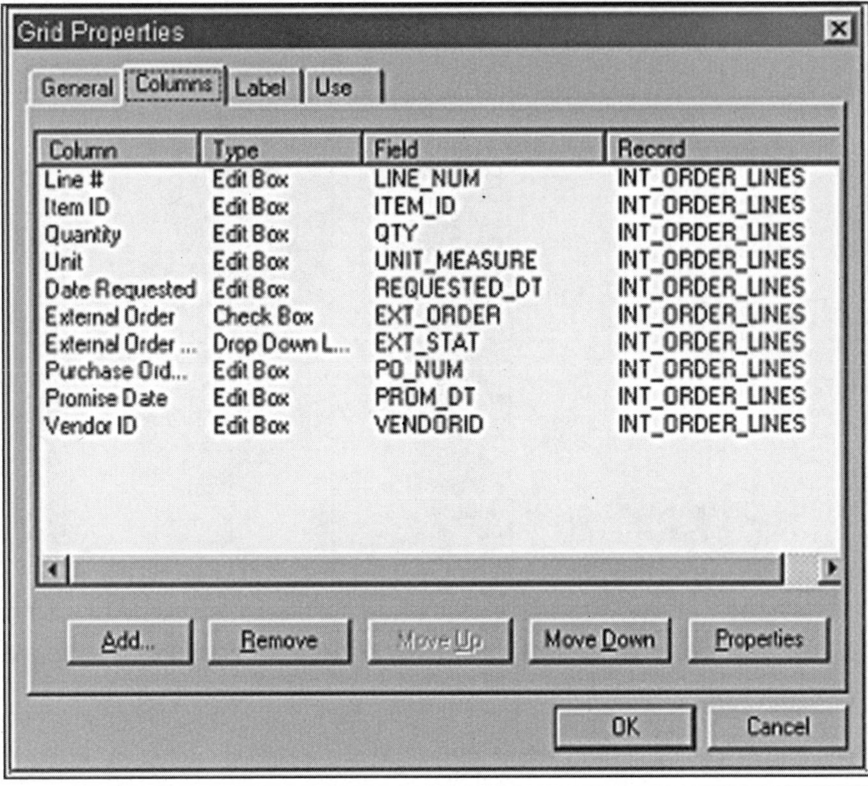

Figure 7-127 COLUMN tab of grid with all the columns added.

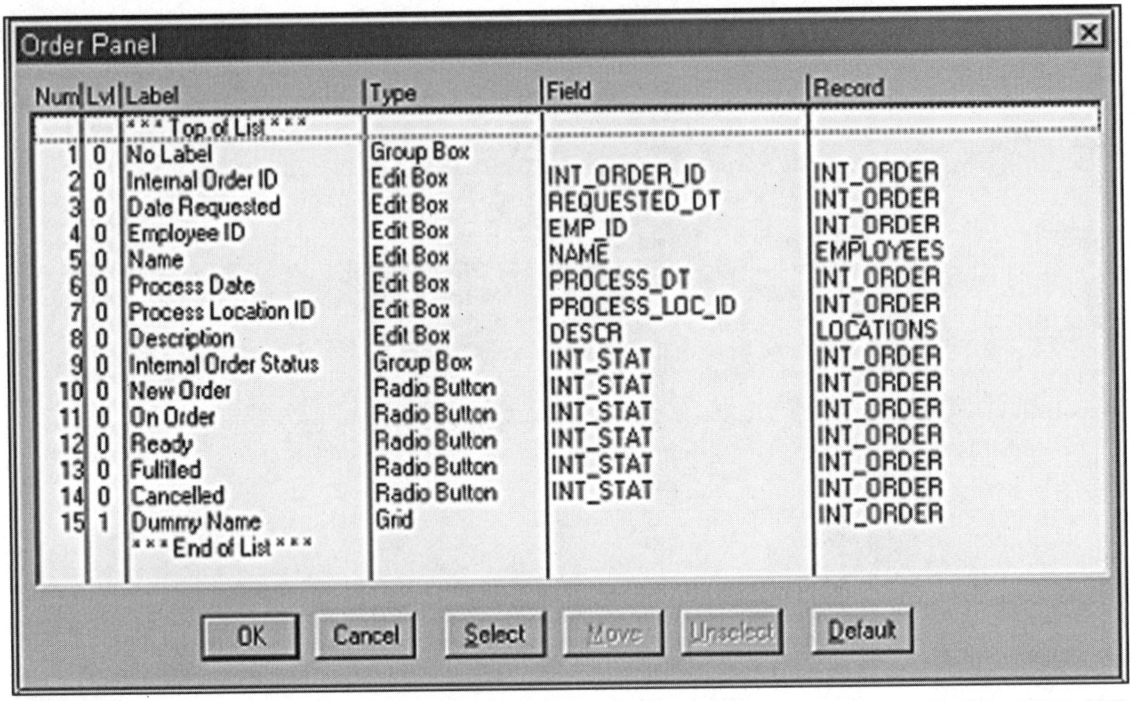

Order Panel

Num	Lvl	Label	Type	Field	Record
		*** Top of List ***			
1	0	No Label	Group Box		
2	0	Internal Order ID	Edit Box	INT_ORDER_ID	INT_ORDER
3	0	Date Requested	Edit Box	REQUESTED_DT	INT_ORDER
4	0	Employee ID	Edit Box	EMP_ID	INT_ORDER
5	0	Name	Edit Box	NAME	EMPLOYEES
6	0	Process Date	Edit Box	PROCESS_DT	INT_ORDER
7	0	Process Location ID	Edit Box	PROCESS_LOC_ID	INT_ORDER
8	0	Description	Edit Box	DESCR	LOCATIONS
9	0	Internal Order Status	Group Box	INT_STAT	INT_ORDER
10	0	New Order	Radio Button	INT_STAT	INT_ORDER
11	0	On Order	Radio Button	INT_STAT	INT_ORDER
12	0	Ready	Radio Button	INT_STAT	INT_ORDER
13	0	Fulfilled	Radio Button	INT_STAT	INT_ORDER
14	0	Cancelled	Radio Button	INT_STAT	INT_ORDER
15	1	Dummy Name	Grid		INT_ORDER
		*** End of List ***			

OK Cancel Select Move Unselect Default

Figure 7-128 Order Panel for the Internal Order panel.

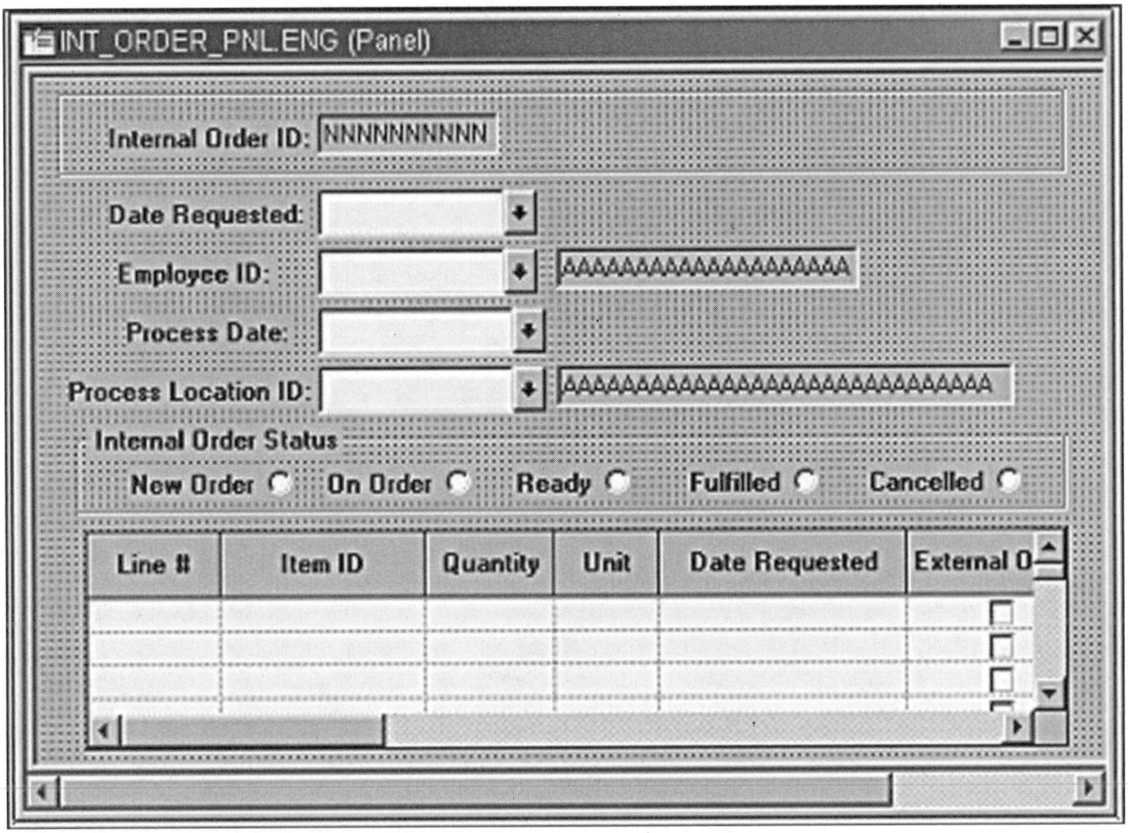

INT_ORDER_PNL.ENG (Panel)

Internal Order ID: NNNNNNNNNN

Date Requested:

Employee ID: AAAAAAAAAAAAAAAAAAAAA

Process Date:

Process Location ID: AAAAAAAAAAAAAAAAAAAAAAAAAAAAAA

Internal Order Status

New Order On Order Ready Fulfilled Cancelled

Line #	Item ID	Quantity	Unit	Date Requested	External O

Figure 7-129 Complete Internal Order panel.

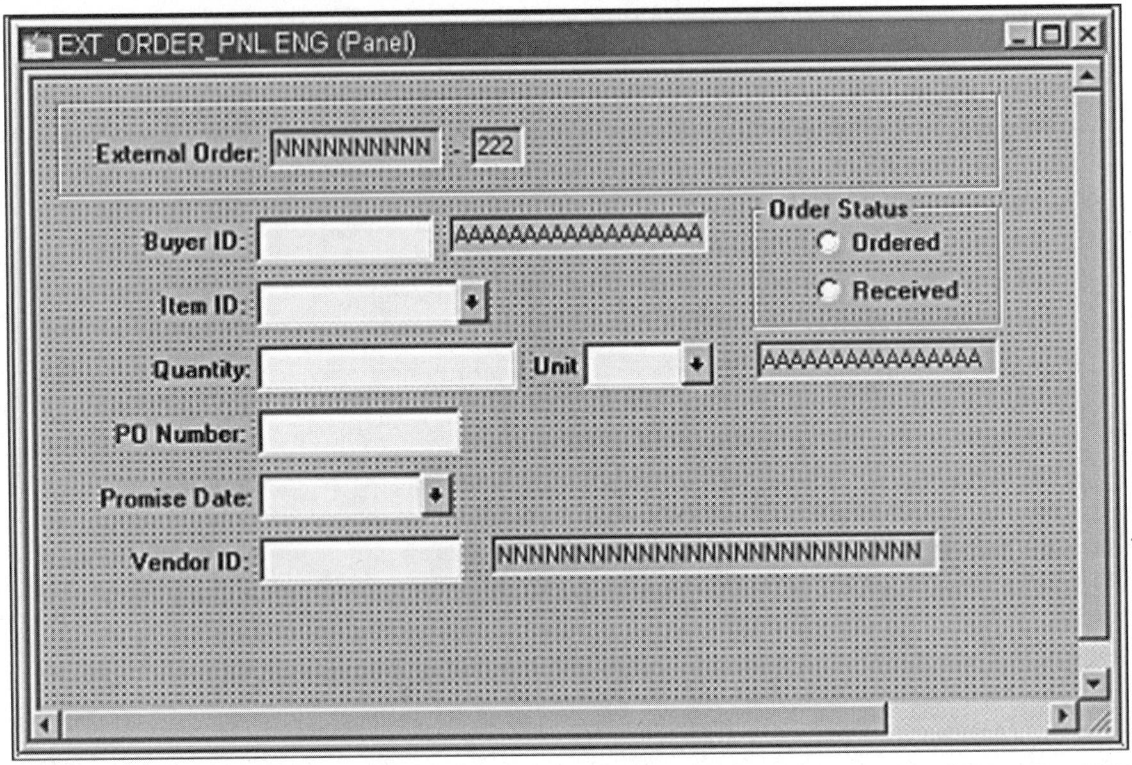

Figure 7-130 Complete External Order panel.

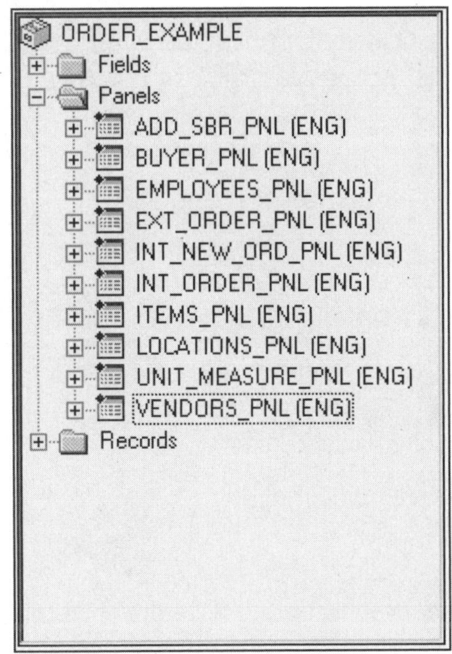

Figure 7-131 Project Workspace with Panel folder expanded.

CHAPTER 8

Panel Groups

Definition of a Panel Group

This chapter, the shortest in the book, covers the easiest PeopleSoft building block. Panel groups are simply a way to organize one to many panels that all share the same key structure. If you recall, when we built all of our panels, we organized them all with their keys grayed out at the top of the panel. If we had multiple panels all related to a specific business object, we would organize them into one panel group. Panel groups effectively create tabbed windows. Moreover, in doing this they allow us to present much more than can be displayed on one panel. A good example of how you might use a panel group is shown in Figure 8-1. This example has been copied from the purchasing module and displays a purchase order inquiry panel group. All of the panels share the same key of business unit, PO number, change order number, and vendor id. Moreover, all of the panels are logically grouped together to create one purchase order. Each panel of the panel group is represented by a tab.

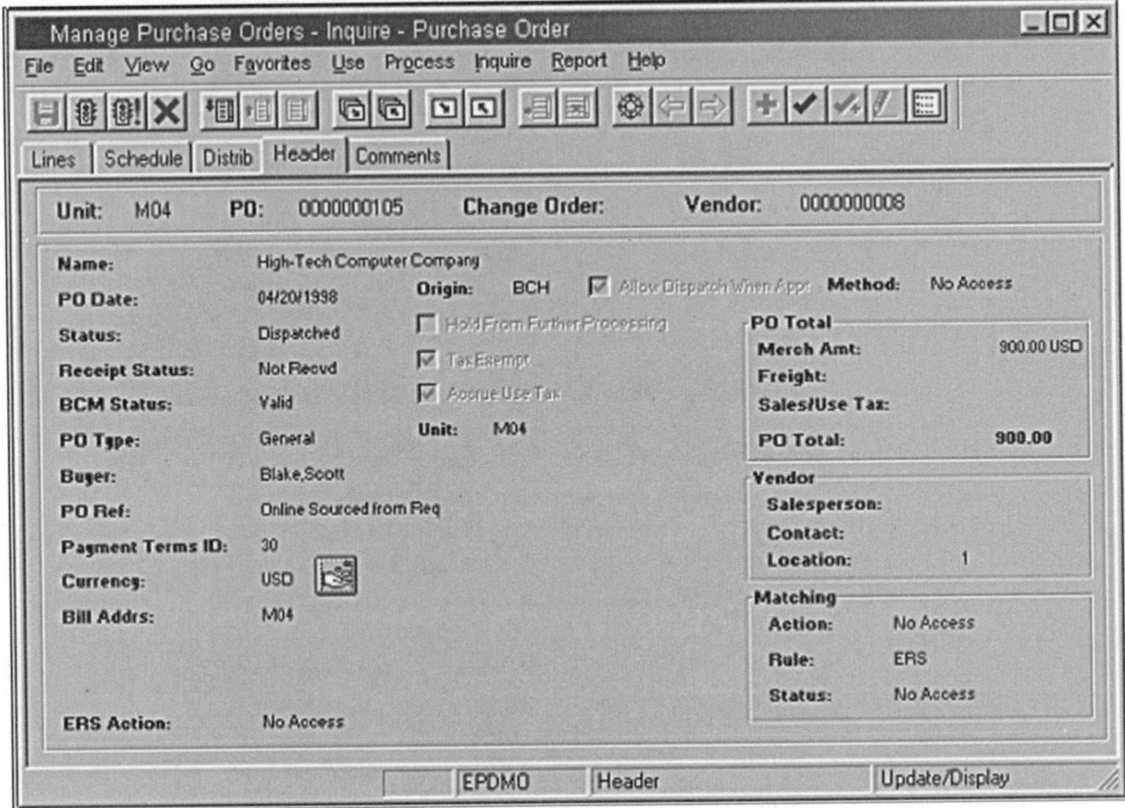

Figure 8-1 Purchase order panel group.

How we define our panel groups will be directly related to how they are displayed in the menu navigation and the actual windows in PeopleSoft. The previous example of a purchase order inquiry showed the tab order starting with LINES, then SCHEDULE, DISTRIBUTION, HEADER, and COMMENTS. If we look at the panel group definition in Figure 8-2, we will see that all of those panels were included into the panel group definition in that same order. In addition, this order is also the same as shown in Figure 8-3, which displays the actual menu used to navigate to this panel group.

When we create panel groups, you must set the search record before you can save the panel group. The search record needs to be the main record that the key fields are taken from for all the panels associated with the panel group. In addition to setting the search record, when you open

PO_INQUIRY.GBL (Panel Group)

	Panel Name	Item Name	Hidden	Item Label	Folder Tab Label
1	PO_LINE_INQ	LINES	☐	&Lines	
2	PO_SCHED_INQ	PO_SCHED_INQ	☐	&Schedule	
3	PO_DISTRIB_INQ	PO_DISTRIB_INQ	☐	&Distrib	
4	PO_HDR_INQ	HEADER	☐	&Header	
5	PO_COMMENTS_IN	COMMENTS	☐	&Comments	

Figure 8-2 Purchase order panel group definition.

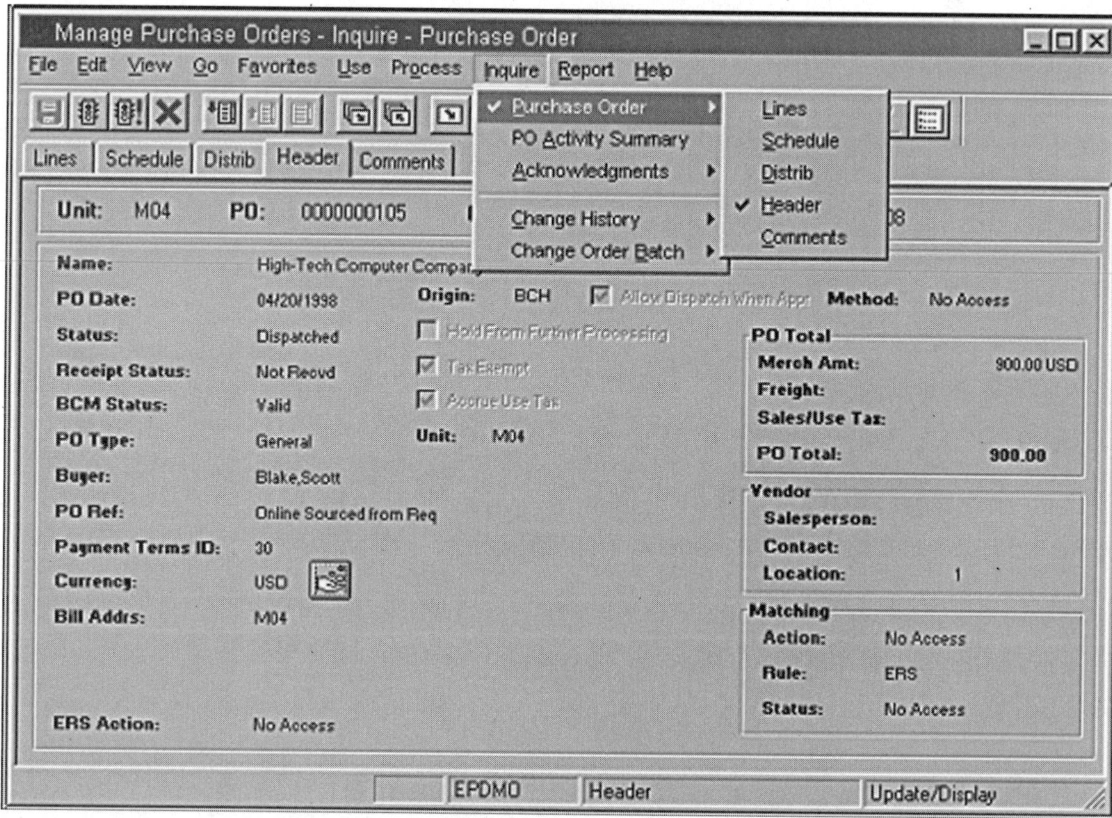

Figure 8-3 Purchase order panel group menu.

the Panel Group Properties dialog, it is also important to check off which actions will be allowed to be performed on the panel group. Figure 8-4 shows the Panel Group Properties dialog for the PO Inquiry panel group. Please note that the search record is `PO_SRCH2`, which is actually a Query View record. Note also that the only action available is UPDATE/DISPLAY. This is not to say that you are able to actually update data that is being displayed. It is only meant to say that you would not be adding any new key values. The fact that this is an inquiry-only panel group is actually set up in the Security Administrator.

Before we begin creating our own panel groups, I would like to highlight a couple of essential points:

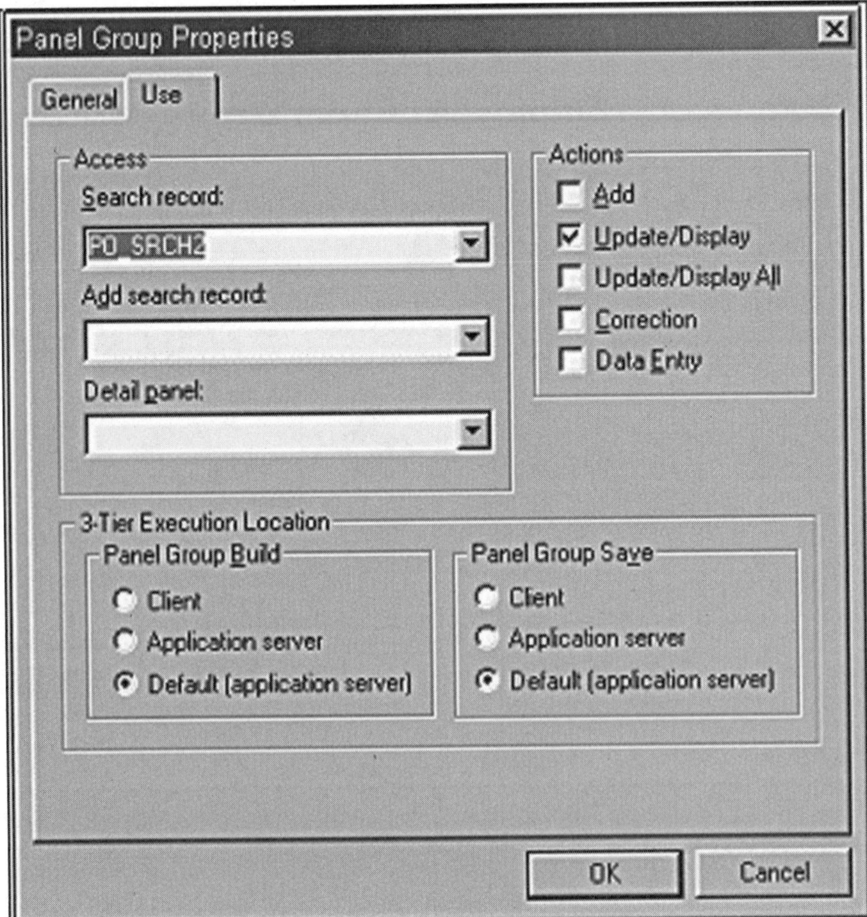

Figure 8-4 Purchase Order Panel Group Properties dialog.

- All panels must belong to a panel group. The only real choice you have here is whether you are going to have more than one belong to the same panel group.
- When you have multiple panels in the same panel group, all the data for each panel are retrieved during an update/display action, which means that everything, including Translate Table data, will be buffered when you initiate the update/display. This can be an essential factor in determining what panels you might want to deploy via an intra/internetwork mechanism. If you are trying to web deploy a large panel group, the system time required to serve the Java panels and all the data might be too long.

Example Panel Groups

Employees Panel Group (EMP_PNL_GRP)

The Employees panel group will contain only the Employees panel. The key fields that make up the key section of the Employees panel are taken from the lookup record EMPLOYEES. Therefore, EMPLOYEES will be its search record. EMPLOYEES is effective dated; therefore, we are going to allow ADD, UPDATE/DISPLAY and UPDATE/DISPLAY ALL, and CORRECTION.

To create our new panel group, press the NEW icon or go to the File menu and select NEW. When the new dialog is displayed, select PANEL GROUP and press OK. Next, with the Panel folder open in the Project Workspace, select the EMPLOYEES_PNL by holding the left mouse button down. Then drag the cursor over the new empty panel group definition and release the mouse button. Figure 8-5 shows the Application Designer while the drag-and-drop operation is taking place.

The panel group definition should now look the same as the one in Figure 8-6. The only thing we need to change in this panel group before we set the Panel Group Properties is the ITEM label, which directly relates to what will be displayed on the menu. Since it is normal windows programming practice to provide alternate key strokes for menu actions, we are going to change the default ITEM label. Tab into the field or use your mouse and change the default to &Employees. The & (ampersand) placed before the E will allow the user to type ALT + E to navigate to the EMPLOYEES_PNL. Figure 8-7 displays the panel group definition with its correct ITEM label.

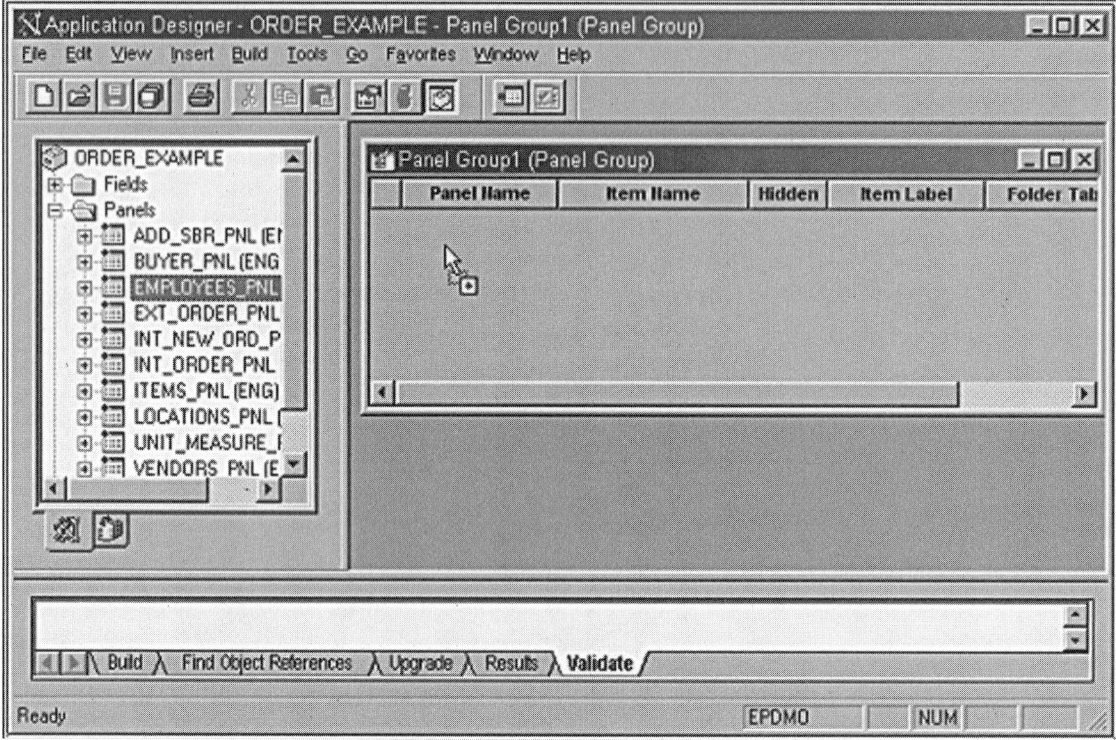

Figure 8-5 Drag-and-drop method for adding a panel to a panel group.

Panel Group1 (Panel Group)

	Panel Name	Item Name	Hidden	Item Label	Folder Tab
1	EMPLOYEES_PNL	EMPLOYEES_PNL	☐	Employees Pnl	

Figure 8-6 Employees panel group definition with default ITEM label.

Panel Group1 (Panel Group)

	Panel Name	Item Name	Hidden	Item Label	Folder Tab
1	EMPLOYEES_PNL	EMPLOYEES_PNL	☐	&Employees	

Figure 8-7 Employees panel group definition with completed ITEM label.

Now we are going to need to set the panel group properties. Press the PROPERTIES icon or go to the File menu and select OBJECT PROPERTIES. When the Panel Group Properties is displayed, select the USE tab and proceed to enter the search record and associated actions. As stated earlier, the Employees panel group search record will be EMPLOYEES, and the actions will be ADD, UPDATE/DISPLAY, UPDATE/DISPLAY ALL, and CORRECTION. Figure 8-8 shows the correct settings for the Employees panel group properties. If yours match, please save your panel group and insert it into your project.

Buyer Panel Group (BUY_PNL_GRP)

The next panel group we are going to create is for the Buyer panel. The Buyer panel's search record is BUYER_VW. Similar to the PO inquiry example we saw earlier, this panel will be read-only. Therefore, we are going to set the action to UPDATE/DISPLAY only. Remember that the read-only attribute will be set in the Security Administrator.

To create our new panel group, press the NEW icon or go to the File menu and select NEW. When the New dialog is displayed, select PANEL GROUP and press OK. Next, with the Panel folder open in the Project Workspace, select the BUYER_PNL by holding the left mouse button down. Then drag the cursor over the new empty panel group definition and release the mouse button.

Now change the ITEM label to &Buyer and then set the panel group properties (see Fig. 8-9). Figure 8-10 shows the completed Buyer panel group.

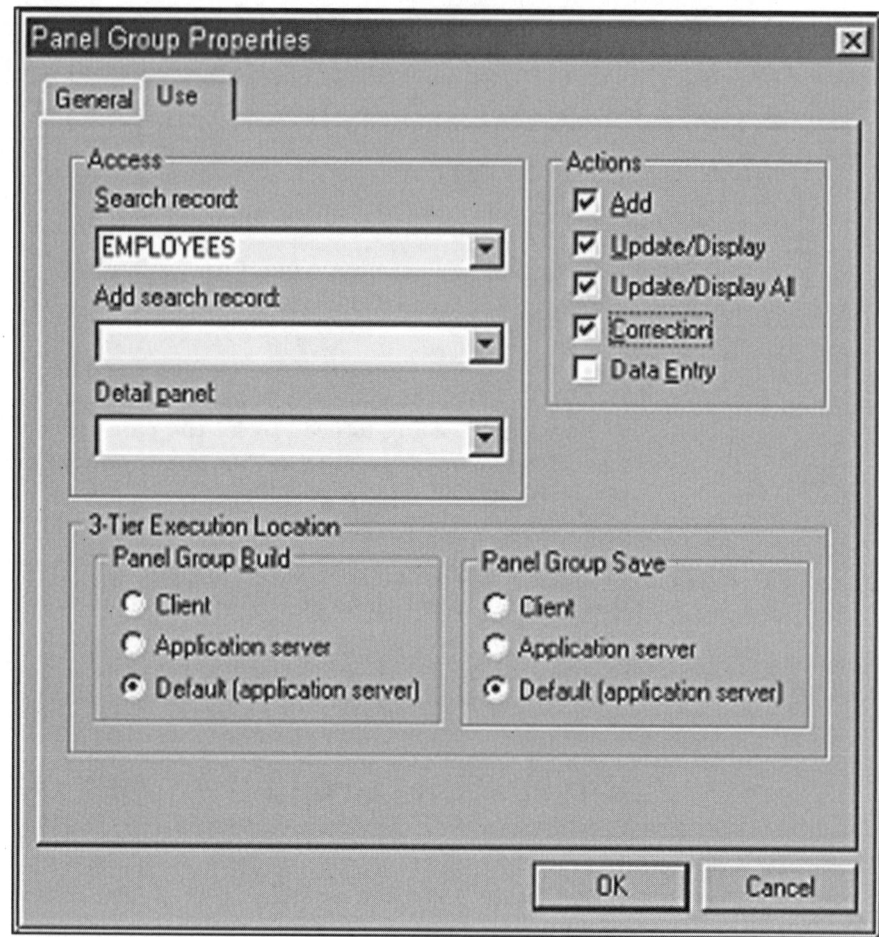

Figure 8-8 Properties of employees panel group.

Items Panel Group (`ITEMS_PNL_GRP`)

The next panel group we are going to create is for our Items panel. Its search record is `ITEMS`, and the actions allowed on the panel are ADD, UPDATE/DISPLAY, UPDATE/DISPLAY ALL, and CORRECTION. Please follow the drag-and-drop method described previously to complete this panel group. When you are finished, your panel groups properties should resemble those in Figure 8-11. In addition, your completed definition should resemble the one in Figure 8-12.

Figure 8-9
Properties of buyer panel group.

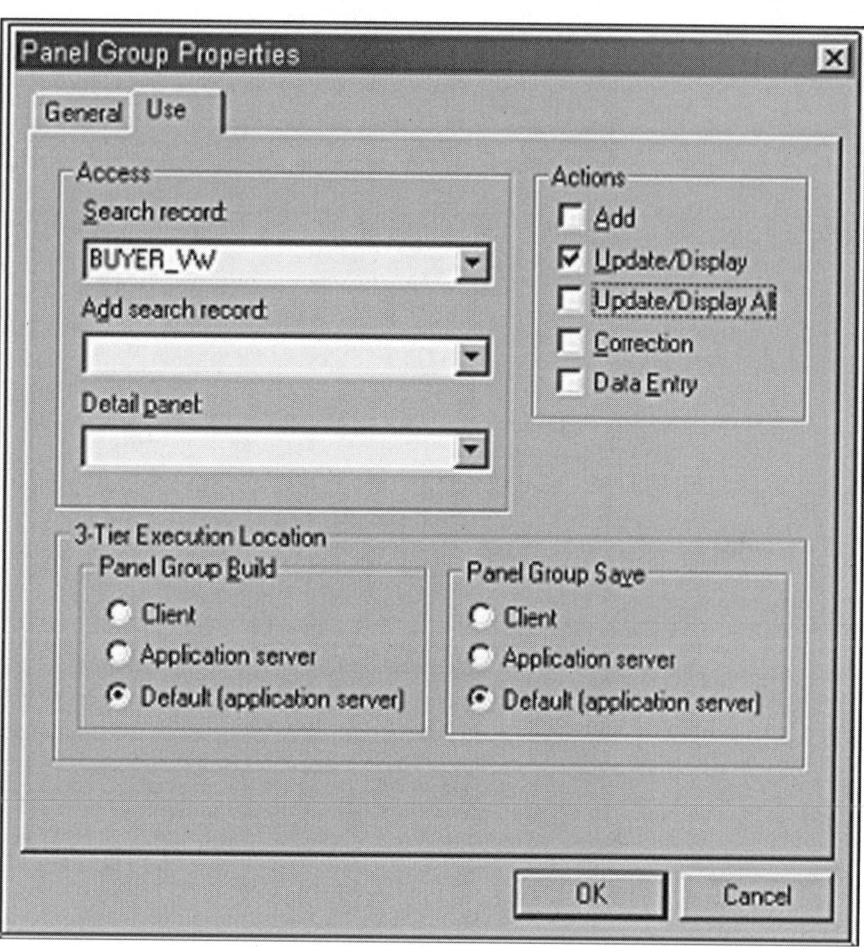

BUY_PNL_GRP.GBL (Panel Group)

	Panel Name	Item Name	Hidden	Item Label	Folder Tab Label
1	BUYER_PNL	BUYER_PNL	☐	&Buyer	

Figure 8-10 Buyer panel group definition.

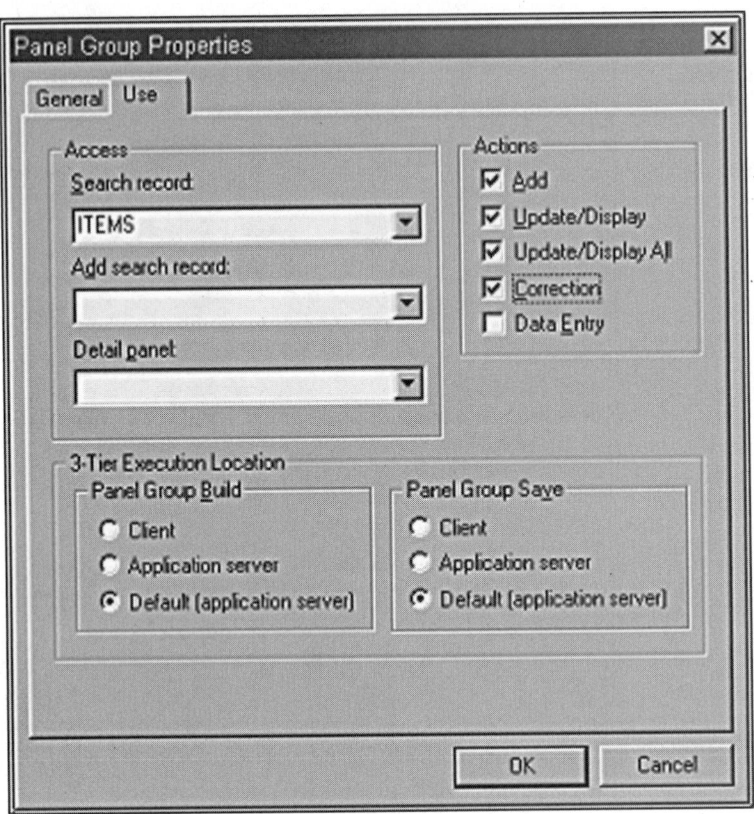

Figure 8-11 Properties of items panel group.

ITEMS_PNL_GRP.GBL (Panel Group)

	Panel Name	Item Name	Hidden	Item Label	Folder Tab Label
1	ITEMS_PNL	ITEMS_PNL	☐	&Items	

Figure 8-12 Items panel group definition.

Locations Panel Group (LOC_PNL_GRP)

The next panel group we are going to create is for our Locations panel. Its search record is LOCATIONS, and the actions allowed on the panel are ADD, UPDATE/DISPLAY, UPDATE/DISPLAY ALL, and CORRECTION. Please follow the drag-and-drop method described previously to complete this panel group. When you are finished, your panel groups properties should look like those in Figure 8-13. In addition, your completed definition should resemble the one in Figure 8-14.

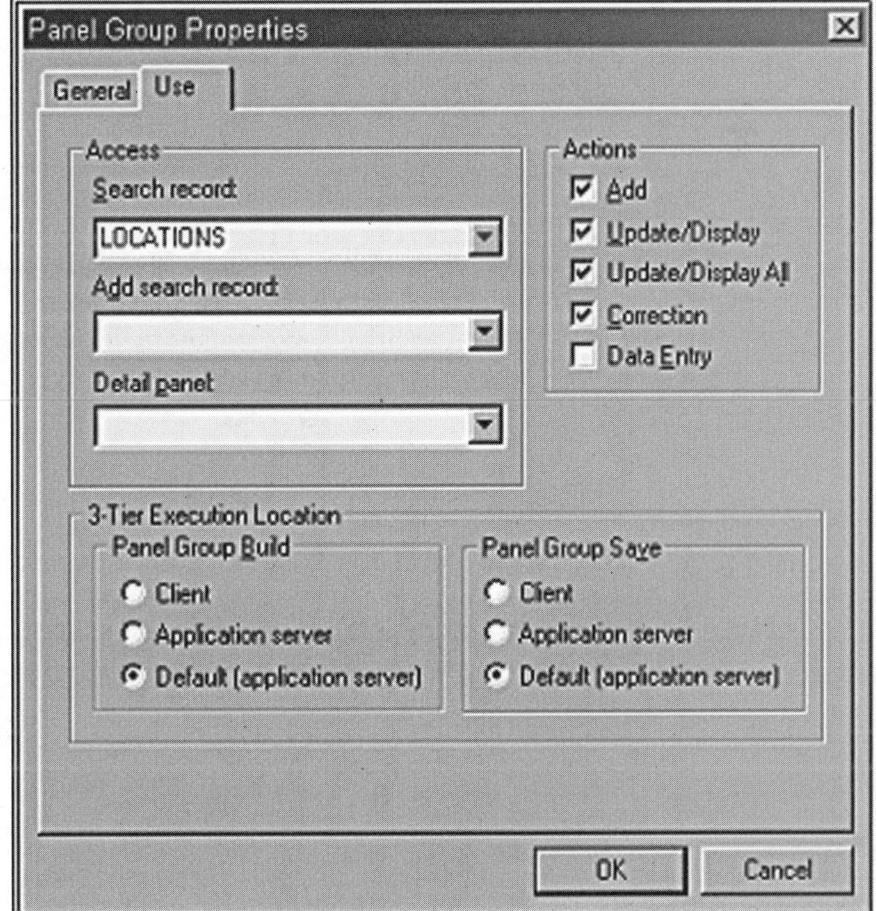

Figure 8-13 Properties of locations panel group.

LOC_PNL_GRP.GBL (Panel Group)

	Panel Name	Item Name	Hidden	Item Label	Folder Tab Label
1	LOCATIONS_PNL	LOCATIONS_PNL	☐	&Locations	

Figure 8-14 Locations panel group definition.

Units of Measure Panel Group (UNITS_PNL_GRP)

The next panel group we are going to create is for our Units of Measure panel. Its search record is UNIT_MEASURE, and the actions allowed on the panel are ADD, and UPDATE/DISPLAY. Please follow the drag-and-drop method described previously to complete this panel group. When you are finished, your panel groups properties should look like those in Figure 8-15. In addition, your completed definition should resemble the one in Figure 8-16.

Vendors Panel Group (VENDORS_PNL_GRP)

The next panel group we are going to create is for our Vendors panel. Its search record is VENDORS, and the actions allowed on the panel are ADD, UPDATE/DISPLAY, UPDATE/DISPLAY ALL, and CORRECTION. Please follow the drag-and-drop method described previously to complete this panel group. When you are finished, your panel groups properties should look like those in Figure 8-17. In addition, your completed definition should resemble the one in Figure 8-18.

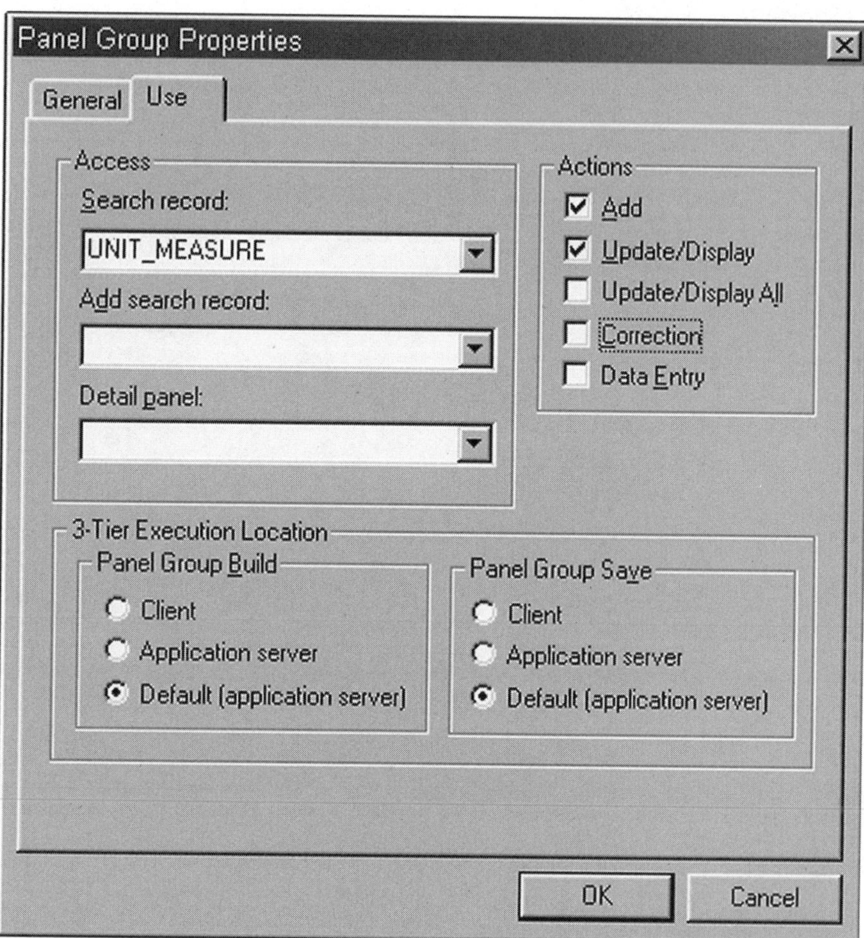

Figure 8-15 Properties of Units of Measure panel group.

UNITS_PNL_GRP.GBL (Panel Group)

	Panel Name	Item Name	Hidden	Item Label	Folder Tab Label
1	UNIT_MEASURE_PN	UNIT_MEASURE_PNL	☐	&Units of Measure	

Figure 8-16 Units of Measure panel group definition.

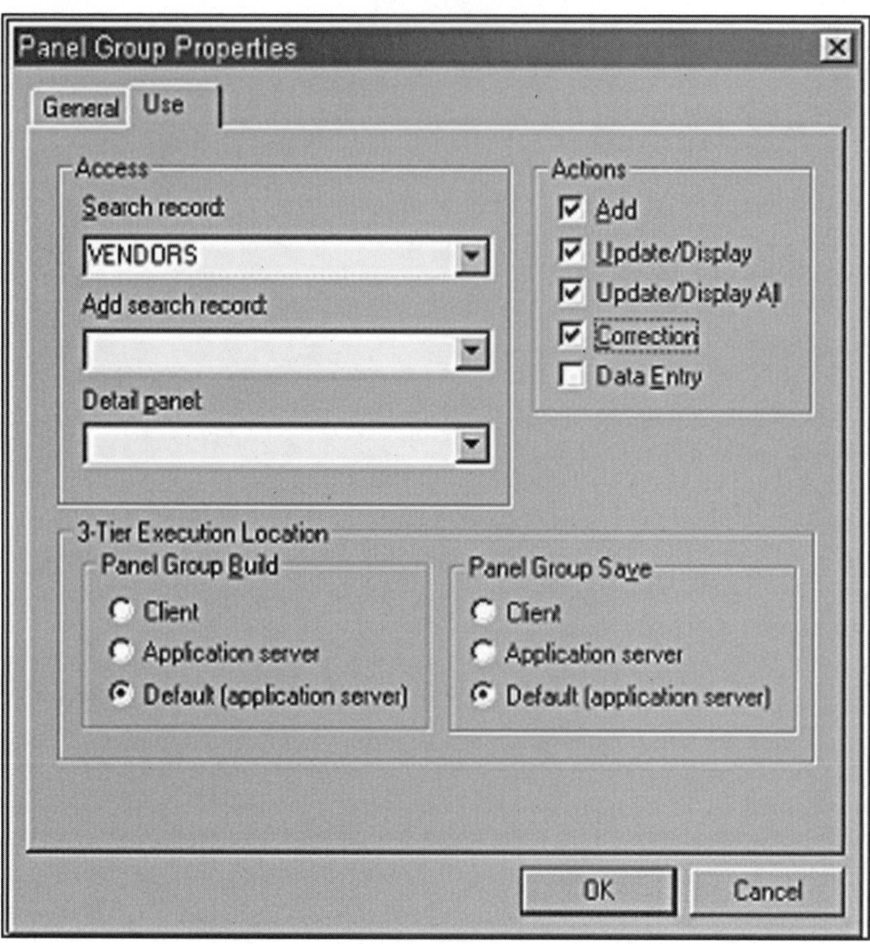

Figure 8-17 Properties of Vendors panel group.

VENDORS_PNL_GRP.GBL (Panel Group)

	Panel Name	Item Name	Hidden	Item Label	Folder Tab Label
1	VENDORS_PNL	VENDORS_PNL	☐	&Vendors	

Figure 8-18 Vendors panel group definition.

New Internal Order Panel Group (NINT_PNL_GRP)

The next panel group we are going to create is for our New Internal Orders panel. Its search record is INT_ORDER, and the only action allowed on the panel is ADD. To create this panel, please follow the drag-and-drop method described previously to complete this panel group. When you are finished, your panel groups properties should look like those in Figure 8-19. In addition, your completed definition should resemble the one in Figure 8-20.

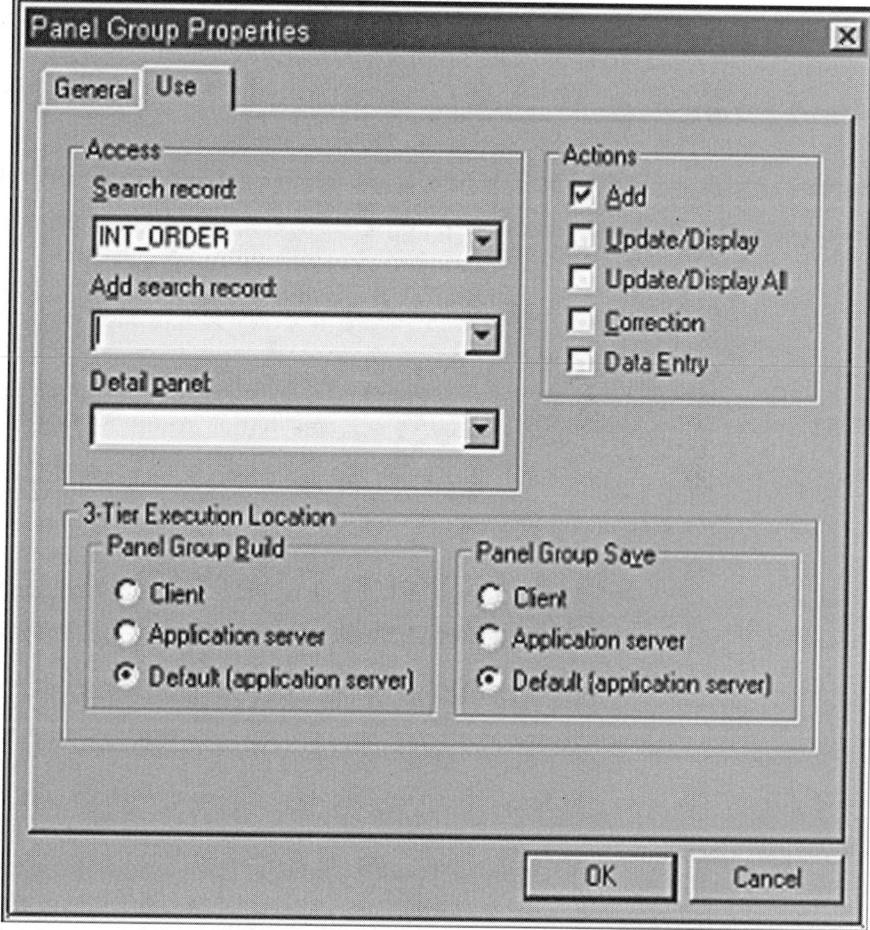

Figure 8-19 Properties of New Internal Order panel group.

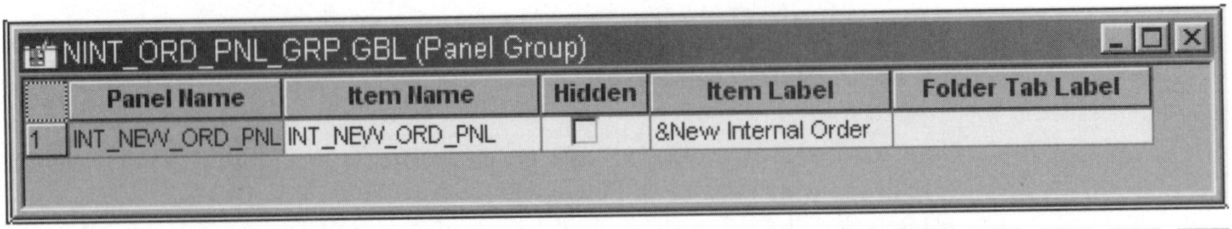

NINT_ORD_PNL_GRP.GBL (Panel Group)

	Panel Name	Item Name	Hidden	Item Label	Folder Tab Label
1	INT_NEW_ORD_PNL	INT_NEW_ORD_PNL	☐	&New Internal Order	

Figure 8-20 New Internal Order panel group definition.

If desired, you can experiment later by separating out the INT_ORDER_LINES, record from this panel and the next two panel groups onto its own panel. Then you could add the lines panel to each of the panel groups. If you do this, please remember to add the FOLDER label text on the panel group definition beside the ITEM label. The FOLDER label is the text that will appear on the tabs when the panel group is displayed.

Warehouse Internal Order Panel Group (WINT_PNL_GRP)

The next panel group we are going to create is for our Internal Orders panel. Its search record is INT_ORDER, and the only action allowed on the panel is UPDATE/DISPLAY.

To create this panel, please follow the drag-and-drop method described previously to complete this panel group. When you are finished, your panel groups properties should look like those in Figure 8-21. In addition, your completed definition should resemble the one in Figure 8-22.

Buyers External Order Panel Group (BEXT_PNL_GRP)

The next panel group we are going to create is for our External Orders panel. Its search record is EXT_ORDER_VW, and the only action allowed on the panel is UPDATE/DISPLAY.

To create this panel, please follow the drag-and-drop method described previously to complete this panel group. When you are finished, your panel groups properties should look like those in Figure 8-23. In addition, your completed definition should resemble the one in Figure 8-24.

When you have completed all the panel group definitions, your Project Workspace should resemble the one in Figure 8-25.

Figure 8-21 Properties of Warehouse Internal Order panel group.

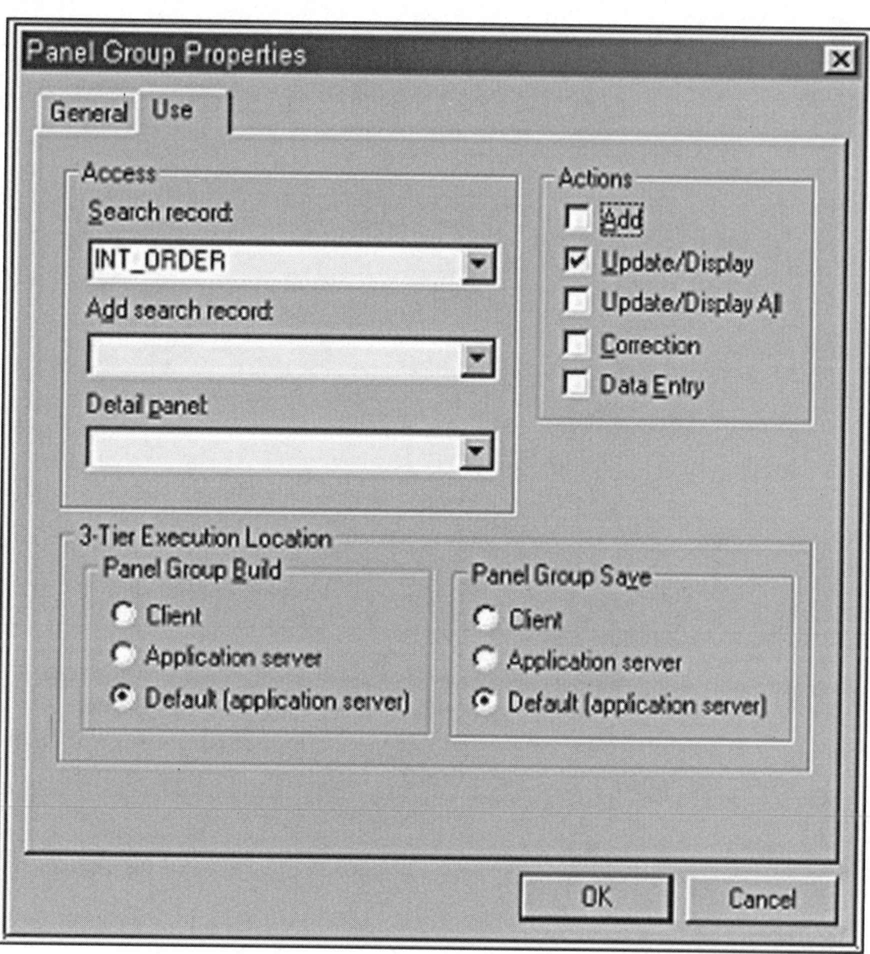

WINT_PNL_GRP.GBL (Panel Group)

	Panel Name	Item Name	Hidden	Item Label	Folder Tab Label
1	INT_ORDER_PNL	INT_ORDER_PNL	☐	&Internal Order	

Figure 8-22 Warehouse Internal Order panel group definition.

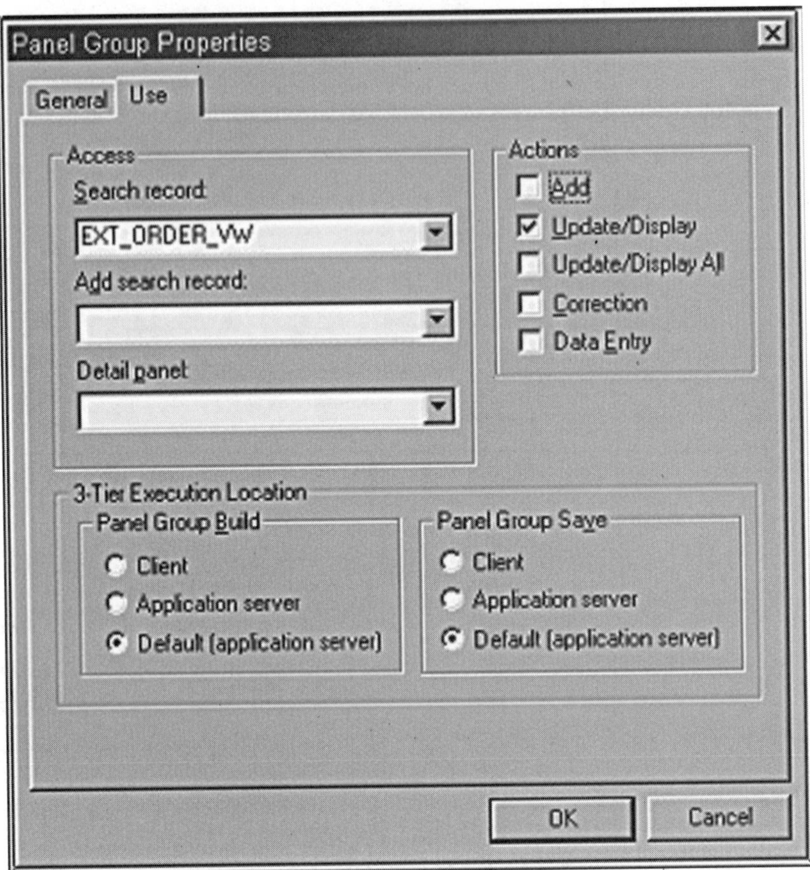

Figure 8-23 Properties of Buyers External Order panel group.

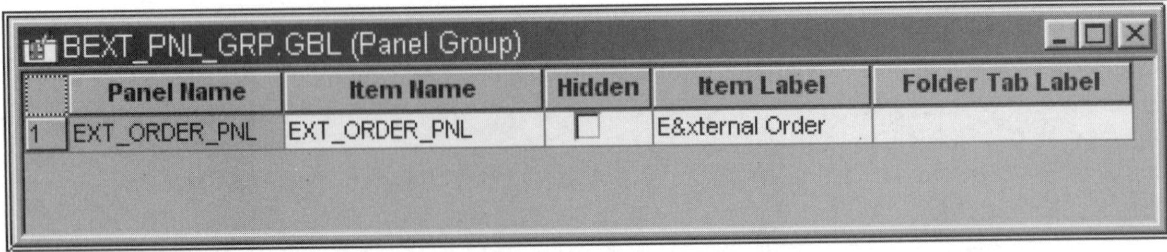

Figure 8-24 Buyers External Order panel group definition.

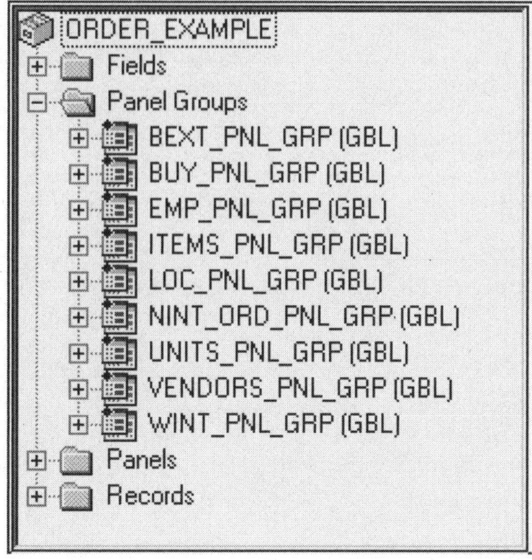

Figure 8-25 Project Workspace with Panel Group folder expanded.

CHAPTER 9

Menus

As mentioned in Chapter 1, menus are the main method of navigating through PeopleSoft applications. Chapter 1 discussed menus from the user's perspective. This chapter discusses menus from the developer's perspective. The developer creates the menus that the users utilize to navigate through the PeopleSoft applications. The developer can create menu groups and standard menus or can create popup menus. Popup menus appear when the mouse is right-clicked. Their purpose is to run PeopleCode programs or to allow the user to quickly get to another panel group. Menu groups and standard menus are accessed from the GO menu bar. Their purpose is to allow the user to get to an application's panel in order to gain access to the data in the database.

This chapter first discusses opening a standard menu and details all the options associated with standard menus. It then discusses how to open a popup menu and details the differences between popup menus and standard menus in terms of the options available. Next, this chapter shows the generic process of creating a menu and, finally, creates the specific menus required in implementing our internal order example.

Menu Groups and Standard Menus

Menu groups and standard menus are accessed from the GO menu bar. When the GO menu bar is clicked, a drop-down list is displayed. This list can contain standard menus, and it can contain menu groups. A *menu group* consists of two or more standard menus. A menu group has a right arrowhead next to its name. If the user moves the mouse toward the right arrowhead, a cascade menu appears. The cascade menu consists of all the standard menus making up the menu group. There is no right arrowhead next to a standard menu. Figure 9-1 illustrates the GO menu bar, a menu group, and a list of standard menus making up the selected menu group.

The preceding description illustrates what the user sees and how the user selects a menu group and finally a standard menu. Now let's look at things from the developer's perspective.

Opening a Standard Menu Definition

First, the developer can open an existing menu for viewing purposes or for modifying purposes. To open an existing menu, the developer must choose FILE, OPEN, and once the Open Object dialog box is displayed, select MENU from the object type drop-down list. The developer can type in selection criteria and then click the SELECT push button. A list of all the menus is displayed. Figure 9-2 shows an Open Object dialog box with an object type of menu. Note that you can type in a string in the NAME box or choose all menus, standard, or popup in the TYPE box. Regardless of what is entered for Selection Criteria, a list of all menus matching the criteria is displayed on the lower section of the screen.

The developer then double-clicks on one of the existing menus and the menu is opened. Figure 9-3 shows what a menu looks like when it is first opened. The grayed-out items are system-defined, and the black items on the menu were created by the developer who created this

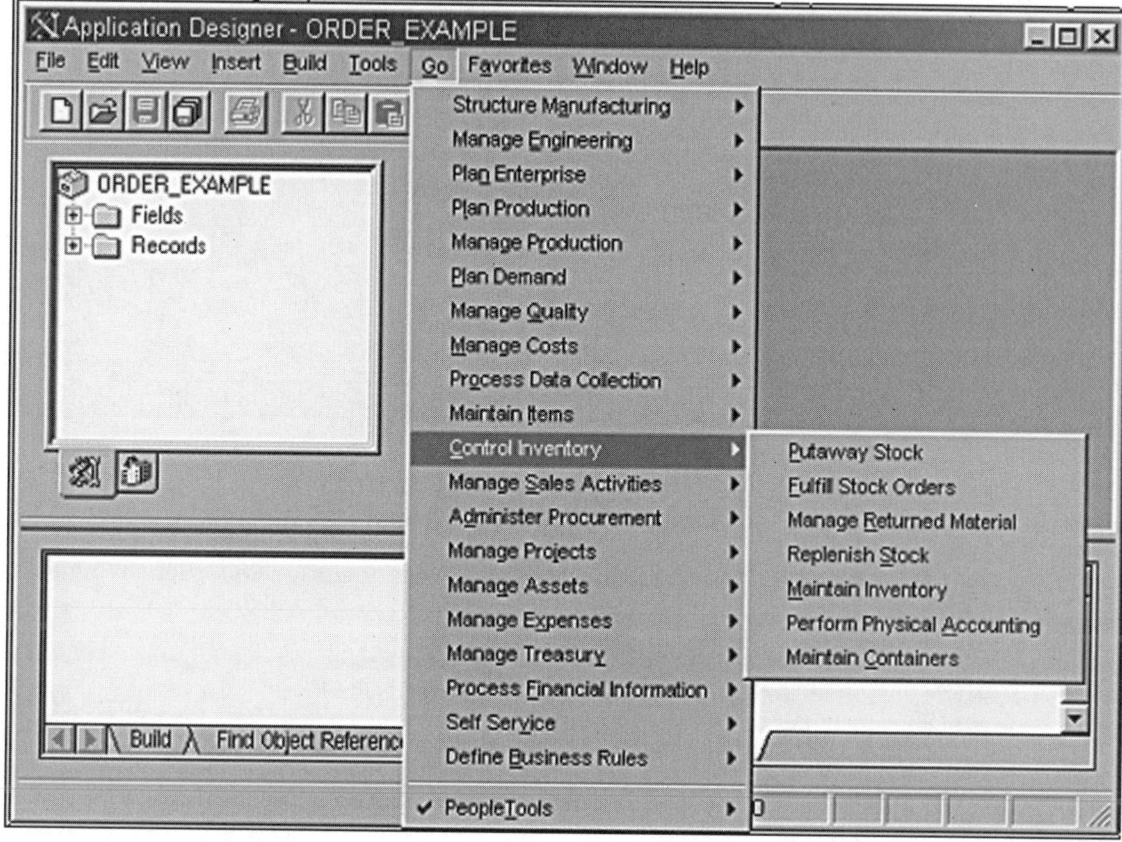

Figure 9-1 GO menu bar consisting of menu groups with a menu group selected. The cascaded menu is a list of the standard menus in the selected menu group.

menu. The developer can click on the empty rectangle on the menu bar to add a new menu bar label. In addition, the developer can click on a menu bar label and the items making up that menu bar are displayed. Figure 9-4 shows the same menu after one of the menu bar labels is clicked on. You can click on the empty rectangle at the bottom of the list to add another menu item. Instead of clicking on the empty rectangle, the developer could also drag and drop a panel group from the Project Workspace area to the empty rectangle. This would quickly add the panel group to the menu as a menu item. Regardless of which way you add a menu item to the menu, be sure to save the menu and the project.

In addition, the developer can right-click and a popup menu will appear. The popup menu differs slightly depending on whether you right-

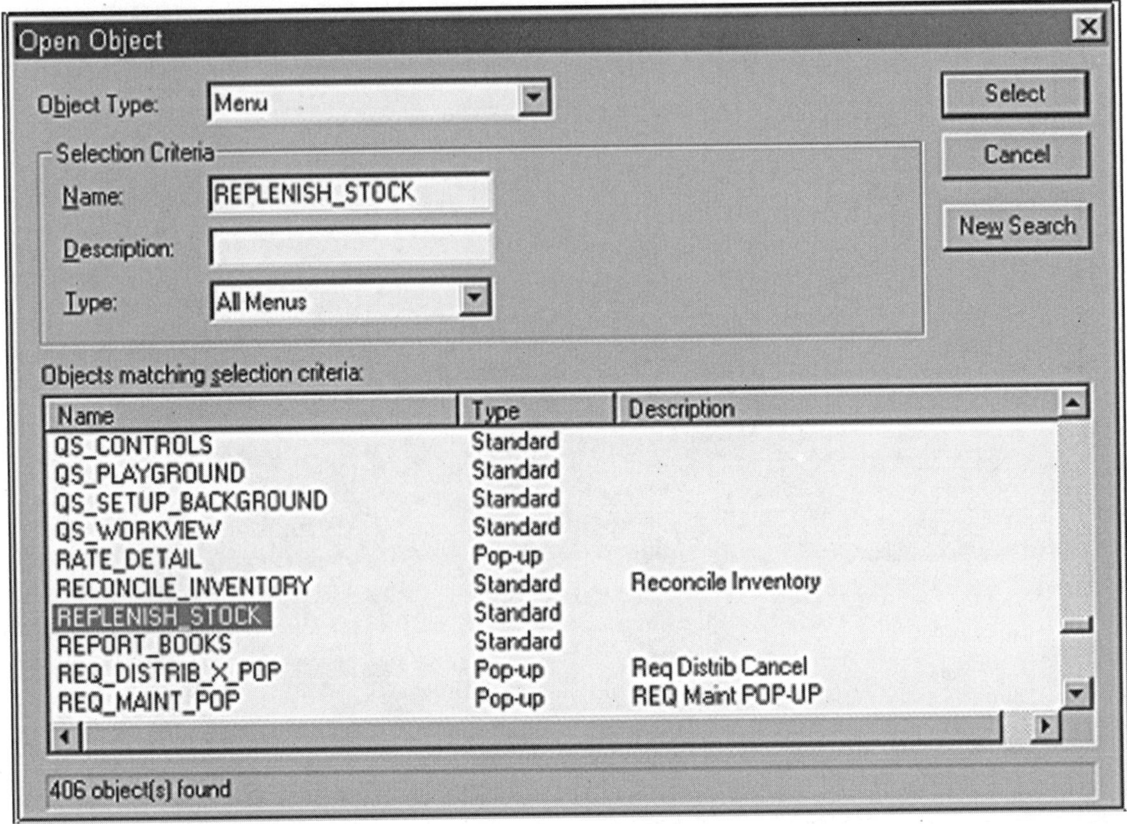

Figure 9-2 Open Object dialog box with object type of Menu.

click on a bar item or on a menu item. If a bar item is right-clicked on, then the popup menu allows the user to view the definition, bring up the Bar Item Properties screen, or bring up the Menu Properties screen. Figure 9-5 shows the popup menu that appears when the mouse is right-clicked on a bar item. If a menu item is right-clicked on, then the popup menu allows the user to view the definition, bring up the Menu Item Properties screen, or bring up the Menu Properties screen. Figure 9-5*a* shows the popup menu that appears when a menu item is right-clicked on.

Menu Properties

If the developer chooses Menu Properties, the Menu Properties dialog box appears as shown in Figure 9-6. This screen has two tabs on it: the GENERAL tab and the USE tab. The GENERAL tab allows the developer to

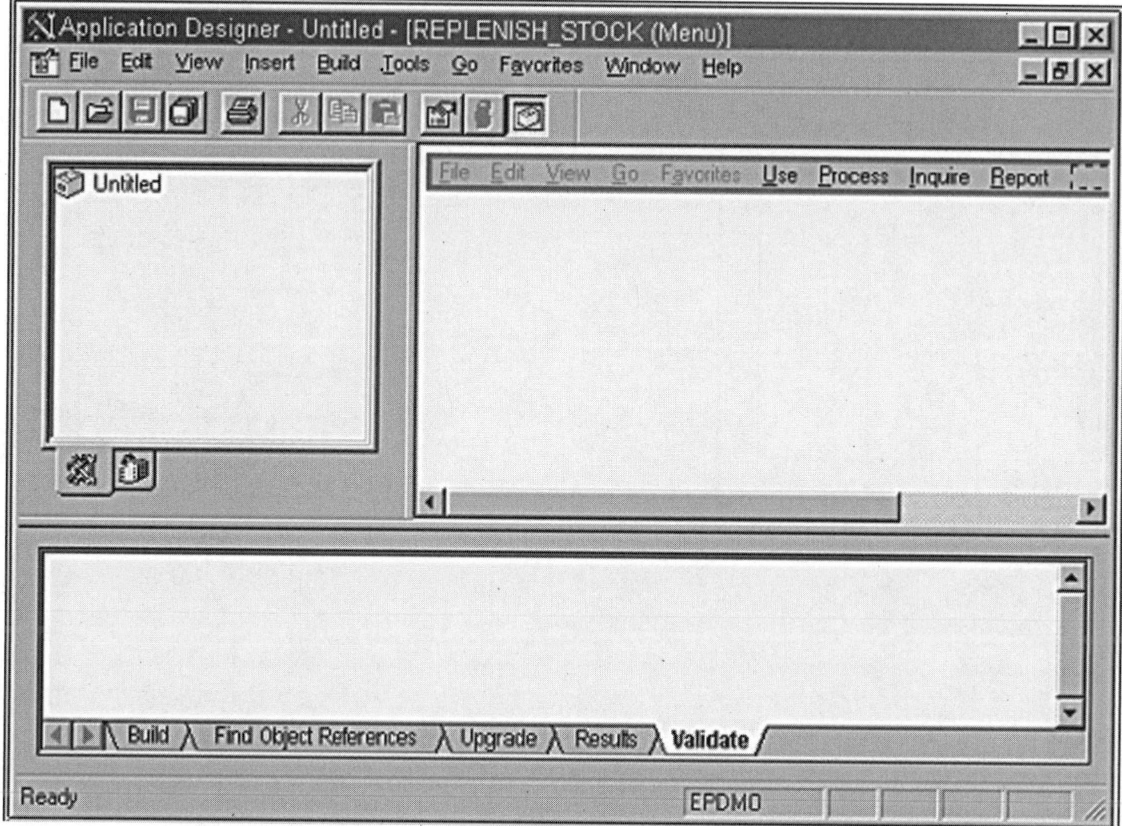

Figure 9-3 An open standard menu.

enter a brief description and some comments related to the menu. It also contains information related to the last date and time the menu was updated and by which operator. Figure 9-6 shows the GENERAL tab.

Figure 9-7 shows the USE tab, which allows the developer to do the following:

- Enter or modify the menu label. If an ampersand is entered in front of the menu label name, then a keyboard shortcut is created for this menu.
- Add the menu to a new or existing menu group. To add the menu to a new menu group, simply type the name of the new menu group in the menu group field of the USE tab. To add the menu to an existing menu group, select one from the displayed list of

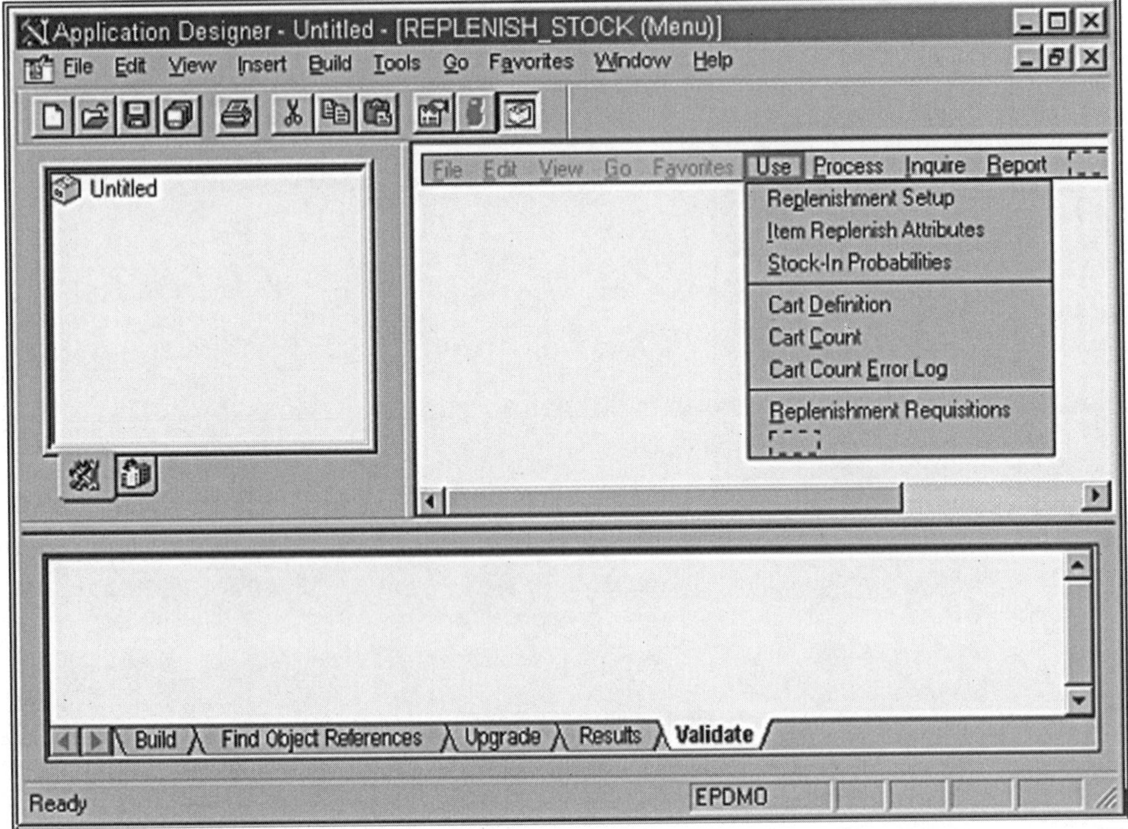

Figure 9-4 Same open menu with a menu bar label clicked on.

menu groups. An ampersand in front of the menu group creates a keyboard shortcut for the menu group. If the menu is not part of a menu group, the menu group field should be left blank. This will place the menu label of the menu on the GO menu bar instead of the name of a menu group.

- Control the order the menu appears in the menu group's cascade menu. You can choose to have the menu names sort in alphabetical order or by sequence number. If sequence number is selected, the developer must enter a value in the sequence number field. All menus being sorted by sequence number will be sorted by ascending sequence number. You can have menus sorted first by sequence number and then alphabetically if desired. The menus

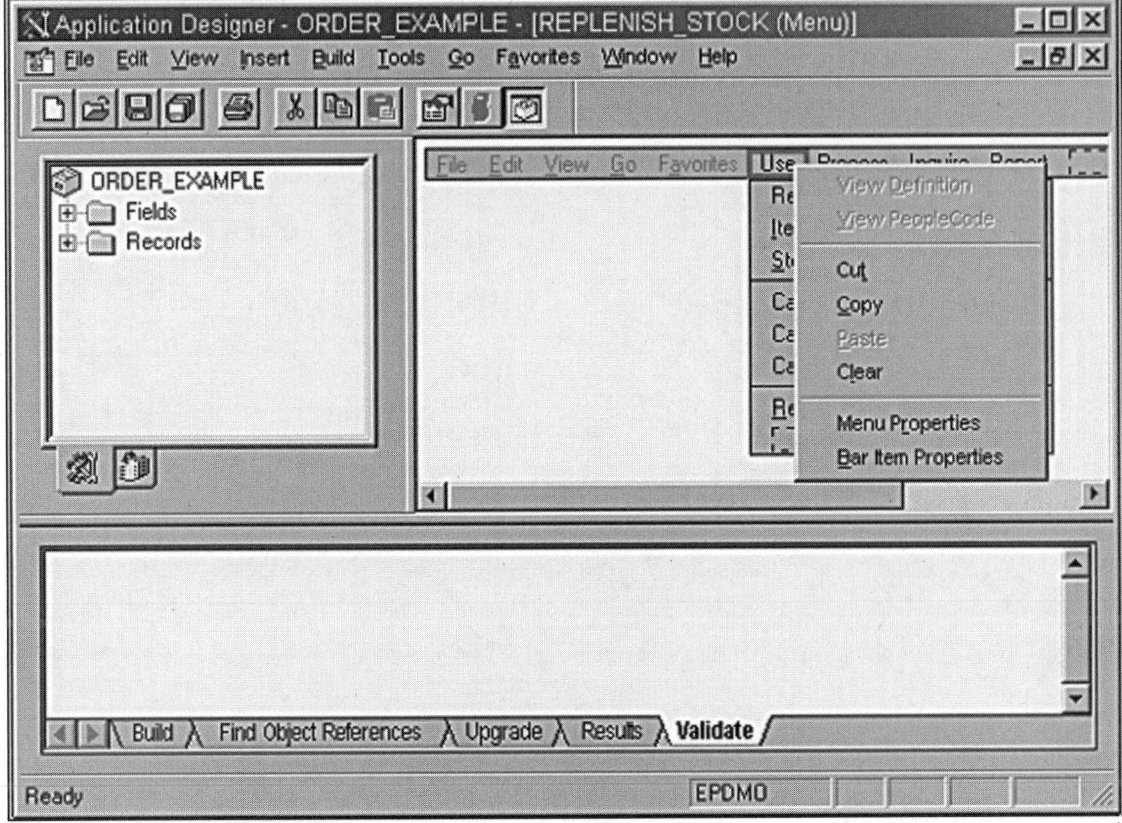

Figure 9-5 A popup menu appears when you right-click the mouse on a bar item.

that are to be sorted alphabetically are assigned a sequence number of 9999. This is the highest sequence number that can be assigned. Thus, if you want a combination sort, the sequence number of the items sorted by sequence number should be less than 9999. This causes them to be listed before any alphabetical-order items.

- Control the order the menu group appears in the GO menu bar. You can choose to have the menu group names sort in alphabetical order or by sequence number. If sequence number is selected, the developer must enter a value in the sequence number field. The sequence numbers will be sorted in ascending order. You can have menu groups sorted first by sequence number and then

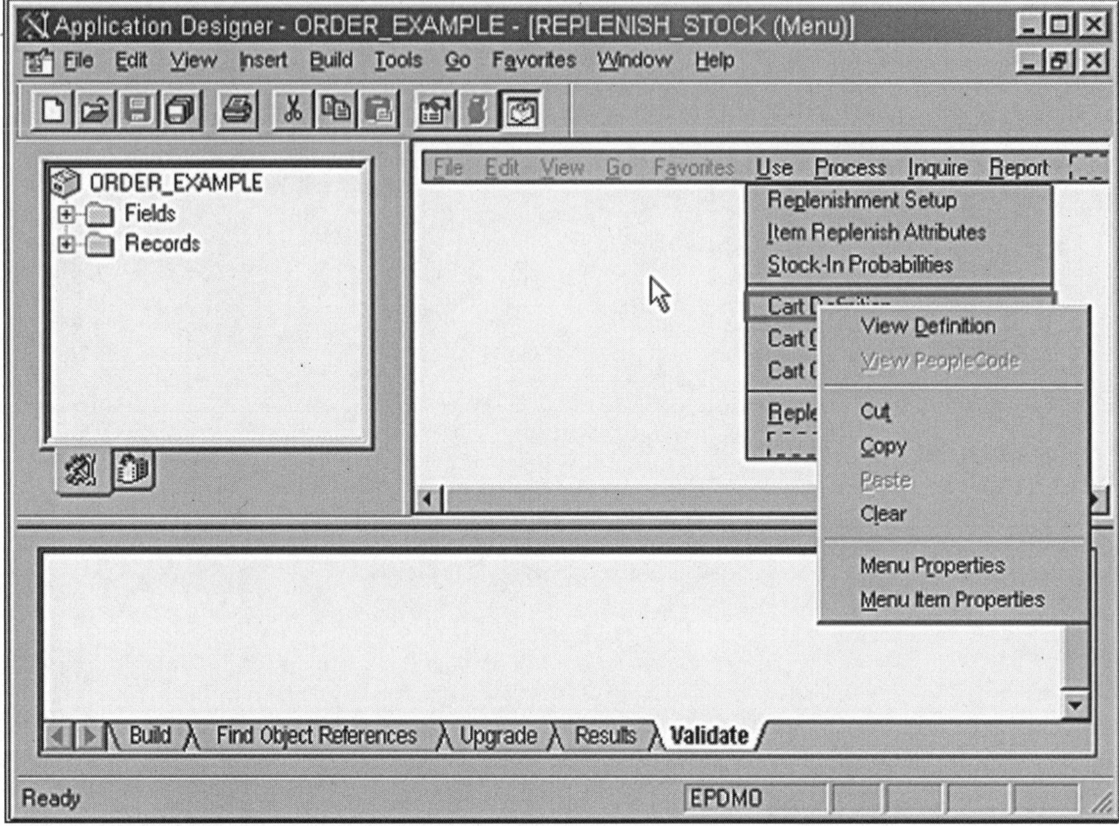

Figure 9-5*a* A popup menu appears when you right-click the mouse on a menu item.

alphabetically if desired. The menu groups that are to be sorted alphabetically are assigned a sequence number of 9999. This is the highest sequence number that can be assigned. Thus, if you want a combination sort, the sequence number of the items sorted by sequence number should be less than 9999. This causes them to be listed before any alphabetical order items.

- Add a separator line. When this is checked, a separator line is displayed below the menu or menu group name.

After all the changes are made on the GENERAL tab and on the USE tab of the Menu Properties dialog box, the developer must select OK. In addition, the developer must SAVE the menu definition by selecting FILE, SAVE.

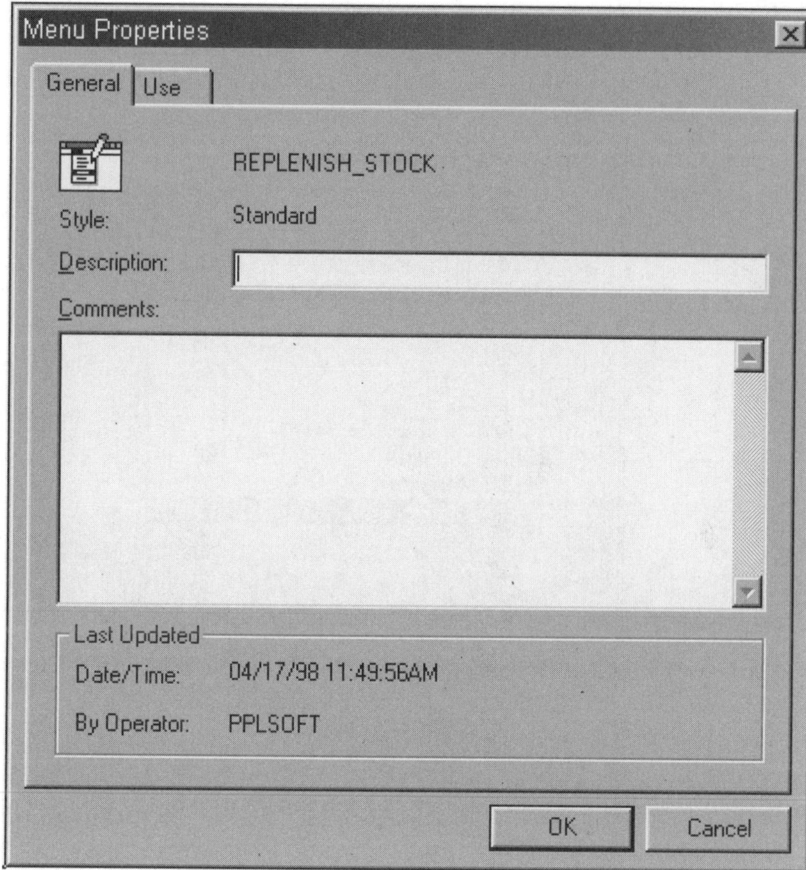

Figure 9-6 The GENERAL tab of the Menu Properties dialog box.

Note that, while at an open menu definition, the developer can also get to the Menu Properties dialog box by selecting FILE, OBJECT PROPERTIES or by pressing the ALT + ENTER keys.

Bar Item Properties

Remember that when the mouse was right-clicked, a popup menu appeared. We just discussed the screens that appear when the MENU PROPERTIES option was selected. Now let's see what happens when the BAR ITEM PROPERTIES option is selected. Figure 9-8 shows the popup menu with BAR ITEM PROPERTIES selected. Figure 9-9 shows the Bar Item Properties dialog box for the USE bar item. This Bar Item Properties dialog box will also be displayed if the developer simply double-clicks on a

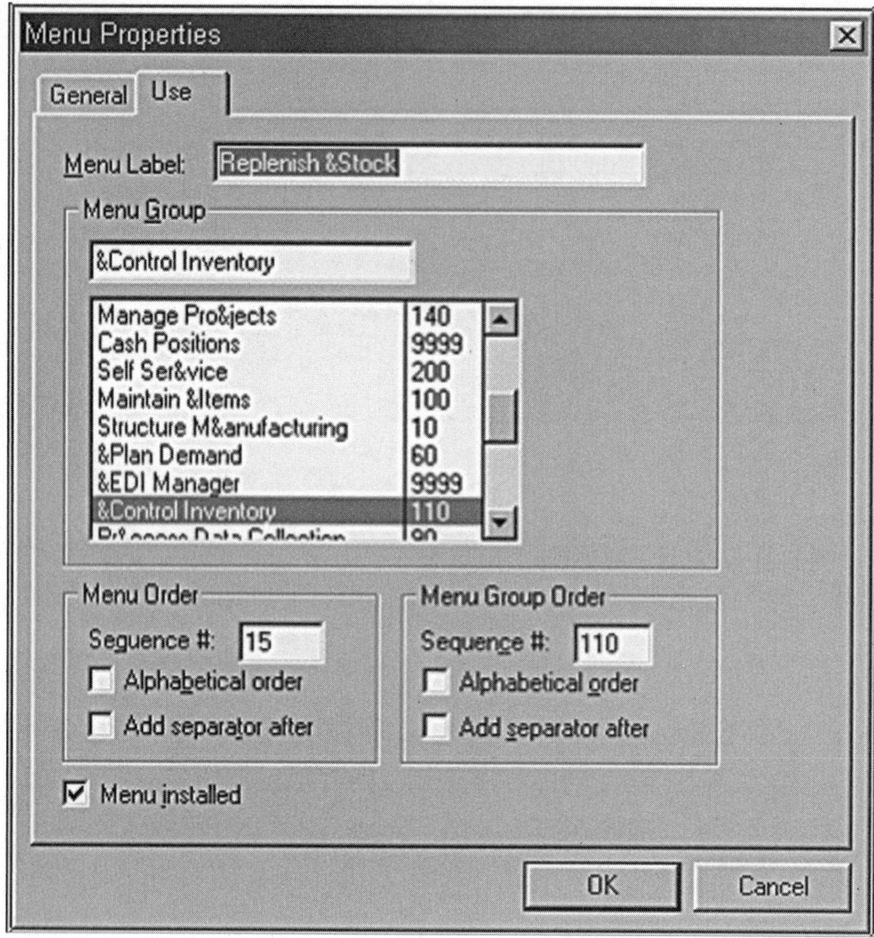

Figure 9-7
USE tab of the Menu Properties dialog box.

bar item. In this case, if the developer clicked on the USE bar item, the exact dialog box would have appeared.

The Bar Item Properties dialog box allows the developer to display or modify the bar item's name and label. Click OK when the name and label are satisfactory.

Menu Item Properties

When an item in a standard menu is double-clicked, the Menu Item Properties dialog box appears. (This dialog box also appears when the right mouse is clicked on a menu item and MENU ITEM PROPERTIES is selected from the popup menu.)

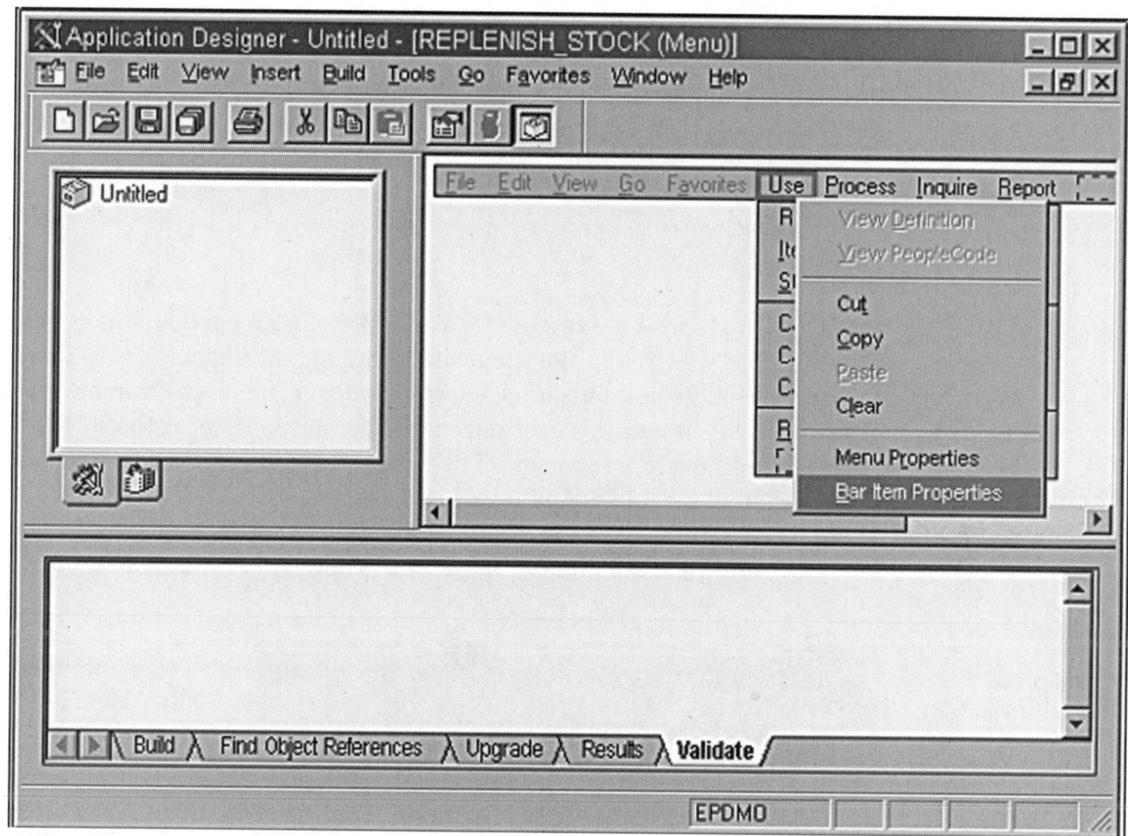

Figure 9-8 Popup menu with BAR ITEM PROPERTIES selected.

Bar Item Properties

Bar Item

Name: USE

Label: &Use

OK Cancel

Figure 9-9 Bar Item Properties dialog box.

The Menu Item Properties dialog box displays the name and text label of the menu item. These can be modified if desired. In addition, this dialog box allows the developer to select the type of menu item. For a standard menu, the menu items can be one of the following types:

- Panel group
- PeopleCode
- Separator

Figure 9-10 shows an example of a Menu Item Properties dialog box. The example shown has the menu item defined as a panel group since the panel group radio button is selected. This is the most common type of menu item. (When the user clicks on this menu item in the application, a panel group is opened.) The developer can click on the SELECT push button to get a list of panel groups.

Note that the menu item name is the name that is displayed in the Security Administrator under the Menu View. This is used to give an

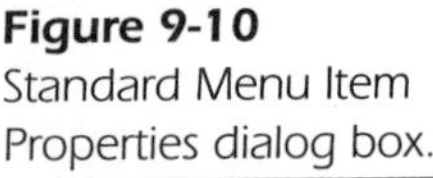

Figure 9-10 Standard Menu Item Properties dialog box.

operator access to the panel group. The label is the text that appears on the menu that the user sees and clicks on. The panel group name is the actual name of the panel group.

After viewing or modifying the Menu Item Properties dialog box, the developer should select the OK push button and then SAVE the menu definition.

Popup Menus

In addition to standard menus and menu groups, the developer can create popup menus. A popup menu appears when the user right-clicks the mouse on a field of a panel that was set up to have a popup menu. The purpose of popup menus is to transfer the user to another panel group in the application or to run a PeopleCode program.

Opening a Popup Menu Definition

Let's look at how the developer opens an existing popup menu. Select FILE, OPEN from the menu bar and set the type of menu to POPUP. Select a popup menu from the list of displayed popup menus available by clicking on one and then pushing the SELECT push button. Refer to Figure 9-11.

Figure 9-12 shows an open popup menu definition.

Menu Properties

The developer can display the Menu Properties dialog box for a popup menu by selecting FILE, OBJECT PROPERTIES or by right-clicking the mouse and selecting MENU PROPERTIES. The MENU PROPERTIES dialog box is shown in Figure 9-13. Note that for popup menus there is only one tab. The GENERAL tab is the only tab on the popup Menu Properties dialog box. This dialog box is the same as that for standard menus with the exception that the style is set to POPUP. This dialog box contains the POPUP menu name, description, comments, style, date and time last updated, and the operator who last updated it.

Bar Item Properties Note that there is no bar item properties dialog box for popup menus.

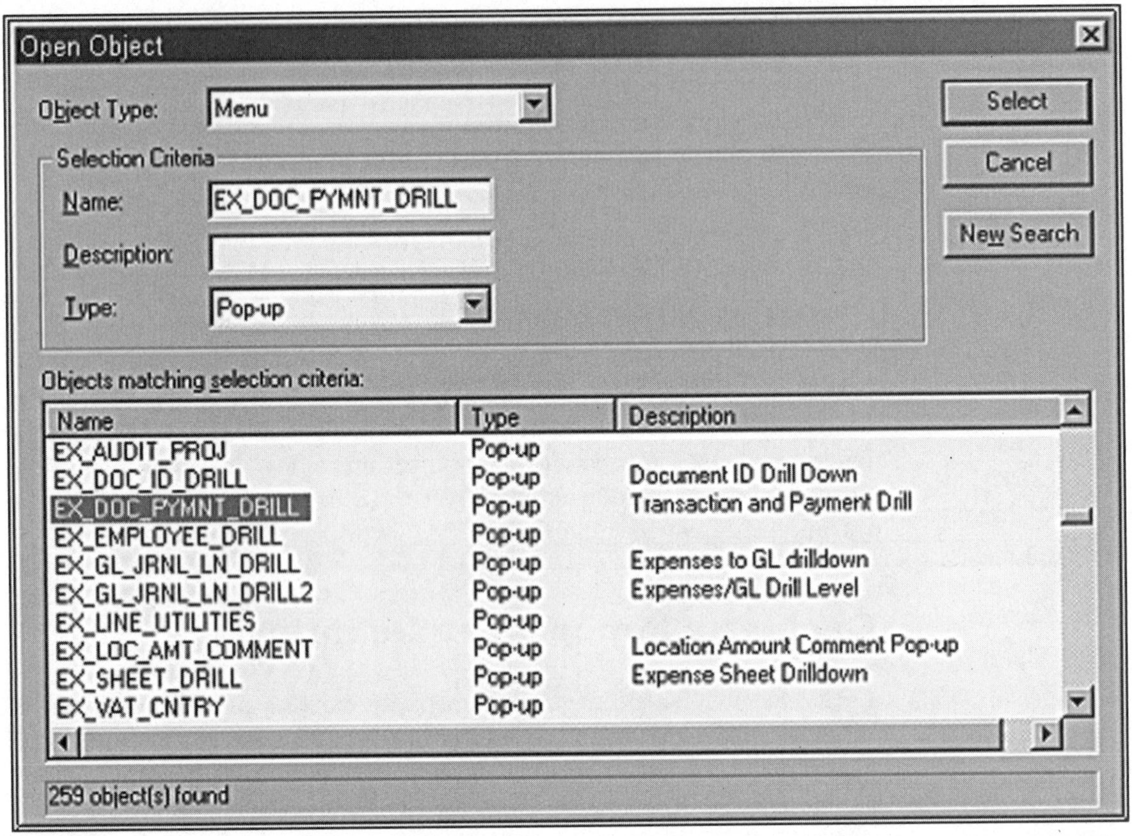

Figure 9-11 Opening an existing popup menu.

Menu Item Properties Double-click on a menu item, and the Menu Item Properties dialog box is displayed as shown in Figure 9-14.

When the Menu Item Properties dialog box is displayed for popup menus, the type field can be set to

- Transfer
- PeopleCode
- Separator.

Remember that the type field for standard menus could be Panel Group, PeopleCode, or Separator. Therefore, the popup menu cannot access panel groups. Instead, they can transfer the user to another

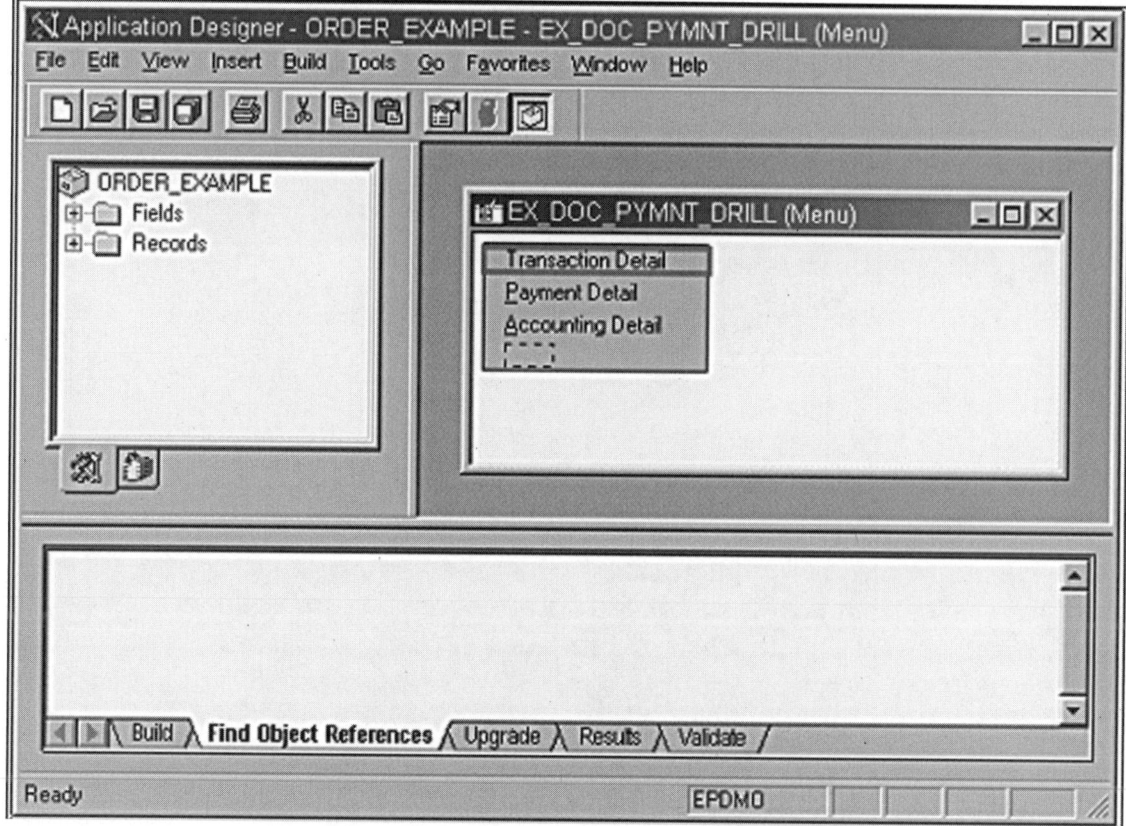

Figure 9-12 Open popup menu definition.

panel group in the same application or run PeopleCode. The developer can get to the Menu Item Properties dialog box by right-clicking the mouse and getting a popup menu and then selecting MENU ITEM PROPERTIES. Other ways to get to this dialog box are to click on the PROPERTIES Icon or select EDIT, MENU ITEM PROPERTIES. The PROPERTIES icon is displayed in Figure 9-15.

Figure 9-16 illustrates an example of when PeopleCode is selected for the type. In this case the DEFINE TRANSFER push button is grayed out. When Transfer is selected, the DEFINE TRANSFER push button is available as an option as shown in Figure 9-17. When the DEFINE TRANSFER push button is clicked, Figure 9-18 appears. This figure shows an example of the Transfer Properties dialog box.

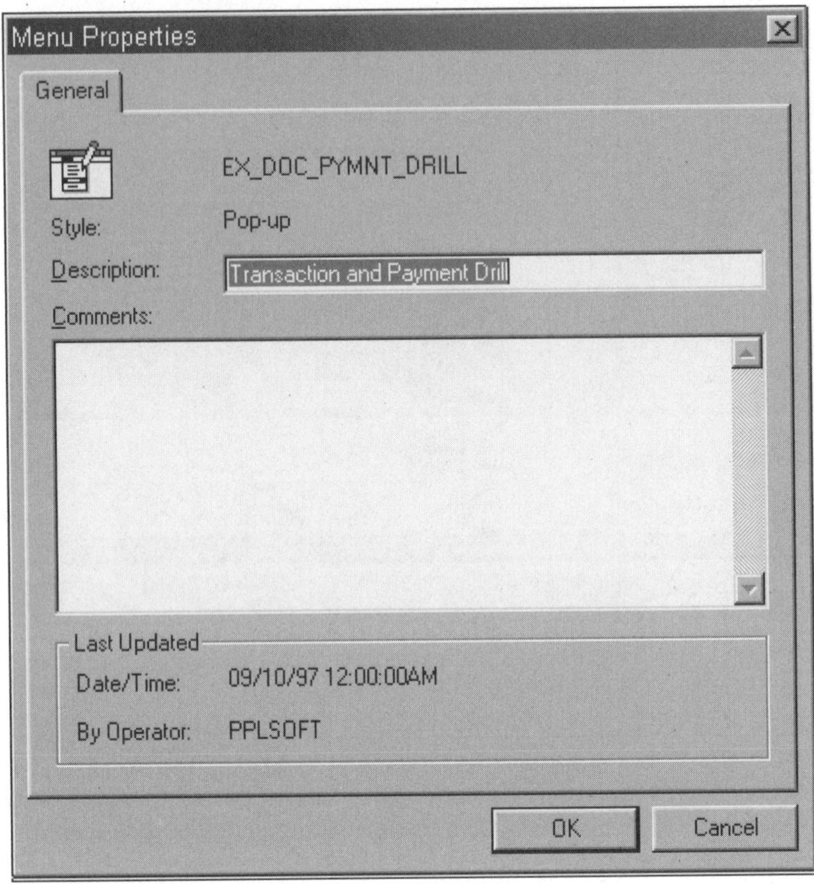

Figure 9-13 Menu Properties dialog box for a popup menu.

The Transfer Properties dialog box allows the developer to enter the menu name, panel group, and panel that the user will transfer to if the item in the popup menu is clicked on. It also defines what action will be performed when the user gets to that panel. The Transfer Properties dialog box has a transfer type group that allows the developer to choose between reusing the current window or using a new window with the current window minimized. In addition, the developer can decide whether to use data from the current panel in the search dialog. Once all the transfer information is entered, the developer should push the OK pushbutton. When all changes are made to the menu, the menu should be saved.

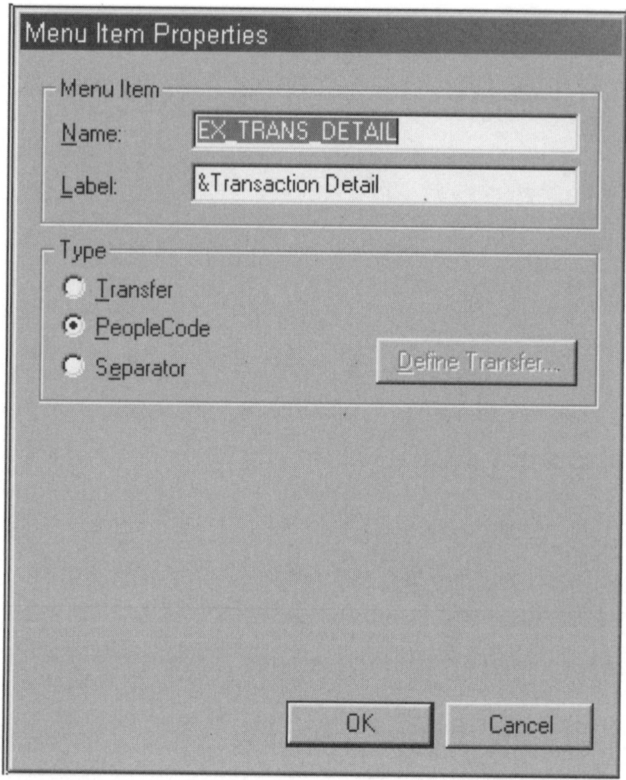

Figure 9-14
Menu Item Properties dialog box.

Figure 9-15
PROPERTIES icon. Click on this icon to get the Menu Item Properties dialog box to appear.

Creating New Menus

To create a new menu, perform the following generic steps:

1. Select FILE, NEW. When the NEW dialog box appears, select MENU as shown in Figure 9-19.

   Click on the OK push button, and the New Menu dialog box (see Fig. 9-20) will appear.

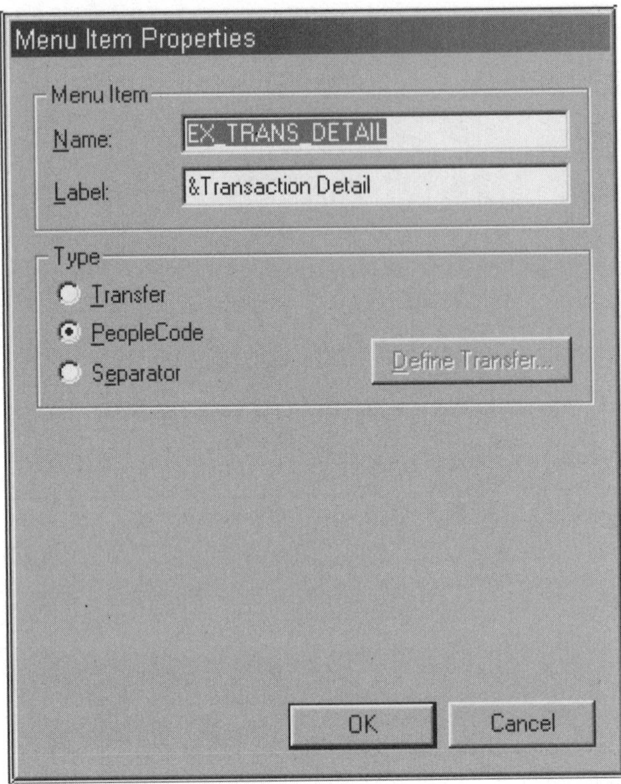

Figure 9-16 Popup Menu Item Properties dialog box when PeopleCode is selected as the type.

2. On the New Menu dialog box, select the menu type of the menu you wish to create. The choices are standard or popup. Click on the OK push button.

Steps for Creating Standard Menus

1. If the menu type selected is standard, a blank menu definition is opened as shown in Figure 9-21. The dotted rectangle indicates where the menu item would be added.
2. Double clicking the rectangle causes the Bar Item Properties dialog box to be displayed as shown in Figure 9-22. Enter a name for the new menu and enter the text that will appear in the bar item and then press OK. Figure 9-23 shows the Bar Item Properties dialog box with entered values for the name and label.

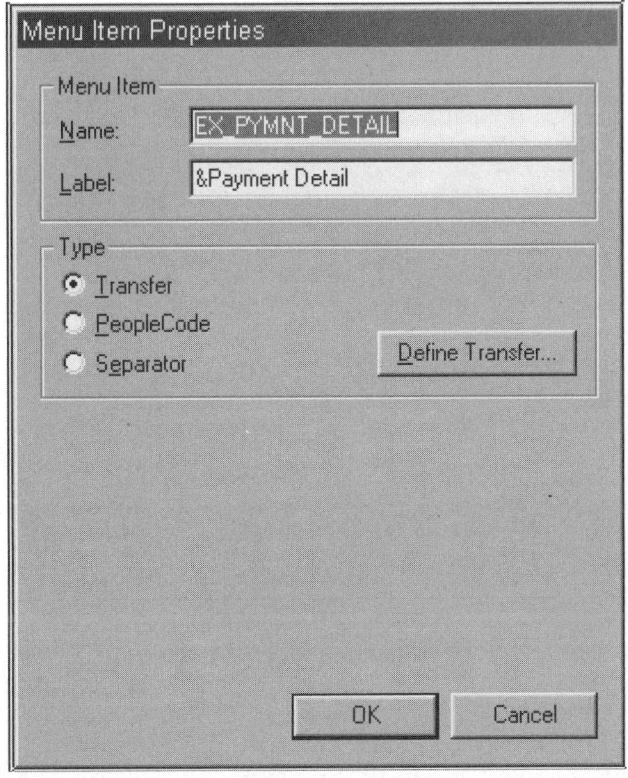

Figure 9-17
Popup Menu Item Properties dialog box when Transfer is selected.

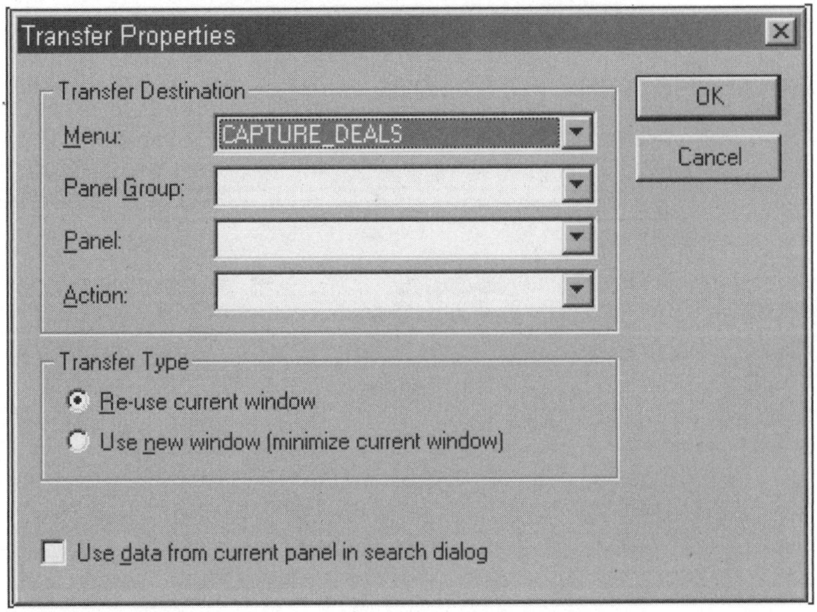

Figure 9-18
Transfer Properties Dialog Box. This appears when the DEFINE PROPERTIES button is clicked.

Figure 9-19
New dialog box with MENU selected.

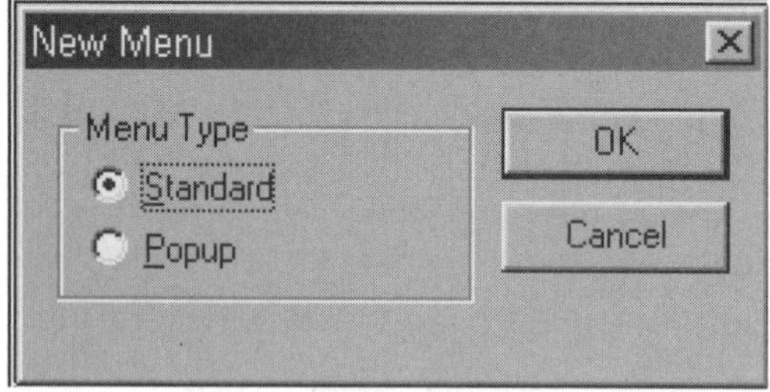

Figure 9-20
New Menu dialog box.

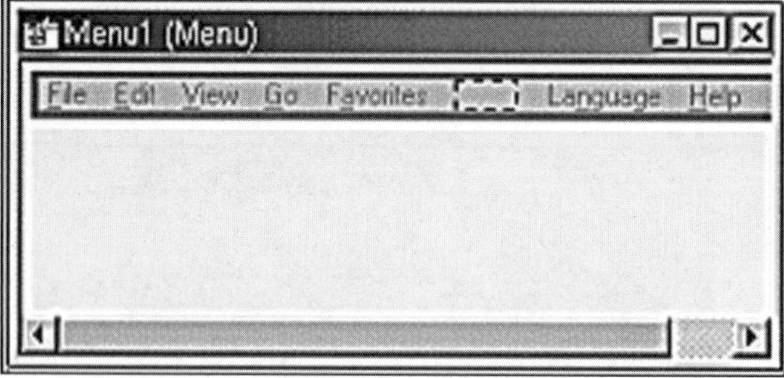

Figure 9-21
Blank menu.

Bar Item Properties
Bar Item
Name: MENUITEM1
Label:
OK Cancel

Figure 9-22
Blank Bar Item Properties dialog box.

Figure 9-24 shows the menu with the new bar item EXAMPLE displayed. At this point, there are no menu items under the new bar item EXAMPLE. Now the next rectangle on the bar is where you would add another new bar item in the same way.

3. Now that you have a new bar item, you must add menu items to the bar item. To do so, bring up the Menu Item Properties dialog box. The easiest way is to double-click on the rectangle below the bar item. In this case, double-click on the rectangle below the bar item EXAMPLE. The blank Menu Item Properties dialog box is displayed as shown in Figure 9-25. Enter the menu item's name and enter the text that will appear in the window. Select the panel group radio button and then select the panel group that this menu item will access when it is clicked on by the user. (Otherwise, select the PeopleCode radio button or Separator radio button if that is the type of menu item desired.) Figure 9-26 shows the Menu Item Properties dialog box filled in with some data. Alternately, the developer could have dragged and dropped a panel

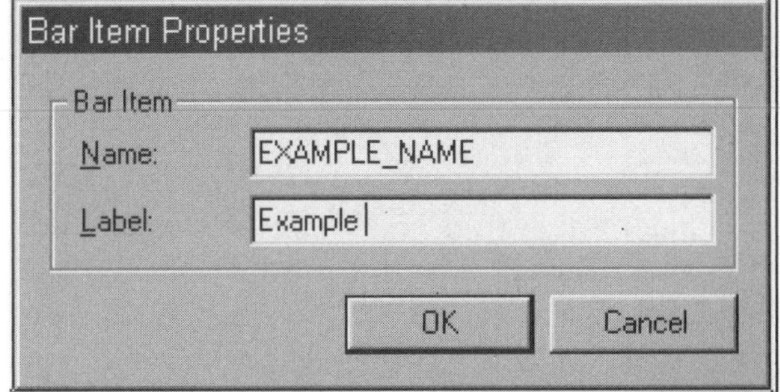

Figure 9-23 Bar Item Properties dialog box with newly entered values.

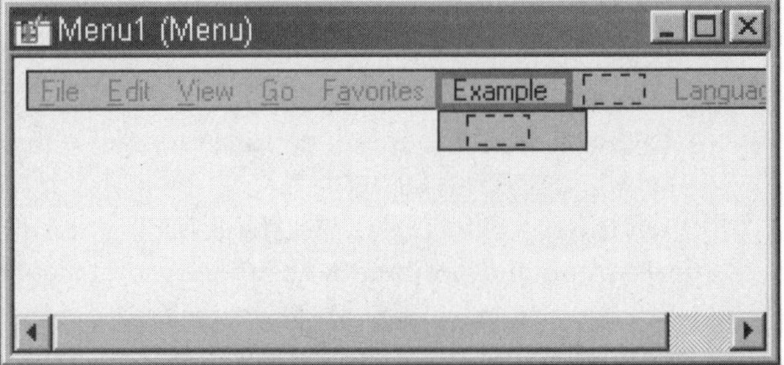

Figure 9-24 Menu definition with the new bar item.

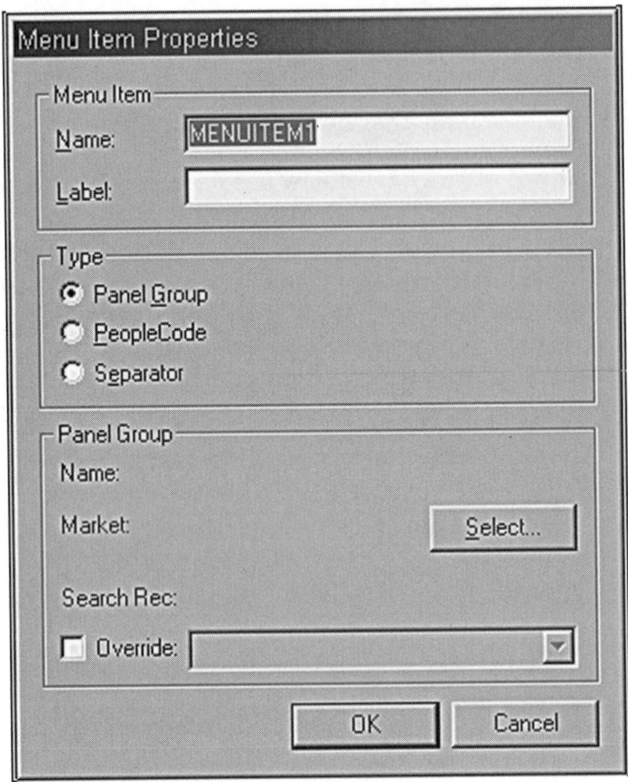

Figure 9-25 Blank Menu Item Properties dialog box when creating a standard menu.

group definition from the Project Workspace over to the rectangle. The menu definition with the newly defined menu item is shown in Figure 9-27.

4. Bring up the Menu Properties dialog box by selecting FILE, OBJECT PROPERTIES in order to set the menu properties.

   Again, other ways to get to the Menu Properties dialog box are

   - To click the PROPERTIES icon.
   - Press ALT + ENTER.
   - Double-click on the menu definition.
   - Right-click on the menu definition to get a popup menu and select MENU PROPERTIES.

   On the GENERAL tab of the Menu Properties dialog box, enter a description and comments about the menu as shown in Figure 9-28.

   On the USE tab of the Menu Properties dialog box, enter the menu label and the menu group that this menu will be in, if any.

Figure 9-26
Menu Item Properties dialog box when selecting Panel Group as the type of menu item.

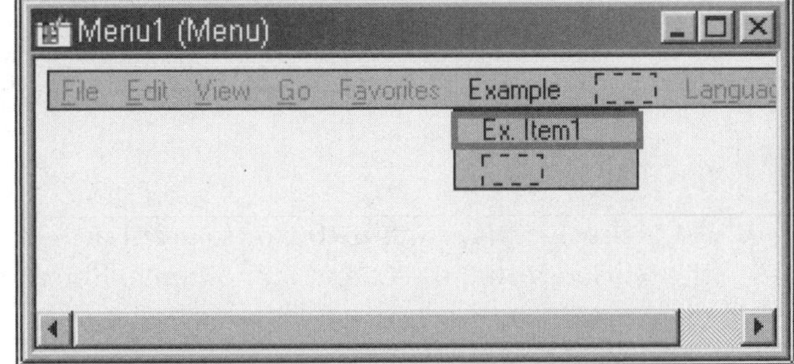

Figure 9-27
Menu definition with newly created menu item.

Set the menu order and the menu group order. Click OK to accept the changes you made. Refer to Figure 9-29.

5. Save the menu by selecting FILE, SAVE and entering the name of the menu in the Save As dialog box as shown in Figure 9-30. Click on the OK push button.

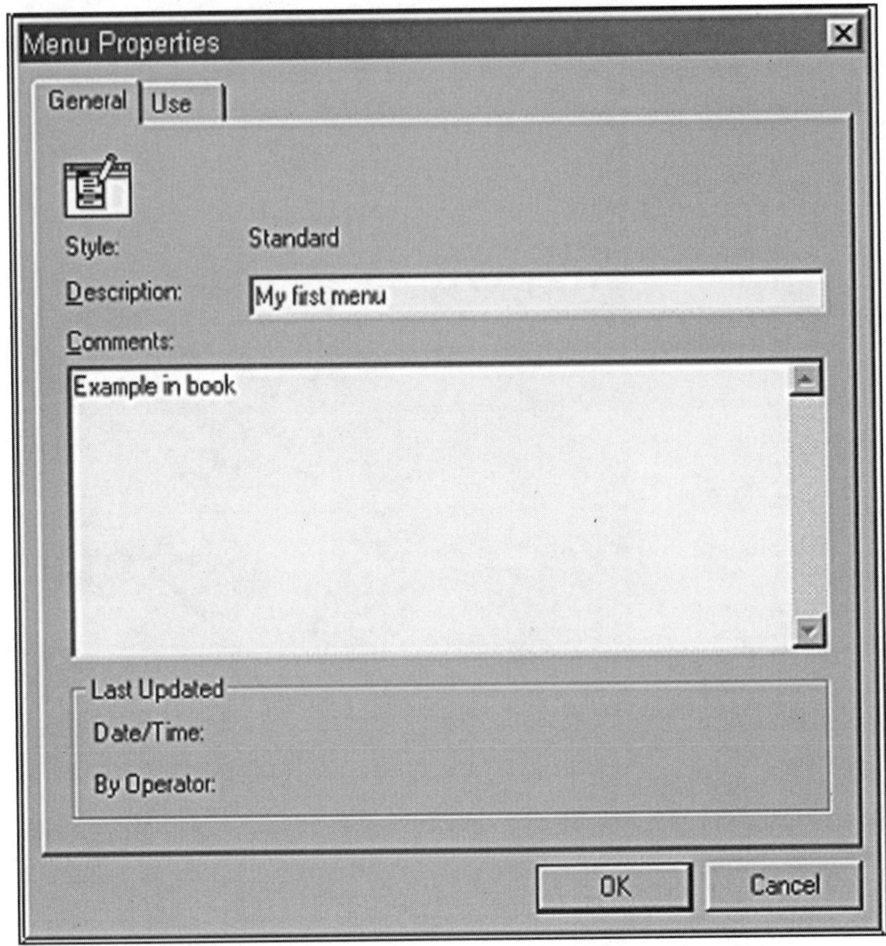

Figure 9-28 GENERAL tab of the Menu Properties dialog box.

6. Go to the Security Administrator to grant access to the users for the newly created menu and menu items. Refer to Chapter 11 for more detail on the Security Administrator.

Steps for Creating Popup Menus

1. Select FILE, NEW from the menu bar and when the New dialog is displayed, select MENU and then click on OK.

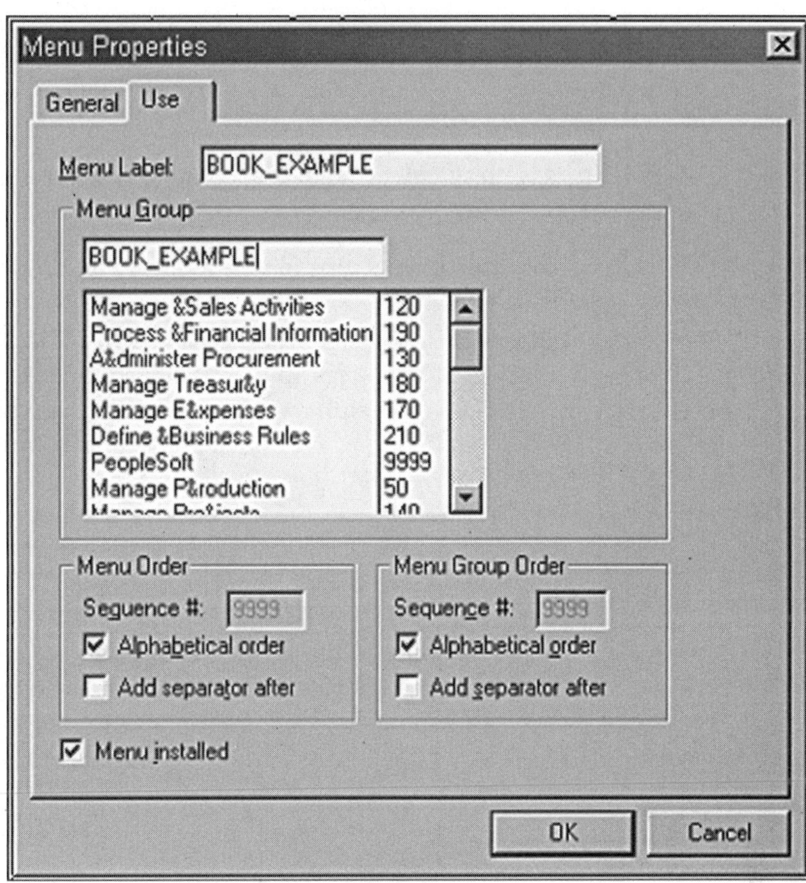

Figure 9-29
USE tab of Menu Properties dialog box.

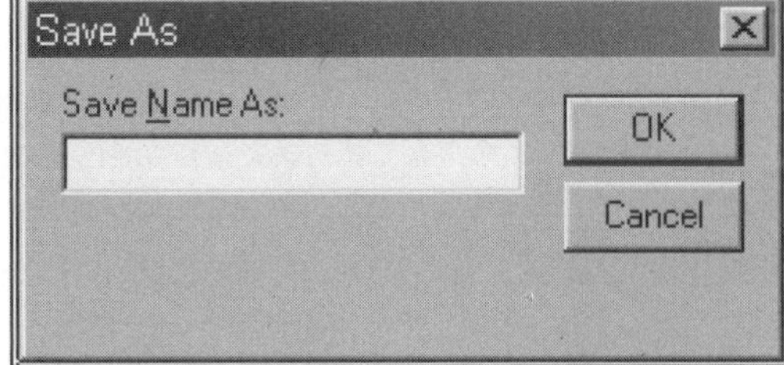

Figure 9-30
Save As dialog box.

2. At the New Menu dialog box, select the POPUP radio button and click on the OK push button as shown in Figure 9-31.
3. A blank popup menu definition is opened and displayed. Figure 9-32 shows a blank popup menu definition. Clicking on the rectangle brings up the Menu Item Properties dialog box as shown in Figure 9-33.
4. Choose the desired type for the menu item: Transfer, PeopleCode, or Separator.
   - If Transfer is selected, the Transfer Properties dialog box is displayed. The developer must enter the transfer destination, which consists of the menu, panel group, panel, and action that the user will jump to when this menu item is selected off the popup menu. Figure 9-34 shows the Transfer Properties dialog box.
   - If PeopleCode is selected, click on the OK pushbutton of the Menu Item Properties dialog box. Then right-click on the menu item that was defined to be of type PeopleCode. This brings up a popup menu. Click on the VIEW PEOPLECODE selection to bring up the PeopleCode editor. Enter the PeopleCode program.
   - If Separator is selected, simply click on the OK pushbutton. Then, move the separator to the desired position in the list of menu items.

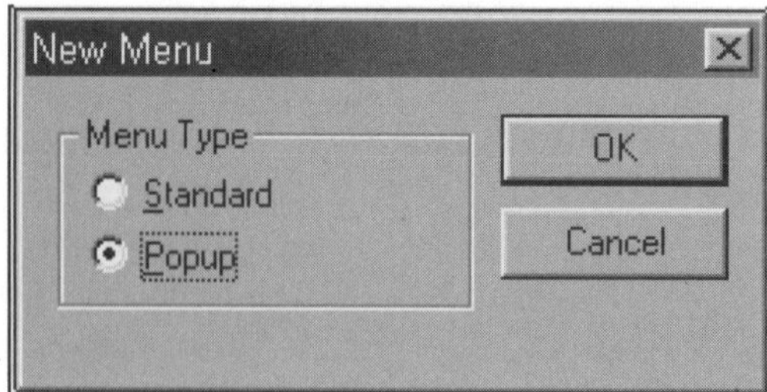

Figure 9-31 New Menu dialog box with POPUP selected.

Figure 9-32 Blank popup menu definition.

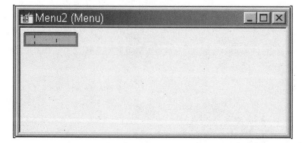

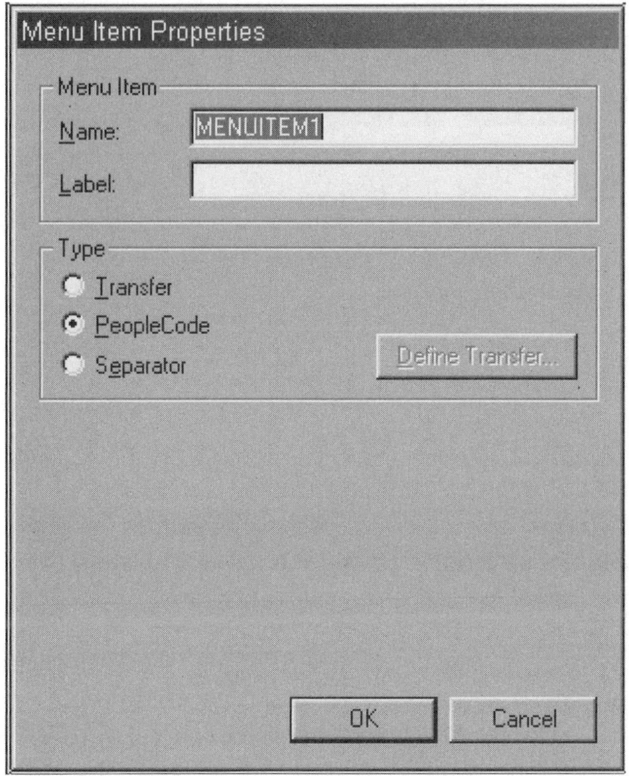

Figure 9-33 Menu Item Properties dialog box displayed when POPUP menu is selected.

Transfer Properties

Transfer Destination

Menu: CAPTURE_DEALS

Panel Group:

Panel:

Action:

OK

Cancel

Transfer Type

Re-use current window

Use new window (minimize current window)

Use data from current panel in search dialog

Figure 9-34 Transfer Properties dialog box.

5. Regardless of which transfer type the menu item is defined as, the next step in creating a popup menu is to associate the popup menu with a field on a panel. To do so, the panel containing the panel field that is to be associated with the popup menu must first be opened. Then, go to the Panel Field Properties dialog box by double-clicking on the panel field. On the USE tab of the Panel Field Properties dialog box, select the popup menu name that was just created. This will associate the new popup menu with the selected field on this panel. After the popup menu is selected, click on the OK pushbutton and then save the panel definition by selecting FILE, SAVE.

Example Menus (Our Example)

Now we are ready to create the menus for our example application. Since our example program is relatively small, we are going to need only one standard menu. Each of our panel groups will be menu items on our new standard menu. In our example menu (`Our_Example`), let's begin by selecting FILE, NEW from the menu bar and when the New dialog is displayed, select MENU and then click on OK. At the New Menu dialog box, select the standard menu radio button and click on the OK. With the new empty menu displayed in the Object Workspace, we are then going to create two new menu bar items. First, double-click on the empty box located to the immediate right of the grayed-out FAVORITES menu bar item. When the Bar Item Properties dialog is displayed, add the name `USE` and label `&Use` to the dialog. Figure 9-35 shows the Bar Item Properties dialog for our `USE` bar item. Next, double-click on the empty box located to the immediate right of the grayed-out `USE` menu bar item. When the Bar Item Properties dialog is displayed, add the name `INQUIRE` and label `&Inquire` to the dialog. Figure 9-36 shows the Bar Item Properties dialog for our `INQUIRE` bar item. Figure 9-37 shows the new menu with the `USE` and `INQUIRE` for items.

Employees Menu item

We can now begin placing our panel groups onto the menu. With the Panel Group folder expanded in the Project Workspace, drag and drop the Employees panel group onto the new menu under the `USE` menu bar.

Figure 9-35
USE Bar Item Properties dialog.

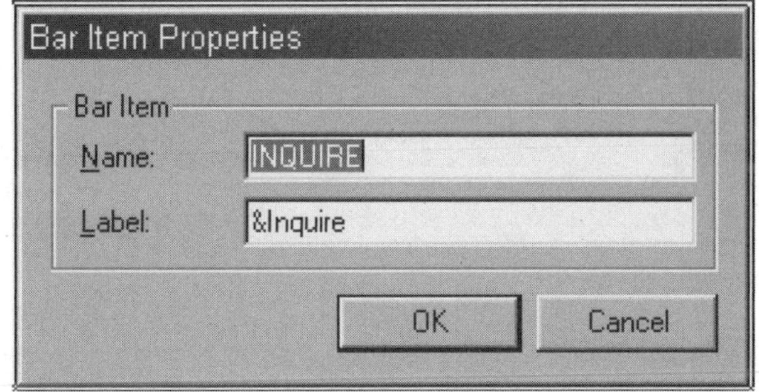

Figure 9-36
Inquire Bar Item Properties dialog.

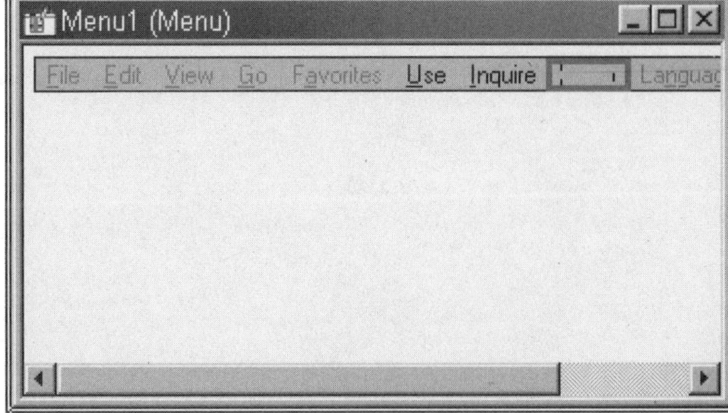

Figure 9-37
New Menu with USE and INQUIRE Bar Items.

Next, double-click on the new menu item. When the Menu Item Properties dialog is displayed, change the label to `&Employees` and press OK. Figure 9-38 shows the Menu Item Properties dialog for the Employees menu item. Figure 9-39 shows the menu after the insert.

Buyers Menu item

We are now going to create our Buyers menu item. When we set up the panel group for our Buyers, we decided that it was going to be a read-only panel. Therefore, we are going to place it under the `INQUIRE` menu

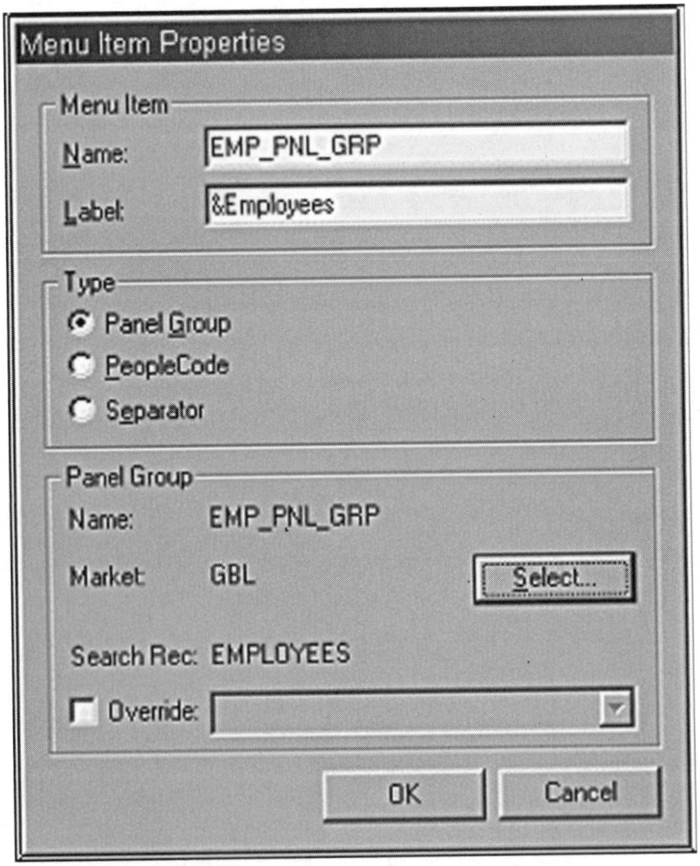

Figure 9-38 Employees Menu Item Properties dialog.

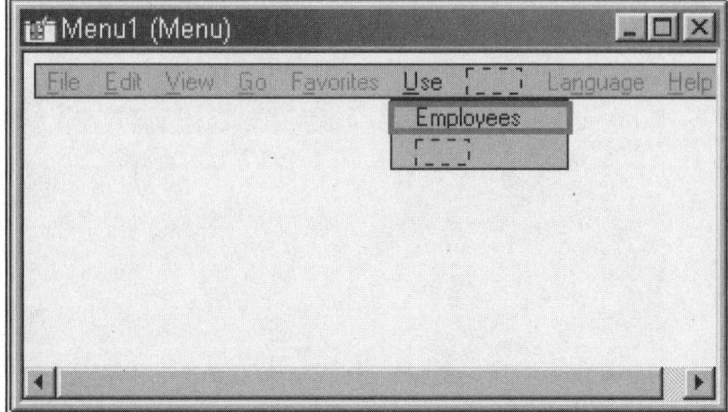

Figure 9-39
Menu with Employees menu item.

bar. Now drag and drop the Buyers panel group and place it under the `INQUIRE` menu bar. Next, double-click on the new menu item. When the Menu Item Properties dialog is displayed, change the label to `&Buyers` and press OK. Figure 9-40 shows the Menu Item Properties dialog for the Buyers menu item. Figure 9-41 shows the menu after the insert.

Items Menu item

We are now going to create our Items menu item. With the Panel Group folder expanded in the Project Workspace, drag and drop the Items panel group onto the new menu under the `USE` menu bar. Next, double-click on the new menu item. When the Menu Item Properties dialog is displayed, change the label to `&Items` and press OK. Figure 9-42 shows the Menu Item Properties dialog for the Items menu item. Figure 9-43 shows the menu after the insert.

Locations Menu item

We are now going to create our Locations menu item. With the Panel Group folder expanded in the Project Workspace, drag and drop the Locations panel group onto the new menu under the `USE` menu bar.

Figure 9-40 Buyers Menu Item Properties dialog.

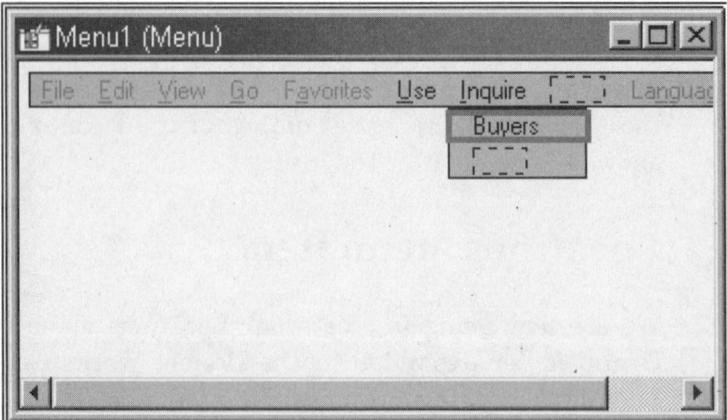

Figure 9-41 Menu with Buyers menu item.

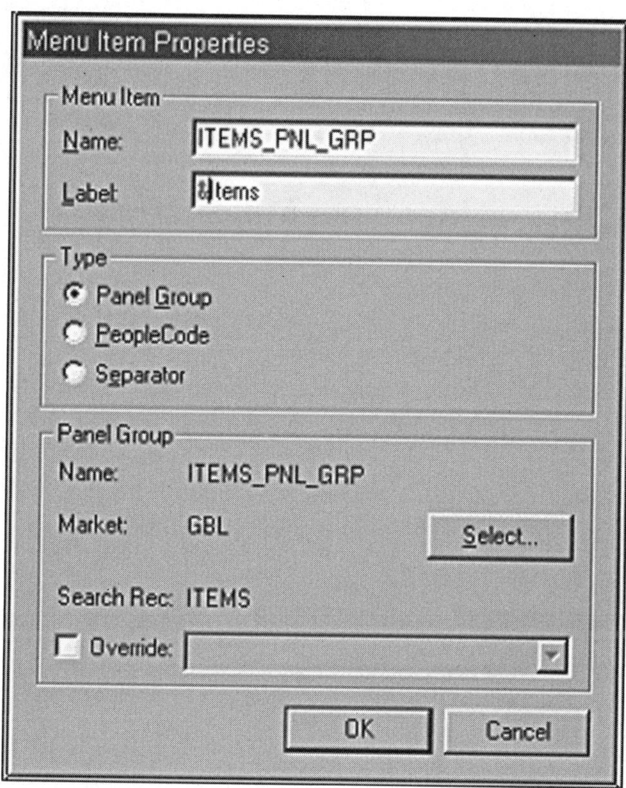

Figure 9-42
Items Menu Item Properties dialog.

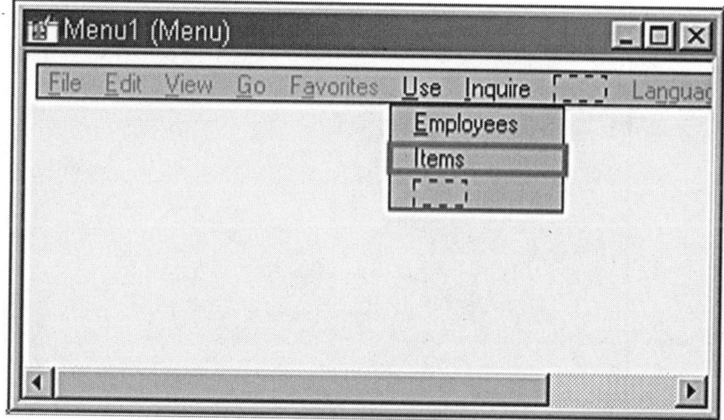

Figure 9-43
Menu with Items menu item.

Next, double-click on the new menu item. When the Menu Item Properties dialog is displayed, change the label to `&Locations` and press OK. Figure 9-44 shows the Menu Item Properties dialog for the Locations menu item. Figure 9-45 shows the menu after the insert.

Units of Measure Menu Item

We are now going to create our Units of Measure menu item. With the panel group folder expanded in the Project Workspace, drag and drop the Units of Measure panel group onto the new menu under the `USE` menu bar. Next, double-click on the new menu item. When the Menu Item Properties dialog is displayed, change the label to `&Units of Measure` and press OK. Figure 9-46 shows the Menu Item Properties dialog for the Units of Measure menu item. Figure 9-47 shows the menu after the insert.

Figure 9-44 Locations Menu Item Properties dialog.

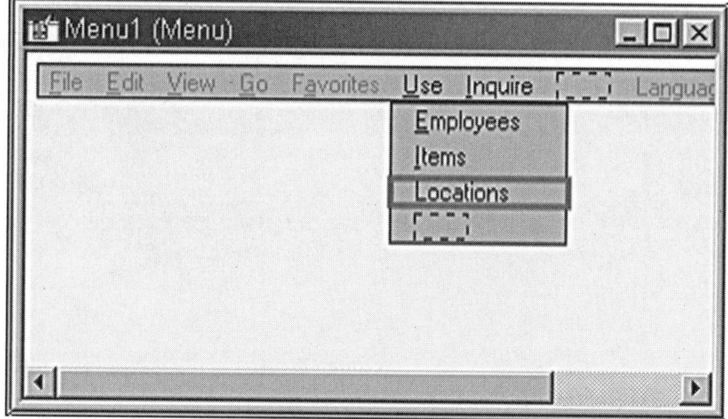

Figure 9-45 Menu with Locations menu item.

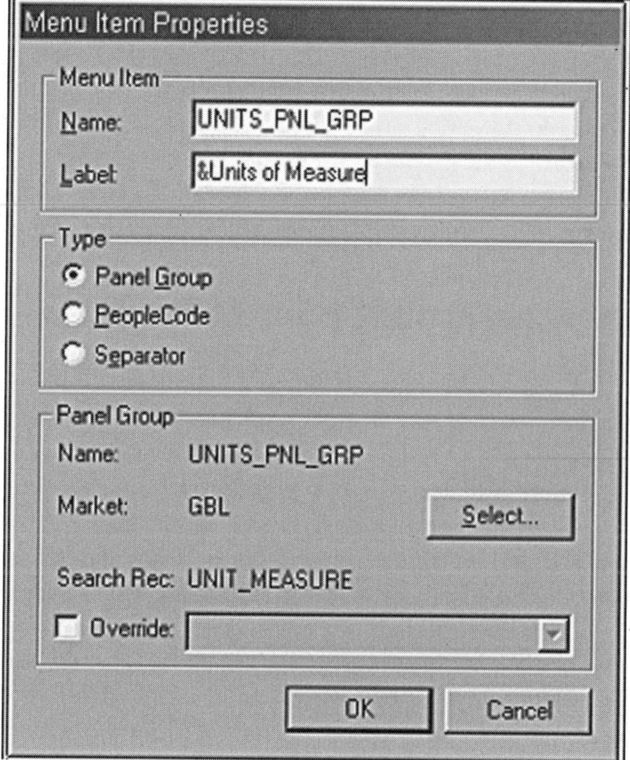

Figure 9-46 Units of Measure Menu Item Properties dialog.

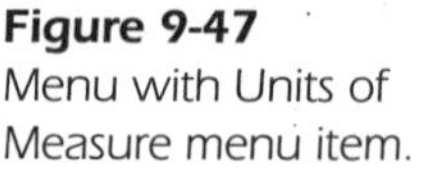

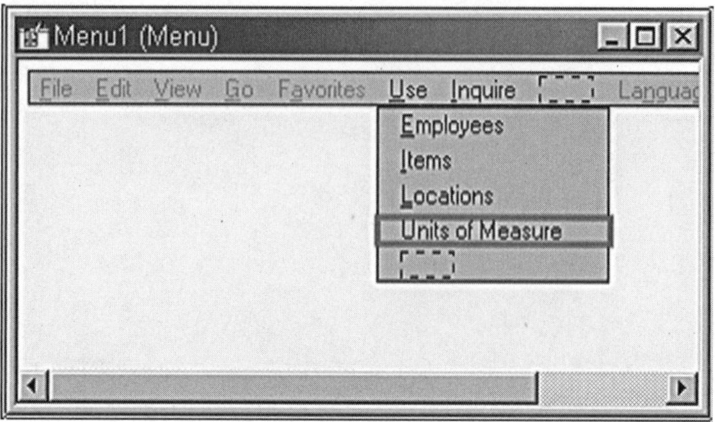

Figure 9-47
Menu with Units of Measure menu item.

Vendors Menu Item

We are now going to create our Vendors menu item. With the Panel Group folder expanded in the Project Workspace, drag and drop the Vendors panel group onto the new menu under the `USE` menu bar. Next, double-click on the new menu item. When the Menu Item Properties dialog is displayed, change the label to `&Vendors` and press OK. Figure 9-48 shows the Menu Item Properties dialog for the Vendors menu item. Figure 9-49 shows the menu after the insert.

New Internal Order Menu Item

We have now completed all the menu items for all our lookup panels. Before we add our main panel groups, we are going to place a menu separator to visually make the distinction between the different menu items. To add a separator, just double-click on the empty box below the Vendors menu item. When the Menu Item Properties dialog is displayed, select the separator radio button and press OK. Figure 9-50 shows the Menu Item Properties for the separator placed after the Vendors menu item.

We are now ready to create our New Internal Order menu item. With the Panel Group folder expanded in the Project Workspace, drag and drop the New Internal Order panel group onto the new menu under the

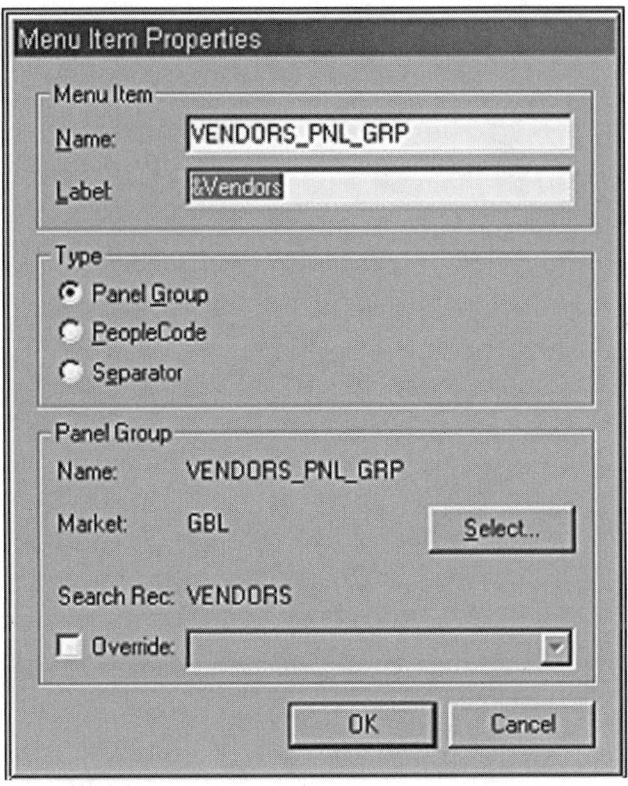

Figure 9-48
Vendors Menu Item Properties dialog.

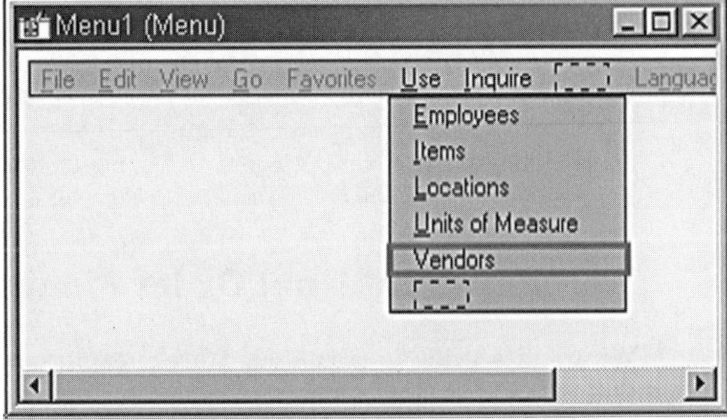

Figure 9-49
Menu with Vendors menu item.

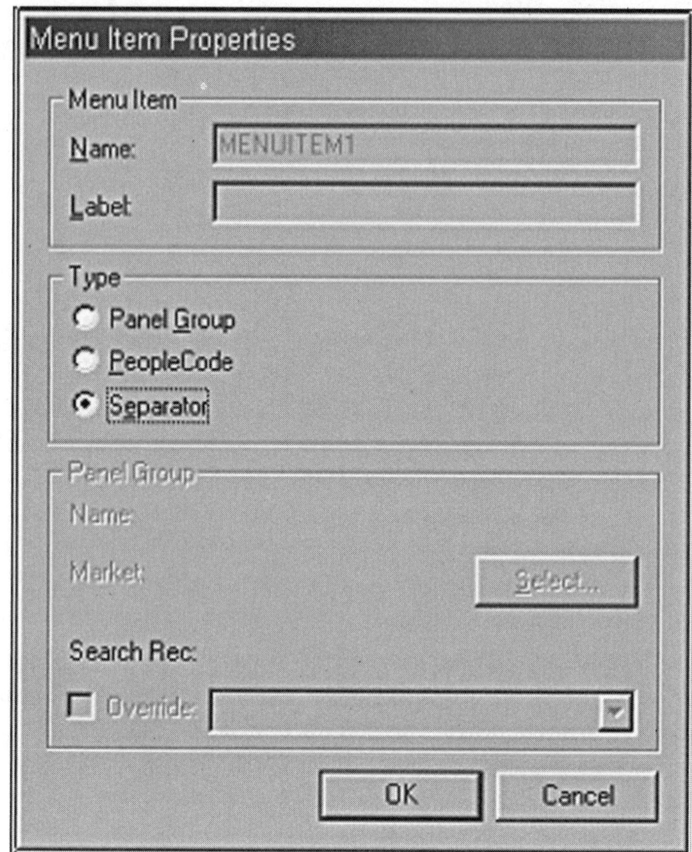

Figure 9-50
Menu Item Properties for separator placed after Vendors menu item.

USE menu bar. Next, double-click on the new menu item. When the Menu Item Properties dialog is displayed, change the label to `&New Internal Order` and press OK. Figure 9-51 shows the Menu Item Properties dialog for the New Internal Order menu Item. Figure 9-52 shows the menu after the insert.

Warehouse Internal Order Menu Item

We are now going to create our Warehouse Internal Order menu item. With the Panel Group folder expanded in the Project Workspace, drag and drop the Warehouse Internal Order panel group onto the new menu

Figure 9-51 New Internal Order Menu Item Properties dialog.

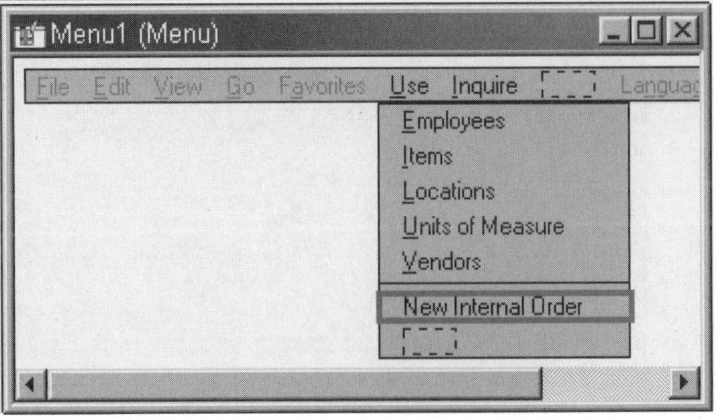

Figure 9-52 Menu with New Internal Order menu item.

under the `USE` menu bar. Next, double-click on the new menu item. When the Menu Item Properties dialog is displayed, change the label to `&Warehouse Internal Order` and press OK. Figure 9-53 shows the Menu Item Properties dialog for the Warehouse Internal Order menu item. Figure 9-54 shows the menu after the insert.

Buyers External Order Menu Item

We are now going to create our Buyers External Order menu item. With the Panel Group folder expanded in the Project Workspace, drag and drop the Buyers External Order panel group onto the new menu under the `USE` menu bar. Next, double-click on the new menu item. When the Menu Item Properties dialog is displayed, change the label to `&Buyers External Order` and press OK. Figure 9-55 shows the Menu Item Prop-

Figure 9-53 Warehouse Internal Order Menu Item Properties dialog.

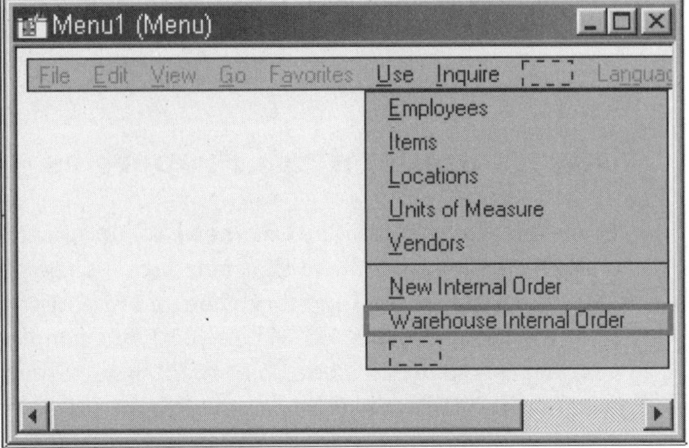

Figure 9-54 Menu with Warehouse Internal Order menu item.

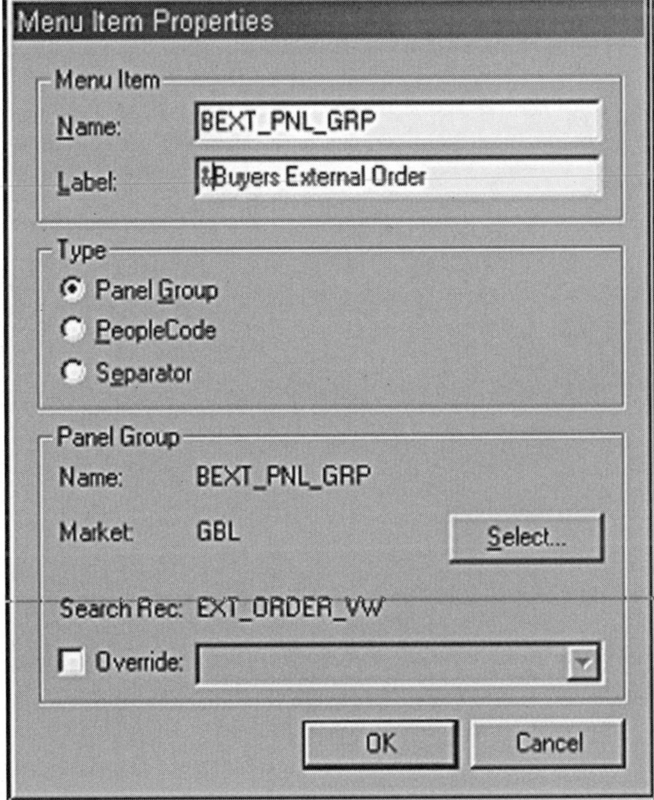

Figure 9-55 Buyers External Order Menu Item Properties dialog.

erties dialog for the Buyers External Order menu item. Figure 9-56 shows the menu after the insert.

Our Example Menu Properties

Before we save our menu, we need to set the menu label and menu group. Our menu will have the same label as the group, `&Our Example`. Since we are not setting more than one menu to the group, our menu label will not be displayed. When you have completed the menu properties, you can save the menu as `OUR_EXAMPLE` and insert it into your project. Figure 9-57 shows the Menu Properties dialog for `OUR_EXAMPLE`. Figure 9-58 shows the Object Workspace with the menu inserted.

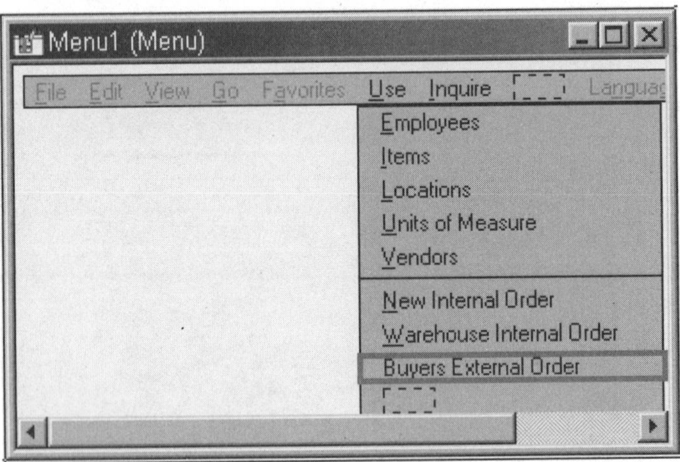

Figure 9-56 Menu with Buyers External Order menu item.

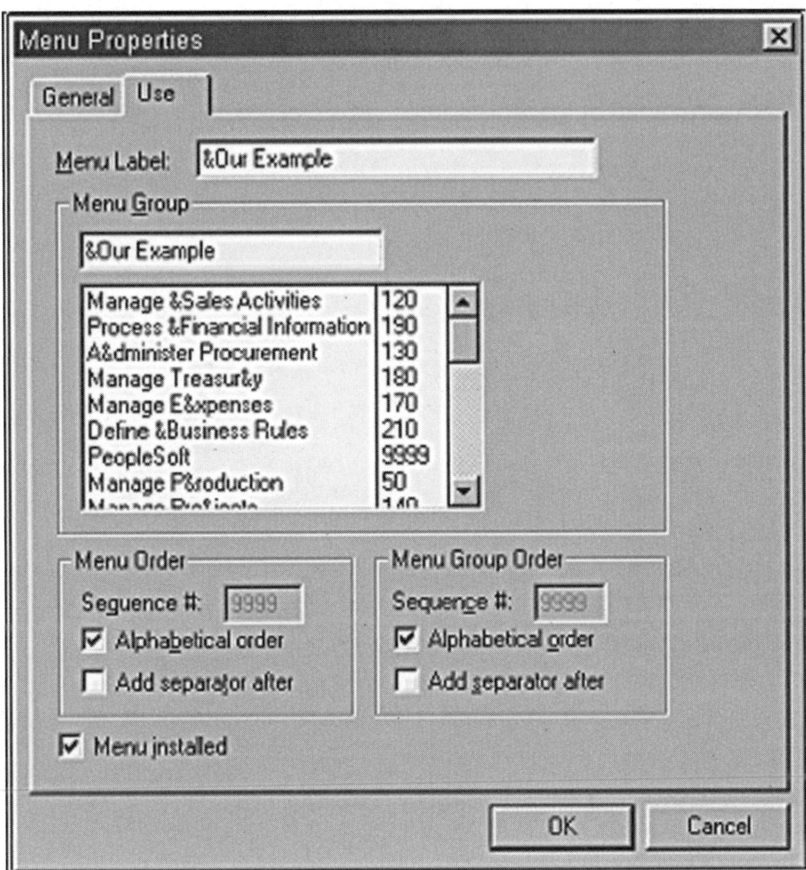

Figure 9-57
MENU PROPERTIES USE tab.

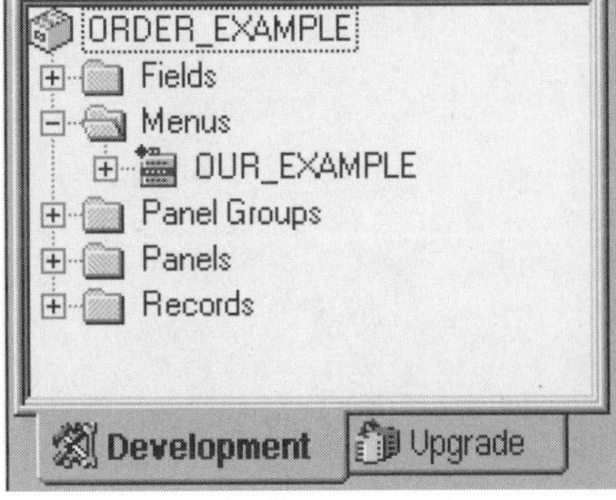

Figure 9-58
Project Workspace with Menus folder expanded.

CHAPTER 10

Granting Access to the User

Now that all the objects in the Warehouse Ordering example have been created, the next step is to grant the user access to these objects. PeopleSoft can do such things as restrict the menu items that a user or a group (class) of users has access to, restrict the times at which they are permitted to sign in, and restrict the process groups. The *Security Administrator* is the PeopleSoft tool that performs these functions. It does so via two types of security definition:

- Operator security definitions
- Class definitions

All users must have an operator security definition in order to sign on to a PeopleSoft system. The *operator security definition* consists of items such as

- Operator id
- Password
- Employee id
- Language preference
- Menus this user has access to
- Times at which the user is permitted to sign on
- Business process groups the user has access to, etc.

A *class definition* does not have an operator id or password. Instead, users are linked to a class definition. In this way, many users can have access to the same set of menus and sign-on times, and so on.

Security Administrator

To get to the Security Administrator while in the Application Designer, select GO, PEOPLETOOLS, SECURITY ADMINISTRATOR as shown in Figure 10-1.

The Security Administrator allows the user to perform the following functions:

1. View an existing operator security definition
2. Create a new operator security definition
3. Create or view a class definition
4. Use the class definition

Viewing an Existing Operator Security Definition

To view an existing operator security definition while in the Security Administrator, select FILE, OPEN. Choose the desired operator id or class name from the list of existing security definitions. Figure 10-2 shows the Open Operator/Class dialog box.

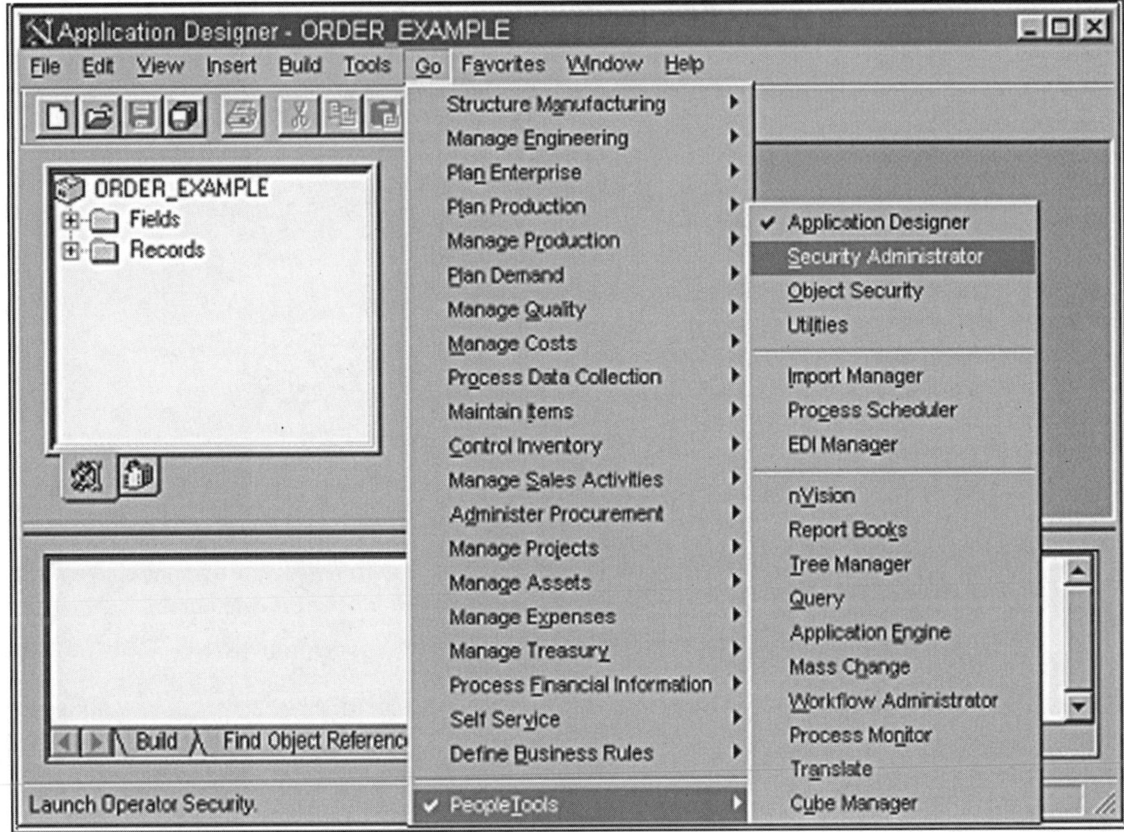

Figure 10-1 Illustration of procedure for gaining access to the Security Administrator.

Each security definition is made up of general attributes, menu items to which it has access, valid sign-on times to the database, and process groups. In addition, an operator security definition also may contain a class.

Once the security definition is displayed, the user can view each section of the definition by selecting one icon from the Navigation list on the left side of the screen. The following icons appear in the Navigation list for an operator: GENERAL, MENU ITEMS, SIGN-ON TIMES, PROCESS GROUPS, and CLASSES. If a class is opened, then CLASSES is not available in the Navigation list since a class can't be part of another class.

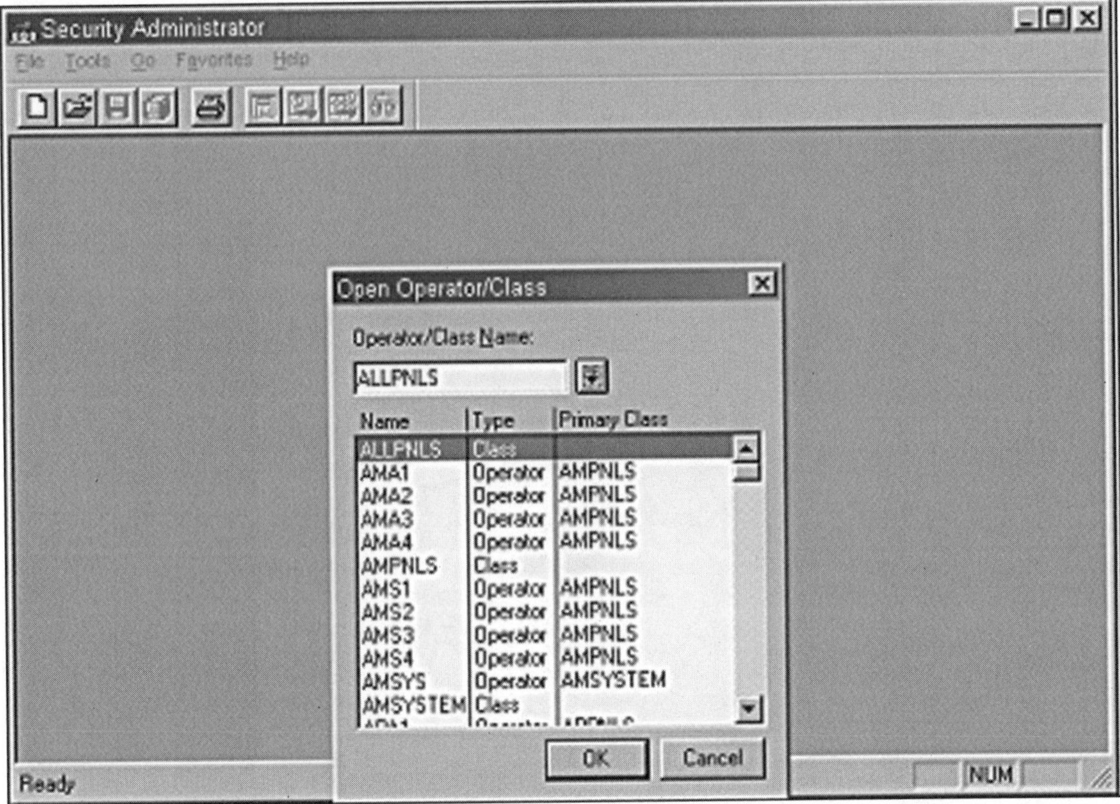

Figure 10-2 Open Operator/Class dialog box.

General View of a Security Definition Figure 10-3 shows the general view of an existing class. The *general* view is the default view when a security definition is open. This is true regardless of whether the security definition is operator or class. To get to this view, the user could also have double-clicked on the GENERAL icon in the Navigation list.

The general view for a class security definition differs from the general view of an operator security definition. They both contain security definition type and description. However, the class general view contains general attributes and the operator general view contains operator attributes. The general attributes include the

1. *Business process map.* This selection is the business process map that will be displayed when PeopleSoft is started by a user belonging to the defined class.

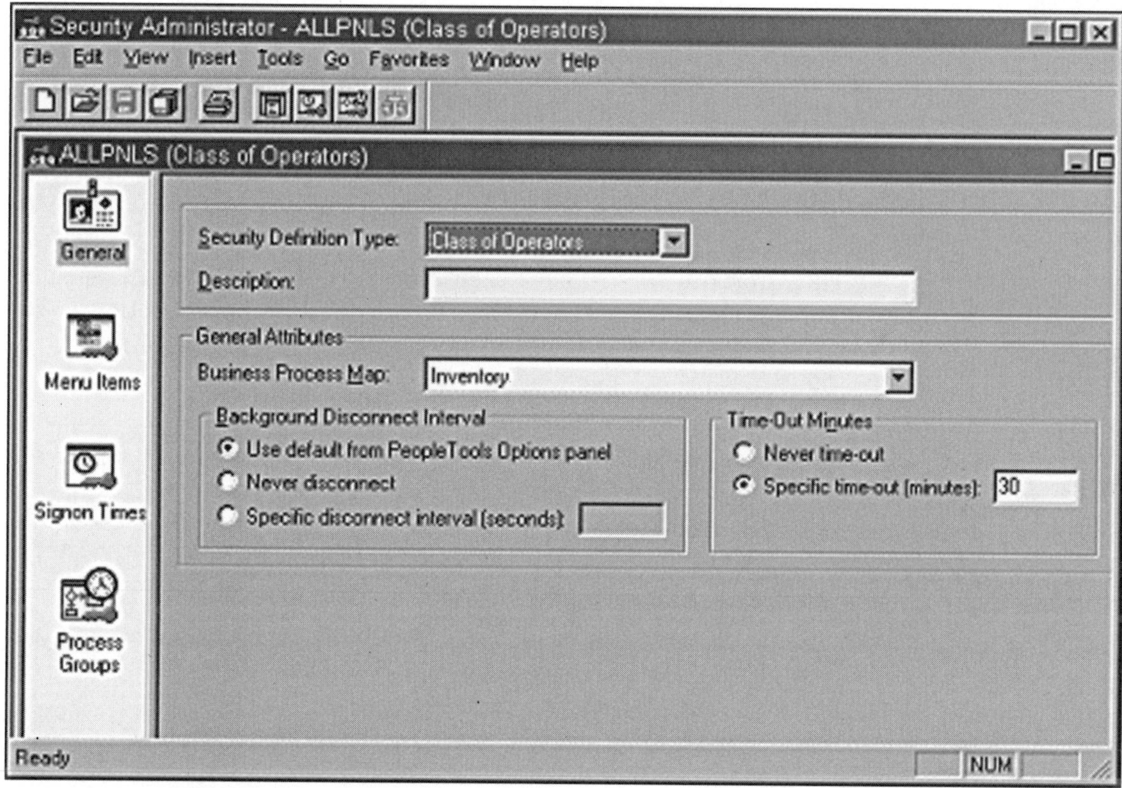

Figure 10-3 General view of an existing class.

2. *Background disconnect interval.* Selections are "Use default from PeopleTools," "Never disconnect," or "Specific disconnect interval [seconds]."
3. *Timeout minutes.* This is the number of minutes before an inactive operator is automatically signed out of PeopleSoft.

The operator attributes include the

1. *Operator password.* Operator password for signing on to PeopleSoft; must be in uppercase letters.
2. *Confirm password.* Also must be uppercase letters.
3. *Employee id.* Optional field.
4. *Language preference.* Optional field.
5. *Access profile.* The access profile is the id and password to the

database. To edit, delete, or add an access profile, select TOOLS, ACCESS PROFILES.

These attributes cannot be modified if the new operator is part of an existing class.

Figure 10-4 shows the general view of an operator security definition. Note that the screen shows operator attributes and also that the icon list contains CLASSES.

The alternate way to view each section of the definition is to select VIEW from the toolbar. Therefore, to select the general section of the security definition, click on VIEW, GENERAL as shown in Figure 10-5.

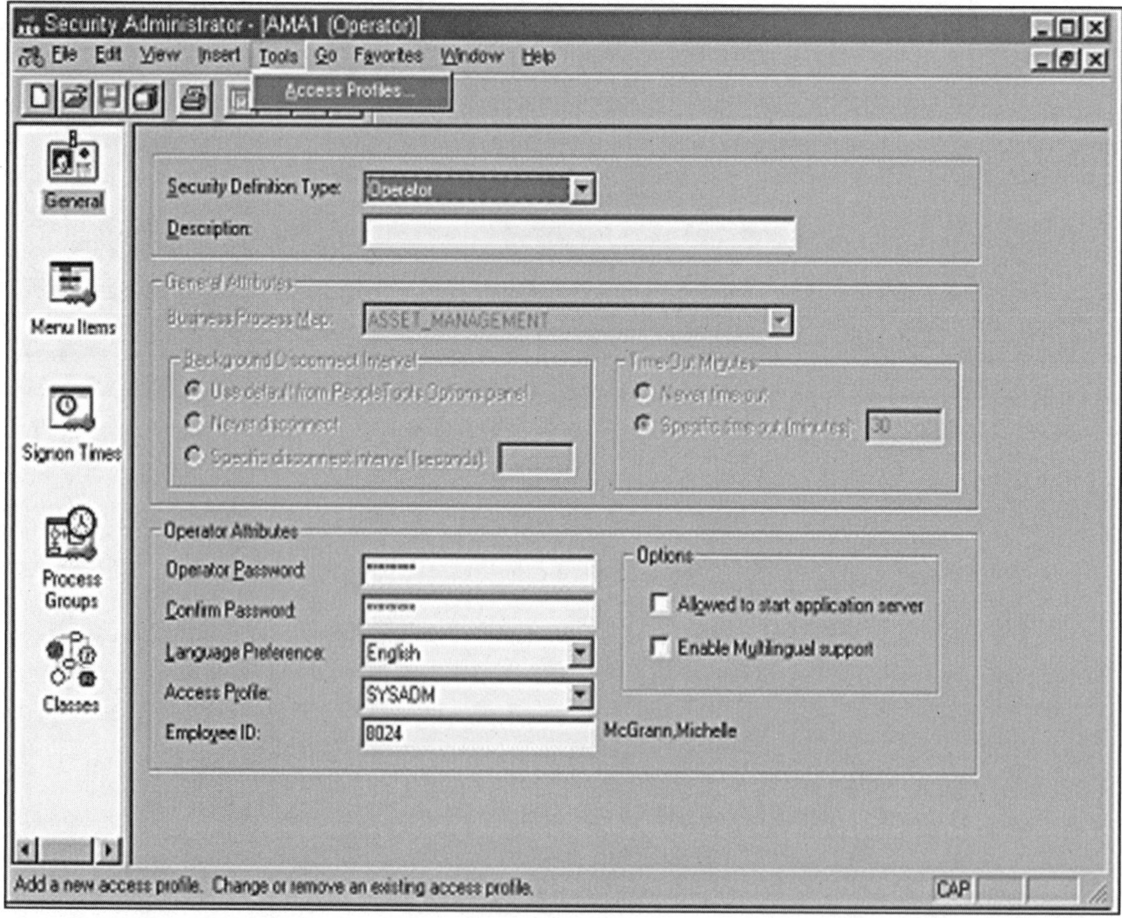

Figure 10-4 General view of an operator security definition.

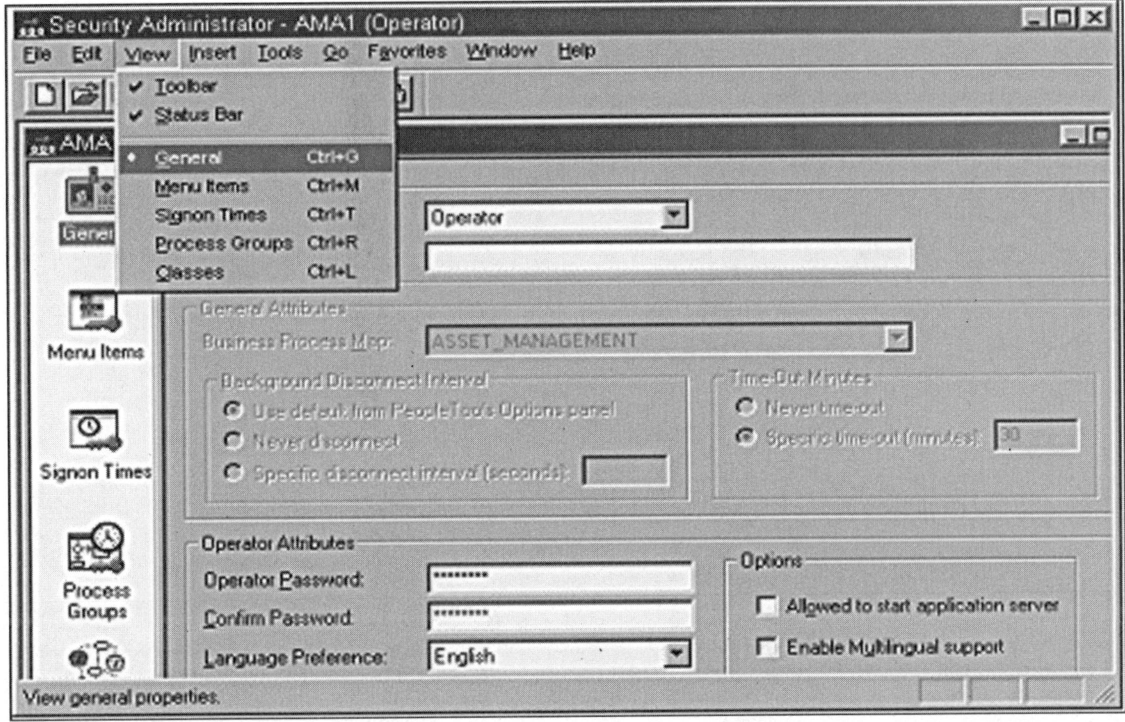

Figure 10-5 Alternate way to display general section of a security definition.

Menu Items View of a Security Definition To get to the Menu Items view, the user should either select VIEW, MENU ITEMS from the menu bar or double-click on the MENU ITEMS icon in the Navigation list. Figure 10-6 shows the menu item section of a security definition. This screen looks the same for an operator security definition as it does for a class security definition. It simply contains the list of menus to which the operator or the class has access.

Each menu that is displayed in the menu items view can be double clicked on to get more information on which components of the menu are actually accessible to the operator or to the class of operators; thus, an operator does not necessarily have access to an entire menu. It may have access only to certain panels in that menu. Even when the operator has access to a panel, the actions it has access to may be limited as well. Figure 10-7 shows in detail a menu to which an existing operator security definition has access. The portion of the detail menu that is highlighted is what the operator has access to. Note that the screen shown in Figure 10-7

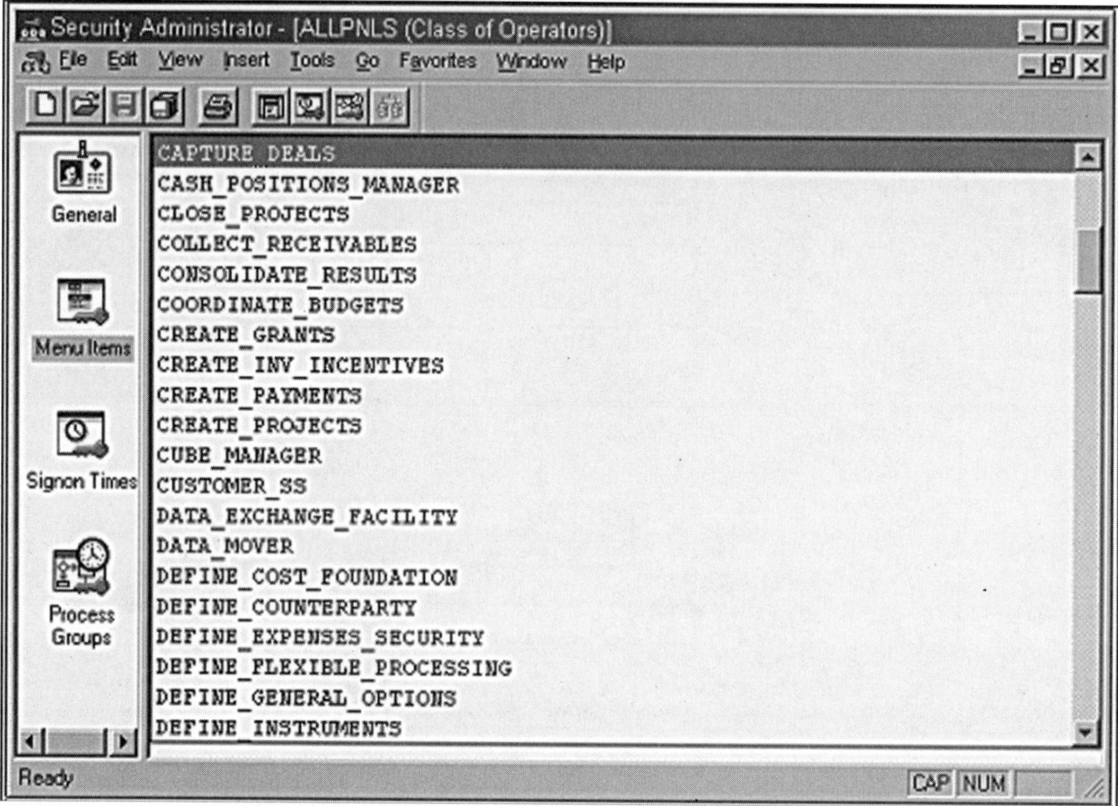

Figure 10-6 Menu items view.

appears for the majority of the menus except when viewing access to the Application Designer menu.

Instead, when the Application Designer is selected from the list of available menus, the Application Designer Access dialog is displayed. The Application Designer Access dialog contains two tabs: the OBJECT TYPES tab and the TOOLS tab.

All the object types are listed on the OBJECT TYPES tab. This list includes

- Business process
- Business process maps
- Fields
- Menus

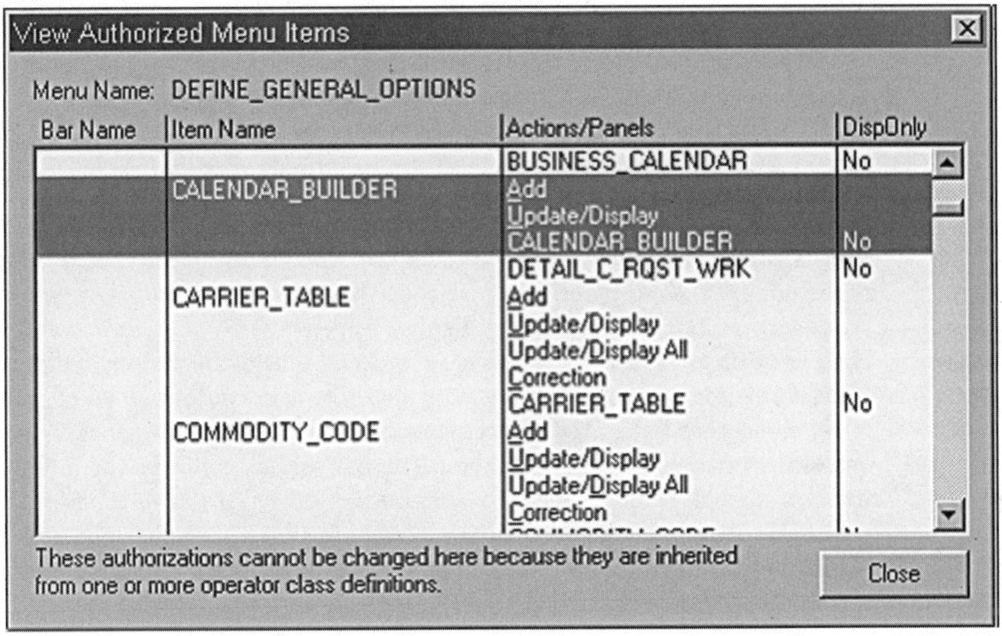

View Authorized Menu Items

Menu Name: DEFINE_GENERAL_OPTIONS

Bar Name	Item Name	Actions/Panels	DispOnly
		BUSINESS_CALENDAR	No
	CALENDAR_BUILDER	Add	
		Update/Display	
		CALENDAR_BUILDER	No
		DETAIL_C_RQST_WRK	No
	CARRIER_TABLE	Add	
		Update/Display	
		Update/Display All	
		Correction	
		CARRIER_TABLE	No
	COMMODITY_CODE	Add	
		Update/Display	
		Update/Display All	
		Correction	

These authorizations cannot be changed here because they are inherited from one or more operator class definitions.

Close

Figure 10-7 View authorized menu items.

- Panels
- Panel groups
- Projects
- Records

Next to each object type is an access level. The access level can be No Access, Read-Only Access, or Full Access for all objects. The object type of fields has an access level of Update Translates Only in addition to the previously mentioned three. The object type of record has an additional access level of Data Admin Only.

The access levels are defined below:

1. *No Access.* This access level indicates that no object of this type may be opened.
2. *Read-Only Access.* This access level indicates that objects of this type may be displayed for viewing purposes but may not be edited.
3. *Full Access.* This access level indicates that objects of this type may be opened, viewed, and edited.

4. *Update Translate Only.* This access level applies only to fields. It indicates that only Translate Table values can be edited.
5. *Data Admin Only.* This access level applies only to records. It indicates that only Data administration attributes found in the TOOLS, DATA ADMINISTRATION menu can be edited.

Figure 10-8 shows what the OBJECT TYPES tab of the Application Designer Access dialog box looks like. The user can choose to modify the access types one at a time by clicking on the down arrow next to each object type's access box. A drop-down display appears with that field's valid choices. Simply click on the access type to make the new selection. Repeat this for each object type. Alternately, a user could instead choose to set the access for all the object types at one time by double-clicking on one of the buttons in the Set All box. The Set All box contains the following buttons: FULL ACCESS, READ ONLY, and NO ACCESS. If one of the Set All buttons is double-clicked on, all the object types will be set to the same value. The user can then go and modify any changes to a specific object

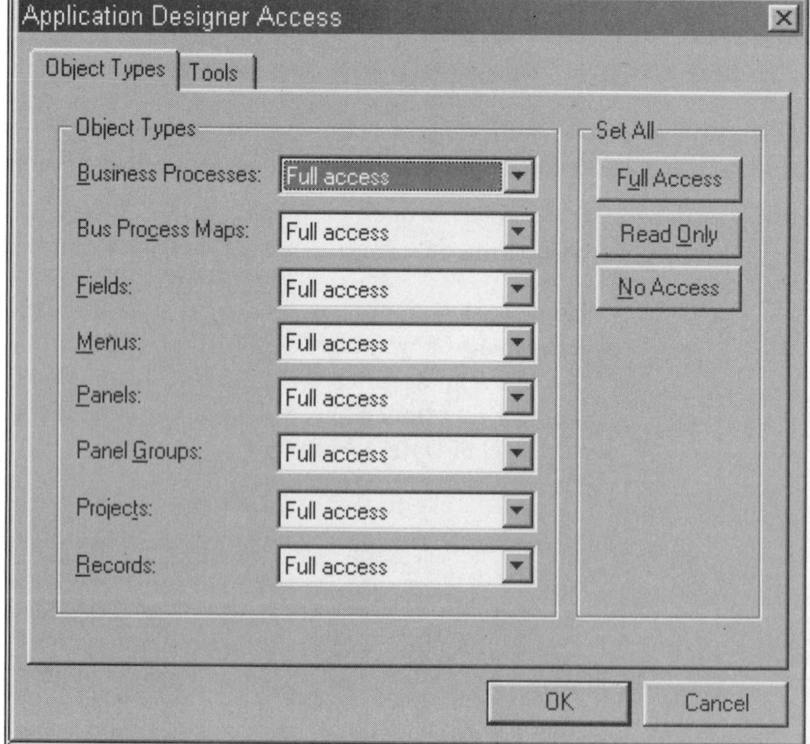

Figure 10-8 OBJECT TYPES tab of the Application Designer Access dialog box.

type. For example, since the Data Admin Only access is not available for other object types, the user would need to go and set this manually should this access type be desired.

The Application Designer Access dialog box also contains a TOOLS tab (see Fig. 10-9). The TOOLS tab displays the current access values of the following Tools menu items and some miscellaneous items as well:

- Change Control
- Upgrade
- Build/Data Admin
- System Colors
- Styles
- Field Formats
- Default Toolbar

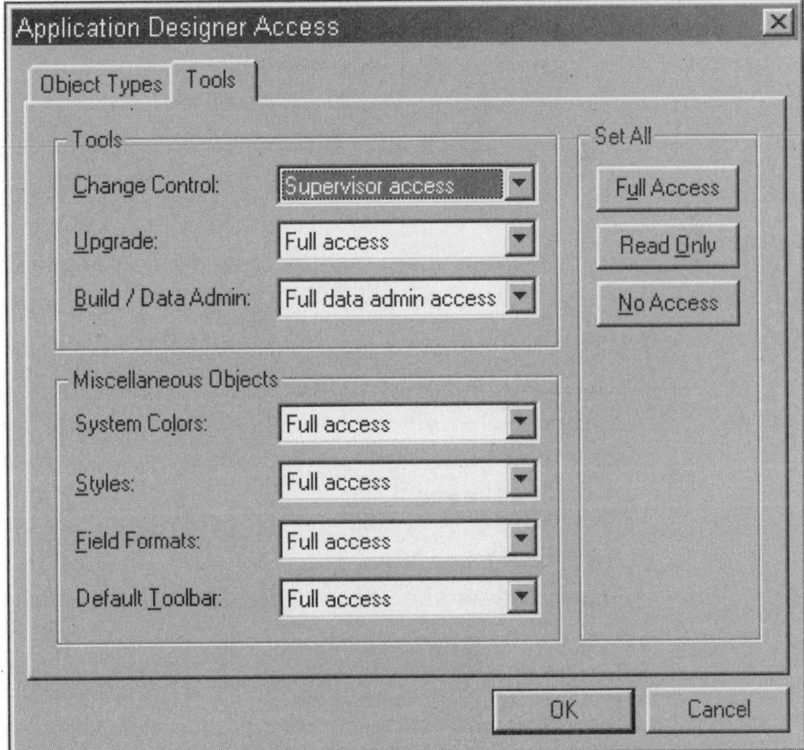

Figure 10-9
TOOLS tab of the Application Designer Access dialog box.

The valid access levels differ for these menu items. Therefore, each item is discussed in detail here.

The Change Control menu item access level can be set to Restricted Access, Developer Access, or Supervisor Access. *Restricted Access* prohibits users from locking or unlocking objects. *Developer Access* allows the user to lock only those objects not already locked and vice versa. *Supervisor Access* permits locking or unlocking of any object regardless of whether the user locked the object. Note that access level for this item controls the user's access to the TOOLS, CHANGE CONTROL menu.

The Upgrade menu item access level can be set to Full Access or No Access. The access level for this item controls the user's access to the TOOLS, UPGRADE Menu.

The Build/Data Admin access level can be set to No Access, Build Scripts Only, Build Online, or Full Data Admin Access. The access level selected applies to both the Build menu items and the TOOLS, DATA ADMINISTRATION menu items:

- *No Access* means that the user has no access to either of these menu items.
- A *Build Scripts Only* access level means that the user can use Build but not Execute SQL Now or Execute and Build Script and can't use TOOLS, DATA ADMINISTRATION.
- An access level of *Build Online* means that the user can use all Build menu items but cannot use the TOOLS, DATA ADMINISTRATION menu items.
- An access level of *Full Data Admin Access* means that the user can use all Build menu items as well as all TOOLS, DATA ADMINISTRATION menu items.

The Miscellaneous Objects of system colors, styles, field formats, and default toolbar all can have the following access levels: No Access, Read-Only Access, or Full Access. These levels were discussed earlier with respect to the object type access levels. The definitions are the same here.

Sign-on Times View of a Security Definition To view the Sign-on Times section of a security definition, either select VIEW, SIGN-ON TIMES from the menu bar or double-click on the SIGN-ON TIMES icon in the Navigation list. The setup shown in Figure 10-10 will appear.

The Sign-on Times view lists all the days and the times of the day that an operator or class of operators may sign on to the system.

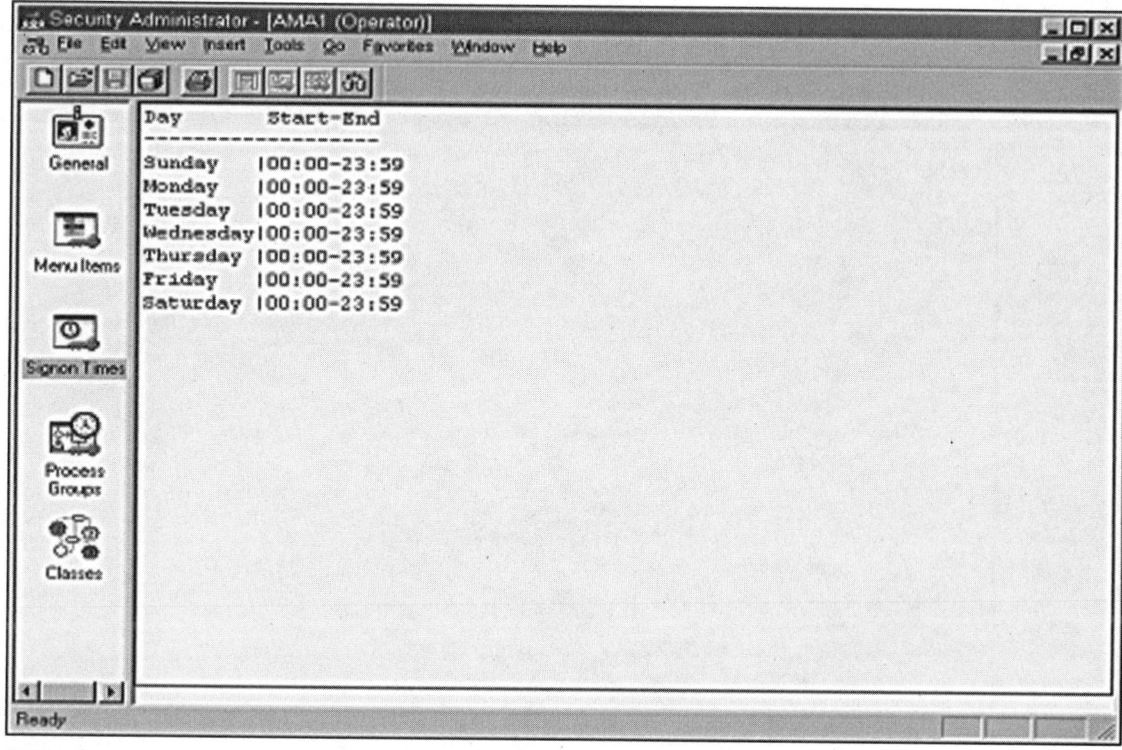

Figure 10-10 Sign-on Times view.

Process Groups View of a Security Definition To view the Process Groups section, select VIEW, PROCESS GROUPS from the menu bar or double-click on the PROCESS GROUPS icon. Figure 10-11 shows the Process Groups view.

Classes View of a Security Definition To view the Classes section of the security definition, select VIEW, CLASSES from the menu bar or double-click on the CLASSES icon in the Navigation list. The list of operator classes of which this operator is a member will be displayed. This view allows the user to select the primary class for this operator. Figure 10-12 shows the Classes view.

The Background disconnect interval, timeout minutes, business process map, and process profile are all inherited from an operator's primary class.

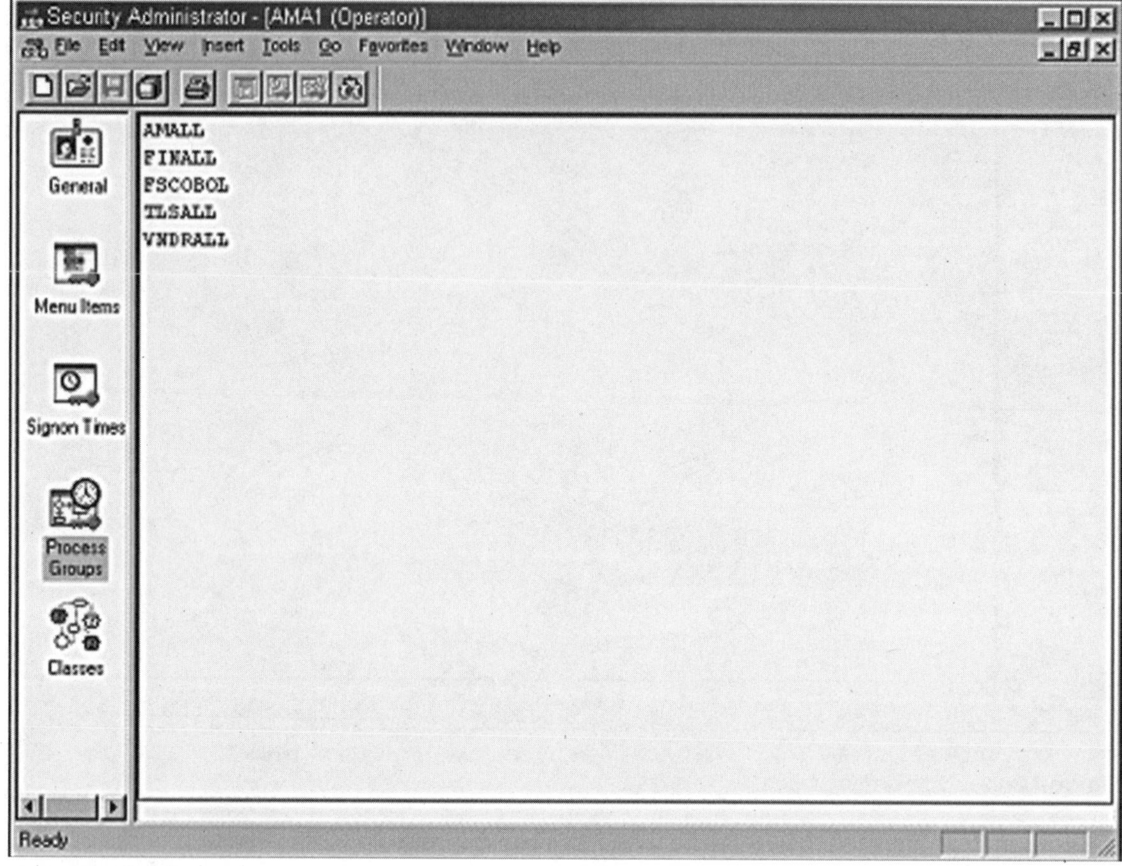

Figure 10-11 Process Groups view.

Creating a New Operator

1. From the Security Administrator, either select NEW from the file menu or press the NEW toolbar icon. With the GENERAL icon selected from the Navigation icon list displayed along the left margin of the window, proceed to
   - Set the security definition type to OPERATOR
   - Enter a description of the operator you are creating
   - Set the background disconnect specifications
   - Set the timeout specifications
   - Set the operator attributes

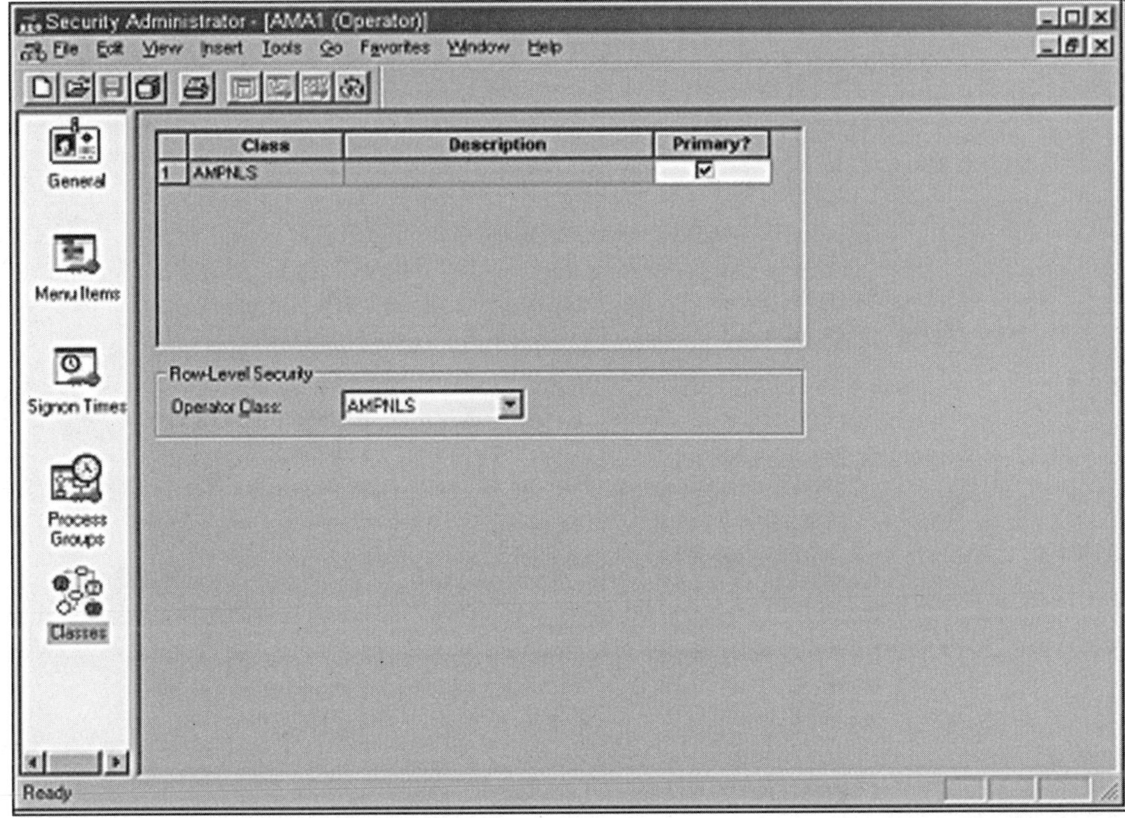

Figure 10-12 Classes view.

2. Next you can set the menus and actions to which your new user will have access:
   - Click on the MENU ITEMS icon in the Navigation list.
   - Select INSERT, MENU ITEMS from the toolbar.
   - Double-click on the new menu name from the list.
   - Select the appropriate actions the new user may execute.
3. Next, the sign-on times must be set for the new operator:
   - Click on the SIGN-ON TIME icon in the Navigation list.
   - Select INSERT, SIGN-ON TIME. The default values of 24 hours a day, 7 days a week will be displayed. Double-click on one of the days and an authorized sign-on screen comes up with start time and end time. Modify the time and click on OK. To delete a day, highlight the day and hit the DELETE button.

4. Now, the process groups which the new operator will have access to should be selected. To do this
   - Choose INSERT, PROCESS GROUP. All the process groups not in the security profile will be displayed.
   - Highlight one group at a time and double-click on OK to select the process group for the new operator.
5. Finally, the new operator must be saved. To do so, select FILE, SAVE. A Save Operator Profile screen will appear and prompt you for the operator profile id name (if all fields are filled in properly). Otherwise, errors will appear to inform you certain operator must be filled in prior to saving the operator id.
6. After the operator id is saved, it is wise to test if the operator was created properly. To do so, sign-off of PeopleTools and sign back in as the new operator. Ensure the new operator has access to everything you selected.

An alternate way to create a new security definition is to open an existing definition and save it using FILE, SAVE AS. Once it is under a new name, open it again and modify it and save it when all changes are complete.

Creating Class Definitions

Class definitions are a way to set and use one security definition for several operators. Class definitions are created the same way as operator definitions with two exceptions:

1. When creating a class, the security definition type (listed under the General Attributes section) should be set to CLASS OF OPERATORS (rather than OPERATOR).
2. The Security Administrator does not allow linking a class with another class. Therefore, the CLASS entry does not appear when creating a class definition.

After all the general attributes, menu items, sign-on times, and process group sections are filled, it is necessary to save the class definition id by selecting FILE, SAVE. The class definition id name should be no longer than eight characters long.

Using Class Definitions

To use your newly created class definition (i.e., to link the class definition with an operator security definition), simply open an operator id and select the CLASSES icon from the Navigation list. A list of available classes will appear. Then double-click on the desired class(es) and SAVE the operator security definition.

Note that an operator security definition can be linked to more than one class. When this occurs, the operator security definition will be assigned a primary class. An operator will inherit certain attributes only from its primary class. The attributes inherited from the primary class only are process profile, business process map, timeout minutes, and background disconnect interval. The remaining attributes that make up the operator security definition will be inherited from *all* its classes.

Example Operators and Classes

We are now at the final step before we can begin testing our example. We now need to give access to the menus we created in the previous chapter. For our example application, we are going to create three new classes and then three new operators which will be associated with them.

Administrator Class

The first class we are going to create is an Administrator class (`ADMIN`) that has access to all the menus and panels we created. To begin, select the FILE, NEW menu option or press the NEW icon from within the Security Administrator. When the new untitled child window is displayed, it should initially be showing the "general" view of an operators definition. Since we want to create a new class, we are going to select CLASS OF OPERATORS from the Security Definition type drop-down list box. Next, we are going to type "Administrators for Our Example" in the description. Figure 10-13 shows the general view with our entries.

In order to give this class access to the panels we created, we need to insert our menu into this definition's menu items and then set full access to it. Press the INSERT MENU ITEMS icon from the toolbar. When the Insert Menu Name dialog is displayed, select `OUR_EXAMPLE` and press OK. Figure 10-14 shows the Menu Name dialog.

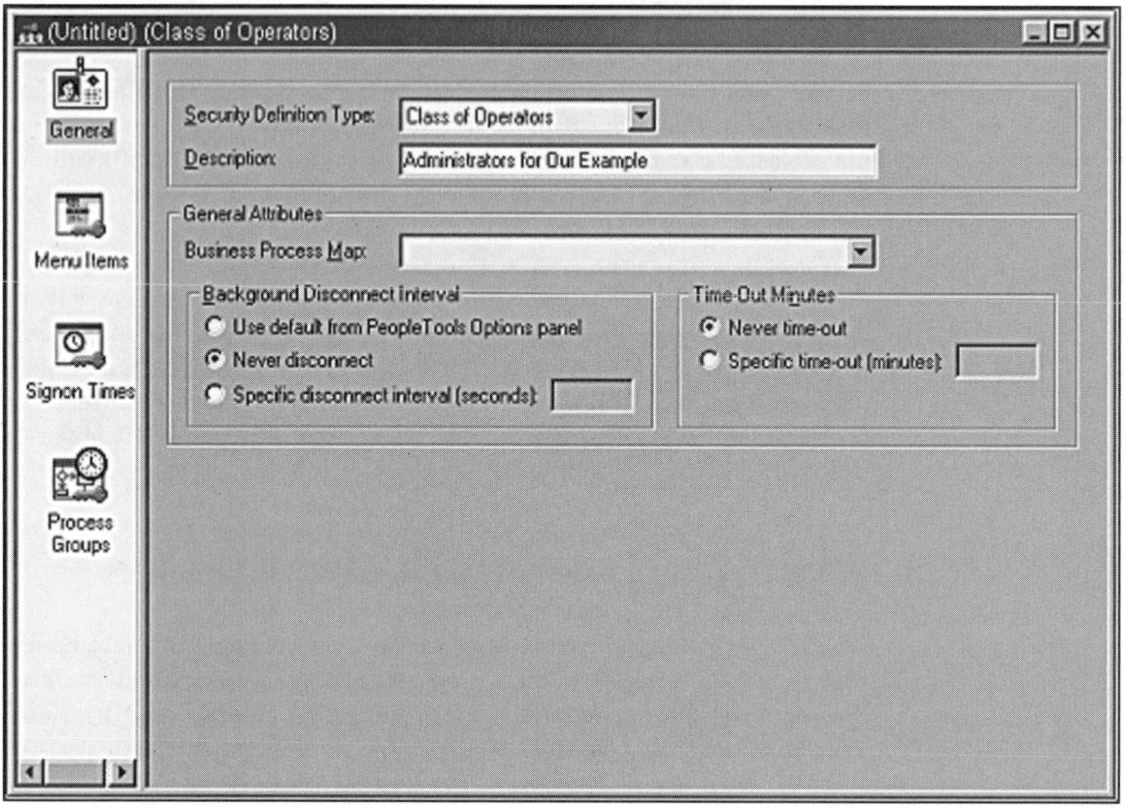

Figure 10-13 General class view.

The Select Menu Items dialog will then be displayed. Since this class will have full access to this menu, press the SELECT ALL button in the lower left and then press OK. All the menu items should have highlighted before you exited the dialog. Figure 10-15 shows the Menu Items dialog with all the items selected. Before you save the class definition, select the last line on the Menu Items dialog and change the Buyers Inquire menu to DISPLAY ONLY.

If all is correct, please save the class as `ADMIN` and continue.

End User Class

The next class we are going to create is for the end users of our example. The End User class (`EUSER`) will be used for all the employees who are initiating internal orders. To begin, select the FILE, NEW menu option or

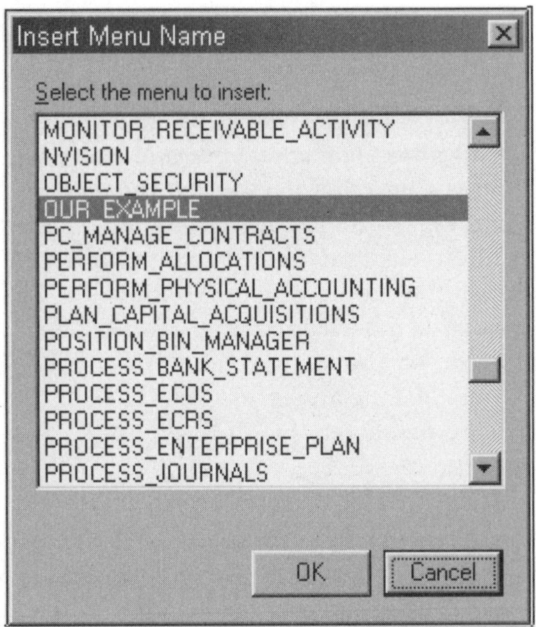

Figure 10-14 Insert Menu Name dialog.

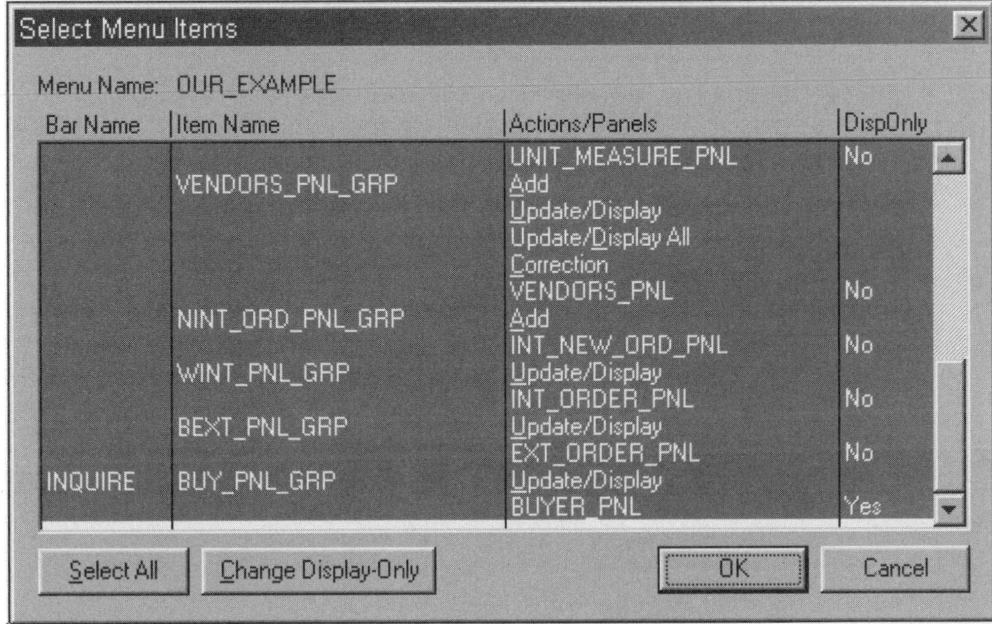

Figure 10-15 Select Menu Items dialog for the Administrators class.

press the NEW icon from within the Security Administrator. When the new untitled child window is displayed, it should initially be showing the general view of an operator's definition. Just as in the previous example, select CLASS OF OPERATORS from the Security Definition type drop-down list box. Next, we are going to type "End Users for Our Example" in the description. We are also going to set disconnect times for this class. Figure 10-16 shows the general view with our entries.

The menu access that we are going to allow for the End User class is full control for the new internal order and read-only access to the Warehouse Internal Order panel. To set this up, press the INSERT MENU ITEM icon on the toolbar. When the Menu Name dialog appears, select `OUR_EXAMPLE` and press OK. The Select Menu Items dialog should now be displayed. Scroll down until you see the New Internal Order panel group, `NINT_ORD_PNL_GRP`. With the left mouse button,

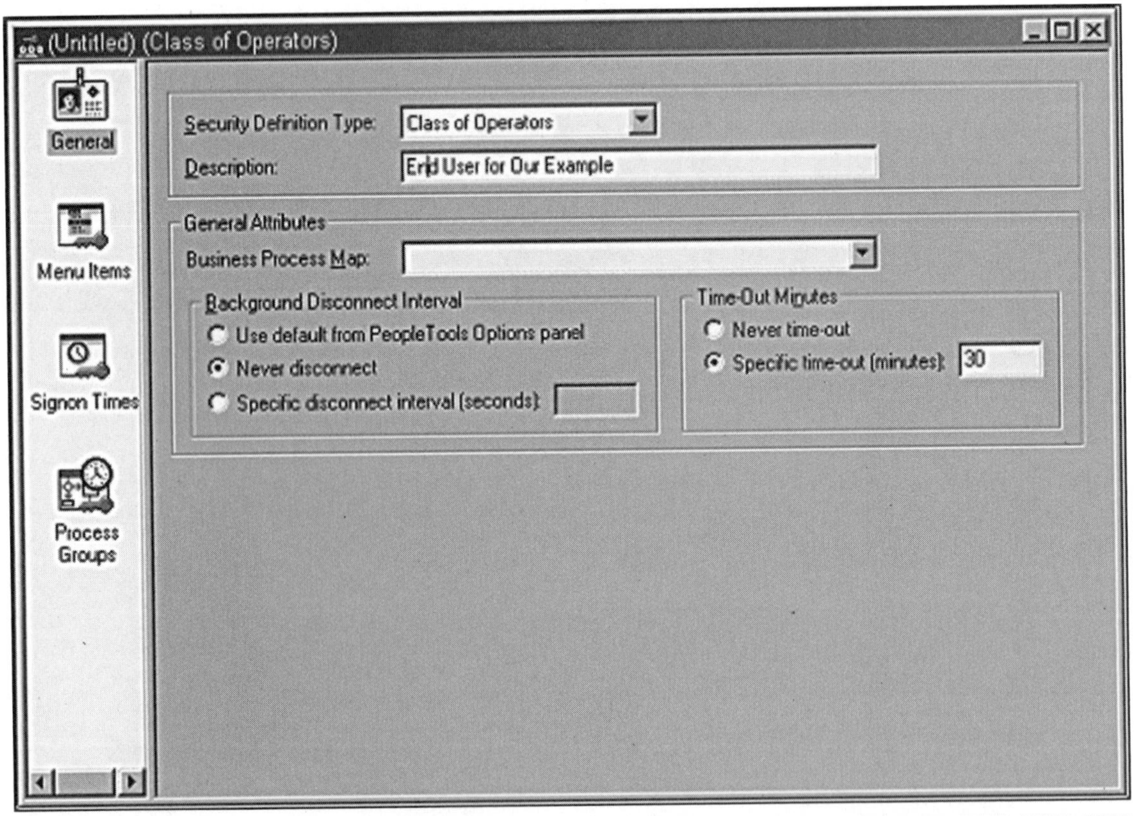

Figure 10-16 General view for the End User class.

select it and the next four lines. This causes NINT_ORD_PNL_GRP and WINT_PNL_GRP to be highlighted which means user class has access to these panel groups. The last step here is to make the Warehouse Internal Order panel group read-only (display-only). To do this, double click on the 'NO' which appears in the DISPONLY column of the WINT_PNL_GRP row. This causes the 'NO' to toggle to 'YES' which makes this panel group Display only. Another way to do this is to focus on the last two lines of the four lines and press the CHANGE DISPLAY ONLY button. Make sure that you leave the line highlighted. When you are done, your dialog should look like the one in Figure 10-17. If yours matches the figure, press OK.

The last thing we are going to do for this class is to limit the sign-on times to Monday through Saturday from 6:00 A.M. to 4:59 P.M. To accomplish this we can delete the default day for Sunday and then double-click on each of the other days and change the start and end times. Figure 10-18 shows the Authorized Sign-on Time dialog that will be displayed when you double-click on the days with the correct entry for Monday. Figure 10-19 shows the completed Sign-on Times view.

If all is correct, please save the class as EUSER and continue.

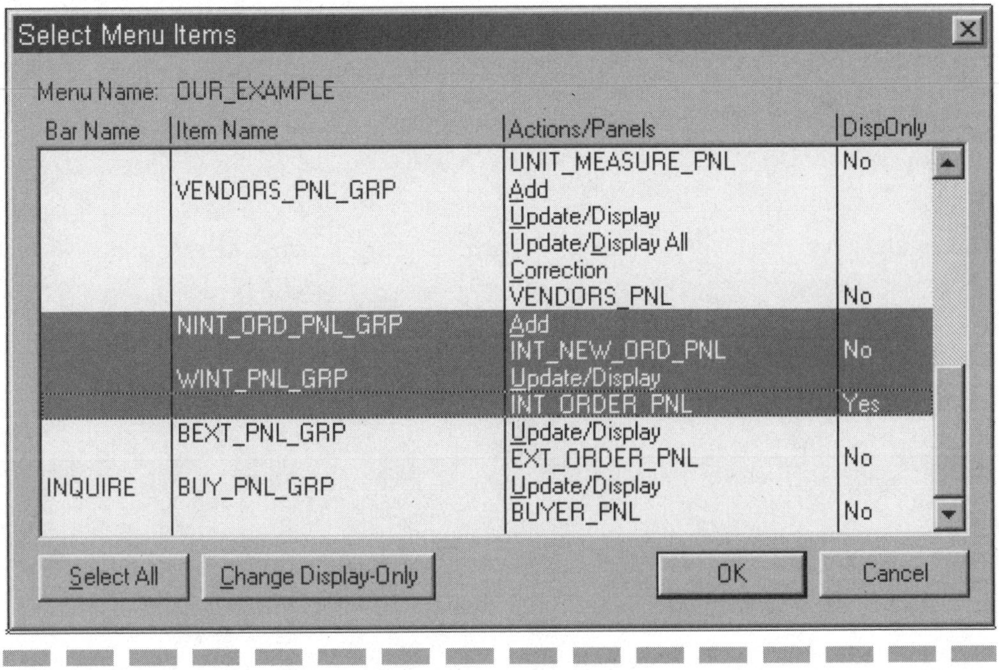

Select Menu Items

Menu Name: OUR_EXAMPLE

Bar Name	Item Name	Actions/Panels	DispOnly
		UNIT_MEASURE_PNL	No
	VENDORS_PNL_GRP	Add	
		Update/Display	
		Update/Display All	
		Correction	
		VENDORS_PNL	No
	NINT_ORD_PNL_GRP	Add	
		INT_NEW_ORD_PNL	No
	WINT_PNL_GRP	Update/Display	
		INT_ORDER_PNL	Yes
	BEXT_PNL_GRP	Update/Display	
		EXT_ORDER_PNL	No
INQUIRE	BUY_PNL_GRP	Update/Display	
		BUYER_PNL	No

Select All | Change Display-Only | OK | Cancel

Figure 10-17 Select Menu Items dialog for the End User class.

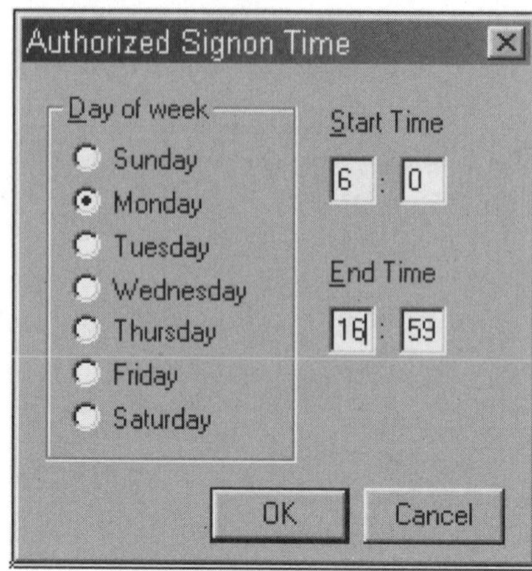

Figure 10-18 Authorized Sign-on Time dialog for End User class.

```
(Untitled) (Class of Operators)

General
Menu Items
Signon Times
Process Groups

Day        Start-End
-------------------
Monday    |06:00-16:59
Tuesday   |06:00-16:59
Wednesday|06:00-16:59
Thursday  |06:00-16:59
Friday    |06:00-16:59
Saturday  |06:00-16:59
```

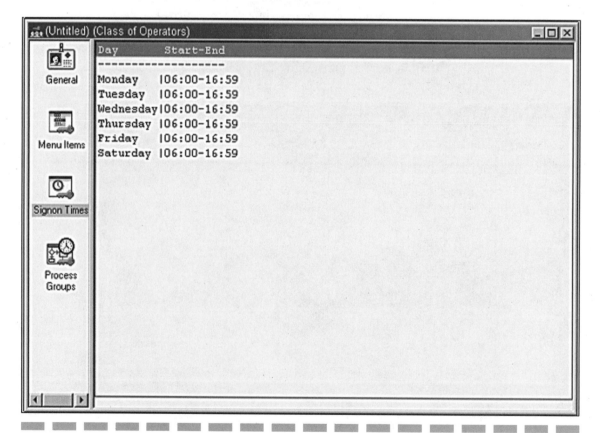

Figure 10-19 Sign-on times for End User class.

Warehouse User Class

The next class we are going to create is for the warehouse users of our example. The Warehouse User class (`WUSER`) will be used for all the employees who fulfill internal orders. To begin, select the FILE, NEW menu option or press the NEW icon from within the Security Administrator. When the new untitled child window is displayed, it should initially be showing the general view of an operators definition. Just as in the previous example, select CLASS OF OPERATORS from the Security Definition Type drop-down list box. Next, we are going to type "Warehouse User for Our Example" in the description. Figure 10-20 shows the general view with our entries.

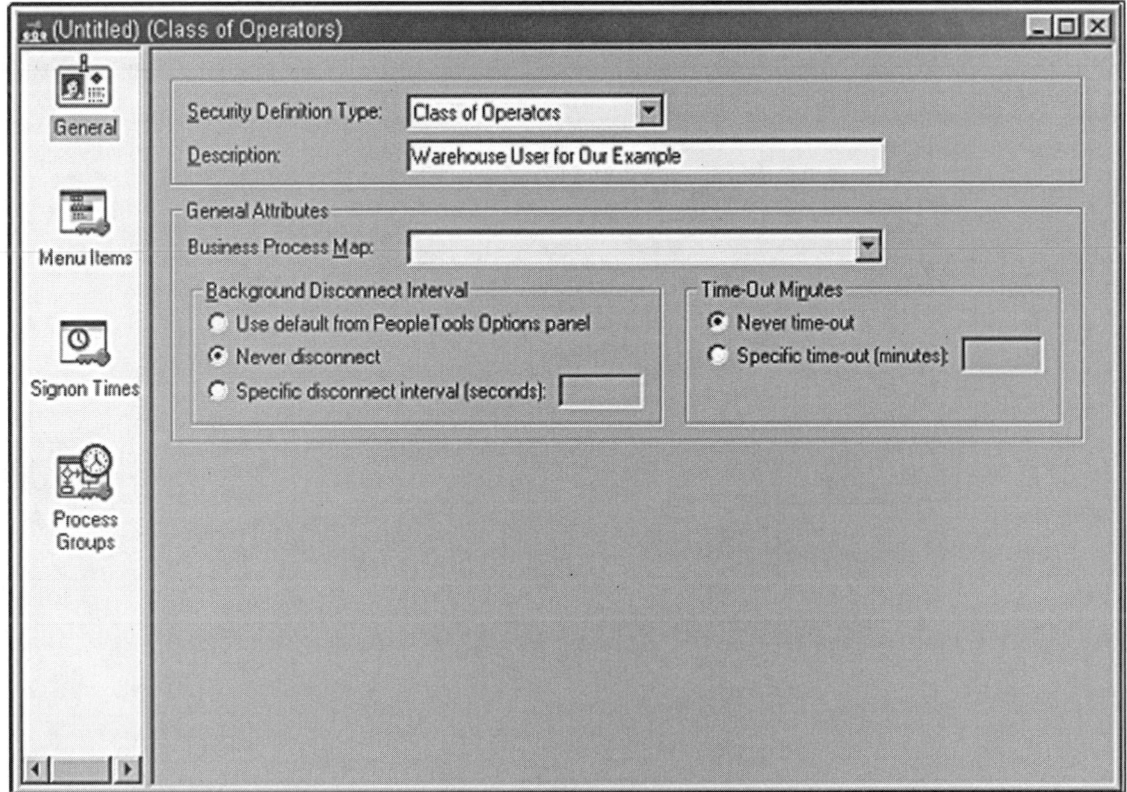

Figure 10-20 General view for the Warehouse class.

The menu access that we are going to allow for the Warehouse User class is full control for the Internal Order panel. To set this up, press the INSERT MENU ITEM icon on the toolbar. When the Menu Name dialog appears, select OUR_EXAMPLE and press OK. The Select Menu Items dialog should now be displayed. Scroll down until you see the New Internal Order panel group, WINT_PNL_GRP. With the left mouse button, select it and the next line. When you are done, your dialog should look like the one in Figure 10-21. If yours matches the figure, press OK.

If all is correct, please save the class as WUSER and continue.

Buyer Class

The final class we are going to create is for the buyers of our example. The Buyers class (BUYER) will be used for all the employees who handle internal orders. To begin, select the FILE, NEW menu option or press the NEW icon from within the Security Administrator. When the new untitled child window is displayed, it should initially be showing the "general"

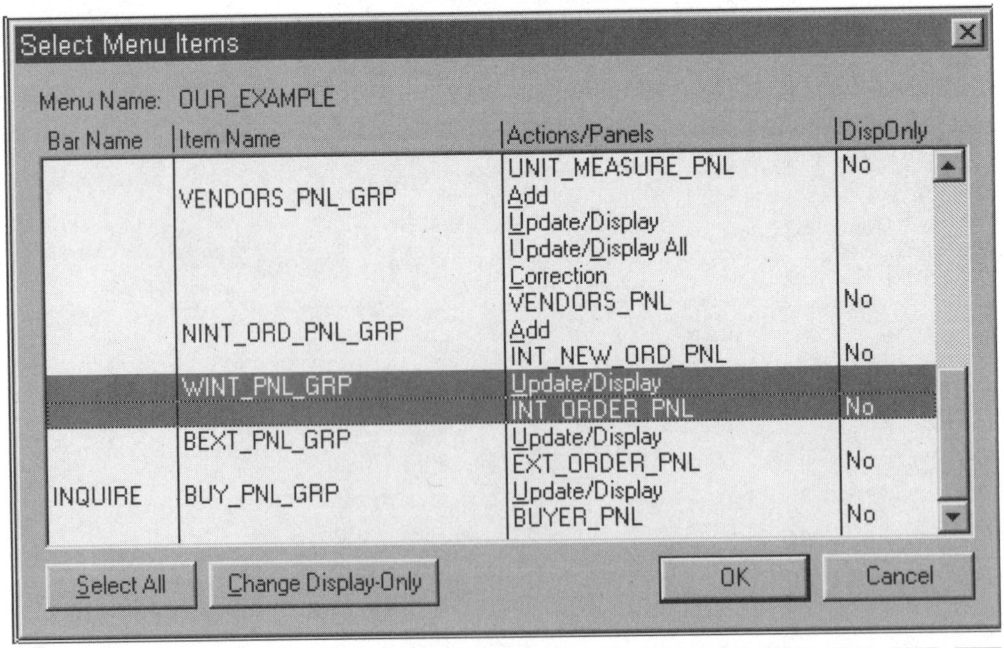

Select Menu Items

Menu Name: OUR_EXAMPLE

Bar Name	Item Name	Actions/Panels	DispOnly
		UNIT_MEASURE_PNL	No
	VENDORS_PNL_GRP	Add	
		Update/Display	
		Update/Display All	
		Correction	
		VENDORS_PNL	No
	NINT_ORD_PNL_GRP	Add	
		INT_NEW_ORD_PNL	No
	WINT_PNL_GRP	Update/Display	
		INT_ORDER_PNL	No
	BEXT_PNL_GRP	Update/Display	
		EXT_ORDER_PNL	No
INQUIRE	BUY_PNL_GRP	Update/Display	
		BUYER_PNL	No

Select All | Change Display-Only | OK | Cancel

Figure 10-21 Select Menu Items dialog for the Warehouse User class.

view of an Operators definition. Just as in the previous example, select CLASS OF OPERATORS from the Security Definition Type drop-down list box. Next, we are going to type "Buyers for Our Example" in the description. Figure 10-22 shows the general view with our entries.

The menu access that we are going to allow for the Buyers class is full control for the External Order panel. To set this up, press the INSERT MENU ITEM icon on the toolbar. When the Menu Name dialog appears, select OUR_EXAMPLE and press OK. The Select Menu Items dialog should now be displayed. Scroll down until you see the External Order panel group, BEXT_PNL_GRP. With the left mouse button, select it and the next line. When you are done, your dialog should look like the one in Figure 10-23. If yours matches the figure, press OK.

If all is correct, please save the class as BUYER and continue.

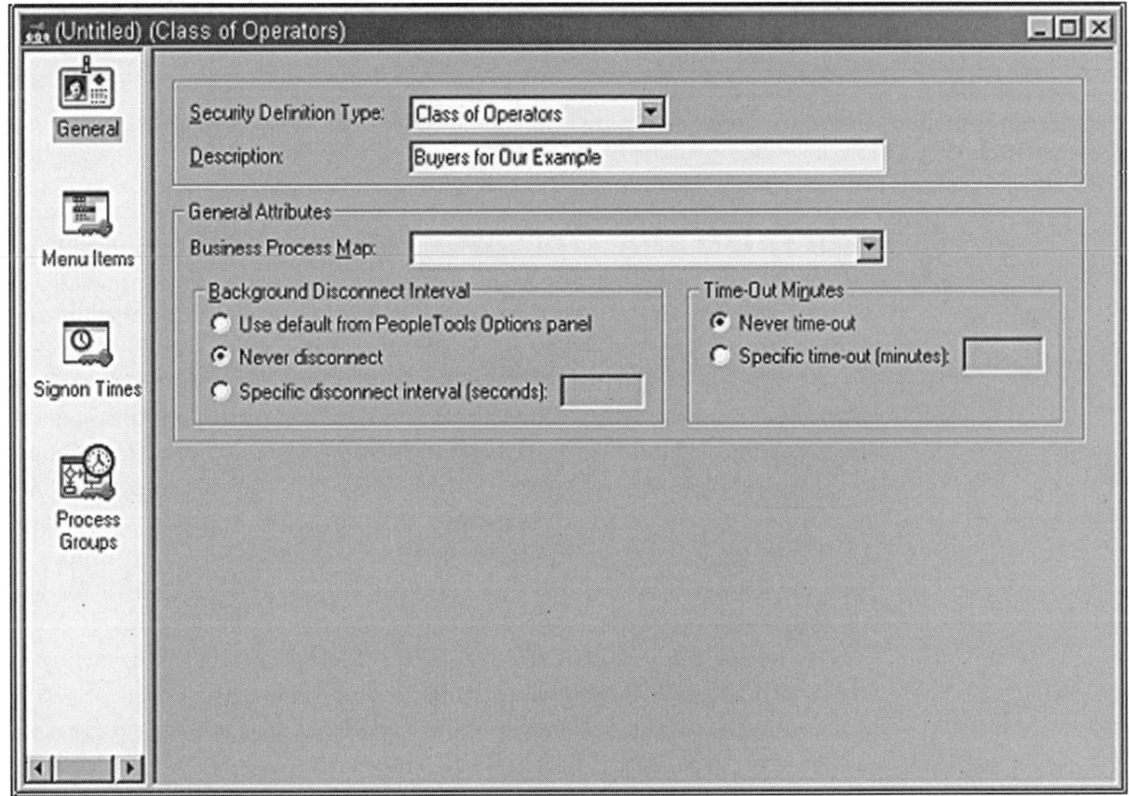

Figure 10-22 General view for the Buyers class.

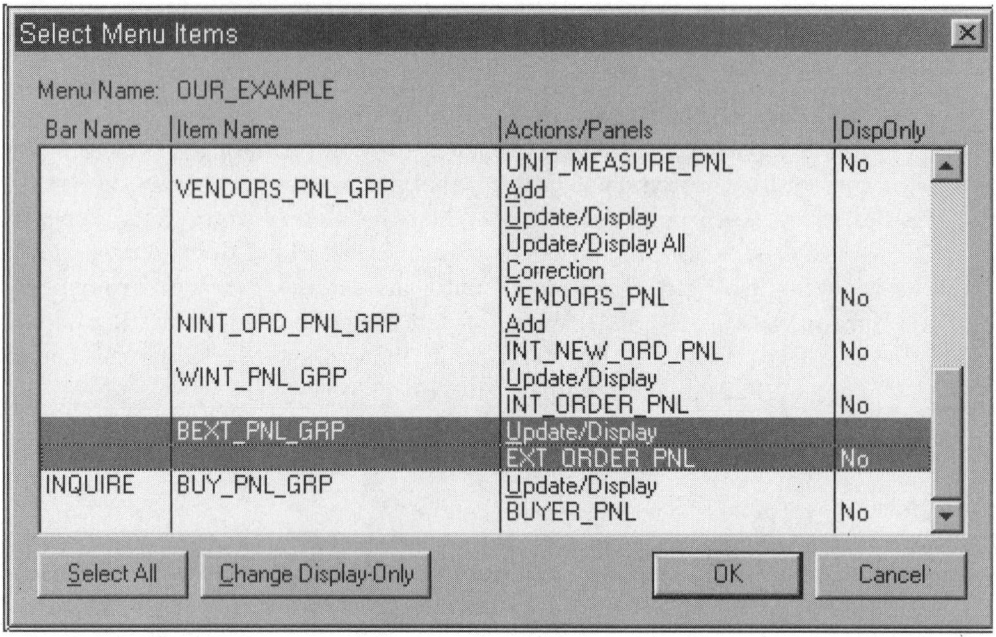

Select Menu Items

Menu Name: OUR_EXAMPLE

Bar Name	Item Name	Actions/Panels	DispOnly
		UNIT_MEASURE_PNL	No
	VENDORS_PNL_GRP	Add	
		Update/Display	
		Update/Display All	
		Correction	
		VENDORS_PNL	No
	NINT_ORD_PNL_GRP	Add	
		INT_NEW_ORD_PNL	No
	WINT_PNL_GRP	Update/Display	
		INT_ORDER_PNL	No
	BEXT_PNL_GRP	Update/Display	
		EXT_ORDER_PNL	No
INQUIRE	BUY_PNL_GRP	Update/Display	
		BUYER_PNL	No

Select All | Change Display-Only | OK | Cancel

Figure 10-23 Select Menu Items dialog for the Buyer class.

Administrator Operator

All that is left to do now is to create four new operators and associate the classes we just created to them. The first operator we are going to create is ADMIN01. Select the FILE, NEW menu option or press the NEW icon from within the Security Administrator. When the new untitled child window is displayed, it should initially be showing the "general" view of an operators definition. Enter "Administrator 01 for Our Example" in the description. Next, set the password to ADMIN01 and enter the access profile. Since we are using SQLBase as our database, our access profile is SYSADM. Figure 10-24 shows the General view with our entries for the Administrator operator.

Now all we need to do before we save this operator is to associate it with the ADMIN class that we already created. Select the INSERT CLASSES icon from the toolbar. When the Insert Classes dialog is displayed, select ADMIN and press OK. Figure 10-25 shows the Insert Classes dialog. When that is complete, the Classes view will be displayed with the ADMIN class. Figure 10-26 shows the completed Classes view. Save the operator as ADMIN01 and continue.

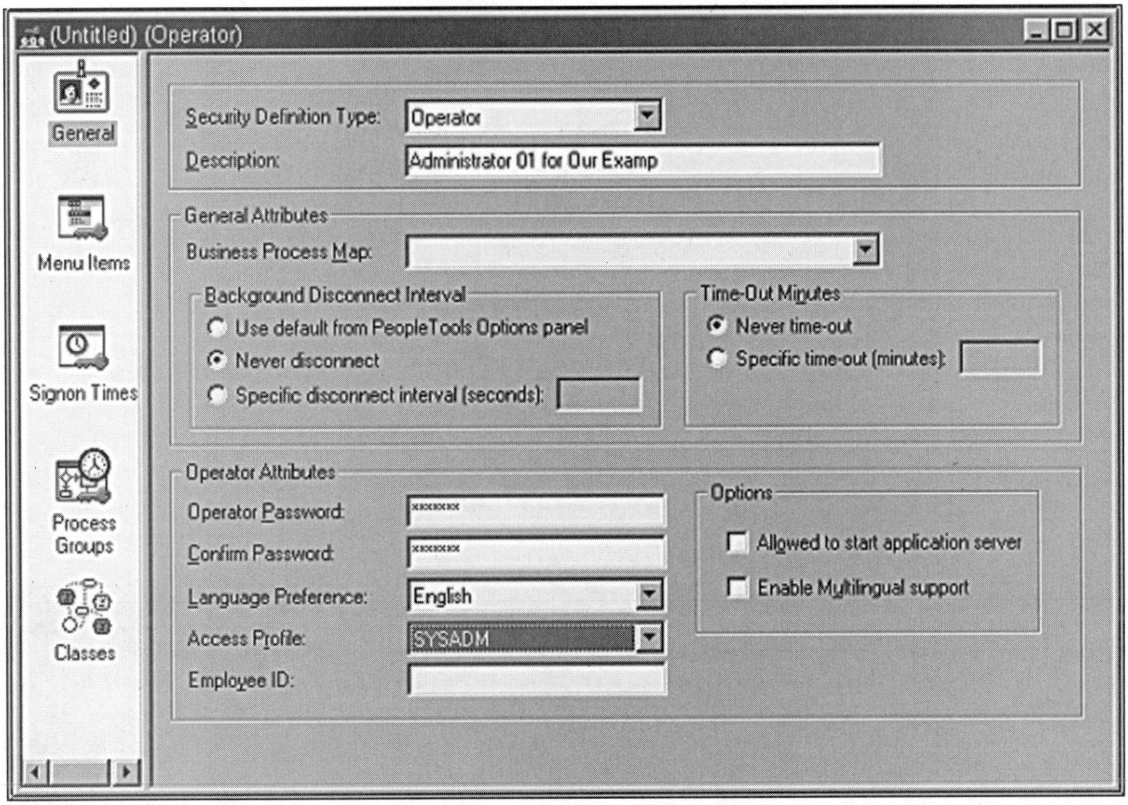

Figure 10-24 General view for Administrator operator.

End User Operator

The next operator we are going to create is EUSER01. Select the FILE, NEW menu option or press the NEW icon from within the Security Administrator. When the new untitled child window is displayed, it should initially be showing the "general" view of an operators definition. Enter "End User 01 for Our Example" in the description. Next, set the password to EUSER01 and enter the access profile. Since we are using SQLBase as our database, our access profile is SYSADM. Figure 10-27 shows the general view with our entries.

Now all we need to do before we save this operator is to associate it with the EUSER class that we already created. Select the INSERT CLASSES icon from the toolbar. When the Insert Classes dialog is displayed, select

Figure 10-25 Insert Classes dialog for Administrator operator.

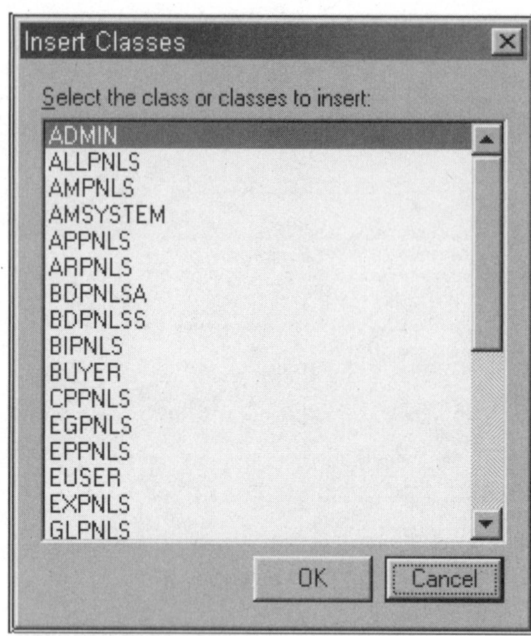

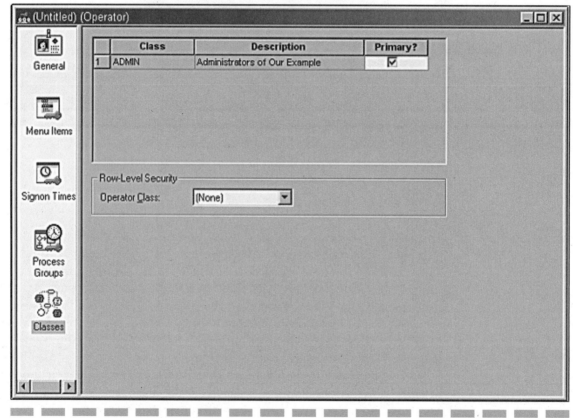

Figure 10-26 Classes view for Administrator operator.

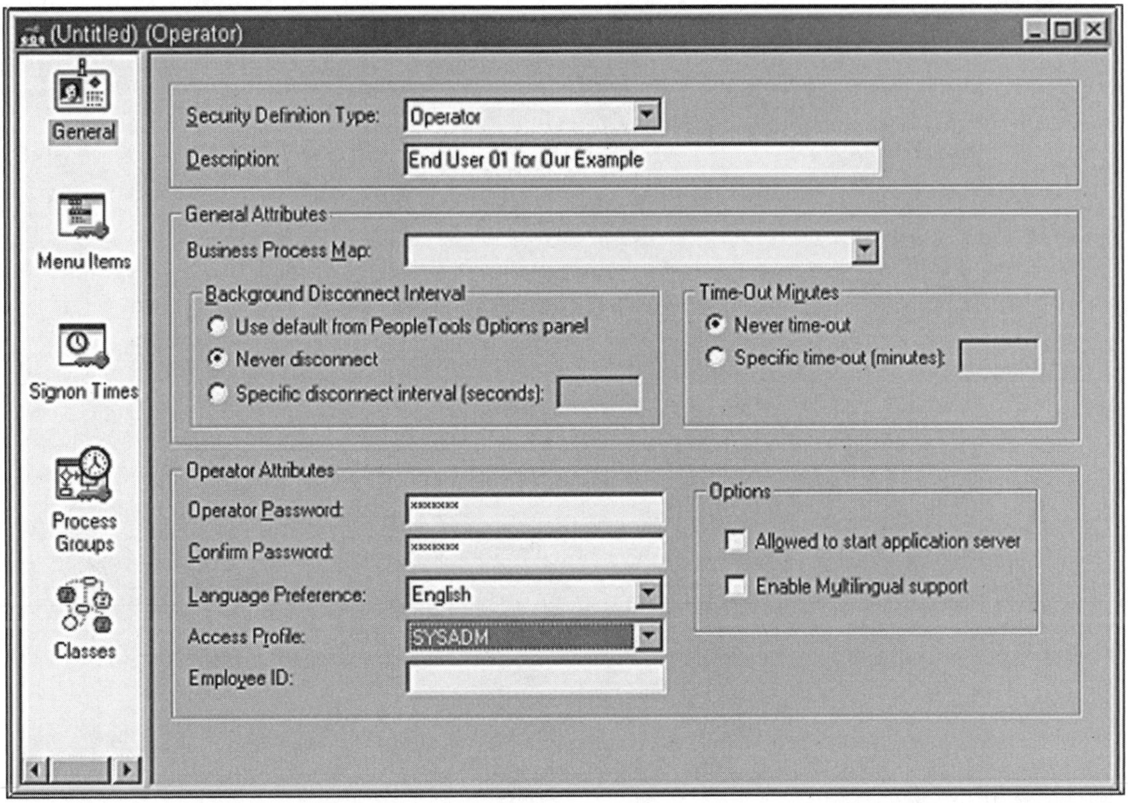

Figure 10-27 General view for End User operator.

EUSER and press OK. When that is complete, the Classes view will be displayed with the EUSER class. Figure 10-28 shows the completed Classes view. Save the operator as EUSER01 and continue.

Warehouse User Operator

The next operator we are going to create is WUSER01. Select the FILE, NEW menu option or press the NEW icon from within the Security Administrator. When the new untitled child window is displayed, it should initially be showing the "general" view of an operators definition. Enter "Warehouse User 01 for Our Example" in the description. Next, set the password to WUSER01 and the access profile. Since we are using SQL-

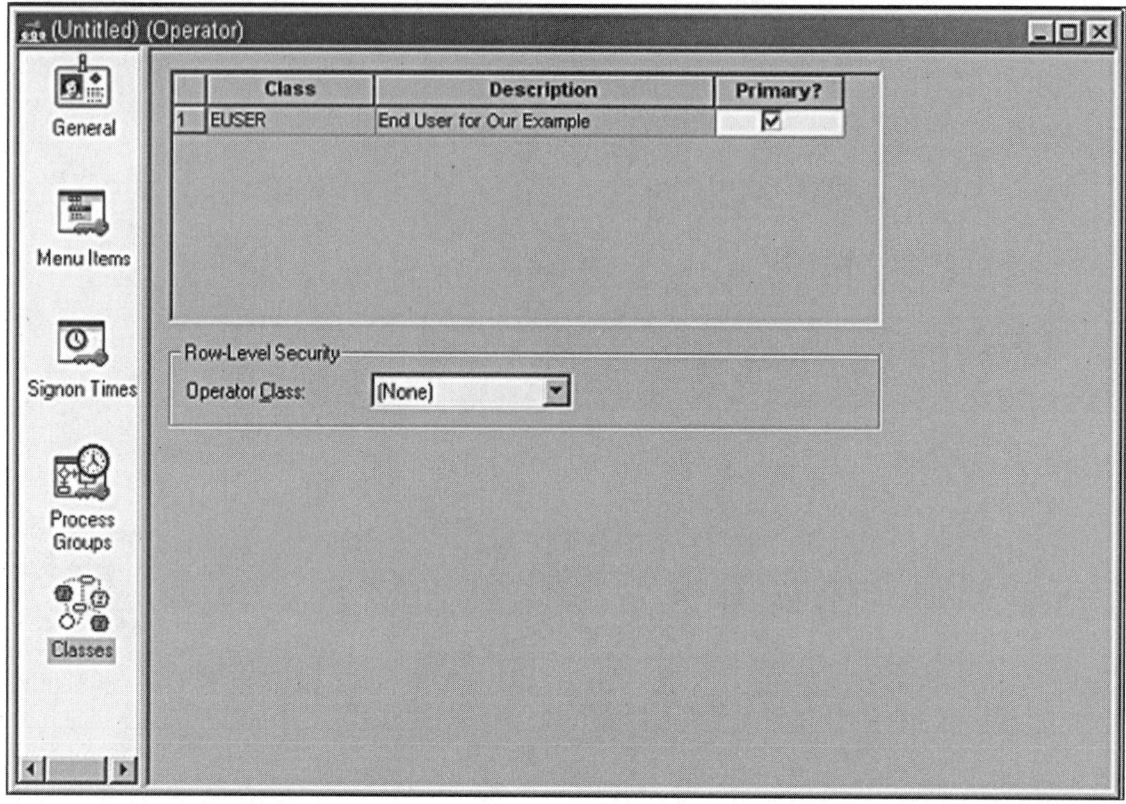

Figure 10-28 Classes view for End User operator.

Base as our database, our access profile is SYSADM. Figure 10-29 shows the General view with our entries.

Now all we need to do before we save this operator is to associate it with the WUSER class that we already created. Select the INSERT CLASSES icon from the toolbar. When the Insert Classes dialog is displayed, select WUSER and press OK. When that is complete, the Classes view will be displayed with the WUSER class. Figure 10-30 shows the completed Classes view. Save the operator as WUSER01 and continue.

Buyer Operator

The last operator we are going to create is BUYER01. Select the FILE, NEW menu option or press the NEW icon from within the Security Administra-

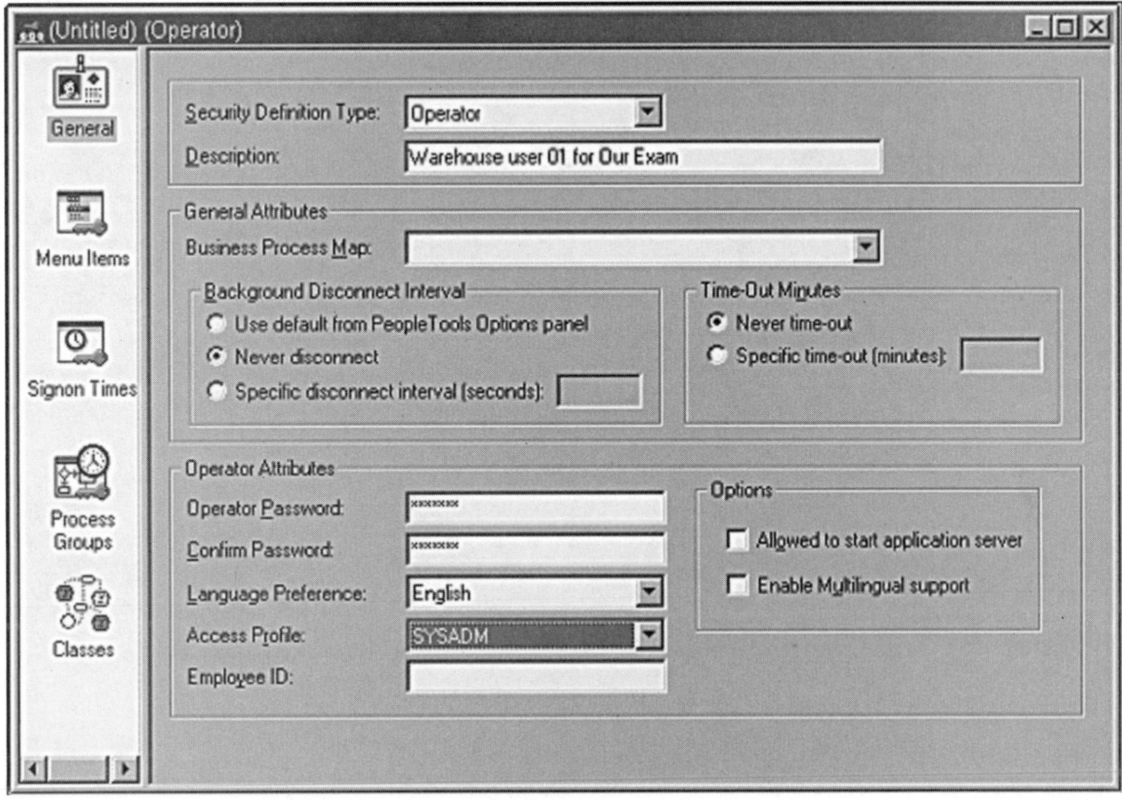

Figure 10-29 General view for Warehouse User operator.

tor. When the new untitled child window is displayed, it should initially be showing the "general" view of an operators definition. Enter "Buyer 01 for Our Example" in the description. Next, set the password to `BUYER01` and the access profile. Since we are using SQLBase as our database, our access profile is `SYSADM`. Figure 10-31 shows the general view with our entries.

Now all we need to do before we save this operator is to associate it with the `BUYER` class that we already created. Select the INSERT CLASSES icon from the toolbar. When the Insert Classes dialog is displayed, select `BUYER` and press OK. When that is complete, the Classes view will be displayed with the `BUYER` class. Figure 10-32 shows the completed Classes view. Save the operator as `BUYER01`.

That's all for the operators and classes we are going to set up for our

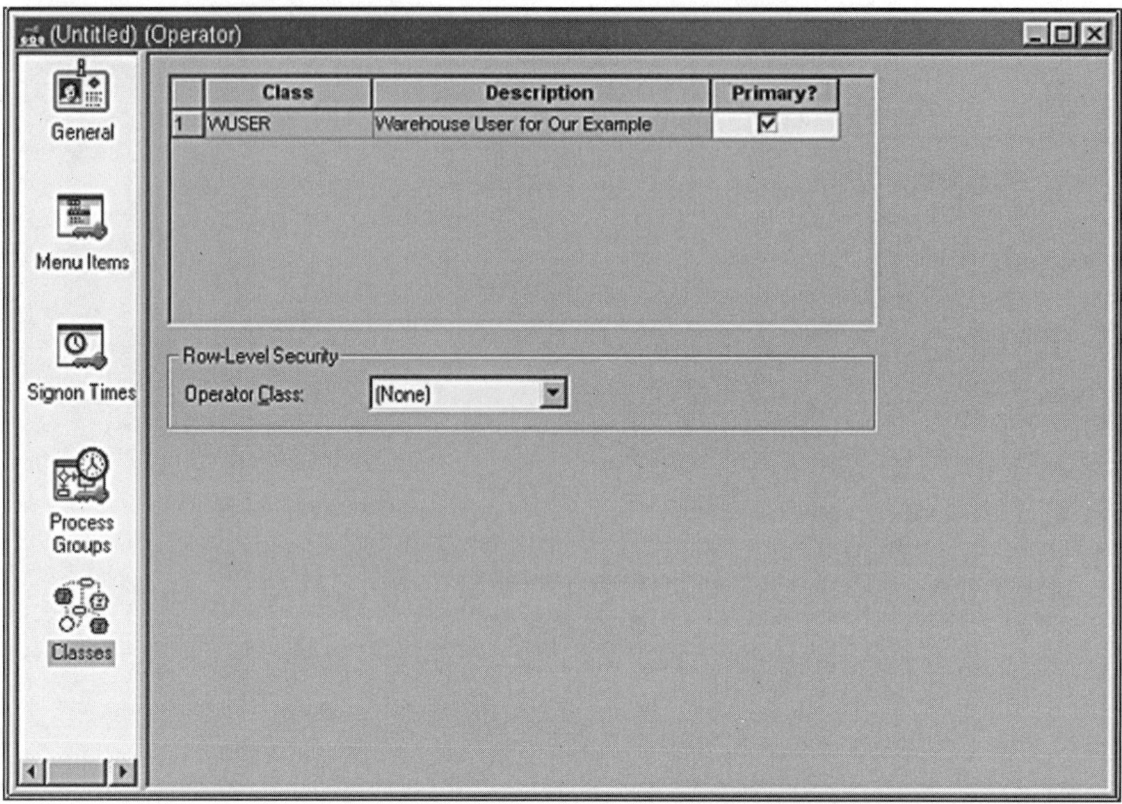

Figure 10-30 Classes view for Warehouse User operator.

example. The next chapter recaps the steps we took to finish the first pass at the application and shows the menus and panels that each of these users will see when they log in.

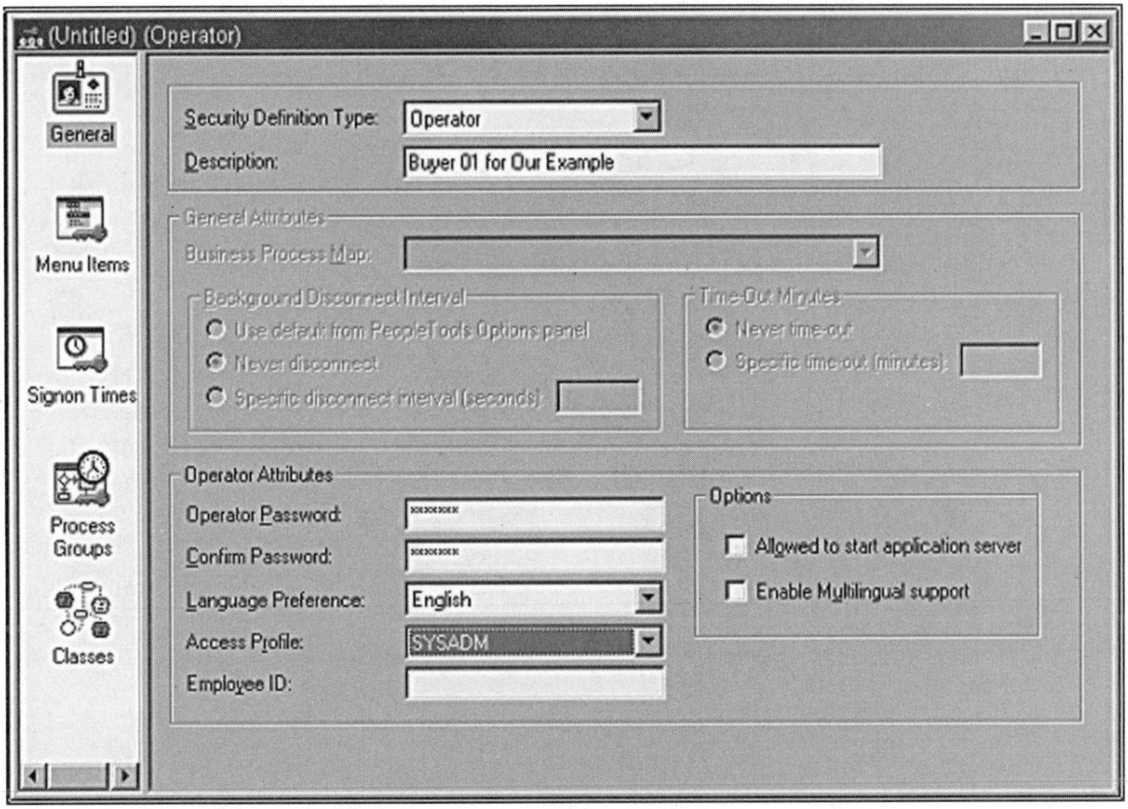

Figure 10-31 General view for the Buyer operator.

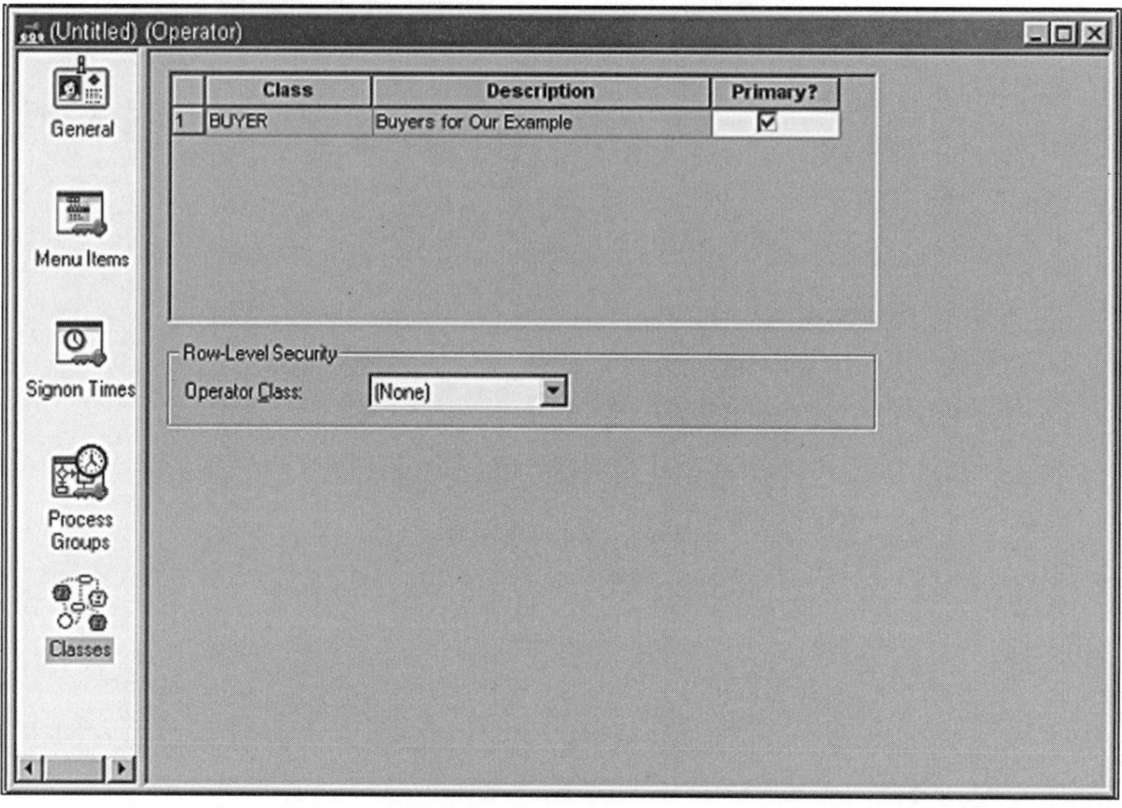

Figure 10-32 Classes view for the Buyer operator.

CHAPTER 11

Application Overview

If you have followed all the steps laid out in the example sections of this book, congratulations; you now have your first PeopleSoft application. This chapter briefly recalls the steps that were followed and shows the results of your hard work.

Development Steps

Steps in the development process (see Fig. 11-1 for a summary) are as follows:

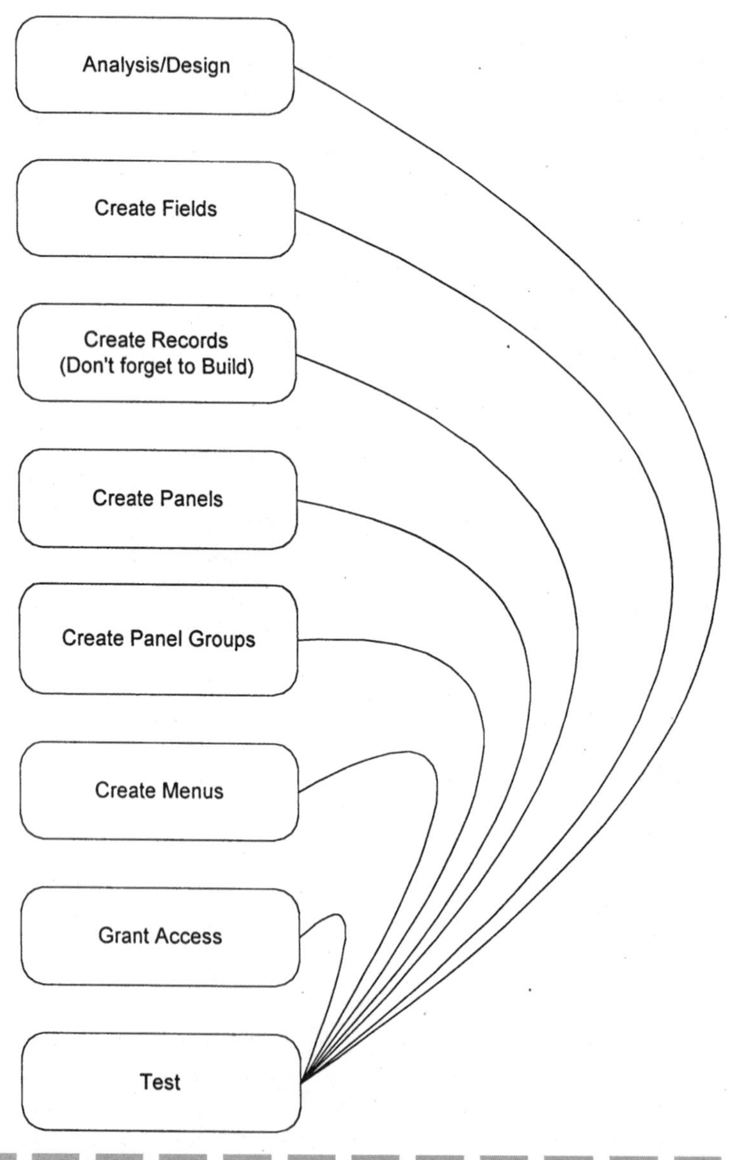

Figure 11-1 Simple PeopleSoft development process.

Analysis/design	Define the problem. Picture the solution. In Chapters 3 and 4 we discussed the internal and external ordering processes.
Create fields	In Chapter 5 we explored fields and then created all the ones we would need.
Create records	Chapter 6 detailed records. Don't forget to build your records. This is a problem for many new PeopleSoft developers.
Create panels	Very similar to many other windows programming environments, panel development is explored in Chapter 7.
Create panel groups	Panel groups combine several panels that all share the same search record. Chapter 8 detailed panel groups.
Create menus	Menus are the main way of navigation in PeopleSoft. Menus allow users to select actions to perform on their panel groups. Chapter 9 was dedicated to menus.
Grant access	Before you can test any of your new panels, you must first give access to the menu that is associated with each. Chapter 10 shows you how to create both classes of operators as well as operators and give them access to menus.
Test	Testing in PeopleSoft is a very iterative process. If anything does not work the way you want it to, you might have to return to any of the previous steps and follow them again. This chapter shows you how the screens should look for our application after this first pass. If your screens do not operate properly, the first place to check is to see if you built the records. If they still do not work, look for your local PeopleSoft cache and delete it.

The rest of this chapter consists of figures that depict the example application that we developed. Go ahead, enter data for all the lookup records, and then try to enter a new internal order. Experiment with all the panels and operators you created. The next section concentrates on enhancing our application. If you have made it this far and your applications resemble those in Figures 11-2 to 11-11, congratulations. If you are having some problems, please review and follow the screen movies on the CD-ROM.

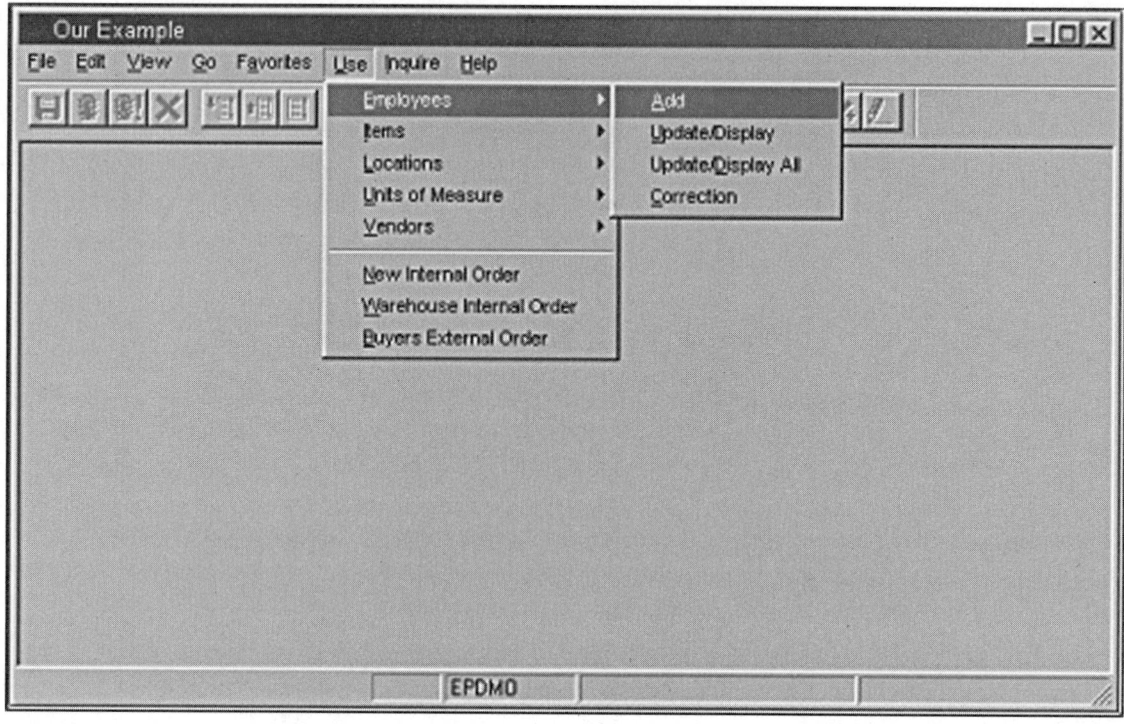

Figure 11-2 Use menu for `ADMIN01`.

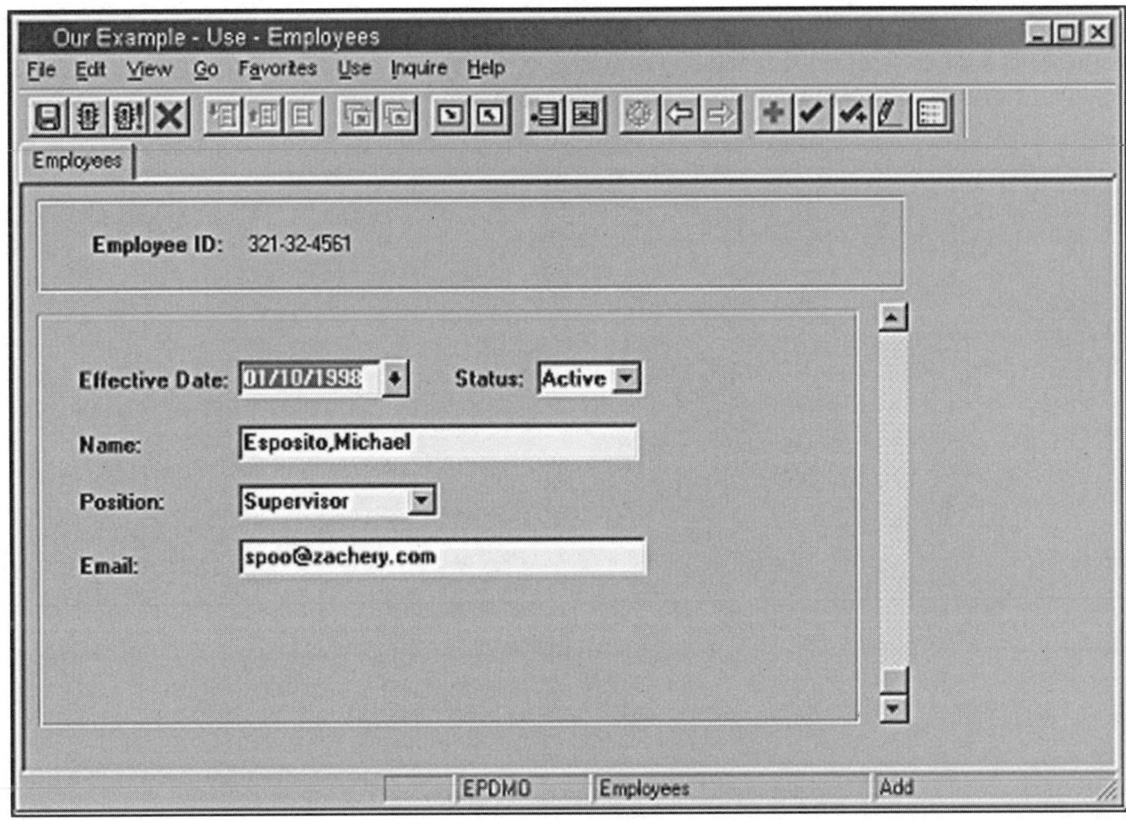

Figure 11-3 Employees Add panel.

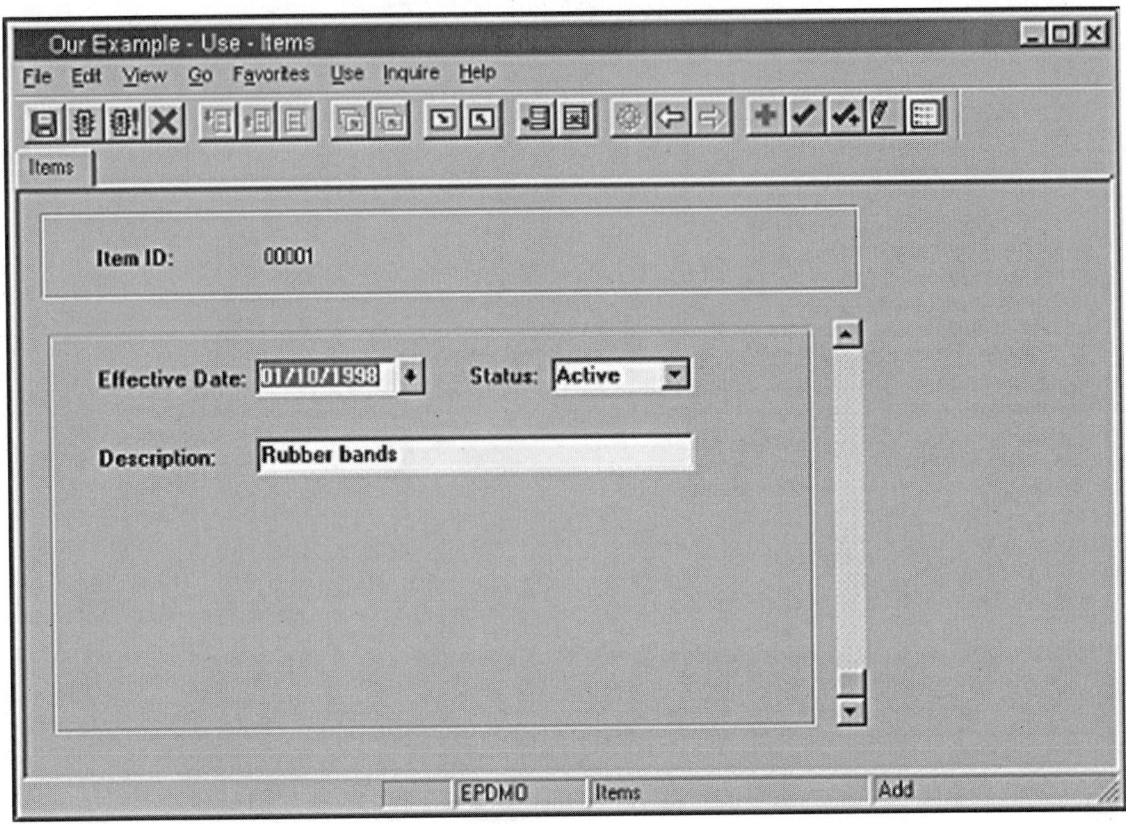

Figure 11-4 Items Add panel.

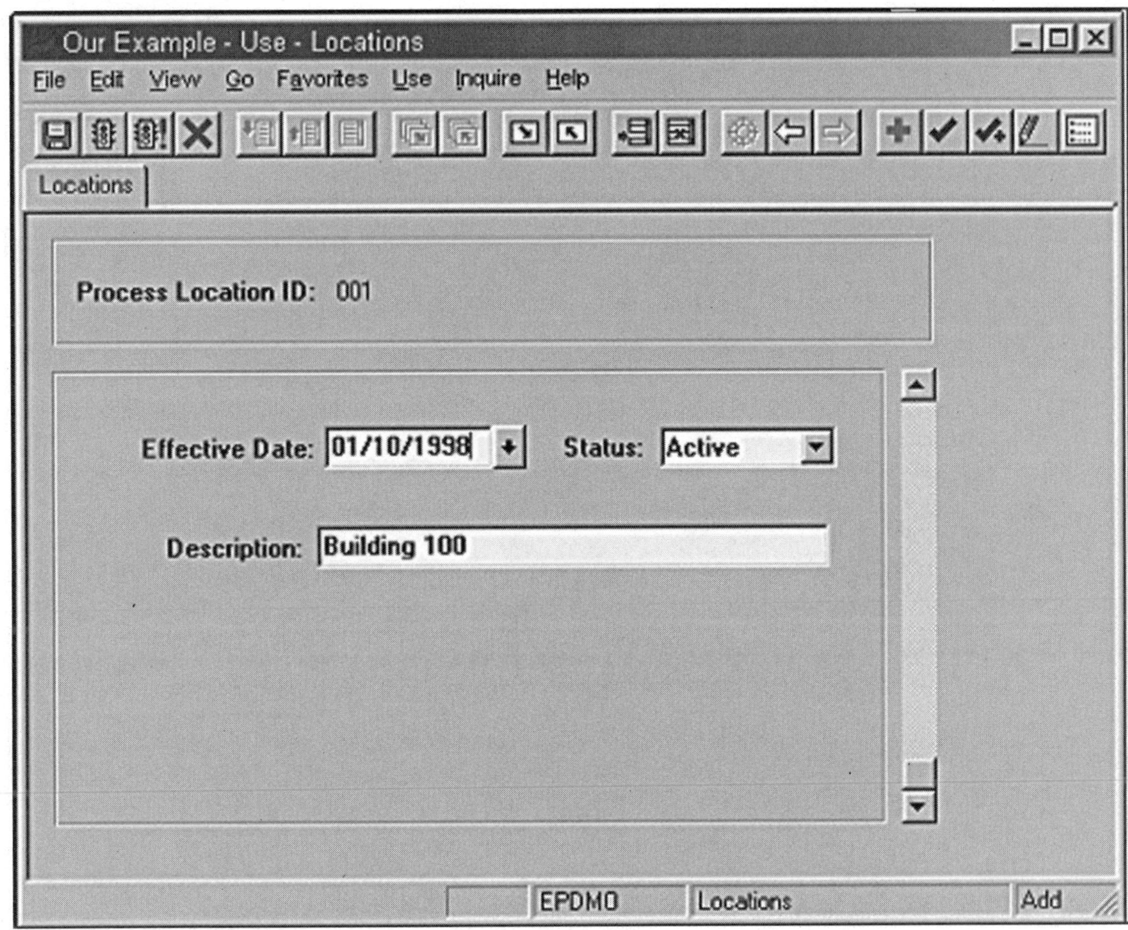

Figure 11-5 Locations Add panel.

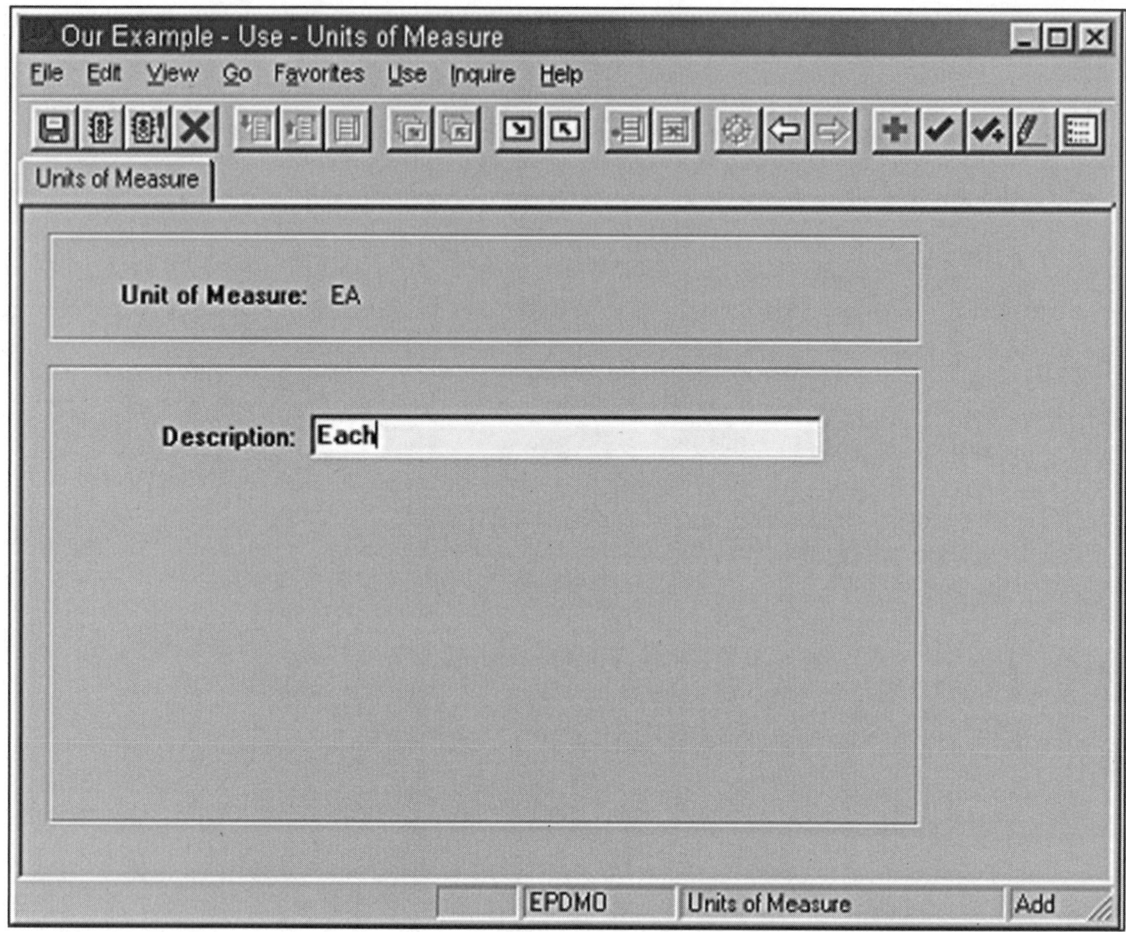

Figure 11-6 Units of Measure Add panel.

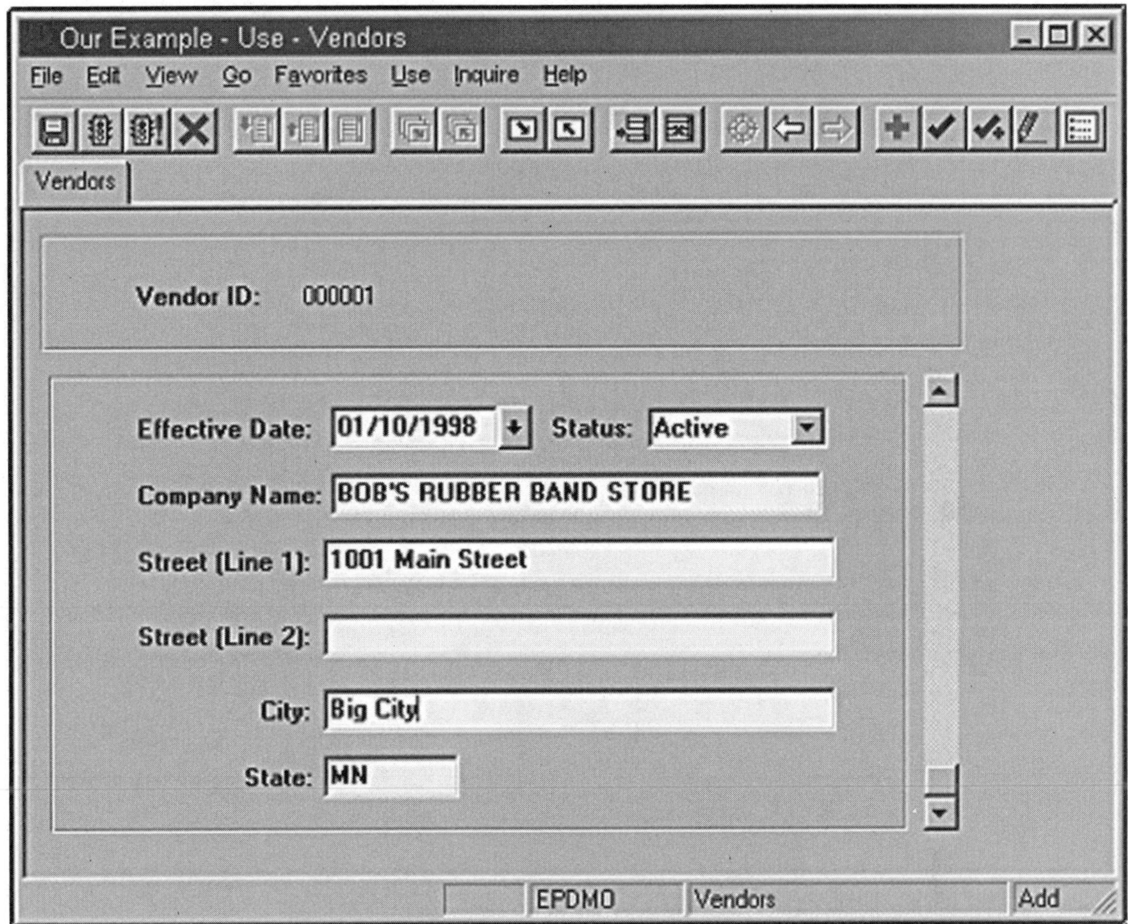

Figure 11-7 Vendors Add panel.

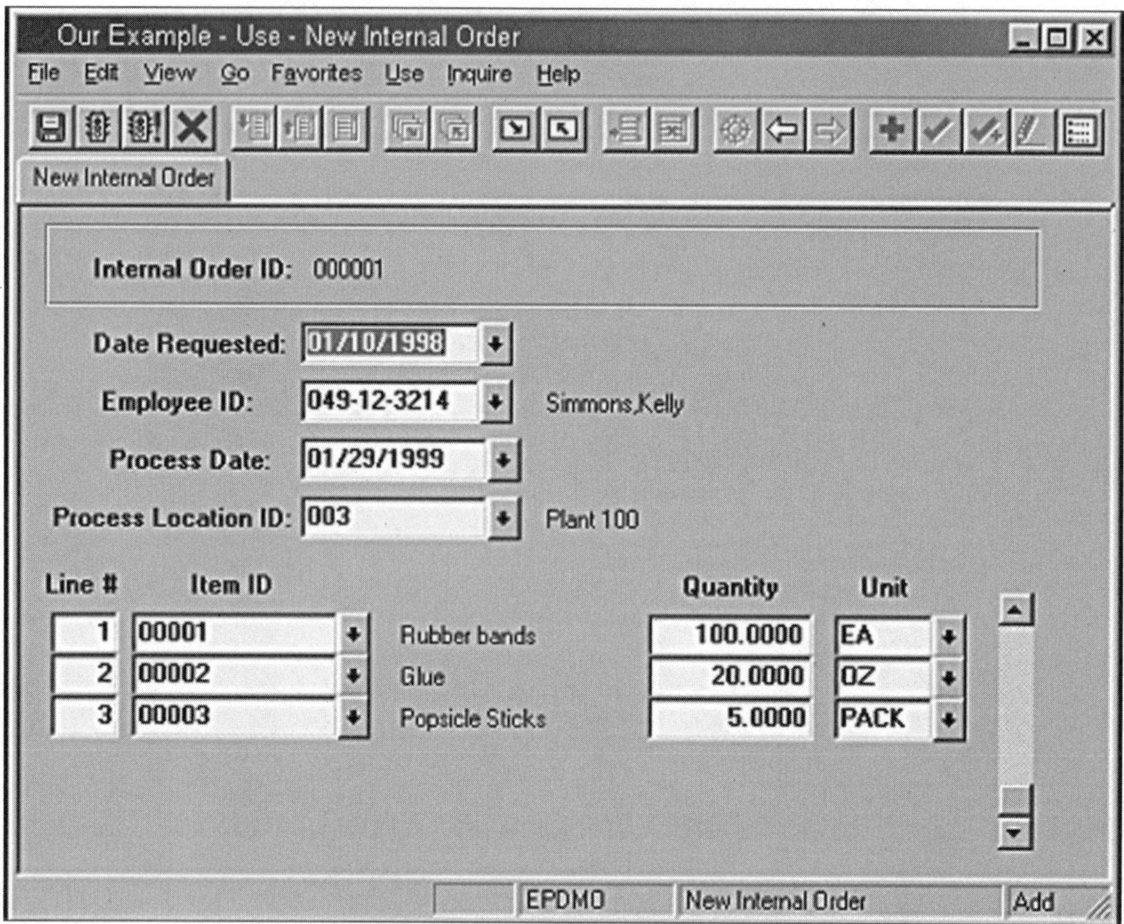

Figure 11-8 New Internal Order Add panel.

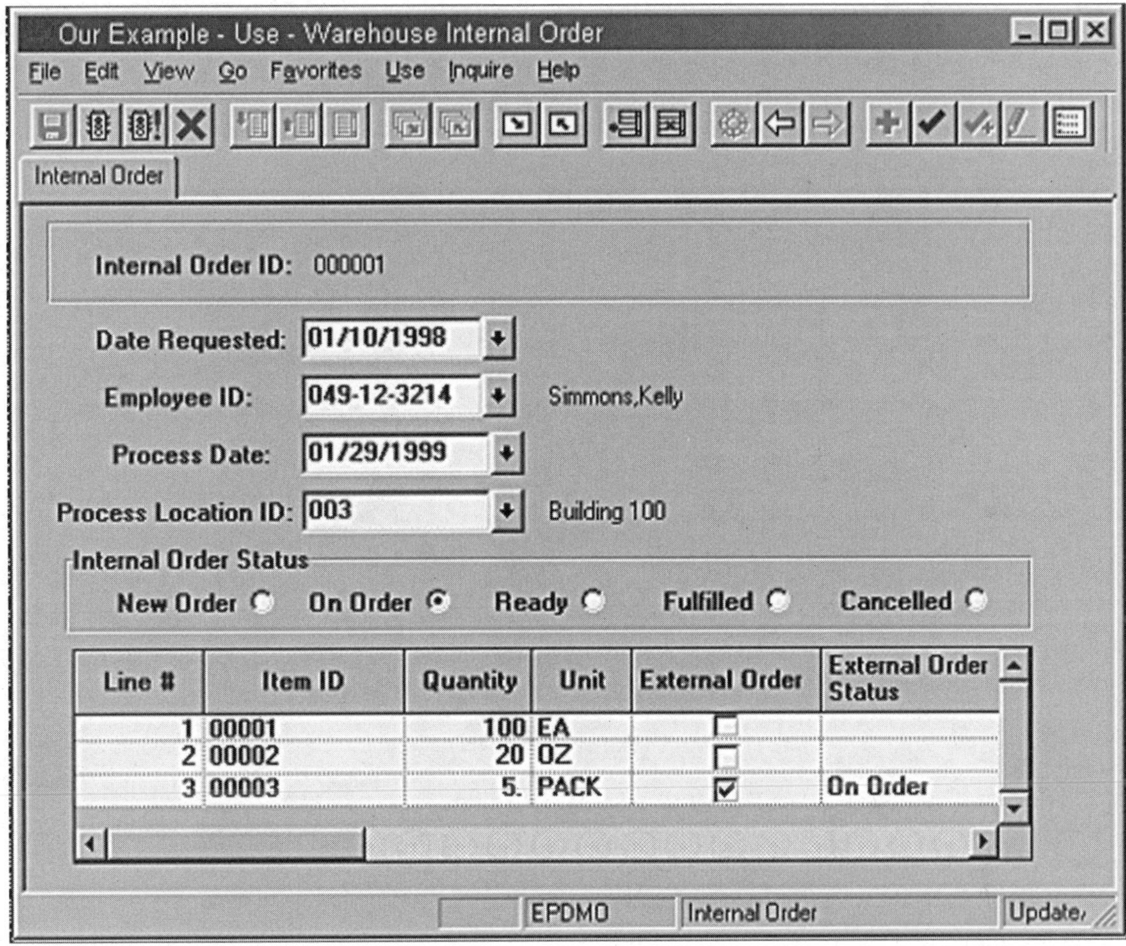

Figure 11-9 Warehouse Internal Order Add panel.

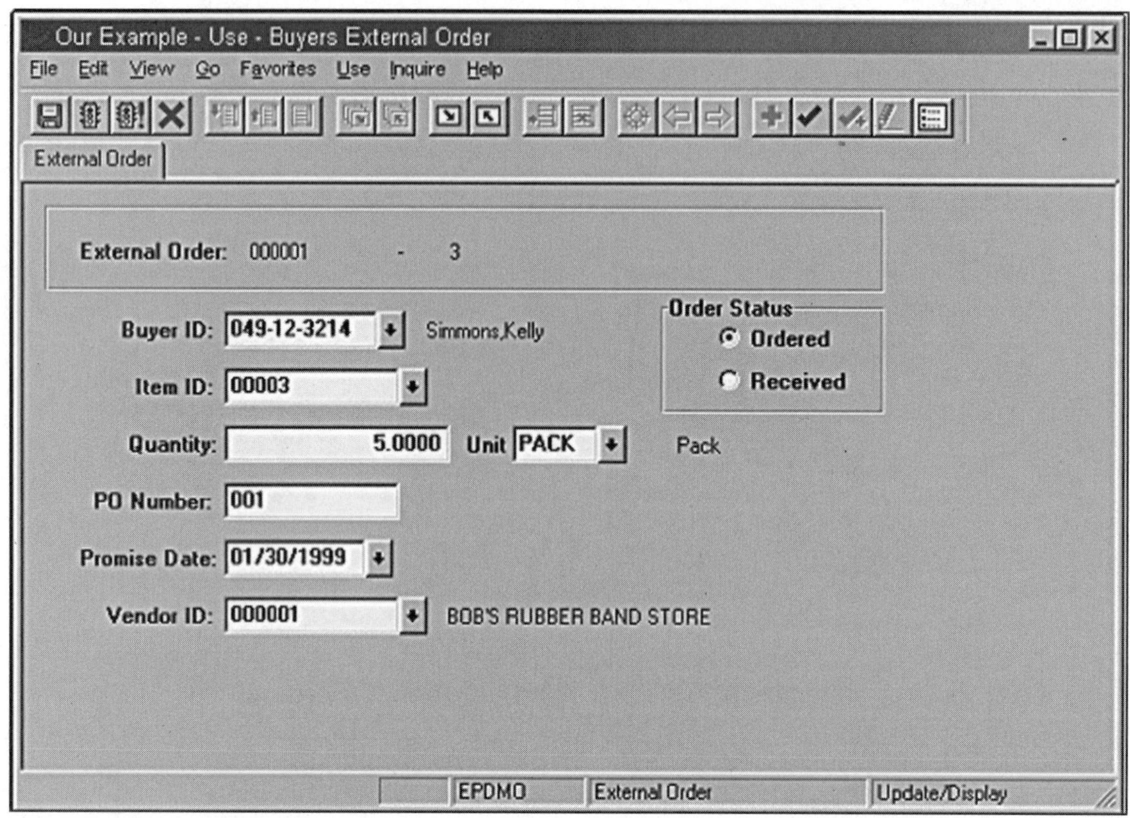

Figure 11-10 Buyers External Order Add panel.

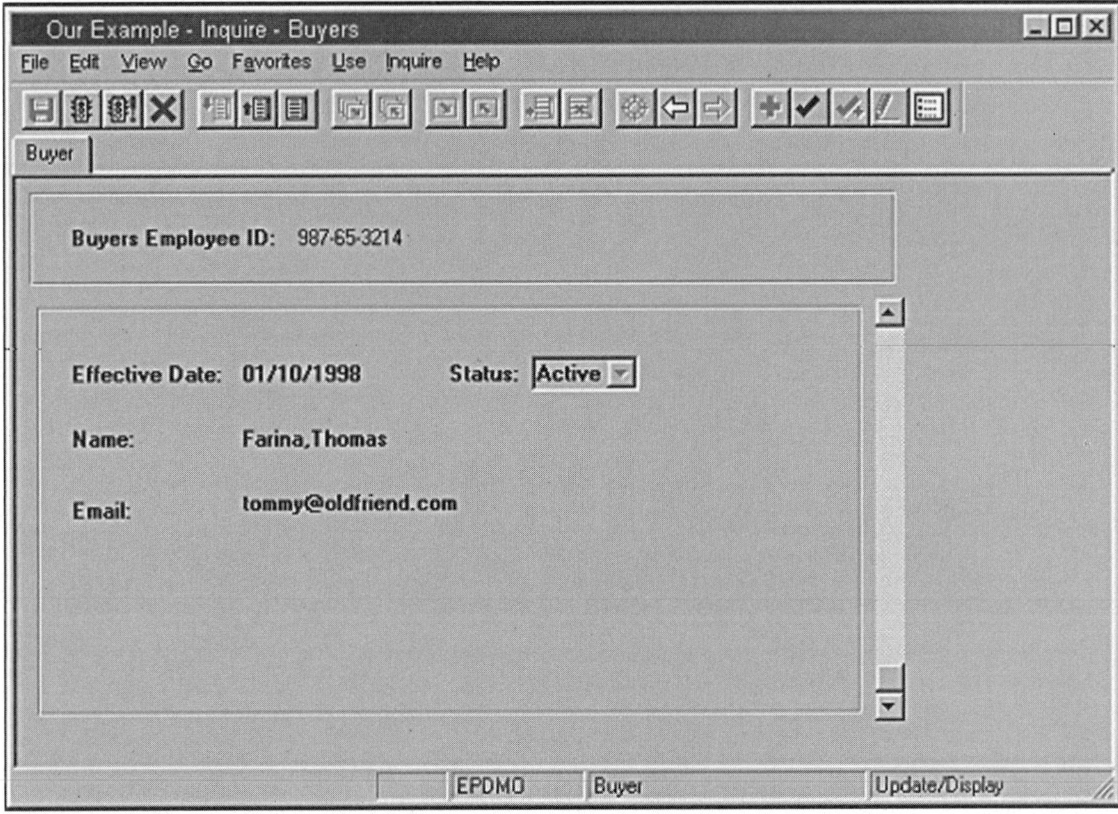

Figure 11-11 Buyers Inquire panel.

CHAPTER 12

Introduction to PeopleCode

PeopleSoft's PeopleCode is a fourth-generation language (4GL) that allows developers to customize and enhance the basic operation provided with panel creation. This chapter starts by introducing PeopleSoft's event model. It is very different from the Windows event model that many Windows programming languages use. PeopleSoft's event model is record-centric, not windows-control-centric. This means that you should not be looking for clicked events on controls that you placed on your panel. Instead, you look at the PeopleCode events found in the record associated with the control field.

After the event model has been detailed and the events have been defined, we will then review how you can use and create PeopleCode. Finally, we will use our newfound PeopleCode knowledge to enhance our Warehouse Ordering example.

PeopleSoft Event Model

PeopleSoft's event model, shown in Figure 12-1, starts with six different actions. The following six actions trigger PeopleCode events:

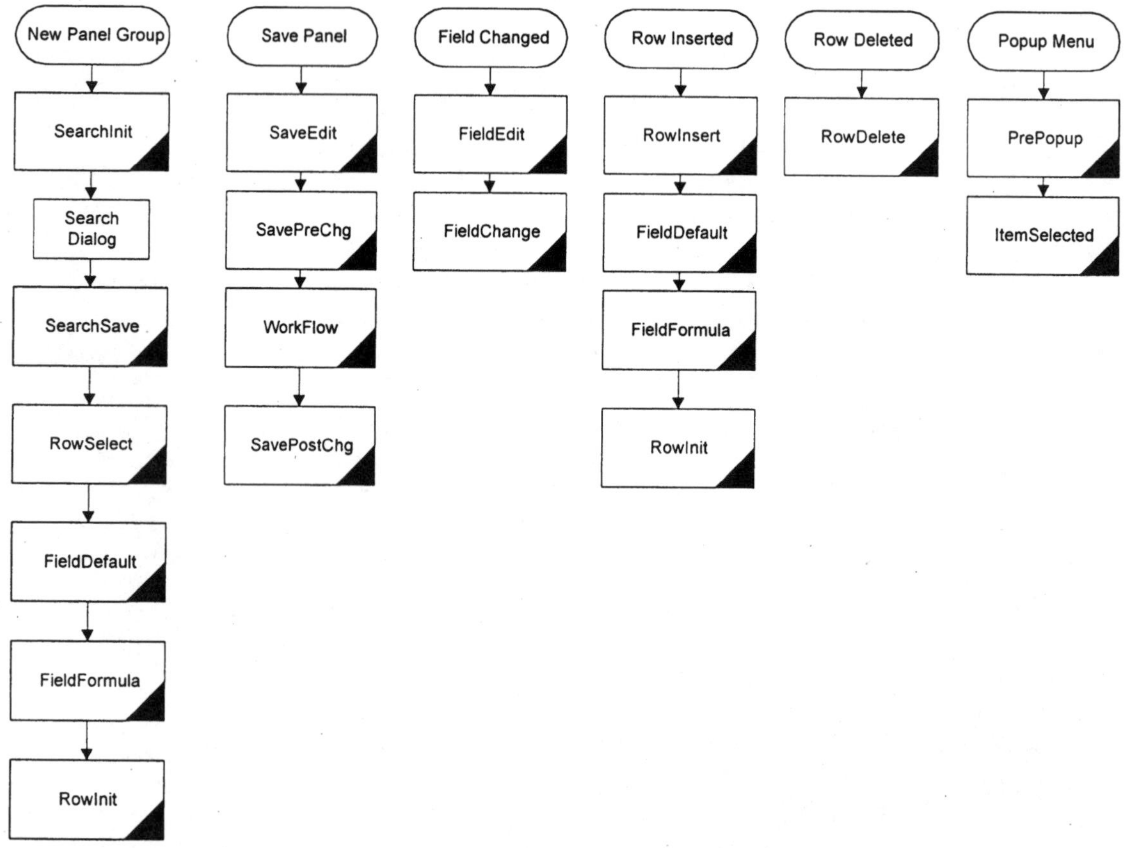

Figure 12-1 PeopleSoft Event Model.

1. *A new panel group.* Any action requiring a new search record group.
   - `SearchInit`. This event occurs before the Search dialog is displayed. PeopleCode can be added here to set defaults for the search keys.
   - `SearchSave`. This event occurs after the user presses the OK button on the Search dialog. PeopleCode can be added here to edit the values that were entered into the Search dialog screen.
   - `RowSelect`. This event occurs as the application selects rows of data. PeopleCode can be added here to filter data before they are displayed in the panel.
   - `FieldDefault`. This event occurs for each field before the row read from the database is displayed. PeopleCode can be added here to set default values.
   - `FieldFormula`. This event is triggered very often. PeopleSoft does not recommend placing code in this event. This event is used mainly in derived records that are used as functional libraries (`FUNCLIBs`).
   - `RowInit`. This event occurs for each new row of data that are returned or created. This event is occurs at the row level; therefore it does not matter what field you place the PeopleCode in.
2. *Save panel.* The user saves the panel.
   - `SaveEdit`. This event occurs when a panel group is saved. PeopleCode can be added here to edit multiple field values that might depend on each other.
   - `SavePreChg`. This event occurs when a panel group is saved. PeopleCode can be added here to perform last-minute logic before the record is saved.
   - `WorkFlow`. This event occurs when a panel group is saved. PeopleCode can be added here to trigger business process events.
   - `SavePostChg`. This event occurs after the record has been updated to the database. PeopleCode can be added here to save data to other records that are not a part of the current panel group.
3. *Field changed.* Field value is changed.
   - `FieldEdit`. This event occurs when a field is changed. PeopleCode can be added here to verify the new value.
   - `FieldChange`. This event occurs when a field is changed. PeopleCode can be added here to execute logic based on the new value.

4. *Row insert.* The user inserts a detail row.
   - `RowInsert`. This event occurs when a new row of data is inserted (F7). PeopleCode can be added *here for additional* `RowInit` *logic.*
   - `FieldDefault`. This event occurs for each field before the row read from the database is displayed. PeopleCode can be added here to set default values.
   - `FieldFormula`. This event is triggered very often. PeopleSoft does not recommend placing code in this event. This event is used mainly in derived records that are used as functional libraries (`FUNCLIBs`)
   - `RowInit`. This event occurs for each new row of data that are returned or created. *This event occurs at the row level;* therefore it does not matter what field you place the PeopleCode in.
5. *Row delete.* The user deletes a detail row.
   - `RowDelete`. This event occurs when a row of data is deleted (F8). PeopleCode can be added here to validate the deletion or to use the data that will be deleted to perform additional logic.
6. *Popup menu.* The user initiates a popup menu.
   - `PrePopup`. This event occurs only when a popup menu is accessed that was created in the Application Designer. Standard PeopleSoft menus do not trigger this event. PeopleCode can be added here to add or disable menu items in the popup menu.
   - `ItemSelected`. This event occurs each time a menu item is selected. For popup menus, the PeopleCode can access the panel's records and therefore PeopleCode can be added to perform a user-defined process associated with the menu item that was selected.

PeopleCode Language Syntax

As mentioned earlier, PeopleCode is PeopleSoft's proprietary language, which is used to enhance and develop PeopleSoft Applications. As with any other language, precise syntax must be followed for it to be understood. This section reviews the basic syntax that is used to create PeopleCode functionality.

Comments

Comments are an important part of any computer language. They allow us to detail in human language exactly what we are doing in the computer's language. PeopleCode utilizes C's comment structure. When `/*` is encountered, everything after that is a comment and is therefore disregarded by the PeopleCode processor. To end the comment section an `*/` must be entered.

```
/* Everything after this point is a comment
   still a comment */
```

Variable Data Types and Scope

PeopleSoft variables can have either a local or global scope. *Local variables* maintain their values for the life of the PeopleCode program in which they were defined. *Global variables maintain their values throughout the entire PeopleSoft session.* PeopleSoft values fall into the following data types:

- Any
- Number
- String
- Boolean
- Date
- Datetime
- Time
- Object

If a variable is not declared, its data type is set to Any and its scope is set to Local. To declare a variable, you can state its data type and scope. An `&` (ampersand) always precedes variables. The following code snippet shows a couple different variable definitions:

```
Local Number &ID
Global String &OpPreference
```

Control Statements

PeopleSoft includes many of the standard programming control structures. The following list highlights the available control structures and their proper syntax.

- *IF/THEN/ELSE.* The IF/THEN/ELSE control acts the same as it does in all the other computer languages. If the expression evaluates to TRUE, then the program control is passed to the lines immediately after the THEN. If the expression evaluates to FALSE, then the control passes to the line after the ELSE. If there is no ELSE, the control passes to the line after the `End-If`.

```
If  <True Condition> Then
           ...
{Else}
           ...
End-If;
```

- *EVALUATE (case).* The EVALUATE control statement is the same as either a case or a switch statement that you might already be familiar with. Remember to use `Break` to force the control to exit the EVALUATE control structure.

```
Evaluate <Expression 1>
       When < = or ! = or <> or < or <=or > or >= > <Expression 2>
            ...
       When < = or ! = or <> or < or <=or > or >= > <Expression 3>
             ...
             Break;
       When < = or != or <> or < or <=or > or >= > <Expression n>
             ...
             Break;
       When-other
             ...
End-Evaluate;
```

- *FOR loop.* The FOR loop performs just as you might imagine it might. For a specific number of times the process repeats the PeopleCode that is included in the FOR loop. If you specify a `Step` amount, the counter amount will be increased by that amount each time the loop is processed. A default value of 1 is used if no `Step` value is given.

```
FOR <counter> = 1 to 10
      {Step n}
      ...
```

```
End-for;
```

- *REPEAT UNTIL loop.* The REPEAT UNTIL loop processes the PeopleCode inside its loop until its UNTIL expression evaluates to TRUE. The REPEAT UNTIL loop will process its logic at least one time.

```
REPEAT
    ...
UNTIL  < expression >;
```

- *WHILE loop.* Unlike the REPEAT UNTIL loop, the WHILE loop checks its expression first. If it does not evaluate to TRUE, its PeopleCode will not be executed.

```
WHILE  < expression >
    ...
END-WHILE;
```

Functions

PeopleCode allows you to use the following types of function:

- Standard built-in functions.
- Internal PeopleCode functions.
- External PeopleCode functions.
- External Non-PeopleCode Functions.

Declaring Functions Functions that are not defined in the PeopleCode program that is referencing them must be declared before they can be used. By convention, all functions are declared at the top of the PeopleCode program along with any variable declarations.

```
Declare Function <Functions name> PeopleCode < Record.Field >
FieldFormula;
```

Calling Functions All functions are called the same way.

```
FUNCTION({PARM1, PARM2,...});
```

If the function returns a value, it must be called as an expression.

```
&RETURNVAR = FUNCTION({PARM1, PARM2,...});
```

Creating Functions PeopleCode functions that are created to be used externally to the PeopleCode program they are defined in are by convention saved in records that begin with FUNCLIB in a field's FieldFormula event. Whether you are creating an internal function or a function library, the following syntax will be used:

```
FUNCTION <function name> ( <parm1>, <parm2>, ...)
     ...
END-FUNCTION;
```

If your function is required to return a value, the following syntax should be used:

```
FUNCTION <function name> ( <parm1>, <parm2>, ...)  returns <data
type>;
     ...
     return <Expression>;
END-FUNCTION;
```

PeopleCode Example

We are now going to implement a couple of PeopleCode changes to our order example. The enhancement that we are going to develop deals with the automatic numbering (autonumbering) of many of our applications' identification numbers. These modifications will highlight many of the essential features of PeopleCode, including how to create and use a function library.

Following the logic that is used throughout the delivered PeopleSoft function libraries, in order to have autonumbering, we are going to need a counter record, a derived function record, and modifications in the RowInit event of all the fields that we are going to autonumber.

Counter Record

For this example we are going to only use the Item id, Vendor id, and Internal Order id. To allow us to implement the autonumbering functionality, we are going to create a one-row table that will store the last value used for each of our fields. A new record definition with our fields must be created. Figure 12-2 shows the record definition that we are going to use for the counter record.

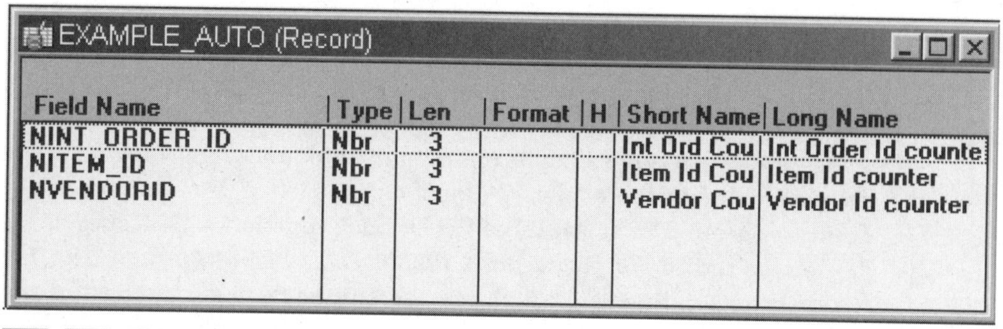

EXAMPLE_AUTO (Record)

Field Name	Type	Len	Format	H	Short Name	Long Name
NINT_ORDER_ID	Nbr	3			Int Ord Cou	Int Order Id counte
NITEM_ID	Nbr	3			Item Id Cou	Item Id counter
NVENDORID	Nbr	3			Vendor Cou	Vendor Id counter

Figure 12-2 EXAMPLE_AUTO record definition.

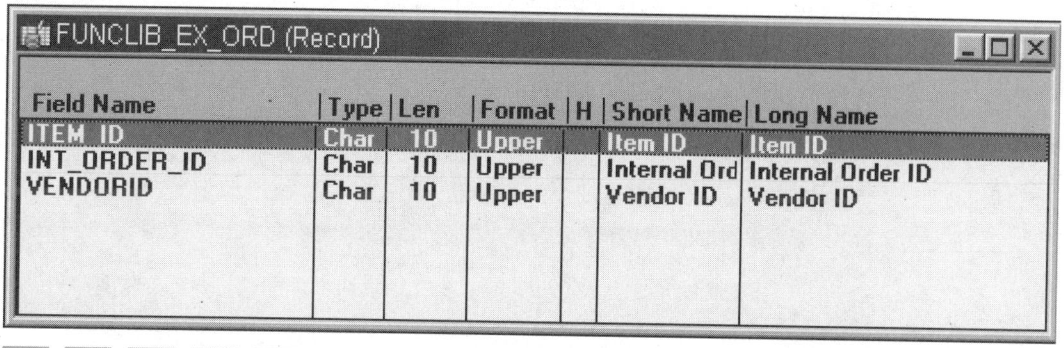

FUNCLIB_EX_ORD (Record)

Field Name	Type	Len	Format	H	Short Name	Long Name
ITEM_ID	Char	10	Upper		Item ID	Item ID
INT_ORDER_ID	Char	10	Upper		Internal Ord	Internal Order ID
VENDORID	Char	10	Upper		Vendor ID	Vendor ID

Figure 12-3 Function library record definition.

After you have added the fields to the record and saved it as EXAMPLE_AUTO, do not forget to build the table. After the table has been built, you can enter the following SQL insert statement using any of the SQL tools that work with your database. After you have committed the insert into the database we will then be ready to use the counter record in our PeopleCode.

```
insert into PS_EXAMPLE_AUTO values(1,1,1);
```

Function Library

We are now ready to begin creating a new derived record that we will use as our function library (FUNCLIB). All you need to do here to begin is to save the previous panel as FUNCLIB_EX_ORD. Figure 12-3 shows the new function library. Before we begin creating our functions there is one last step. Open the Records Properties dialog and change the type to `Derived/Work`. Figure 12-4 shows the TYPE tab of `FUNCLIB_EX_ORD`'s Record Properties dialog.

We are now ready to begin coding our autonumbering functions. We are going to add two PeopleCode functions to each of the `FieldFormula` events associated with the three fields. Each function will be specific for its field or record. *To begin, press the PEOPLECODE VIEW button with the record in focus.* Figure 12-5 shows the empty PeopleCode view of the record.

With the PeopleCode view open, double-click on the `Ffo` column of the `ITEM_ID` field. The PeopleCode editor will now be displayed with the field set to the `ITEM_ID` field displayed in the left drop-down list box

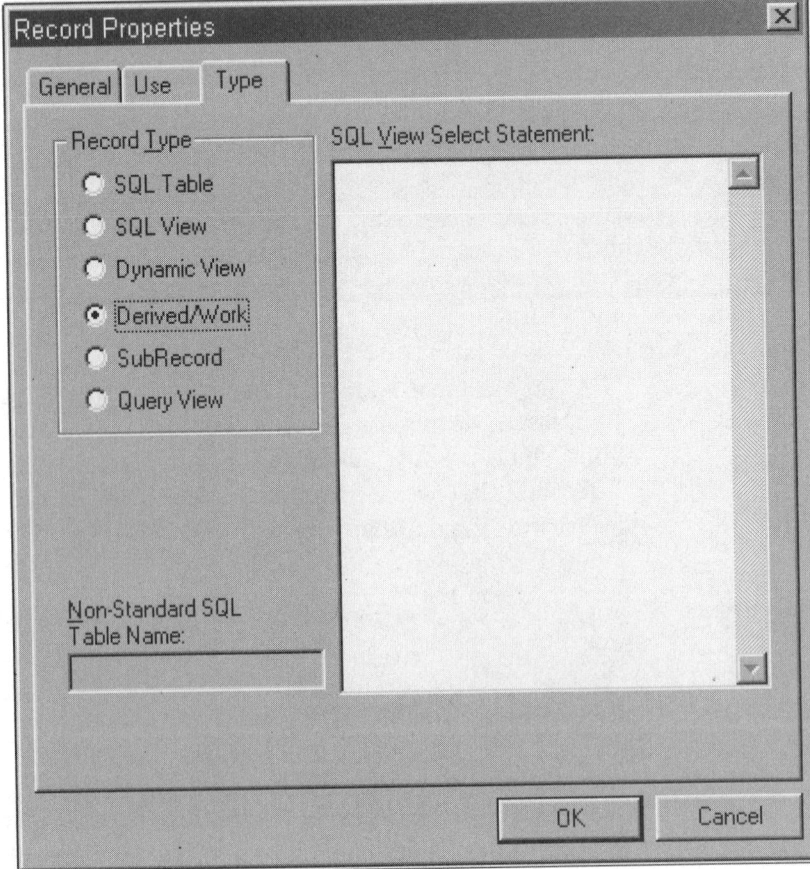

Figure 12-4 `FUNCLIB_EX_ORD` Record Properties dialog.

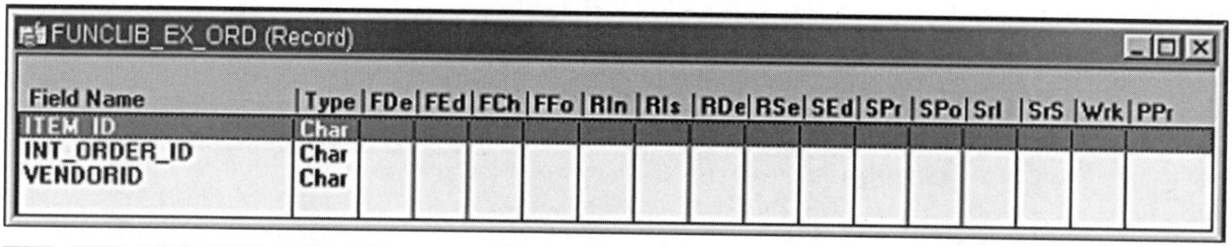

FUNCLIB_EX_ORD (Record)

Field Name	Type	FDe	FEd	FCh	FFo	RIn	RIs	RDe	RSe	SEd	SPr	SPo	SrI	SrS	Wrk	PPr
ITEM_ID	Char															
INT_ORDER_ID	Char															
VENDORID	Char															

Figure 12-5 FUNCLIB_EX_ORD empty PeopleCode view.

and FieldFormula displayed in the right drop-down list box. We can now begin creating our new function. Type the following code snippets into the respective events. The two functions we are going to be adding consist of a verify function that checks the uniqueness of the new identification number (id) and another function that retrieves the latest id and adds one to it.

```
/* FieldFormula Event for FUNCLIB_EXAMPLE_AUTO.ITEM_ID */
/* try_again
*  Example PeopleCode Function
*/
Function try_again(&ID) Returns boolean;
   SQLExec("select count(ITEM_ID) from PS_ITEMS WHERE ITEM_ID = :1",
&COUNT, &ID);
   If &COUNT < 1 Then
      Return False;
   Else
      Return True;
   End-If;
End-Function;

/* get_next_item_id
*  Example PeopleCode Function
*/
Function get_next_item_id() Returns number;
   &LOOP = True;
   Repeat
      SQLExec("select NITEM_ID from PS_EXAMPLE_AUTO", &IT_ID);
      &IT_ID = &IT_ID + 1;
      &ITEM_ID = &IT_ID;
      SQLExec("update PS_EXAMPLE_AUTO set NITEM_ID = :1", &IT_ID);
      &LOOP = try_again(&ITEM_ID);
   Until &LOOP = False;
   Return &IT_ID;
End-Function;

/* FieldFormula Event for FUNCLIB_EXAMPLE_AUTO.INT_ORDER_ID */

/* try_again
*  Example PeopleCode Function
```

```
*/
Function try_again(&ID) Returns boolean;
   SQLExec("select count(INT_ORD_ID) from PS_INT_ORDER WHERE
INT_ORD_ID = :1", &COUNT, &ID);
   If &COUNT < 1 Then
      Return False;
   Else
      Return True;
   End-If;
End-Function;

/* get_next_int_order_id
*  Example PeopleCode Function
*/
Function get_next_int_order_id() returns number;
   &LOOP = True;
   Repeat
      SQLExec("select NINT_ORDER_ID from PS_EXAMPLE_AUTO",
&IT_ORDER_ID);
      &IT_ORDER_ID = &IT_ORDER_ID + 1;
      &INT_ORDER_ID = &IT_ORDER_ID;
      SQLExec("update PS_EXAMPLE_AUTO set NINT_ORDER_ID = :1",
&IT_ORDER_ID);
      &LOOP = try_again(&IT_ORDER_ID);
   Until &LOOP = False;
return  &INT_ORDER_ID;
End-Function;

/* FieldFormula Event for FUNCLIB_EXAMPLE_AUTO.VENDORID */

/* try_again
*  Example PeopleCode Function
*/
Function try_again(&ID) Returns boolean;
   SQLExec("select count(VENDORID) from PS_VENDORS WHERE VENDORID =
:1", &COUNT, &ID);
   If &COUNT < 1 Then
      Return False;
   Else
      Return True;
   End-If;
End-Function;

/* get_next_vendorid
*  Example PeopleCode Function
*/
Function get_next_vendorid() Returns number;
   &LOOP = True;
   Repeat
      SQLExec("select NVENDORID from PS_EXAMPLE_AUTO", &VNDORID);
      &VNDORID = &VNDORID + 1;
      &VENDORID = &VNDORID;
      SQLExec("update PS_EXAMPLE_AUTO set NVENDORID = :1",
&VNDORID);
      &LOOP = try_again(&VNDORID);
   Until &LOOP = False;
   Return &VENDORID;
End-Function;
```

FUNCLIB_EX_ORD (Record)

Field Name	Type	FDe	FEd	FCh	FFo	RIn	RIs	RDe	RSe	SEd	SPr	SPo	SrI	SrS	Wrk	PPr
ITEM_ID	Char				Yes											
INT_ORDER_ID	Char				Yes											
VENDORID	Char				Yes											

Figure 12-6 `FUNCLIB_EX_ORD` PeopleCode view.

Figure 12-6 shows the PeopleCode view after you have entered the PeopleCode into the `FieldFormula` events for each field. The only new topic that you might have noticed in the PeopleCode that you just entered was the SQLExec function. SQLExec is very powerful. It enables you to perform selects, inserts, updates, and deletes to the PeopleSoft database instance to which you are connected. Since many PeopleSoft Operator ids use a database profile of a database system administrator, usually very few database-level constraints are placed on the PeopleSoft user. Therefore, developers need to be very careful when using SQLExec. The syntax for SQLExec is as follows.

1. **SQLExec** (`SQL Command`, `Bind Variables`, `Output`)
   - `SQL Command` `Select, Insert, Update, or Delete.`
   - `Bind Variables` `:1, :2, :3, ...`
   - `Output` `:1, :2, :3, ...`
2. **SQLExec with update, insert, and delete SQL commands can be run only in the following events:**
   - `SavePreChange`
   - `WorkFlow`
   - `SavePostChange`

Record Modification

We are now ready to modify our original records to have them call the function library we just created. Let's start by editing the `SavePreChange` event for items. Open the Items record definition. Select the PeopleCode view and then double-click on the `SPr` column. When the PeopleCode editor opens, type in the following PeopleCode:

```
/* SavePreChg for ITEMS.ITEM_ID
*
* Example PeopleCode
*/
Declare Function get_next_item_id PeopleCode FUNCLIB_EX_ORD.ITEM_ID
FieldFormula;

If ITEM_ID = "NEXT" Or
      ITEM_ID = "next" Or
      ITEM_ID = "Next" Then
   &ITEM = get_next_item_id();
   ITEM_ID = &ITEM;
End-If;
```

After you have entered the PeopleCode for the Item id, proceed with the final two PeopleCode record modifications:

```
/* SavePreChg for VENDORS.VENDORID
*
* Example PeopleCode
*/
Declare Function get_next_vendorid PeopleCode FUNCLIB_EX_ORD.VENDORID
FieldFormula;

If VENDORID = "NEXT" Or
   VENDORID = "next" Or
   VENDORID = "Next" Then
   &VENDOR = get_next_vendorid();
 VENDORID = &VENDOR;
End-If;

/* SavePreChg for INT_ORDER.INT_ORDER_ID
*
* Example PeopleCode
*/
Declare Function get_next_int_order_id PeopleCode
FUNCLIB_EX_ORD.INT_ORDER_ID FieldFormula;

If INT_ORDER_ID = "NEXT" Or
 INT_ORDER_ID = "next" Or
 INT_ORDER_ID = "Next" Then
   & INT_ORDER = get_next_int_order_id();
 INT_ORDER_ID = &INT_ORDER;
End-If;
```

With the record modifications complete, you are now ready to begin testing your work. Figures 12-7 through 12-9 show an example of adding a new vendor with automatic numbering.

You are now ready to begin customizing the code you already entered. A nice feature might be to pad the characters. Many more enhancements can be applied to our example application. Please take the time to try a few of them on your own.

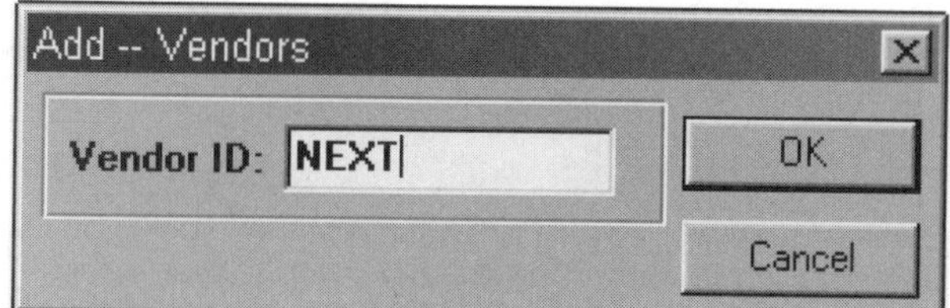

Figure 12-7
Add Vendors dialog.

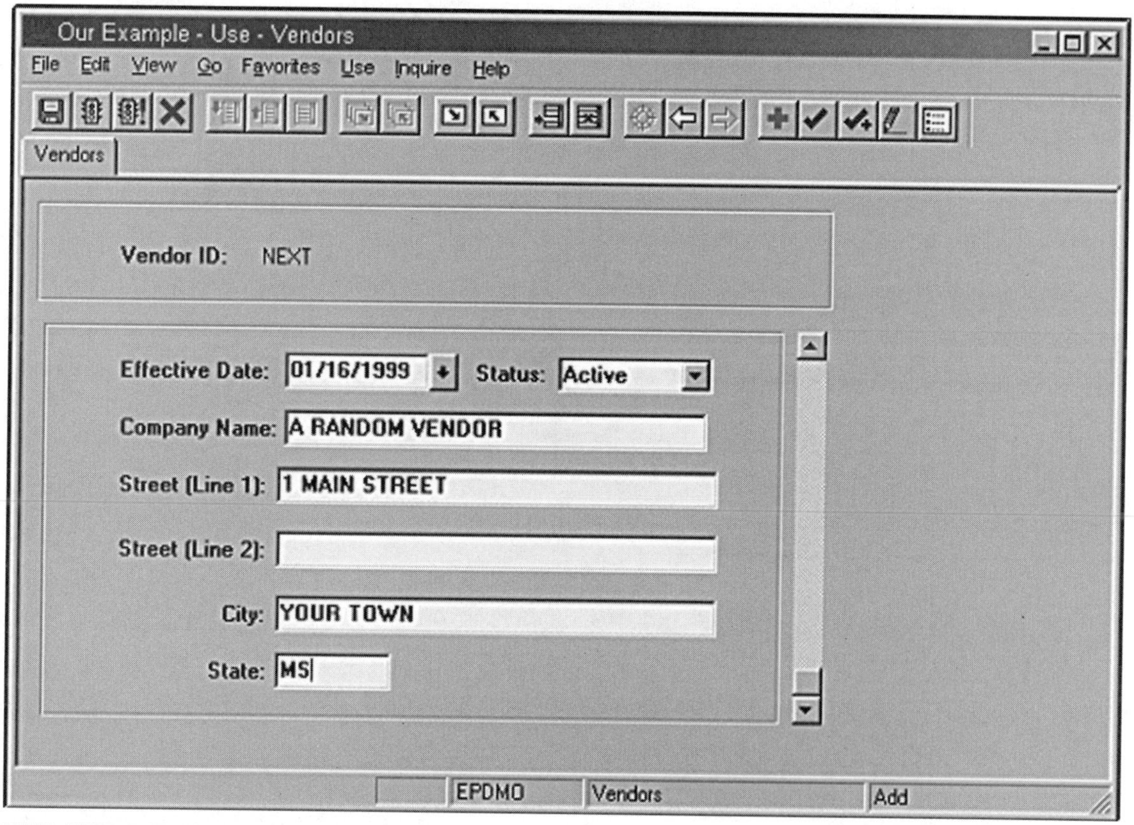

Figure 12-8 Vendors panel.

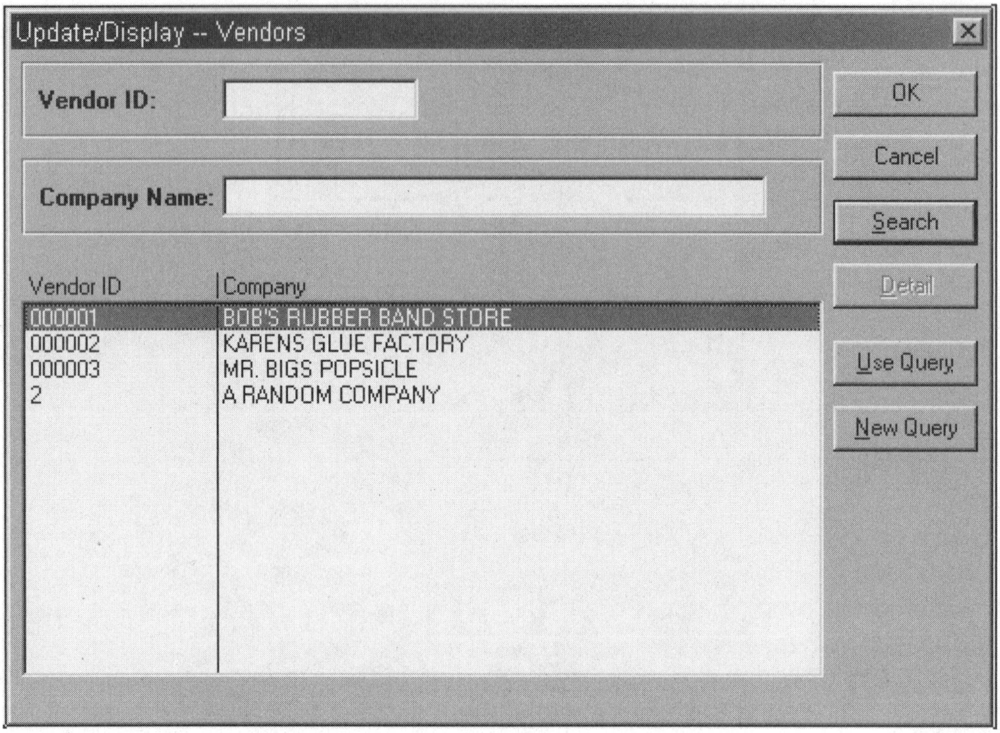

Figure 12-9 Update/Display dialog for Vendors.

PART 4

Query and Reporting Tools

In this part of the book we review PeopleSoft Query, Crystal Reports, PeopleSoft NVision, the Process Scheduler, and SQR. Chapter 14 discusses Query, Crystal Reports, and nVision. Chapter 15 discusses PeopleSoft's Process Scheduler and how PeopleSoft panels interact with SQR programs via run control tables. Chapter 15 discusses what SQR is and how to execute SQR programs. In addition, Chapter 15 discusses in detail how to program with SQR as well as cover most of the commands and features and many of the options available to those commands. *This is not intended to be a complete SQR language reference manual.*

CHAPTER 13

Query, Crystal Reports, and nVision

PeopleSoft Query

PeopleSoft Query allows the user access to the data in the database without utilizing SQL statements. To get to PeopleSoft Query from the Application Designer, select GO, PEOPLETOOLS, QUERY. This brings up the initial Query screen shown in Figure 13-1.

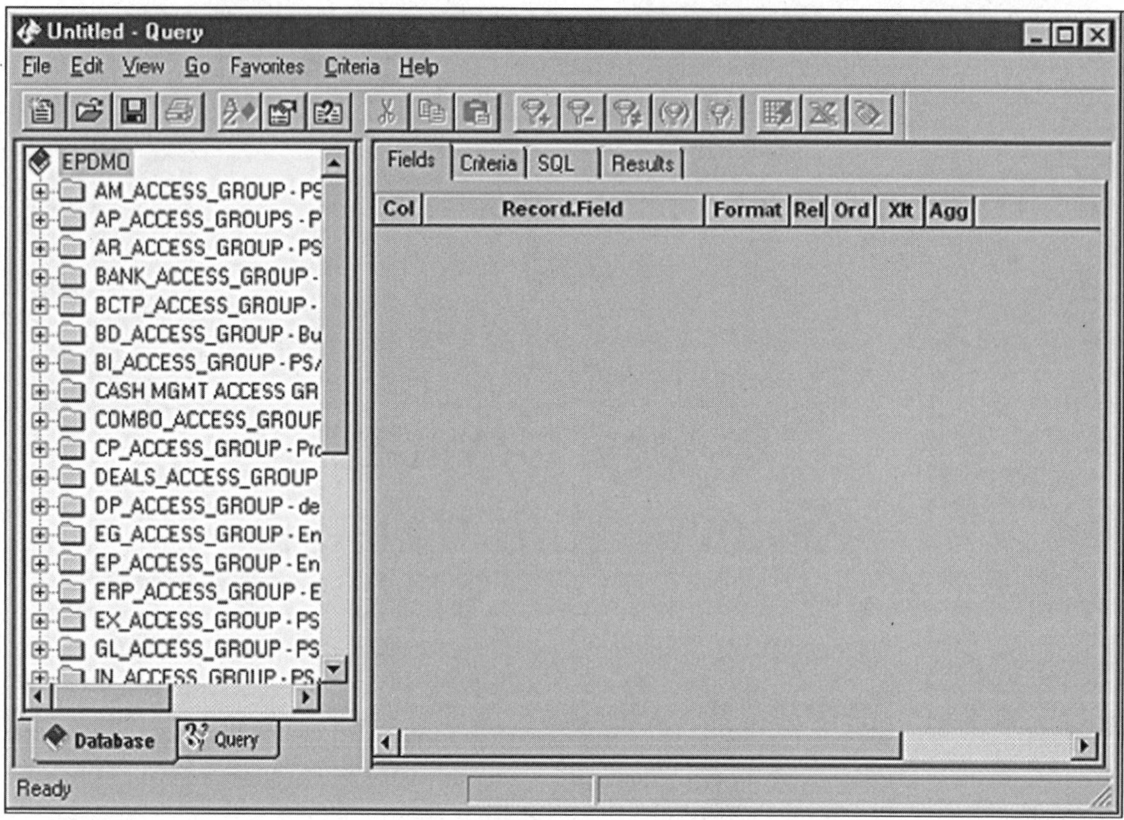

Figure 13-1 Initial screen of PeopleSoft Query.

This initial screen is divided into two sections. The left section is called the *component view* and the right section is called the *designer view*. The left section (component view) has two tabs at the bottom of the screen: the DATABASE tab and the QUERY tab. When the DATABASE tab is selected, a list of all records (database tables) the user has access to is displayed. When the QUERY tab is selected, the current query is displayed. The right section (designer view) contains four tabs: the FIELDS tab, the CRITERIA tab, the SQL tab, and the RESULTS Tab.

PeopleSoft Query allows queries to be created and saved so that they can be run again by the same operator or by another operator.

Running an Existing Query

To run a query

1. Select FILE, OPEN and select the query from the list of available queries.
2. Select FILE, RUN and the query will be run. When a query is run, the results are displayed on the RESULTS tab.

Creating a Query

To create a query, perform the following steps:

1. Select the record(s) (or tables). To do this be sure that the DATABASE tab is selected. Then select a record from the list of records on the left side of the screen by double-clicking on the record name. A record could also be selected by dragging it to the right side of the screen into the designer view or by selecting EDIT, ADD RECORD for the first record or EDIT, NEW JOIN for other records. Once a record is selected, the QUERY tab will automatically be displayed to show that the record was added to the query. An alias is assigned to the selected record at the top of the query tree. For example, Figure 13-2 shows the database tab and record `REPLEN_RQST_INV`, which is selected by selecting EDIT, ADD. Once the record is selected, the QUERY tab is displayed as shown in Figure 13-3. Note that there is `A` = REPLEN_RQST_INV at the top of the query tree. The `A` is the alias for `REPLEN_RQST_INV`. If another record is selected, its alias would be `B` (see Fig. 13-4).
2. Select the fields from the selected records. To do this go to the QUERY tab and double-click on each field desired in the query one at a time. The fields are displayed on the right side of the screen (designer view) as shown in Figure 13-5. The view preferences are set to display fields in the select list only. See note below on preferences. To remove a field from the query, double-click on the column number on the FIELD tab.

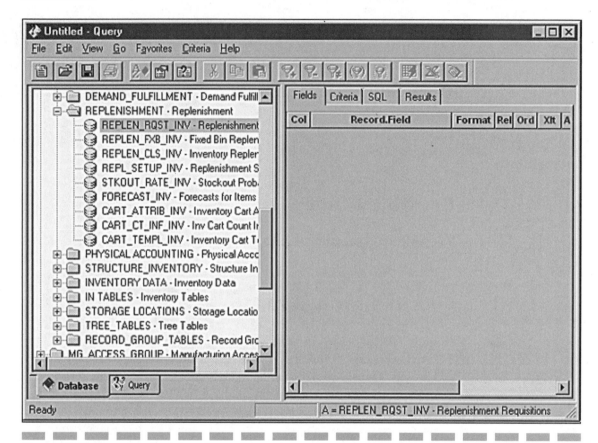

Figure 13-2 DATABASE tab of Query's component view with a record selected for a query.

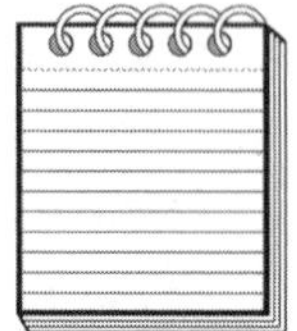

NOTE: *To change what is displayed in the component view or designer view, the user can modify the view preferences by selecting* VIEW, PREFERENCES. *There are three tabs on the Preferences dialog box: the* GENERAL *tab, the* COMPONENT VIEW *tab, and the* DESIGNER VIEW *tab. The* GENERAL *tab allows the user to select autojoin. The* COMPONENT VIEW *tab allows the user to turn the show access groups option on or off. The* DESIGNER VIEW *tab allows the user to specify what fields are displayed in the designer section of the screen and how they are sorted. The fields displayed can be all the fields in the selected record, the fields in the select list, the fields in the order by SQL clause, only the fields with selection criteria, or all fields. The fields can be sorted by record, field, column order, field name, or order by. The* DESIGNER VIEW *tab also allows the user to select whether*

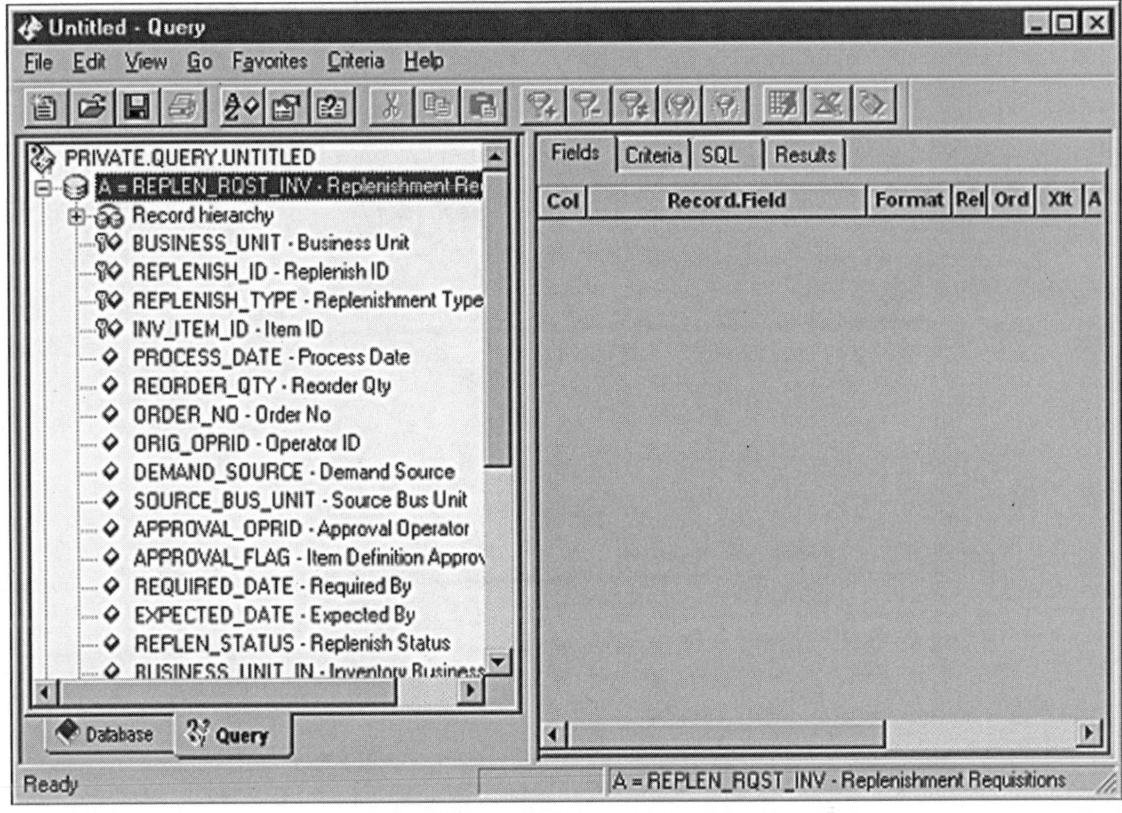

Figure 13-3 The QUERY tab is automatically displayed when a record is selected.

to show row headings in the RESULT tab and whether to run the query when the RESULT tab is selected. Figure 13-6 shows the DESIGNER VIEW tab of the Preferences dialog box.

3. Enter any selection criteria required for the query on the CRITERIA tab. Selection criteria limit the number of rows returned by the query. This is basically the WHERE clause of the select statement in SQL. To enter selection criteria, you must be on the CRITERIA tab and then follow the steps below:
   - Select the field that will be used in the selection criteria by dragging it from the component view section of the screen and dropping it onto the CRITERIA tab under expression 1.

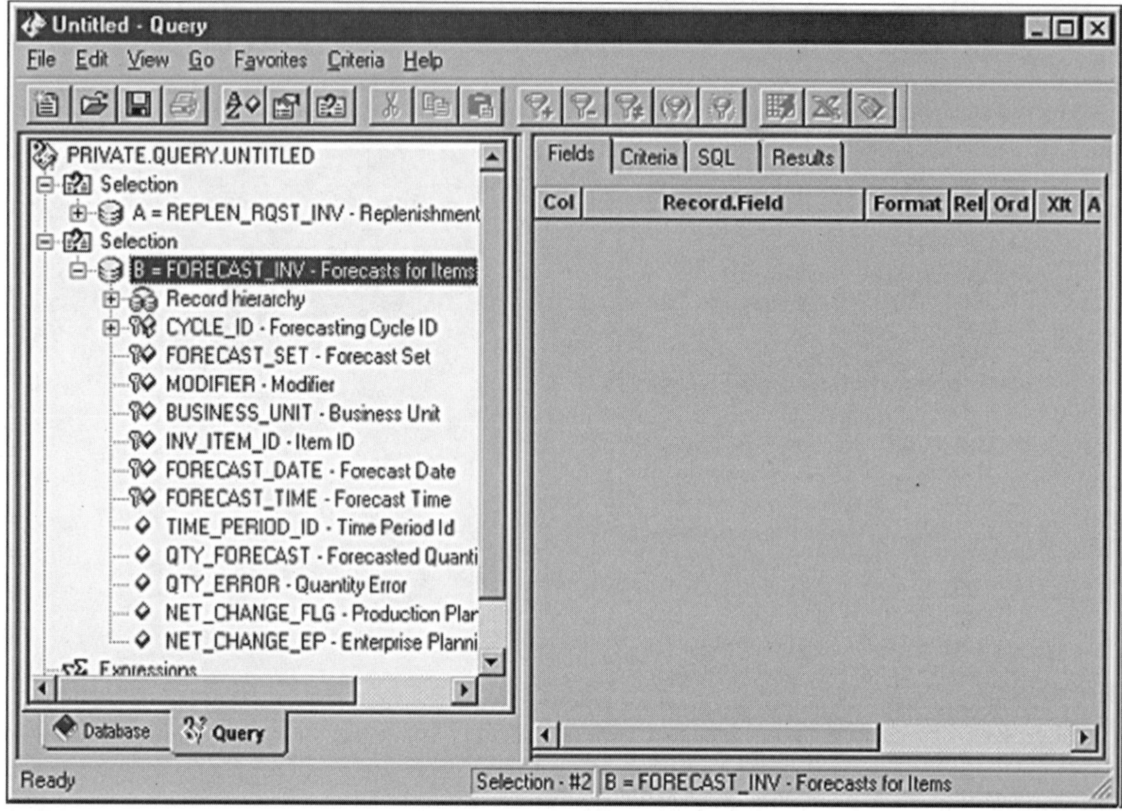

Figure 13-4 The QUERY tab with two records selected.

- Select the operator (equal to, not equal to, greater than, etc.) from the operator drop-down list.
- Right-click on the expression 2 field of the criteria, and a popup menu will appear that allows you to enter what type of value expression 2 will be. The choices are field, expression, constant, subquery, or prompt as shown in Figure 13-7. Once the type is selected, then the value for expression 2 is entered. Entering this value varies depending on what type was selected. Figure 13-8 shows what happens when a type of constant was selected. The Constant dialog that is displayed allows you to enter a value for the criteria. Figure 13-9 shows the completed CRITERIA tab.
- Verify the SQL by moving to the SQL tab. Figure 13-10 shows the completed SQL.

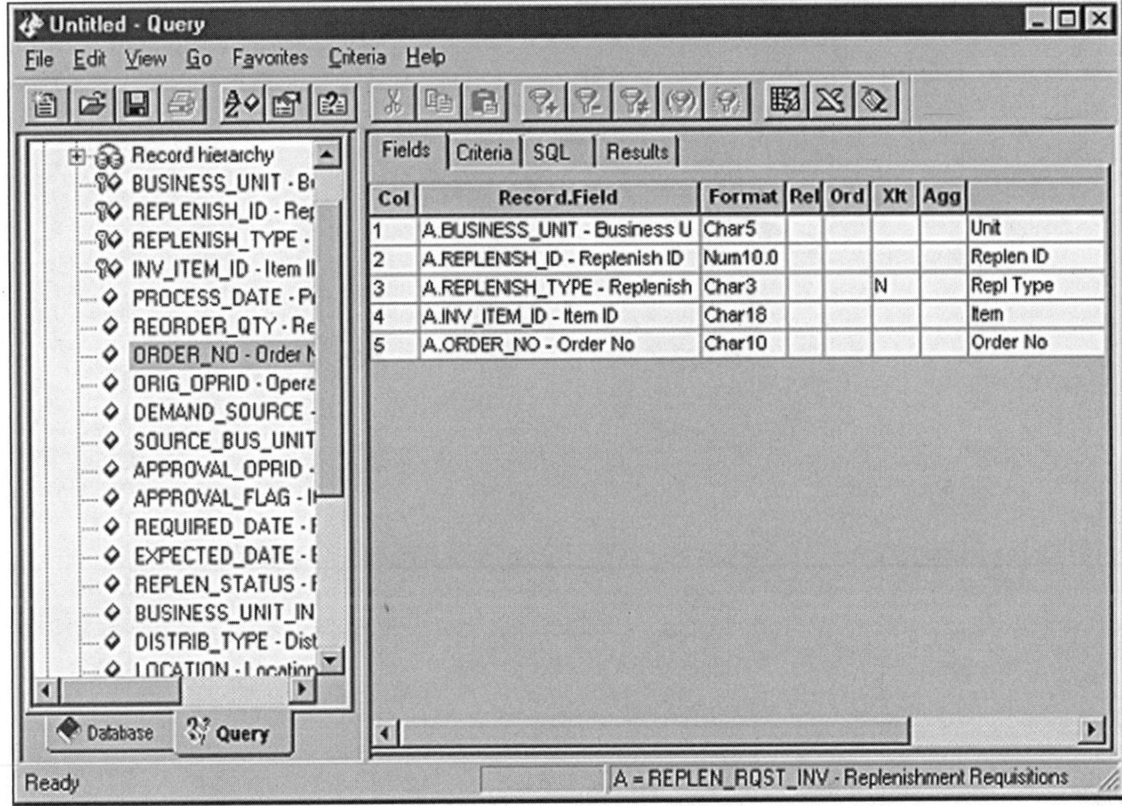

Figure 13-5 The FIELDS tab of the designer view displays the fields selected for the query.

- Run the query to view the results. Move to the RESULTS tab and press the RUN QUERY icon.

4. Save the query by selecting FILE, SAVE AS. The Save Query As dialog box appears as shown in Figure 13-11. Enter the name of and a description of the query and click on OK.

Running the Newly Created Query

The query can be run so that the results are displayed on the RESULTS tab, the results are passed to Crystal Reports, or the results are passed to Microsoft Excel depending on which RUN option is selected from FILE.

If you run the query by selecting FILE, RUN CURRENT QUERY, the output of the query is displayed on the RESULTS tab as shown in Figure 13-12.

Figure 13-6 The DESIGNER VIEW tab of the Preferences dialog box.

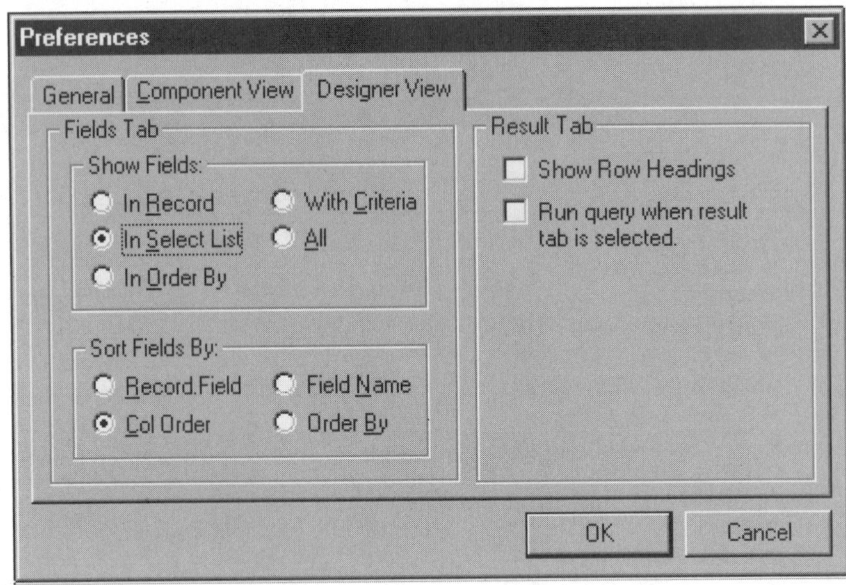

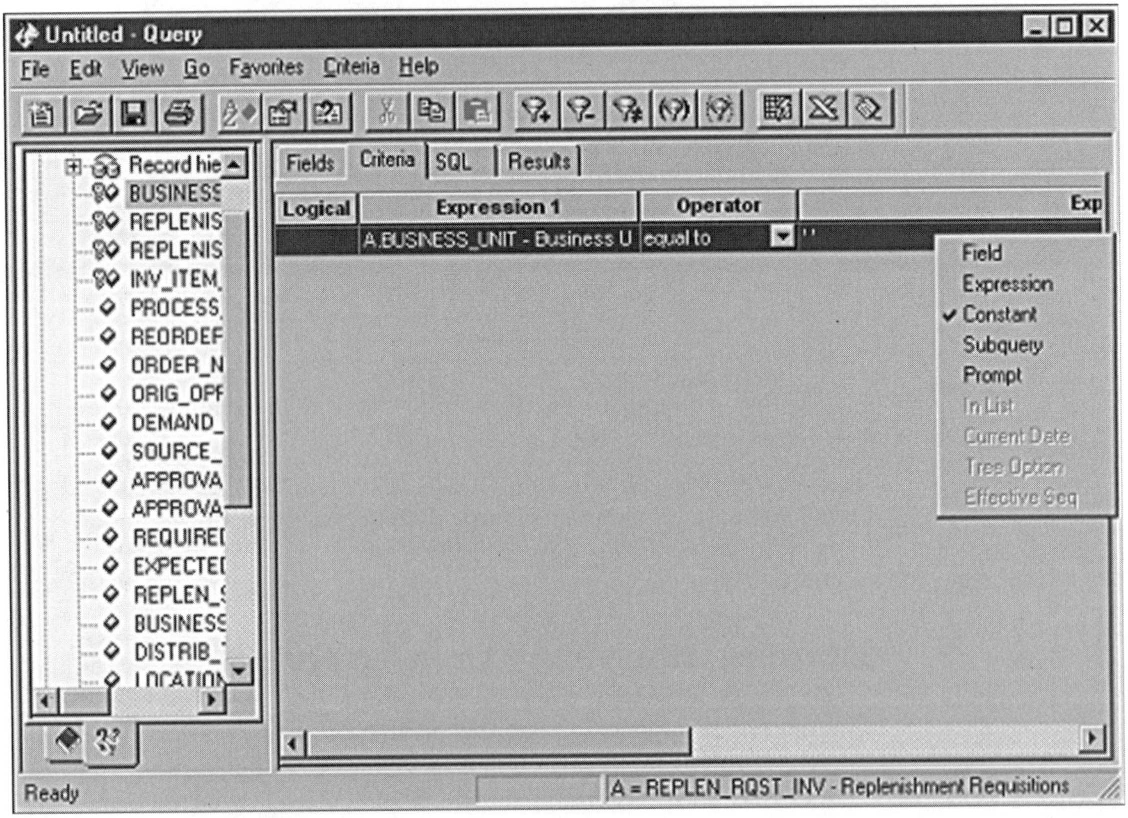

Figure 13-7 Entering selection criteria.

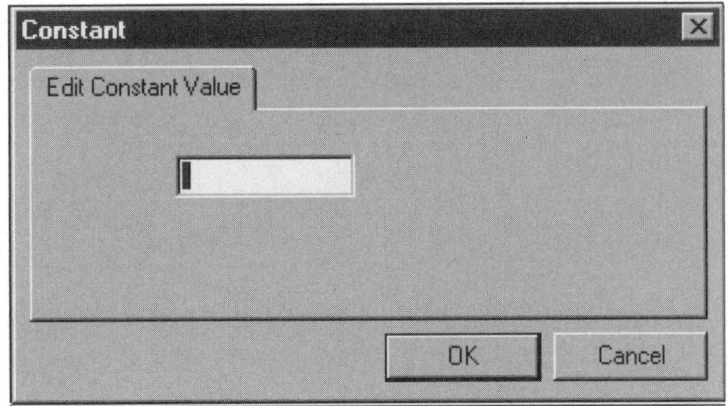

Figure 13-8 Entering a constant value for expression 2 of the selection criteria.

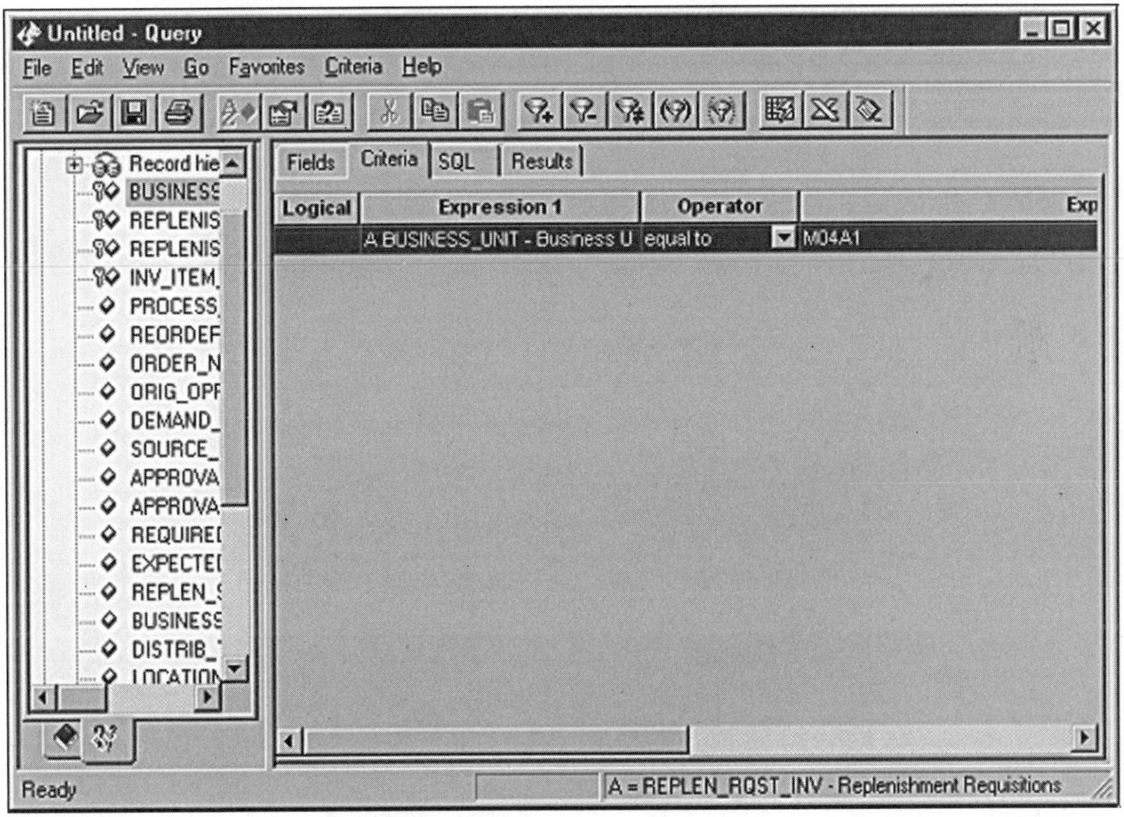

Figure 13-9 The selection criteria is set up.

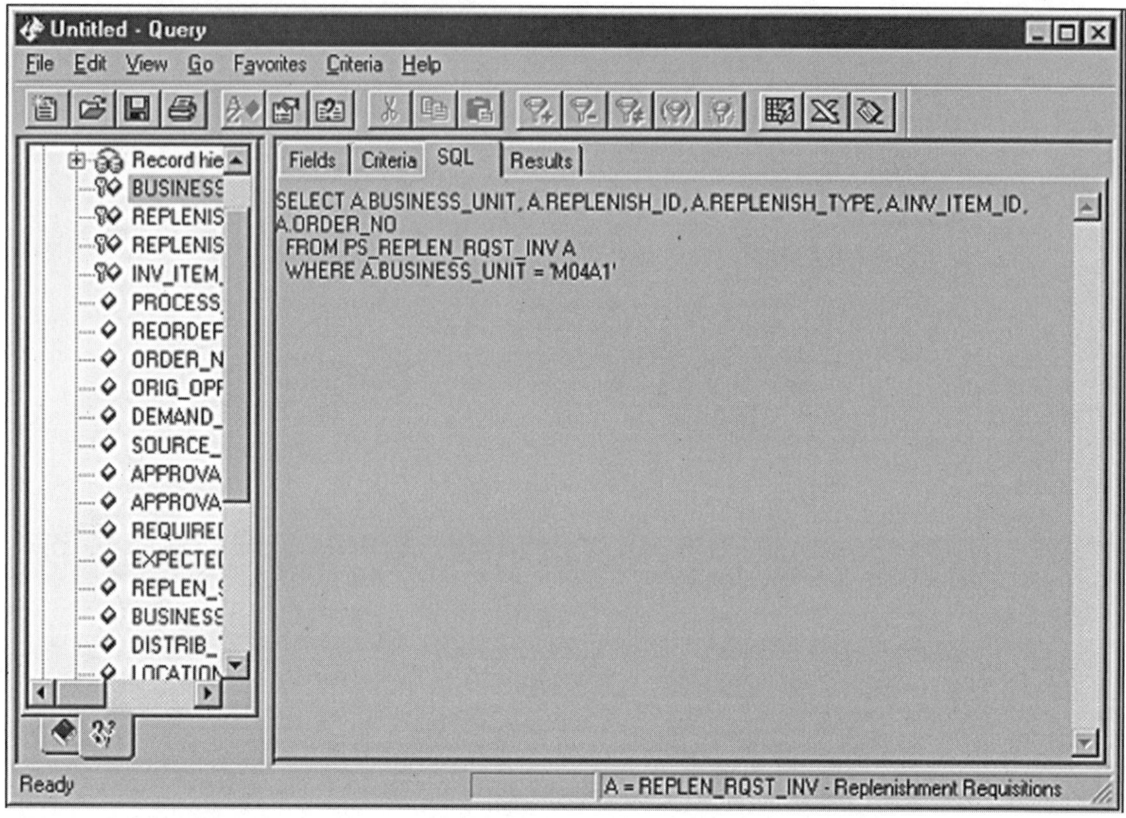

Figure 13-10 The SQL tab shows the SQL for this query.

Figure 13-11 The Save Query As dialog box.

Save Query As

Owner: PRIVATE

Type: QUERY

Query Name: OUR_EXAMPLE

Description:

OK Cancel

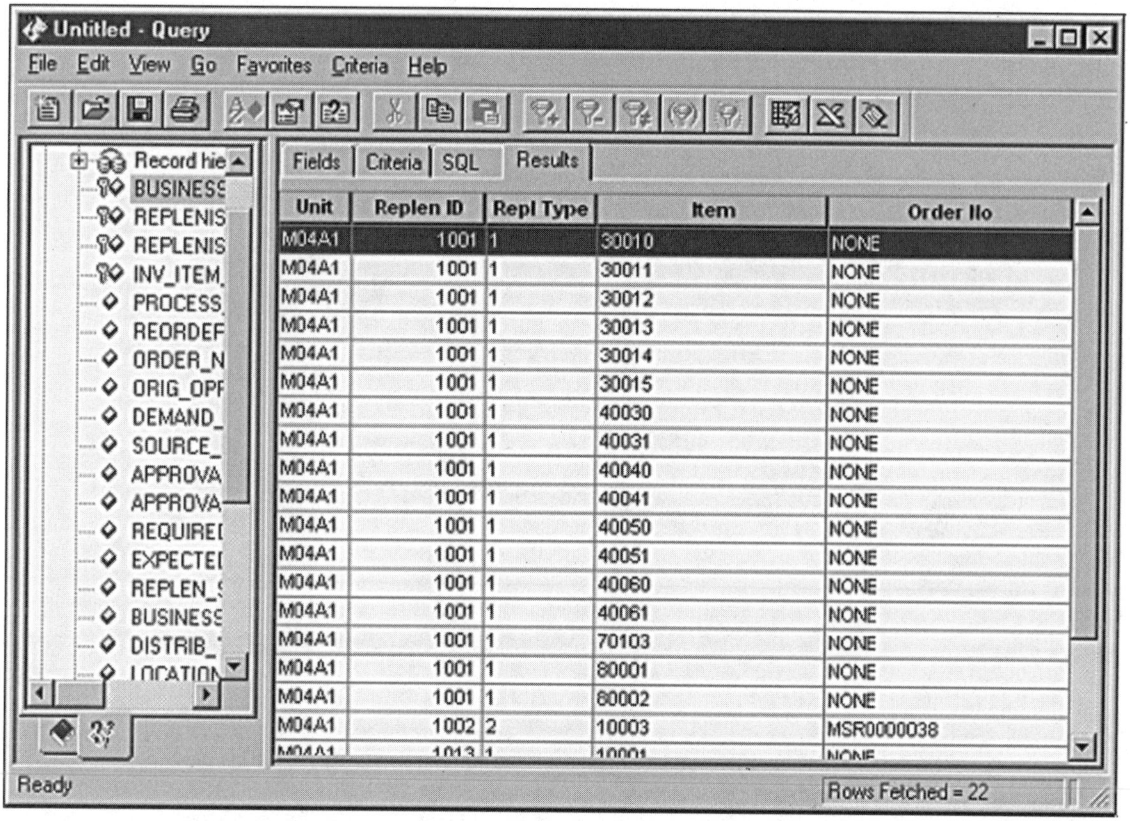

Figure 13-12 The RESULTS tab shows the output of the query.

Formatting Query Output on the RESULT Tab

If the field name on the QUERY tab is double clicked on, the Field Properties dialog box appears as shown in Figures 13-13 through 13-16. The Field Properties dialog box allows the user to format the output of the query.

The Field Properties dialog box has four tabs: COLUMN# tab, HEADING tab, ORDER BY tab, and AGGREGATE tab. You can change the field properties as desired.

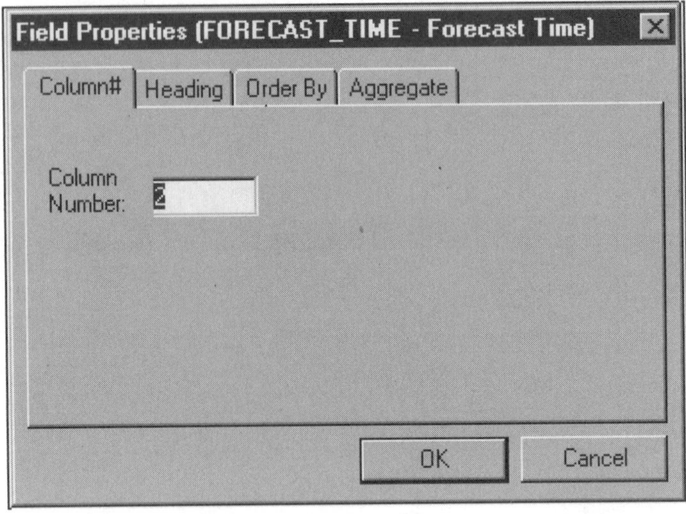

Figure 13-13 COLUMN# tab of the Field Properties dialog box.

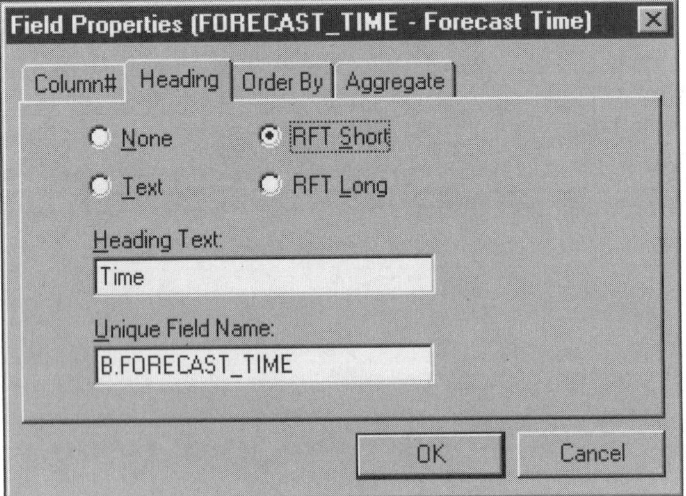

Figure 13-14 HEADING tab of the Field Properties dialog box.

Crystal Reports

The results from the query run by PeopleSoft Query can be passed to Crystal Reports by selecting FILE, RUN TO CRYSTAL instead of FILE, RUN CURRENT QUERY. When the query above is run by selecting RUN TO CRYS-

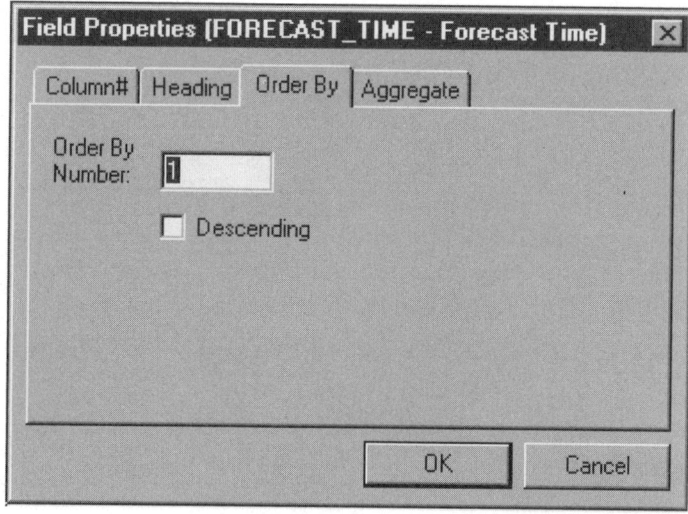

Figure 13-15 ORDER BY tab of the Field Properties dialog box.

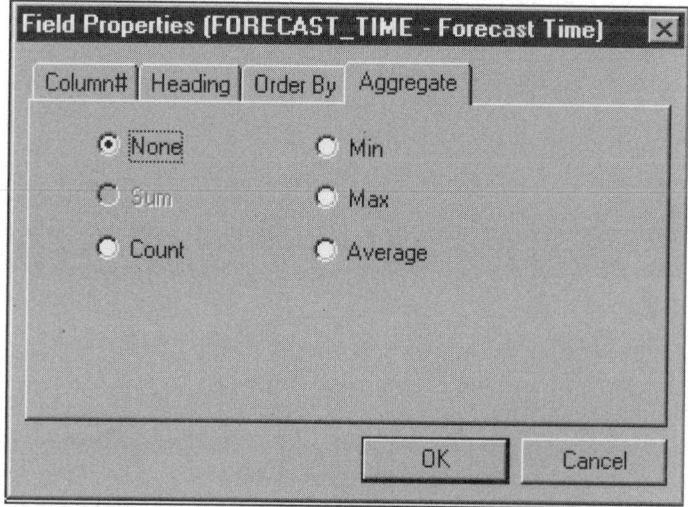

Figure 13-16 AGGREGATE tab of the Field Properties dialog box.

TAL, a report template is created as shown in Figure 13-17. Notice that all the fields from the query named OUR_EXAMPLE are displayed on this template.

The report header, page header, report footer, and page footer can be modified as desired using Crystal Reports menu options.

The report can be viewed in print preview by selecting FILE, PRINT

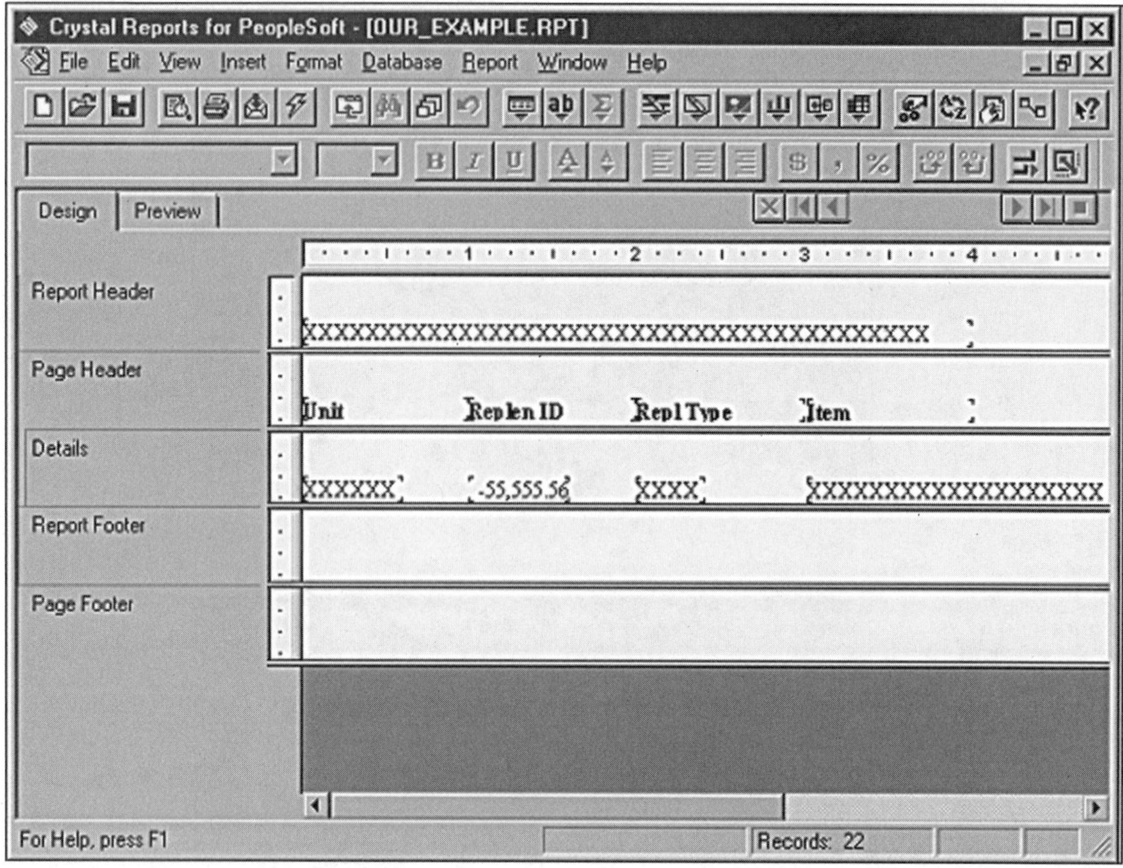

Figure 13-17 Crystal Report template of OUR_EXAMPLE query.

PREVIEW. The report, including the detailed rows of data, appears on the screen as shown in Figure 13-18.

When the report is to your satisfaction, save it and print it.

Exporting Queries to Microsoft's Excel

The results from the query can also be passed to Microsoft's Excel via PeopleSoft's nVision by selecting FILE, RUN TO EXCEL. When nVision is run, it automatically launches Microsoft Excel. Once in Excel, the user

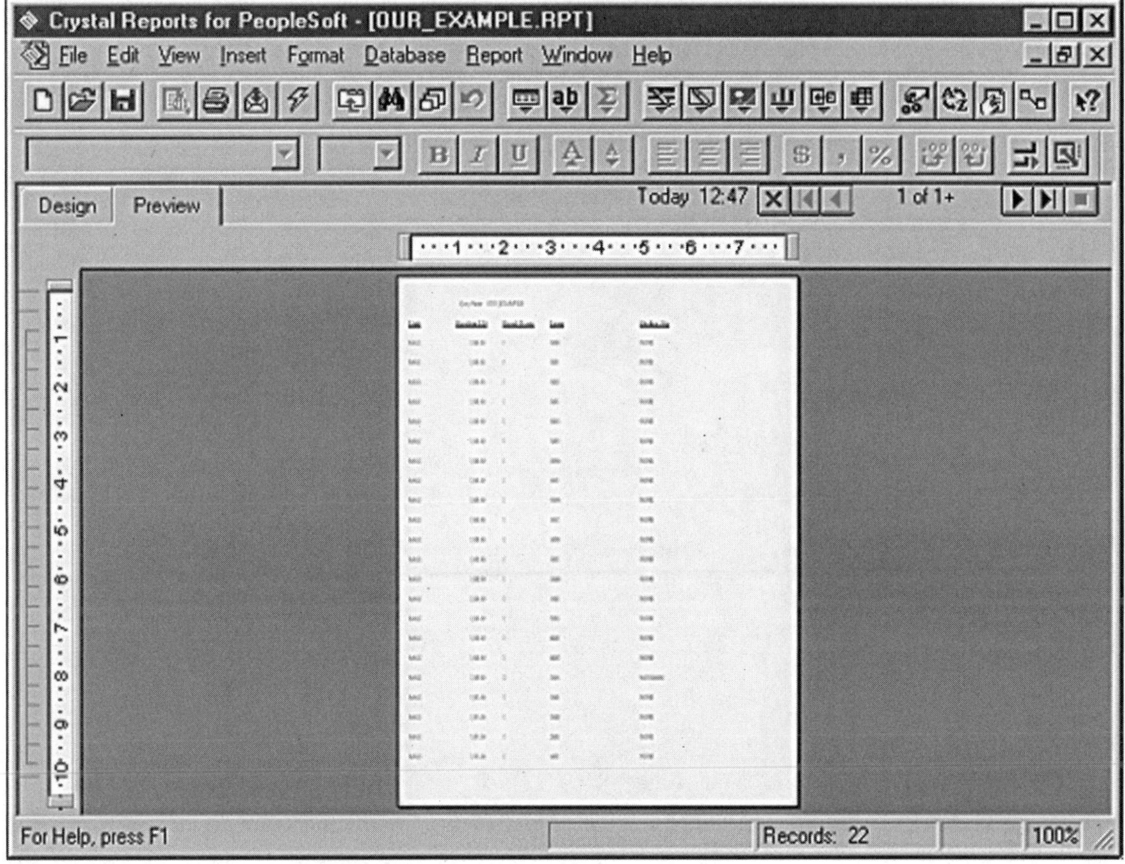

Figure 13-18 Crystal reports print preview of the report.

can work on the Excel spreadsheet as desired utilizing all of Microsoft Excel's features. See Figure 13-19.

nVision can also be run from PeopleTools by selecting GO, PEOPLETOOLS, NVISION.

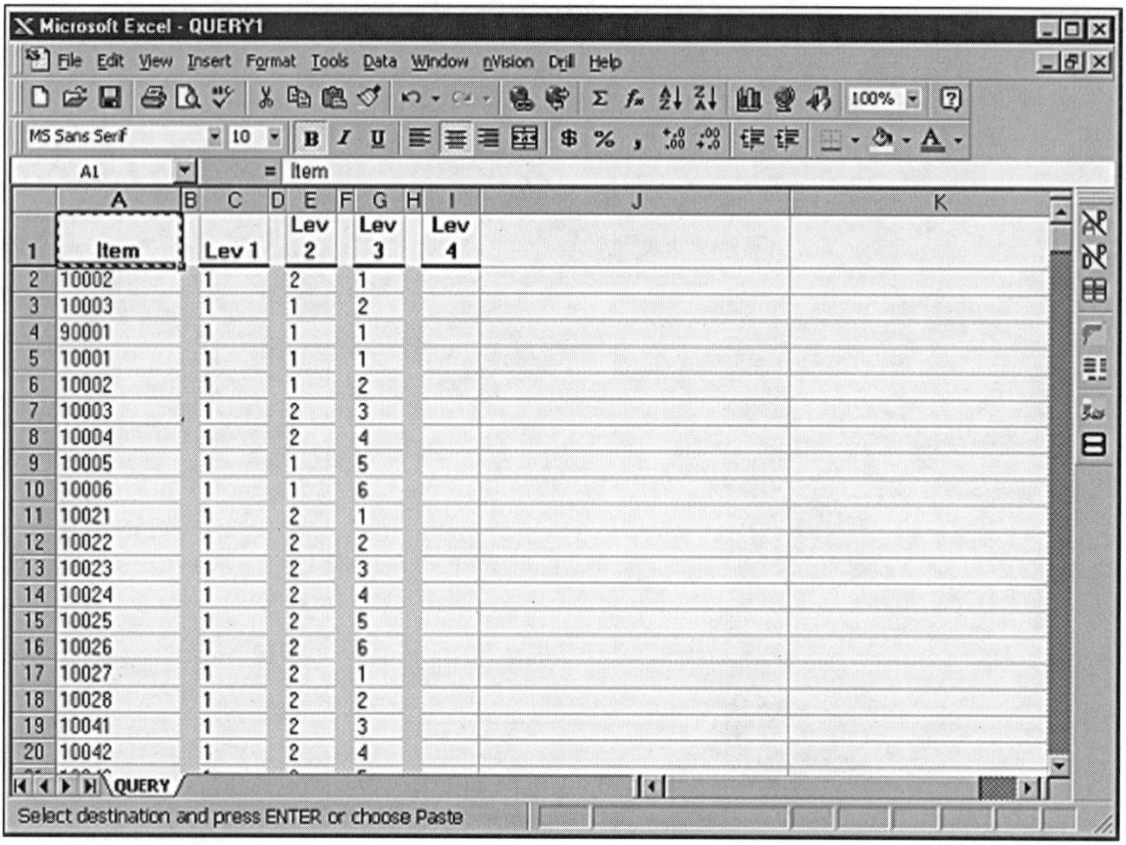

Microsoft Excel - QUERY1

	A	C	E	G	I
1	Item	Lev 1	Lev 2	Lev 3	Lev 4
2	10002	1	2	1	
3	10003	1	1	2	
4	90001	1	1	1	
5	10001	1	1	1	
6	10002	1	1	2	
7	10003	1	2	3	
8	10004	1	2	4	
9	10005	1	1	5	
10	10006	1	1	6	
11	10021	1	2	1	
12	10022	1	2	2	
13	10023	1	2	3	
14	10024	1	2	4	
15	10025	1	2	5	
16	10026	1	2	6	
17	10027	1	2	1	
18	10028	1	2	2	
19	10041	1	2	3	
20	10042	1	2	4	

QUERY

Select destination and press ENTER or choose Paste

Figure 13-19 Query exported to Excel via nVision.

CHAPTER 14

Process Scheduler

This chapter discusses the Process Scheduler from the perspective of the developer.

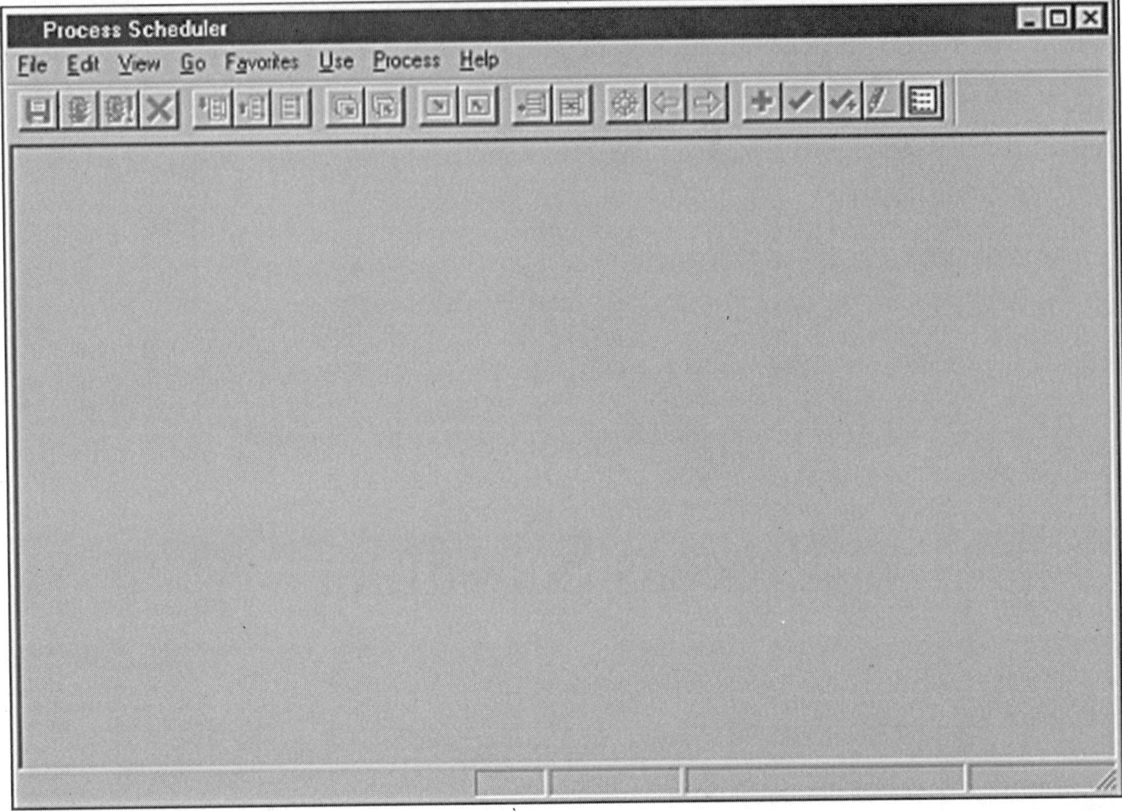

Figure 14-1 Initial screen displayed when the Process Scheduler is displayed.

In order to launch the Process Scheduler, select START, PROGRAMS, PEOPLESOFT, PEOPLETOOLS. Sign on, and once in the Application Designer, select GO, PEOPLETOOLS, PROCESS SCHEDULER. Figure 14-1 shows what the initial Process Scheduler screen looks like.

We will now discuss the Use menu.

Use menu

The Use menu contains the following menu options:

- Process types
- Process definitions

- Process servers
- Job definitions
- Process system

At any time, the CANCEL icon can be clicked on to return to the main Process Scheduler screen.

Process Types

Refer to Figure 14-2 to see the Use menu. In this figure, PROCESS TYPES is selected. The developer can select to add a process type or to update and/or display a process type. There must be a unique process type for

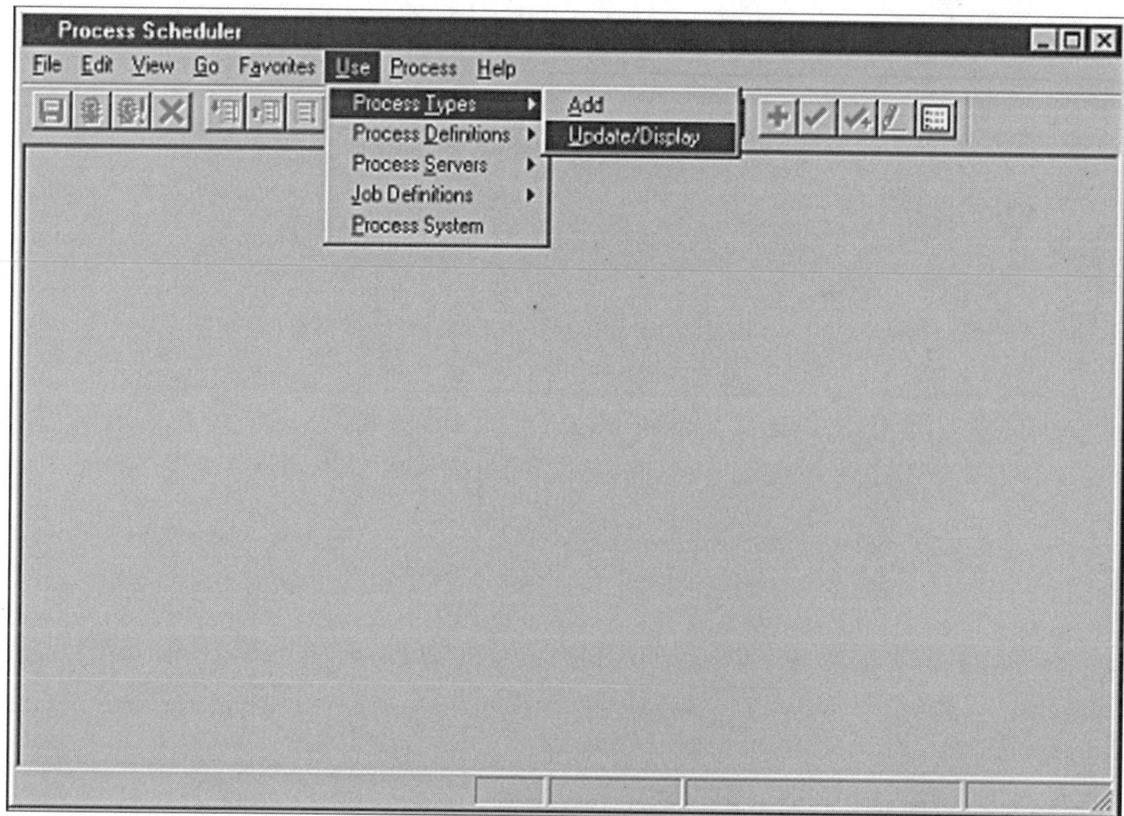

Figure 14-2 Use menu of the Process Scheduler.

each database and operating system combination. Since many process types are available with PeopleSoft, this step may not be required for your system since your combination of database and operating system may already be included in the existing process types. However, should you need to add one or wish to modify an existing one, select PROCESS TYPES off the Use menu and choose ADD or UPDATE/DISPLAY. We will discuss UPDATE/DISPLAY here.

When UPDATE/DISPLAY PROCESS TYPE is selected, the Update/Display Process Types dialog box appears as shown in Figure 14-3. The developer must enter the process type, the operating system platform, the database platform, and a process type description. To view the valid values for each input, click on the down arrow next to the field. For example,

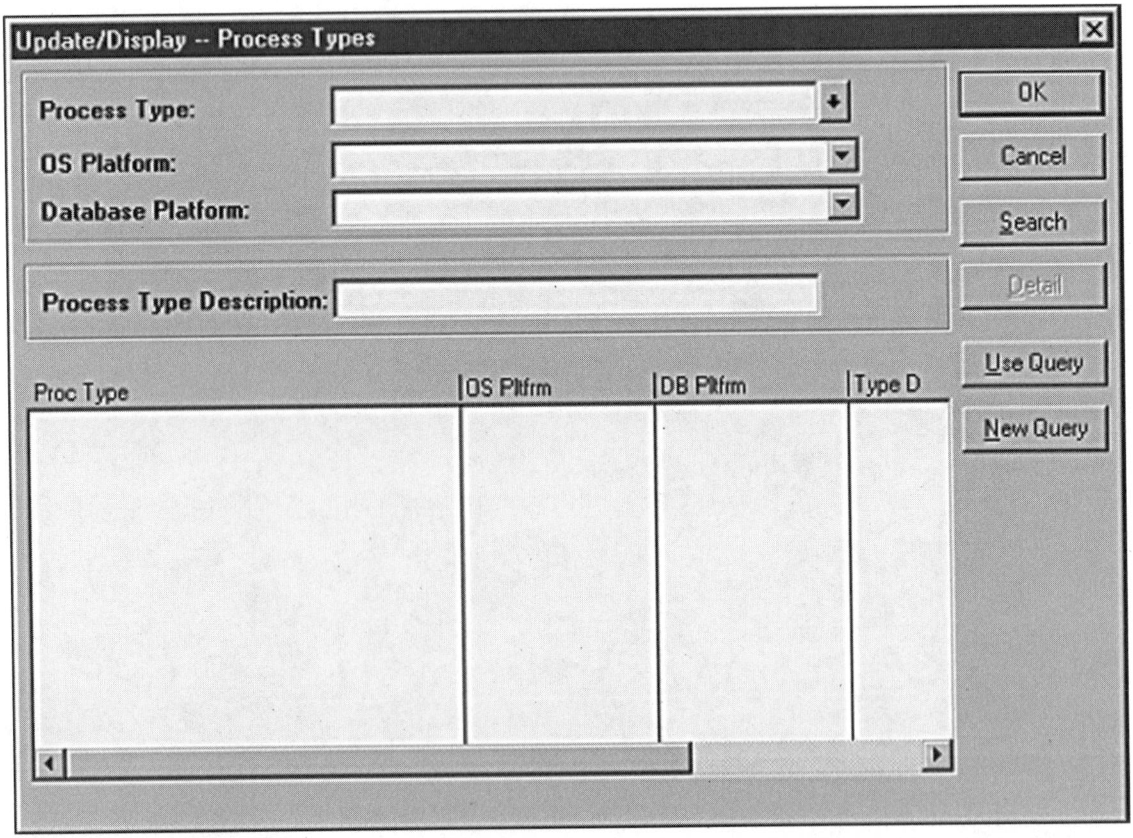

Update/Display -- Process Types

Process Type:
OS Platform:
Database Platform:
Process Type Description:

OK
Cancel
Search
Detail
Use Query
New Query

Proc Type	OS Pltfrm	DB Pltfrm	Type D

Figure 14-3 Update/Display Process Types dialog box.

the valid values for the process type field appear in the Valid Values dialog box as shown in Figure 14-4. The valid values include Crystal, COBOL SQL, SQR process, and SQR report. The operating system platforms include UNIX, VMS, and NT. The database platform values include Sybase, ORACLE, DB2, etc.

If we select SQR Report as the process type, the Update/Display Process Type dialog box appears with the selected process type. The developer must click on SEARCH, and the screen will be updated as shown in Figure 14-5. Select the desired process type definition from the list in the window and double-click. Figure 14-6 shows the TYPE DEFINITION tab that is displayed next.

The TYPE DEFINITION tab allows the developer to define the command-line path and executable that will be run, the working directory path, and the output destination for the process type definition being modified. In addition, SQR parameters can be set up by clicking on the SQR PARMS button. Figure 14-7 shows the SQR Parameters dialog box, which allows the developer to enter the SQR connect string, SQR flags, SQR run control parameters, search path, and SQT working directory. Figure 14-8 shows the Operating System Parameters dialog box that appears when the OS PARMS button is clicked on.

Figure 14-4
Valid values for the Process Type field.

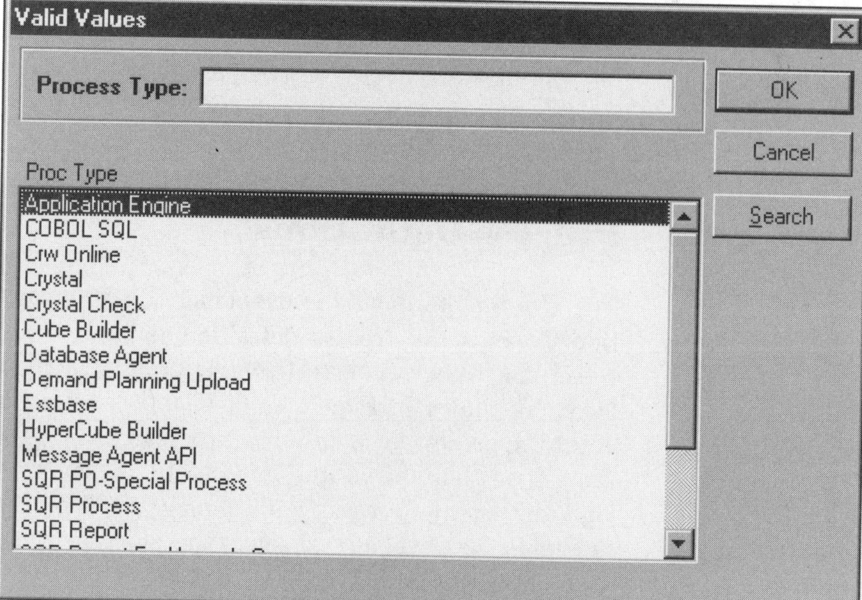

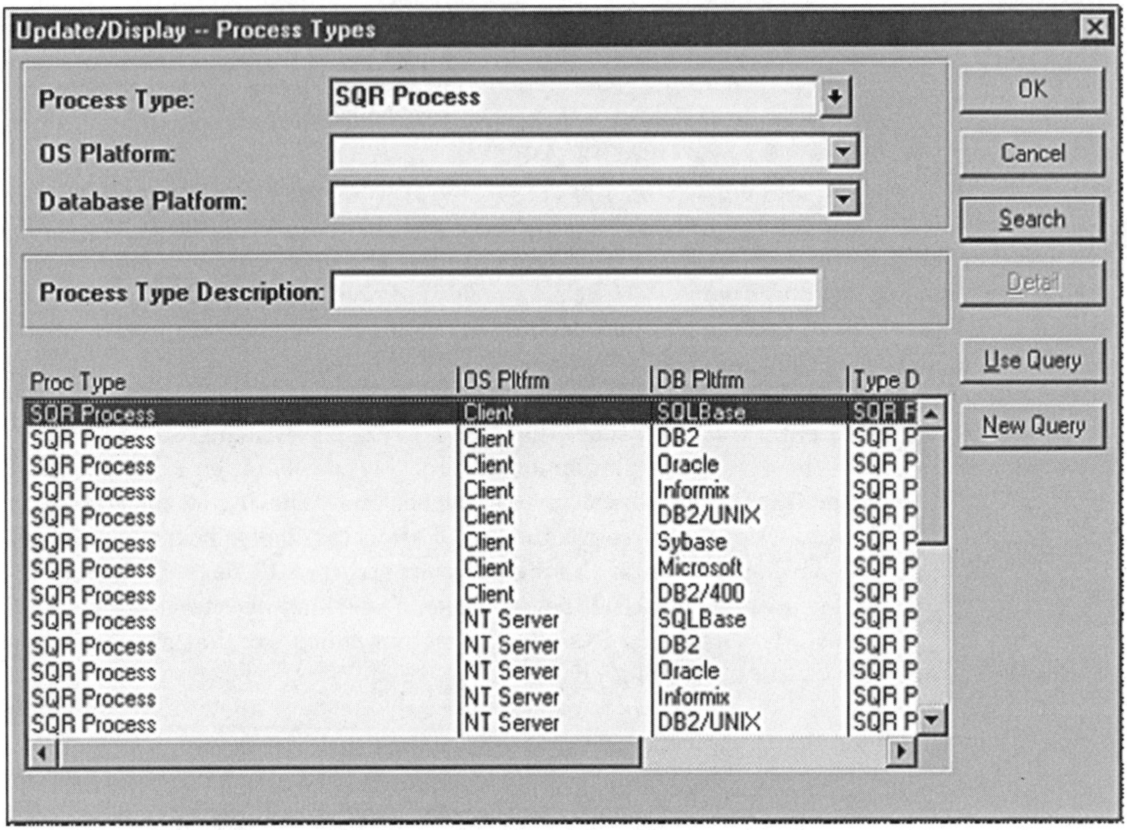

Figure 14-5 List of process types is displayed in the window after the process type field is selected from the Valid Values dialog.

Process Definitions

The Use menu allows the developer to add or modify a process definition. To get to the Process Definition dialog box of the Process Scheduler, select USE, PROCESS DEFINITION, PROCESS DEFINITION (ADD or UPDATE/DISPLAY), as shown in Figure 14-9. If ADD is selected, the developer must enter the process type and new process name in the Add Process Definitions dialog box shown in Figure 14-10. If UPDATE/DISPLAY is selected, the Update/Display Process Definitions dialog box (Fig. 14-11) is displayed to enable the developer to select the process type and search for all the

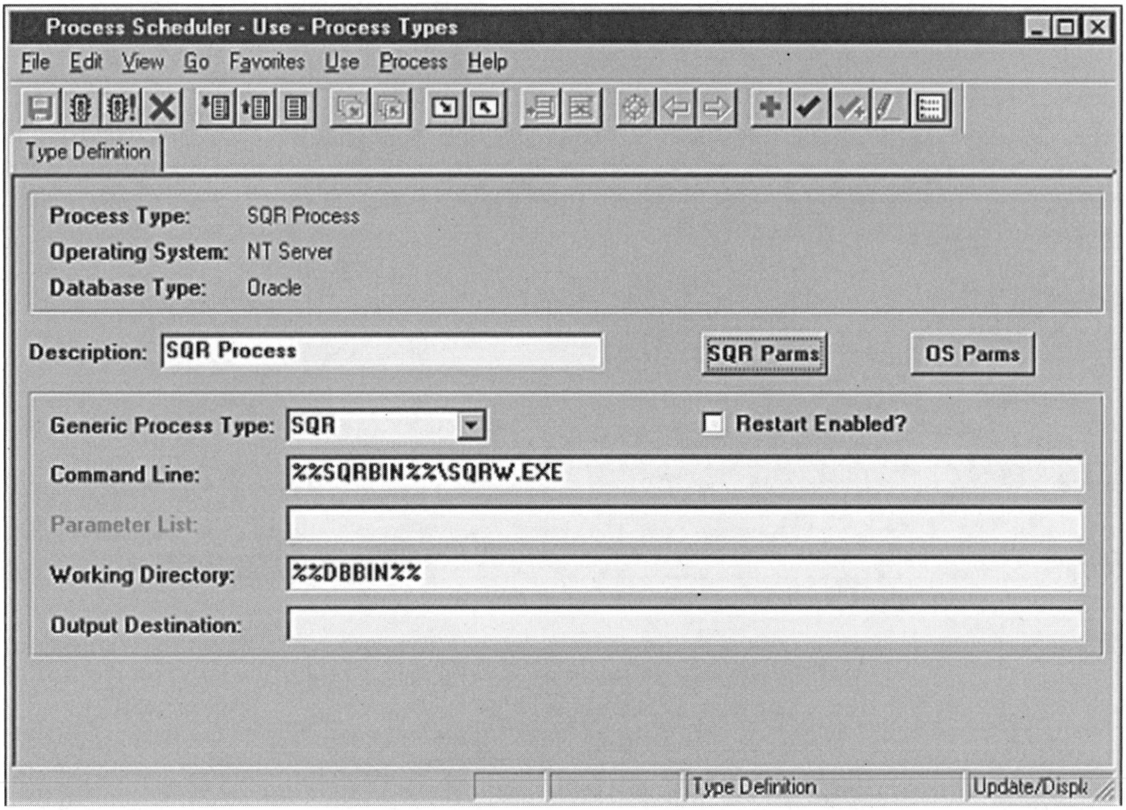

Figure 14-6 Type definition.

Figure 14-7 SQR Parameters dialog box appears when the SQR PARMS button is selected.

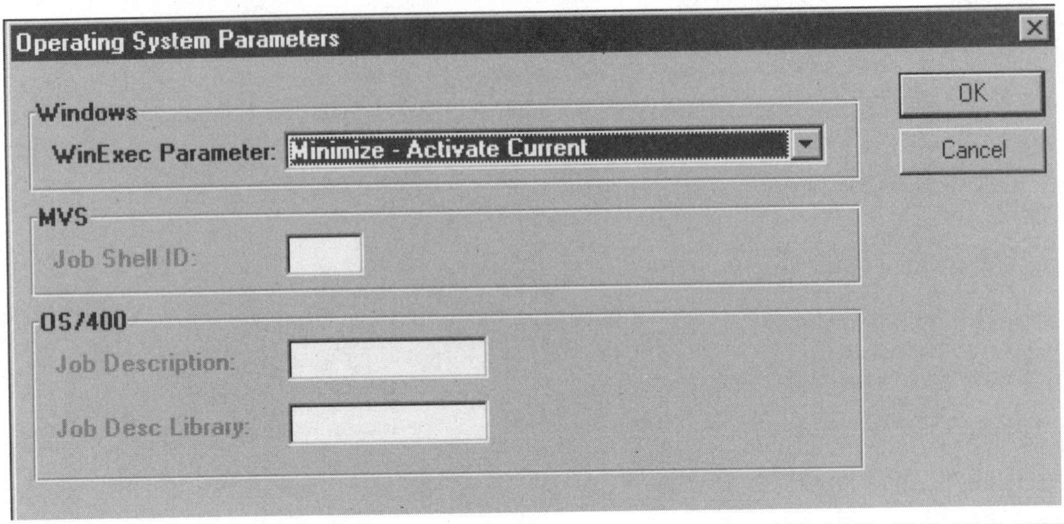

Figure 14-8 Operating System Parameters dialog box appears when OS PARMS button is selected.

existing process definitions of that type. Select the process definition from the list and click on OK.

Once OK is selected, the PROCESS DEFINITIONS tab is displayed as shown in Figure 14-12. This tab shows the process type and the process name. In this case, the process type is SQR Report and the process name is `POPO005`. This means that the SQR program that will be executed must be in a file named `POPO005.SQR`. The SQR program must be found in one of the search directories in the Configuration Manager's SQR search path parameters. Otherwise, the program will not be run.

In addition, this tab allows the developer to enter the following:

- *Description.* Short description of what the process does.
- *Process class.* Select a process class from the drop-down list.
- *Priority.* The priority of the process. This is used to determine which processes will be executed first if more than one process is on the queue.
- *Run location.* This is the default run location. It can be set to CLIENT, SERVER, or BOTH. This run location overrides the one set up in the run location on the Process Scheduler Request dialog. If the run location is set to BOTH here, the one on the Process Scheduler Request dialog box will be used.

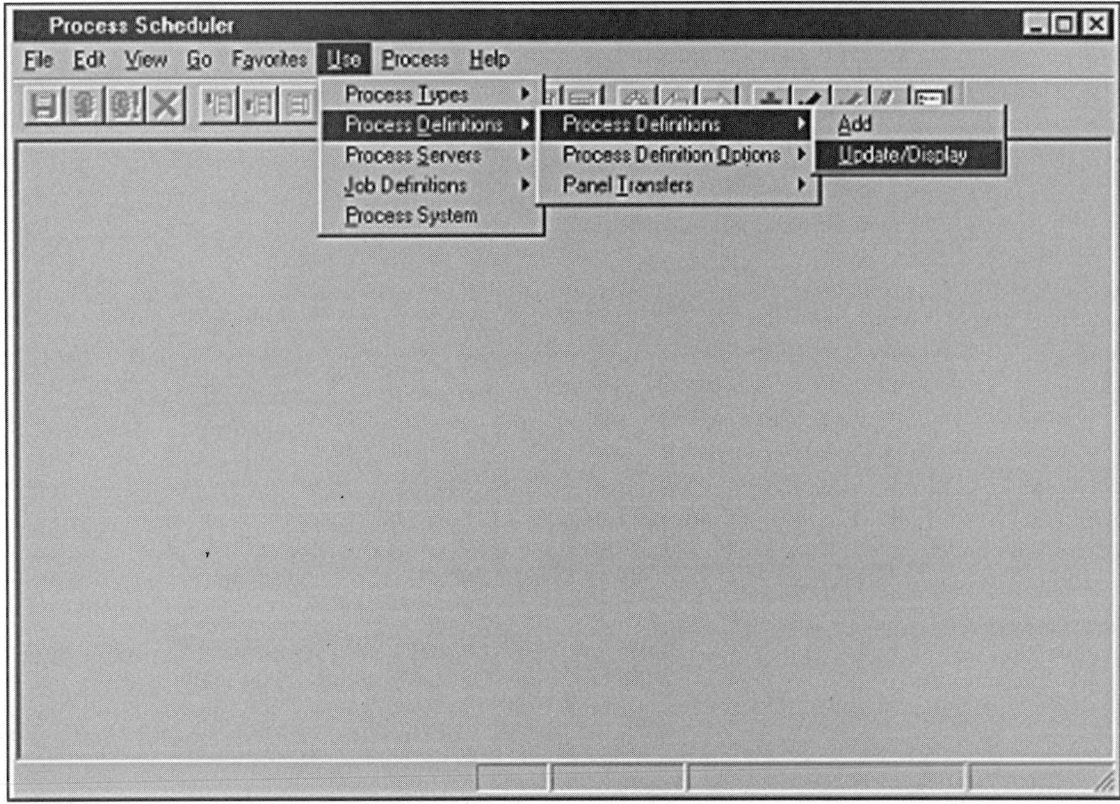

Figure 14-9 Getting to the Process Definitions screen of the Process Scheduler.

Add -- Process Definitions

Process Type:

Process Name:

OK

Cancel

Figure 14-10 The Add Process Definitions dialog box.

- *Server name.* If the run location is set to SERVER, the server name can be entered. This would normally be left blank to allow the system to run it on the first available server. The server name would be entered only if it is desired to limit which server this process can run on.

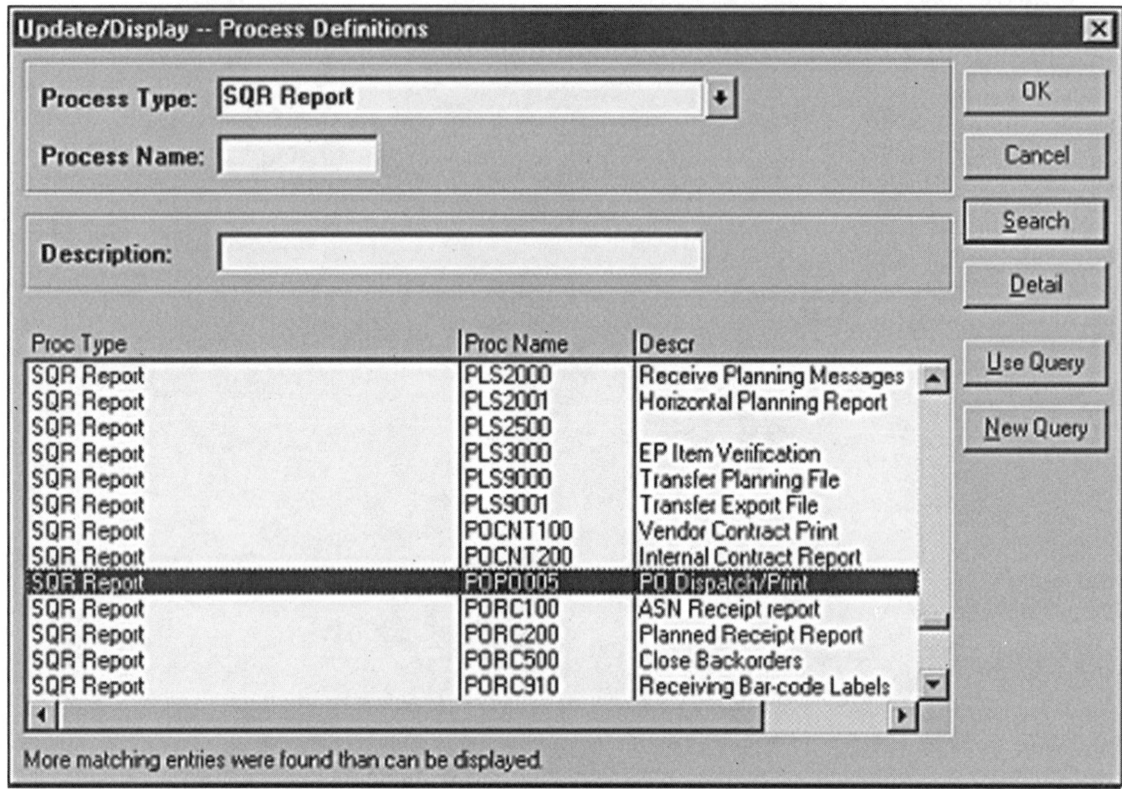

Figure 14-11 The Update/Display Process Definitions dialog box. Select a process type and click SEARCH for a complete list of available process definitions.

- *Log client request.* Logs each time the process is run on a client workstation. Default is ON.
- *SQR run time.* Creates a `.SQT` and uses the SQT working directory defined in the process type.
- *Long description.* Long description of the process.
- *Panel groups.* Enter the panel groups from the drop-down list. The panel groups selected will be the only places that the process being defined can run from.
- *Process security groups.* Enter the security groups that can have access to this process.

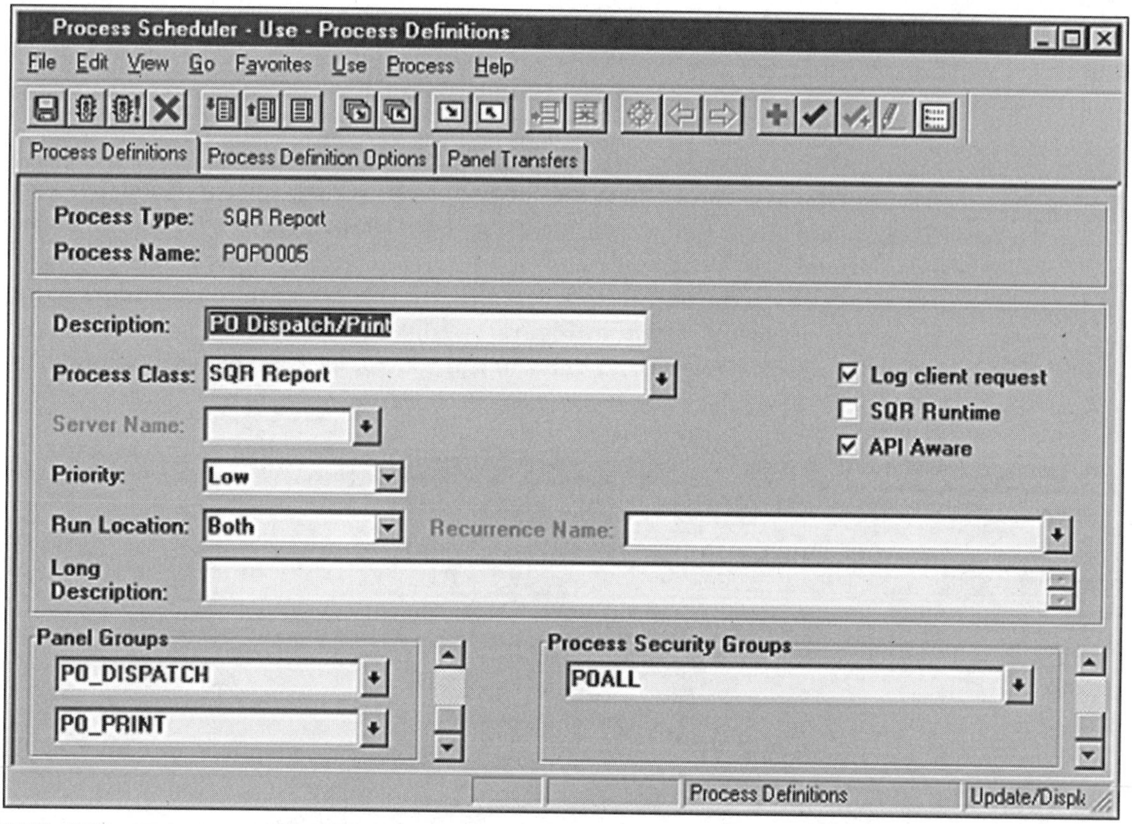

Figure 14-12 The PROCESS DEFINITIONS tab of the Process Definitions dialog box.

In the example shown in Figure 14-12, the process that will be run is a SQR program named `POPO005.sqr`. The panel groups that can run process `POPO005.SQR` are named `PO_DISPATCH` and `PO_PRINT`. Both of these panel groups are process panel groups. This means that in order to get to them off the menu bar, you must select `PROCESS`. A process panel group has a primary key of operator id and run control. PeopleSoft utilizes run controls to pass parameters from the PeopleSoft application to the process.

Let us leave the Process Scheduler for a moment and bring up the actual panel group `PO_DISPATCH` in the Application Designer so that it will be clear how all this ties in with each other. To get to the `PO_DISPATCH` panel group from the Application Designer, select GO,

ADMINISTER PROCUREMENT, MANAGE PURCHASE ORDERS. Then, from the MANAGE PURCHASE ORDERS screen, select PROCESS, DISPATCH PURCHASE ORDERS. Figure 14-13 shows how to get to the `PO_DISPATCH` process panel group of the Purchasing Application.

Once there, ADD or UPDATE/DISPLAY can be selected. When Dispatch Purchase Orders ADD is selected from the menu, the Add Dispatch Purchase Orders dialog box appears as shown in Figure 14-14. This dialog box asks for a run control id.

Once a run control id is entered, the Dispatch Purchase Orders panel is displayed as shown in Figure 14-15. Note that the primary key on the panel is the operator id and the run control id. Both are grayed out. The

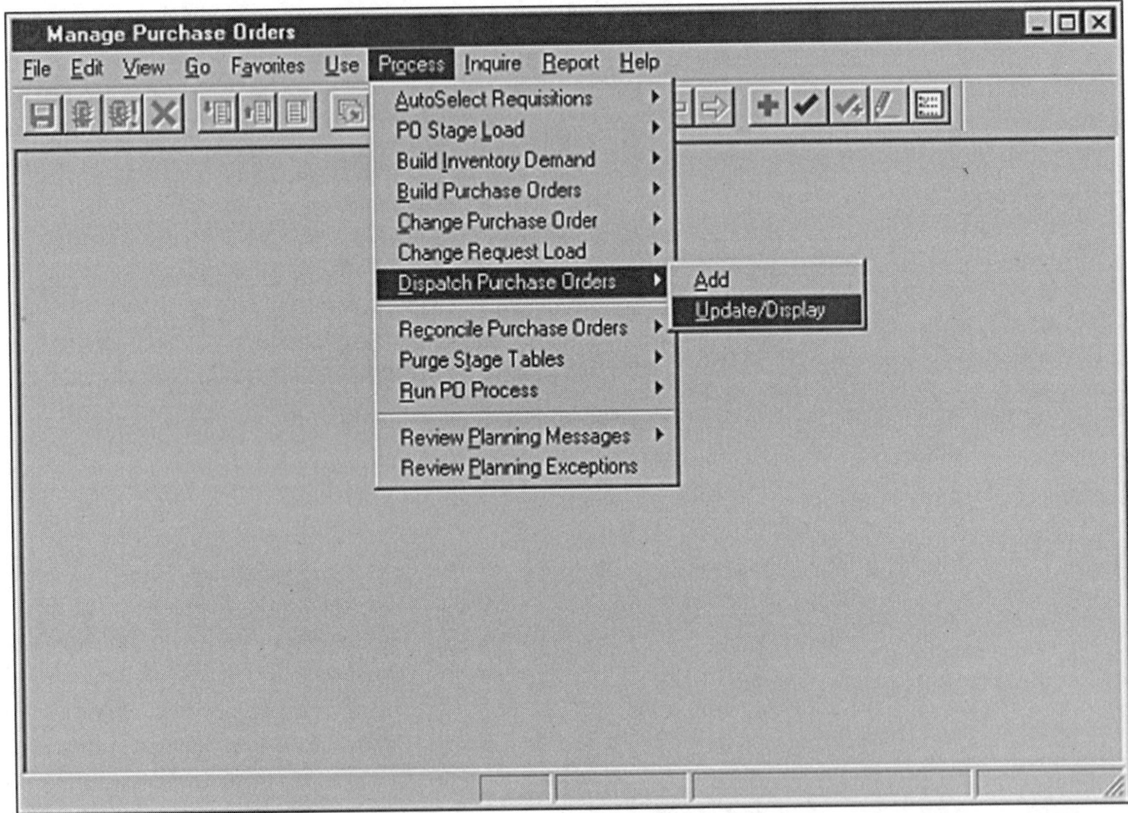

Figure 14-13 Selecting a Process Panel group from the menu bar.

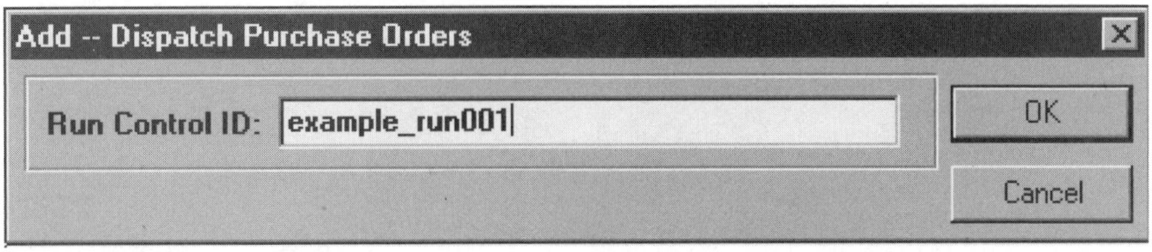

Figure 14-14 Add Dispatch Purchase Orders dialog box.

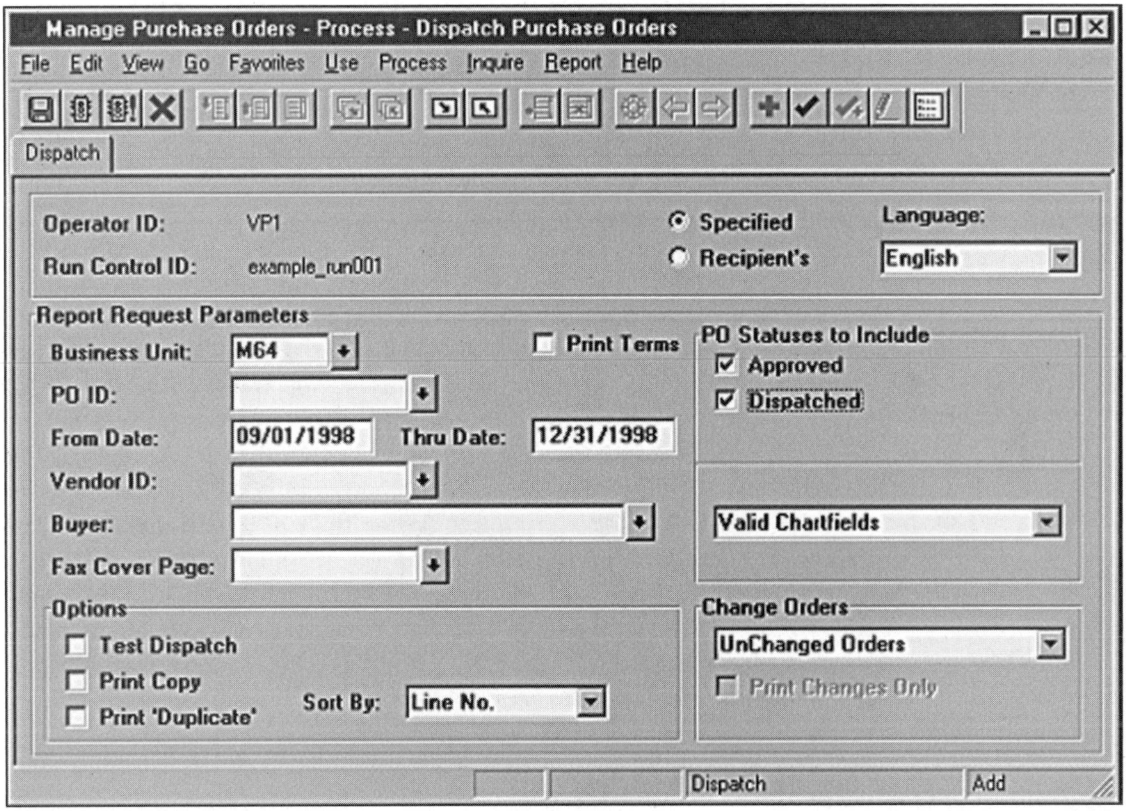

Figure 14-15 Dispatch Purchase Orders panel. Initially the data cells are blank. The user enters the specific data desired to run the report on.

Figure 14-16
RUN icon from the toolbar.

run control id is `example_run001` because that was just entered on the Add Dispatch Purchase Orders dialog box. The next step is to enter the specific data desired for generating the report as shown in Figure 14-15. When the parameters are saved, the data entered will be written to the run control table `ps_run_cntl_pur` by the `PO_DISPATCH` panel group with the operator id and run control id as the primary key.

Once the parameters for this run control are saved in the run control table, you can press the RUN icon (Fig. 14-16) from the toolbar to initiate the `PO_dispatch` process. The primary key of the panel that you just *updated will be passed to `POPO005.sqr` as a parameter.* The `sqr` program can then utilize the operator id/run control to query the run control table to extract the parameters that were just set. `POPO005` allows you to define such things as from/to date that can be used as a filter as well as what status to include in your dispatch. The `sqr` program utilizes the'ask' command to retreve the command line parameters that are passed from the Process Scheduler. In order to send these parameters to an `SQR` program from PeopleSoft, predefined PeopleSoft metastrings must be utilized. In the Process Scheduler, you must enter the metastring of the desired parameters into the `SQR` Parameter Field on the Process Definition options tab of the Process Definitions Dialog Box. For example, the metastring for operator's SignOn Id is %%OPRID%% and for Run Control ID is %%RUNCNTLID%%. When the run icon is clicked on, the Process Scheduler Request dialog box appears as shown in Figure 14-17.

Once all the scheduling information is satisfactory, click OK to queue the process. The status of the queued process can be checked in the Process Monitor as shown in Figure 14-18. To get to the Process Monitor, select GO, PEOPLETOOLS, PROCESS MONITOR.

Process Servers

From the Use menu, it is possible to ADD or UPDATE/DISPLAY process servers. If UPDATE/DISPLAY is selected, the Update/display Process Servers dialog box (Fig. 14-19) will appear. Select a server and click OK. The SERVER DEFINITION tab will appear as shown in Figure 14-20. This allows server-specific information to be updated.

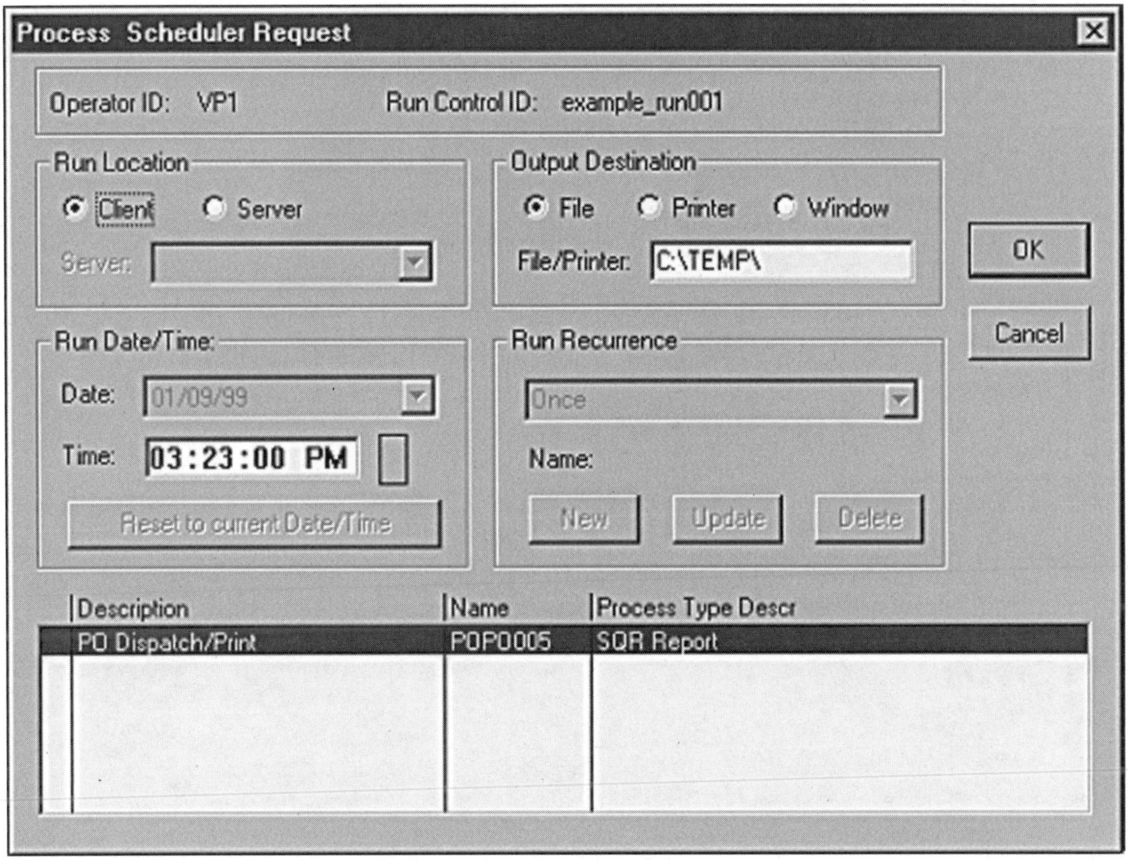

Figure 14-17 Process Scheduler Request shows the name of the process that will be scheduled.

Process Job Definitions

A *job* consists of one or more scheduled processes. To create a job go to the Use menu, select USE, JOB DEFINITIONS, JOB DEFINITIONS, ADD. When the Add Job definition dialog appears, enter the Process Job Name and press OK. Figure 14-21 shows the Add Job Definitions dialog.

After OK is clicked, the JOB DEFINITION tab is displayed as shown in Figure 14-22. A description of the job, the server name the job should run on, the process class, the run mode, the job priority, the recurrence, and the process type and process name of each process in the job can be selected on this tab. In order to enter more than one process in the job, press the F7 key or click on the INSERT ROW button from the toolbar.

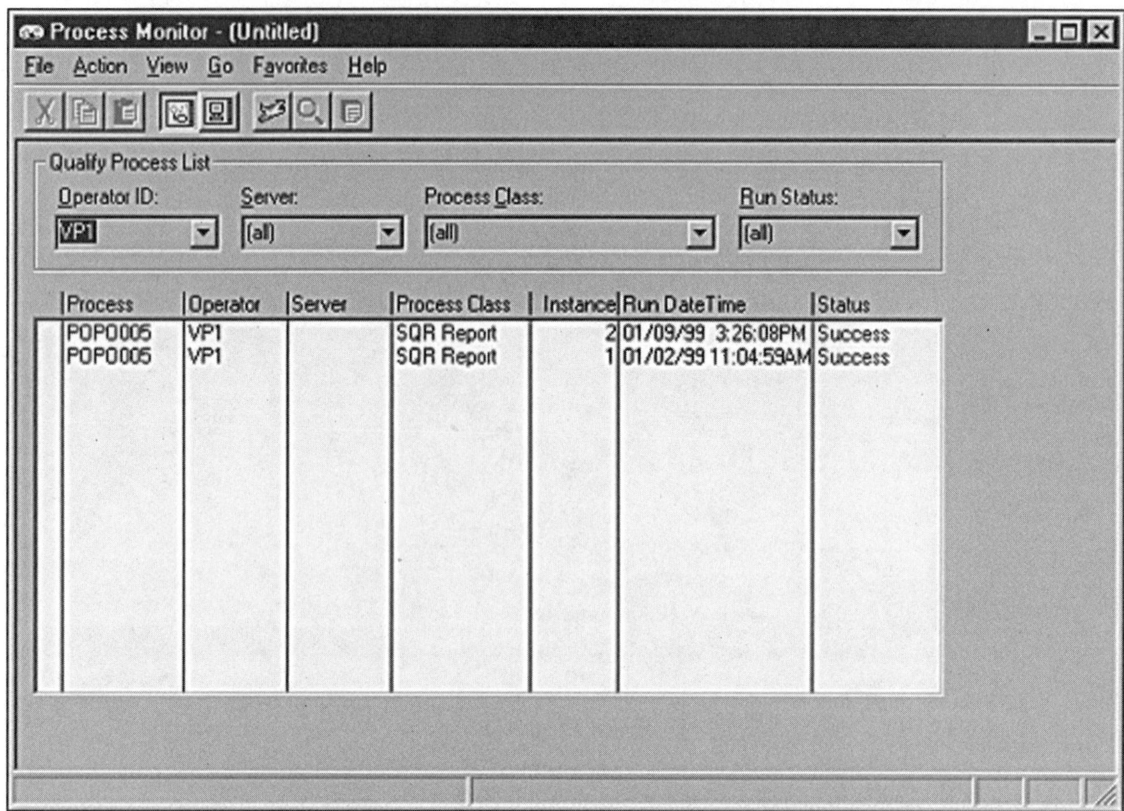

Figure 14-18 Process Monitor shows the status of the SQR report.

Process System

From the Use menu, select USE, PROCESS SYSTEM. This displays Figure 14-23, which allows the Last Process Instance and the Default Operating System to be modified.

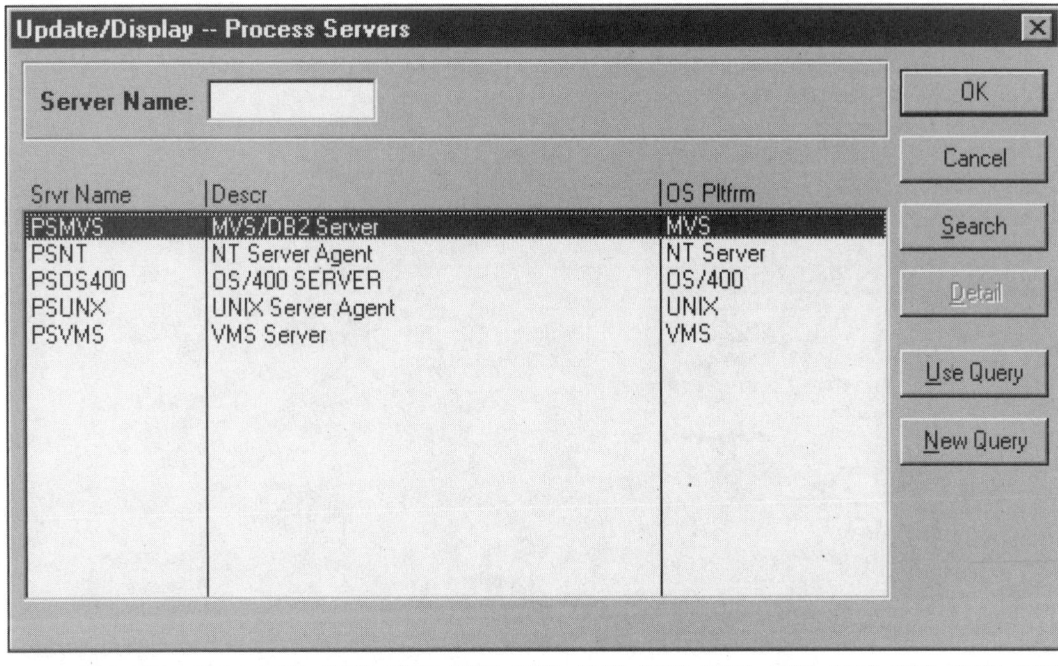

Figure 14-19 Update/Display Process Servers.

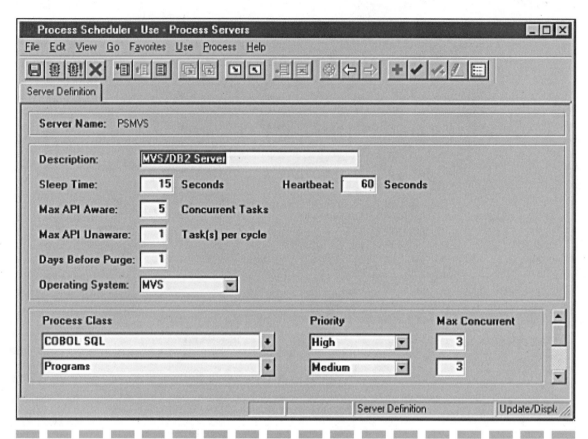

Figure 14-20 SERVER DEFINITION tab defines server information.

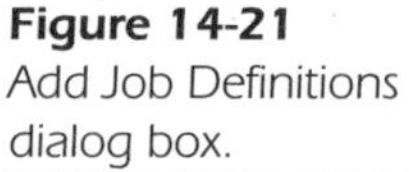

Figure 14-21 Add Job Definitions dialog box.

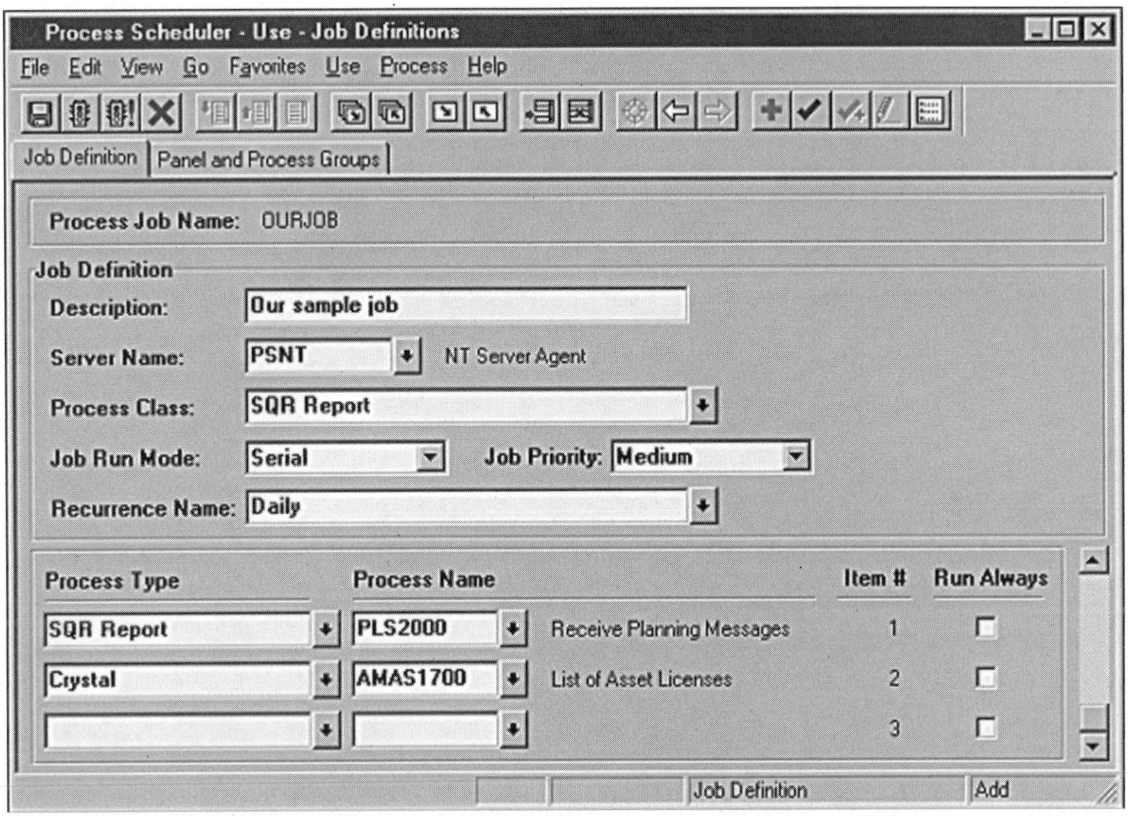

Figure 14-22 JOB DEFINITION tab.

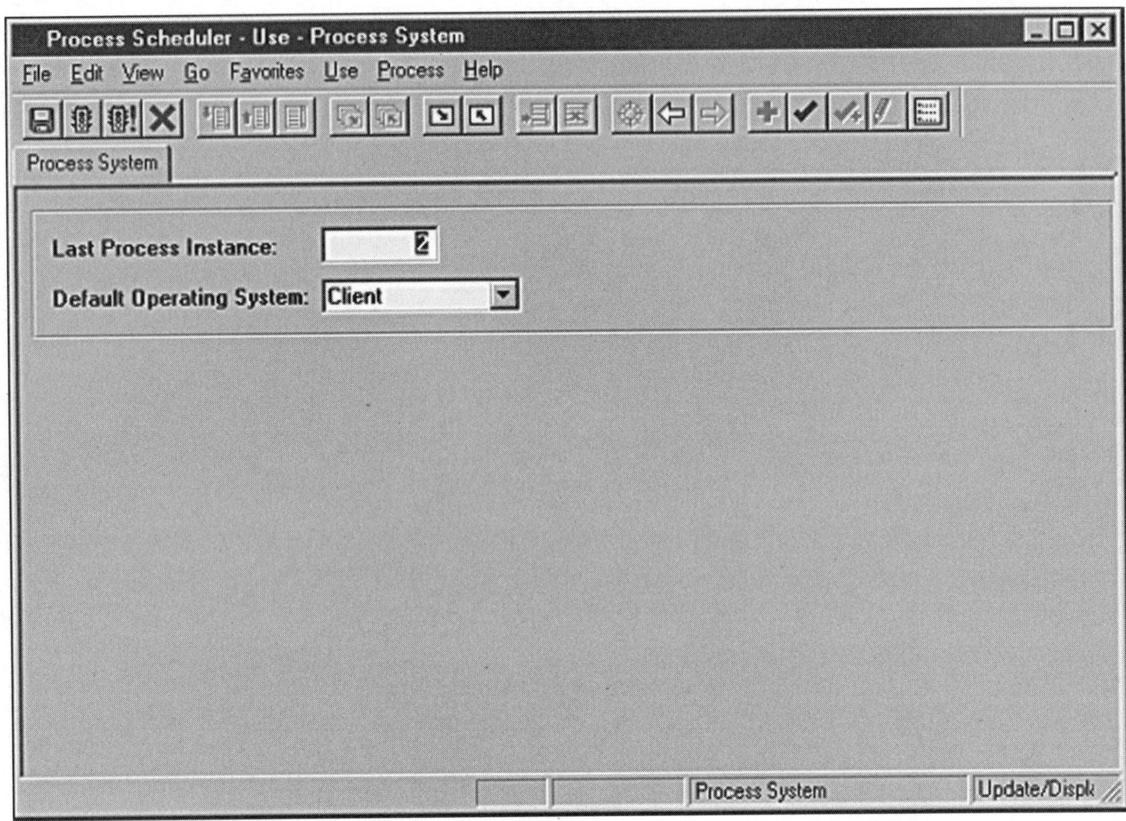

Figure 14-23 PROCESS SYSTEM tab.

CHAPTER 15

SQR

SQR Defined

SQR is a software package produced by SQRibe Technologies and it is included in the PeopleSoft package. SQR allows you to write programs that produce reports. SQR is geared toward creating reports that are a scheduled type of report usually run in batch processing mode. The type of report created is not an ad hoc graphical user interface type of report run on the fly by a user. Instead, these reports are programmed, and the intent is that they will be run at specific times during the day or week; and typically a lot of data are being reported on in these reports. Day-end processing is an example of when SQR reports would be used. One very useful feature of SQR is that it allows multiple reports to be created with only one pass through the data. SQR is also used for importing data into the database or exporting data out of the database.

Executing SQR Programs

An SQR program can be run either outside or inside PeopleSoft. While outside PeopleSoft, an SQR program can be run from a command line. Inside PeopleSoft, SQR can be run directly off the PeopleSoft submenu or as a scheduled process in the Process Scheduler.

Executing SQR from the Command Line

SQR programs can be run from a command line. The syntax for executing an SQR program from a command line follows:

```
SQR programname connectivity flags arguments @file
```

where

- `Programname` is the name of your program.
- `Connectivity` is the information needed to sign on to your database. It varies depending on the type of database it is. For example, if the database is Sybase, then *connectivity* refers to the username and password needed to sign on to your database.
- Flags are the option flags. Each flag should have a hyphen in front of it. If the flag has an argument, the argument should come immediately following the flag without any spaces between. For example, `-Eerrorfile.dat` `-E` is the save errors to a file flag; `errorfile.dat` is the name of file that the errors will be saved to. Note there is no space between the flag (`-E`) and the argument (`errorfile.dat`).

A subset of the available flags that can be used follows:

`-A`	Appends the output to an existing output file.
`-B`	Indicates the number of rows to retrieve from database.
`-CB`	Causes the communication box to be used when running from Windows.
`-DEBUG`	Causes the compiler to compile any lines preceded by `#DEBUG`.
`-E`	Writes errors to the error file specified.
`-F`	Writes the output to the file specified.
`-I`	Used to list the directories to be searched on a `#include` if the file to be included is not in the current directory.

`-KEEP`	Causes SQR to generate a `.SPF` file as well as a `.LIS` file when running a report.
`-NOLIS`	No `.LIS` file is generated. Instead, `.SPF` files are generated.
`-PRINTER:LP`	Creates a `.LIS` file that can be printed to a line printer.
`-PRINTER:HP`	Creates a `.LIS` file that can be printed to an HP LaserJet.
`-PRINTER:HT`	Creates an HTML (HyperText Markup Language) `.LIS file`.
`-PRINTER:PS`	Creates a PostScript (Adobe) `.LIS` file.
`-PRINTER:WP`	Creates a Windows (Microsoft) `.LIS` file.

- Arguments are any arguments being passed into the program.
- `@file` is the name of a file that contains arguments to the SQR program. This file must have one argument on each line.

Generally, SQR reports would be run in batch mode. To do this, a command procedure, shell script, or batch file would be created which would contain the SQR command lines. In this way, many SQR reports could be started one after another without an operator manually running each one.

Executing SQR from the PeopleSoft Submenu

SQR programs can be run from PeopleSoft by selecting START, PROGRAMS, PEOPLESOFT, SQR. This brings up the Windows SQR dialog box as shown in Figure 15-1. (If SQR is not showing up in the PeopleSoft submenu, then it is necessary to go to the CLIENT SETUP tab of the Configuration Manager and check the SQR box of the Shortcut Link group.) *While it is possible to run SQR programs from the Windows SQR dialog box, this would probably be used only to run non-PeopleSoft SQR programs since run controls cannot be used here.*

To run an SQR program from the SQR dialog box, the user must enter the following:

- Full path of the SQR program in the report name field.
- The name of the database being used.
- The username and password to sign on to the database.
- Any report flags and arguments needed for the report to run properly.

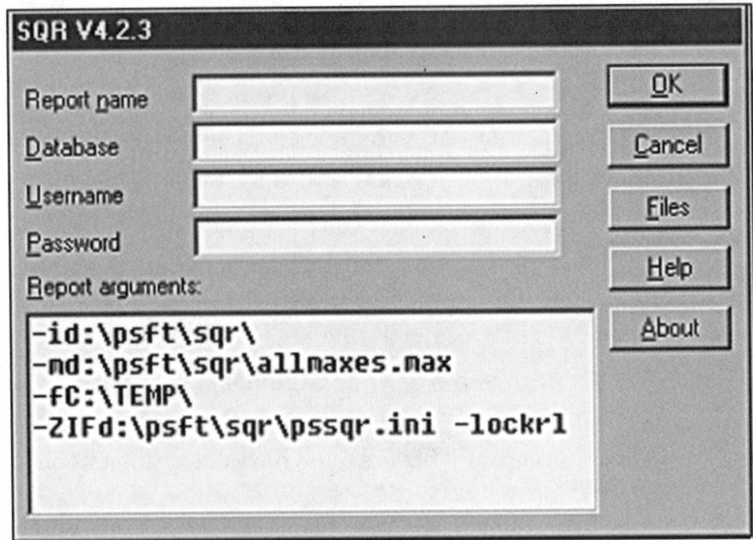

Figure 15-1 SQR dialog box appears so that the user can run an SQR report from the PeopleSoft submenu.

Executing SQR from the Process Scheduler

SQR programs can be scheduled in the Process Scheduler as discussed in the previous chapter.

Output from an SQR Program

The output from your SQR program is usually created in the directory where it is being run, and it is named `program.lis` unless the `-F` flag is being used. The path of the output file can be specified with the `-F` flag along with the name of the output file.

Programming in SQR

SQR Variables

There are several different types of SQR variables:

- *Numeric*. Numeric variables must start with a #. A numeric variable can be of type decimal, float, or integer. The precision of a numeric variable is 38 digits.

- *String.* A string variable must start with a $. The text string can be of any length. The null string is between single quotes.
- *Column.* A column variable starts with a &. Column variables are filled from the database when a select statement is being performed.
- *Reserved.* Reserved variables are controlled by SQR automatically. #page-count is an example of a reserved variable that SQR maintains for you. There is a separate reserved variable for each report of a multireport program.
- *Date.* Date variable.

Scope of Variables All variables are global unless they are specifically being passed as arguments to a procedure with a colon in front of the variable or they are in a local procedure. A local procedure has the key word *local* on it.

If there happens to be a global variable and local variable with the same name, in order to refer to the global variable in the local procedure, #_, $_, or &_ must be in front of the variable. For example, if #x is a global variable and there is a local procedure test that has a local variable #x, then, to refer to the global variable while in procedure test, it must be referred to as #_x.

Declaring Variables It is not required to explicitly declare variables in SQR. If variable $a is not declared, then it is a string variable because of the $ in front of it. However, it is possible to explicitly declare variables via DECLARE-VARIABLE. The syntax to DECLARE-VARIABLE follows:

```
DECLARE-VARIABLE
[ DEFAULT-NUMERIC = {DECIMAL | FLOAT | INTEGER  ]
[ DECIMAL [ ( prec_lit ) ] num_var ]
[ FLOAT num_var ]
[ DATE date_var ]
[ INTEGER num_var ]
[ TEXT string_var ]

END-DECLARE
```

The DECLARE-VARIABLE can be only in a BEGIN-SETUP section or the first line of a local procedure. It can be used to set the default of a numeric variable to decimal, float, or integer. It is also used to declare variables to a certain type. For example, the following DECLARE-VARIABLE sets the numeric default to decimal, declares variables #Y and #Z to be integer, and declares $BIRTHDATE to be type DATE.

```
BEGIN-SETUP
 DECLARE-VARIABLE
  DEFAULT-NUMERIC = DECIMAL
  INTEGER  #Y #Z
  DATE  $BIRTHDATE
 END-DECLARE
END-SETUP
```

SQR Sections

An SQR program is made up of many different sections. One section controls what the heading of the report will look like. Another section controls the footer of the report. There is a setup section, a program section, and a procedure section.

Heading The heading section is an optional section. It contains a BEGIN-HEADING as the first line and an END-HEADING as the last line. This section defines what the heading of the report(s) will look like. Typically inside the heading section, there would be print statements that would print such information as the title of the report, the current date, the page number, and column labels. The BEGIN-HEADING line defines the number of lines the heading will consist of on the report. In addition, if the program is going to produce multiple reports, there can be a separate heading for each report. To define a separate heading for each report being produced by the program, the FOR-REPORTS qualifier must be used on the BEGIN-HEADING line. If the FOR-REPORTS qualifier is not included on the BEGIN-HEADING line, then the heading is by default for all the reports being created in the program. An example heading section follows:

```
BEGIN-HEADING 4 FOR-REPORTS=(REPORT1, REPORT2, REPORT5)
 PRINT 'Our first Report' (1) Center
 PRINT $current-date (2,1)
END-HEADING
```

The BEGIN-HEADING line above indicates that the heading will be four lines long and that the heading defined in this heading section will apply to reports named REPORT1, REPORT2, and REPORT5. The heading will print out "Our first Report' centered on line 1 of the heading portion of the report. The current date will be displayed in row 2, column 1. The $current-date is a reserved SQR variable that is maintained by SQR. There will be two blank lines in the header since the header is defined to be four lines long. More information on creating multiple reports will be discussed later in this chapter. For now, just keep in mind in order to use the FOR-REPORTS qualifier, DECLARE-REPORT and USE-REPORT must be used in other sections of the SQR program.

The heading section can also contain logic statements such as if and else. Calls to procedures are legal in the heading section as are print commands. Again, keep in mind that the heading section is not a required section of the SQR program.

Note that there are three areas on a report page: the heading, the body of the report, and the footing of the report. Each of these areas will have its own line numbers. Thus, even though the heading area starts at line 1, the body area will start at line 1 and the footing area will start at line 1 as well.

Footing The footing section is also an optional section. The footing section contains a BEGIN-FOOTING as the first line and an END-FOOTING as the last line. This section defines what the footer of the report(s) will look like. The BEGIN-FOOTING line defines the number of lines the footer will consist of on the report. In addition, if the program is going to produce multiple reports, there can be a separate footer for each report. To define a separate footer for each report being produced by the program, the FOR-REPORTS qualifier must be used on the BEGIN-FOOTING line.

The footing section can contain logic statements, calls to procedures, and print commands. Anything that is legal in the heading section of the SQR program is also legal in the footing section.

Setup The setup section is an optional section. This section begins with a BEGIN-SETUP line and ends with an END-SETUP line. This section is the only place that allows the developer to declare reports, charts, images, layouts, printer, and procedure via the DECLARE-REPORT, DECLARE-CHART, DECLARE-IMAGE, DECLARE-LAYOUT, DECLARE-PRINTER, and DECLARE-PROCEDURE commands.

The ASK command can only appear in the setup section also. No logic statements are allowed in this section. In addition to the above-mentioned commands that can appear only in this section, the setup section can also have the following commands which can appear in other SQR sections as well:

```
ALTER-LOCALE, BEGIN-SQL, DECLARE-VARIABLE, LOAD-LOOKUP, CREATE-ARRAY.
```

The setup section is executed at compile time.

Program The program section is a required section of an SQR program. This section is executed first when the program is run. The first line of this section is the BEGIN-PROGRAM line, and the last line is the END-PROGRAM line. This section can contain logic statements and procedure calls. Use caution when including BEGIN-SQL or BEGIN-SELECT statements in this section. Depending on the version of SQR that is being run, these statements may not be allowed in the program section. Since version 4 of SQR, the BEGIN-SQL and BEGIN-SELECT statements are allowed in the program section. It seems that many SQR programmers usually only put procedure calls in the program section and do the bulk of the processing inside the procedures even though most any SQR command could be placed in the program section. This is a matter of style.

To call a procedure, you use the DO command. The following SQR code contains a BEGIN-PROGRAM statement, a couple calls to procedures, and the END-PROGRAM statement:

```
BEGIN-PROGRAM
 DO MAIN
 DO CLEANUP
END-PROGRAM
```

Each SQR command must be on its own line and can be indented if desired. Remember that if the command is going to the database (e.g., BEGIN-SELECT, each line must be in column 1.

Procedure The procedure section is an optional section of the SQR program. It can have arguments if desired. The procedure can be called in the BEGIN-PROGRAM section of the SQR program or it can be called from another procedure. The procedure section can have any SQR command in it. The procedure section starts with a BEGIN-PROCEDURE and ends with an END-PROCEDURE. If the procedure is to be a local procedure it can have a keyword LOCAL on it. Procedures are by default global.

```
BEGIN-PROCEDURE test LOCAL (ARG1,ARG2, ARG3)

END-PROCEDURE
```

SQR Print Command

Every SQR report requires print commands. The print command prints what will be on the report. The syntax of the print command follows:

```
PRINT VARNAME (ROWPOS,COLPOS,WIDTH) [format command] [format command]
```

where

`Varname`	The name of the variable to be printed.
`ROWPOS`	The row position where the data will start.
`COLPOS`	The column position where the data will start.
`WIDTH`	The width of the field to be printed.
`FORMAT COMMAND`	Several format commands can be in a print command, including `BOLD`, which will make the text being displayed appear in boldface print. Print format commands are discussed later in this chapter.

Note that there must be a space between the variable name and the left paren. If this space is missing, a compile error will result. This is a very common error.

An example of a simple print statement follows:

```
PRINT $NAME (2,10,30)
```

In this example, the value stored in the text variable `NAME` will be printed in row (or line number) 2, column 10 with a width of 30. Note that it is a text variable because it has a `$` in front of it.

In addition to printing the value of a variable, a literal string can also be printed. The literal must be between single quotes. An example of a literal print command follows:

```
PRINT 'THIS IS AN EXAMPLE' (1,1,30)
```

In this example, the text `THIS IS AN EXAMPLE` will print at line 1, column 1 with a width of 30. Note that if the width position is left out of the print command, the length required to print the actual value will be used.

The row position and column position are unique to each section of the report. The report consists of the header, the body of the report, and the footer. Therefore, each section of the report has a line 1 column 1 and a current print position.

Absolute versus Relative Print Position A print command can have absolute positions or relative positions. The examples in the previous section contain *absolute* positions. This is because the row, column, and width are all set to a particular value without a sign in front of them. A couple more examples of absolute printing follow:

```
PRINT 'MY ADDRESS IS '(5,1,14)
PRINT &ADDRESS (5,16,25)
```

These print commands will print the text MY ADDRESS IS on line 5, column 1 with a width of 14. The value of the column variable &ADDRESS is printed on line 5, column 16 with a width of 25.

Relative printing refers to printing the value of a variable or literal in a location on the report that is relative to the cursor's current print position. When a print command is relative, there is usually a positive or negative sign in front of it or the position is blank. The following few examples illustrate relative printing:

```
PRINT 'MY ADDRESS IS '(+1,5)
PRINT &ADDRESS (,+30)
```

In these examples, the same text MY ADDRESS IS is printed, but this time it is printed one line down from where the current print cursor is located starting in column 5. The actual value of &ADDRESS is printed on the same line as MY ADDRESS IS since the row column is blank. It starts in the last column printed plus 30. Therefore, it starts in column 48 since MY ADDRESS IS starts in column 5 and ends in column 18.

Note that if the row or column had a minus sign in front of it, it would mean go up x number of lines or over x number of columns.

Explicit versus Implicit Printing A print command can be explicit or implicit. An explicit print command is one where the word PRINT is actually there. The following example, as well as the examples in the previous section, is an explicit print command:

```
PRINT 'THIS IS AN EXPLICIT PRINT COMMAND'(1,1)
```

An implicit print command is a print command where the word PRINT is not actually necessary. This is used only in select paragraphs where the columns being selected are to be printed. An example of a select paragraph where the columns are printed follows:

```
BEGIN-SELECT
EMPLOYEE (1,1)
ADDRESS (,+25)
CITY (,+20)
FROM EMPTABLE
END-SELECT
```

Format Commands The print command has the following format commands:

BOLD	Prints the printed text in bold.
BOX	Draws a box around the printed text.
NOP	Noprint—stops the text from being printed.
CENTER	Centers the text on the specified line.
CODE-PRINTER	Causes the printer to print something special.
SHADE	Draws a shaded box around the printed text.
EDIT	Edits the text before it is printed.
UNDERLINE	Underlines the text to be printed.
FILL	Fills the line(s) specified with a specific character or string.
MONEY	Causes the numeric variable to be printed using the `MONEY_EDIT_MASK` in the current locale.
NUMBER	Causes the numeric variable to be printed using the `NUMBER_EDIT_MASK` in the current locale.
WRAP	Wraps at word spaces.
ON-BREAK	Very useful format command that helps with reports that need to have subtotals, etc. when a change occurs in the data. This format command is discussed in much greater detail later in this chapter.

Here are a few examples of the print command with format commands:

```
PRINT &SOC_SEC_NUM (1,) EDIT 'xxx-xx-xxxx'  BOLD CENTERED

PRINT #WINNING_AMT (,+10) EDIT $999,999.99

PRINT 'This is your life' (1,) CENTER
```

EDIT MASKS There are numeric, text, and date edit masks. For each type of edit mask, there are certain characters in the edit mask. Each character has a different meaning, so the output will be printed in the desired way.

The more common edit mask characters are listed below.

Numeric Edit Mask Characters	Representation
9	Digit
8	Left-justified
0	Retain leading zeroes
$	Place dollar sign when printing data
.	Place a period in this location when printing data
,	Place a comma in this location when printing data
MI	Place a minus at the end of the number.

Text Edit Mask Characters	Representation
X	Place character when printing data
B	Place blank in this location when printing data
~	Drop this character when printing data

Date Edit Mask Characters	Representation
Y	Digit of the year
DAY	Name of day
D	Day of week (1-7)
DD	Day of month (1-31)
MONTH	Full name of month
MON	Abbreviated name of month
MM	Month (01-12)
AM PM	A.M. or P.M.
HH	Assumes 24-h clock unless A.M. or P.M. is indicated.
SSSSS	Seconds past midnight (0-86399).

SQR Database Access

The main reason for using SQR is to write a report on the data from your database. This section discusses the essentials for accessing the database via SQR. SQR enables us to perform both Data Definition Language (DDL) and Data Manipulation Language (DML) SQL statements against the database. DDL includes both SQL create and alter statements. DML includes insert, update, and delete SQL statements. All of these can be performed in an SQR SQL paragraph. SQR also provides a specialized paragraph for SQL selects. SQR selects are only used for selecting data out of the database.

BEGIN-SELECT and END-SELECT The BEGIN-SELECT statement begins the select paragraph, and the END-SELECT ends the select paragraph. The select paragraph selects columns of data from the database. In other words, the select paragraph retrieves the data from the database and stores them in column variables. The select statement is read-only. It retrieves the data from the database but does not allow the data in the database to be modified. In addition, since the data are being read from the database one row at a time, logic can be performed on each row because SQR statements are allowed in a select paragraph. An example program follows:

```
BEGIN-PROGRAM
DO MAIN
END-PROGRAM

BEGIN-PROCEDURE MAIN
BEGIN-SELECT
EMPLOYEE_NAME (+1,1)
DEPARTMENT
START_DATE    (,35)
SALARY        (,+15)
   ADD 1 TO #EMP_COUNT
FROM EMPLOYEE_TABLE
WHERE DEPARTMENT=1000
ORDER BY SALARY
END-SELECT
END-PROCEDURE
```

As we stated earlier, the program section will be executed first. Therefore, the first thing that happens is the procedure main will be executed. In procedure main, there is a select paragraph. The columns being retrieved from the database are EMPLOYEE_NAME, DEPARTMENT, START_DATE, and SALARY. These column names are the exact column names that appear in the database table EMPLOYEE_TABLE. The rows that will be returned will be those that have a department number of 1000. The rows will be returned by ascending salary. This program will create a report that prints out the rows of matched data. If the data are to be printed on the report, the parentheses must appear next to the column name that indicates the row and column number that this piece of data should be printed on. The report created by this program will print out the employee name in the next row after where the cursor is currently located and in column 1. The department number will not be printed since there are no parentheses next to it. The start date will be printed on the same row as employee name but in column 35. The salary will be printed on the same row, but 15 column positions away from the end of the start date. Note that all the columns in the BEGIN-SELECT paragraph start in column 1. This is mandatory if the select paragraph is to run without error. Note also that the line that is adding 1 to the EMP_COUNT is indented. This line is an SQR statement, and it must be indented. In other words, the actual lines representing the SQL statement being sent to the database must be in column 1. There must be no commas between the column names. All other statements must be indented. Note the variable #EMP_COUNT. This represents a numeric variable. If we chose to, we could use the column variables of &EMPLOYEE_NAME, &DEPARTMENT, &SALARY, or &START_DATE. These variables are filled with the data retrieved from the table in the database.

It is possible to use dynamic SQL in this section.

BEGIN-SQL and END-SQL Statements The BEGIN-SQL statement is the first line of an SQL paragraph, and the END-SQL is the last line of an SQL paragraph. The SQL paragraph is used for any SQL statement except the select statement. Unlike the select paragraph which is read-only on the data in the database, the SQL paragraph can modify the database via such SQL statements as create, alter, insert, delete, or update. The syntax to the SQL statements is whatever the database being used requires. The SQL paragraph can contain more than one SQL statement, but the statements must be separated by a semicolon. Note that it is not good practice to have more than one statement in the SQL paragraph because if one SQL statement fails, the next one will be executed, anyway. Even if the ON-ERROR qualifier is used on the BEGIN-SQL statement to trap errors, it may not always be clear which of the

SQL statements in the paragraph failed. It is good practice to always use the ON-ERROR qualifier to trap errors.

The following program has an insert statement inside the SQL paragraph. It also has ON-ERROR on the BEGIN-SQL line. If an error occurs when performing the insert statement, procedure INSERT_CLASS_ERROR will be executed automatically.

```
BEGIN-PROGRAM
 DO PROC1
END-PROGRAM

BEGIN-HEADING 3
 PRINT 'COLLEGE CLASS ENTRY' (1) CENTER BOLD
 PRINT $CURRENT-DATE (2) CENTER
END-HEADING

BEGIN-PROCEDURE PROC1
INPUT $CLASS_DATE 'ENTER THE DATE' TYPE=DATE
INPUT $CLASS_TIME 'ENTER THE TIME'
INPUT $CLASS 'ENTER THE CLASS'

BEGIN-SQL ON-ERROR=INSERT_CLASS_ERROR
INSERT INTO APPTS(CLASS_DATE, CLASS_TIME, CLASS)
VALUES ($CLASS_DATE, $CLASS_TIME, $CLASS)
END-SQL
END-PROCEDURE

BEGIN-PROCEDURE INSERT_CLASS_ERROR
PRINT 'ERROR IN PROC1' (+1)
PRINT $SQL-ERROR (+1,1)
END-PROCEDURE
```

Control Structures

This section discusses the different control structures that are included in the SQR language.

IF...ELSE...END-IF An example using an IF control structure follows:

```
BEGIN-SELECT
EMP_NAME
SALARY
START_DATE
NUM_VAC_WKS
 IF (&SALARY <70000)
   DO ADD_WEEK_VACATION
   DO GIVE_COPY_OF_THIS_BOOK
   PRINT &EMP_NAME (+1,1)
   PRINT &START_DATE (,+20)
   PRINT &SALARY (,+10)
   PRINT &NUM_VAC_WKS (,+15)
```

```
  ELSE
    DO GIVE_BIG_STOCK_OPTIONS
  END-IF
FROM EMP_TABLE
END-SELECT
```

In this example, each row of data returned from the employee table is checked to determine if the salary of the employee is less than $70,000.00. If it is less than $70,000.00, then the procedures ADD_WEEK_VACATION and GIVE_COPY_OF_THIS_BOOK are called and some of the data are printed to a report. Otherwise, the salary is greater than or equal to $70,000.00 and the ELSE is processed. When the ELSE is processed, the procedure GIVE_BIG_STOCK_OPTIONS is called.

There is no THEN in this control structure. If one is added, an error will occur. In addition, each key word must be on its own line. Do not place the ELSE on the same line as the IF. An ELSE clause is not required but is allowed. There is no ELSE IF allowed in SQR. It is okay to have several levels of IF statements. The following examples are also valid IF control structures. In the first example below, there is no ELSE clause. If the numeric variable #ERRORCOUNT = 3, the literal TOO MANY BAD TRIES is printed out to the report.

```
IF (#ERRORCOUNT=3)
  PRINT 'TOO MANY BAD TRIES'(+1,1)
  STOP
END-IF
```

This next example illustrates how to nest some IF statements:

```
IF ($MAKE = 'AMERICAN')
  IF ($CARTYPE = 'FORD')
    LET #FORD_COUNT = #FORD_COUNT + 1
  ELSE
    LET #NON_FORD_COUNT = #NON_FORD_COUNT + 1
  END-IF
ELSE
  IF ($CARTYPE = 'MERCEDES')
    PRINT 'GOOD CHOICE' (+1, 1)
    LET #MERC_COUNT = #MERC_COUNT + 1
  END-IF
END-IF
```

WHILE...END-WHILE The WHILE...END-WHILE control structure loops through the code inside the WHILE construct while the expression on the WHILE line is true. Once the expression on the WHILE line is no longer true, the next line to be executed is the line following the END-WHILE. A WHILE loop can also be exited using the BREAK command. Once the BREAK is reached, the next line of code to be executed is the line following the END-WHILE. An example program containing a WHILE...END-WHILE construct is shown below:

```
BEGIN-PROGRAM
 DO MAIN
END-PROGRAM

BEGIN-PROCEDURE MAIN
LET $CARTYPE = 'FORD'
WHILE ($CARTYPE <> 'MERCEDES')
 DO MERCEDES_SALES_PITCH
 LET #COUNT = #COUNT + 1
 INPUT $YESNO 'Would you buy a Mercedes now that you have heard the
sales pitch (Y/N)?'
 IF ($YESNO = 'Y')
   LET $CARTYPE = 'MERCEDES'
 ELSE
   IF (#COUNT = 5)
     PRINT 'You are a tough customer' (+1,1)
     BREAK
   END-IF
 END-IF
END-WHILE
PRINT 'FIRST LINE EXECUTED AFTER WHILE LOOP'(+1,1)
END-PROCEDURE
BEGIN-PROCEDURE MERCEDES_SALES_PITCH
 PRINT 'MERCEDES IS A GREAT CAR. BUY IT'(+1,1)
END-PROCEDURE
```

In this example, the text variable $CARTYPE is not equal to MERCEDES, so the code inside the WHILE will be executed. It will continue to be executed as long as $CARTYPE is not equal to MERCEDES (note that the WHILE condition is checked only at the top of the WHILE loop). The procedure MERCEDES_SALES_PITCH is called each time, and the number of times the procedure is called is incremented with each pass through. The INPUT command is used to ask the users whether they would buy a Mercedes now that they have heard the sales pitch. The users' responses are stored in the text variable $YESNO. If Y was entered, then $CARTYPE is set to MERCEDES. Each time the END-WHILE is reached, the execution of the program jumps back up to the WHILE condition. Each time the WHILE is executed, the condition is checked. If the condition is still true, the code inside the WHILE will again be executed. In this case, once Y is entered and the variable $CARTYPE is set to MERCEDES via the LET command, the WHILE condition will no longer be true and the next line that would be executed would be the print command just below the END-WHILE. This example also illustrates the use of the BREAK command. If the user answers N (no) to buying a Mercedes 5 times, then the BREAK command is executed. This breaks you right out of the WHILE loop, and the next line to be executed is the print command just below the END-WHILE.

EVALUATE...END-EVALUATE The EVALUATE construct is equivalent to a case or switch statement in other programming languages. It has much better performance than several nested IF statements. An EVALUATE construct is made up of the EVALUATE line, WHEN expressions with the code to be executed should the value of the variable in the EVALUATE match the WHEN value, a WHEN-OTHER section, and an END-EVALUATE statement. Each WHEN must be on its own line. There should be a BREAK between the WHEN sections. If no BREAK is present, then the next WHEN section will be evaluated. Should the value of #NUMCARS be modified inside a WHEN section that does not have a BREAK command inside it, it is possible that the code inside other WHEN sections may be executed. This may be your intention, and if so, it is legal. However, leaving the BREAK command out more than most often would be a bug that you did not intend to do.

An example illustrating an EVALUATE control structure follows:

```
BEGIN-PROGRAM
 DO MAIN
END-PROGRAM

BEGIN-PROCEDURE MAIN
INPUT #NUMCARS 'Enter the number of cars your household currently
owns:' TYPE=integer
EVALUATE #NUMCARS
 WHEN = 0
   DO MERCEDES_SALES_PITCH
   LET #ZEROCARS = #ZEROCARS + 1
   BREAK
 WHEN = 1
   LET #ONECAR = #ONECAR + 1
   BREAK
 WHEN = 2
   LET #TWOCARS = #TWOCARS + 1
   BREAK
 WHEN = 3
   LET #THCARS = #THCARS + 1
   BREAK
 WHEN-OTHER
   PRINT 'DO YOU LIVE AT A USED CAR DEALERSHIP'(+1,1)
   PRINT 'OR ARE YOU A PEOPLESOFT CONSULTANT?'( +1,1)
 END-EVALUATE
END-PROCEDURE
BEGIN-PROCEDURE MERCEDES_SALES_PITCH
 PRINT 'MERCEDES IS A GREAT CAR. BUY IT'(+1,1)
END-PROCEDURE
```

In this example, the user is prompted to enter the number of cars currently at their household via the INPUT command. The value they entered is stored in the numeric variable #NUMCARS. On the basis of the value of #NUMCARS, only one of the WHEN sections will be executed. Once the code in the WHEN section is executed, the BREAK command will execute, which causes the next line to be executed to be the line immediately following the END-EVALUATE.

More Commands

DO Command The DO command is used to call a procedure. We have seen procedures being called via the DO command in several of the previous examples. The syntax of the DO command is simply the word DO followed by the procedure name to be called. For example, if it is desired to call procedure MAIN, the command would be

```
DO MAIN
```

The call to the procedure may be either with or without arguments. This call to procedure MAIN is without arguments. An example of a DO command calling a procedure with arguments follows:

```
DO SENDVAL(#VALUE1, #VALUE2)
```

This DO command is calling procedure SENDVAL and passing two arguments to it: #VALUE1 and #VALUE2. In this example, after procedure SENDVAL is executed, the #VALUE1 and #VALUE2 variables will remain whatever the values were before SENDVAL was executed even if procedure SENDVAL changed their values. In other words, these variables are sent by reference, not by value. If we wanted to send these variables by value, we would need to put a colon in front of them. To be clear, if the value of #VALUE1 or #VALUE2 were modified in procedure SENDVAL and we wanted this new value to be available to the calling procedure, then the variables must have a colon in front of them. The DO command should look as follows:

```
DO SENDVAL(:#VALUE1, :#VALUE2)
```

GOTO Command The GOTO command causes the execution of the program to jump to the specified label. The syntax of the GOTO command is the word GOTO followed by a label name. The GOTO command allows you to jump either backward or forward. In the following example, if the value of the number of cars currently at your household is greater than 4, the execution of the program jumps back up to label NEXTINPUT and the next line executed is to prompt the user to reenter the number of cars.

```
BEGIN-PROGRAM
DO MAIN
END-PROGRAM

BEGIN-PROCEDURE MAIN
NEXTINPUT:
INPUT #NUMCARS 'Enter the number of cars currently at your household:'
TYPE=integer
IF (#NUMCARS > 4)
 PRINT 'ERROR: VALUE MUST BE LESS THAN OR EQUAL TO 4'(+1,1)
 GOTO NEXTINPUT
END-IF
INPUT $YESNO 'Do you want to buy a Mercedes?'
END-PROCEDURE
```

The GOTO command and the label must be in the section of the program and in the same paragraph as well.

STOP Command The STOP command forces the SQR program to stop executing. Typically, you would print out some errors prior to the STOP command so that the user would understand why the program came to a halt. In addition, the QUIET option can be used so that SQR abort messages will not be displayed.

```
IF (#VALUE > 4)
 PRINT 'ERROR: VALUE MUST BE LESS THAN OR EQUAL TO 4'(+1,1)
 STOP QUIET
END-IF
```

BREAK Command The BREAK command is used to break out of the EVALUATE or the WHILE control structures. Refer to the EVALUATE section and the WHILE section of this chapter for more information.

EXIT-SELECT Command The EXIT-SELECT command works identically to the BREAK command. Both are unconditional exits to a control structure. The EXIT-SELECT is used only in the SELECT paragraph, whereas, the BREAK command is used to unconditionally exit out of the EVALUATE and

WHILE constructs. A program follows which contains an EXIT-SELECT statement to exit out of the select statement if the number of employees living in Ohio is greater than 100.

```
BEGIN-PROGRAM
DO MAIN
END-PROGRAM

BEGIN-PROCEDURE MAIN
BEGIN-SELECT
NAME
STATE
 IF (&STATE ='OH')
   PRINT &NAME (+1,1)
   PRINT &STATE (,35)
   ADD 1 TO #OH_EMPS
 END-IF
 IF (#OH_EMPS > 100)
   PRINT 'MAX OHIO EMPLOYEES ALLOWED'(+1,1)
   EXIT-SELECT
 END-IF
FROM EMPLOYEE_TABLE
END-SELECT
END-PROCEDURE
```

LET Command The LET command is an SQR assignment statement. We have seen it several times in the previous program examples. The syntax of the LET command follows:

```
LET destination_variable = expression
```

The expression can be as simple as a number or a single variable. The types of the variable do not have to be the same because SQR handles conversion of the variables to prevent the occurrence of errors. The expression can be very complex and made up of operands, operators, and functions. Parentheses can be used to override existing precedence rules. Some LET command examples follow:

```
Let #tax = #price * #tax
Let #var1 = (#a + #b + #c) / 100
Let #var2 = abs(#var1) + exp(#var1 * 2)
Let $string = $string || $string1 || string2
```

OPERATORS The following is a list of operators. The operators are listed by highest precedence first.

<table>
<tr><th>Operator</th><th>Description</th></tr>
<tr><td>||</td><td>Concatenate strings or dates</td></tr>
<tr><td>+,-</td><td>Sign prefix (positive or negative)</td></tr>
<tr><td>^</td><td>Exponent</td></tr>
<tr><td>*,/,%</td><td>Multiply, divide, remainder</td></tr>
<tr><td>+,-</td><td>Plus, minus</td></tr>
<tr><td>>, <, >=, <=, =, <>, !=</td><td>Comparison operators: greater than, less than, greater or equal to, less than or equal to, equal, not equal to, not equal to</td></tr>
<tr><td>not</td><td>Logical NOT</td></tr>
<tr><td>and</td><td>Logical AND</td></tr>
<tr><td>or, xor</td><td>Logical OR, XOR (exclusive OR)</td></tr>
</table>

Functions Functions can be part of an expression. A subset of the functions that SQR supports in a LET command follow:

Function	Description
abs	Returns the absolute value of the variable specified; let #dabsvar = abs(#dvar)
acos	Returns the arccosine of the variable specified
ascii	Returns the ASCII value for the first character in the string specified
asin	Returns the arcsine
atan	Returns the arctangent
cos	Returns the cosine
cosh	Returns the hyperbolic cosine of the variable specified
dateadd	Returns a date after adding (or subtracting) the specified units to the specified date value
delete	Deletes the file specified
e10	Returns the value of 10 raised to the value specified
exists	Determines if the file specified exists
exp	Returns the value of *e* raised to the value specified
log	Returns the natural logarithm of the specified value
log10	Returns the base^{10} logarithm of the variable specified

Function	Description
mod	Returns the fractional remainder
rad	Returns a value expressed in radians of num_value which is expressed in degrees
Rename	Renames the first file name to the new filename
sign	Returns a -1, 0, or + 1 depending on the sign of specified variable's value
sin	Returns the sine of the specified variable
sinh	Returns the hyperbolic sine of the specified variable
tan	Returns the tangent of the specified variable
tanh	Returns the hyperbolic tangent of the specified variable

ADD Command The ADD command adds a value to a variable The variable on the right is the one being modified. The ROUND = xx option can be used to round the result. The digits on the right side of the decimal point are rounded to the number of digits specified with xx. This ROUND option only applies to decimal or float results.

In the following example 1 is added to the numeric variable #NUMVAR:

```
ADD 1 TO #NUMVAR
```

This is more efficient than the let command:

```
LET #NUMVAR = #NUMVAR + 1.
```

The following ADD command adds the raise amount to the salary. Therefore, #salary will now be equal to #salary + #raise.

```
ADD #raise to #salary.
```

SUBTRACT Command The SUBTRACT command subtracts from a variable. The variable on the right is the one being modified. The ROUND = xx option can be used to round the result. The digits on the right side of the decimal point are rounded to the number of digits specified with xx. This ROUND option only applies to decimal or float results.

The following SUBTRACT command subtracts 2 from the variable #HOURLY_RATE. The result of the subtraction is stored in #HOURLY_RATE.

```
SUBTRACT 2 FROM #HOURLY_RATE
```

The following SUBTRACT command subtracts #PENALTY from #TAX_REFUND. The result is stored in #TAX_REFUND.

```
SUBTRACT #PENALTY FROM #TAX_REFUND
```

MULTIPLY Command The MULTIPLY command multiplies one variable times another. Again, the variable on the right side is the destination variable. The ROUND = xx option can be used on the multiply command to round the result. The digits on the right side of the decimal point are rounded to the number of digits specified with xx. This ROUND option applies only to decimal or float results.

The following example multiplies #SALES_TAX_RATE * #TOTAL. The result is stored in variable #TOTAL, and the number of decimal places is 2.

```
MULTIPLY #SALES_TAX_RATE TIMES #TOTAL ROUND=2
```

DIVIDE Command The DIVIDE command divides one number into another. Again, the ROUND=xx option can be used.

The following DIVIDE command divides #total by 98.75 and stores the result into #total (#total = #total / 98.75):

```
divide 98.75 into #total
```

INPUT Command The INPUT command is a screen input/output (I/O) command. It prompts the user and reads the user's response into a variable. The syntax of the INPUT command follows:

```
INPUT variablename ['prompt'] [TYPE=typevalue ] [MAXLEN=value]
[FORMAT=] [NOPROMPT]
```

where

Variablename	This variable will hold the input value entered by the user.
Prompt	The prompt to be displayed on the screen must be in single quotes. If a prompt is not specified, the default prompt is Enter $variablename.
NOPROMPT	Use of this qualifier stops any prompt from being displayed to the screen.
TYPE	Specifies the data type of the input. The data type of the input variable can be CHAR, TEXT, NUMBER, INTEGER, or DATE.

	If TYPE is not included in the INPUT command, the default is CHAR or TEXT. When TYPE is included on the INPUT command, the user will be prompted again if the value entered does not match the specified type.
MAXLEN	Maximum length of the input. When used on the INPUT command, this causes the user to be prompted again if the value entered is greater than the maximum length allowed. Note that MAXLEN should always be used when the data entered will be used in a table insert.
FORMAT	This qualifier is used to set the desired date format. If the format of the date entered by the user does not match the format specified with the FORMAT qualifier, then the user will be prompted again to reenter.

A sample program using the INPUT command follows:

```
BEGIN-PROGRAM
 DO LIST_EMPS
END-PROGRAM

BEGIN-PROCEDURE LIST_EMPS
INPUT #DEPT_NUM 'Enter the dept number to search for: ' MAXLEN=2
TYPE=INTEGER
BEGIN-SELECT
EMP_NAME    (+1,1)
DEPT_NO  (  ,25,5)
SALARY   (  ,40)
FROM EMPLOYEE_TABLE
WHERE DEPT_NO = #DEPT_NUM
END-SELECT
END-PROCEDURE
```

ASK Command The ASK command is a screen input/output (I/O) command also. It sets substitution variables. The substitution variables are set at compile time. The ASK command is allowed in the SETUP section only. The ASK command must be used in an SQR program if it is desired to receive parameters from the Process Scheduler. Refer to Chapter 14 for more information. The syntax of the ASK command is

```
ASK sub-var (prompt)
```

where

```
sub-var is the substitution variable
prompt is an optional prompt that is
       displayed if the value for sub-var was
       not on the command line or in an argument
       file
```

DISPLAY Command The DISPLAY command is used to display data to the screen rather than to the output report as with the print command. The DISPLAY command can use the same EDIT commands as the print command. Each DISPLAY command causes the data to be displayed on a new line of the screen. This can be suppressed via the NOLINE option of the DISPLAY command.

The following example displays 123-4567 onto the screen because of the edit mask.

```
display'1234567' xxx-xxxx
```

The following two display commands cause the text HOW ARE YOU? to be displayed on one line. This is accomplished because of the NOLINE option on the first DISPLAY command.

```
DISPLAY 'HOW ARE ' NOLINE
DISPLAY 'YOU?'
```

MOVE Command The MOVE command moves one variable to another. It can be used to convert to another variable type since the source variable and destination variable can be different types. It can edit the field also.

Some examples follow:

```
MOVE 45 TO #AGE
MOVE 'LYNN' TO $FIRSTNAME
MOVE '123456789' TO $SOCSECNUM XXX-XX-XXXX
```

STRING Command The STRING command concatenates a list of variables or literals into a single text variable. The data being concatenated are separated by the delimiter specified in the STRING command. The delimiter can be a combination of symbol(s) and character(s). However, whatever the delimiter is defined to be, it cannot occur in the data.

The following example concatenates the data shown, separates it by a colon, and stores it into variable $WININFO:

```
STRING $winner_name $selling_agent $state $amt_won BY ':' INTO
$WININFO
```

The result of this STRING command would set $WININFO to the following string. Note that the data are separated by a colon. This is because the delimiter was set to colon in the preceding STRING command.

```
John Doe:Cumberland Farms:Massachusetts:100000.00
```

UNSTRING Command The UNSTRING command performs the opposite function of the STRING command. It separates the data in a text variable into separate variables based on the delimiter specified.

To unstring $WININFO above into separate variables, perform the following UNSTRING command:

```
UNSTRING $WININFO BY ':' INTO $winner_name $selling_agent $state
$amt_won
```

Be sure that when unstringing the text variable, the variables to set are in the proper order.

Arrays

SQR supports arrays. To create an array in SQR, use the CREATE-ARRAY command.

```
CREATE-ARRAY NAME = arrayname SIZE = nn
FIELD = name:type [:occurs ][= {init_value_txt_lit|_num_lit}]
```

where

NAME = arrayname	Specifies the name of the array.
SIZE = nn	Defines the number of elements in the array.
FIELD	Specifies the name of the field; the type of the field, and the number of occurrences of the field. The valid types of the field are DECIMAL, FLOAT, INTEGER, NUMBER, CHAR, and DATE.

The CREATE-ARRAY commands must be inside the BEGIN-SETUP section. The following example creates an array named CARS that has 500 elements. The elements of the array are referenced from 0 to 499. The fields that are in the CARS array are CARYEAR, which is a number and is initialized to -1. MAKE is a character and is initialized to None. MODEL is a character and is initialized to Undefined. INSTOCK is a number, which two occurrences both are intialized to -1. INSTOCK will be referenced by INSTOCK(0) or INSTOCK(1) depending on which occurrence is being referenced.

```
BEGIN-SETUP
CREATE-ARRAY NAME=CARS SIZE=500
 FIELD=CARYEAR:NUMBER=-1
 FIELD=MAKE:CHAR='None'
 FIELD=MODEL:CHAR='Undefined'
 FIELD=INSTOCK:NUMBER:2=-1
END-SETUP
```

To reset the values in the array to their initial values, use the CLEAR-ARRAY command. Arrays are accessed with the GET and PUT commands. Other commands that can manipulate arrays are ARRAY-ADD, ARRAY-SUBTRACT, ARRAY-MULTIPLY, and ARRAY-DIVIDE.

CLEAR-ARRAY Command The CLEAR-ARRAY command clears the array. If there were initial values, the array is set to the initial values that were set up in the CREATE-ARRAY command. The syntax of the CLEAR-ARRAY command follows:

```
CLEAR-ARRAY {NAME = arrayname}
```

where NAME = arrayname specifies the name of the array to be cleared or initialized.

For example, the following CLEAR-ARRAY command initializes the CARS array:

```
CLEAR-ARRAY NAME=cars
```

GET Command The GET command retrieves data from an array and stores them in a variable. The syntax of the GET command follows:

```
GET var  FROM arrayname(element) fieldname(occurrence)
```

A couple of GET examples follow. The following example places the value stored in the #X element of array CARS field CARYEAR into variable $year:

```
GET $year FROM CARS(#X) CARYEAR
```

The next example places the first occurrence of INSTOCK of the first element of array CARS into variable $number. Remember that the elements of the array are referenced from 0 to 499. Therefore, the first element is in the 0 position. Occurrences of a field are also referenced starting with 0.

```
GET $number FROM CARS(0) INSTOCK(0)
```

PUT Command The PUT command places data into an array. The syntax of the PUT command follows:

```
PUT variable INTO arrayname (element) field (occurrence)
```

The following example puts the value of numeric variable #X into the #A element of CARS in the INSTOCK(1) field.

```
PUT #X INTO CARS(#A) INSTOCK(1)
```

On-Break

ON-BREAK is an option of the print command (both implicit and explicit prints). It is a very useful tool for creating reports which are sorted by a field. Each time the field changes conditional processing can be performed. The syntax of the ON-BREAK print qualifier follows:

```
ON-BREAK [PRINT = {ALWAYS|CHANGE|CHANGE/TOP-PAGE|NEVER}]
[SKIPLINES =]
[AFTER = procedure name]
[BEFORE = procedure name]
[SAVE = variable]
[LEVEL = nn]
```

The PRINT = qualifier specifies when to print the break field. The default is when the field changes. It can be set to ALWAYS so that the field is printed for every detail line. It can be set to CHANGE/TOP-PAGE, which will print the field each time it changes as well as when it appears at the top of a new page. It can be set to NEVER, in which case the field would never be printed. SKIPLINES = specifies the number of lines to skip when the field value changes. AFTER = specifies a procedure that should be called after the field changes. BEFORE = specifies a procedure that should be called before the field changes. SAVE = var name specifies the name of the variable to save the previous field value to. LEVEL = nn specifies the variable that the break will be occurring on. LEVEL = 1 indicates that the break will occur on the first column of the select.

The best way to explain how ON-BREAK works is to start with an example. Let's say we want to produce a report that for each music category, prints the music category, the sales in descending order, and the name of the artist who made the sales. Once the music category changes, we want to print out the total sales for the last music category before printing out the next category sales information. The output should resemble the following:

MUSIC CATEGORY	SALES	ARTIST NAME
ROCK	$ 5000.00	The Rolling Stones
	$ 2450.00	U2
	$ 1300.00	Steve Miller
TOTAL FOR ROCK	$ 8750.00	
MUSIK CATEGORY	SALES	ARTIST NAME
HARD ROCK	$ 3000.00	AC/DC
	$ 100.00	Pat Boone
TOTAL FOR HARD ROCK	$ 3100.00	
MUSIK CATEGORY	SALES	ARTIST NAME
POP	$ 2850.00	Celine Dion
	$ 1600.00	Rod Stewart
	$ 1500.00	Tina Turner
	$ 1250.00	Elton John
	$ 1250.00	Carol King
TOTAL FOR POP	$ 8450.00	
TOTAL SALES FOR ALL MUSIC CATEGORIES	$20,300.00	
PAGE COUNT	1.0	

The program which can produce the music report is listed below:

```
BEGIN-FOOTING 3
PRINT 'PAGE COUNT '(+1,1)
PRINT #PAGE-COUNT (,+10)
END-FOOTING

BEGIN-PROGRAM
 DO MAIN
 PRINT 'TOTAL SALES FOR ALL MUSIC CATEGORIES'(+1,1)
 PRINT #TSALES (,35) EDIT $99999.99
END-PROGRAM

BEGIN-PROCEDURE MAIN
BEGIN-SELECT
CATNAME (+1,1) ON-BREAK LEVEL=1 SAVE=$CATNAME AFTER=PRINTOT
BEFORE=PRINTHEAD
SALES (,25) EDIT $99999.99
ARTISTNAME (,35)
 LET #SALES = #SALES + &SALES
 LET #TSALES = #TSALES + &SALES
FROM MUSIC
ORDER BY CATNAME, SALES DESC
END-SELECT
END-PROCEDURE

BEGIN-PROCEDURE PRINTOT
```

```
 LET $OUT = 'TOTAL FOR '||$CATNAME
 PRINT $OUT (+1,1)
 PRINT #SALES (,25) EDIT $99999.99
 LET #SALES = 0
 NEXT-LISTING
END-PROCEDURE

BEGIN-PROCEDURE PRINTHEAD
 PRINT 'MUSIC CATEGORY'(+1,1) UNDERLINE
 PRINT 'SALES' (,25) UNDERLINE
 PRINT 'ARTIST NAME'(,35) UNDERLINE
END-PROCEDURE
```

Note the ON-BREAK qualifier on the implicit print statement in the select paragraph. It looks like this:

```
CATNAME (+1,1) ON-BREAK LEVEL=1 SAVE=$CATNAME AFTER=PRINTOT
BEFORE=PRINTHEAD
```

It has several qualifiers on it. The LEVEL = 1 qualifier means that the break will occur on the category name variable (CATNAME) since this is the first variable in the select. The BEFORE = PRINTHEAD qualifier means that before each break, call procedure PRINTHEAD. Procedure PRINTHEAD prints out the column labels of MUSIC CATEGORY, SALES, and ARTIST NAME. The AFTER = PRINTOT qualifier means that after each break occurs, procedure PRINTOT will be called. The SAVE = $CATNAME means that each time the category changes, the previous category name will be stored in variable $CATNAME.

This program selects category name, sales, and artist name from the table MUSIC. It is ordered by the music category name and sales in descending order. The first thing this program does is call procedure MAIN. Once in MAIN, the first thing this program does is call procedure PRINTHEAD to print the column labels. Then the first row of category name, sales, and artist name is selected from the table MUSIC. The variable $catname will be set to ROCK and then the first row of data (The Rolling Stones) will be printed. It will continue printing the detailed data under the music category of ROCK and adding up the sales for this category in variable #SALES. It is also accumulating the total sales for all categories in variable #TSALES. Once the category changes to HARD ROCK, the AFTER procedure PRINTOT will be processed. Since $catname was set to ROCK, $OUT is set to TOTAL FOR ROCK and is printed along with the sales (#SALES). Then #SALES is cleared and a NEXT-LISTING is done. (NEXT-LISTING puts the cursor on a new line and resets the line count to 1.) Again, the save variable will be set to the new music category value. Therefore, $catname will now be HARD ROCK. The

BEFORE procedure PRINTHEAD is called again to print the column labels. If there is a SKIPLINES qualifier, the number of lines specified would now be skipped. The detail lines in the HARD ROCK category will be printed and the #sales variable will be adding up the sales for the HARD ROCK category now. This will continue until a break in the level 1 variable CATNAME occurs again. When another break occurs, the AFTER procedure is called again to print TOTAL FOR HARD ROCK etc. and to set #sales to 0. The save variable is now set to POP. The BEFORE procedure PRINTHEAD is called to print the column labels. The detail lines in the POP category will be printed and the sales for the POP category will be updated. This will continue until the select is complete. After the select is complete, the AFTER procedure is called again. Finally, procedure MAIN is complete and the program is back in the BEGIN-PROGRAM paragraph. This is where TOTAL SALES FOR ALL MUSIC CATEGORIES is printed out.

Multiple Reports

It is possible to have the same program output to many different reports. The reports will each be in a separate output file. The first step to handling multiple reports in a program is to declare the reports in the BEGIN-SETUP section. For example, in the following setup section, two reports are declared: the DETAIL report and the SUMMARY report.

```
BEGIN-SETUP
DECLARE-REPORT DETAIL
END-DECLARE

DECLARE-REPORT SUMMARY
END-DECLARE
END-SETUP
```

Once the report names are declared, the USE-REPORT is used to make a report current. The print commands print to the current report.

```
USE-REPORT DETAIL
PRINT 'THIS PRINT WILL BE PRINTED ON THE DETAIL REPORT'(+1,1)
PRINT 'THIS PRINT WILL ALSO BE PRINTED ON THE DETAIL REPORT'(+1,1)
USE-REPORT SUMMARY
PRINT 'THIS PRINT WILL BE PRINTED ON THE SUMMARY REPORT'(+1,1)

USE-REPORT DETAIL
PRINT 'THIS PRINT WILL BE PRINTED ON THE DETAIL REPORT '  (+1,1)
```

In addition, each report can have its own header and footer by listing the report names in the FOR-REPORTS = qualifier of the BEGIN-HEADING or BEGIN-FOOTING lines.

```
BEGIN-HEADING 3 FOR-REPORTS=(DETAIL)
 PRINT 'MAJOR'(+1,1)
 PRINT 'GRADE POINT' (,+10)
 PRINT 'STUDENT NAME'(,+10)
END-HEADING

BEGIN-HEADING 3 FOR-REPORTS=(SUMMARY)
 PRINT 'MAJOR'(+1,1)
 PRINT 'AVERAGE GRADEPOINT'(,+10)
 PRINT 'HIGH GRADEPOINT'(,+10)
 PRINT 'LOW GRADEPOINT' (,+10)
END-HEADING
```

Flat Files

SQR language contains the ability to process flat files. A flat file is an ASCII or text file or a tape containing ASCII or text files. The data in the database can be exported to a flat file or imported from a flat file. The SQR commands that perform these functions are the OPEN command, the READ command, and the WRITE command.

Opening a Flat File via the OPEN command The OPEN command is used to open a flat file. The syntax of the OPEN command follows:

```
OPEN filename AS filenum accesstype
{FOR-READING|FOR-WRITING|FOR-APPEND}
{RECORD = record length [:FIXED|:FIXED_NOLF|:VARY]}
[STATUS = numbervar ]
```

where

filename	The name of the flat file to be opened.
filenum	The logical unit number of the flat file to be opened.
accesstype	Access type must be set to FOR-READING, FOR-WRITING, or FOR-APPEND.
FOR-READING	The file is opened for sequential read.
FOR-WRITING	A new file is opened for writing.
FOR-APPEND	The file is opened and new data are written at the end of the existing data.

Record length	This is the length of the record. If the record type is FIXED, the record length is the length without the terminator. If the record type is VARY, the record length is the maximum length of the record. The default record type is VARY. The maximum record length that can be opened is 32767.
STATUS = #var	The #var is a variable that will store the status of the OPEN command. The OPEN command is successful when the #var value is 0. If #var is -1, then the OPEN command failed. Use of the STATUS qualifier is highly recommended because otherwise if the OPEN command fails, the program will just simply come to a halt.

Some OPEN command examples follow. The following example opens the file CUSTOMER.DAT for reading. This file will have a record length of 80, and the record length will be 80 fixed. The status variable to check is called #STAT. The logical unit number assigned to this file is 2. This logical unit number must then be used in the READ or WRITE commands to access this file.

```
OPEN 'CUSTOMER.DAT' AS 2 FOR-READING RECORD=80:FIXED STATUS=#STAT
IF #STAT != 0
   PRINT 'OPEN ERROR  ON CUSTOMER.DAT'(+1,1)
   STOP
END-IF
```

The following example opens the file stored in string variable $FILE_NAME. The logical unit number assigned to this file is 1. The file is opened for writing and the maximum record length is 132. The status variable is #ST.

```
OPEN $FILE_NAME AS 1 FOR-WRITING RECORD=132:VARY STATUS=#ST
IF #ST <> 0
 !process errors as desired
END-IF
```

The following example opens the file EMPLOYEE.DAT. The logical unit number assigned to this file is 3. The file is opened for appending and the record length is 80 fixed length with no line delimiters. The status variable is #OPEN_STATUS.

```
OPEN 'EMPLOYEE.DAT' AS 3 FOR-APPENDING RECORD=80:FIXED_NOLP
            STATUS=#OPEN_STATUS
IF #OPEN_STATUS=-1
  PRINT 'OPEN ERROR ON FILE EMPLOYEE.DAT'(+1,1)
END-IF
```

Reading a Flat File via the READ Command The READ command reads a record from a flat file and stores it into SQR variable(s). The syntax of the READ command is

```
READ logical-unit-number INTO variables STATUS = #var
```

where

`Logical-unit-number`	The number assigned to the file in the open command.
`Variables`	Variable or variables in which the record data from the flat file will be stored; the `:length` option can be used when filling the variables.
`STATUS = #var`	The `#var` is a variable that will store the status of the READ command. The read command is successful when the `#var` value is 0. Otherwise a system error number will be stored in `#var`. It is highly recommended to use the `STATUS` qualifier because otherwise if the READ command fails, the program will simply come to a halt.

The `#end-file` reserved SQR variable is 1 when the end of the flat file is reached and there are no more data to read. The data from the flat file can be read into text or numeric variables.

A few examples follow. The first two examples are similar. They are reading from a flat file containing customer information. In fact, the same information is contained in both files. The difference is that in the first example, the data in the file are not delimited. Instead, the length of each field is known and the READ command is using the `:length` option when storing the data in each variable. In the second example, the entire record of 80 characters long is being stored in string variable `$cust_var`. The UNSTRING command is used to separate the data which is comma-delimited in the file into separate variables.

```
READ 2 INTO $CUSTNAME:20 $ADDR:20 $CITY:10 $STATE:2 $ZIP:5
$ITEMBOUGHT:23

READ 2 INTO $CUST_VAR:80
UNSTRING $CUST_VAR BY ',' INTO $CUSTNAME $ADDR $CITY $STATE $ZIP
$ITEMBOUGHT
```

In this example, the flat file contains text data and numeric data. The record is read and the first two characters are stored in the text variable `$PROCCODE`. The next 10 characters in the file are stored in the numeric variable #VALUE. The next character is stored in the numeric variable #FLAG, and the next nine characters are stored in text variable $DEPT.

```
READ 1 INTO $PROCCODE:2 #VALUE:10 #FLAG:1 $DEPT:9
```

Finally, there is a short program which determines if the file customer.dat exists by using the EXISTS command. If it does exist, the file is opened for reading with a varied record length of 132. Otherwise, an error is displayed and the program is stopped via the STOP command. The status variable #iostat is checked to determine if the open was successful. Again, if the open was unsuccessful, the program is stopped via the STOP command. Next, the program will go into the WHILE loop and continue reading from the customer.dat file until there are no more records to read. No more records is determined by checking the #end-file variable. If #end-file is 1, then the BREAK command breaks us out of the WHILE loop. The UNSTRING command is used to break up the comma-delimited file into variables $name, $addr1, $city, $state, and $phone. The data are printed to the report for each record that was read from the file.

```
begin-program
 do main
end-program

begin-procedure main
if exists('customer.dat')=0
open 'customer.dat' as 1 for-reading status=#iostat record=132
else
  display 'File customer.dat does not exist: exiting'
  stop quiet
end-if
if #iostat=-1
  display 'Error opening file customer.dat'
  stop quiet
end-if

while 1 = 1
  read 1 into $cust_var:132
  if #end-file
   break ! no more records to read
  end-if
  unstring $cust_var by ',' into $name $addr1 $city $state $phone

  print $name (,+10)
  print $addr1 (,+25)
  print $city  (,+25)
  print $state (, +12)
  print $phone (, +12)
end-while
close 1
end-procedure
```

In this program, the data that were read in from the flat file could be inserted directly into the database table if desired by placing the following BEGIN-SQL paragraph into the while loop of the program:

```
BEGIN-SQL
INSERT INTO CUSTOMER_TABLE (NAME, ADDRESS, CITY, STATE, PHONE) VAL-
UES ($NAME, $ADDR1, $CITY, $STATE, $PHONE)
END-SQL
```

Writing to a Flat File via the WRITE command The WRITE command writes data stored in SQR variable(s) to a flat file. The file must be opened for writing in order to write to the file.

The syntax of the WRITE command is

```
WRITE logical-unit-number FROM variables STATUS = #var
```

where

`Logical-unit-number`	The number assigned to the file in the open command.
`Variables`	Variable(s) that will be written to the flat file; the `:length` option can be used and if so, the value will be truncated or filled to meet the length.
`STATUS = #var`	The `#var` is a variable that will store the status of the WRITE command. The WRITE command is successful when the `#var` value is 0. Otherwise a system error number will be stored in `#var`. Use of the `STATUS` qualifier is highly recommended because otherwise if the WRITE command fails, the program will simply come to a halt.

A few examples follow. The first two examples are similar. They involve writing customer information to a flat file. In fact, the same information will be written to both files. The difference is that in the first example, the variables are written directly to the file. The second example utilizes the STRING command.

The STRING command concatenates them together separated by commas into text variable $CUST_VAR. Then $CUST_VAR is written directly into the file.

```
WRITE 2 FROM $CUSTNAME:20 $ADDR:20 $CITY:10 $STATE:2 $ZIP:5 $ITEM:23
```

and

```
STRING $CUSTNAME $ADDR $CITY $STATE $ZIP $ITEMBOUGHT BY ','
INTO $CUST_VAR
WRITE 2 FROM $CUST_VAR
```

APPENDIX A

CONFIGURATION MANAGER

To start the Configuration Manager, simply select START, PROGRAMS, PEOPLETOOLS, CONFIGURATION MANAGER.

The Configuration Manager allows the user to change configuration settings that PeopleTools uses when it is running. It is a dialog box containing tabs. Each tab contains several settings grouped together by function. Each tab contains an OK button, a CANCEL button, an APPLY button, and a HELP button. When you double-click on the OK button, the changes that were made to the settings are saved and the Configuration Manager is closed. The CANCEL button cancels any changes and closes the Configuration Manager. The APPLY button saves the changes made to the settings and allows the user to remain in the Configuration Manager. The HELP button brings up Help screens pertinent to the tab currently being displayed. The changes made to the settings do not take effect until PeopleTools is restarted.

A description of the Configuration Manager tabs follows:

STARTUP Tab

The STARTUP tab allows the operator to modify the following PeopleSoft settings:

1. *Initial window.* The screen name entered here is the first screen that will appear after the user has logged into PeopleSoft successfully.
2. *Sign-on defaults.* This section contains the default values of the database type, application name, server name, database name, and operator id that appear on the sign-on screen. The defaults (with the exception of passwords, of course) appear automatically to facilitate user sign-on; users will not need to type any values in unless they prefer to sign on to something other than the default.
   - Database type is the type of the relational database management system being used. For example, some selections would be SQLbase or ORACLE.

- Application name is the application's server name. This is required only if the user entered APPSRV when selecting the database type. This indicates that instead of signing on to a database, the user is signing on to an application server. To sign on to an application server, the application server must be registered on the APPLICATION SERVERS tab of the Configuration Manager.
- Server name is the default database server name.
- Database name is the default database name that the user will utilize when PeopleSoft is running.
- Operator id is the PeopleSoft operator id. The operator id is set up in the Security Administrator.

3. *Operator can override.* This section contains *operator can override database type*, *operator can override database name*, and *operator can override operator id*. When there is a check next to database type, this indicates that a specific user may enter a different database type when signing on to PeopleSoft. If it is not checked, the user can sign on only to the default database type set up for that user. The same is true for *operator can override database name*. When override database name is not checked, the operator can log in only to the default database set up for that user.
4. *Server logon security.* This feature allows setting a database password outside of PeopleSoft. It behaves differently depending on the database type.

To make the changes, click on the OK button. To exit without making changes, click on the CANCEL button. The changes made will not take effect until PeopleSoft is exited and reentered.

An example of a STARTUP tab is shown in Figure A-1.

DISPLAY Tab

The Display screen allows the operator to configure the general format of PeopleSoft screens. It allows the operator to modify the following PeopleSoft settings:

1. *Panel display.* This group of settings contains display size, panel sizing, show panel in navigator, highlight popup menu fields, and show database name.

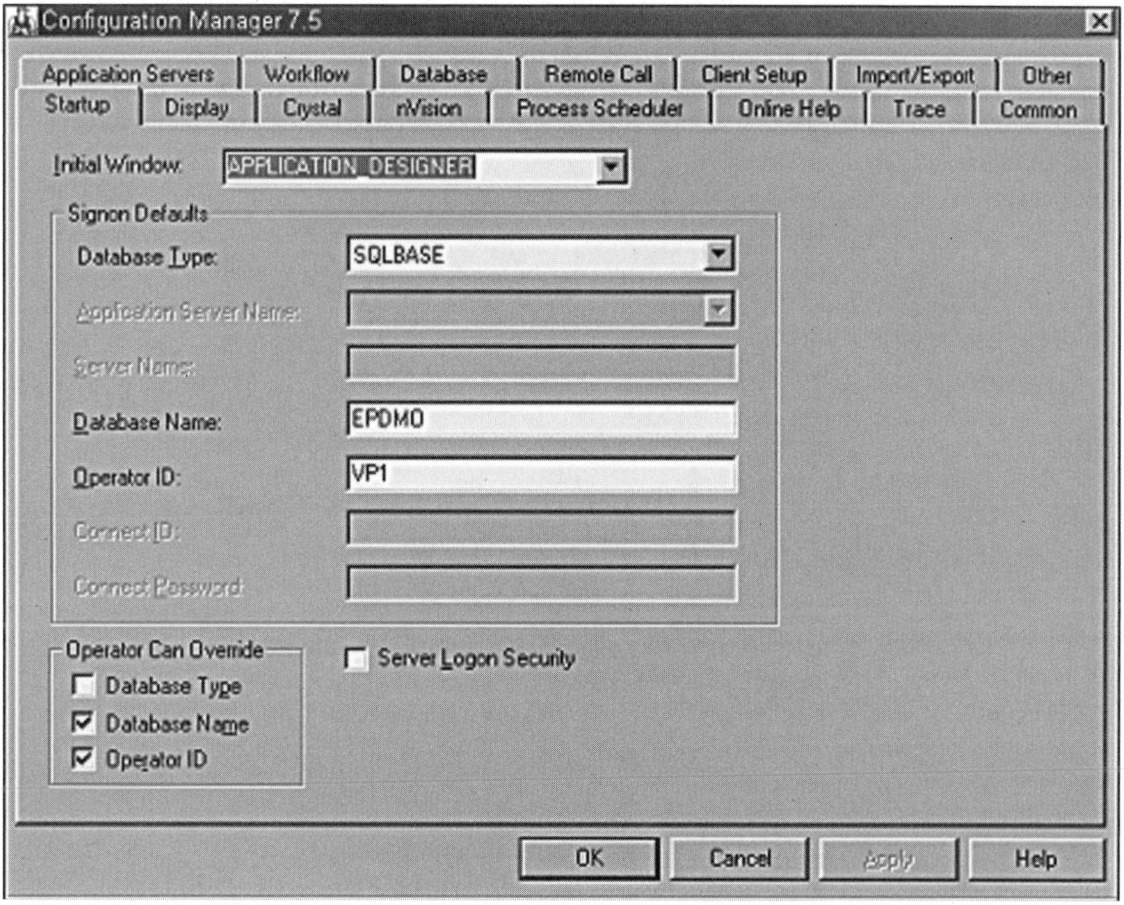

Figure A-1 STARTUP tab.

- *Display size.* This is the width × height of the screen in pixels. If a value is blank or zero, the default size will be 640 × 480. This display size will affect all the PeopleSoft windows.
- *Panel sizing.* This can be set to CLIP or SCALE. When a larger screen is opened in a smaller window, the screen will be cut off on the right side and on the bottom of the screen if CLIP is selected. However, if SCALE is selected, the larger screen will be resized so that all its contents will fit in the smaller window.
- *Show panel in navigator.* When selected, this means that the user will see the panel view and the tree view of a business process on the same window.

- *Highlight popup menu fields.* Fields associated with popup menu will be highlighted when this option is checked.
- *Show database name.* When selected, this means that the status bar at the bottom of the screen will display the current database name.

2. *Navigator display.* The Navigator display can be set to ON, OFF, or FIRST. When it is set to ON, the Business Process Navigation display is always displayed when a menu group is opened. If it is set to FIRST, the Business Process Navigation display will be displayed only the first time. If it is set to OFF, the only way for the Business Process Navigation display to be displayed is if the user manually does so by selecting VIEW, NAVIGATION, BUSINESS PROCESS in the application.

An example of the DISPLAY tab of the Configuration Manager is illustrated in Figure A-2.

CRYSTAL Tab

The CRYSTAL tab of the Configuration Manager allows the user to modify the following setting groups: crystal directories and options.

1. *Crystal directories.* This section consists of `CRYSTAL EXEs` Path and Default Crystal Reports. The `CRYSTAL EXEs` Path is the directory where the `CRYSTAL` report executables are located. The Default Crystal Reports is the default directory in which the Crystal Reports will be stored on creation.
2. *Options.* The options that can be set up in the Configuration Manager are *use trace during execution* and *report columns*.
   - If use trace during execution is selected, a trace file must be entered on the CRYSTAL tab. This file is where the trace statements will be written during the execution of the Crystal Report.
   - If report columns is checked, the Crystal Report will be created with column numbers. Otherwise, there will not be column numbers on the report.

   An example of the CRYSTAL tab is illustrated in Figure A-3.

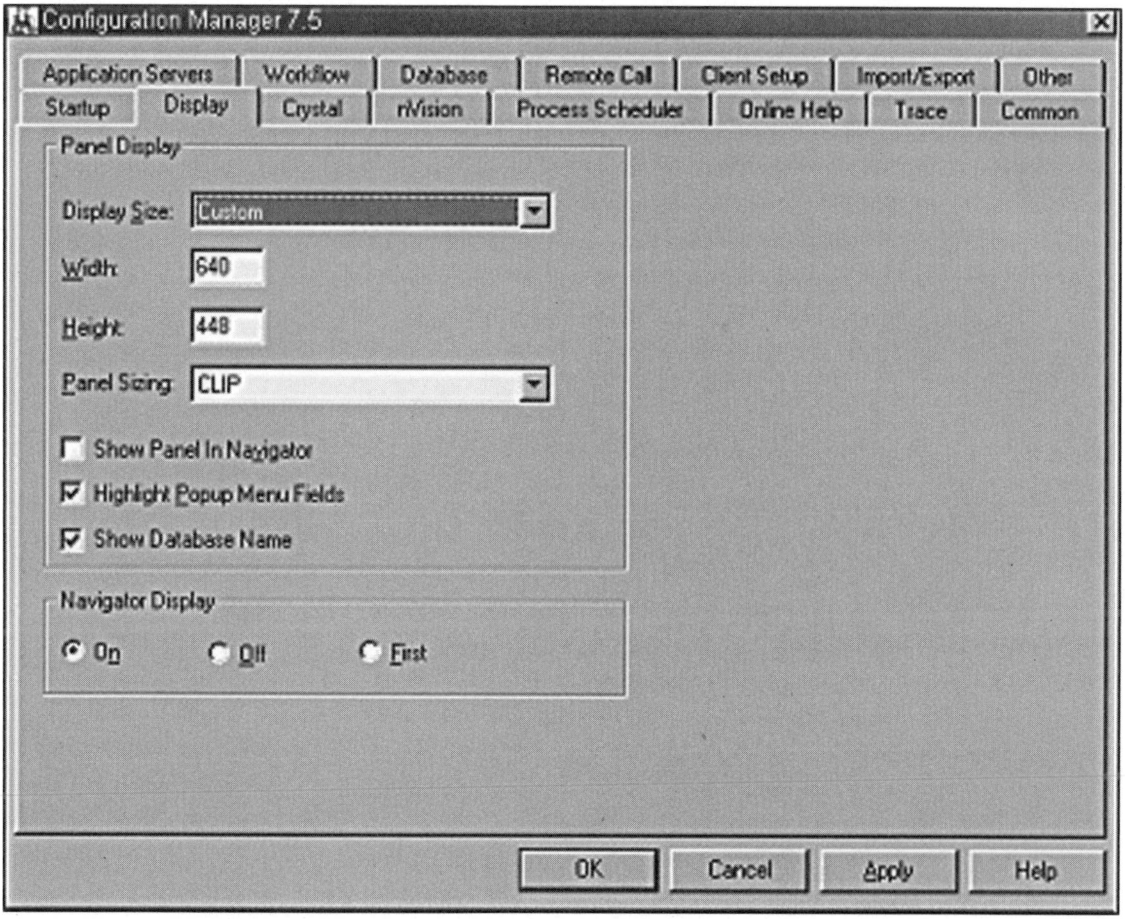

Figure A-2 DISPLAY tab.

NVISION Tab

The NVISION tab allows the user to configure which spreadsheet application is being used, space between query columns, and directory paths.

The spreadsheet application must always be set to EXCEL. The *space between query columns* setting specifies the number of blank characters between output columns.

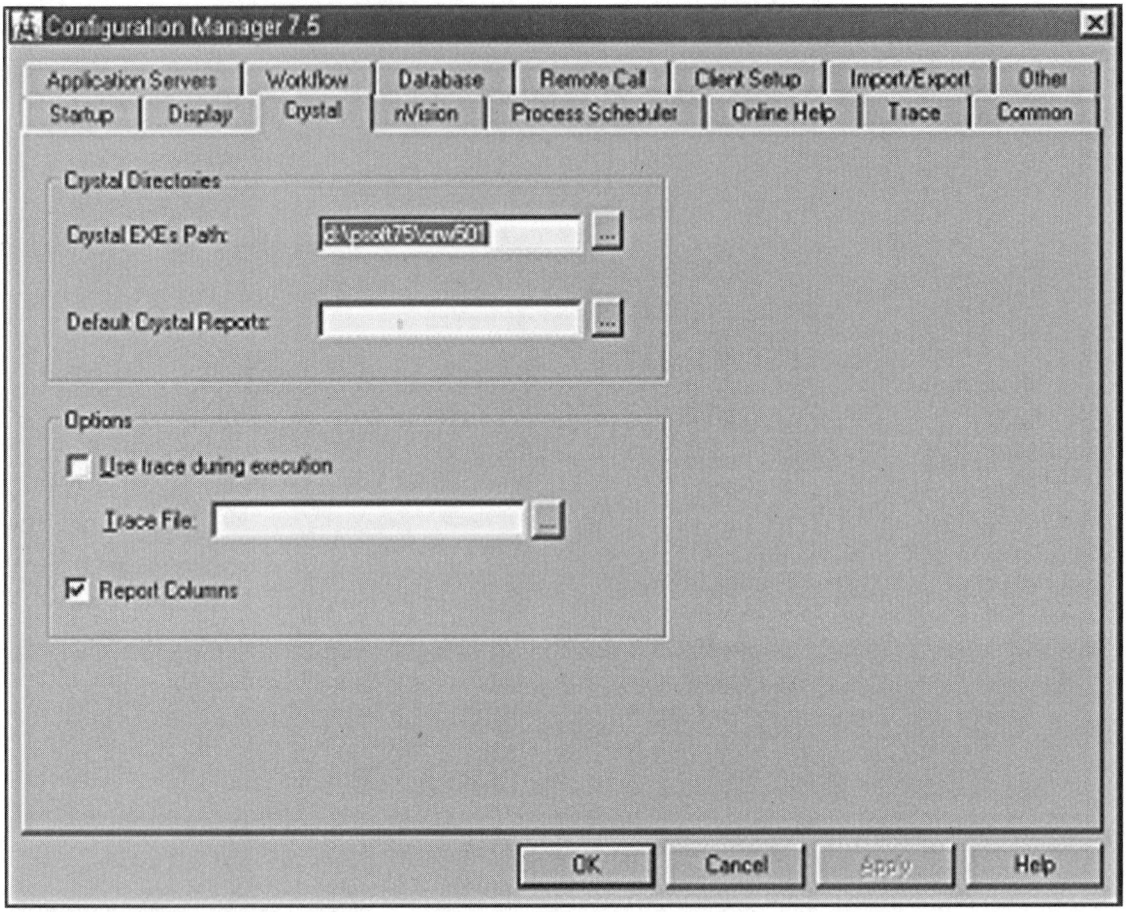

Figure A-3 CRYSTAL tab.

The directory paths group of settings allows the setup of the Excel installation directory, the customization macros directory, the report layouts directory, the drilldown layouts directory, the report instance directory, and the query templates directory.

1. *EXCEL installation directory*: location of Microsoft Excel executables
2. *Customization macros*: directory location of nVision macros
3. *Report layouts*: location of nVision report layouts
4. *Drilldown layouts*: location of layouts

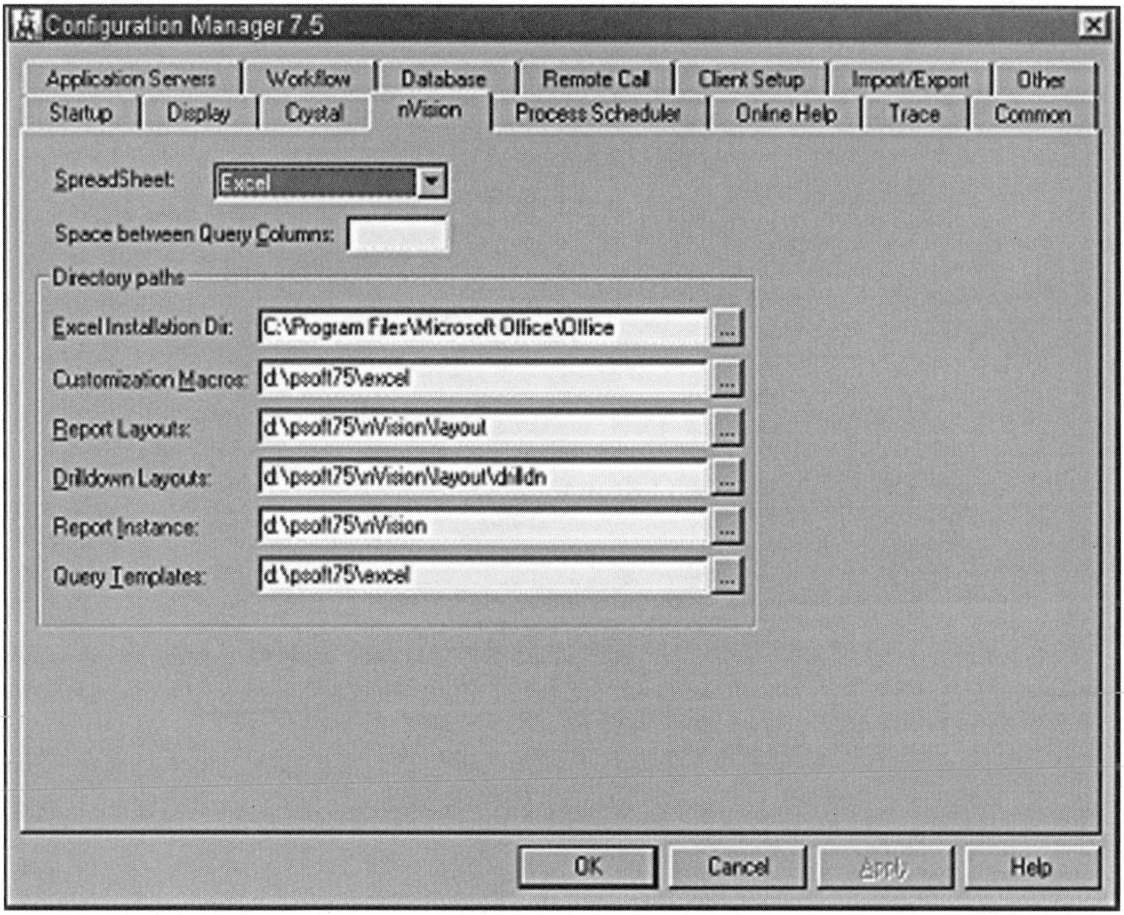

Figure A-4 NVISION tab.

5. *Report instance*: location of report instance
6. *Query templates directory*: location of Excel's `QUERY.XLT` file

An example of an NVISION tab is displayed in Figure A-4.

PROCESS SCHEDULER Tab

The PROCESS SCHEDULER tab (Fig. A-5) allows the user to set up all the directories that the Process Scheduler uses. The following directories can be set up:

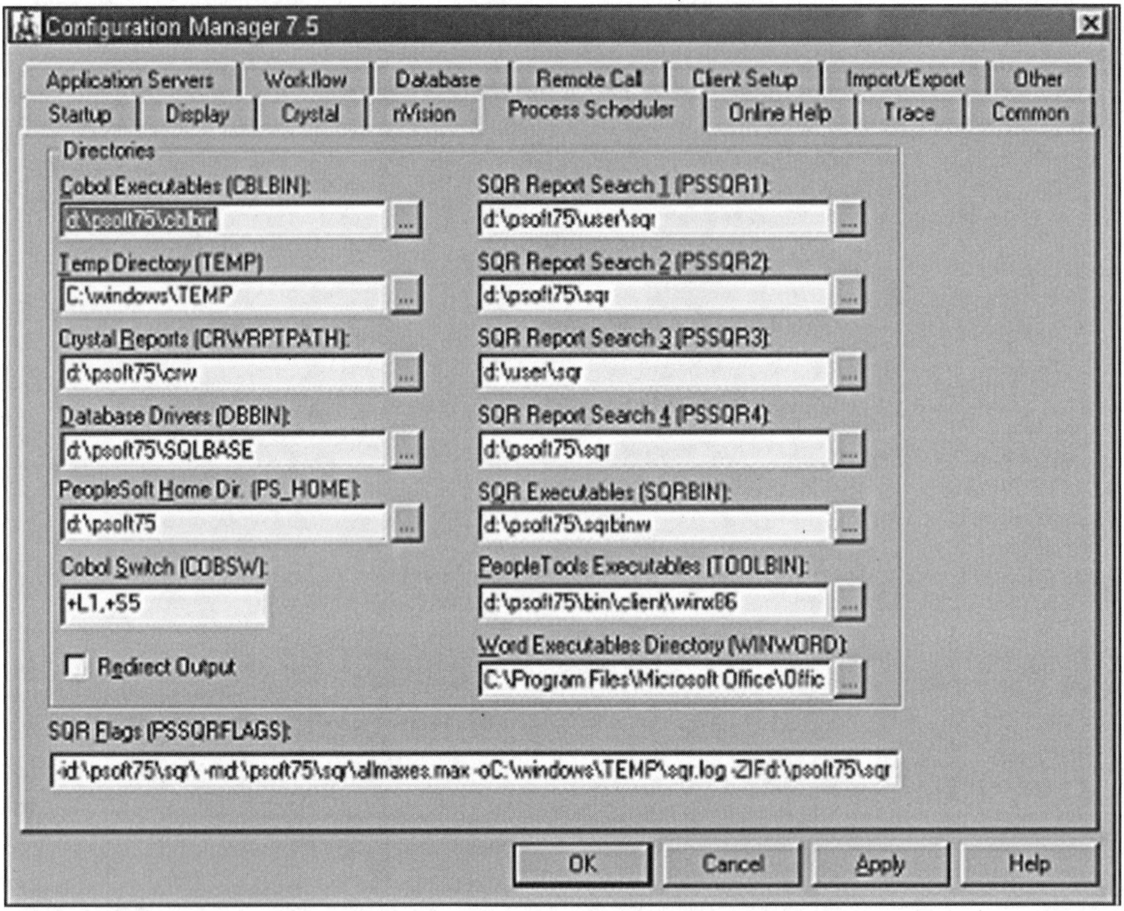

Figure A-5 PROCESS SCHEDULER tab.

1. *COBOL executables* (CBLBIN). This is the directory path where the COBOL executables are located.
2. *Temp directory* (TEMP). This is the directory path for the temporary directory.
3. *Crystal reports* (CRWRPTPATH). This is the directory path where the Crystal Reports are created.
4. *Database drivers* (DBBIN). This is the directory path where the database drivers are located.

5. *PeopleSoft home directory* (PS_HOME). This is the top-level PeopleSoft directory.
6. *COBOL switch* (COBSW). This is a setting used for determining what type of messages appear on the screen when COBOL programs are running. It is used when debugging your program. The default for this setting is +L5, +S5.
7. *SQR Report Search 1* (PSSQR1). This is the first directory path that the SQR executables will use to find SQR reports.
8. *SQR Report Search 2* (PSSQR2). This is the second directory path that the SQR executables will use to find SQR reports.
9. *SQR Report Search 3* (PSSQR3). This is the third directory path that the SQR executables will use to find SQR reports.
10. *SQR Report Search 4* (PSSQR4). This is the fourth directory path that the SQR executables will use to find SQR reports.
11. *SQR executables* (SQRBIN). This is the directory path where the SQR executables are located.
12. *PeopleTools executables* (TOOLBIN). This is the directory path where the PeopleTools executables are located.
13. *WORD executables directory* (WINWORD). This is the directory path where the Microsoft Word executables are located.

In addition to the directory paths, the following can also be set up on the PROCESS SCHEDULER tab:

1. *Redirect output box.* When checked, allows the user to send the output messages to a log file rather than just to the screen. The log file will be located in the user's %TEMP%\PS_HOME\DBNAME directory.
2. *SQR flags.* These are the option flags needed for SQR reports to be started by the Process Scheduler. The following options must be entered:

-i	This flag is used to indicate the path to the SQC files.
-o	This flag is used to indicate the path and name of the log file.
-f	This flag is used in front of the output path.
-ZIF	This flag is used to indicate the path to the SQR.INI.
-m	This flag is used to indicate the path to the ALLMAXES.MAX.

ONLINE HELP Tab

The ONLINE HELP tab allows the setup of the following:

1. *NFO Files Path.* This is the directory path where PeopleBooks are located (i.e., files with the extension .NFO).

2. *PeopleBooks Search Order.* This is the order in which the .NFO files will be searched.

3. *PeopleBooks Viewer.* This is the full path to VIEWS.EXE.

4. *Help Viewer.* This is the full path to PSHLP.EXE.
5. *Function keys.* The following three function keys can be set up by the user to execute the PeopleBooks viewer, to execute the help viewer, to execute Windows help, or to be unassigned:

   F1
   SHIFT +F1
   CTRL +F1

An example of the ONLINE HELP tab is displayed in Figure A-6.

TRACE Tab

The TRACE tab allows the user to select SQL trace options and PeopleCode trace options. It also allows the user to select the online trace file.

An example of the TRACE tab is displayed in Figure A-7.

COMMON SETTINGS Tab

The COMMON SETTINGS tab changes the language default, cache files default directory, and data mover directories; the Data Mover directories group consists of the input directory, output directory, and log directory:

- *The language default.* The language in which the menus and panels are displayed. The default language is English.
- *Cache files default directory.* The parent directory path of the cache files for your database. In this section, there is a PURGE

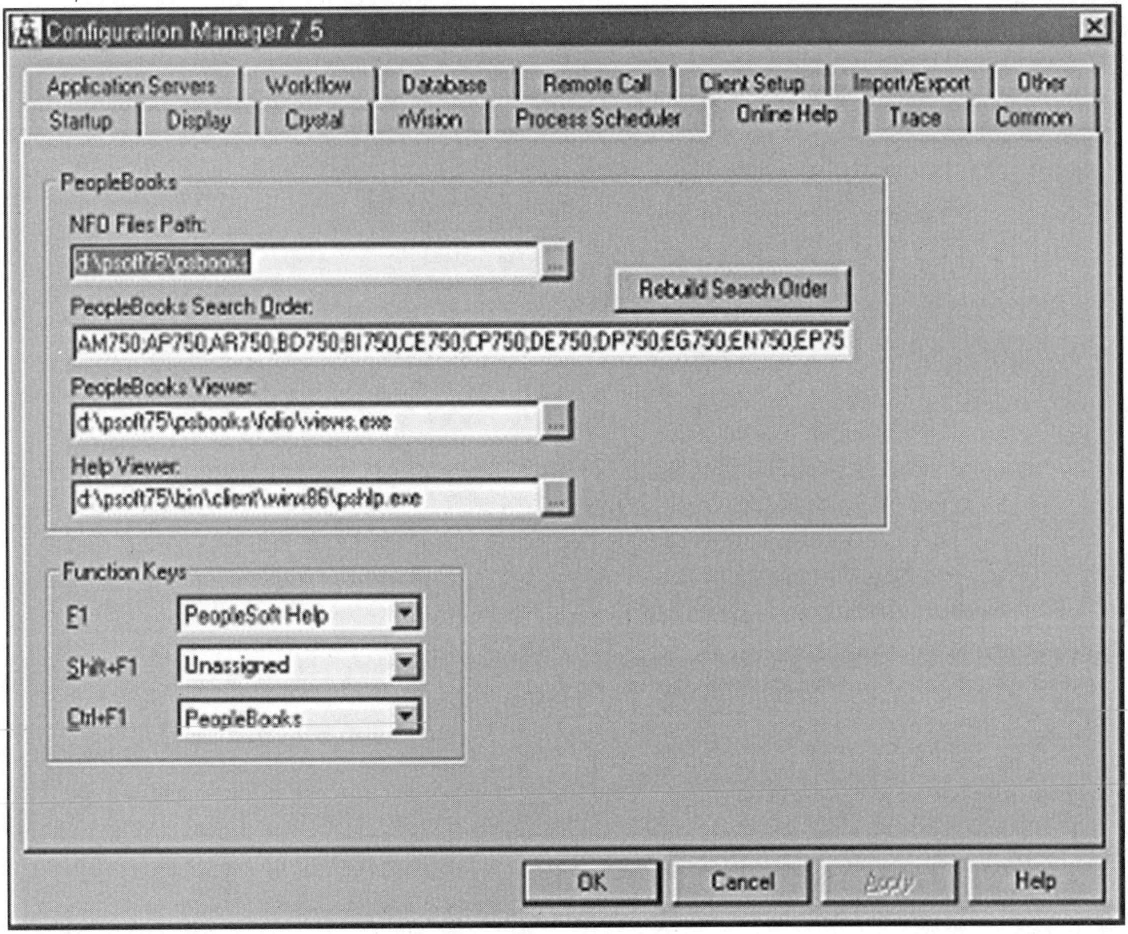

Figure A-6 ONLINE HELP tab.

CACHE DIRECTORIES button. If this button is double-clicked on, the user can choose to delete a cache directory from a list of existing cache directories or delete all cache directories. There is a different cache directory for each database.

- *Data mover input directory*. This is the path of the Data Mover input data files (files with an extension of `.DB`)
- *Data mover output directory*. This is the path where Data Mover will put the scripts it creates.

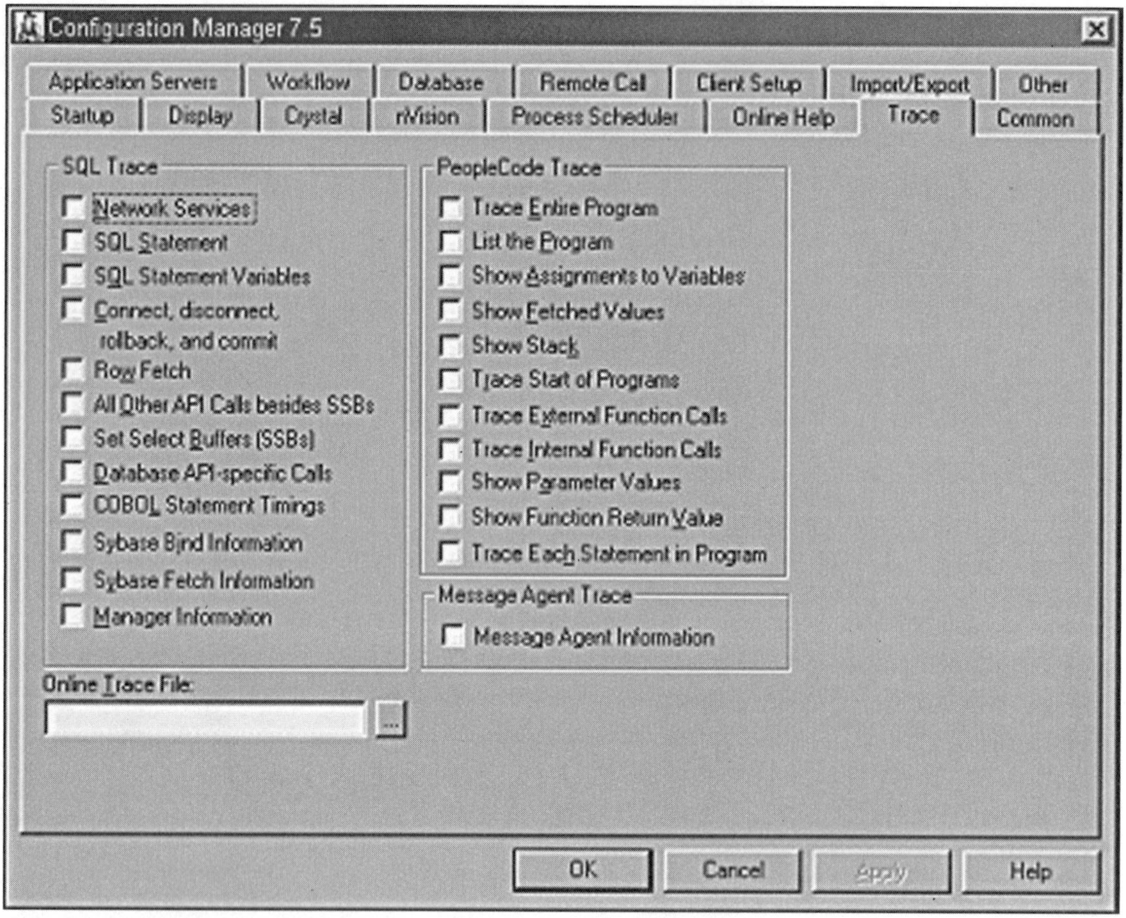

Figure A-7 TRACE tab.

- *Data mover log directory*. This is the path of the Data Mover Log files.

An example of the COMMON SETTINGS tab is displayed in Figure A-8.

OTHER Tab

The OTHER tab allows the operator to enter the quality server settings. These settings include the local data directory and the SQR output directory:

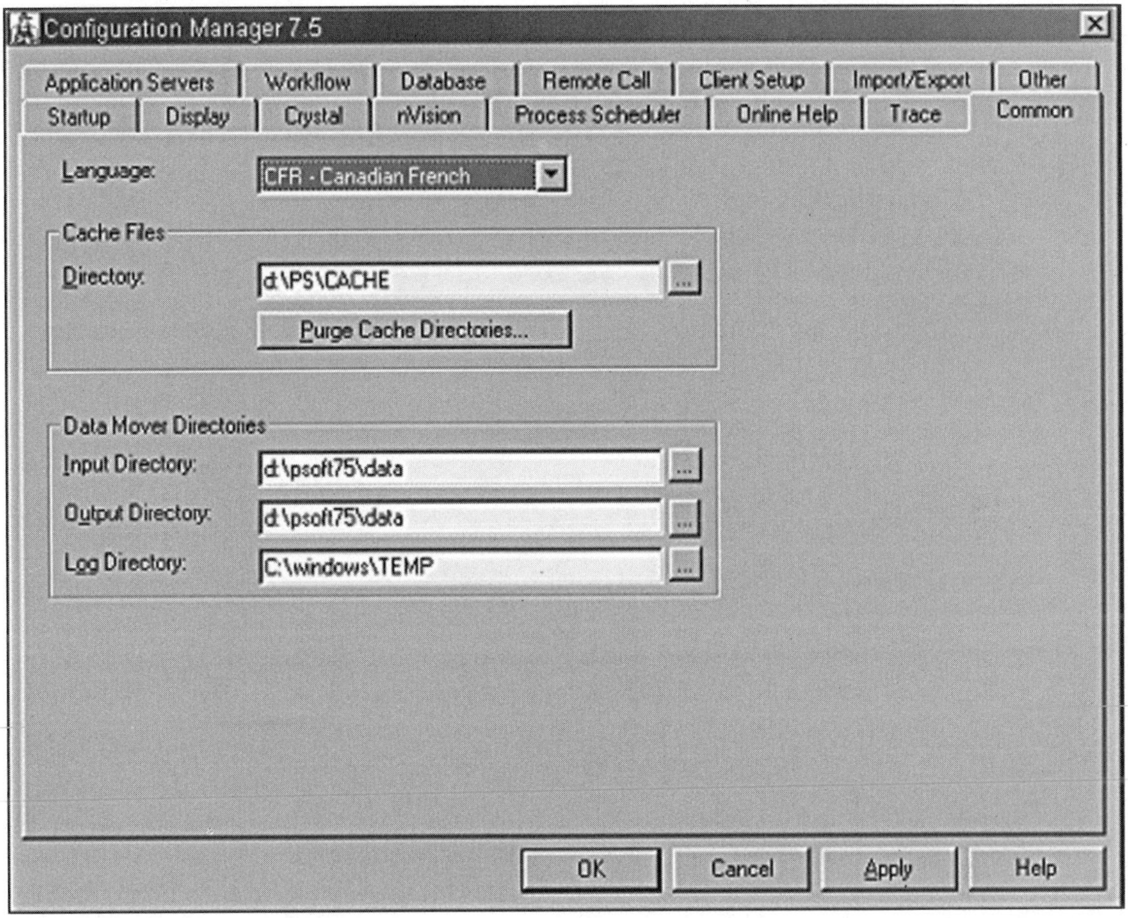

Figure A-8 COMMON SETTINGS tab.

- *Local data directory.* The path where the analysis data files are located.
- *SQR output directory.* The path the SQR uses to write to the analysis data files.

An example of the OTHER tab is displayed in Figure A-9.

IMPORT/EXPORT Tab

The Import/Export screen allows the user to save the configuration settings recently set up to a file for later use (export). (It is essential that

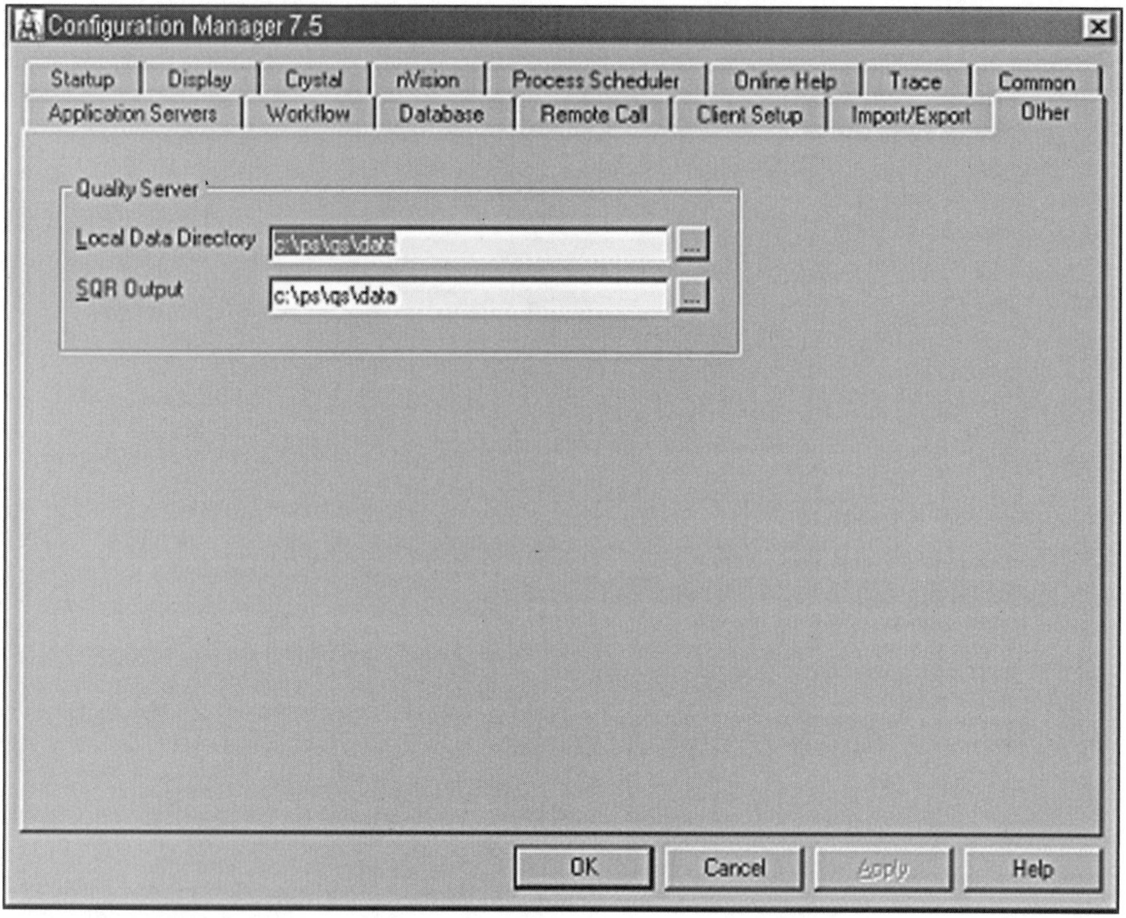

Figure A-9 OTHER tab.

the user select the APPLY button prior to selecting to EXPORT. Otherwise, any changes made in this session would not be saved to the export file.) After the EXPORT key is selected, the user will be asked to enter the name of the export file. This file would then be imported to configure another workstation for a different user if desired. When it is desired to import from a file, the user must select a file from a list. Once the file is opened, the settings in that file will be in effect. An example of the IMPORT/EXPORT tab is displayed in Figure A-10.

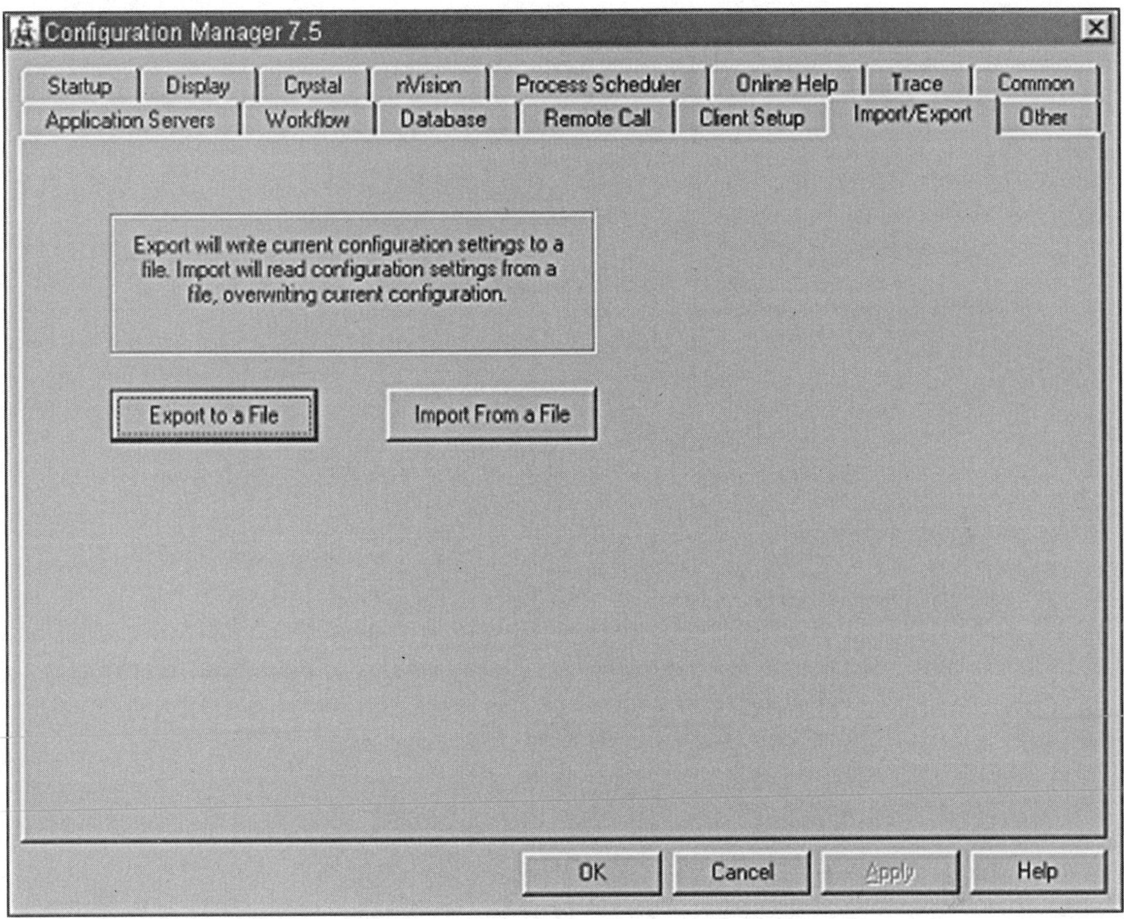

Figure A-10 IMPORT/EXPORT tab.

CLIENT SETUP Tab

The CLIENT SETUP tab allows the operator to modify the following settings related to the workstation:

1. *Shortcut links.* When any of the following boxes are checked, a shortcut is created on the workstation which only needs to be double-clicked on to invoke the process:

- PeopleTools
- Application Designer
- Configuration Manager
- Data Mover
- Uninstall Workstation
- PeopleTools RPT Converter
- PeopleBooks
- SQA Robot Setup
- SQR

2. *ODBC setup.* These options are *Install ODBC driver Manager 3.0* and *Install PeopleSoft ODBC driver*. These options should be selected to run the PeopleSoft Open Query application. However, if your client already has ODBC drivers installed, then the first of these two options is not necessary. If you do select it, your ODBC Driver Manager may be overwritten.
3. *Three-tier minimal install.* Copy three-tier client to local drive. When checked, the user must enter the local directory where the three-tier files will be installed.
4. *Install workstation box.* This box must be checked to have the shortcut links created, ODBC setup performed, and three-tier minimal install performed.

Click on the OK or APPLY button prior to exiting this screen for the settings to be saved. Figure A-11 shows an example CLIENT SETUP tab.

REMOTE CALL Tab

The REMOTE CALL tab is illustrated in Figure A-12. It allows the user to modify Remote Call Client Configuration Parameters. These parameters consist of

1. *Timeout time.* The time in seconds that Tuxedo's Remote Call will kill its child COBOL process.
2. *Debugging options.* When running Remote Call in debug mode, the user can choose to redirect the standard output and standard error of the COBOL process to a log file. If this is desired, the Redirect Output box should be checked. Also, if the user wishes to save the COBOL input file, the Support COBOL animation box should be checked. This means that the input file can be used with the COBOL animator.

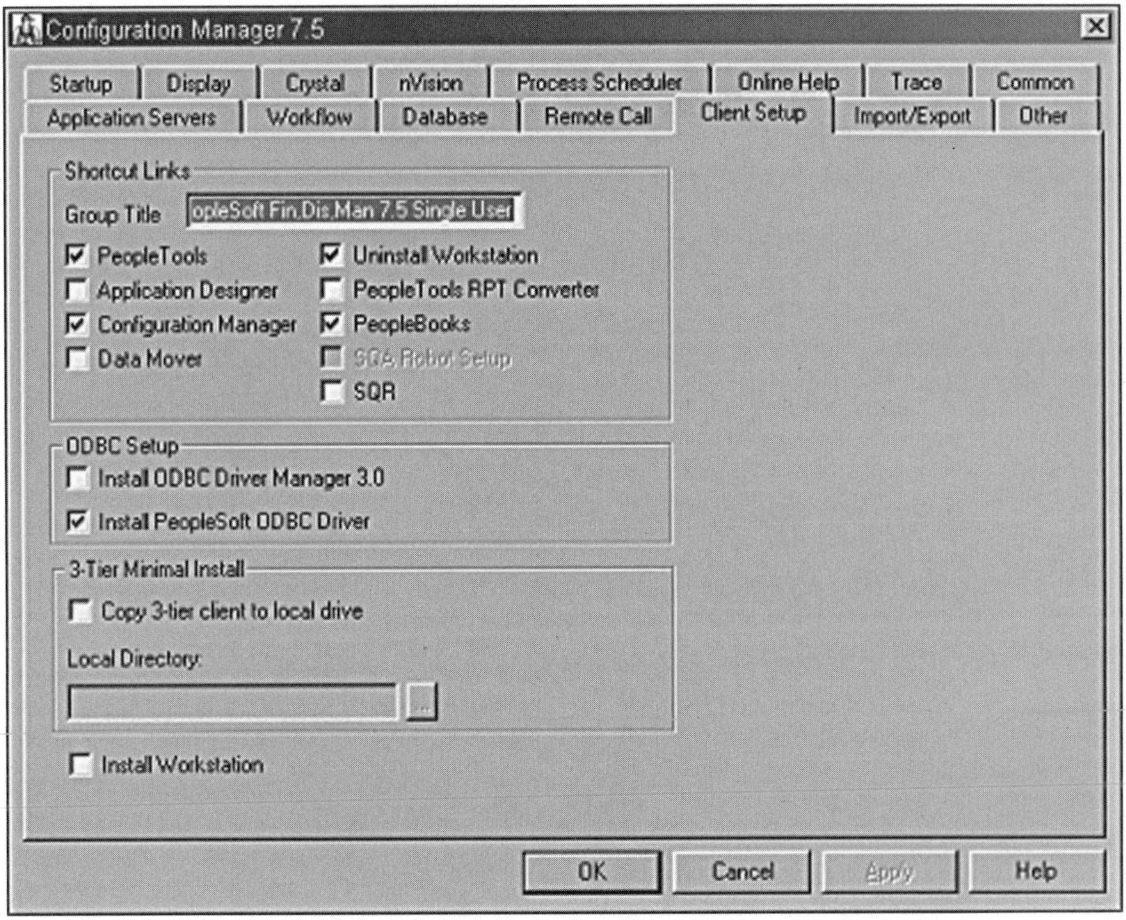

Figure A-11 CLIENT SETUP tab.

3. *Show window state.* This refers to whether the COBOL process window should be normal, minimized, or hidden.

DATABASE Tab

The DATABASE tab (Fig. A-13) allows the user to modify the following:

1. *DB2 input message size in bytes.* Maximum size of the DB2 input message buffer.

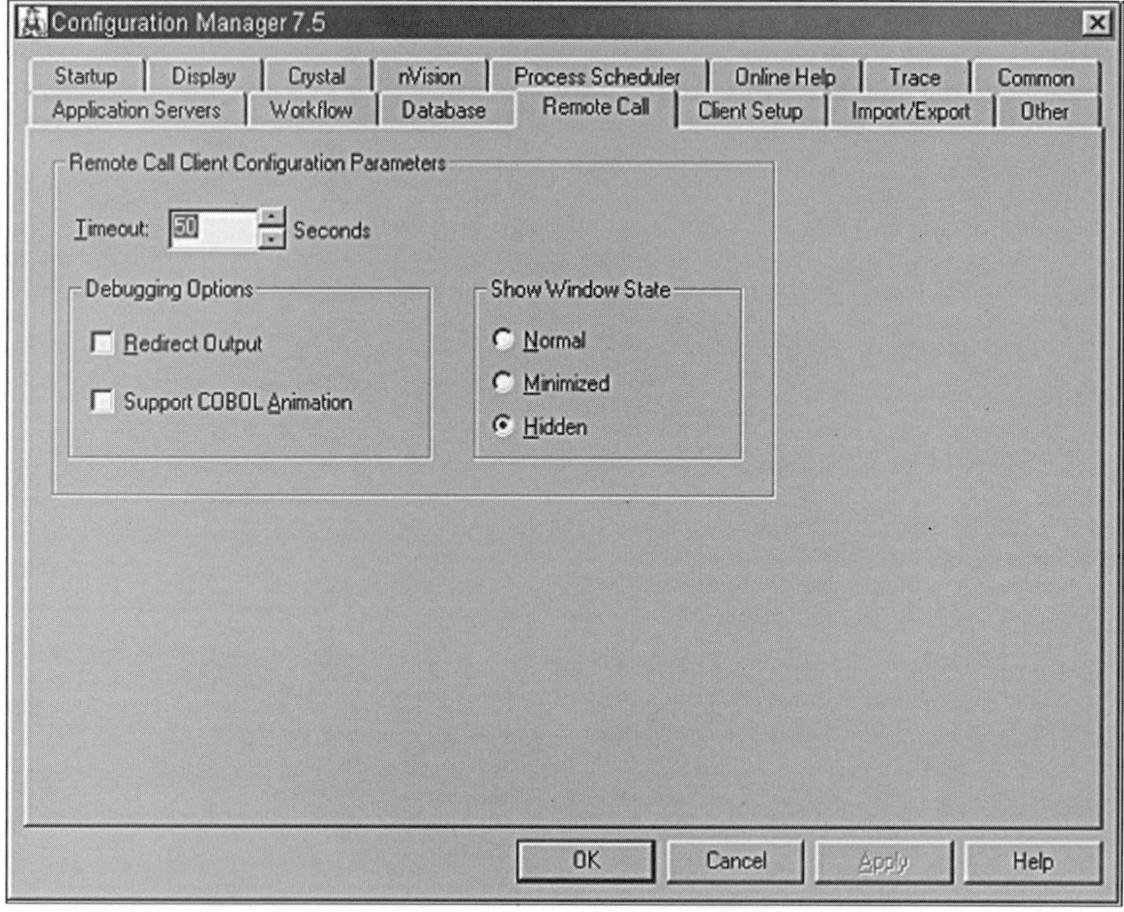

Figure A-12 REMOTE CALL tab.

2. *DB2 output message size in bytes.* Maximum size of the DB2 output message buffer.

3. *Sybase packet size.* TCP (Transmission Control Protocol) packet size is the packet size used in TCP/IP (TCP/Internet Protocol) communication with the Sybase server. Default is 512.

4. *Application designer image conversion.* Allows user to select the desired image conversion option. The options are "Convert and shrink images to platform limit," "Convert and shrink images to image size limit," "Don't convert, but shrink images to image size

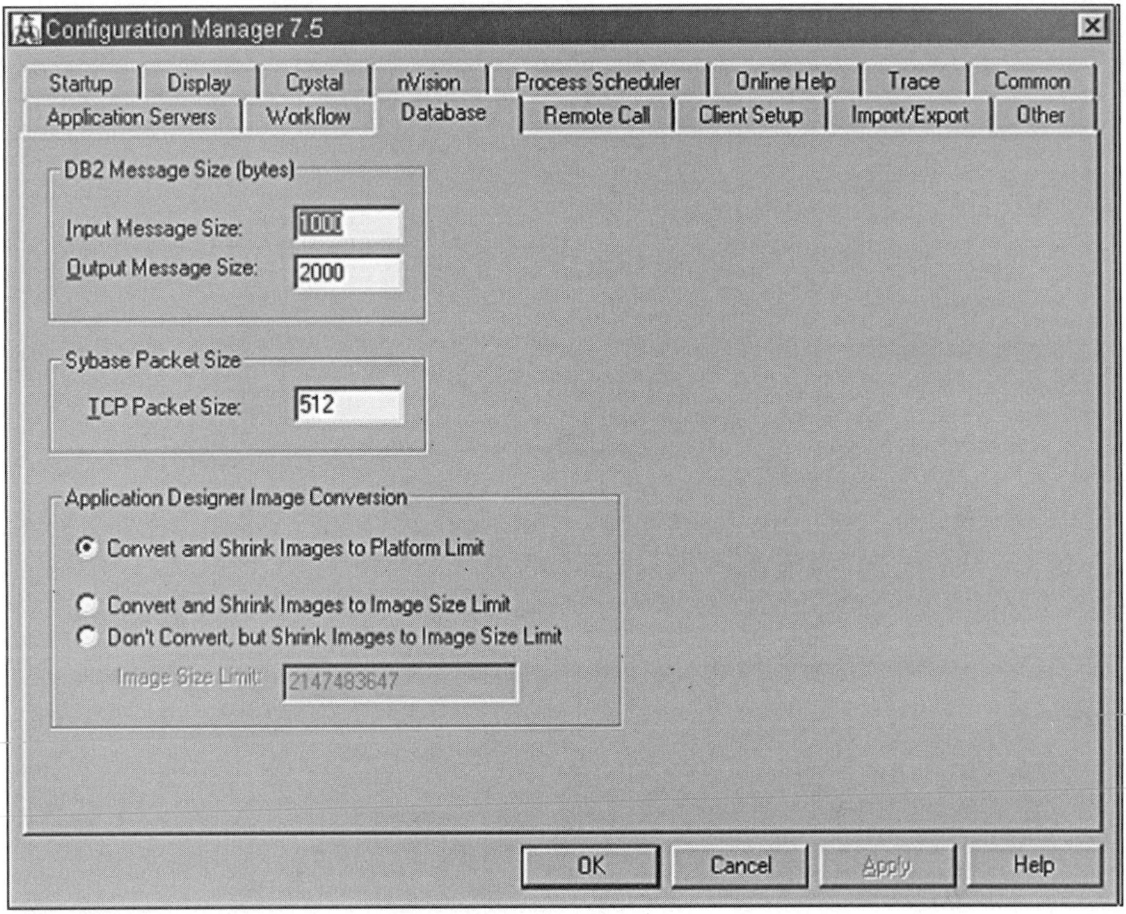

Figure A-13 DATABASE tab.

limit." These options are necessary when a new version of PeopleTools is put on your machine. The old images are not compatible with the newer version. Hence, the images need to be converted.

WORKFLOW Tab

The Workflow Tab (Fig. A-14) of the Configuration Manager allows the user to set up settings related to automated workflow. *Automated workflow* is when certain things automatically happen in the system. For

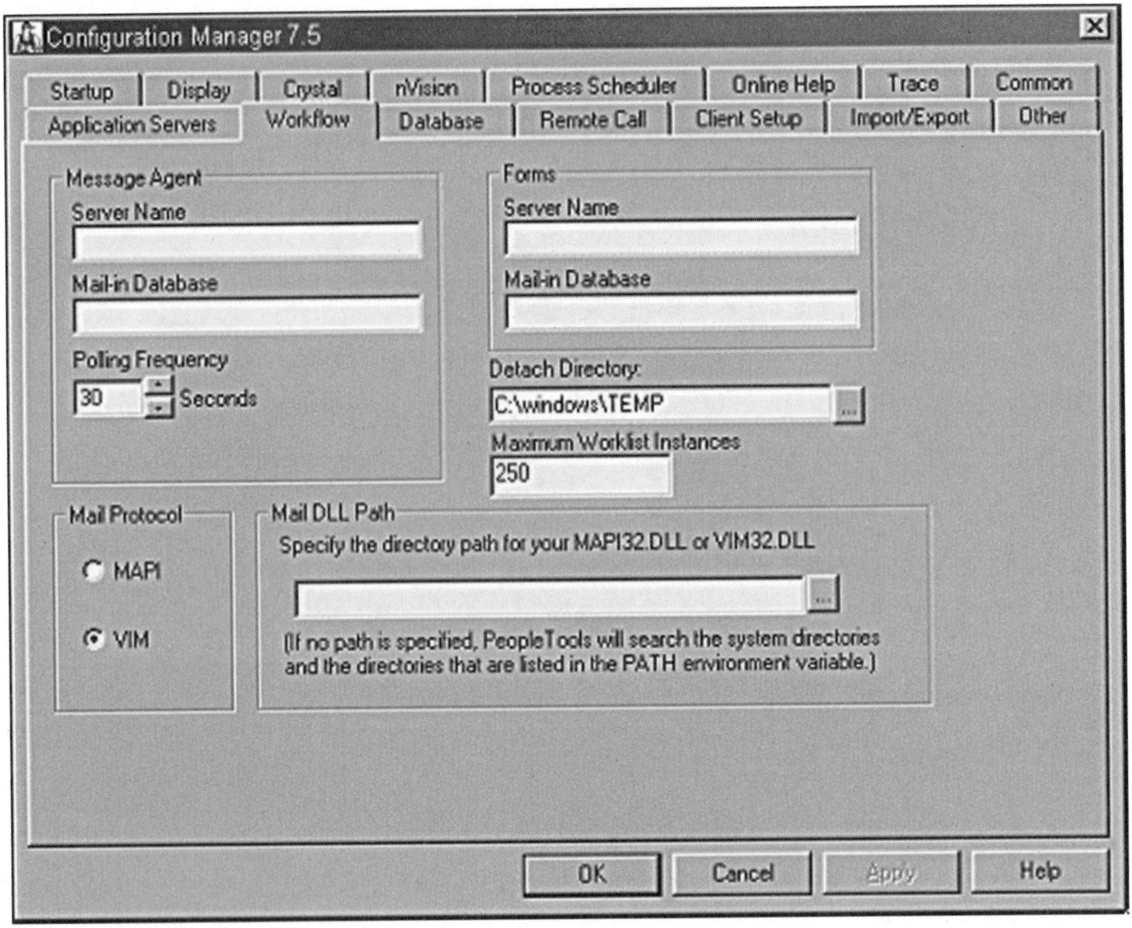

Figure A-14 WORKFLOW tab.

example, when an employee orders an item, a form may be automatically sent out to another employee for approval or an email message may be sent out. The following workflow settings are set up in the Configuration Manager on the WORKFLOW tab:

1. *Message agent settings.* Server name, mail-in database, and polling frequency make up the message agent section.
   - *Server name.* The server where the Lotus Notes mail-in database is located.
   - *Mail-in database.* The name of the Lotus Notes mail-in database where the Lotus Notes forms are sent.

- *Polling frequency.* Length of time in seconds that the mail-in database is checked to see if any new forms are waiting to be processed.

2. *Forms.* Server name and mail-in database make up the forms section.
   - *Server name.* The Lotus Notes server where the forms are defined.
   - *Mail-in database.* The database name where the forms are defined.
3. *Detach directory.* The directory where any attachments on the forms are placed and where any files not delivered are placed.
4. *Maximum worklist instances.* Maximum number of worklists displayed.
5. *Mail protocol.* Mail protocol can be MAPI (Messaging Application Program Interface) or VIM (Vendor Independent Messaging Interface). Choose the mail protocol currently being used on the your system.
6. *Mail DLL path.* The location of the mail DLL.

APPLICATION SERVERS Tab

The *Application Servers* Tab allows the user to set up the following settings:

1. *Application server name.* The name of the application server on which PeopleSoft will be running.
2. *Machine name or IP address.* This is the IP address of the Application Server. The same IP address must be in the `PSAPPSRV.CFG` file
3. *Port number.* This is the port number of the Application Server. The value entered here must be the same as the one entered in the `PSAPPSRV.CFG` file.
4. *Tuxedo connect string.* A string that allows the client to connect to another server.
5. *SET button.* SET places the application server name on the top of the screen so that another application server can be set up. Don't

forget to select APPLY or OK to save the Application Server set up prior to exiting the Configuration Manager. Don't be fooled into thinking that because the Application Server is displayed on the top of the screen, it is saved. Again, it is saved only if APPLY or OK has been selected.

6. *DELETE button.* Deletes an application server setup.

Figure A-15 illustrates the APPLICATION SERVERS tab.

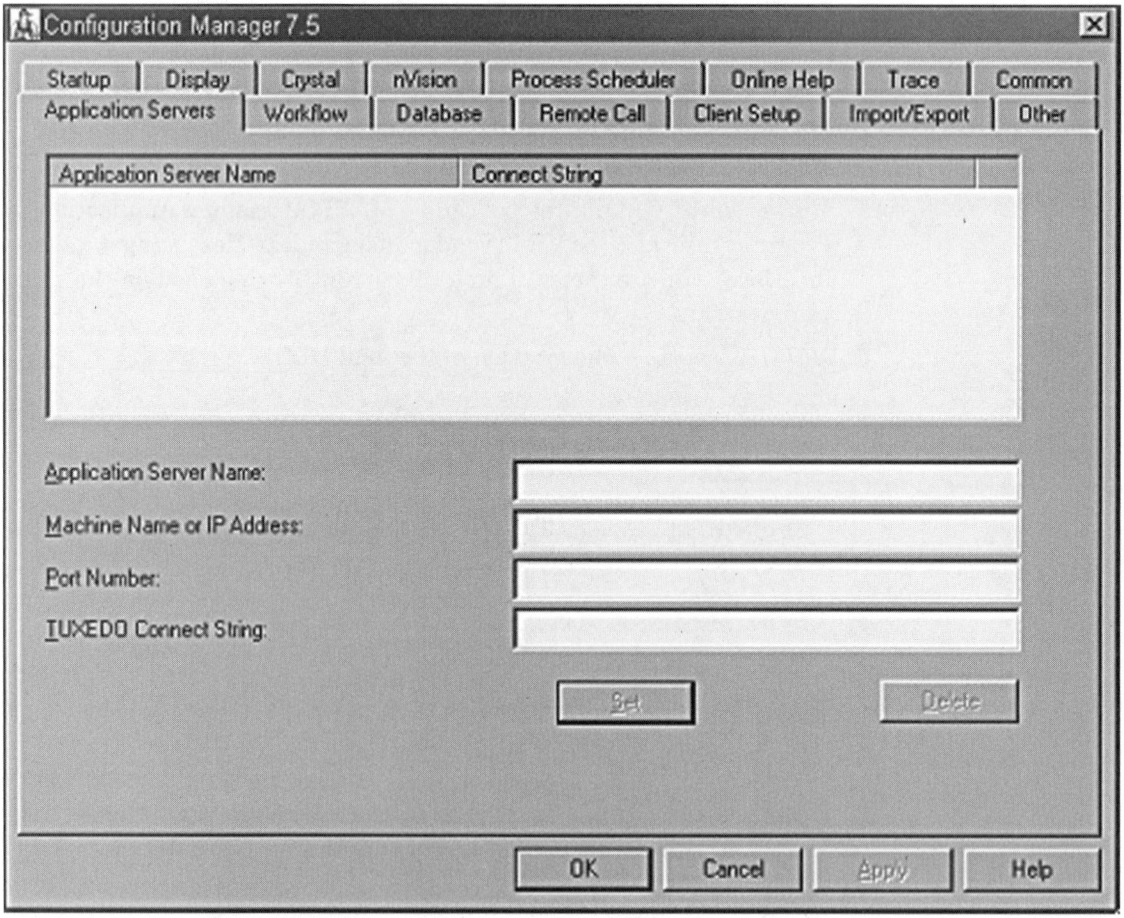

Figure A-15 APPLICATION SERVERS tab.

APPENDIX B

APPLICATION DESIGNER IN UPGRADE MODE

The Application Designer can be run in Development mode and in Upgrade mode. In the Project Workspace of the Application Designer, there are two tabs. The left tab is the Development tab and the right tab is the Upgrade Mode tab. The Application Designer is used to develop a project when the development tab in the Project Workspace is selected. The Application Designer is in Upgrade Mode when the Upgrade tab is selected. Upgrade mode means that the project will be upgraded from development and testing into production. When the project is upgraded to production for example, objects in the project residing in the testing database (source database) are copied to the production database (target database).

Click on the Upgrade tab to view the Application Designer in Upgrade Mode. Once this is done, the Upgrade View is displayed. Refer to Figure B-1 to see what the Upgrade View looks like. The Upgrade View contains a folder for all the object types that can be upgraded. When an object folder is double clicked on, the Upgrade Definition Window for that object type appears as shown in Figure B-2.

The Upgrade Definition Window displays all the objects of that type. For each object, it displays information such as the name, source, target, action, upgrade, and done. The source column displays the status of this object in the source database. The target column displays the status of this object in the target database. The status column values can be 'changed', 'unchanged', or 'absent'. The action column is the action that will take place on this object when it is upgraded to the target database. The possible actions are 'Add', 'Delete', or 'Replace'. The upgrade box must be checked if the user wishes to upgrade this object into the target database. The Done column indicates whether the object has been upgraded to the target database. The Done flag can be cleared in order for the object to be copied over again. The user can modify these settings as desired. The user can also run comparison reports on the source and target databases to be sure of what actions he or she wants to do during the upgrade. To run comparison reports, the user should select TOOLS, UPGRADE, COMPARE AND REPORT. The objects in the source database and the target database should be locked during the comparison process and the Upgrade process.

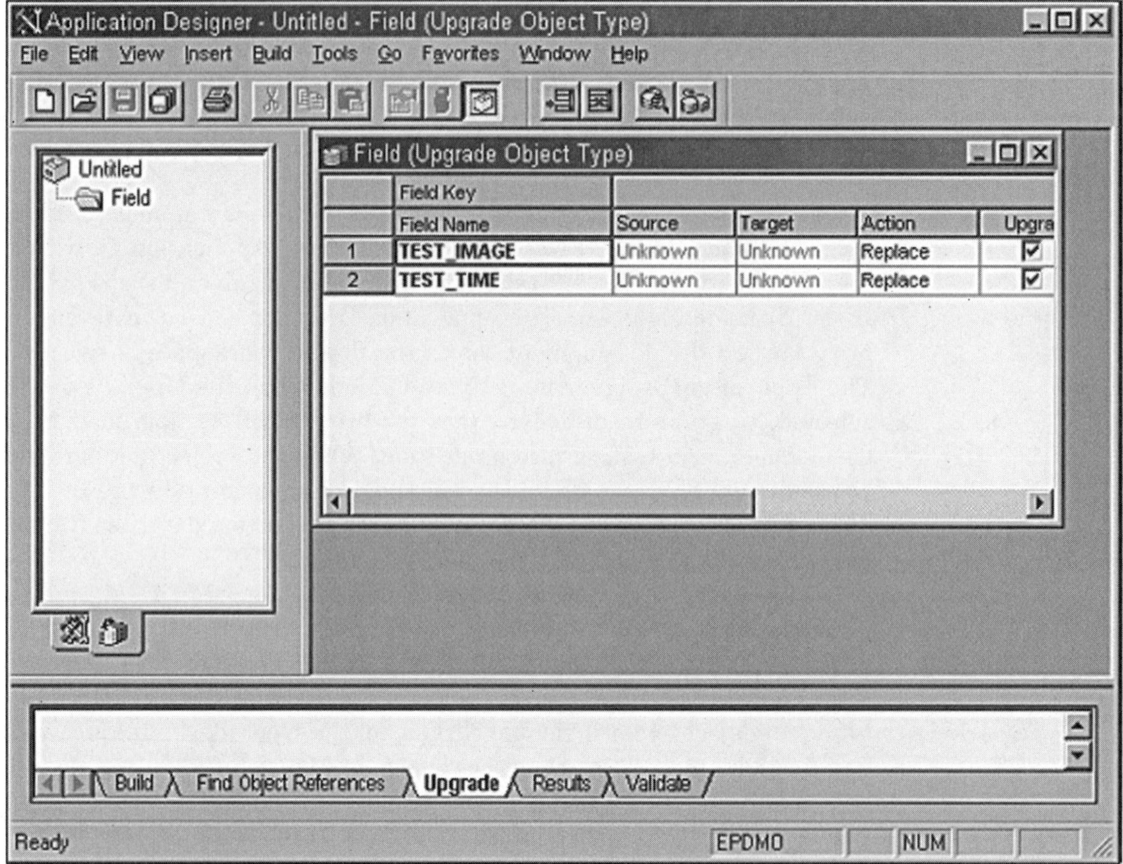

Figure B-1 Upgrade View of the Application Designer.

Field (Upgrade Object Type)

	Field Key					
	Field Name	Source	Target	Action	Upgrade	Done
1	TEST_IMAGE	Unknown	Unknown	Replace	☑	☐
2	TEST_TIME	Unknown	Unknown	Replace	☑	☐

Figure B-2 Upgrade Definition Window.

To copy a project from the source database to the target database the user should select TOOLS, UPGRADE, COPY. When this is selected, the user must sign on to the target database. Figure B-3 shows the target database sign-on dialog. Figure B-4 shows the Copy dialog that is displayed during the Upgrade. The user selects which object types to be

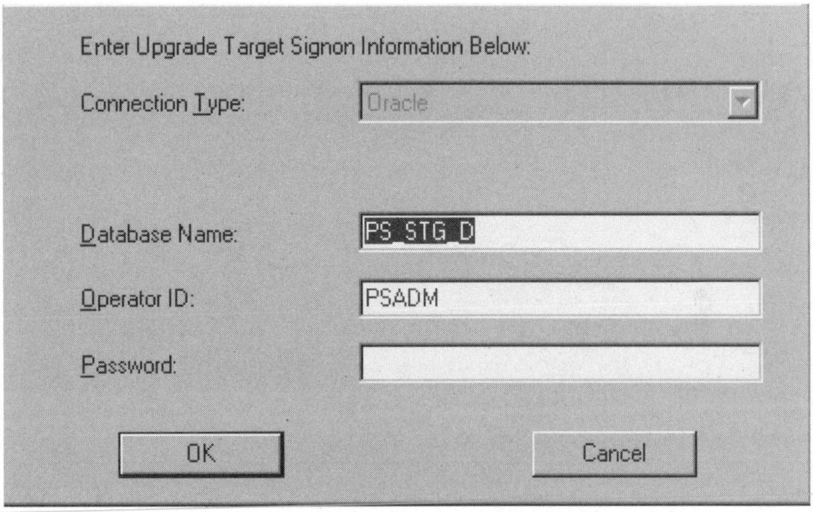

Figure B-3 Target database sign-on dialog.

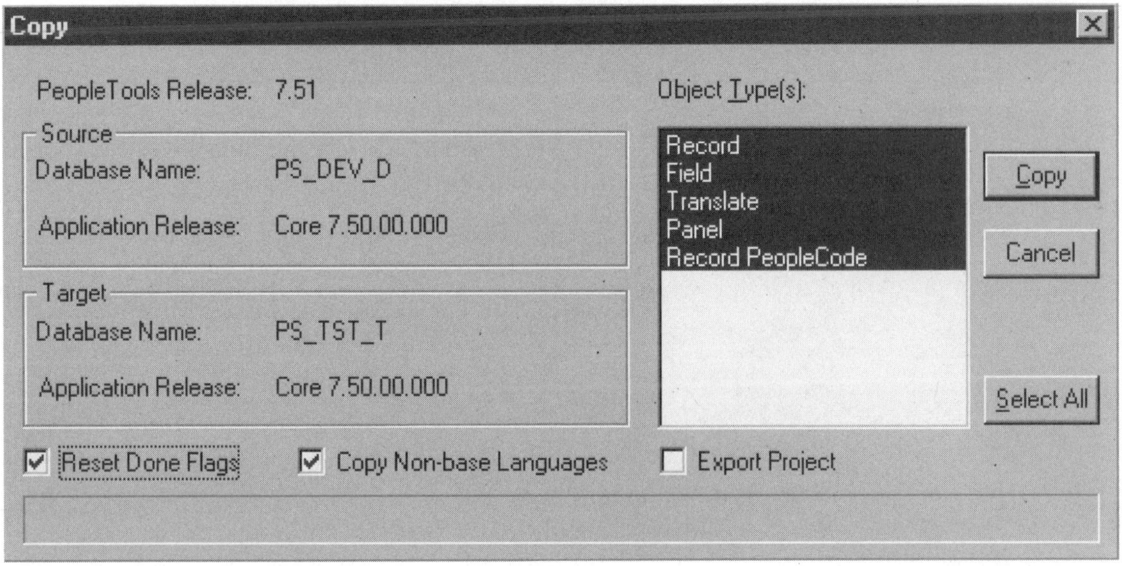

Figure B-4 Copy Dialog displayed during the Upgrade Process.

copied and then starts the copy by clicking on the 'COPY' button. An indicator will appear to show the progress of the copy. When the copy is complete and all is well, it is necessary to stamp the target database. To do this, select TOOLS, UPGRADE, STAMP DATABASE. Enter the new customer release number and double click on the STAMP button. Figure B-5 shows the Stamp Database Dialog box.

Figure B-5 Stamp database dialog box.

INDEX

D

E

F

G

I

N

O

P

T

U

About the Authors

Richard Gillespie is a software consultant for Pfizer, where he is designing and implementing a multiple business unit PeopleSoft 7.5 Inventory and Purchasing System. A graduate of PeopleSoft's development training programs, he has consulted for such clients as Cigna, Aetna, MicroPatent, and the Connecticut Department of Labor. He has broad experience in programming in many languages.

JoAnn Gillespie is a consulting software engineer at GTECH, a company that develops lottery systems. She currently works on Y2K issues. A graduate of Westfield State College, she has 14 years of experience in all aspects of system development. Her expertise includes SQR and spans many developing environments and programming languages.

SOFTWARE AND INFORMATION LICENSE

The software and information on this diskette (collectively referred to as the "Product") are the property of The McGraw-Hill Companies, Inc. ("McGraw-Hill") and are protected by both United States copyright law and international copyright treaty provision. You must treat this Product just like a book, except that you may copy it into a computer to be used and you may make archival copies of the Products for the sole purpose of backing up our software and protecting your investment from loss.

By saying "just like a book," McGraw-Hill means, for example, that the Product may be used by any number of people and may be freely moved from one computer location to another, so long as there is no possibility of the Product (or any part of the Product) being used at one location or on one computer while it is being used at another. Just as a book cannot be read by two different people in two different places at the same time, neither can the Product be used by two different people in two different places at the same time (unless, of course, McGraw-Hill's rights are being violated).

McGraw-Hill reserves the right to alter or modify the contents of the Product at any time.

This agreement is effective until terminated. The Agreement will terminate automatically without notice if you fail to comply with any provisions of this Agreement. In the event of termination by reason of your breach, you will destroy or erase all copies of the Product installed on any computer system or made for backup purposes and shall expunge the Product from your data storage facilities.

LIMITED WARRANTY

McGraw-Hill warrants the physical diskette(s) enclosed herein to be free of defects in materials and workmanship for a period of sixty days from the purchase date. If McGraw-Hill receives written notification within the warranty period of defects in materials or workmanship, and such notification is determined by McGraw-Hill to be correct, McGraw-Hill will replace the defective diskette(s). Send request to:

Customer Service
McGraw-Hill
Gahanna Industrial Park
860 Taylor Station Road
Blacklick, OH 43004-9615

The entire and exclusive liability and remedy for breach of this Limited Warranty shall be limited to replacement of defective diskette(s) and shall not include or extend to any claim for or right to cover any other damages, including but not limited to, loss of profit, data, or use of the software, or special, incidental, or consequential damages or other similar claims, even if McGraw-Hill has been specifically advised as to the possibility of such damages. In no event will McGraw-Hill's liability for any damages to you or any other person ever exceed the lower of suggested list price or actual price paid for the license to use the Product, regardless of any form of the claim.

THE McGRAW-HILL COMPANIES, INC. SPECIFICALLY DISCLAIMS ALL OTHER WARRANTIES, EXPRESS OR IMPLIED, INCLUDING BUT NOT LIMITED TO, ANY IMPLIED WARRANTY OF MERCHANTABILITY OR FITNESS FOR A PARTICULAR PURPOSE. Specifically, McGraw-Hill makes no representation or warranty that the Product is fit for any particular purpose and any implied warranty of merchantability is limited to the sixty day duration of the Limited Warranty covering the physical diskette(s) only (and not the software or in-formation) and is otherwise expressly and specifically disclaimed.

This Limited Warranty gives you specific legal rights; you may have others which may vary from state to state. Some states do not allow the exclusion of incidental or consequential damages, or the limitation on how long an implied warranty lasts, so some of the above may not apply to you.

This Agreement constitutes the entire agreement between the parties relating to use of the Product. The terms of any purchase order shall have no effect on the terms of this Agreement. Failure of McGraw-Hill to insist at any time on strict compliance with this Agreement shall not constitute a waiver of any rights under this Agreement. This Agreement shall be construed and governed in accordance with the laws of New York. If any provision of this Agreement is held to be contrary to law, that provision will be enforced to the maximum extent permissible and the remaining provisions will remain in force and effect.